FREQUEN... ...CE OF LINGUISTIC STRUCTURE

TYPOLOGICAL STUDIES IN LANGUAGE (TSL)

A companion series to the journal "STUDIES IN LANGUAGE"

Honorary Editor: Joseph H. Greenberg
General Editor: Michael Noonan
Assistant Editors: Spike Gildea, Suzanne Kemmer

Editorial Board:

Volumes in this series will be functionally and typologically oriented, covering specific topics in language by collecting together data from a wide variety of languages and language typologies. The orientation of the volumes will be substantive rather than formal, with the aim of investigating universals of human language via as broadly defined a data base as possible, leaning toward cross-linguistic, diachronic, developmental and live-discourse data.

Volume 45

Joan Bybee and Paul Hopper (eds.)

Frequency and the Emergence of Linguistic Structure

FREQUENCY AND THE EMERGENCE OF LINGUISTIC STRUCTURE

Edited by

JOAN BYBEE
University of New Mexico

PAUL HOPPER
Carnegie Mellon University Pittsburgh

JOHN BENJAMINS PUBLISHING COMPANY
AMSTERDAM/PHILADELPHIA

™ The paper used in this publication meets the minimum requirements of American National Standard for Information Sciences — Permanence of Paper for Printed Library Materials, ANSI Z39.48-1984.

Library of Congress Cataloging-in-Publication Data

Frequency and the emergence of linguistic structure / edited by Joan Bybee, Paul Hopper.
    p.   cm. -- (Typological studies in language, ISSN 0167-7373; v. 45)
    Includes bibliographical references and index.
    1. Frequency (Linguistics). 2. Grammar, Comparative and general. I. Bybee, Joan. II. Hopper, Paul. III. Series.
P128.F73F74   2001
415--dc21   00-051912
ISBN 90 272 2947 3 (Eur.) / 1 58811 027 3 (US) (Hb; alk. paper)
ISBN 90 272 2948 1 (Eur.) / 1 58811 028 1 (US) (Pb; alk. paper)   CIP

John Benjamins Publishing Co. • P.O.Box 36224 • 1020 ME Amsterdam • The Netherlands
John Benjamins North America • P.O.Box 27519 • Philadelphia PA 19118-0519 • USA

Contents

Part III: Phrases and constructions

Part IV: General

Acknowledgements

The articles in this volume are revised versions of papers given to an invitational symposium held at Carnegie Mellon University in May 1999. Our thanks are due to David Kaufer, Chair of the English Department, and Peter Stearns, Dean of Humanities and Social Sciences, at CMU for their generosity in providing funding and in placing department and college facilities at our disposal during the conference. We also wish to thank Chris Werry, then a graduate student in rhetoric at CMU, for his efficiency and hard work in coordinating the local arrangements. We would also like to thank the participants, most of whom traveled from far and wide to attend and share their ideas.

A substantial portion of the task of copy-editing and editorial assistance was undertaken by Catie Berkenfield, of the University of New Mexico, whose thoroughness and patience carried the project through in good form. The editors and contributors alike owe Catie a special note of thanks. Funding from Robert and Elizabeth Bybee with matching funds from the Exxon Foundation covered the costs of editorial assistance. Finally, the editors are grateful to the contributors for producing excellent papers for the symposium and for allowing them to be published here.

Introduction to frequency and the emergence of linguistic structure

JOAN BYBEE and PAUL HOPPER

1. Introduction

A legacy of the structural tradition in linguistics is the widespread acceptance of the premise that language structure is independent of language use. This premise is codified in a variety of theoretical distinctions, such as *langue* and *parole* (Saussure 1916) and competence and performance (Chomsky 1965). A further premise of this legacy is that the study of structure is a higher calling than the study of usage and is a potentially more promising avenue for uncovering the basic cognitive mechanisms that make human language possible.

In contrast, outside linguistics it is widely held that cognitive representations are highly affected by experience. In humans and non-humans detailed tracking of probabilities leads to behavior that promotes survival (Kelly and Martin 1994). Even within linguistics, certain usage-based effects permeate the general lore that practitioners and theoreticians accept: unmarked members of categories are more frequent than marked members (Greenberg 1966); irregular morphological formations with high frequency are less likely to regularize; regular patterns have a wider range of applicability; and high frequency phrases undergo special reduction. Many of these effects had been catalogued and described by George K. Zipf in a pioneering work from the 1930s, *The Psycho-Biology of Language* (Zipf 1965 [1935]). Zipf is known these days chiefly for his "law" that the length of a word is inversely proportional to its frequency and his explanation through the "principle of least effort." While this aspect of Zipf's work is often criticized (see, for example, Miller 1965), he anticipated many of the themes of more recent investigations of the relationship between frequency and structure, such as the fusion of pronouns with auxiliaries in forms like *we're, you'll*, etc. and their significance for the genesis of inflection (Zipf 1965 [1935], 247–51). Zipf coined the term "dynamic philology" for the quantitative study of language change and its relevance for linguistic structure.

Zipf's work in linguistics was taken up only sporadically in the discipline as linguists focused their attention on the theoretical questions of how to define the structural units of language exclusively through local combinatorial possibilities. However, by the 1980s, a number of linguists had begun to think of linguistic structure (grammar) as a response to discourse needs, and to consider seriously the hypothesis that grammar comes about through the repeated adaptation of forms to live discourse (Hopper 1979; Givón 1979; Givón (ed.) 1983; Hopper and Thompson 1980, 1984; Du Bois 1985). The parallel question of how experience with language as reflected in frequency could affect cognitive representations and categorization and thus the internalized grammar of language users also began to occupy researchers at this time in both linguistics (Bybee 1985) and psychology (Rumelhart and McClelland 1986). A related development, symptomatic of the increasing impatience with studies of individual "competence" and growing suspicion regarding the reliability of intuitions as a source of data, was the rise in the 1990s of the new field of corpus linguistics. Starting from trends that had begun with "computational linguistics" going back as far as the 1950s, corpus linguistics has been made possible by the exponential increase in data storage and high-speed processing. While the corpus is the prime tool for frequency studies in general, with many linguists it also serves as a heuristic for new facts about linguistic structure. One especially important claim coming out of corpus studies is that the dividing line between grammar and lexicon, which has been virtually a dogma in linguistics, cannot be sustained (see Stubbs 1996: 36–9 for discussion from the perspective of the Hallidayan strain in corpus linguistics, also Langacker 1987, Hopper 1987, Poplack, this volume, Bybee, this volume, Hallan, this volume, and others). Time and again the operation of linguistic rules has been found to be limited by lexical constraints, sometimes to the point where a construction is valid only for one or two specific words.

Increasingly, then, in many quarters structure has come to be seen not as a holistic autonomous system but as something more fluid and shifting. An influential concept here has been that of *emergence* (Hopper 1987, 1998, 1988, 1993), understood as an ongoing process of *structuration* (Giddens 1984). Structuration in recent sociology refers to "the conditions which govern the continuity and dissolution of structures or types of structures" (Giddens 1977: 120). Emergence in this sense is distinct from *ontogenesis*, which refers to the origins and development—the history—of an existent organism or of a system. By contrast, emergent structures are unstable and are manifested stochastically. The fixing of linguistic groups of all kinds as recognizably structural units (word and phrase units) is an ongoing process; it is the result at any point in time of the "constant resystematization" of language (Coseriu 1954). From this perspective, mental representations are seen as provisional and temporary states of affairs that are sensitive, and constantly adapting themselves, to usage. "Grammar" itself and associated theoretical postulates like "syntax" and "phonology" have no autonomous existence beyond local storage and real-time processing (Hopper 1987; Bybee, this volume). The notion of language as a monolithic system has had to give way to that of a language as a massive collection of heterogeneous *constructions*, each with affinities to different contexts and in constant structural adaptation to usage (Langacker 1987).

The notion of emergence constitutes a break with standard ideas about grammar that envisage it as a fixed synchronic system. It relativizes structure to speakers' actual experience with language, and sees structure as an on-going response to the pressure of discourse rather than as a pre-existent matrix (Hopper 1988; Ochs, Schegloff, and Thompson 1997). It follows that accounts of grammatical (and phonological) structure must take note of how frequency and repetition affect and, ultimately, bring about form in language (Bybee 1985, to appear; Bybee *et al.* 1994). Now work on the notion that frequency of exposure and use is an important factor in the establishment and maintenance of linguistic structure has begun to branch out in many directions. One of the goals of this book is to represent some of the findings of this research.

1.2 Contents of the volume

The papers in this volume build on these two strands of research into language use—the heuristic of frequency and the metalinguistic principle of emergence—to illustrate certain general principles that are robustly documented by empirical investigations of various sorts: distribution in natural conversation, diachronic change, variability, child language acquisition, and experimentation. Two major principles are addressed here:

1. The distribution and frequency of the units of language are governed by the content of people's interactions, which consist of a preponderance of subjective, evaluative statements, dominated by the use of pronouns, copulas and intransitive clauses.
2. The frequency with which certain items and strings of items are used has a profound influence on the way language is broken up into chunks in memory storage, the way such chunks are related to other stored material and the ease with which they are accessed.

Each of the chapters of this volume treats several issues related to these two principles, so that organizing them thematically has been difficult. The organization we have settled is:

I.   **Patterns of Use.** These are papers that deal with patterns of occurrence of morphosyntactic structures in natural conversation;
II. **Word-level frequency effects,** that is, the papers that deal with the direct and indirect effects of frequency of use on change and structure at the word level;

III. Phrases and constructions, which contains papers that demonstrate that many of the same principles found at the word level also operate in multi-word sequences; and

IV. General. In this category are placed papers that reference and model multiple phenomena and therefore do not fit easily into the first three categories.

2. Patterns of use in natural discourse

2.1 Use of natural discourse data

By definition, any study that deals with tokens (as opposed to types) takes as its data base extended samples of natural language, whether these be written language or transcriptions of speech. It might seem that discourse data are simply an extension of the data from intuition, differing only or primarily in quantity but otherwise consistent in structure with forms retrieved through introspection. However, a number of authors in the present volume have drawn attention to what Scheibman (this volume) terms the "slippage" between standard ideas about grammaticality and the facts presented by natural data. Poplack (this volume) finds that the grammar of the subjunctive and conditional in the spoken vernacular French of Canada is quite different from that of the norms dictated for Metropolitan French by the Académie Française. On the other hand, the official grammar fails to note the significant role of lexical constraints in these constructions in the vernacular, where a small number of verbs and main/subordinate verb combinations decisively dominate the grammatical picture. In fact, virtually none of the meanings or functions attributed to the Future or the Subjunctive in official French appear to any significant degree in Canadian French. She echoes a conclusion that has been reached by numerous students of vernacular French (Bauche 1928; Bally 1966 [1932]; Ashby 1977; Lambrecht 1981; etc.), namely that modern spoken French has moved radically beyond the official written language that still forms the basis for structural grammatical studies.

Poplack echoes a theme in frequency studies that is repeated in several of the papers in this volume: there is a very serious mismatch between the results of quantitative studies and grammatical accounts—both descriptive and normative—that rely exclusively on imaginary data. Hallan, commenting on the disparity between the standard view of the prepositional phrase consisting of PREPOSITION + NOUN as the normal context for the category Preposition in English and the markedly late appearance of this pattern in child language, concludes that this prototype is engendered in the course of schooling for literacy. Hallan goes even further in suggesting that the availability of large corpora might call for a general reassessment of grammatical categories. In this she follows Sinclair's assertion that "even major parts of speech are not as solidly founded as they might be" (Sinclair:1992: 14, cited in Stubbs 1996: 39).

Hopper and Thompson also note some fundamental differences between linguistic structure as it is posited on the basis of imagined configurations and that of utterances in live conversational contexts. They note that lexical frames for verbs that specify their possible argument structures in advance of usage are often violated in practice, and that the more frequent a verb type, the less predictable the number of arguments; a rare verb like *to elapse* is limited to a single argument, whereas a common verb like *to get* appears in discourse with one, two, or three of the traditional arguments depending on the speaker's need. Scheibman, arguing for the centrality of subjective expression in conversational English, points out that this role of subjectivity is in opposition to the privileging of referential language in standard linguistic analysis.

2.2 Subjectivity

By their nature, all frequency studies are based on usage in some measure. Scholars differ, however, in the degree to which discourse figures as a central part of the study rather than as the site for statistical studies. For a number of contributors, especially those concerned with morphological and phonological questions, the interpretation of contextual meaning is largely irrelevant, since what is at issue for them is type or transitional frequency. For others, it is essential that quantitative work should be combined with a more or less close reading of textual data. Scheibman, for example, shows in detail how the personal, expressive nature of spoken discourse manifests itself in what would be, from the point of view of canonical linguistics, skewed distributions of pronouns and tenses. She stresses that common categories such as third person singular are frequent not because discourse is naturally referential (quite the contrary), but because this category conflates several subtypes, usually evaluative, such as *it* in *it isn't fair*. She shows through careful text counts that the relatively high frequency of first and second person singular pronouns is owed to their collocation with verbs of cognition (*I think*, etc.) She concludes that interactive discourse favors "those subject-predicate combinations that permit speakers to personalize their contributions . . ." Further evidence of the frequency of subjectifying elements is the high frequency of modal verbs in the corpus examined in Krug's contribution to the volume. Modal verbs provide the speaker's evaluation or perspective on the situation described by the main verb (Scheibman 2000).

Poplack adds another dimension to this same theme, that of Variation Theory, which seeks to identify the different contexts that give rise to the choice of one or another variant of a form. She shows that these contexts can be quite elaborate, and include a strong element of lexical preference and a less clear influence of type and token frequency. Poplack's domain of study is that of the Irrealis in Canadian French. She shows that robust collocations between the main-clause verb and the verb of the subordinate clause have pesisted over long periods of time, and she thus provides historical proof of storage units that transgress the clause boundary.

Thompson and Hopper, in their study of transitivity in spoken discourse, point to incompatibilities between standard accounts of clause structure based on intuitions and the less rigid structure of utterances in conversational contexts. They show that high transitivity in the sense of Hopper and Thompson 1980, which is often taken as the prototype for fully exemplified argument structure, is rare or absent in normal utterances. More generally, the argument structure frames for verbs predicted by theories of the "mental lexicon" are only recoverable for natural discourse to the degree that the verb is unusual. For the more common verbs such as *to get* exceptions and special uses abound to the point of invalidating a priori schemata.

Hallan tackles the problem of "prepositions" or "path morphemes" and their ontogenesis. Tracing the development of such forms as *on* and *over* from their earliest attestations in infants' utterances, she challenges the standard ideas about "prepositions" and the cognitive models of the preposition that are based on a prototype of prenominal forms with locative meanings.

A diachronic perspective on frequency effects is presented by Smith in his study of the English anterior aspect. Smith looks at the distribution of *to be* and *to have* as auxiliaries of the anterior aspect (*I am gone* vs. *I have gone*) in the earliest Old English texts, and makes the point that earlier attempts at synchronic semantic analyses of the distribution have not worked because the synchronic distribution represents a system in flux, caught up in the beginnings of a process whereby the *have* forms are bit by bit encroaching on the *be* forms. Smith hypothesizes that type frequency is a better predictor of the eventual victor in a competition between two forms than token frequency, based on the role of type frequency in morphological productivity (MacWhinney 1978; Bybee 1985). Although the textual frequency of the two auxiliaries is about equal in Old English, the number of verbs construed with *have* (i.e., the type frequency) is by far preponderant. On the other hand, he suggests, high frequency tokens of the less frequent competing types will be the last to succumb to the specialization process. (Poplack, however, finds that for two of her three variables, the future and the imperfect, productivity is not robustly predicted by either type frequency or token frequency, and speculates that other factors may be at work.)

Berkenfield and Bush adopt a more "micro" perspective on discourse in their studies of the "morphophonetics" of English *that* and cross-word boundary palatalization respectively. Berkenfield examines the descendents of the Old English demonstrative pronoun *thæt* in its functions as demonstrative pronoun, as demonstrative adjective, as complementizer, and as relativizer from the point of view of the relationship between vowel quality and frequency. She shows strikingly that vowel reduction, as measured by both vowel length (in microseconds) and quality (F1 value), and token frequency go hand in hand with increasing grammaticization. She concludes that "sub-phonemic" distinctions are nonetheless available to speakers in discriminating morphosyntactic functions, a result of some significance for our notions of phonology and phonetics (see also Bybee [this volume, and to appear]).

In another paper influenced by Bybee's "Usage-based Phonology," Bush studies the palatalization of segments across word boundaries in, for example, "would you" > [wudju] as opposed to the absence of such palatalization in sequences such as "good you" (which had been noted by earlier researchers). Bush invokes *transitional probability*, the degree of likelihood that one word will be followed by a specific collocate. He concludes that the discourse "chunking" of lexical words creates units that may behave in every respect like unitary words, permitting the application of processes that are otherwise word-internal (see Bybee 2000a). His study indicates that frequency of cooccurrence significantly drives assimilation whether words are function or content words. Palatalization in conversation is not restricted to the pronoun *you* as suggested by some studies, nor is it possible to predict its occurrence with reference to constituent structure. Pairs of words that are frequently used together, whatever their apparent constituency and status as lexical or grammatical (*don't you, told you, that you, last year*), are more likely to show effects of coarticulation than words that are used together less often.

In most or all of these studies the speech act and its participants have a central role. Most utterances are evaluative in the sense of either expressing a judgement or presenting the world from the perspective of the self or on interlocutor. Referential utterances of the kind that figure so prominently in "syntactic" studies, with their lexical nouns and single-word verbs, are in fact rare in natural discourse. They favor third-person constative utterances, ones that typically indicate a shift of the focus of the discourse away from its immediate existential context and into the realm of unwitnessed, objective, remote events (Hopper 1997). Natural discourse is concerned with the here-and-now world of the speaker and the hearer, and with the contingencies (imperatives, conditionals, possible worlds) that proceed directly from it. Natural discourse is, in other words, preeminently *subjective* (Scheibman, this volume, and Scheibman 2000). If grammar is emergent from commonly used sequences, it is natural to expect that that such sequences will comprise the core of grammaticalized structures, and therefore that grammar—the internalized aggregate of formations from usage—will move into increasingly subjective spheres (Traugott 1989; Traugott and Koenig 1991). This point is implicit or explicit in a number of papers in which functional areas like modality, transitivity, and aspect figure.

3. Units of usage

A mainstay of linguistic analysis is the identification of recurring units in the continuous stream of speech. Thus we identify features, segments, syllables, morphemes, words, phrases, clauses and so on, on the basis of distribution and with reference to phonetic and semantic features. The problems with attempting to exhaustively and discretely divide utterances into these units are well-known: classificational difficulties include the issues of diphthongs, affricates, extra-syllabicity, empty morphs, clitics, auxiliary verbs, and subordinate clauses, yet the reality of these recurring units is attested to by their patterns of use, including use in novel utterances. An important motivation for identifying these units is to assign them to lexical storage or to describe their structure in terms of grammatical rules. It has been assumed that language users come up with the same analysis as linguists do and that the most economical treatment of this complex system would postulate a small number of storage units and a set of rules for their combination. Thus it is usually assumed that morphemes or words are units of storage and access, while larger units are produced by combinatory rules.

Recently evidence from a variety of research traditions has been brought forward to question the economy of storage and the separation of lexicon from grammar (Hopper 1987; Langacker 1987; Stubbs 1996; etc.). The model that is emerging to replace the old conception postulates that to a large extent, the units of usage ARE the units of storage and access. As people do not speak in isolated morphemes or words, in many cases the units of memory and processing contain multiple morphemes and even multiple words (see Wray and Perkins 2000). The categorization in storage of units of use forms a network based on the user's experience with language, and from this network, recurrent patterns emerge (Bybee 1998).

What sorts of units might we expect to find in storage? We are largely restricted to answering this question for English, since so much more research has been concentrated on this language than on any others. First, the traditional unit of noun phrase does occur in conversation, and NPs are often independent intonation units (Ono and Thompson 1994; Croft 1995). NPs almost always include determiners (*a/an* or *the*) and the phonological alternations that are characteristics of these determiners suggest that DET + NOUN is a storage unit (Bybee, to appear).

Verbs in most languages are multi-morphemic units (given the widespread occurrence of inflection on verbs), but in English verbal expressions are typically dispersed over multiple words. Hopper 1991 cites examples of VERB + PARTICLE, VERB + ADVERB, VERB + PREPOSITION, VERB + NOUN, AUX + VERB in which the VERB element is not readily separable from other parts of the functional group. Examples are *wake up, speeded up, head straight in, has drifted left, heave a sigh of relief, start exploding, have to quickly decide* and so on.

Other sorts of frequently-occurring snatches of speech that show evidence of autonomy characteristic of stored items are *I don't know, I don't think* (Bybee and Scheibman 1999), *wanna, gotta, gonna,* etc. (Krug, this volume), *you and I* (Boyland, this volume), *did you, didn't you, don't you* (Bush, this volume), *is gone* (Smith, this volume), *come on, over here, over there* (Hallan, this volume). Stubbs (1996: 39), citing Renouf and Sinclair (1991), adds from corpus studies *a couple of, a lot of, an indication of, an element of, be able to, be ready to, too easy to, too close to,* concerning which he comments: "Such items are highly frequent, an integral part of language, yet lie somewhere between word and group." These frequently-occurring sequences include both phrases that can be used in isolation, e.g. *I don't know,* and also parts of constructions that require nouns and verbs to be combined with them to be complete: NP *wanna* VERB, NP *be able to* VERB, NP *gonna* VERB, *did you* VERB, NP *is gone.* Thus many of the storage units we are proposing here are constructions in that they have open slots that take items that share certain properties.

In the model suggested by the papers in this volume (Pierrehumbert, this volume; see also Bybee 1998, to appear) tokens of experience with language are organized into exemplars on the basis of high similarity of phonetic shape and function or meaning, and such exemplars are tagged for their contextual associations, both linguistic and extra- linguistic. Thus tokens of *I* in *I don't know, I don't think, I see, I want* etc. are mapped onto the same representations. This does not prevent a strong link between *I* and *don't* from also being maintained, as *don't* is the second most frequent item to follow *I* (*'m* is the most frequent) (Bybee and Scheibman 1999; Krug 1998). Thus even though complex units (such as *I don't*) are stored and accessed, their component parts are also identified in the categorization and storage process.

A major part of the evidence for the storage of multimorphemic words and multiword phrases and constructions is the fact that, as shown in several of the papers of this volume (see especially, Part 2), both direct and indirect frequency effects can be demonstrated for these units. Linguistic material cannot accrue frequency effects unless the brain is keeping track of frequency in some way; frequency effects cannot be attributed to units unless they are items in storage that are affected by experience. A natural way to track frequency is to postulate that tokens of experience strengthen stored exemplars (Bybee 1985; Pierrehumbert, this volume).

In the following sections, we will discuss the effects of frequency that have been documented in the literature and in the papers of this volume as applying both at the word level and in multi-word sequences and the cognitive mechanisms underlying them.

4. Frequency effects and cognitive mechanisms in emergent grammar

The notion of emergent structure has become important in various branches of the sciences in the last two decades. The basic idea is that what may appear to be a coherent structure created according to some underlying design may in fact be the result of multiple applications or interactions of simple mechanisms that operate according to local principles and create the seemingly well-planned structure as a consequence. MacWhinney (this volume) discusses emergentist theories as they have developed in the physical and biological sciences, and examines the various ways in which emergence can be applied to the study of language. His discussion focuses on neurological models of language learning and representation that proceed from local self-organizing maps to more complex networks that incorporate larger chunks of language, multiple associations among the units of language as well as grounding in the physical and social domains. Such models can accommodate frequency effects, as long as the details about how frequency effects work can be established empirically.

Many of the papers in the current volume are directed towards understanding the multiple ways that frequency of use can effect linguistic behavior. In the following subsections we will discuss these frequency effects focusing on the cognitive mechanisms that bring them about and functional consequences they have for language. These effects are (1) phonological reduction in high frequency words and phrases (4.1); (2) functional change due to high frequency (4.2); (3) frequency and the formation of constructions (4.3); (4) frequency and accessibility (4.4); (5) the retention of conservative characteristics (4.5); and (6) the notion that a stochastic grammar is a result of linguistic knowledge based on experience (4.6).

4.1 Phonological reduction in high frequency words and strings

Recent research has documented a tendency identified in Schuchardt 1885 by which words of higher frequency tend to undergo sound change at a faster rate than words of lower frequency. This effect has been identified for English reduction to schwa (Fidelholtz 1975), schwa deletion (Hooper 1976), t/d deletion (Bybee 2000, Gregory *et al.* 1999), deletion of [ð] in Spanish (Bybee, to appear), the raising of /a/ before nasals in Old English (Phillips 1980), and the raising of /æ/ in San Francisco English (Moonwomon 1992).[1] Among the current papers, the effects of high frequency on reductive change is documented in the chapters by Berkenfield, Bush, Jurafsky *et al.*, Krug, and Phillips; it is also discussed in the chapter by Fenk-Oczlon.

One of the most important consequences of these studies is the finding that sound change is gradual both phonetically and lexically, because this means that very specific phonetic features, probably specified as a range of phonetic variation, are associated with particular lexical items (Hooper 1981; Bybee 2000b, Mowrey and Pagliuca 1995). Any phonological representation that fails to register non-contrastive features is not able to account for this lexically-specific variation. On the other hand, an exemplar model, as proposed in Johnson 1997, which records and organizes in memory distinct phonetic variants of words and phrases, can accommodate lexical variation.

Pierrehumbert (this volume) demonstrates how an exemplar model can be formalized to account for both the perception and production of lexically-specific variation. In addition, she models the effect that a lenition bias or tendency towards reduction can have on a set of exemplars, and the effect of token frequency on reductive processes.

The origins of reduction are in the automatization of neuro-motor sequences which comes about with repetition. This automatization involves the reduction of the magnitude of articulatory gestures and the increased overlap of these gestures (Browman and Goldstein 1992; Mowrey and Pagliuca 1995). Such reductions are systematic across speakers; that is, they do not represent 'sloppy' or 'lazy' speech. Moreover, reduction or lack of reduction are carefully monitored and controlled by the speaker according to the context. As a result, reduction or lack of it can take on pragmatic value.

The role of token frequency in reductive sound change involves the interaction of a complex set of factors. One factor is that automatization is occurring whenever speech is produced, which results in small changes in the magnitude and timing of gestures; frequent words have more opportunity to be affected as they are exposed to these on-line processes more than infrequent words (Moonwomon 1992). Frequent words are also used more in familiar, casual settings, where more reduction is allowed than in formal settings. This also exposes frequent words to more reduction. This point is also made by Dahl (this volume), who points out that a number used as a date, such as "1999", characteristically receives a more reduced articulation than the same number used to denote a quantity or a street address.

In addition, Fowler and Housum (1987) have shown that in reading a narrative, subjects' productions of the second occurrence of a word in the narrative is significantly shorter in overall duration that the first occurrence of the word. The shortening of a word has an effect on all the gestures that comprise the word, decreasing their magnitude and increasing their overlap. Gregory et al. (1999) find a similar effect in conversation, and in addition, report the semantic relatedness of a word in the discourse has a very strong effect on duration. Thus, when the word *coast* occurred in a conversation about weather it was much shorter than when it occurred in a conversation about family budgets.

The speaker seems to be able to gauge how much phonetic information the hearer needs in order to access the correct word. Where the word has occurred before, it is primed and easier to access; where the word is primed by the other words in the context, it is also easier to access. The persistent use of this strategy by speakers leads to the development of a listener strategy by which reduced words are judged to be repetitions and thus part of the background in the discourse (Fenk-Oczlon, this volume). Thus with the reduction the speaker signals that the reduced word is just the same old word as used before, not a new one.

Fenk-Oczlon (this volume) relates these correspondences to information flow: according to her, efficiency demands a relatively constant flow of information. Thus short words should convey less information than longer words. Besides relating to the correspondence between length of word and semantic complexity, this principle makes several predictions about the length of words and their position in discourse ('more frequent before less frequent'), in particular in binomial 'freezes' (frequently conjoined nouns) such as *bread and butter*, *salt and pepper*. By showing a discourse relationship that goes beyond one of mere length-to-frequency, but rather places these in a functional frame, she operationalizes Zipf's "law" and strips it of the standard objection that the law amounts to a tautology (see Miller's introduction to Zipf 1965: v–x).

The paper by Jurafsky *et al.* (this volume) takes into account a number of factors under the Probabilistic Reduction Hypothesis, which includes not just the predictability of a word within a particular discourse, but also its cumulative token frequency and the probability of a word given neighboring words. Jurafsky *et al.* provide useful formulae for calculating the predictability of a word given the previous and following word. They study the top ten most frequent words of English, which are all function words (*a, the, in, of, to, and, that I, it, you*). These words both show more vowel reduction and shorter duration as they are more predictable from the preceding and following word. In contrast, content words ending in /t/ or /d/ were studied for the deletion of their final consonant and here they find that only the frequency of the word containing the /t/ or /d/ predicts the rate of deletion.

Thus Jurafsky *et al.* suggest that function words are more affected by context than the less frequent content words. This in turn indicates that the phonological shapes of function words are more determined by the constructions that they are in, while content words are more independent. In fact, one could argue that function words only occur in constructions and do not have independent representation (unless they are homophonous with a noun or verb). This would mean that function words have multiple representations, since each construction a function word occurs in requires a representation. Berkenfield (this volume) demonstrates that the polysemous function word *that* has different phonetic properties depending upon whether it is functioning as a demonstrative, a complementizer, or a relative clause marker, and that part of this difference is due to the frequency of the different constructions in spoken discourse.

Krug's study (this volume) of the new emerging modals also demonstrates phonological reduction inside frequently occurring chunks: phrases such as *want to*, *have to*, *got to*, *ought to*, *going to* undergo extraordinary reduction, due, at least in part, to the high frequency with which they are used together. His study also underscores the categorizing features of linguistic storage, as he argues that these units are classed together as a new emergent category of modal auxiliary based on their phonological and semantic coherence.

These studies all lead us to consider the nature of the storage and processing units in mental representation. In order for sequences to accrue frequency effects or phonological fusion and reduction, they must exist as units in mental representation. Jurafsky *et al.* take their evidence to indicate that "probabilistic relations between words are represented in the mind of the speaker" (p. 2). By this they do not mean that any words that affect one another are stored as single units, because they distinguish between lexicalization, by which sequences are treated as single words, and probability relations. A possible interpretation of their findings would be that stored words are linked sequentially and that frequency of co-occurrence strengthens these links.

MacWhinney (this volume), while treating many issues in the modeling of emergence in language, discusses the formation of chunks and advocates a distinction between a chunk in perceptual processing and an avalanche, which is a serial string of behavior, such that the triggering of the beginning of the string leads to the firing of all the component pieces.

4.2 Functional change due to high frequency

Functional and semantic change in high frequency strings or constructions is the focus of the recent research in grammaticization (Bybee *et al.* 1994; Hopper and Traugott 1993, among many others). Phonological reduction and fusion in grammaticization are paralleled by semantic generalization and functional shifts. Frequency is one of the factors that conditions functional change. Haiman (1994) argues that repetition is one of the factors behind emancipation, the process by which an instrumental act becomes symbolic through association with a particular outcome. Repetition also conditions bleaching through the process of habituation, wherein an organism ceases to respond at the same level to a repeated stimulus. Dahl (this volume) likens the process to inflation in economics: as strong expressions are increasingly overused, their effect weakens, and newer, stronger expressions must take their place if the same rhetorical effect is to be achieved.

Grammaticization is the mechanism by which structure emerges from language use. Since such a vast literature on the topic now exists, it is not a specific focus for the current volume. However, the paper here by Krug deals with the emerging class of modals in English, which are erstwhile main verbs undergoing grammaticization into a new class of modal auxiliaries.

4.3 Frequency and the formation of constructions

Constituent structure is determined by frequency of co-occurrence (Bybee and Scheibman 1999): the more often two elements occur in sequence the tighter will be their constituent structure. The tightest constituency is the result of two very specific items occurring frequently together. Clear examples are cases in which two words have fused because of their frequent co-occurrence and now behave essentially as single words, e.g. *want to* > *wanna*, *going to* > *gonna*, *I am* > *I'm*, *can not* > *can't*, *do not* > *don't*, *I don't know* > *I dunno*, *would have* > *would've* (Boyland 1996; Bybee and Scheibman 1999; Krug 1998, this volume). In a sense, frequency of use has led to the loss of former constituent boundaries within these strings, in some cases, major constituent boundaries such as that between subject and predicate (*I'm*) or between main clause and subordinate clause (*wanna*). In addition to these cases, which one might want to view as marginal, the kind of constituency normally studied by syntacticians also has its source in language use and frequency of co-occurrence. Thus determiners occur with nouns, auxiliaries with verbs, prepositions with noun phrases and so on. Constructions such as [DET + NOUN], [AUX + VERB], [PREP + NP] are conventionalized through frequent use.

However, grammars (however conceived) do not merely contain the highly schematic representations such as [DET + NOUN] but also many more specific or local representations with very explicit lexical material included. Again, which representations of this sort exist depends almost entirely on frequency of use. Hallan (this volume) shows that the use of specific instances of constructions begins very early in language acquisition; in fact, children acquire very specific instances of constructions and use them quite appropriately long before there is any evidence for the extraction of grammatical principles from the ambient language. For instance, in the Wells corpus the five most frequent uses by all speakers of the word *over*, often regarded as a canonical preposition, do not include a prepositional use. Instead *over there* occurs the most, followed by *over* in phrasal verbs, such as *fall over, knock over* and the phrase *all over (the)*; *over here* is the fifth most frequent use. Similarly the uses of *on* include many fixed expressions and frequent phrases. Not surprisingly, the early uses of *on* are dominated by particular phrasal verb combinations such as *come on, put on, turn on*. Even the prepositional uses of *on* occur with certain nouns, such as *on the floor, on (one's) own, on the bed* and so on. This view of child language makes it clear that children acquire very specific expressions and routines that only later become productive and show evidence of more schematic representation (see also Lieven *et al.* 1997).

Boyland's study shows that hypercorrect forms of English pronouns, specifically the use of *you and I* in object position and the use of *whom* in subject position, are heavily influenced by frequency of use. Boyland shows that it is not just any conjoined pronouns that are used in subject form in object position, but rather that it is *you and I* that are most commonly used hypercorrectly. Her corpus study shows moreover that of all conjoined phrases with *I*, the specific phrase *you and I* is the most frequently occurring. She argues that *you and I* has become a processing unit because of its frequency and that, like other high frequency items, it is easy to access whole. Thus speakers use it as a unit rather than generating two separate pronouns with the conjunction. There is of course no question that speakers know that the phrase *you and I* consists of three words, all of which are used elsewhere, but that does not prevent them from packaging this particular sequence as a unit.

Hypercorrect uses of *whom* are also highly influenced by frequency. Local constructions consisting of preposition + *whom* are the most stable and consistently used. Hypercorrection occurs most commonly in larger syntactic units where *whom* plays different roles at different levels, for instance in *Someone whom he feels is worth listening to has convinced him.* Here the smaller clause, *whom he feels*, determines the case of the relative pronoun. The frequency of *whom* use in such cases reflects the frequency of *whom* use in normal relative clauses: it is most frequent after prepositions, next most frequent as a direct object and least frequent as a subject.

Bybee's paper suggests an understanding of French liaison phenomena as a function of constructions in which certain phonological material is highly entrenched. Liaison consonants appear in DETERMINER + NOUN constructions, CLITIC PRONOUN + VERB constructions, prepositional phrases, and some ADJECTIVE + NOUN constructions. Liaison alternations are maintained most consistently in the higher frequency constructions. The fact that frequency plays a greater role than syntactic constituency in determining liaison is brought home by the fact that the third singular of *être* 'to be', *est*, has a much higher rate of maintaining liaison than any other of the forms of the same verb even in the same construction. Bybee proposes that for each construction with the alternation there are two subschemas, one supplying the consonant before a vowel-initial word and one without the consonant before a consonant-initial word. Because consonant-initial words are twice as frequent as vowel-initial words, the latter construction generalizes, bringing about the loss of the liaison consonant. But her study goes further and raises a more general question about the relationship between syntax and phonology. This relationship has generally been seen as a very indirect one between a set of categories and a set of phonological segments. Bybee suggests instead that liaison in French is neither morphosyntactic nor phonological, but is a frequency effect such that "the higher the frequency of a phrase or construction, the more likely it is to preserve liaison." It follows that constituent structure as it is normally viewed, that is, without reference to the discourse frequency of the set, cannot be causally involved in the loss or preservation of liaison. Speakers, she suggests, CREATE structure by frequent use of certain word combinations, and since each of these words can participate in other collocations, more than one constituent analysis may be possible (for example, *'ll* in *I'll do it* is simultaneously part of *I* and of *do*.)

4.4 Frequency and Accessibility

It has long been known that the speed of lexical access of individual words is highly affected by frequency of use: in lexical decision tasks, subjects identify words much faster if they are of high frequency. Evidence already reviewed here suggests that frequency of use may make access of larger units easier as well. Strings such as *you and I*, *come on*, *fall over*, and common sequences with liaison in French, such as *mes amis* 'my friends', *c'est un* 'it's a', and *l'un avec l'autre* 'with one another' may be more efficiently accessed as units than composed morpheme by morpheme. In more traditional models in which only monomorphemic units are stored, however, no frequency effects in the processing of multi-morphemic units are to be expected.

Hare *et al.* investigate this issue for regular morphologically complex verbs in English. The hypothesis has been put forward that while irregular English verbs have lexical listing and thus show effects of frequency in derived forms, such as the Past tense, regulars are derived by rule and thus their Past tenses can show no frequency effects (Pinker 1991, among others). Hare *et al.* are able to falsify this hypothesis by demonstrating in two different tasks that subjects respond to regular Past tense words in English according to their frequency of use. Their experiments involve homophones in which one word is a regular Past tense form. The first experiment demonstrates that when subjects are asked to write down the word that they heard there is a strong tendency to write the most frequent of the two homophones, even if that is a regular Past tense form. In the second experiment homophones were used for primes in a lexical decision task. The results showed that if the Past tense member of the homophone pair was more frequent, priming effects on the base verb were evident, but if the non-verb homophone was more frequent, reaction times were slower. These experiments show that regular Past tense verbs in English can accrue lexical strength and thus must have a mental representation.

If regular morphologically complex words can be stored in memory even though they are derivable by regular rules, then there is no reason to suppose that lexicon and grammar are separate from one another (Bybee 1998; Hopper 1987; Langacker 1987; Sinclair 1992). Furthermore, the argument can be taken to a higher level: sequences of words that are frequently used can be represented mentally by the same principle.

4.5 Retention of conservative properties in high frequency units

Hooper 1976 pointed out a paradox in the lexical diffusion of sound change versus analogical change: sound change affects high frequency items first, while analogical change affects low frequency items first. This difference reflects distinct motivations and cognitive mechanisms for the two types of change. High frequency words are in the forefront of phonetic reduction because their frequent use exposes them to reductive processes and their reduction reflects their predictability in discourse (see section 4.1); high frequency forms resist analogical change, such as regularization of irregulars, because their frequency makes them easy to access whole and there is no need to re-form them by regular rule. One of the difficulties in the articulation of this theory of lexical diffusion lies in the specification of the set of changes that proceed from low frequency to high frequency items. In this volume, Phillips proposes that the defining characteristic of such changes is their base in lexical analysis, or the analysis of other forms. Thus when *wept* is replaced by *weeped* it is because of a pattern extracted from the analysis of other forms. Phillips' study contains several examples of word-level changes that proceed in this manner. Since high frequency irregulars are highly entrenched and easily accessible, they are the last to undergo such changes. This pattern of lexical diffusion explains why irregularity is situated in the high frequency paradigms of a language.

To our knowledge, the most comprehensive study of the effects of frequency on the maintenance of morphological irregularity is found in the paper by Corbett *et al.* in this volume. These authors examine and classify all the irregularities found in Russian noun paradigms and count the token frequency of the forms with these irregularities in the one-million-word Uppsala corpus. Their results show a consistently strong association of high token frequency with irregularities in the plural forms of the noun paradigms. They also test the hypothesis that irregularity will be found in plurals which have a high frequency relative to their singulars, but the support for this hypothesis in their data is much weaker. It appears that it is not so much paradigmatic relations as pure token frequency that allows irregularity to be maintained.

For linguistic theory the major consequence of the finding that high frequency units are resistant to reformation on the basis of productive patterns is that the resistant units must have storage in memory in order to resist change and in order to be affected by frequency of use. For irregular nouns and verbs this proposition is not very controversial, since most linguists would now agree that irregular forms have lexical listing. However, the same argument is applicable to syntactic or multi-word units, which also maintain irregular or conservative patterns when of high frequency. The resulting implication that high frequency phrases are stored in memory radically changes our notions of the way syntax operates (Bybee and Thompson 1997).

Smith's study in this volume shows that the maintenance of the *be* auxiliary for the resultative/perfect in English occurred only with the most frequent verbs used in this tense. As the *have* auxiliary generalized to more and more verbs, it worked from the least frequent to the most frequent, leaving only *is gone* in Present Day English. Thus the generalization of the *have* auxiliary worked like a regularization process; in order for the high frequency combinations to resist regularization, phrases such as *is come, is gone*, etc. had to have been stored in memory and accessed as units. Bybee's study of French liaison also finds the liaison alternations maintained only in the most frequent constructions, as mentioned above. The loss of liaison is the result of a 'regularization' or the generalization of the construction which does not contain the liaison consonant.

Thus evidence for the storage of auxiliary + verb, determiner + noun, clitic pronoun + verb, and adjective + noun are found in these studies. Poplack's study extends the reach of the storage of specific constructions and phrases even further. Her study of the maintenance of the Subjunctive in Canadian French shows that very specific lexical dependencies can reach across traditional clause boundaries. Only certain high frequency matrix verbs and embedded verbs create the conditions for the appearance of the Subjunctive, suggesting that very specific constructions replete with particular lexical material are accessed to produce the Subjunctive.

4.6 Stochastic grammar

Grammatical generalizations are at their very base variable and probabilistic in nature and derived from the user's experience with language (Pierrehumbert 1994a). Probabilistic knowledge of variation ranges from phonetic detail to word structure to morphosyntactic patterns. Pierrehumbert in this volume demonstrates how phonetic variation can be built into a stochastic grammar.

Frisch *et al.* take up the topic of word structure or phonotactic patterns. Recent research into word and syllable structure has shown that speakers' judgements of acceptability for nonce words corresponds closely to the frequency of those structures in the existing lexicon (Pierrehumbert 1994b; Vitevitch *et al.* 1997). Thus the phonotactic patterns in the lexicon turn out to be good testing ground for the nature of linguistic generalizations. Frisch *et al.* pursue this line of investigation of phonotactic patterns in English and Arabic. They find evidence that subjects use generalizations about existing words at varying levels of abstraction. Their results indicate that subjects used knowledge of natural classes, particularly in making judgements about consonant sequences in Arabic, and that they also used comparison to particular existing words if the nonce word was highly similar to an existing word. Of considerable interest also is their finding for English-speaking subjects, that experience with language changes intuitive judgements: subjects with larger vocabularies judged low probability words as more acceptable than did subjects with smaller vocabularies. Boyland's study also suggests that speaker's intuition and usage can change over time due to exposure to different patterns.

Poplack (this volume) demonstrates that in some cases variability can be quite stable over long periods of time. Her study indicates that morphosyntactic constructions are not in a simple one-to-one relationship with pragmatic or semantic function, but rather that variant constructions for the same function can alternate freely and this variation can be maintained over a long period of time.

In the view of these authors and others in this volume, grammar is not fixed and absolute with a little variation sprinkled on the top, but it is variable and probabilistic to its very core. Patterns of usage and particular choices made by speakers at any given moment are heavily influenced by both immediate and long range experience with language. Intuitions about grammaticality are based on this experience. An utterance is judged as grammatical if it is highly similar to other frequently heard utterances; if an utterance has a part which bears no resemblance to any previously experienced constructions or fixed phrases, it will be judged to be ungrammatical. Clearly, the criteria for such comparisons with past experience are individual, inexact, and scarcely amenable to treatment in terms of precise objective categories.

5. Conclusion

The study of frequency effects in language has important implications for the goals of linguistics. Among other things, it raises the challenging question of how linguists are led to impute structure to any sequence of forms if not on the grounds of their prominence in usage and memory, that is, their usefulness in discourse reflected in their frequency. In other words, what are the alternatives to frequency as an explanation for structure and regularity in language?

One well-known answer to this question involves "intuition," the introspective sense that a sequence conforms to an internalized grammar. But even intuitions could be based on the user's experience with language rather than on an abstract grammar autonomous from language function and use. The dominant paradigms of linguistics assume some such pre-existent holistic grammar as the most important prerequisite for communication. But, as Roy Harris (1990 [1978]: 149) pointed out in his inaugural lecture for the Chair of General Linguistics at Oxford University, such an assumption is suspect on several grounds, in the first place because it is radically at odds with all other forms of social experience. We do not communicate through reference to prior fixed abstract forms, but rather ". . . we create language as we go, both as individuals and as communities, just as we create our social structures, and our forms of artistic expression, our moral values, and everything else in the great complex we call civilisation." Harris calls for ". . . [a movement] away from a study based on the hypothesis of fixed monolithic structures called "languages" which somehow exist independently of whether or how they are brought into use" (Harris 1990 [1978]): 150), and in its place appeals for ". . . a science in which a language is envisaged, not as something which exists as a system over and above the communication situations in which it is manifested, but as a cumulative product of such situations which can be variously exploited to provide a basis for their subsequent renewal."

In Harris' "integrational linguistics" (see Toolan 1996 and Wolf ed. 2000 for extended discussion), language would be studied not as a distinct and separately apprehended "segregated" entity but as an activity blended with the nexus of other activities that form part of communicative situations such as chatting or interviewing. On the one hand, the papers in the present volume may be said to constitute a step in this direction. As a body they support Harris' view of structure as a product rather than a prerequisite of communication. On the other hand, the papers are virtually unanimous in emphasizing the *individual* speaker, focusing on solitary linguistic behavior and cognitive capacities with only fleeting references to the complex of communal experiences which make utterances possible in the first place. But as some of the papers hint, frequency and emergent structure involve more than unmediated linguistic behavior. Situations and their participants are also repetitive phenomena, and linguistic routinization is ultimately inseparable from cultural practices in general. In this respect while these papers retain a link with the standard assumptions of linguistics, they at the same time suggest a basis and a direction for future research.

Notes

1. It is not the case that sound changes divide neatly into those that evince lexical diffusion and those that apply across the board (the Neogrammarian changes) as proposed by Labov 1981 (see Phillips 1984). Nor is it the case that lexical diffusion of phonetically-motivated change is a type of analogy as claimed by Kiparsky 1995 (see Phillips, 1998).

References

Ashby, William. 1977. *Clitic inflection in French: A historical perspective.* Amsterdam: Editions Rodopi NV.

Bally, C. 1966 [1932]. *Linguistique générale et linguistique française*. Fourth Edition. [First published in 1932] Bern: Francke.

Bauche, Henri. 1928. *Le langage populaire. Grammaire, syntaxe, et dictionnaire du français tel qu'on le parle dans le peuple de Paris, avec tous les termes d'argot usuel*. Paris: Payot.

Boyland, Joyce Tang. 1996. *Morphosyntactic Change in Progress: A Psycholinguistic Approach*. Dissertation: Linguistics Department, University of California.

Browman, Catherine P. and Louis M. Goldstein. 1992. Articulatory phonology: an overview. *Phonetica* 49: 155–80.

Bybee, Joan L. 1985. *Morphology: A study of the relation between meaning and form*. Philadelphia: Benjamins.

Bybee, Joan L. 1998. The emergent lexicon. CLS 34.2: *The Panels*. 421–35.

Bybee, Joan. 2000a. Lexicalization of sound change and alternating environments. In *Laboratory V: Language Acquisition and the Lexicon*, Michael Broe and Janet Pierrehumbert (eds.), 250–68. Cambridge: Cambridge University Press.

Bybee, Joan L. 2000b. The phonology of the lexicon: Evidence from lexical diffusion. In *Usage- Based Models of Language*, M. Barlow and S. Kemmer (eds.), 65–85. Stanford: CSLI.

Bybee, Joan. To appear. *Phonology and Language Use*. Cambridge University Press.

Bybee, Joan, Revere Perkins, and William Pagliuca. 1994. *The Evolution of Grammar: Tense, Aspect and Modality in the Languages of the World*. Chicago: University of Chicago Press.

Bybee, Joan, and Joanne Scheibman. 1999. The effect of usage on degree of constituency: the reduction of *don't* in American English. *Linguistics* 37.575- 596.

Bybee, Joan and Sandra Thompson. 1997. Three frequency effects in syntax. BLS 23.65–85.

Chomsky, Noam. 1965. *Aspects of the Theory of Syntax*. Cambridge, Mass: MIT Press.

Coseriu, Eugenio. 1974. *Synchronie, Diachronie und Geschichte* (trans. Helga Sohre). Munich: Fink. ((=International library of general linguistics 3) (*Sinchronía, diachronía y historia; el problema del cambio lingüístico*. Montevideo: Impresora Cordon 1958).

Croft, William. 1995. Intonation units and grammatical structure. *Linguistics* 33.839–82.

DuBois, John. 1985. Competing motivations. *Iconicity in syntax*, John Haiman (ed.), 343–65. Amsterdam: John Benjamins.

Fidelholtz, James L. 1975. Word frequency and vowel reduction in English. CLS 11.

Fowler, Carol A., and Jonathan Housum. 1987. Talkers' signaling of "new" and "old" words in speech and listeners' perception and use of the distinction. *Journal of Memory and Language* 26: 489–504.

Giddens, Anthony. 1977. *Sudies in Social and Political Theory*. London: Hutchinson.

Giddens, Anthony. 1984. *The Constitution of Society: Outline of the Theory of Structuration*. Cambridge: Polity Press.

Givón, T. 1979. *On Understanding Grammar*. New York: Academic Press.

Givón, T. 1983. Introduction to Topic Continuity. In *Topic Continuity in Discourse: A Quantitative Cross-Language Study*, T. Givón (ed.). Amsterdam: John Benjamins. (TSL 3).

Givón, T. (ed) 1983. *Topic Continuity in Discourse: A Quantitative Cross-Language Study*. Amsterdam: John Benjamins. (TSL 3)

Greenberg, Joseph H. 1966. *Language Universals*. The Hague: Mouton.

Gregory, Michelle, William D. Raymond, Alan Bell, Eric Fosler-Lussier and Daniel Jurafsky. 1999. The effects of collocational strength and contextual predictability in lexical production. CLS 35.

Haiman, John. 1994. Ritualization and the development of language. In *Perspectives on grammaticalization*, William Pagliuca (ed.), 3–28. Amsterdam: John Benjamins.

Harris, Roy. 1978. *Communication and Language*. Oxford University Press. Reprinted in *The Foundations of Linguistic Theory. Selected Writings of Roy Harris*, Nigel Love (ed.) 1990, 136–50. London: Routledge.

Hooper, Joan B. 1976. Word frequency in lexical diffusion and the source of morphophonological change. In *Current Progress in Historical Linguistics*, W. Christie (ed.), 96–105. Amsterdam: North Holland.

Hooper, Joan Bybee. 1981. The empirical determination of phonological representations. In *The Cognitive Representation of Speech* Terry Myers, John Laver, and John M. Anderson (eds.), 347–57. Amsterdam: North Holland.

Hopper, Paul J. 1979. Aspect and foregrounding in discourse. In *Discourse and Syntax*, T. Givón (ed.). New York: Academic Press, 213–41.

Hopper, Paul J. 1987. Emergent grammar. BLS 13: 139–57.

Hopper, Paul J. 1988. Emergent Grammar and the A Priori Grammar Postulate. In *Linguistics in Context*, D. Tannen, (ed.), 117–34. (Collected General Lectures from the 1985 LSA Linguistics Institute, Georgetown University.) Ablex Corp.

Hopper, Paul J. 1991. Dispersed verbal predicates in vernacular written narrative. BLS 17. 402–13.

Hopper, Paul J. 1997. Discourse and the category Verb in English. *Language and Communication. Special Issue: The Importance of Theory in Discourse Analysis*. Vol. 17.2: 93–102.

Hopper, Paul J. 1998. Emergent Grammar. In *The New Psychology of Language: Cognitive and Functional Approaches to Language Structure*, Michael Tomasello (ed.), 155–75. Mahwah, NJ/London: Lawrence Erlbaum Associates.

Hopper, Paul J. and Sandra A. Thompson. 1980. Transitivity in grammar and discourse. *Language* 56: 251–99.

Hopper, Paul, and Sandra Thompson. 1984. The discourse basis for lexical categories in universal grammar. *Language* 60: 703–52.

Johnson, Keith. 1997. Speech perception without speaker normalization. In *Talker variability in speech processing*, Keith Johnson and John W. Mullennix (eds.), 145–65. San Diego: Academic Press.

Kelly, Michael H. and Susanne Martin. 1994. Domain-general abilities applied to domain-specific tasks: Sensitivity to probabilities in perception, cognition and language. *Lingua* 92: 105–40.

Kiparsky, Paul. 1995. The phonological basis of sound change. In *The Handbook of Phonological Theory*, John A. Goldsmith (ed.), 640–70. Oxford: Basil Blackwell.

Krug, Manfred. 1998. String frequency: a cognitive motivating factor in coalescence, language processing and linguistic change. *Journal of English Linguistics* 26: 286–320.

Labov, William. 1981. Resolving the Neogrammarian controversy. *Language* 57: 267–308.

Lambrecht, Knud. 1981. *Topic, antitopic and verb agreement in Nonstandard French*. Amsterdam: Benjamins.

Langacker, Ronald. 1987. *Foundations of cognitive grammar, Vol. 1. Theoretical prerequisites*. Stanford: Stanford University Press.

Lieven, Elena, Julian M. Pine and Gillian Baldwin. 1997. Lexically-based learning and early grammatical development. *Journal of Child Language* 24.187–219.

MacWhinney, Brian. 1978. *The acquisition of morphophonology*. Monographs of the Society for Research in Child Development, no. 174, vol. 43.

Miller, George A. 1965. Introduction. In George K. Zipf, *The Psycho-Biology of Language*, i–x. Cambridge: The MIT Press.

Moonwomon, Birch. 1992. The mechanism of lexical diffusion. Paper presented at the Annual Meeting of the Linguistic Society of America, January 1992, Philadelphia.

Mowrey, Richard, and William Pagliuca. 1995. The reductive character of articulatory evolution. *Rivista di Linguistica* 7(1): 37–124.

Ochs, Elinor, Emanuel A. Schegloff, and Sandra A. Thompson, 1996. *Introduction*. Ochs et al., eds., 1–51.

Ochs, Elinor, Emanuel A. Schegloff, and Sandra A. Thompson, eds., 1996. *Interaction and Grammar*. Cambridge: Cambridge University Press. (Studies in Interactional Sociolinguistics 13)

Ono, Tsuyoshi and Sandra A. Thompson. 1994. Unattached NPs in English conversation. BLS 20.

Phillips, Betty S. 1998. Lexical diffusion is NOT lexical analogy. *Word* 49.369–81.

Pierrehumbert, Janet. 1994a. Knowledge of variation. *Papers from the Parasession on Variation*, 30th Meeting of the Chicago Linguistic Society, CLS 30.232–56.

Pierrehumbert, Janet. 1994b. Syllable structure and word structure: a study of triconsonantal clusters in English. In Patricia Keating, ed., *Phonological Structure and Phonetic Form: Papers in Laboratory Phonology III*, 168–90. Cambridge: Cambridge University Press.

Renouf, A. and John McH. Sinclair. 1991. Collocational frameworks in English. In *English Corpus Linguistics*, K. Aijmer and B. Altenberg (eds.), 128–44. London: Longman.

Rumelhart, D. and McClelland, J. 1986. On learning the past tenses of English verbs: Implicit rules or parallel distributed processing? In *Parallel distributed processing: Explorations in the microstructure of cognition*, J. McClelland, D. Rumelhart, and the PDP Research Group (eds.). Cambridge, MA: MIT Press.

Saussure, Ferdinand de. 1916. *Cours de linguistique général*. Paris: Payot.

Scheibman, Joanne. 2000. *Structural Patterns of Subjectivity in American English Conversation*. Doctoral Dissertation. Albuquerque: Department of Linguistics, University of New Mexico.

Schuchardt, Hugo. 1885. Über die Lautgesetze: Gegen die Junggrammatiker. [Translated in: *Schuchardt, the Neogrammarians and the transformational theory of phonological change*, Theo Vennemann and Terence Wilbur (eds.) 39–72. Frankfurt: Athenäum, 1972.]

Sinclair, John McH. 1991. *Corpus, Concordance, Collocation*. Oxford: Oxford University Press.

Sinclair, John McH. 1992. Trust the text. In M. Davies and L. Ravelli (eds.) *Advances in Systemic Linguistics*, 5–19. London: Pinter.

Stubbs, Michael. 1996. *Text and Corpus Analysis*. Oxford: Blackwell.

Toolan, Michael. 1996. *Total Speech: An Integrational Linguistic Approach to Language*. Durham and London: Duke University Press.

Traugott, Elizabeth. 1989. On the rise of epistemic meanings in English: An example of subjectification in semantic change. *Language* 65:31–55.

Traugott, Elizabeth, and Ekkehard Koenig. 1991. The semantics-pragmatics of grammaticalization revisited. In E. Traugott and B. Heine (eds) *Approaches to Grammaticalization, vol. I*, 189–218. Amsterdam: John Benjamins.

Vitevitch, Michael S., Paul A. Luce, Jan Charles-Luce, and David Kemmerer. 1997. Phonotactics and syllable stress: implications for the processing of spoken nonsense words. *Language and Speech* 40: 47–62.

Wolf, George (ed.) 1999. *Special Issue on Integrational Linguistics in the Context of 20th Century Theories of Language. Language and Communication* 19,1. Oxford: Pergamon Press.

Wray, Alison, and Michael R. Perkins. 2000. The functions of formulaic language: an integrated model. *Language and Communication* 20,1:2000, 1–28.

Zipf, George K. 1965. *The Psycho-Biology of Language: An Introduction to Dynamic Philology*. Cambridge, Mass.: The MIT Press. (First published in 1935 by Houghton Mifflin.)

Part I:
Patterns of Use

Transitivity, clause structure, and argument structure: Evidence from conversation*

SANDRA A. THOMPSON and PAUL J. HOPPER

*University of California, Santa Barbara
and Carnegie-Mellon University*

1. Introduction

The nature of the transitivity relationship in a clause and its possible role in communication has intrigued linguists for much of the last three decades. The data base for the study of transitivity, however, has largely been restricted to two sources: constructed sentences and spoken or written narratives. There has been almost no study of how transitive clauses function in spontaneous conversation. Yet conversation is arguably the most basic of all genres (Schegloff 1993, 1996a, 1996b). Bakhtin (1986) regarded it as the primary genre from which all other genres were derived; and Swales (1990) goes so far as to term conversation 'pre-generic', exempt from assignment to any genre. As such, we might expect to find that conversation yields important insights into the discourse correlates of the grammar of transitivity.

This paper has two related aims. First, we would like to argue that conversation, at least in English, is very low in transitivity. In terms of a number of measures of frequency, the role of transitive clauses in everyday conversation is surprisingly small. Second, we would like to show that a close examination of the issues that arise in trying to quantify the transitivity of the clauses in conversational discourse has serious implications for our understanding of the grammar of clauses. We will be especially concerned with what conversational data contribute to our view of transitivity and clause structure, especially what is known as 'argument structure'—the grammar of the verb and its arguments. We will furthermore show how our findings support Hopper's claim that 'the more useful a construction is, the more it will tend to become structuralized, in the sense of achieving cross-textual consistency, and serving as a basis for variation and extension' (1987: 150).

2. Methodological preliminaries

2.1 Scalar transitivity revisited

In Hopper and Thompson (1980), we proposed that many grammatical facts from languages around the world could be accounted for if transitivity were viewed as a continuum. We further provided evidence to support the claim that clauses of relatively high transitivity characterize foreground, as opposed to background, portions of a narrative. In arguing that transitivity is composite and that it is a matter of the grammar of the entire clause, rather than just the relationship between a verb and its object, we introduced ten *component parameters* of transitivity (Hopper and Thompson (1980: 252). From here on, we will use the term Transitivity with a capital T to designate the composite, scalar understanding of this notion as it was introduced in that paper. For each of these Transitivity parameters, a clause could be marked with any number of scalar values. In Table 1 we reprise these parameters, with values 'high' and 'low' as in our original paper.

2.2 The database

We will appeal to these parameters as our argument unfolds. As suggested in our introduction, according to a range of frequency measures, our data show that English conversation is low in Transitivity. To illustrate, we offer the following example from our database. In this excerpt, family members are discussing the type of birthday cake Kendra likes. As can be quickly observed, most of the clauses in this excerpt are very low in Transitivity in the ways outlined in Hopper and Thompson (1980).

Table 1. *The parameters of scalar transitivity (Hopper and Thompson 1980)*

	High	Low
A. Participants	2	1
B. Kinesis	action	non-action
C. Aspect	telic	atelic
D. Punctuality	punctual	non-punctual
E. Volitionality	volitional	non-volitional
F. Affirmation	affirmative	negative
G. Mode	realis	irrealis
H. Agency	A high in potency	A low in potency
I. Affectedness of O	O highly affected	O not affected
J. Individuation of O	O highly individuated	O not individuated

(1) The following transcription conventions are seen (Du Bois *et al.* 1993):

square brackets: overlap
=: length
@: laughter
each line is one prosodic unit

KENDRA: It's a beautiful cake,
                but why do you guys always give me ice cream cakes.
KEVIN: . . . Because [it's the only kind we're not] [allergic to].
MARCI: [Don't you like ice cream]?
KENDRA: [I don't like ice
                                                                           crea=m].

WENDY: . . . Do you like . . frozen yogurt?
KENDRA: . . . I shouldn't blow this out.
      ..
WENDY: Do you like frozen yogurt cakes?
                . . . You don't.
KENDRA: . . . [I don't like]—
KEVIN: [Do you like] shrimp cake?
KEVIN: [Hm].
WENDY: [Do you] like rice cakes?
MARCI: I can give you a rice cake,
                with cheddar on it,
                if you'd like that,
                . . tonight.
KENDRA: I don't want to hur=t you=,
                I mean I like—
                . . Ice [cream's okay],
WENDY: [Well,]
MARCI: [I didn't n-]—
WENDY: we're all [. . just]—
MARCI: You've   [never] told us what you like and don't like,
                [dear,]
KEVIN: [I guess that would be=,
MARCI: you just go off to your roo[=m].
KENDRA: [I think] [I walk around
                all the ti=me],
KEVIN: [your] [fault,
                then].

KENDRA: saying,
　　　　I hate ice cream.
　　　　I hate ice cream.
　　　　It makes me too cold.
KEVIN:　Never.
KENDRA: Ask Kelli.
　　　. . . Call up Kelli right now and ask her.

The intuitive sense that the language of everyday conversation is 'intransitive', as illustrated by this excerpt, is supported by empirical evidence, which we will present in the rest of this section.

Our database consists of 446 clauses from three face-to-face multi-party conversations among friends and family members in American English.[1] All the speakers are relatively well-educated middle-class Caucasian Americans. These clauses were transcribed and coded for a range of Transitivity features, as described below.

2.3 Coding for clause

We begin arguing for our claim that Transitivity in everyday conversation is very low by making explicit how we coded our data. We counted as clauses the following four types of utterances containing a predicate.

2.3.1 All simple clauses were counted as 'clauses'
Examples are:

(2)　*she was there with the baby*
　　 you drove all over Denver

2.3.2 All clauses traditionally viewed as subordinate in English except infinitival complements were counted as 'clauses'
This included the following clause types, with the relevant clauses boldfaced:

• complement clauses (though see 2.3.4 just below)

(3)　*he intimated **that there had been some kind of a business deal***
(4)　*she didn't know **it was from me***

• adverbial clauses

(5)　***because Maureen was visiting***

• relative clauses

(6) *the coffee house chain **that's going to take over the city***

2.3.3 Elliptical clauses following full-fledged clauses were counted as full clauses
There were very few of these in the database; one example is:

(7) A. *I heard Ray howling the blues*
     B. *you did?*

2.3.4 We made a special coding decision about sentences which have traditionally been considered as taking a clausal complement.
As we noted just above, complement clauses were counted as 'clauses'. But they were not counted as participants in the larger sentence of which they are a part. What this means is that a complement clause as in the boldfaced portion of (8) was not counted as an object of a main clause verb *wonder*:

(8) *I was wondering **why I hadn't heard from him***

This is because we take expressions such as *I was wondering* as markers of epistemicity and evidentiality (Thompson and Mulac 1991a, b) and not as main clauses with complement-taking predicates and object complements (as described in Noonan 1985). Thus in (8), our coding system would count *wonder* as a one-participant epistemic/evidential verb, whose one participant is *I*, the whole expression projecting more to come, and thus serving as an epistemic/evidential introducer for the following material. Our coding system would count *why I hadn't heard from him* as a clause (see further discussion of epistemic/evidential expressions below in Section 3.3.3).[2]

We do not have space here to present all the evidence in favor of this claim.[3] This evidence includes the facts that in conversational discourse:

1. most apparently complement-taking predicates do not also occur with NP arguments;
2. most apparent complements occur without complementizers, especially the most frequent ones (see Thompson and Mulac 1991a, b);
3. the most frequent apparently complement-taking predicates reveal phonological and grammatical properties of epistemic and evidential introducers.[4]

Though this coding decision is a departure from Hopper and Thompson (1980), we feel it is a well-justified decision; in any case, since clauses with complements would be very low in Transitivity even if they were counted as 'objects', this decision does not lower the overall Transitivity very much.

3. Findings

In this section we will present our evidence that the clauses in conversational English are low in Transitivity. We will do this by considering a range of measures, and we will address each of the Transitivity parameters.

3.1 Number of participants

We will start with the first transitivity parameter, number of participants, since having two or more participants is central to the traditional notion of Transitivity. If the majority of the clauses in conversation turn out to have two or more participants, then on those grounds alone our claim that conversation is low in Transitivity would be seriously jeopardized.

How many clauses in the database even have two or more participants? Table 2 gives the answer to this question.

Table 2. *Frequency of one-partici-pant and two-participant clauses*

Two participants		One participant	
No.	%	No.	%
121	27	325	73

Table 2 shows that only 27% (121/446) of the clauses in the conversational data have two or more participants. Here are three examples:

(9) a. *I saw **her** at Scott's*
     b. *he told **me** about her*
     c. *yeah **they** put **their** flyer up in phone booths*

The fact, then, that the majority of the clauses in conversation do *not* turn out to have two or more participants provides initial support for our claim that conversation is low in Transitivity.

3.2 Two-participant clauses

The next question we asked was: how high is the Transitivity in these two participant-clauses? Our counts show that even among these 121 two-participant clauses, the Transitivity is low. To support this claim, we consider several Transitivity parameters. A table summarizing our findings is given at the end of this section; here we will discuss each one in turn, though not necessarily in the order shown in Table 1 above.

3.2.1 No High Transitivity clauses

Our first piece of evidence supporting our claim that our conversational database is low in Transitivity is the fact that we found no clauses that could be coded as 'High' for each of the ten Transitivity parameters. The two which come the closest are these:

(10) a. *I sent her a tape of you talking*
      b. *she sent it*

Each of these clauses has two participants, a (human) A, which is high in potency, and an individuated and affected O. Each contains a volitional telic action verb which is affirmative and realis. But they fail on the parameter of punctuality, since 'sending' involves a series of actions that are distributed over time.

So the first point to notice is that there are no clauses of 100 per cent High Transitivity.

3.2.2 V-O compounds

Before discussing the rest of the Transitivity parameters, we wish to note a prominent feature of the grammar of English conversation: V-O compounds. We use the term 'V-O compounds' to refer loosely to combinations of verb plus lexical noun in which one or more of the following features is found:

1. the combination is lexicalized
2. the O is non-referential
3. the V is 'light' or 'low-content' (Chafe 1994)

V-O compounds are rampant in English conversation and have been discussed by a number of grammarians. Typical examples from our database are:

(11) a. *I'll have fun*
      b. *they uh just had a gig at Starbucks*
      c. *your clues make no sense*
      d. *I need to get sleep over the weekend*
      e. *Scott's making some good bucks*
      f. *we gotta get a picture.*
      g. *which is all we have time for*
      h. *wait a minute*
      i. *he has a green card*

These V-O compounds are low in Transitivity because it is difficult to maintain that O is individuated or affected. In fact, for clauses with V-O compounds, it is not clear whether they should even be considered two-participant clauses at all. Thus in (12), we can inquire whether *have fun* is a one-participant intransitive predicate or whether *fun* is the object of transitive *have*:

(12) *I'll **have fun***

For this project, as in Hopper and Thompson (1980), we counted these V-O compounds as 'two-participant' clauses in an effort to be as conservative as possible and to bias against our hypothesis that the degree of Transitivity in our data is low. If we hadn't counted them as two-participant clauses, the number of two-participant clauses would have gone down from 27% to 22%, as 21, or 18%, of the two-participant clauses contain V-O compounds. That is, counting V-O compounds one-participant predicates would have resulted in the figures shown in Table 3.

Table 3. *Frequency of one-participant and two-participant clauses, counting V-O compound clauses as one-participant clauses*

Two participants	One participant
No. %	No. %
100 22	346 78

3.2.3 Kinesis

The second Transitivity parameter is Kinesis, whether or not a predicate names a physical action. The number of predicates that could be argued to name an action in our conversational data is remarkably small. There are 17 predicates, all of which are two-participant verbs. Here are some of the clearest candidates:

(13) *just don't **open your mouth***
       ***shut your eyeballs** (said in jest (this expression from Walt Kelly's 'Pogo' comics) to someone about to receive a surprise birthday present)*

Among the less clear candidates are verbs naming a non-Punctual action which is distributed over time (see 3.2.5 just below), as in:

(14) a. *and they **sold that** (referent is 'car')*
       b. *and **bought two others** (referent is 'cars')*
       c. *K **sent you a taped letter**?*
       d. *I'll just **take my gifts** up to my room, and **open** 'em by myself*

Including even these questionable instances, the number of predicates which could count as high in Kinesis is still very small: 14% of the two-participant clauses. Interestingly, among the 17 action predicates, 12, or 71%, are what we could call 'irrealis', that is, not reporting an event that happened in the past or is currently happening. The examples in (13) above illustrate the 'irrealis' predicates, being future and imperative, while those in (14) illlustrate the 'realis' ones.

What our data show about Kinesis, then, is that

1. kinetic action predicates are rare in our database;
2. in conversation, even kinetic action predicates tend to be low in Transitivity in another respect, either Mode (by being irrealis (Transitivity parameter G)) or Punctuality (by being non-punctual (parameter D)).

3.2.4 Aspect
Another strong measure of the Transitivity of the clauses in our database is that of Aspect. Following Hopper and Thompson (1980), we defined Aspect in semantic rather than morphological terms; thus a clause coded as High for Aspect would be a Telic one, a completed action with an O that is bounded, as in:

(15) a. *he **called me** like eleven o'clock in the morning*
     b. *she **brought that up***

A clause coded as Low for Aspect would be Atelic, i.e., not a completed action with a bounded O, as in:

(16) a. *when he **needed something***
     b. *they **send in their money***

Only 17, or 14%, of the two-participant clauses are Telic. Or, to put it the other way around, most of the two-participant clauses (104, or 86%) are Atelic.

3.2.5 Punctuality
A Punctual event, as described by Hopper and Thompson (1980), has no transitional phase between its inception and its completion. Examples of clauses expressing punctual events in our data include:

(17) *I **saw** her at Scott's*
     ***shut** your eyeballs*
     *just don't **open** your mouth*

In our data, these are the only three clauses expressing Punctual events (0.6% of all the clauses). Examples of non-Punctual two-participant events include:

(18) *he's **had** a couple of engagments*
     *it **sounds** like that*
     *I'd **throw** Kendi **off the trail** (metaphorical)*

So only 0.6% of the two-participant clauses express Punctual events; that is, 99.4% of them express non-Punctual events.

3.2.6 Affectedness of O
The O in most two-participant clauses (101, or 84%) is not affected. Here are two examples of highly affected O:

(19) *can you hand me **a toothpick**?*
       *just don't open **your mouth***

And here are two examples of the much more frequent pattern, where O is not affected:

(20) *I hadn't even seen **her**, for a year*
       *they've known **each other** for . . .*
       *I may have misheard **him***
       *don't you remember **that**?*

3.2.7 Other transitivity parameters
We do not report the figures for Parameter F, 'Affirmation', since this Parameter has not been shown to correlate strongly with other measures of Transitivity.

For three of the other four Parameters listed in Table 1, the clauses in our database are divided about evenly between 'High' and 'Low'; these are:

E. Volitionality (is A volitional?)
G. Mode
J. Individuation of O

That is, about half of the 121 two-participant clauses are high in Volitionality of A (Parameter E). This is because volitional activities (E) are named in about half the two-participant clauses (though overwhelmingly in non-telic or non-punctual frames (see the discussion in 3.2.4. and 3.2.5. above). About 70% of the two-participant clauses are high in Mode (that is, they are 'realis' (Parameter G)). Finally, about half of them are high in Individuation of O (Parameter J), because pronominal Os, which are high in Individuation, are relatively frequent, as in the following examples:

(21) *you can barely see **it***
       *I still have **it** in there*

For the final Transitivity Parameter, namely H., Agency (is A 'potent'), the A's in the two-participant clauses in our database are overwhelmingly human (96/99, or 97%, of expressed A's), so these clauses are all high in 'Agency of A', as defined in Hopper and Thompson (1980), as we would expect.

3.2.8 Interim summary
Table 4 summarizes the results of our investigation of Transitivity Parameters for the minority two-participant clauses in our database.

Table 4. *Low transitivity of two-participant clauses*

'V-O compounds'	18 %
Kinesis: Non-action	86%
Aspect: Atelic	86 %
Punctuality: Non-punctual	98 %
Affectedness: Non-affected O	84 %
Mode: Non-irrealis	70%
Individuation: Non-individuated O	55 %
Volitionality: Non-volitional A	50%
Agency: Potent A	97 %

What we have shown so far, then, is that clauses with 2 Participants are rare in conversation (27%), as represented by our database, and that these are low in Transitivity by a range of measures.

3.3 One-participant clauses

What, then, of the majority of clauses in our conversational database? What kinds of clauses are the 325 one-participant clauses that make up 73% of the database? And what can we learn about grammar by looking at these one-participant clauses?

   Our most revealing finding is that 89% of the one-participant clauses fall into three big groups:

1. Verbal predicates with one participant
2. Copular clauses
3. Epistemic/Evidential Clauses

We will briefly discuss and exemplify each of these.[5]

3.3.1 Verbal predicates with one participant
Approximately one third (38%) of the one-participant clauses in the database are verbal predicates with one participant, as illustrated by the boldfaced predicates in the following examples:

(22) *I've been **sleeping** 10 hours*
     *because Maureen **was visiting***
     I forgot

*they **pay** in advance*
*I don't **remember***
*I was **belly-aching***
*you guys **are supposed to go home** now*

It is intriguing that several of these predicates, such as *visit, forget*, and *remember*, may also occur with two participants in English. What is striking is that for many such verbs, the one-participant use is at least as frequent as the two-participant one. Such considerations have strong implications for the notion of argument structure, to which we will return below.

3.3.2 Copular clauses
Approximately another one third (37%) of the one-participant clauses in the database are copular clauses. That is, they have no lexical verb at all.[6] These fall into three groups:

(a) Predicate adjective clauses (almost half, or 47%, of Copular clauses)

(23) *Trish is **pregnant** again*
      *I'm **excited about it***
      *it was **confidential***

(b) Predicate nominal clauses (1/3, or 35%, of Copular clauses)

(24) *is that just **carbonated water**?*
      *that's **the whole point***
      *Ray's **his manager***

(c) Predicate oblique clauses (1/5, or 19%, of Copular clauses)

(25) *she's still **at home***
      *she's **in here** sobbing*
      *it was **from me***
      *I'd be **on pregnancy vitamins**,*
      *I think I'm **over it** faster than I would be.*

3.3.3 'Epistemic/Evidential clauses'
The final major group of one-participant clauses, accounting for 14% of all of them, are what we are calling epistemic/evidential Clauses, that is, clauses containing epistemic or evidential verbs. Recall that in our discussion of our coding system, we counted such verbs as *know, think, see, figure*, and *remember*, when followed by a clause, as one-participant epistemic/evidential clauses rather than as 'complement-taking predicates', as illustrated by (26).

(26) *I don't see* how French over the phone could be workable
   I dunno if it's worked
   I guess we are
   I remember I was talking to him regularly for a time
   I don't think it's workable
   I can't tell you whether that fear was completely off the wall

Table 5 summarizes our findings for the one-participant clauses in our database.

Table 5. *Types of one-participant clauses*

Verbal predicate clauses		38 %
Copular clauses		37 %
Predicate adjective	47 %	
Predicate nominal	35 %	
Predicate oblique	19 %	
Epistemic/evidential		14%
Other (idioms, 'dispersed predicates' (Hopper 1991, 1995a, 1997a, 1997b)		11%

3.4 Summary of Transitivity Findings for conversation

What the quantitative analysis of our English conversational database reveals is that the vast majority of clauses in English conversation are either one-participant clauses or two-participant clauses with very low Transitivity. These findings have been corroborated by conversation-based research on other languages as well (Ewing 1999 for Cirebon Javanese, Helalsvuo to appear for Finnish, Ono and Sadler ms. for Japanese, and Turk 2000 for Russian). This research shows that the most frequent kind of clause used by speakers in everyday conversational interactions is one that is low in Transitivity.

4. Argument structure

The fact that most of everyday conversational language (to extrapolate from the research on English, Finnish, Japanese, and Russian) consists of clauses of very low Transitivity has a number of implications for the study of grammar. Here we would like to turn to what we think our results suggest for argument structure, that is, the relationship between the verb and its arguments—a central issue in the study of how speakers put clauses together, itself a primary concern of all approaches to the grammar of human languages.

4.1 A brief history of argument structure

The term 'argument structure' has come to be used to refer to how many and what kind of arguments a predicate takes. 'Argument structure' is widely understood in contemporary linguistics as referring to the idea that predicates are listed in the lexicon along with their frames specifying what their obligatory and optional arguments are (Alsina 1996; Dik 1989; Dixon 1991; Dowty 1991; Fillmore 1968, 1986; de Groot 1989; Jackendoff 1990; Langacker 1987; Lazard 1994; Levin 1993; Napoli 1993; Payne 1997; Siewierska 1991; Wechsler 1995; inter alia).

For English, and possibly some other languages, this includes a listing of the alternations that a given verb can participate in, as demonstrated by Levin (1993). For example, speakers of English need to know that the verb *spray* can occur in both of the following frames (Levin 1993:51):

(27) *Jack sprayed paint on the wall*
       Jack sprayed the wall with paint

while the verb *cover* can occur in only the first of these frames:

(28) *June covered the baby with the blanket*
       *June covered the blanket over the baby

and the verb *pour* can occur in only the second of these frames:

(29) *Tamara poured water into the bowl*
       *Tamara poured the bowl with water

We would agree that these are indeed among the facts that speakers of English acquire as they learn to use their language. What we are finding, though, is that (a) such facts are a small fraction of the important facts that speakers need to learn about their language and (b) the apparent importance of such facts may be an artifact of working with idealized data. Discussions of argument structure have to date been based on fabricated examples rather than on corpora of ordinary everyday talk and can be seen as evidence of the 'written language bias' (Linell 1982) in the study of language that has been discussed in much recent literature (Hopper 1992, 1997b; Couper-Kuhlen and Selting 1996:11)

Central to discussions of argument structure has been the idea of 'valence', defined by Croft (1991:99) as 'inherent relationality'. Payne (1997: 169–70) provides a succinct characterization of 'valence', dividing it into two types.

1. 'Semantic valence' is ' the number of participants that must be 'on stage' in the scene expressed by the verb'. 'For example, the verb *eat* in English has a semantic valence of two, since . . . there must be at least an eater and an eaten thing'.

2. 'Syntactic valence' is 'the number of arguments present in any given clause'. 'For example, a given instance of the verb *eat* in English may have a syntactic valence of one or two', so that 'in *have you eaten yet*, the only argument is the eater'.

4.2 Problems with the notion of argument structure

Among the problems with approaching the study of clause grammar from the perspective of argument structure are the following: scenes, predicates with no argument structure, and indeterminate boundaries between 'one-participant' and 'two-participant' predicates.

4.2.1 Scenes
The methodology for determining semantic valence is vulnerable. The linguist introspects about imagined or conceptualized 'scenes' for verbs and who or what must be present or 'on stage' with that verb, as suggested by Payne. Langacker, in discussing the verb *find*, remarks "One cannot conceptualize the [FIND] relationship without conceptualizing the two things functioning as trajector and landmark of that relation" (Langacker 1988: 103, cit. Croft 1991: 63). But corpus-based research has identified both a range of uses and collocations of verbs as well as frequency effects that have not been addressed in the argument structure discussions based on introspection (see below and Tao 2000).

Further, the concept of 'scene' is not applicable at all to many of the predicates in our database because they do not refer to single physical events; for example:

(30) *I forgot*
      they pay in advance
      I can't stand having things in my teeth
      I think I was belly-aching
      she brought that up

Or the notion of 'scenes' may be inapplicable because there is no lexical verb, as shown in (31):

(31) *I'm **excited about it***
      *it was **confidential***
      *that's **the whole point***
      *Ray's **his manager***
      they don't come in green

Even in those instances where imagining a scene for a given verb is relatively straightforward, the scene often has little to do with the way clauses containing that verb actually occur. Two cases in point involve the verbs *remember* and *drive*. We will consider *drive* in Section 4.2.3; here we briefly illustrate our concern by reporting findings involving *remember*.

The English verb *remember* can be considered, among other things, to be a member of the class of cognitive transitive verbs which can take an ordinary noun phrase as an object, as in (32):

(32) *She remembered* **her keys**

That is, its scene involves an animate being who remembers something and an object which is remembered. However, Tao (2000), in an extensive corpus study of the actual everyday usage of the verb *remember*, finds that imagining such a scene is irrelevant to the way in which *remember* is actually used in everyday conversation. Among a number of fascinating results and of particular relevance to our point here is Tao's finding that (a) *remember* rarely takes an object and (b) the environments in which *remember* occurs are unlike those in which other members of the illusory class of cognitive verbs occur. Here is a typical environment for *remember*, from a conversation between a pair of fiancées:

(33) JEFF: **remember,**
     JILL: . . @ @ @
     JEFF: . . you're gonna spend the rest of your life with m=e.

Tao notes that in this example, the verb *remember* is used without any subject, occurs as an imperative, forms an intonation phrase of its own, and is followed by a pause. Syntactically, it is possible to analyze this example as either a verb *remember* followed by a complement clause or as a discourse particle followed by a main clause. Tao suggests that the prosody, rhythm, and pausing all support the second analysis.

Here is another typical environment for *remember*:

(34) LOIS: she probably **remem[bers]**.
     JANICE: [uh Ev] [elyn,
     EVELYN: [I don't **remember**.

In (34), the verb *remember* occurs twice. In the first instance, it has no direct object, occurs in the present tense, and finishes a turn. In the second instance, it occurs with the pronoun *I*, again has no direct object, occurs in the negative in the present tense, and finishes a turn. Tao's quantitative analysis reveals that these are among the highly recurrent properties of instances of *remember* in the data.

In sum, as illustrated by these facts about *remember* in everyday conversation, imagining 'scenes' for verbs does not appear to be a fruitful approach to determining how verbs and arguments are used by real speakers.

4.2.2 Predicates with no argument structure

Our investigation shows that many of the predicates we use in everyday talk cannot be described in terms of argument structure at all. This is because, among the clauses in our database with two participants, a number are 'dispersed verbal expressions' (Hopper 1991, 1995a, 1997a), as in (35):

(35) a. *I don't think you'll be getting much out of that one, Wendo.*
      b. *I think I'm over it faster than I would be.*
      c. *I'd be on pregnancy vitamins,*
      d. *they don't come in green.*

Many of these are lexicalized expressions (Fillmore *et al.* 1988, Pawley and Syder 1983). Some are highly lexicalized, like (35) a—(35) c; some allow 'variables', like (35) d, forming what Fillmore *et al.* call a 'lexically open idiom'. These are learned as units, they haven't been mentioned in discussions of argument structure, and they are difficult to accomodate within an approach to argument structure that is based on verbs' choosing the nouns they occur with.

4.2.3 Indeterminate boundary between 'one-participant' and 'two-participant'
      predicates
Judging from a number of recent studies of natural interactional data from a range of languages, it is hard to escape the conclusion that languages differ markedly in how clearly their predicates can be assigned to the categories of 'one-participant' and 'two-participant' predicates (Dahl 1997, Ewing 1999, Helasvuo to appear, Ono and Thompson 1997, Payne 1985, Tao 1996). In fact, not only do languages differ in this regard, but within a given language, predicates vary with respect to how clearly they specify the nouns they can occur with (see Section 4.3.2).

   Our study of predicates in English conversation suggests that the boundary between these two categories is extremely and perhaps surprisingly fluid. Most linguists are well aware of the 'labile' verbs such as *break*, *boil*, and *melt*, which can occur as either 'one-participant' or 'two-participant' predicates, as shown in these constructed examples:

(36) *I boiled the water for tea*
      The water started to boil

Although we do not question the existence of these verbs in the mental lexicon of speakers of English, we didn't find any examples of these in our conversational data. What we did find, however, which is much more troublesome for a theory of argument structure, are three other types of instances in which the assignment of 'one-participant' vs. 'two-participant' for English would be entirely arbitrary. These are instances of 'object-deletion', instances of verbal expressions with what O'Dowd (1998) has called 'P' words (those which can be analyzed as either prepositions or particles) and V-O compounds. We will discuss each of these in turn.

4.2.3.1 'Object deletion'. The example of *have you eaten yet* was used by Payne (1997) to illustrate the distinction between 'syntactic' and 'semantic' valence. *Eat* is a prototypical example of a verb which may be described as semantically 'requiring' two participants, of which one may be omitted.

Here are some instances from our database of verbs which are commonly imagined to 'take' two 'arguments', but which regularly occur without a second 'argument'.

(37) *it's time to **eat**.*
      *that's the best time to **find out**,*
      *tell me when I can **look**.*
      *you **can tell**,*
      *I'm just **checking***
      *you were **driving** through Denver*
      *and just **think**, you can use the bowl for a washtub.*

Taking an argument structure approach, one could argue that these are 'two-argument' verbs with their 'objects' 'deleted'. This is essentially equivalent to the traditional description of a 'transitive' verb 'used intransitively'. One could equally well argue that these are verbs with two argument structures, one requiring two arguments and one requiring one. As far as we can tell, there is essentially no agreement on this point among researchers; which proposal one favors depends on one's assumptions about argument structure.

We would agree with recent research that suggests that the sense of a verb or predicate is related to the grammatical schemas that it can occur in (Roland and Jurafsky to appear). For example, as Fillmore (1986) has pointed out, very often specific semantic properties accompany the 'intransitive' uses. Thus an example such as (38) has to involve drinking alcohol (not milk, Evian, or Gatorade):

(38) *they went **drinking*** (constructed example)

This research strongly supports the claim which our data also provide evidence for: that among the things speakers know about verbs is the range of forms they collocate with according to the different senses they have. And it stands to reason that the more different types of uses of language speakers are exposed to and participate in, the wider the range of options for a given verb sense they are likely to have encountered and stored. We will return to this issue below.

As is well known, some collocations involving specific verb senses develop lives of their own as general discourse or coherence markers, as have *I mean, y'know,*

I don't know, I think, and *just think* (Kärkkäinen 1998; Östman 1981; Redeker 1991; Scheibman 2000a; Schiffrin 1987; Thompson and Mulac 1991a, 1991b). Tao (2000) shows that this is also a highly persuasive account for the verb *remember*, which occurs in spoken English 24% of the time without any expressed subject and 40% of the time without an expressed object, as we illustrated in Section 4.2.1.

The case of a verb like *drive* is interesting; while *drive* can be used with a second participant, such as *a car, a tractor,* etc., most linguists would not consider that *drive* is a good example of a two-argument verb which can be used with its object 'deleted'. To the extent that they would not, we suggest that this has everything to do with frequency. Although *drive* is not frequent enough in our database for us to gather the relevant data, there are ample indications from other corpora that it is used significantly more frequently as a one-participant verb than as a two-partici- pant verb. (In the Cobuild corpus of spoken British English, only 29 of 259 in- stances of *drive* in the sense of 'drive a vehicle', or 11%, mentioned a direct object.) We suggest that it is this fact that is behind the intuition that *drive* is not basically a two-participant verb. The point is that if frequency plays a role in linguists' intu- itions about the argument structure of a given verb, it makes sense to actually look at what the frequency facts are and build a theory of clause organization around those probabilistic facts.

4.2.3.2 'P' words. There are many instances in the English data where the status of what O'Dowd (1998) calls a 'P' word is indeterminate between 'preposition' and 'particle'. Here are several examples from our database:

(39) *we all want to **play with** them*
      *she has **fit into** the mold*
      ***get on** it*
      *it **sounds like** that*
      *does it **look like** cream soda?*

The analytical question is: what is the 'verb' in such clauses? In the first example, is the 'verb' the one-participant verb *play* with a prepositional phrase or is the 'verb' the two-participant verb *play with* plus an 'object'? As O'Dowd persuasively ar- gues, the answer is both. She shows at length that the standardly cited tests will not resolve the indeterminacy, because the tests give conflicting results.

In fact, the picture is even more complex than this. Such combinations of verb and 'P' words actually fall on a continuum between clearly one-participant and clearly two-participant predicates. Examples such as ***turn off** the lights*, according to their ability to 'pass' a number of the tests referred to just above, could be placed nearer the two-participant end, but unfortunately, most of the examples in our data- base, as indicated in (39), were not nearly this clear. In the coding for our quantification of Transitivity in the first part of this paper, therefore, in the absence of clear evidence of a two-participant 'two-word verb', we coded such clauses as taking one participant.

4.2.3.3 'V-O' compounds.   Recall that in section 3.2.2., we discussed the indeterminacy of the analysis of V-O compounds, such as:

(40) *I'll have **fun***
       *making **some good bucks***
       *we gotta get **a picture.***

As we noted, once again the analytical question is: Is *have fun* an 'intransitive predicate', or is *fun* the 'object' of transitive *have*? Though we adopted a 'conservative' position for this project, counting them as instances of two-participant clauses, they are an excellent case in point for our claim here that the boundary between one-participant and two-participant predicates is very fluid in English talk-in-interaction.

To sum up this sub-section, we suggest that for English, transitivity is often indeterminate; there are many instances in real discourse where it is arbitrary whether we call a verb a 'one-participant' or 'two-participant' predicate. And in fact, in most such instances, this distinction is one for which there is no convincing usage-based evidence.

4.2.4 Summary of problems with the notion of argument structure
In this section, we have shown that there are a number of problems in analyzing conversational English data in terms of a traditional view of argument structure. Our data confirm that methodologically, an introspective approach based on imagined scenes to determine valence will miss much of what speakers are doing in their everyday conversations, and that the majority of the predicates in the data do not lend themselves to being described in terms of a distinction between those taking one vs. those taking more than one argument.

4.3 Toward a usage-based account

Here we will briefly discuss two prominent features of everyday language, as revealed in a conversational corpus, which have strong implications for a theory of how speakers put clauses together when they use everyday language to interact with each other. We will consider the fluidity of categories and what we can learn from considerations of frequency.

4.3.1 Fluidity of categories
As we have argued, the conversational data suggest a very different picture of how speakers store and use the clause-level grammatical resources available to them.

Our study of the degree of Transitivity in conversation shows that the notion of argument structure as outlined above may not be relevant for understanding how humans produce and process language.

Rather, predicate 'meanings' can only be understood as including a vast range of semantic and pragmatic associations regarding the sorts of activities, states, and participants that can invoke their use (see, for example, Aarts and Aarts 1995; Aarts and Meyer 1995; Bybee 1998, to appear; Tao 2000; and Tomasello and Brooks 1998). As pointed out by many researchers recently, including Bybee (1985, 1998, to appear) Bybee *et al.* (1994), Haiman (1994, 1998), Hopper (1987, 1988, 1998), Ono and Thompson (1995), and Weber (1997), these 'meanings' are actually generalizations from many repetitions of *hearing* predicates *used* in association with certain types of human events and situations over the course of a person's lifetime. What appears to be a fixed 'structure' is actually a set of schemas, some more 'entrenched' (Bybee 1985,1998; Langacker 1987) than others, arising out of many repetitions in daily conversational interactions. The way in which verbs and nouns come to pattern is thus an intriguing example of an adaptive self-organizing system (Du Bois 1985; Lewin 1992).

That is, as these studies show, 'argument structure' needs to be replaced by a greatly enriched probabilistic theory capturing the entire range of combinations of predicates and participants that people have stored as sorted and organized memories of what they have heard and repeated over a lifetime of language use. Such a theory, we suggest, will resemble a good unabridged dictionary much more than it will the types of statements of a given verb form's valence that are found in current discussions of argument structure. As indicated in such a dictionary, we know many things about what 'goes with' every verb in the language. And we know something about how to predict what will come after certain kinds of predicate forms (Roland and Jurafsky to appear, Trueswell *et al.* 1993). But what we know may not be stored in very neatly distinguishable categories. Thus the evidence suggests that a clause such as that in (41) may not be stored as either 'intransitive verb + prepositional phrase' or as 'transitive verb + object'; it has characteristics of both:

(41) *we all want to **play with** them*

The human brain is masterfully adept at categorizing and sorting and our data confirm the claim that grammatical categories are very much like everyday categories (Edelman 1992; Labov 1973; Lakoff 1987; Taylor 1995). Evidence for the reality of grammatical categories is abundant in the conversational data. For example, when speakers meet a new instance, they have a sense of what to do with it, in something like the way that they know they can sit in a beanbag 'chair'. They can treat a new verb, such as *e-mail*, like prototypical members of the class of verbs, and even of the subclass of verbs which participates in the 'ditransitive construction' (see 4.3.2). We argue that these categories are formed by the same kinds of processes as everyday categories are—from the constant process of cognitive sorting, distilling, and generalizing from frequent encounters in daily living.

We could say, then, that what we think of as grammar is a complex of memories we have of how our speech community has resolved communicative problems. 'Grammar' is a name for the adaptive, complex, highly interrelated, and multiply categorized sets of recurrent regularities that arise from doing the communicative work humans do. In other words, the sense of a verb or predicate is related to the lexico-grammatical schemas that it can occur in and argument structure can be seen as essentially a subset of these schemas.

4.3.2 Argument structure and frequency

As suggested above in our discussion of *drive*, there is a growing body of evidence supporting the hypothesis that what has been understood as argument structure has much to do with frequency in actual language use. The data show that how verbs collocate with nouns is not a fixed property of items in the mental lexicon but is in fact highly variable. We discuss three ways in which this variability is related to frequency, looking first at extensions, or novel creations, then at the frequency of individual verb forms, and finally at the role of frequency in hypothesizing constructional schemas as an important part of speakers' grammatical resources.

4.3.2.1 'Extensions'.

Goldberg (1995) argues in favor of speakers' knowledge of constructional templates in addition to individual verbs and their meanings, basing her arguments on the ability of speakers to extend the use of a verb with a new constructional template, as in the much-discussed example *She sneezed the napkin off the table*. Here are some actual examples from a wider range of interactional contexts than we are considering for this paper:

(42) *We can't sample you* (said by a nurse-practitioner to a patient, meaning that she couldn't give her any samples of a specific medication)

(43) *Have they sampled you yet?* (said by a nurse-practitioner meaning 'Have they taken a sample from you yet?')

(44) *Even my mother was campaigning me* (former Senator Alfonse d'Amato in a radio interview, November 1998)

(45) *We don't minutes this meeting* (said by department chair, meaning that for a faculty meeting at which students are being discussed, no minutes should be taken)

(46) *You can send me $5 to the department* (e-mail from student to former student not in residence) (*send* usually not treated as a 'four-argument' verb)

(47) *That house hasn't **appraised** yet* (said by a realtor about a house that hadn't been appraised)

These examples illustrate two important points about frequency and argument structure. First, the degree to which any of these might be viewed as 'novel' varies from one individual to another, based entirely on his/her prior linguistic experience. Second, in our view, to the extent that they are novel, such uses of verbs nicely illustrate the fluidity of the information we have stored regarding the meanings of verbs and what participants they can go with. With several hearings, they lose their novelty; thus the dividing line between stored 'argument structures' and 'extensions' can be seen to be constantly changing under the influence of everyday language use.

In fact, it is very interesting that the 'extensions', as Goldberg points out, happen in accordance with constructional patterns that are already highly frequent (Bybee and Thompson 2000). Thus, in the case of *e-mail*, discussed above, what Bybee calls the high 'type frequency', or large class membership (see Bybee 1998, to appear, Bybee and Thompson 2000) of verbs of sending and communicating is what allows a new such verb, like *e-mail*, to be used in the highly frequent 'ditransitive construction' (Goldberg 1995).

4.3.2.2 Frequency of verbs.   But frequency effects are even more conspicuous when we note that predicates vary greatly in the extent to which they specify what Payne (1997) describes as the 'number of participants that must be 'on stage'. And strikingly, the extent to which a predicate seems to be imaginable in terms of 'participants on stage' at all is a function of frequency.

Specifically, we can predict that the more frequent a verb is, the less likely it is to have any fixed number of 'argument structures'. To illustrate this, we can consider the verb form *get*, which is the most frequent verbal form in conversation (apart from *have* and *be*), according to Biber *et al.* (1999) and Krug (this volume). *Get* is a prime example of a verb with no easily imagined obvious argument structure, precisely because it is used in so many lexicalized 'dispersed' predicates and specific constructions (Bybee 1998, to appear; Fillmore *et al.* 1988; Hopper 1991, 1995a, 1997a, b), as shown in the following examples from our database:

(48) ***got** sick*
      *don't **get** wet*
      *you guys are **getting** ashes all over me*
      ***getting** good rest*
      *we gotta **get** a picture*
      ***get** that out of my mouth*
      *I don't think you**'ll be getting much out of** that one*

The next most frequent eight verb forms in English conversation, according to Biber *et al.*, are equally difficult to assign 'argument structures' to, for exactly the same kinds of reasons. These are *say*, *go*, *know*, *think*, *see*, *come*, *want*, and *mean*. Some of these are found frequently in lexicalized expressions and discourse markers (Jucker and Ziv 1998; Kärkkäinen 1998; Lenk 1997; Scheibman this volume, 2000a, b, to appear; Thompson and Mulac 1991 a, b). The data show very clearly that the most frequent verbs in the language have no 'argument structures', but occur in a wide range of lexicalized expressions that must be learned.

As a corollary, we can also predict that the predicates for which a relatively fixed argument structure seems intuitively the clearest are extremely infrequently used in real interactions, verbs such as those frequently found in the pages of the argument structure literature, e.g., *elapse*, *spray*, *load*, *empty*, *fill*, *swarm*.

In fact, Napoli (1993) suggests that what she calls 'high-information verbs' (those which can be used only in very restricted contexts) impose clear roles on their 'arguments', that is, they have relatively clear 'argument structures', while 'low-information verbs' (those which put few limitations on the contexts in which they can be used) have a range of possible 'argument structures'. We feel that this is a very important insight, but that it is not an arbitrary fact about 'verbs' in the 'lexicon' that has to be learned by speakers. Rather, it is a fact about *language use*. That is, what Napoli discusses intuitively in terms of 'high' and 'low' 'information' is what can be described empirically in terms of low vs. high *token frequency*. A 'high information verb' is one which can be used only in very restricted contexts and, thus, has low token frequency. That, we argue, is precisely why it is easier to imagine the range of participants it goes with than with verbs of high token frequency, what Napoli calls 'low information verbs'.

So we would suggest that what has been discussed as 'valence' and 'argument structure' may be better captured by an empirical usage-based theory which embraces the range of clausal contexts in which predicates and verbs can be used, without trying to imagine scenes and participants. What appears to be 'structure' is in fact better viewed, not as a set of abstract principles, but as a limited spreading of systematicity from remembered individual words, phrases, and small sets. The research referred to above in 4.3.1 represents a start towards such an empirical usage-based theory of clause structure (e.g., Aarts and Aarts 1995; Aarts and Meyer 1995; Biber *et al.* 2000; Bybee 1998, to appear; Tao 2000; and Tomasello and Brooks 1998).

4.3.2.3 Argument structure and constructions.   Fillmore *et al.* and their colleagues have argued convincingly for the importance of a notion of 'construction' (Fillmore 1988, 1989; Fillmore *et al.* 1988; Fillmore and Kay 1993; Goldberg 1995; Goldberg *et al.* manuscript; Goldberg 1998; Taylor 1998). Goldberg

(1995: 3) proposes what she calls 'argument structure constructions', 'a special subclass of constructions that provides the basic means of clausal expression in a language'.

- Ditransitive   *Pat faxed Bill the letter*
- Caused Motion   *Pat pushed the pen off the table*
- Resultative   *She kissed him unconscious*
- Intransitive Motion   *The fly buzzed into the room*
- Conative (X directs action at Y) *Sam kicked Bill*

Intriguingly, these are vanishingly rare in our database.[7] Only 'Ditransitive' occurs at all, and even it is very rare, appearing ten times in our data, that is, in 2% of the clauses, with the following verbs and frequencies, and an example of each:

tell   4   *you didn't tell me that*
send   3   *I sent her a tape of you talking*
give   2   *she had given me the tape recorder*
hand   1   *can you hand me a toothpick?*

The construct of 'construction' captures significant regularities about the distribution of meaning between verbs and arguments, as well as regularities in patterning that are independent of particular verbs. However, our numbers do raise questions about how these five argument structure constructions can be 'a special subclass of constructions that provides the basic means of clausal expression in a language'. We think our data show the importance of looking at the recurrent patterns in everyday interactions in order to know what constructions speakers are using and storing (Ono and Thompson 1995, Bybee 1998). Not only does it appear that people make use of a very wide variety of lexico-grammatical constructions, but in fact, the favorite constructions in conversational English, rather than argument structure constructions, are:

- Intransitive Verbal Clauses
- Copular Clauses
- Epistemic/Evidential Clauses

4.4 Summary

In this section we have suggested that the low transitivity of conversational language has strong implications for the study of what has been described in terms of argument structure. To capture what speakers do know about how to put everyday clauses together, we need to move toward a theory that is based on what speakers actually do and on what the data tell us about how speakers are sorting, categorizing, and storing the generalizations they make about what they hear and say every day.

5. Conclusions and implications

In this paper we have shown that, by a variety of measures, the clauses in English conversation are very low in Transitivity. We have outlined the support for this claim and we have discussed some of the implications of its validity for the study of what has come to be known as argument structure. In conclusion, we would like to touch on two related issues.

The first of these issues is the question of clause types. Starting perhaps with the work of Tesnière 1959, much attention has been paid in the functional grammatical literature to such aspects of clause grammar as the marking for grammatical relations in highly Transitive clauses and to voice and 'valency-changing' operations. This research has focused on what Andrews (1985) calls Primary Transitive Verbs and 'operations' on clauses with such verbs (Payne 1997). We would be the first to acknowledge the range of facts that have emerged from assuming highly Transitive clauses to be the starting point for the study of grammatical relations and voice and valency-changing operations; at the same time, we are struck by the fact that most of the attention in current functional linguistics, not to mention more structurally oriented research, is currently being given to patterns whose instantiations are vanishingly rare in ordinary talk. Since clauses of extremely low Transitivity are far and away the most frequent kind in ordinary everyday interactions, this suggests that more attention be given to studies of the grammar of one-participant clauses, as seen in such work as Bentivoglio (1992), Bentivoglio and Weber (1986), Dryer (to appear), Du Bois (1987), Durie (1987, 1988), Dutra (1987), Fox (1995), Hengeveld (1990, 1992), Kärkkäinen (1996), Naro and Votre (1999), Ono et al. (2000), Stassen (1997), and Verhaar (1990).

Having discussed low Transitivity at some length, we would now like to briefly consider the second issue: high Transitivity. In Hopper and Thompson (1980), we referred to clauses of high Transitivity as 'cardinal' Transitive clauses, on analogy with cardinal vowels. At that time, we did not consider relative frequencies, but some fascinating recent research suggests that 'cardinal', or 'maximally filled out' constructional schemas may be instantiated quite rarely in actual language use (Ewing 1999, Hopper 1997b). Our data can also be interpreted in this way: there is evidence that a 'cardinal' Transitive schema is known to speakers, but the conditions under which it would be appropriate to instantiate such a schema occur with strikingly low frequency. Clauses of low Transitivity are far more useful in the intersubjective interpersonal contexts that make up most of our talking lives.

Our findings regarding the low Transitivity of most of the clauses in conversational language have much to do with what has been described as 'genre'. We do not have the space to delve here into the relationship between genre and interaction, but we follow Miller (1984) in taking genre as inherently social, in that it has to do with language use (see Bazerman 1997, Biber 1988, Biber and Finegan 1994, and Mayes 1999 for useful discussion).

Clearly what speakers know about the clauses of their language has everything to do with the kinds of language they have participated in and been exposed to during their lifetimes. For many speakers of English this includes a wide range of forms of written language as well as a range of interactional styles and registers. This means that they have stored and can process and retrieve many more patterns than are evident in the data we have collected.

Of the many different ways in which language can be used, we are considering only one in this paper, everyday face-to-face conversation, which is itself of course not a unified 'genre', as Swales (1990) notes. Our findings regarding the low Transitivity of the clauses in conversation suggest one way in which this particular kind of language use can be viewed: the low Transitivity in our conversational data is to a considerable extent determined by the kinds of things we are doing when we talk with friends and acquaintances. We do not seem to talk much about events, let alone actions (as Hopper 1991, 1997a has also shown), but rather, our talk is mostly about 'how things are from our perspective'. Our data show that we describe states, reveal our attitudes, ascribe properties to people and situations, and give our assessments of situations and behavior. As discussed at some length in Dahl (1997), Hopper (1991, 1995a, 1997a), Iwasaki 1993, Scheibman (this volume, 2000b), and Stein and Wright (1995), these are reflections of *subjectivity* in our everyday use of language; these are the ways in which we display our identities, convey who we are to others, express our feelings and attitudes, and check our views of the world with our community-mates.

Intriguingly, even in genres in which we might expect a higher proportion of clauses of high Transitivity, we find that expectation not borne out by the data. Even in the written narratives analyzed for Hopper and Thompson (1980), the number of 'foreground' clauses of high Transitivity was consistently much lower than the number of 'background' clauses of low Transitivity. And Hopper (1991) has described a vernacular written action narrative in which there are almost no clauses which report a past-time action initiated by a volitional agent affecting a patient. Instead, even the actions are expressed as evaluated, non-punctual, modalized, and distributed events and the narrative is also full of evaluative and image-projecting clauses, many of which are very low in Transitivity. Such clauses of high Transitivity that do occur seem to be used for reporting events in a highly non-subjective, in fact distancing, manner.

In discussing the implications of Transitivity for argument structure, we have suggested, based on evidence from everyday talk in one language, that argument structure is much more variable than is usually granted in the literature on the grammar of clauses. We hope to have made a convincing case for the following points:

(a) In contrast to the highly Transitive examples which form the basis of most discussions of clause grammar, including argument structure, case-marking, person-marking, and voice, ordinary conversation abounds in clauses of very low Transitivity, typically consisting of only one participant.
(b) The data from English conversation provide robust support for the view that predicates within a language differ widely, partly because of their differential frequency, in how clearly they specify what arguments they can go with.
(c) Much of everyday conversation consists of one-participant clauses and prefabricated constructions and expressions, challenging the idea, popular in discussions of argument structure, that verbs 'choose' the arguments that go with them.

We have tried to demonstrate the close connection between the goals, motives, and purposes of everyday conversation in one cultural setting and the grammatical resources that speakers in this setting draw upon to accomplish their interactional goals. We hope to have shown that the degree of Transitivity of the utterances people use in everyday interaction, and indeed the very nature of clause grammar itself, is tightly related to what they are *doing* with their talk. More broadly, we hope to have made a case for favoring closely examining real interactional communication over imagining semantic interpretations of de-contextualized utterances as a basis for theorizing about the nature of lexico-grammatical knowledge. To know how lexico-grammar works to convey what speakers mean, we have to know what they are doing in the actual everyday linguistic situations in which they find themselves.

Notes

* We are grateful to the following people for helpful discussion of the ideas in this paper: Yung-O Biq, Susanna Cumming, Michael Ewing, Barbara Fox, Ritva Laury, Tsuyoshi Ono, Joanne Scheibman, Michael Tomasello, Sebastião Votre, and especially Joan Bybee. We hope they agree with the way this paper has turned out, but if they don't, it's our responsibility.

1. We are grateful to John W. Du Bois, Director of the Corpus of Spoken American English, and to Steven Albert and Joanne Scheibman for the data from these three conversations.

2. We found no instances of what could be analyzed as 'clausal subjects' in our data.

3. For further discussion of this view of complement clauses, see Thompson (to appear.)

4. In addition to Thompson and Mulac (1991a, 1991b), Kärkkäinen (1998), and Thompson (to appear) for English, the reader is referred to Englebretson (2000) for an in-depth discussion divorcing complement clauses from argument structure in conversational Indonesian and to Tao (2000) for a discussion of *remember* in English as an epistemic/evidential introducer.

5. For further discussion of the implications of these types of predicates, see Scheibman (this volume).

6. This finding is nearly identical to what Dahl (1997) found for Swedish conversation and for the conversational portions of the London-Lund corpus of British English.

7. We are well aware that such constructions may appear with higher frequency in other kinds of linguistic uses, such as written texts. In fact, data from child language, as noted by Michael Tomasello and Patricia Clancy (p.c.), suggest that activity-oriented language, with more two-participant predicates, and more instances of argument structure constructions, is much more characteristic of children's talk than of adults' (see Berman 1993, Clancy to appear, Tomasello and Brooks 1998).

References

Aarts, J. and Aarts, F. 1995. *Find* and *want*: a corpus-based case study in verb complementation. In Bas Aarts and Charles F. Meyer (eds.), *The verb in contemporary English*, 159–82. Cambridge: Cambridge University Press.

Aarts, Bas and Charles F. Meyer (eds.) 1995. *The Verb in Contemporary English*, 159–82. Cambridge: Cambridge University Press.

Alsina, Alex. 1996. *The Role of Argument Structure in Grammar: Evidence from Romance*. Stanford: CSLI Publications.

Andrews, Avery. 1985. The major functions of the noun phrase. In T. Shopen (ed.), *Language Typology and Syntactic Description*, Vol. I: 62–154. Cambridge: Cambridge University Press.

Bakhtin, M. M. 1986. The problem of speech genres. Speech Genres and Other Late Essays. Translated by Vern W. McGee, and edited by Caryl Emerson and Michael Holquist, pp. 60–102. Austin: University of Texas Press.

Bazerman, Charles. 1997. The life of genre, the life of the classroom. In Wendy Bishop and Hans Ostrom (eds.), *Genre and Writing*, 19–26. Portsmouth, NH: Boynton/Cook-Heinemann.

Bentivoglio, Paola. 1992. Linguistic correlations between subjects of one-argument verbs and subjects of more-than-one-argument verbs in spoken Spanish. In P. Hirschbühler and K. Koerner (eds.), *Romance Languages and Modern Linguistic Theory*, 11–24. Amsterdam: Benjamins.

Bentivoglio, Paola and Elizabeth G. Weber. 1986. A functional approach to subject word order in spoken Spanish. In Osvaldo Jaeggli and Carmen Silva-Corvalán (eds.), *Studies in Romance Linguistics*, 23–40. Dordrecht: Foris.

Berman, Ruth. 1993. Marking of verb transitivity by Hebrew-speaking children. Journal of *Child Language* 20: 641–69.

Biber, Douglas. 1988. *Variation Across Speech and Writing*. Cambridge: Cambridge University Press.

Biber, Douglas and Edward Finegan. 1994. *Sociolinguistic Perspectives on Register*. New York: Oxford University Press.

Biber, Douglas, Stig Johansson, Geoffrey Leech, Edward Finegan, and Susan Conrad. 1999. *Longman Grammar of Spoken and Written English*. London: Longman.

Bybee, Joan. 1985. *Morphology: A Study of the Relation Between Meaning and Form*. Amsterdam: Benjamins.

Bybee, Joan. 1998. The emergent lexicon. CLS 34: The Panels, 421–35.

Bybee, Joan. To appear. Mechanisms of change in grammaticization. In Richard Janda and Brian Josephs (eds.), *A Handbook of Historical Linguistics*. Oxford: Blackwell.

Bybee, Joan and Sandra A. Thompson. 2000. Three frequency effects in syntax. Berkeley Linguistic Society 23. 378–88.

Bybee, Joan, William Pagliuca, and Revere Perkins. 1994. *The Evolution of Grammar: Tense, Aspect and Modality in the Languages of the World*. Chicago: University of Chicago Press.

Chafe, Wallace. 1994. *Discourse, Consciousness, and Time: The Flow and Displacement of Conscious Experience in Speaking and Writing*. Chicago: University of Chicago Press.

Clancy, Patricia. To appear. The acquisition of argument structure.

Couper-Kuhlen, Elizabeth and Margret Selting. 1996. Towards an interactional perspective on prosody and a prosodic perspective on interaction. In Elizabeth Couper-Kuhlen and Margret Selting (eds.), *Prosody and Interaction*, 11–56.

Croft, Wiliam. 1991. *Syntactic Categories and Grammatical Relations. The Cognitive Organization of Information*. University of Chicago Press.

Dahl, Östen. 1997. Egocentricity in discourse and syntax. http://www.ling.su.se/staff/oesten/egocentric.

Dik, Simon. 1989. *The Theory of Functional Grammar. Part 1: The Structure of the Clause*. Dordrecht: Foris.

Dixon, R.M.W. 1991. *A New Approach to English Grammar, on Semantic Principles*. Oxford: Clarendon Press.

Dowty, David. 1991. Thematic proto-roles and argument selection. *Language* 67: 547–619.

Dryer, Matthew. To appear. Clause types. In Timothy Shopen (ed.) *Language Typology and Syntactic Description*, second edition. Cambridge: Cambridge University Press.

Du Bois, John W. 1985. Competing motivations. In John Haiman (ed.), *Iconicity in Syntax*, 343–65. Amsterdam: Benjamins.

Du Bois, John W. 1987. The discourse basis of ergativity. *Language* 63: 805–55.

Du Bois, John, Stephan Schuetze-Coburn, Danae Paolino, and Susanna Cumming. 1993. Outline of discourse transcription. In Jane A. Edwards and Martin D. Lampert (eds.), *Talking Data: Transcription and Coding Methods for Language Research*, 45–89. Hillsdale, NJ: Lawrence Erlbaum.

Durie, Mark. 1987. Grammatical relations in Acehnese. *Studies in Language* 11.2: 365–99.

Durie, Mark. 1988. Preferred argument structure in an active language. *Lingua* 74: 1–25.

Dutra, Rosalia. 1987. The hybrid S category in Brazilian Portuguese. *Studies in Language* 11.1: 163–80.

Edelman, Gerald M. 1992. *Bright Air, Brilliant Fire: On the matter of the Mind.* New York: BasicBooks.

Englebretson, Robert. 2000. *Complementation Strategies in Colloquial Indonesian Conversation.* PhD dissertation, University of California Santa Barbara.

Ewing, Michael. 1999. *The Clause in Cirebon Javanese Conversation.* PhD dissertation, University of California Santa Barbara.

Fillmore, Charles J. 1968. The case for case. In Emmon Bach and Robert T. Harms (eds.), *Universals in Linguistic Theory,* 1–88. New York: Holt, Rinehart and Winston.

Fillmore, Charles J. 1986. Pragmatically controlled zero anaphora. BLS 12: 95–107.

Fillmore, Charles J. 1988. The mechanisms of 'construction grammar'. BLS 14: 35–55.

Fillmore, Charles J. 1989. Grammatical construction theory and the familiar dichotomies. In R. Dietrich and C.F. Graumann (eds.), *Language Processing in Social Context,* 17–38. Amsterdam: Elsevier.

Fillmore, Charles J. and Paul Kay. 1993. Construction grammar. Unpublished manuscript, University of California, Berkeley.

Fillmore, Charles J., Paul Kay, and Mary C. O'Connor. 1988. Regularity and idiomaticity in grammatical constructions. *Language* 64: 501–38.

Fox, Barbara A. 1995. The category 'S' in English conversation. In W. Abraham, T. Givón, and S. Thompson (eds.), *Discourse grammar and typology,* 153–78. Amsterdam: Benjamins.

Goldberg, Adele. 1995. *A Construction Grammar Approach to Argument Structure.* Chicago: University of Chicago Press.

Goldberg, Adele. 1998. Patterns of experience in patterns of language. In Michael Tomasello (ed.), *The New Psychology of Language,* 203–20. Mahwah, NJ: Lawrence Erlbaum.

Goldberg, Adele, Nitya Sethuraman and Devin Casenhiser. Ms. Learning argument structure generalizations. University of Illinois.

de Groot, Casper. 1989. *Predicate Structure in a Functional Grammar of Hungarian.* Dordrecht: ICG Printing.

Helasvuo, Marja-Liisa. To appear. When discourse becomes syntax: Noun phrases and clauses as emergent syntactic units in Finnish conversational discourse. Amsterdam: Benjamins.

Hengeveld, Kees. 1990. Semantic relations in non-verbal predication. In J. Nuyts, A. M. Bolkestein, and C. Vet (eds.), *Layers and Levels of Representation in Language Theory,* 101–22. Amsterdam: Benjamins.

Hengeveld, Kees. 1992. *Non-verbal Predication: Theory, Typology, Diachrony.* Berlin: Mouton.

Hopper, Paul J. 1987. Emergent grammar. BLS 13, 139–57.

Hopper, Paul J. 1991. Dispersed verbal predicates in vernacular writing. BLS 17: 402–13.

Hopper, Paul J. 1992. Times of the sign. *Time and Society* 1,2: 223–38.

Hopper, Paul J. 1995a. Dispersed verbal predicates in vernacular written narrative. In Akio Kamio (ed.), *Directions in Functional Linguistics,* 1–18. Amsterdam: Benjamins.

Hopper, Paul J. 1995b. The category 'event' in natural discourse and logic. In W. Abraham, T. Givón, and S. Thompson (eds.), *Discourse Grammar and Typology*, 139–50. Amsterdam: Benjamins.

Hopper, Paul J. 1997a. Discourse and the category 'verb' in English. *Language and Communication* 17.2: 93–102.

Hopper, Paul J. 1997b. When 'grammar' and discourse clash: the problem of source conflicts. In Joan Bybee, John Haiman, and Sandra A. Thompson (eds.), *Essays on Language Function and Language Type*, 231–47. Amsterdam: Benjamins.

Hopper, Paul J. 1998. Emergent grammar. In Michael Tomasello (ed.), *The New Psychology of Language*, 155–75. Mahwah, NJ: Lawrence Erlbaum.

Hopper, Paul J. and Sandra A. Thompson. 1980. Transitivity in grammar and discourse. *Language* 56: 251–99.

Iwasaki, Shoichi. 1993. *Subjectivity in Grammar and Discourse*. Amsterdam: Benjamins.

Jackendoff, Ray. 1990. *Semantic Structures*. Cambridge, MA: MIT Press.

Jucker, Andreas H. and Yael Ziv (eds.) 1998. *Discourse Markers: Descriptions and Theory*. Amsterdam: Benjamins.

Kärkkäinen, Elise. 1996. Preferred argument structure and subject role in American English conversational discourse. *Journal of Pragmatics* 25.5: 675–701.

Kärkkäinen, Elise. 1998. *The Marking and Interactional Functions of Epistemic Stance in American English Conversational Discourse*. PhD dissertation, UC Santa Barbara.

Labov, William. 1973. The boundaries of words and their meanings. In C.-J. Bailey and Roger Shuy (eds.), *New Ways of Analyzing Variation in English*. Georgetown: Georgetown University Press.

Lakoff, George. 1987. *Women, Fire, and Dangerous Things*. Chicago: University of Chicago Press. 1987.

Langacker, Ronald. 1987. *Foundations of Cognitive Grammar*. Stanford: Stanford University Press.

Langacker, Ronald. 1988. The nature of grammatical valence. In Brygida Rudzka-Ostyn (ed.) *Topics in Cognitive Linguistics*, 91–125 Amsterdam: Benjamins.

Lazard, Gilbert. 1994. *L'actance*. Paris: Presses Universitaires de France.

Lenk, Uta. 1997. *Marking Discourse Coherence: Functions of Discourse Markers in Spoken English*. Tübingen: Gunter Narr Verlag.

Levin, Beth. 1993. *English Verb Classes and Alternations*. Chicago: University of Chicago Press.

Lewin, Roger. 1992. *Complexity: Life at the Edge of Chaos*. New York: Collier Books.

Linell, Per. 1982. *The Written Language Bias in Linguistics*. Linköping: University of Linköping.

Mayes, Patricia. 1999. *Linguistic Reflections of Social Structure and Culture: A Comparison of Japanese and American Cooking Class Genres*. PhD dissertation, UC Santa Barbara.

Miller, Carolyn R. 1984. Genres as social action. *Quarterly Journal of Speech* 70: 151–67.

Naro, Anthony J. and Sebastião J. Votre. 1999. *Discourse Motivations for Linguistic Regularities: Verb/Subject Order in Spoken Brazilian Portuguese*. Probus 11: 75–100.

Napoli, Donna Jo. 1993. *Syntax*. Oxford: Oxford University Press.

Noonan, Michael. 1985. Complementation. In Timothy Shopen (ed.), *Language Typology and Syntactic Description*, Vol. II, 42–139. Cambridge: Cambridge University Press.

O'Dowd, Elizabeth M. 1998. *Prepositions and Particles in English: A Discourse-functional Account*. Oxford: Oxford University Press.

Ono, Tsuyoshi and Misumi Sadler. Ms. The status of 'canonical' transitive clauses in Japanese conversation.

Ono, Tsuyoshi and Sandra A. Thompson. 1995. What can conversation tell us about syntax? In Philip W. Davis (ed.), *Descriptive and Theoretical Modes in the Alternative Linguistics*, 213–71. Amsterdam: Benjamins.

Ono, Tsuyoshi and Sandra A. Thompson. 1997. Deconstructing 'zero anaphora'. BLS 23.

Ono, Tsuyoshi, Sandra A. Thompson, and Ryoko Suzuki. 2000. The pragmatic nature of the so-called subject marker *ga* in Japanese: evidence from conversation. *Discourse Studies* 2.1: 55–84.

Östman, Jan-Ola. 1981. *You Know: A Discourse-Functional Approach*. Amsterdam: Benjamins.

Pawley, Andrew and Frances H. Syder. 1983. Two puzzles for linguistic theory: nativelike selection and nativelike fluency. In Jack C. Richards and Richard W. Schmidt (eds.), *Language and Communication*, 191–267. London: Longman.

Payne, Doris. 1985. Degrees of inherent transitivity in Yagua verbs. IJAL 51: 19–37.

Payne, Thomas. 1997. *Describing Morphosyntax*. Cambridge: Cambridge University Press.

Redeker, Gisela. 1991. Linguistic markers of discourse structure. *Linguistics* 29: 1139–72.

Roland, Douglas and Daniel Jurafsky. To appear. Verb sense and verb subcategorization probabilities. In Suzanne Stevenson and Paola Merlo (eds.), *Papers from the 1998 Cuny Sentence Processing Conference*. Amsterdam: Benjamins.

Schegloff, Emanuel. 1993. Reflections on language, development, and the interactional character of talk-in-interaction. *Research on Language and Social Interaction* 26.1: 139–53.

Schegloff, Emanuel. 1996a. Issues of relevance for discourse analysis: contingency in action, interaction, and co-participant context. In Eduard H. Hovy and Donia R. Scott (eds.), *Computational and Conversational Discourse*. New York: Springer.

Schegloff, Emanuel. 1996b. Turn organization: one direction for inquiry into grammar and interaction. In Elinor Ochs, Emanuel Schegloff, and Sandra A. Thompson (eds.), *Interaction and Grammar*. Cambridge: Cambridge University Press.

Scheibman, Joanne. 2000a. *I dunno* . . . a usage-based account of the phonological reduction of *don't* in American English conversation. *Journal of Pragmatics* 32: 105–24.

Scheibman, Joanne. 2000b. *Structural Patterns of Subjectivity in American English Conversation*. PhD dissertation, University of New Mexico.

Schiffrin, Deborah. 1987. *Discourse Markers*. Cambridge: Cambridge University Press.

Siewierska, Anna. 1991. *Functional Grammar*. London: Routledge.

Stassen, Leon. 1997. *Intransitive Predication*. Oxford: Clarendon Press.

Stein, Dieter and Susan Wright (eds.), 1995. *Subjectivity and Subjectivization*. Cambridge: Cambridge University Press.

Swales, John. 1990. *Genre Analysis: English in Academic and Research Settings*. Cambridge: Cambridge University Press. (The Cambridge Applied Linguistics Series)

Tao, Hongyin. 1996. *Units in Mandarin Conversation: Prosody, Discourse, and Grammar*. Amsterdam: Benjamins.

Tao, Hongyin. 2000. Discovering the usual with corpora: the case of *remember*. In Simpson, Rita and John Swales (eds.), *Selected Papers from the North American Symposium on Corpora and Applied Linguistics*. Ann Arbor: University of Michigan Press.

Taylor, John R. 1995. *Linguistic Categorization* (second edition). Oxford: Clarendon Press.

Taylor, John R. 1998. Syntactic constructions as prototype categories. In Michael Tomasello (ed.), *the New Psychology of Language*, 177–203. Mahwah, NJ: Lawrence Erlbaum.

Tesnière, L. 1959. *Elements de syntaxe structurale*. Paris: Klinksieck.

Thompson, Sandra A. To appear. Object complements and conversation: Towards a realistic account.

Thompson, Sandra A. and Anthony Mulac. 1991a. The discourse conditions for the use of complementizer *that* in conversational English, *Journal of Pragmatics* 15: 237–51.

Thompson, Sandra A. and Anthony Mulac. 1991b. A Quantitative Perspective on the Grammaticization of Epistemic Parentheticals in English. In Elizabeth Traugott and Bernd Heine (eds.), *Grammaticalization* II, 313–39. Amsterdam: Benjamins.

Tomasello, Michael and Patricia J. Brooks. 1998. Young children's earliest transitive and intransitive constructions. *Cognitive Linguistics* 9.4: 379–95.

Trueswell, John C., Michael K. Tanenhaus, and Christopher Kello. 1993. Verb-specific constraints in sentence processing: separating effects of lexical preference from garden-paths. *Journal of Experimental Psychology* 19.3: 528–53.

Turk, Monica. 2000. *Word Order in Russian Conversation: A Quantitative Study*. MA Thesis, UC Santa Barbara.

Verhaar, John. 1990. How intransitive is intransitive? *Studies in Language* 14.1: 93–168.

Weber, Thilo. 1997. The emergence of linguistic structure: Paul Hopper's emergent grammar hypothesis revisited. *Language Sciences* 19.2: 177–96.

Wechsler, Stephen. 1995. *The Semantic Basis of Argument Structure*. Stanford: CSLI Publications.

Local patterns of subjectivity in person and verb type in American English conversation*

JOANNE SCHEIBMAN

Old Dominion University

1. Linguistic subjectivity

In his introduction to the volume, *Subjecthood and subjectivity*, John Lyons (1994) remarks that interest in linguistic subjectivity is currently fashionable and, indeed, in the last several years, there have been many studies highlighting ways in which speakers use language to express their perceptions, feelings, and opinions in discourse (=subjectivity) and how such expressive motivations and strategies conventionalize and interact with linguistic structure (=subjectification). Verhagen (1995: 116) suggests that the most usual mode of expression in language is in fact a subjective one—that "the presence of some argumentational orientation is the default situation in natural language"—and he notes that even lexical items like *expensive* and *tall* orient an addressee towards a particular conclusion and are not solely informative.

In a discussion of linguistic subjectivity, Benveniste (1971: 225) writes: "Language is marked so deeply by the expression of subjectivity that one might ask if it could still function and be called language if it were constructed otherwise". He characterizes subjectivity as the ability of speakers to view themselves as subjects and he discusses how common grammatical categories, in particular, person (in the form of personal pronouns), contribute to this expressive capacity of speakers. Benveniste notes that the first person singular pronoun is a rich source of subjectivity in language in that it explicitly refers to the speaker and he discusses meaning distinctions present in utterances that contain the same verb but contrast in subject. For example, *I* with verbs such as *feel*, *believe*, and *suppose* typically express the speaker's attitude regarding a subsequent piece of discourse or an event in the current context; on the other hand, when these same verbs occur with the third person singular subjects *she* or *he*, there is an impression that what is conveyed is descriptive or informative.

Many linguists have noted interactions between subjective phenomena and linguistic structure. For example, Iwasaki (1993) demonstrates how speakers' perspective influences tense and clause chaining in Japanese narratives. Thompson and Mulac (1991) report on the grammaticization of main clause predicates *I think* and *I guess* as epistemic parentheticals in English. And Scheibman (2000a) reports that the negative auxiliary *don't* consistently appears in a reduced form when it occurs in its most frequent context—in the collocation *I don't know*–where it primarily functions as an epistemic downtoner or politeness marker (see also Tsui 1991). In an analysis of English written narrative, Hopper (1991, 1997) observes that simple verbs (single lexical items) are relatively rare in discourse and that much more common are dispersed predicates, especially in high involvement language use. In an investigation of egocentric expressions and generic pronouns in Swedish conversation (linguistic elements that refer to speech act participants), Östen Dahl (1997) finds that utterances making reference to discourse participants, particularly the speaker, are frequently occurring in conversation. And an important contribution to work in linguistic subjectivity, proposed and elaborated by Elizabeth Traugott, is the phenomenon of subjectification in grammaticization processes whereby, over time, meanings often become increasingly based in speakers' attitudes towards what they are saying (e.g., Carey 1995, Traugott 1995).

Notwithstanding the ubiquity of subjective expression in discourse (e.g., the conveying of mental states, affect, preference, evaluation), the propositional, or referential, function of language (=the communication of information and ideas) has often been elevated in discussions of the functions of language (e.g., Jakobson 1960) and promoted in the practice of linguistic analysis itself. Silverstein (1976: 14) claims that pure reference (descriptive language) likely plays a minor communicative role cross-culturally, though it has "formed the basis for linguistic theory and linguistic analysis in the Western tradition". To illustrate, the notion of compositionality—that grammatical and lexical bits contribute to the meanings of propositions (e.g., English -*s* contributes the meaning of 'more than one' to some argument of a proposition)—reflects the referential mode that has predominantly characterized linguistic analysis. As analysts, we tend to segment and slot linguistic material based on its structural and semantic contribution to what we *envision* as the expression of some proposition. And it is not illogical to proceed in this fashion given that linguistic form is substantive and manipulable, and because, analytically speaking, language is a reifier of linguistic, social, and cognitive activity as well as a site for on-the-fly interactions and negotiations of meaning.

In his discussion of linguistic signs of self-alienation, John Haiman (1995: 214) points out that "speakers using language in general are alienated from the emotions they describe if they control them sufficiently to use language to describe them". So in some sense language presents a paradox—human expression is inherently subjective, but in using a conventional code, we objectify this expression. Given, then, that language always represents a speaker's interpretation of the world, investigating linguistic structure from the perspective that all language is subjective to varying degrees (as opposed to assuming fundamental propositionality) may not only contribute to the characterization of linguistic subjectivity itself, but may enhance what we know about the grammaticization of meaning and interaction in context.

2. Emergence of linguistic structure and usage-based linguistics

One of the most important contributions to recent linguistic scholarship is the set of theories and practices that view language structure as rooted in usage—thus treating it as dynamic in both its manifestation and in its development and change. In his classic paper, "Emergent grammar", Paul Hopper (1987) argues that linguistic form is neither fixed nor aprioristically determined; rather structure is shaped (e.g., often in prefabricated chunks) by discourse use and this process is itself ongoing. Hopper notes that, "the more useful a construction is, the more it will tend to become structuralized, in the sense of achieving cross-textual consistency, and serving as a basis for variation and extension" (1987: 150).

This general usage-based framework illustrated by Hopper's work and formulated and elaborated by many linguists (e.g., Bybee 1998, Haiman 1998) emphasizes the role of frequency, or repetition, in the formation of what we call grammar. This theoretical orientation subsumes several overlapping lines of linguistic research, such as diachronic and synchronic investigations of grammaticizing material (e.g., Bybee, et al. 1994, Thompson and Mulac 1991), repetition and the ritualization of linguistic form (e.g., Bybee to appear, Haiman 1998), the impact of social interaction on grammatical structure (e.g., Ford 1993, Fox 1987, Ono and Thompson 1995), and studies of cognitive processing mechanisms affiliated with frequency and storage leading to the conventionalization of form (e.g., Boyland 1996, Bybee and Scheibman 1999, Krug 1998). As is true within any theoretical framework, not all researchers in these related fields uniformly agree on the various factors claimed to influence the development of grammatical and lexical constructions (nor, if they do, the ranking of these factors). What appears to unite these various approaches is a common goal of connecting larger, analytically delineated patterns (=linguistic structure) with the sounds, gestures, and timing characteristic of local usage activities.

2.1 Local patterning

Given this idea that both lexical and discursive substance (in context) form the basis for grammatical organization (i.e., that what we know as grammar arises from both the conventionalization and creativity of human interaction), then how successful may analysts expect to be in explaining global patterns of linguistic form and function when confronted with the often interdependent and opaque elements of complex local activities? Relative to more formal (=aprioristic) theoretical approaches, one wonders whether the practice of usage-based linguistics brings with it—aside from obvious differences in classification and analysis of naturally-occurring data that this kind of work entails—a less global type of linguistic generalization, or perhaps a shift in expectation regarding our capacity to generalize, simply because of the natural complexity of the material serving as input to (the description of) linguistic patterns (cf. Hopper 1997).

If interactive and lexical material direct grammar and conventionalization of form occurs within specific social and linguistic contexts (e.g., Bybee 1998), then we should expect to find differences in behavior (distribution, function) among members of the same grammatical and lexical categories (e.g., we shouldn't be surprised to find that the subject pronouns in English occur in distinct linguistic and interactional environments and fulfill different functions in discourse, even given their common membership in the grammatical class of person) (cf. Bybee 1985). If grammar emerges from linguistic and interactive contexts, then tracking linguistic categories within these individual contexts becomes important. Local patterns, then, contribute to the formation of more global patterns. However, it might not always be possible to find reliable, unified explanations for global structural organization of linguistic form for several reasons: (1) because of the unique nature of component contributions (i.e., that the whole is neither equal to nor derivable from the sum of its parts); (2) because of limitations of extant analytical categories that have typically been delineated without having been derived from natural discourse data; and (3) because there are factors that are invariably unaccounted for in any analysis. Another potential obstacle to fully accounting for global linguistic patterns is suggested by recent work on the emergence of complex adaptive systems. Simply stated, complex adaptive systems characterize the behavior of biological organisms (along with their attendant social and cognitive organizations and structures; e.g., political systems, financial markets, thinking, learning, and language) as collective entities that function by schematizing and adapting to experiences in order to function/persist in the world. And, notably, complex adaptive systems themselves have the capacity to engender greater complexity (Gell-Mann 1994). With respect to language structure, then, it is possible that some global patterns have themselves emerged from the complexity of more local systems and may not be transparently reducible to their input (tokens of usage).

2.2 Global and local patterns in conversation

In a database of American English conversation to be described in the next section, the majority of all predicates are formally present tense (64%). Yet there is no overarching functional or linguistic explanation readily available to account for this pattern. However, in looking at morphological tense of these predicates in relationship to frequently co-ocurring subjects and semantic verb types, local collocational patterns emerge. For utterances with a first person singular (1s) or a second person singular (2s) subject, the present tense frequently occurs with verbs of cognition (e.g., *I don't know*, *I think*, *you know*), but for clauses with third person singular subjects (3s), the present tense is found most frequently with inanimate subjects (*it*, *this*, *that*) in relational predicates (copular clauses) (e.g., *that's okay*, *it's overwhelming*). By looking at local structural patterns (the frequent combinations of linguistic material in discourse), we may facilitate understanding of the more global trends characterizing conventionalized linguistic structure.

The intersection of the two general theoretical issues discussed above—(1) that all language (in particular, spontaneous conversation) is subjective in that it is fundamentally used by speakers to express their perceptions, feelings, and opinions, and (2) that conventionalized linguistic structure, or grammar, emerges from repetition, or frequency of use, of (sequences of) lexical and grammatical elements in natural discourse—suggests a general hypothesis that linguistic items (constructions of all sizes) that commonly appear in conversation are those that participate in subjective expression. In other words, we would expect greater co-occurrence of elements whose combinations lend themselves to conveying speaker point of view than those whose combinations do not (e.g., after Benveniste 1971, verbs of cognition would more frequently appear with a first person singular subject than with a third person singular).

As part of evaluating this general hypothesis—that we should see associations between frequently occurring structures in conversation and semantic and pragmatic expression of subjectivity—this study will examine relations among person, semantic verb type, and tense in a corpus of American English conversation in order to target the most common subject-verb type combinations in spoken discourse. Section 3 describes the database and provides brief definitions of the categories and codes used in this work and, in Section 4, major distributional patterns in the database are presented. Sections 5 through 7 focus on the most frequent combinations of person (first person singular, second person singular, and third person singular, respectively) and verb type. And finally, Section 8 provides discussion of some of the theoretical issues pertinent to the analysis.

3. Description of the database[1]

The data for this study consist of nine audiotaped informal conversations among friends and/or family members. Eight of the nine tapes with their transcripts were provided courtesy of the Corpus of Spoken American English at the University of California, Santa Barbara and one tape was recorded and transcribed by me.[2] Transcription conventions follow the Du Bois *et al.* (1993) system and intonation units appear on separate lines. In all, eighty minutes of conversation were coded for analysis—ten minutes from each of seven tapes and five minutes from each of two tapes—representing the speech of 33 adult speakers of American English, 21 women and 12 men. The corpus consists of 2,172 utterances—finite clauses with expressed subjects and main verbs; not included are utterances such as *he couldn't.*

3.1 Subject

Subjects are tagged first person singular (*1s*), second person singular (*2s*), third person singular (*3s*), first person plural (*1p*), second person plural (*2p*),and third person plural (*3p*).[3] Coding is based on the form of the subject, so in cases where there is a mismatch between form and meaning/function, it is the form of the subject that is coded. For example, English speakers often use a second person singular subject generically to refer to their own experience, as in (1).[4] In these cases, the subject is coded *2s* (cf. Dahl's 1997 discussion of the egocentricity of generic pronouns in Swedish).

(1) I had a terrible flu.[5]
     I keep having like,
     feeling good, X-wise,
     it's just,
     you feel it shift in your body.   G16–3–8

3.2 Main verb type

In order to assess the subjectivity of subject-verb combinations in English conversation, it was necessary to classify main verbs by semantic type because it is not possible, for example, to discuss the frequent co-occurrence of mental verbs (e.g., verbs of cognition) with first person singular subjects without specifying these semantic classes in advance. The purpose in coding verb type was not to create an exhaustive taxonomy of English verbs; such a task alone could fill the pages of several volumes. Rather, the intent was to establish a useful number of semantic groupings of verbs based on extant systems in the literature to be able to discern general patterns of subject-verb co-occurrence in conversation.

The classification system for verb type is based on Halliday's general taxonomy of verbal processes in English which models three general processes of human experience: being, sensing, and doing (Halliday 1994). Table 1 provides a summary

Table 1. *Main verb types*

Verb Type	Description	Examples
Cognition	cognitive activity	*know, think, remember, figure out*
Corporeal	bodily gestures, bodily interaction	*eat, drink, sleep, live, smoke*
Existential	exist, happen	*be, have, sit, stay, happen*
Feeling	emotion, wanting	*like, want, feel, need, bother, enjoy*
Material	concrete and abstract doings and happenings	*do, go, take, teach, work, use, play, come*
Perception	perception, attention	*look, see, hear, find, notice*
Perception/ Relational	perception (subject not senser)	*look, smell, sound*
Possessive/ Relational	possession (x has a)	*have, get*
Relational	processes of being (x is a, x is AT a)	*be, get, be like* (descriptive), *become*
Verbal	saying, symbolic exchange of meaning	*say, talk, mean, tell, ask, go* (quotative), *be like* (quotative)

of the 10 semantic classes used for coding in this study. The values *cognition, existential, feeling, material, perception, relational*, and *verbal* are taken directly from Halliday; the *corporeal* class—verbs referring to bodily gestures and activities—is from Dixon (1991). The double-codes *perception/relational* and *possessive/relational* emerged during the coding process. In keeping with the goal of tracking subjective expression in conversation, this system allows for more sensitive distinctions among verbs having to do with speakers' states and processes (e.g., feeling, thinking, speaking, perceiving, bodily gestures and activities) than for more general external actions which are grouped under one super class, *material*, subsuming a diverse collection of verbs expressing both abstract and concrete activities.

Though one of the goals of classifying main verbs semantically was to hold lexical items steady while looking at their variable uses in discourse, it was simply not possible to consistently assign a single lexical item the same code. Polysemy—whether due to variation in linguistic contexts, pragmatic contexts, or shifts in semantic roles of arguments in the clause—occasionally required coding the same phonological form as more than one verb type. For example, the presence or absence of an experiencer subject determined whether the verb *feel* is coded as a verb of *feeling* or *perception/relational*, respectively (e.g., *and you would think they would feel that stuff* vs. *this arm feels like lead*). Similarly, the verb *be* may be coded as *relational* or *existential*. Other examples include *tell* which typically represents a *verbal* process but is coded as a verb of *perception* when it follows the modals *can* and *can't*; and *call* is tagged as a *material* process in (2) but a *verbal* one in (3).

(2) and he **called** looking for Jeannie and,   F3–44
(3) what's the other one **called**.   H7–21

3.3 Tense

Tense is coded as it is morphologically marked/unmarked on the finite verb in the utterance. The values are *present, past, modal* (for clauses with central modals where formal marking of time reference is typically abnormal).[6]

4. Global frequency patterns in the data

Table 2 summarizes the most frequently occurring subjects in the database of English conversation. Third person singular occurs as the subject of utterances in 931 out of the total 2,172 clauses, or in 43% of the tokens; the next most common subject is first person singular in 28% of the items. Second person singular subjects account for 15% of the data and 10% of clauses appear with third person plural subjects. Notably, 64% of all utterances in the corpus are present tense and this pattern persists for all subject pronouns, though the ratio of present to past (and to modal) varies by person.

Table 3 outlines the distribution of semantic verb types with respect to subject. The most frequent verb class is relational (typically copular constructions). These

Table 2. *Utterances by person and tense* (n=2,172)

	Present	Past	Modal	Total	Percent
1s	346	191	80	617	28.41
2s	229	48	58	335	15.42
3s	626	239	66	931	42.86
1p	35	21	10	66	3.04
2p	3	1	1	5	0.23
3p	145	50	23	218	10.04
Total	1,384	550	238	2,172	100.00
Percent	63.72	25.32	10.96	100.00	

Table 3. *Utterances by person and verb type* (n=2,172)*

	1s	2s	3s	1p	2p	3p	Total
Cognition	195	110	15	6	0	14	340
	31.60%	32.84%	1.61%	9.09%	0.00%	6.42%	15.65%
Corporeal	24	7	30	1	1	3	66
	3.89%	2.09%	3.22%	1.52%	20.00%	1.38%	3.04%
Existential	12	6	62	3	0	8	91
	1.94%	1.79%	6.66%	4.55%	0.00%	3.67%	4.19%
Feeling	19	9	10	2	0	5	45
	3.08%	2.69%	1.07%	3.03%	0.00%	2.29%	2.07%
Material	141	90	176	30	2	100	539
	22.85%	26.87%	18.90%	45.45%	40.00%	45.87%	24.82%
Perception	27	19	6	10	0	2	64
	4.38%	5.67%	0.64%	15.15%	0.00%	0.92%	2.95%
Perception/rel	0	0	35	0	0	4	39
	0.00%	0.00%	3.76%	0.00%	0.00%	1.83%	1.80%
Possessive/rel	21	31	29	5	0	16	102
	3.40%	9.25%	3.11%	7.58%	0.00%	7.34%	4.70%
Relational	50	41	497	6	2	45	641
	8.10%	12.24%	53.38%	9.09%	40.00%	20.64%	29.51%
Verbal	128	22	71	3	0	21	245
	20.75%	6.57%	7.63%	4.55%	0.00%	9.63%	11.28%
Total	617	335	931	66	5	218	2172
	100%	100%	100%	100%	100%	100%	100.00%

*Individual percentages below utterance counts refer to person (e.g., 31.60% of items with 1s subjects occur with verbs of cognition). The right-hand column shows the percentage of each verb type in the corpus (e.g., 11.28% of all semantic verb types are verbal).

account for 30% of the predicates and 497 of these relational verbs (497/641), or 78%, have third person singular subjects. The next most frequent verb class is the material type—a large heterogeneous group of lexical items whose meanings fall under the general processes of *doing* and *happening* (Halliday 1994); these items make up 25% of all utterances. The third most frequent verb type in the corpus is verbs of cognition (16% of the total) and, notably, 57% of these tokens co-occur with first person singular subjects. Finally, predicates designating verbal processes account for 11% of the main verb types and 52% of these appear with first person singular subjects.

Sections 5, 6, and 7 highlight local patterns in the data contributing to the general distributional trends introduced in this section as regards the subjective (e.g., epistemic, evaluative) functions of the most frequently occurring subject-verb combinations. The organization of the analysis is based on the three most frequent subjects in the corpus (Section 5: first person singular, Section 6: second person singular, and Section 7: third person singular), and summaries are provided at the end of the sections. For each person, discussion will focus on the most commonly occurring verb types (relational, material, cognition, verbal) and how the most frequent structural patterns are tied to subjective expression.

5. First person singular subjects

First person singular is the prototypical site for expression of speaker point of view and the second most frequently occurring subject in this corpus. As summarized in Table 3, Section 4, *I* most often appears with verbs of cognition (32% of 1s subjects), material verbs (23% of 1s subjects), and verbal processes (21% of 1s subjects). The remaining 24% of first person singular subjects are spread among the other verb types (except perception/relational, which only occurs with third person subjects).

5.1 Verbs of cognition with 1s subjects

As noted, verbs in this group account for 32% of all predicates with first person subjects. Moreover, 57% (195/340) of all verbs of cognition themselves co-occur with a first person singular subject and 32% of these cognition predicates have second person singular subjects (see Section 6.1 for discussion). Table 4 presents the distribution of verbs of cognition preceded by first person singular subjects. Of the 195 1s + verb of cognition tokens, 131, or 67%, are present tense and 50 items, or 26%, are past tense.

The most frequent lexical verb in this present tense group is *know* (n=52) and 77% of these items occur in the construction *I don't know*, which exhibits a range of semantic and pragmatic functions in conversation (Scheibman 2000a). The second and third most frequent combinations of first person present tense subjects with verbs of cognition are tokens of the collocations *I think* (n=44) and *I guess* (n=17), respectively; the majority of these function as epistemic clauses (e.g., **I think** *a lot of it might be national temperament*) (Thompson and Hopper this volume, Thompson and Mulac 1991).[7] Eighty-nine percent, then, of all present tense 1s + verb of cognition combinations are formulaic expressions such as *I think*, *I don't know*, and *I guess*, and these expressions function epistemically or serve to mitigate assertion

Table 4. *Verbs of cognition with first person singular subjects* (n=195)

	Present	Past	Modal	Total
believe	1		3	4
catch		1		1
figure	1	1		2
figure out	1	5		6
find out	3	1	2	6
forget	2	2		4
guess	17			17
imagine			1	1
know	52	3	1	56
learn		1	1	2
realize	1	2		3
remember	2	2	1	5
suppose	1			1
think	48	31	5	84
wonder	2	1		3
Total	131	50	14	195

or disagreement in conversation. These are subjective functions that organize expression of the speaker's point of view in conversation; they are not being used to inform participants of the speaker's cognitive activities.

On the other hand, only 26% of cognition verbs with 1s subject (n=50) are morphologically marked past tense and the only frequent lexical verb in this group is *think* (n=31). As is true for the frequent 1s + verb of cognition combinations in the present tense, past tense tokens also tend to personalize the speaker's contribution as opposed to providing propositional information. The most frequent collocation with *think* in the past is *I thought* (n=23) and it is often the case that these utterances are not expressing past time reference. For example, the speaker uttered (4) at the moment an overhead light spontaneously went on in the room, so her use of the past tense has present relevance. In other words, she was not conveying something she *thought* in the past except as it frames the current situation.

(4) **I thought** we got our electricity fixed.   L16–49a

And finally, with respect to verbs of cognition that appear with other subjects —aside from the large number of these predicates that occur with second person singular subjects (see Section 6.1)—there are only 35 tokens of this verb type appearing with non-first person (and non-second person) singular subjects. Fifteen of these occur with third person singular human subjects (*s/he* or lexical NPs) and often these assertions that relate to another person's mental state are tempered by the speaker, as in (5), in which the speaker uses the epistemic parenthetical *I think* to soften his statement.

(5) **he thought I think** he'd have to pull it in second gea=r.   F6–35a

Additionally, six utterances with cognitive predicates have first person plural subjects and 14 co-occur with the third person plural pronoun *they*. In this latter group, all but two of the utterances have subjects which are referentially generic. In (6), for example, *they* refers to an imprecisely delineated group of people. In general, speakers hesitate to make assertions about other people's awareness, unless these statements are mediated (hedged) or if the subject entities are generically construed, as is the case below.

(6) **they don't know** what they're doing?   R12–17a

5.2 Material verbs with 1s subjects

Recall that material verbs designate processes of doing and happening, or "processes of the external world" (Halliday 1994: 107). In the database, material verbs are the second largest class of verbs and also the group containing the most lexemes (168 different lexical verbs). Furthermore, material verbs constitute the second largest verb class for utterances with first person singular subjects—23% (n=141) of 1s clauses contain material verbs. With regard to linguistic subjectivity, an interesting question surfaces related to the high frequency of this verb class with 1s subjects: if *I* is the prototypical site for a speaker's evaluative and organizing expression, then why does this subject pronoun so frequently occur with predicates referring to propositional events and activities? The rest of this section will present observations relevant to the patterning of this group in an effort to investigate this issue as it relates to the hypothesis in Section 2.1—that the most frequent constructions we see in discourse should be those that are linked to subjective expression.

For *I* + verbs of cognition utterances, the high frequency of the group is related to the high frequency of *I* plus particular lexical items in the group (e.g., *I think*, *I (don't) know*, *I guess*, *I thought*) This is not the situation for *I* + material verbs. The most frequently occurring lexical verbs in the 1s + material verb group are neither terribly frequent nor terrifically lexical: *go* (n=19), *do* (n=15), *get* (n=13). In other words, there are no frequently repeated, conventionalized expressions in this group; there are 65 lexical verbs in this group and 141 individual tokens, compared to the 1s + verb of cognition group which contains 15 lexical verbs and 195 individual items. The combination of *I* with these more propositional verbs (those that make reference to events in the world) may not be useful enough in discourse to form conventionalized grammatical or pragmatic constructions.

An interesting observation about this group, however, is that 1s + material verb is one of the few subject-verb type combinations in the corpus where there are more tokens in the past tense (the typical site of reporting of events and activities) than in the present; that is, 43% (n=60) of the items in this group are past tense and 31% (n=44) are present tense (see Table 7, Section 6.2). And these 1s + material verb past tense utterances do seem to function as conveyors of propositional information concerning the speaker's experiences, as illustrated in (7) and (8). However, given that the most frequent verbs in this group are basic English verbs (e.g., *do*, *get*), the level of propositionality (i.e., referential informativity) of even these material predicates is relatively general.

(7) **I** just **went** to some local doctor,   D10–42
(8) **I did** well, on the first block.   G13–38

Of the 44 present tense material verbs with *I* subjects in the corpus, 25 of these contain some type of intermediate function verb in their predicates (e.g., *gonna*, *want to*, *need*, *try to*) as in (9) and (10). These modal-like elements tend to mediate the propositionality of the predicate by personalizing the event, or activity, designated by the main verb—in essence, making the predicate more subjective.

(9) **I need to get** sleep over the weeke=nd.   A6–41b
(10) I wanna go out lambada dancing with you=.   L18–45

Another subgroup within the present tense material verbs with first person singular subjects (9 of the 44) are those predicates that express habitual meaning. In (11), the speaker is discussing the general state of her relationship with her boss at work.

(11) and **I** don't **play** that game.   G18–8

Though habitual expressions convey information, they also serve as generalizations. And generalizing, by definition, is not specifically informative and is always potentially evaluative.

Related to the frequent presence of intermediate function verbs (e.g., quasi modals, semi-auxiliaries) with present tense predicates with material verbs discussed above is the distributional fact that 26% (n=37) of all 1s + material verb items have predicates that contain a modal auxiliary. Moreover, throughout the corpus, central modals consistently (in all subjects) occur more frequently with material verbs than with other semantic verb types. Again, this suggests that in interactive discourse, even the most potentially informative predicate types are structurally integrated into the speaker's point of view (in this case by the presence of modal expressions).

5.3 Verbs of verbal process with 1s subjects

The fourth most common verb type in the corpus is the group of verbal processes; this class not only includes verbs of saying but also other symbolic processes such as meaning (Halliday 1994). Notably, first person singular subjects account for over half of all verbal process predicates in the corpus (128/245, or 52%) and 76% of these (97/128) occur in the present tense. Table 5 presents the distribution of verbal process verbs occurring with first person singular subjects in the data.

Table 5. *Verbs of verbal process with first person singular subjects* (n=128)

	Present	Past	Modal	Total
ask		2	1	3
be like (quotative)	4		1	5
bet	3		1	4
go			2	2
mean	78			78
propose		1		1
put		1		1
say	4	9		13
show	1			1
sound	1			1
suggest			1	1
swear	2			2
talk		5		5
tell	3	8		11
Total	96	26	6	128

Most striking about this group is that 61% of all tokens (78/128) and 81% of present tense tokens (78/96) are instances of the collocation *I mean*. Schiffrin (1987) characterizes *I mean* as a discourse marker that prefaces expansion/explanation of speakers' contributions or intentions in conversation. As is true for *I think* and *I guess*, *I mean* also acts as an epistemic clause (cf. Thompson and Hopper this volume) as in (12).

(12) **I mean** Rene and Anne were very sweet.   C11–38a

Worth noting is that the lexical verb *mean* only occurs with non-first person singular subjects seven times in the database: four times with the subjects *this* and *that* and three times with *you* (e.g., *what do you mean*).

5.4 Summary of first person singular subjects

In a corpus of spoken American English conversation, the first person singular pronoun functions as the subject of 28% of the utterances. Clauses with 1s subjects account for 57% of the verbs of cognition, 52% of the verbs of verbal process, and 26% of material verbs. Within the category of utterances with 1s subjects itself, 32% of these appear with verbs of cognition, 23% with material verbs, and 21% with verbal process predicates; that is, 75% (464/617) of 1s subjects occur with these three verb types. The high frequency of *I* with present tense verbs of cognition and verbal processes is attributable to the high frequency of individual routinized expressions that personalize and organize the speaker's contribution (e.g., *I think*, *I mean*). Even for cognitive verbs in the past tense, the most frequent item is *I thought* which neither conveys information about past events nor even typically designates past time reference.

With respect to material verbs, the situation is different from the cognition and verbal types discussed above. The high frequency of this verb class may be an artifact of the broad delineation of the category—that this group includes many lexical verbs. Even so, it is notable that there are no highly frequent verbs in this particular group, and that the most common lexical items are basic verbs in English that form low content, nonreferential verb-object combinations (Thompson and Hopper this volume), or dispersed predicates (Hopper 1991), as opposed to contributing to more semantically informative clauses. Additionally, the data suggest that material verbs in general co-occur more frequently with expressions of modality indicating that even when participants are relating events in the world, this information is mediated by the speaker's subjective, or evaluative, stance.

6. Second person singular subjects

Utterances with second person singular subjects are the third most frequent subject type in the database. They account for 15% (n=335) of the total and only 14% (48/335) of *you* subjects occur with past tense predicates. With respect to the most frequent verb types, 2s utterances make up 32% of all verbs of cognition and 17% of material verbs. Within the category of second person singular itself, 33% of the tokens (110/335) co-occur with verbs of cognition and 27% (90/335) with material verbs. The combinations of *you* with these two most frequent verb types will be the topics of Sections 6.1 and 6.2.

6.1 Verbs of cognition with 2s subjects

Table 6 presents the distribution of cognitive verbs with second person singular

Table 6. *Verbs of cognition with second person*
singular subjects (n=110)

	Present	Past	Modal	Total
find out		1		1
know	98	2		100
know better			1	1
learn		1		1
make up			1	1
remember			1	1
think	1	2	1	4
think about	1			1
Total	100	6	4	110

subjects. Quite clearly the frequency of this subject with this verb type is due to the conversational frequency of one item—the formulaic *you know*, which accounts for 98/110 or 89% of the total utterances in this group.

You know fulfills automated, interactive (=organizational) functions in conversation. Schiffrin (1987) discusses specific uses of *you know* in conversation and narrative; one function of the expression is that of allowing speakers to check in with other participants to make sure they share relevant background knowledge during the talk. Schiffrin also observes that in conversational narrative, *you know* occurs with evaluative utterances to encourage hearers to attend to (agree with?) speakers' assessments. In (13), the speaker is justifying her distancing from her brother during a period when he had a disruptive drug habit; *you know* in this episode appears to solicit support for her stance, illustrating the interactive evaluative function of this expression suggested by Schiffrin.

(13) but you have to—
      you have to at one point let go.
      you can't constantly be torn,
      . . (H) just to=rn to pie=ces,
      by=,
      you know=,
      somebody like tha=t.   D23–1

However, a functional distinction between *you know* serving as a metalinguistic check on the sharing of information by participants versus the expression's garnering support for the speaker's evaluative stance is not easy to determine, in part due to the more general problem of distinguishing informativeness from evaluativeness in linguistic utterances. Therefore, in (13), it is ambiguous whether the speaker's *you know* is guiding the participants to attend to the relevant facts of the story or to the speaker's own assessment of the facts.

6.2 Material verbs with 2s subjects

Twenty-seven percent (90/335) of clauses with second person singular subjects contain material verbs. As is true for first person singular utterances with material verbs, there are no highly frequent lexical verbs in this group; rather, the frequency of the type comes from the large number of lexical verbs in the category (51 types, 90 tokens in this case). Table 7 shows the distribution of tense and modal auxiliaries for material predicates with 1s, 2s, and 3s subjects. Recall that central modals occur more frequently with material verbs than with other verb types. It was suggested in Section 5.2, regarding utterances with 1s subjects and material verbs, that speakers tend to personalize these more propositional predicates with modal expressions.

Table 7. *Material verbs by 1s, 2s, and 3s and tense* (n=409)

Subject	Present	Past	Modal	Total
1s	44	60	37	141
	31.21%	42.55%	26.24%	100.00%
2s	44	19	27	90
	48.89%	21.11%	30.00%	100.00%
3s	83	70	23	176
	47.16%	39.77%	13.07%	100.00%
Total	172	150	87	409
Percent	42.05%	36.67%	21.27%	100.00%

Table 7 shows that predicates with 1s and 2s subjects have a greater proportion of modals than do 3s subjects. It appears, then, that when speakers are addressing another speech act participant directly, they often mediate their assertions towards the addressee by using a modal element, as in (14).

(14) **you can use** this for your muffins.   A13–20

Because of interpersonal considerations (e.g., negative politeness strategies), these second person singular utterances containing material verbs and modal elements reflect a kind of interactive subjectivity—in that the speaker expresses a subjective, or empathetic, construal of the other person's agentivity.

Table 7 also shows that almost half of the 2s + material verb clauses occur in the present tense (n=44), and there appears to be little evidence of an informative, or

propositional, character to these utterances. This group of 2s present tense material
process clauses includes: (a) interrogatives and other questions; (b) utterances with
subjects that are best categorized as generic (i.e., not specifically referential), often
conveying first person singular reference (e.g., (15) in which the speaker is describing his own reaction); or (c) "subordinate" clauses following evaluative or epistemic
"main" clauses as in (16) and (17), respectively.

(15) it smells like **you're walking** past a d=umpster.   D18–28b

(16) that's good **you're getting** r- good rest.   A6–42b

(17) I think **you ought to change** doctors.[8]   D10–38b

    There are only 19 utterances with second person singular subjects with material
verbs in the past tense. The major difference between this past tense group and the
much more frequent present tense material clauses is that in these past tense 2s
material utterances (with the exception of one hypothetical clause), all the subject
pronouns refer to discourse participants (i.e., they are not generic). In two ways,
then, the informative, or propositional nature of these past tense items is mediated
structurally as discussed for the present tense: (a) almost half of the group are questions and (b) several of the tokens are subordinate clauses preceded by epistemic
expressions and evaluatives (e.g., *I thought* **you** *already* **brought** *the cake in. well,
glad* **you** *stopped i=n,*). There are also a few clauses in this past tense group that are
direct assertions about the subject, illustrated in (18) and (19).

(18) but . . . . **you wrote**,
     Z's aging again,   G17–8

(19) **you met** Benno,   D20–5

6.3 Summary of second person singular subjects

Second person singular subjects are the third most frequent group of utterances in
the database; they make up 15% of the corpus (n=335). The two most frequent verb
types occurring with *you* subjects are verbs of cognition (33%) and material verbs
(27%). Proportionally, there is less past tense with 2s predicates and more frequent
occurrence of modal auxiliaries than for other subjects in the corpus.

    Eighty-nine percent of 2s verbs of cognition (and 29% of all 2s utterances) are
tokens of the fixed expression *you know*. These, of course, are all present tense.
Forty-nine percent of 2s material verbs are also present tense; this group consists of
questions, utterances with generic *you* reference (often interpreted as first person),
and so-called subordinate clauses prefaced by epistemic and evaluative clauses. In
all of these present tense forms, speakers personalize and situate their utterances in

relation to another speech act participant. Moreover, the use of generic *you* found in many 2s utterances allows speakers to make generalizations, which are themselves forms of evaluation. Almost a third of second person subjects with material predicates also contain a modal auxiliary. This permits speakers to mediate direct assertion about a speech act participant and expresses a kind of interactive subjectivity which may be viewed as an empathetic negative politeness strategy.

There are very few past tense predicates with second person singular subjects (6 tokens with verbs of cognition and 19 tokens with material verbs). Given that the past tense is typically an important vehicle for conveying propositional information (e.g., through narrated events), it is not surprising that English speakers use it infrequently with second person subjects due to face issues. Though there are not many past tense tokens of material verbs in this group, one characteristic that distinguishes them from their present tense counterparts is that the past tense subjects are much more likely to be referential (i.e., refer to a speech act participant) than generic.

7. Third person singular subjects

Third person singular is the most frequent subject in the corpus; it accounts for 43% (931/2172) of all utterances. Sixty-seven percent of these clauses (626/931) are present tense, 26% (239/931) are past tense, and 7% of these predicates (66/931) contain modal auxiliaries. Third person singular, however, is a much more complex member of the English category person than are first and second person singular subject pronouns (though the latter two are not without functional variation). This is because 3s includes several subject types which differ in animacy and referentiality and this affects their distribution in relation to verb type and tense.

Table 8 presents counts of third person subject types by tense. Overall, the most frequent subjects are *s/he*, *it*, lexical noun phrases, and *that*. For 3s clauses, present tense is much more frequent than past; however, we see that for the human subject *s/he*, there is proportionally more past tense than for the other subject types (present: 50%, past: 41%). For 3s subjects with inanimate referents, such as *it*, *that*, and *this*, there is a larger proportion of present tense than past tense. There seems to be a general trend in these data, with the exception of second person singular which is 68% present and 14% past, that subjects with human referents (*I*, *s/he*, and some lexical NPs) co-occur with a greater proportion of past tense predicates than do inanimate subjects.

In the next Section, I will investigate the high frequency of third person singular subjects with relational verbs, specifically, the frequency of referentially non-human subjects with this verb type. The relational verb class is the most frequent

Table 8. *Third person singular subject types* (n=931)

3sg Subj type	Present	Past	Modal	Total	Percent 3 sg
s/he	125	101	23	249	26.72
	50.20%	40.56%	9.24%	100.00%	
it	163	51	16	230	24.57
	70.87%	22.17%	6.96%	100.00%	
lexical NP	103	57	15	175	18.88
	58.86%	32.57%	8.57%	100.00%	
that	117	16	12	145	15.56
	80.69%	11.03%	8.28%	100.00%	
there	40	10	0	50	5.36
	80.00%	20.00%	0.00%	100.00%	
this	38	0	0	38	4.08
	100.00%	0.00%	0.00%	100.00%	
what	28	3	0	31	3.33
	90.32%	9.68%	0.00%	100.00%	
who	7	1	0	8	0.86
	87.50%	12.50%	0.00%	100.00%	
they	3	0	0	3	0.43
	100.00%	0.00%	0.00%	100.00%	
one	2	0	0	2	0.21
	100.00%	0.00%	0.00%	100.00%	
Total	626	239	66	931	
Percent	67.24	25.67	7.09	100.00	100.00

verb type in the database and occurs with over half (53%, 497/931) of all utterances with 3s subjects.

7.1 Relational verbs with 3s subjects

Relational processes are processes of being. Halliday (1994: 119) explains that "[i]n relational clauses, there are two parts to the 'being': something is being said to 'be' something else. In other words, a relation is being set up between two separate entities." Relational processes may be schematically represented as: "*x* is *a*" "*x* is at *a*" (where "is at" represents "is at, in, on, about", etc.), or "*x* has *a*" (Halliday 1994: 119).[9] In English, relational verbs overwhelmingly appear as predicate nominal, predicate adjective, or predicate oblique clauses, as illustrated in (20). There are, however, other verbs besides *be* that express relations between two entities, as in (21).

(20) *Predicate nominal clause*
     this is . . a raging bureaucracy,   R13–6
     Predicate adjective clause
     that's terrible.   D13–25
     Predicate oblique clause
     he's still out there.   M7–29

(21) this tractor's going sour on him.   F6–44

Recall that relational processes are the most frequent verb type in the corpus; they account for 30% of the data (641/2172). Seventy-eight percent (497/641) of all subjects occurring with relational verbs are third person singular and 79% of these 3s relational clauses are present tense. In contrast, 1s subjects occur with relational verb types in only 8% of the utterances, 2s subjects in 9%, and 3p subjects in 7%. Moreover, within this super category of third person singular subject, relational predicates account for 53% of the tokens (497/931).

Table 9 (see p. 82) shows the distribution of relational verb processes for 3s subject types. Notably, the most frequent subjects that combine with these predicates are *it*, *that*, and lexical noun phrases, that is, primarily subjects with inanimate referents.[10] Recall also from Table 8, that with respect to 3s subjects as a whole, the most frequent types are *s/he* and *it*, but for relational predicates, 3s human subject pronouns account for only 12% (59/497) of this type.

In both English and Swedish corpora of conversation, Dahl (1997) also finds that egocentric (speech act participants) and non-speech act participant animate subjects rarely occur with copular clauses. He notes that, distributionally, "[t]he differences between copular and non-copular clauses both with regard to animacy and egocentricity are striking" (Dahl 1997: 24). Given that structure emerges from what speakers commonly do in discourse, then what activities or proclivities of speakers in interaction might account for there being so many relational expressions with non-human subjects (in particular, *it* and *that*) in English conversation?

In many approaches to linguistic analysis, third person singular past tense is considered the representative site for reporting—for narrating events and conveying information about the world and the people acting in it. In a discussion of the English verb with respect to discrepancies between decontextualized sentences grammarians make up and the structures actually found in discourse, Hopper observes:

> Clearly if one is going to make up a sentence in order to illustrate a grammatical phenomenon, the impulse will be to select a perspective that is remote, third person, distant

from involvement, unwitnessed, and so on. In taking such sentences to be the norm for English, we implicitly exclude emotional involvement from grammatical analysis, and impart to the verb a privilege which its relatively lowly status in natural discourse does not seem to merit. We are thus in danger of instating an unnatural and highly marked type of utterance as the basis for English grammar.   (Hopper 1997: 243)

And, indeed, with respect to 3s relational predicates, there is a "clash" between the traditional referential mode of grammatical description and what is proto-typically found in English discourse. The most frequent third person singular utterance in English conversation is not a structure with clipped, informative, telic, past tense verbs, such as *Robin turned on the lights, sat down by the fire and ate two pieces of pizza*. Rather, the third person singular utterances we see most often are expressions such as: *it's just dry skin, that's true, feminist really is a dirty word, that's funny*, or *but that's probably her personality*. That is, the most frequent verb

Table 9. *Relational verbs with third person singular subject types* (n=497)

3sg Subj type	Present	Past	Modal	Total	Percent 3 sg
s/he	45	11	3	59	11.85%
	76.27%	18.64%	5.08%	100.00%	
it	112	34	9	155	31.12%
	72.26%	21.94%	5.81%	100.00%	
lexical NP	57	20	5	82	16.47%
	69.51%	24.39%	6.10%	100.00%	
that	102	13	7	122	24.50%
	83.61%	10.66%	5.74%	100.00%	
there	10	2	0	12	2.41%
	83.33%	16.67%	0.00%	100.00%	
this	31	0	0	31	6.22%
	100.00%	0.00%	0.00%	100.00%	
what	28	1	0	29	5.82%
	96.55%	3.45%	0.00%	100.00%	
who	5	0	0	5	1.20%
	100.00%	0.00%	0.00%	100.00%	
one	2	0	0	2	0.40%
	100.00%	0.00%	0.00%	100.00%	
Total	392	81	24	497	
Percent	78.87%	16.30%	4.83%	100.00%	100.00%

types in this corpus are relational predicates, in particular, those with third person singular inanimate subjects. Functionally, these relational clauses index attitude and, less frequently, place. Even clauses that might be characterized as descriptive, such as (22), are in fact evaluative. This example was uttered by a mother who was trying to convince her daughter that the vacuum cleaner she bought her for her birthday was high quality. In other words, it is an evaluation. Note also the presence of the amplifier *all*.

(22) It's all metal,   A19–5

Similarly, the speaker of (23) is describing the dance floor in a bar he goes to. One might argue that he is simply conveying information to the other participants. But he is not relating a description of the bar's layout; rather, he is conveying his opinion of the dance floor and this is emphasized by the intensifier *too* and the modality adverb *though*.

(23) the dance floor's too small in that place though,   L18–31

Relational predicates, then, tend to be evaluative (surely, to varying degrees). In these conversational utterances, it appears as though the conveying of information is rarely (if ever) purely descriptive. The frequency of these clause types reflects what speakers are commonly doing in conversation—they are evaluating and situating attitudes, events, and places. In short, they are personalizing their discourse using these copular constructions.

And finally, a few provisional comments concerning the preponderance of inanimate subjects with relational verbs are in order. The two most frequent subjects occurring with these predicates are *it* (155/497, or 31% of the relationals) and *that* (122/497, or 25% of the relationals) and the majority of the clauses appearing with these subjects are predicate adjectives and predicate nominals. Though there are certainly differences in uses of *it* and *that*, both of these subjects are referentially versatile for speakers; that is they may refer to an entity, an event or state, or a piece of discourse.[11] Moreover, *it* and *that* are subjects (also *there*) that in some usages, in some grammatical treatments, might be characterized as nonreferential, or empty, indicating that in particular constructions they may be more grammaticized than the other third person singular subjects.[12] This generality of reference of these inanimate pronouns may grant speakers great freedom in referring to a variety of discursive and grammatical phenomena to personalize their utterances. Similarly, the demonstrative pronouns (which also include *that*) are subjective in that they tacitly make reference to the speaker; thus they are referentially flexible as well. In a discussion of deictic pronouns and other similar elements, Benveniste writes:

These signs are always available and become "full" as soon as a speaker introduces them into each instance of his discourse. Since they lack material reference, they cannot be misused; since they do not assert anything, they are not subject to the condition of truth and escape all denial. Their role is to provide the instrument of a conversion that one could call the conversion of language into discourse.   (Benveniste 1971: 219–20)

Therefore, both deictic and nondeictic 3s inanimate subjects may appear frequently with these relational clauses precisely because they are highly grammaticized and exhibit pragmatic and contextual flexibility in their reference. When these expressions are subjects in English, speakers use them to situate a discursive focus, or starting point, for their evaluations—the substance of which is played out in the relational predicates (see Chafe 1994 for discussion of English subjects as starting points).

8. Conclusions

Though this study is primarily an investigation into the structure of subjective expression as it manifests in frequently occurring subject-predicate combinations in English conversation, this work (because of its method and use of conversational data) has implicitly tested characterizations of morphosyntactic and semantic categories as they are instantiated in spontaneous discourse. Frequency counts of subject-verb type patterns reveal three global trends: (1) the most frequent subjects in the corpus are (in order) third person singular, first person singular, and second person singular; (2) the most frequent verb types are (again, in order) relational, material, cognition, and verbal; and (3) the majority of predicates are present tense. Though these generalizations function as theoretical guides, they are not on their own research questions (at least not in their present form). One reason for not automatically treating these global patterns as empirically testable hypotheses is that there is always slippage between the fitness of linguistic categories (e.g., person, verb type, tense, third person singular subject) as they have been traditionally characterized and the actual conversational utterances that instantiate them. Such a situation argues for the analysis of local (=contextualized) patterns in grammatical investigations.

For example, third person singular is the most frequent subject in the corpus because it is composed of several subtypes, and these subtypes pattern differently with respect to their animacy and referentiality and also with respect to surrounding grammatical and lexical material. So as regards English conversation—depending on the goals of the investigation—third person singular may not be a coherent or useful grammatical category on its own. Similarly, in this database, 64% of all utterances are present tense, but it is well known that there are many meanings assigned to the English present tense (e.g., state present, habitual present, historical present, generic) (Comrie 1985, Quirk et al. 1985) and that these meanings may also shift depending on the verb (type), predicate, or interactive context. Thus present tense in English discourse is also a super category and is best analyzed in individual contexts.

There are, however, traditional grammatical categories that are more harmonious with usages in conversation than the preceding examples (i.e., they "work" for conversation) such as first person singular subjects, verbs of cognition, and past tense. A constant thorn in the sides of researchers using conversational data to investigate grammar (or vice versa) is the fact that referentially-based descriptions of linguistic categories exhibit varying degrees of fitness when applied to data from interactive discourse. One way to mediate this challenge is to be guided by global frequency patterns but then to analyze constructions locally, or contextually, in order to evaluate the usefulness and, if necessary, to modify referentially derived analytical categories.

Given the role of frequency in the emergence of conventionalized structure in interaction, subjective patterning manifests uniquely in different contexts. With first person and second person singular subjects we find highly frequent lexical colloca- tions with pragmatic import, in particular with verbs of cognition and, for first per- son, with verbal process predicates as well (e.g., *I guess, I don't know, you know, I mean*). Moreover, text counts indicate that the high use of these conventionalized 1s and 2s expressions is in large part responsible for the frequency of these catego- ries as a whole (e.g., 1s, 2s, verbs of cognition), as well as for the individual verb lexemes (e.g., *know, think,* and *mean* are the second, fourth, and fifth most frequent lexical verbs, respectively, in the database).

For both first person and second person singular subjects, we also find functional continuity among different usage contexts. That is, the majority of clauses with 1s subjects, including the grammaticized epistemic collocations, consistently commu- nicate the speaker's subjective stance (e.g., modality, evaluation, generalization) and these often have discourse management function as well. For 2s utterances, there is a paucity of structures promoting direct assertion (even with material verbs where it would be most expected) and when speakers use *you* referentially (=to refer to a speech act participant vs. generically), they are usually asking questions or mediat- ing their assertions with modal expressions. In general, then, 2s utterances reflect an interactive, or empathetic, subjectivity on the part of the speaker toward the addressee.

With respect to third person singular utterances, highlights from the data indicate that 44% of the tokens in this super category are subjects with nonhuman referents co-occurring with relational predicates (most commonly, the highly grammaticized *it* and *that*). It was suggested that these primarily copular clauses allow speakers to index their opinions and attitudes as opposed to being informatively descriptive. A question still to be explored, however, is the relationship between referentiality of subject and the expression of subjectivity. One wonders, for example, how these bleached, shifting (often deictic), inanimate subjects contribute to the expression of evaluation in these relational predicates?

In looking at the most frequent combinations of subject and verb type in English conversation, it appears that the prototypical structures of English clauses do not seem geared to objective relating of events. If high transitivity may be taken as a premiere example, or a grammatical prototype, of propositional or referential communication (=the conveying of unmediated descriptive information or facts about multiple participants and events in the world), then we know that frequency of these expressions is quite low in English conversation (Thompson and Hopper this volume). Instead, what we find most commonly in interactive discourse are those subject-predicate combinations that permit speakers to personalize their contributions, index attitude and situation, evaluate, and negotiate empathetically with other participants.

Notes

* I would like to thank Melissa Axelrod for several sensible discussions about this work. Without her input and encouragement, the data analyzed and presented in this paper might still be languishing in their respective cells in an Excel spreadsheet. Of course, any errors in analysis or interpretation are my own.

1. This database is a subset of a larger one which consists of 37 coding fields; see Scheibman (2000b) for detailed discussion of terms and coding categories.

2. I would like to acknowledge the Corpus of Spoken American English at the University of California, Santa Barbara for permission to use these recorded conversations and transcripts.

3. There are very few *2p* subjects (n=5). They are *you guys*, *you both*, and one case of *you* where it was clear that the speaker was referring to a married couple.

4. Bolding highlights the parts of utterances under discussion; numbers following examples locate utterances in the database.

5. The following transcription symbols are used in this paper: . final transitional continuity; , continuing transitional continuity; ? appeal transitional continuity; — truncated utterance; = lengthening; .. pause; (H) inhalation; X indecipherable.

6. Future tense is not coded. *Will* is classified as a modal and *gonna/going to* as an intermediate function verb (verbs that semantically and/or morphosyntactically fall somewhere between the broad categories of auxiliary and main verb in English) (see Quirk *et al.* 1985:136 ff.).

7. Four tokens of *I+think* are present progressive.

8. Note that this utterance also contains *I think* plus the marginal modal *ought to*.

9. However, in this study, "*x* has *a*" clauses are grouped separately in a verb class called possessive/ relational and are not included in the larger relational group discussed here.

10. Only 24 of the 82 lexical NP subjects with relational verbs have human referents and five of these are generic (e.g., *somebody, a person*). This means that 70% (58/82) of these lexical NP subjects also have nonhuman referents.

11. Though *it* is coded as discourse referential only 9 times in the corpus, *that* serves the same function 46 times.

12. Bolinger (1977) suggests that *it* is always referential (ambient *it*) in that it refers to the environment. Responding to claims that the pronoun is nonreferential, he writes, "Our mistake has been to confuse generality of meaning with lack of meaning" (85).

References

Benveniste, E. 1971. *Problems in General Linguistics*. (Translated by M. E. Meek). Coral Gables, FL: University of Miami Press.

Bolinger, D. 1977. *Meaning and Form*. London/New York: Longman.

Boyland, J.T. 1996. "Morphosyntactic change in progress: a psycholinguistic approach. Berkeley". Doctoral Dissertation, UC Berkeley.

Bybee, J. 1985. "On the nature of grammatical categories: a diachronic perspective". In *Proceedings of the Second Eastern States Conference on Linguistics*, S. Choi (ed.), 17–34.

Bybee, J. 1998. "The emergent lexicon". *CLS 34: The Panels*. Chicago: Chicago Linguistic Society, 421–35.

Bybee, J. To appear. "Mechanisms of change in grammaticization: the role of frequency". In *Handbook of Historical Linguistics*, R. Janda and B. Joseph (eds.). Oxford: Blackwell.

Bybee, J., Perkins, R. and Pagliuca, W. 1994. *The Evolution of Grammar: Tense, Aspect, and Modality in the Languages of the World*. Chicago: University of Chicago Press.

Bybee, J. and Scheibman, J. 1999. "The effect of usage on degrees of constituency: the reduction of *don't* in English". *Linguistics* 37:575–96.

Carey, K. 1995. "Subjectification and the development of the English perfect". In *Subjectivity and Subjectivization: Linguistic Perspectives*, D. Stein and S. Wright (eds.), 83–102. Cambridge: Cambridge University Press.

Chafe, W. 1994. *Discourse, Consciousness, and Time*. Chicago: University of Chicago Press.

Comrie, B. 1985. *Tense*. Cambridge: Cambridge University Press.

Dahl, Ö. 1997. *Egocentricity in Discourse and Syntax*. http://www.ling.su.se/staff/oesten/ egocentric.

Dixon, R.M.W. 1991. *A New Approach to English Grammar, on Semantic Principles*. Oxford: Clarendon Press.

Du Bois, J., Schuetze-Coburn, S., Cumming, S. and Paolino, D. 1993. "Outline of discourse transcription". In *Talking Data: Transcription and Coding in Discourse Research*, J.A. Edwards and M.D. Lampert (eds.), 45–89. Hillsdale, NJ: Lawrence Erlbaum.

Ford, C.E. 1993. *Grammar in Interaction: Adverbial Clauses in American English Conversations*. Cambridge: Cambridge University Press.

Fox, B.A. 1987. *Anaphora and the Structure of Discourse*. Cambridge: Cambridge University Press.

Gell-Mann, M. 1994. *The Quark and the Jaguar: Adventures in the Simple and the Complex*. New York: W. H. Freeman.

Haiman, J. 1995. "Grammatical signs of the divided self: A study of language and culture". In *Discourse Grammar and Typology: Papers in Honor of John W. M. Verhaar*, W. Abraham, T. Givón and S.A. Thompson (eds.), 213–34. Amsterdam/Philadelphia: John Benjamins.

Haiman, J. 1998. *Talk is Cheap: Sarcasm, Alienation, and the Evolution of Language*. New York: Oxford University Press.

Halliday, M.A.K. 1994. *An Introduction to Functional Grammar*, 2nd Edition. London: Edward Arnold.

Hopper, P.J. 1987. "Emergent grammar". *Berkeley Linguistics Society* 13:139–57.

Hopper, P.J. 1991. "Dispersed verbal predicates in vernacular written narrative". *Berkeley Linguistics Society* 17:402–13.

Hopper, P.J. 1997. "When 'grammar' and discourse clash: the problem of source conflicts". In *Essays on Language Function and Language Type*, J. Bybee, J. Haiman and S.A. Thompson (eds.), 231–47. Amsterdam/Philadelphia: John Benjamins.

Iwasaki, S. 1993. *Subjectivity in Grammar and Discourse: Theoretical Considerations and a Case Study of Japanese Spoken Discourse*. Amsterdam/Philadelphia: John Benjamins.

Jakobson, R. 1960. "Concluding statement: linguistics and poetics". In *Style in Language*, T.A. Sebeok (ed.) 350–77. New York: John Wiley & Sons and The Technology Press of Massachusetts Institute of Technology.

Krug, M. 1998. "String frequency: a cognitive motivating factor in coalescence, language processing, and linguistic change". *Journal of English Linguistics* 26:286–320.

Lyons, J. 1994. "Subjecthood and subjectivity". In *Subjecthood and Subjectivity: the Status of the Subject in Linguistic Theory*, M. Yaguello (ed.) 9–17. Paris: Ophrys.

Ono, T. and Thompson, S.A. 1995. "What can conversation tell us about syntax?". In *Descriptive and Theoretical Models in the Alternative Linguistics*, P.W. Davis (ed.), 213–71. Amsterdam/Philadelphia: John Benjamins.

Quirk, R., Greenbaum, S., Leech, G. and Svartvik, J. 1985. *A Comprehensive Grammar of the English Language*. London: Longman.

Scheibman, J. 2000a. "*I dunno* . . . A usage-based account of the phonological reduction of *don't* in American English conversation". *Journal of Pragmatics* 32:105–24.

Scheibman, J. 2000b. "Structural patterns of subjectivity in American English conversation". Doctoral Dissertation, University of New Mexico.

Schiffrin, D. 1987. *Discourse Markers*. Cambridge: Cambridge University Press.

Silverstein, M. 1976. "Shifters, linguistic categories, and cultural description". In *Meaning in Anthropology*, K.H. Basso and H.A. Selby (eds.), 11–55. Albuquerque: University of New Mexico Press.

Thompson, S.A. and Hopper, P.J. This volume. "Transitivity and clause structure in conversation". In *Frequency and the Emergence of Linguistic Structure*, J. Bybee and P. Hopper (eds.), Amsterdam/Philadelphia: John Benjamins.

Thompson, S.A. and Mulac, A. 1991. "A quantitative perspective on the grammaticization of epistemic parentheticals in English". In *Approaches to Grammaticalization, Volume II: Focus on Types of Grammatical Markers*, E.C. Traugott and B. Heine (eds.), 313–29. Amsterdam/Philadelphia: John Benjamins.

Traugott, E.C. 1995. "Subjectification in grammaticalisation". In *Subjectivity and Subjectivization: Linguistic Perspectives*, D. Stein and S. Wright (eds.), 31–54. Cambridge: Cambridge University Press.

Tsui, A.B.M. 1991. "The pragmatic functions of *I don't know*". *Text* 11:607–22.

Verhagen, A. 1995. "Subjectification, syntax, and communication". In *Subjectivity and Subjectivization: Linguistic Perspectives*, D. Stein and S. Wright (eds.), 103–28. Cambridge: Cambridge University Press.

Paths to prepositions?
A corpus-based study of the acquisition of a lexico-grammatical category*

NAOMI HALLAN

Chemnitz University of Technology, Germany

1. Introduction

In this paper I discuss the use of data from large corpora of natural language to investigate the behavior of a group of multifunctional words in British English. I will examine findings relating to the acquisition of these different functions by children and their use in adult speech.

1.1 The role of introspection in linguistic research

The growing body of data available from modern corpus linguistics (e.g., Sinclair 1991a, Francis *et al.* 1996, Stubbs 1996) is beginning to make clear that the type of linguistic knowledge accessed by introspection is by no means the same as that used by speakers and writers when they produce language.

Fillmore (1992) points out that the two types of linguistic knowledge, that gained through introspection and that observed in large bodies of natural language data, should complement one another. Indeed, the patterns observable in corpus studies are not always accessible to intuition and the structures which our intuition leads us to believe are possible may not always occur in a given body of data, due to accidents of text selection. Croft (1998) cautions that introspection can only be a guide to constraints on possible forms. It cannot, on its own, predict what will in fact occur.

There is an additional problem with introspection, which is that none of the introspectors are unbiased. Whether we like it or not, all members of our academic communities have been influenced, and perhaps even conditioned, by the prescriptive teaching we have received about our mother tongue in the course of our primary and secondary education. We make sometimes unquestioning assumptions about the structure of our native tongue. We are not always conscious that what we claim we *would* say is perhaps what we feel we *should* say (cf. Labov 1972, 1973).

One field in which the dependence on introspection may have led scholars to plausible but unsupported conclusions is the modeling of linguistic relationships and categories, which has become increasingly important in the field of cognitive linguistics in recent years. Lakoff and Johnson (1980), Langacker (1987), Johnson (1987) are just a few of the important works in this field, which laid the ground rules for an approach to the mental representation of different linguistic categories, both semantic and syntactic, which blossomed in the 1980s and shows no sign of flagging today. Two fundamentals of this approach are:

(a) the idea of such representations and the categories they portray as *embodied*, grounded in a mental model of the world that is ineluctably shaped by the fact the we experience it through the perceptual filters and kinetic properties of our bodies;

(b) the growing evidence from psychological research, particular the work of Rosch and her colleagues (for instance Rosch 1973, 1978), which provided support for the notion that many mental categories are based on a central reference point—a prototype, with central members of the category most nearly resembling the prototype and peripheral members having perhaps only a few of its properties.

Prepositions have always attracted a lot of attention in this approach because of the perception and modelling of spatial relationships, and their early development from bodily perception (for instance H.H. Clark, 1973). Since Brugmann's (1983) model of the highly polysemous *over*, the models have proliferated, for instance Lakoff (1987), Schulze (1987), Vandeloise (1994), Taylor (1995), Dirven (1995), among others.

The recognition that human beings are embodied communicators, with all that this implies for the human communication system, and the application of psychological findings to explanations in linguistics seem to me to be valuable and constructive. However, the essentially introspection-driven nature of many analyses by the authors mentioned above and by their colleagues diminishes the value of their theses. The psychological insights which they so creatively apply have been tested by experiment and observation. Their applications, however, depend on the introspections of individual native-speakers, who for all their extensive training and pre-eminent status in the field, should not be exempt from the basic requirement of scientific endeavor, that they find a way of testing their hypotheses. This discontent is of course not uniquely mine: Sandra and Rice (1995) have given it detailed expression. In addition the techniques of modern corpus linguistics now make it

possible to test at least some of the hypotheses of these models and this is what I try
to do in the research described here.

1.2 An implicit assumption

Most of the models of prepositional structures referred to in Section 1.1 start with
the (often implicit) assumption that the use of word forms such as *on*, *in*, or *over* as
spatial prepositions is primary. This arises almost automatically from the basic
assumption of the whole cognitive approach, that spatial perception itself is primary
(see for instance Brugmann 1983: 2–3, 54). The examples invented to support the
argumentation (or informally elicited, in the case of Taylor, 1995), all involve what
is held to be the basic, prototypical use of a word such as *over*, in sentences such as:

(1) The plane flew over the field (Brugmann 1983: 19)
(2) Boris climbed over the wall (Brugmann 1983: 21)
(3) The lamp hangs over the table (Taylor 1995: 110)

Similar types of examples are invented in the discussions of other prepositions and
in most of the others that have been published. There seems to be little awareness
that the large amount of available language data might tell us what speakers and
writers actually do with the word forms in question.

These word forms, which Bowerman (1996) calls *path morphemes*, are clearly
multi-functional in English. Bowerman's study is primarily concerned with the
acquisition of locative semantics, in a language with path morphemes, like English,
and one without, like Korean. My concerns here are somewhat different, but I will
adopt her term for two reasons. First, the study for which she uses it is in part concerned with countering preconceptions about the very necessity of this word-class.
Other languages besides Korean, in other language families, make little or no use
of this class of grammatical morpheme (cf. Levinson 1996). There is not necessarily
anything fundamental about prepositions.

Second, the assumption that the prepositional use of these words is in some way
primary, or "central" in prototypical terms, is testable, but has not yet been widely
tested. Central members of basic level categories are learned first by children building up their mental model of the world (Rosch 1973). They are frequently taught by
caregivers through ostensive definition: we point to the brown furry creature sniff-
ing round the lamp-post and say "look, doggie!". Thus, the linguistic terms for the
basic level categories and their central members are the first acquired: *dog*, *cat*, and
rabbit come before *mammal*, or *spaniel*, *tortoiseshell*, or *lop-ear*. If the prepositional use of a path morpheme is central in its category, one would expect it to
be acquired before the adverbial or particle use. If it is central in adult language,
one might well expect it to occur more frequently than other uses. By choosing the

neutral term *path morpheme* to refer to word forms which can apparently function as prepositions, particles, adverbs, and even adjective complements, I avoid assumptions about which function is more "basic" or "central" and which others may be derived from it.

This paper describes some findings from a long-term project intended to examine evidence of the different functions of path morphemes in both language acquisition data and adult conversational data. I will describe the results for only two path morphemes—*over* and *on*. Before doing so, however, I will briefly discuss the attitudes to and uses of path morphemes in British English.

2. The misrepresented word class

Linguistic prescriptivism has always been important in Britain and Cameron (1995) provides a cogent account of the social and political aspects of this important theme of British life. Traditionally, one of the popular targets of the grammar police has always been the so-called "stranded preposition":

(4) The man I had the argument with.
(5) Someone you can depend on.

The "correct" form of such sentences is supposed to be:

(6) The man with whom I had the argument.
(7) Someone on whom you can depend.

I am not alone among native speakers of British English in finding these "corrections" stilted and even pompous-sounding, particularly in (7). The reason for the awkwardness of the "correct" versions is that they are based on a false assumption, at least in the case of (7). This is that the path morphemes in these sentences function entirely as prepositions.

The origin of this assumption goes back to the belief, already current several hundred years ago, that Latin should serve as the model for the correct grammar of any language. An account of early prescriptivist developments in the approach to this part of English grammar can be found in Claridge (2000). The path morphemes in sentences like (4) and (5), and in verb groups like *fall over*, are much more closely bound to the verb than those in examples (1–3). Early grammarians had recognized this and were prepared to attribute a variety of functions to path morphemes, but later these were assigned to the preposition class, since their Latin equivalents function only as prepositions.

The result is that generations of educated speakers of British English have believed that these words *are* prepositions, and that the only correct use is that shown

in sentences like examples (1–3). Claridge (2000) also discusses present-day attitudes to these structures, which can be characterized as more negative than neutral.
They are generally regarded as suitable only for casual speech, and the prescriptions
against "stranded prepositions" are generally accepted. There is no way of knowing
how much of the general assumption of primarily prepositional function for path
morphemes may not be due to an unconscious adherence to the prescriptivism
which is so deeply entrenched in our culture.

Material for teaching foreign learners of English (for instance Sinclair 1991b,
Murphy 1994, Soars and Soars 1986–97) shows considerable inconsistency in the
presentation of constructions with path morphemes. Few authors adopt any sort of
specific terminology, or go beyond the catalogue approach in their account of usage.
This could be viewed as another symptom of the ambivalence towards these structures among educated mother-tongue speakers. Experience suggests that the issue
of how to teach this important part of English usage adequately is to a large extent
simply side-stepped where English is taught in schools. In view of the frequency of
these structures and the vital function of path morphemes in forming them, the re-
luctance to accept their legitimacy is remarkable.

2.1 Multi-word lexemes

In fact, much recent corpus-based research has served to demonstrate that verb-path
morpheme combinations are only one type of structure in which meaning is spread
over several word forms. Work by Altenberg and Eeg-Olofsson (1990), Lancashire
(1992), Stubbs (1996), and Moon (1998), among others, supports a view of language structure that began to emerge some time ago, that fixed expressions, multi-
word verbs, fixed phrases, and many other types of extended lexical unit (ELU) are
essential and highly frequent building blocks of both spoken and written English
(Pawley and Syder 1983). There is much evidence that meaning is often carried by
such associations of several words, rather than composed additively from the individual meanings of the word forms involved (Sinclair 1991a, Francis et al. 1996).
A frequent lexical item may collocate with a whole group of semantically or affec-
tively related words to form a semantic prosody (Sinclair 1991a, Louw 1993, Stubbs
1995): individual members of the set may be rare, but as a group they may form a
substantial part of speakers' repertoires of utterances. It is becoming clear that despite the emphasis on the creative use of language in recent decades, a surprisingly
large proportion of what speakers and writers produce consists of such "prefabricated" ELUs (Kjellmer 1991)—even the most creative writers are no exception
(Lancashire 1992). Evidence from psycholinguistics and phonology supports the
view that language is interpreted, stored, and accessed in larger units than words
(Bybee 1998). The existence of such chunks is recognized in second language learn-

ing, as well as in first language acquisition. Recent research confirms that many utterance fragments are first learned by the young child as unanalyzed wholes and only later are broken into grammatical and lexical components (Lieven *et al.* 1997).

To some extent, the failure to consider the role of path morphemes in ELUs may be the result of the focus on the creative aspect of language use mentioned above. The use of ELUs implies the routine use of ready-made combinations of words, which are on the borderline between grammatical structures and lexical items (Bybee 1998)—hence the use of the term *lexicogrammar*, made popular by Sinclair and others in corpus-based lexicography. It is difficult to accommodate them in the traditional framework with its divided responsibilities, where lexis carries much of the content and syntax and morphology convey most of the relationships.

Multi-word verbs, which have been a feature of the English language for several centuries, as Claridge (2000) points out, merit more attention than they have received. In particular, if they are frequently and competently used by adult speakers, then they must have been acquired by these speakers along with all the other structures of their language in their early childhood. Examination of a corpus of acquisition data should throw some light on how this process takes place. The meanings of path morphemes as they are used in multi-word verbs are not necessarily the supposedly primary locative ones. Although much ingenuity can be expended on proposing possible derivations, it seems unlikely that these meanings would be developed via such derivation during the acquisition process. Should this be the case however, there should be some evidence of this in a reasonably large corpus of such data. Such data should allow us to judge to what extent the introspectively derived prototype models correspond to what happens in real life.

In Section 3, I shall describe the results of a pilot study, in which I examined the uses of *over* to and by children acquiring British English as their first language. In the sections that follow, I will examine adult conversational data for *over* and another path morpheme, *on*. I will analyze the data for *on* from the child language and see what conclusions can be drawn about the acquisition of the different functions of this word and for other members of the category.

3. The child data

The Wells Corpus (Wells 1981, 1986) is available for research through the CHILDES databank (MacWhinney 1991), which is a large and continuously growing collection of recordings and transcriptions of child language, donated by scholars all over the world. The corpus consists of recordings of spontaneous speech by 32 children, 16 girls and 16 boys, born in the Bristol area in the second half of 1972. The children were recorded for a day every three months between the ages of 18 months and 3 years 6 months, and again at almost five years, giving a total of ten age-band samples. They wore a radio microphone harness with a range of about 100 meters over their clothes, and random 90 second samples were recorded automatically onto a tape recorder placed in another part of the house, so that the children and their entourage were not aware when recording was taking place. The microphones allowed the children to move freely through house and garden and picked up all speech in the children's presence, whether addressed to the children or not. In all about 90 minutes of material was recorded for each child in each session and the full range of daily activities are represented: meal times, bath times, toilet training, solitary and group play, story reading, 'helping' mother, misbehavior and punishment, accidents, and occasional episodes of illness. The transcriptions contain contextual information, provided by the parents when they listened to the recordings afterwards, which makes interpretation of the often elliptical utterances much easier. The advantage of the method is clear: the recordings provide us with genuine spontaneous speech in a completely naturalistic setting. Of course this has a drawback —there is often a great deal of background noise, but the quality is on the whole more than adequate.

The corpus contains about 395,000 words. This is very large compared with some of the data collections which serve as the basis for descriptions of language acquisition. Many of these smaller corpora are transcriptions of only one or two children or else of short sessions with a larger number of children. The Wells Corpus offers the opportunity to generalize about the behavior of many children in the same community. Of course the children come from a variety of social backgrounds and this is evident in the parents' speech, especially to other adults, but there is less variation in the speech addressed to the target children, principaly because there is little or no variation across the group in the topics and situations they talk about.

Although the corpus may be large by child language standards, it is of course very small in corpus linguistic terms. The first modern corpora in the 1960s had one million words, and today hundreds of millions are not unusual (Sinclair 1991). Biber (1993) shows that the earliest corpora such as the Brown Corpus (Kučera and Francis 1967) and the LOB corpus (Johansson *et al.* 1978), both of which contain a million words, are large enough to provide reliable data about very frequent function words such as prepositions. In fact samples from individual texts of as few as 200 words can be taken together to provide reliable data on prepositional phrases (Biber 1993: 249–52). This suggests that the collection of 90-second samples in the Wells corpus can provide an adequate basis for the type of investigation I am undertaking here.

4. The pilot study

The first stage of the investigation was an analysis of the uses of *over* in the Wells Corpus. I originally used data from only 16 children, and compared my findings with data from a small corpus of written and spoken English (about 2.3 million words) collected by Professor Michael Stubbs at Trier University, Germany. The results of this study (Hallan 1996) showed clearly that the distribution of the uses and meanings of *over* in both corpora diverged significantly from the claims made in the cognitive linguistics models. As a result, I began the current investigation by repeating the analysis of *over* for the whole of the Wells Corpus.

The original classification was closely based on the meanings discussed by Brugman (1983). However, given the small number of examples, only 333 in the whole corpus, this level of detail was difficult to justify—many of the categories contained only one or two examples. In addition, in the present study I am interested in function as much as meaning, so I have adopted a 'mixed' classification here. Some of the items are related to meaning, and some to function or syntactic structure. Here I have made use of the categories defined in Soars and Soars (1986–97). The associations of verbs with path morphemes are grouped on the basis of frequent structures. They are discussed under the general heading of 'multi-word verbs', the term favored by Claridge (2000) and which I also use. The structures are given names which are also found in other grammar books:

(a) *Fall over* and similar structures are 'phrasal verbs without an object', and the path morphemes are described as adverbs.

(b) The type exemplified by example (8) are 'phrasal verbs with an object':

(8) I put up the picture/I put the picture up/I put it up

Again the path morphemes are described as adverbs, and attention is drawn to the fact that only noun objects, but not pronouns, can change position—although no explanation for the possible movement of noun objects is given.

(c) The third type of structure is the type exemplified in (4), which are 'prepositional verbs', and the only comment on the structure is that they always have an object, which must always follow the "preposition" even when it is pronominal.

(d) The last structure described is the type that Winston Churchill is supposed to have caricatured in a marginal note on a speech corrected by an aide: "This is the sort of thing up with which I will not put":

(9) a. I will not put up with this sort of thing.
     b. This is the sort of thing I will not put up with.

These are called 'phrasal-prepositional verbs'.[1]

I use this classification, not because it is especially good, but because it makes clear the different functions of the path morphemes in the different constructions, and because it is relatively well-known. The results of the pilot study are shown in Figure 1.

The 'central' uses of *over* are exemplified by sentences of the type given in examples (1–3) above. These are considered in all the cognitive models to be in some way basic or prototypical. As can be seen, there were in fact very few uses of this type. These were mostly produced by adults or older children, and rarely addressed to the target children. There were a few uses by the target children, one from a five-year-old, and others in recited nursery rhymes, which cannot be considered productive use (but might count as fixed expressions). 'Metaphorical' uses, also infrequent, included time expressions such as *over the weekend* and uses such as *worried over X*. These were only produced by adults and older children, and seldom addressed to the target children. Of more interest were the examples of *all over (the)*, more than 10% of the whole, and almost all addressed by mothers (or more rarely fathers) to the target children or their siblings. The children themselves produced this expression, although much less frequently, but were clearly learning its use by ostensive definition, mostly in a context of dirt, mess, spilt food or drink, or improper use of color pencils.[2]

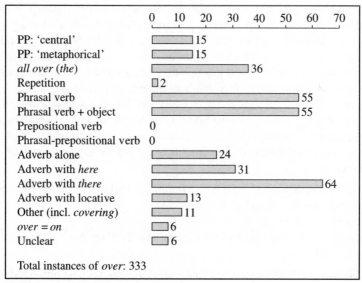

Figure 1. Uses of over *by all speakers in the Wells corpus*

More interesting was the fact that over 50% of all uses were either in phrasal verbs such as *fall over*, phrasal verbs with a direct object, such as *knock X over*, or in the locative adverbial *over there*. The last is especially interesting, as together with the less frequent *over here* it seems to be used to provide ostensive definitions related to personal as well as spatial deixis. The instruction given in (10) tells the child to move towards the speaker: it has the force of "come to me":

(10) Come over here (passim)

While utterances of the type shown in (12) and (13) direct the child's activities and attention to places which are neither in the speaker's sphere of influence, nor in the child's:

(11) Put X over there (passim)
(12) What's that over there? (passim)

Not surprisingly, the children are already using *over there* to direct the attention of their mothers and other care-givers from the earliest recordings.

It should be noted however that the first use need not be strictly spatial: the child quite possibly understands *over here* as bridging the separation between the speaker and hearer, between first and second person, while still experiencing this separation as interpersonal rather than focussing on its spatial extent. Similarly *over there* would refer to something which is associated with neither the speaker or the hearer, thus playing the role of third person. The *over* in these expressions, which are most probably acquired as unanalyzed units, is not prepositional: explanations which depend on postulating unexpressed prepositional objects are unsatisfactory for this stage of development, since the children do not yet construct prepositional phrases. They may not even apply for adults, who use these expressions so frequently (cf. Table 1 below) that one can well imagine that they are still treating them as ELUs. However *over* in this use is clearly a path morpheme, encoding as it does the notion of movement from proximal to distal, or vice versa. It seems plausible to me that the use of adverbial *over* to signify the bridging of the deictic gap is the next stage of a development which leads on to a *consciousness* of the deictic gap as an *obstacle*, and then to a consciousness of the *contents* of the deictic gap as something which can be gone over:

(13) *JON: Jonathan want come over Mummy 3. *MOT: No.*JON: Jonathan want come over Mummy.
      (repeated twice more)
      *MOT: No.*JON: Jonathan want come over 2.*JON: No. *JON: Mummy said no' Mummy 10.[3]

      (Jonathan, 1;11,29, trying to climb the safety gate keeping him out of the room where his mother is working)

A later stage is exemplified in:

(14) *BEN: I can get over gates.
      *BEN: but not down.*BEN: just fall 3.*BEN: not like Mummy.
      (Age-band 8: Benjamin, 3;2,29)

Only when the *contents* of the deictic gap are treated as a point of reference, a landmark, for defining the path of some moving entity (a trajector) will "canonical" prepositional phrases occur. In fact the main production of prepositional phrases by the target children is with *over* in the sense of "covering", which is treated as a derived sense in the cognitive models, and which I have included in the "other" category.

(15) *IRI: Just go over the cot won't it ?
      (Age-band 10: Iris, 4;8,4, putting her doll to bed)

As can be seen, this use is not very frequent. The uses of *over* in situations where *on* might seem more appropriate are mostly produced by older siblings:

(16) *RIC: xxx I xxx some mud [?] over it.
      (Age-band 2: Richard, elder brother of Harriet, 1;9,1, complaining about the state of his bat after his sister has played with it.)

The conclusion I draw from this evidence is that during the pre-school period *over* does not behave like a central member of the traditional class of prepositions, either in the speech of care-givers or in that of the target children. The first uses the children acquire are adverbial, followed by the particle function in phrasal verbs. The earliest prepositional uses are in a set of expressions with the form *all over X*, and in the sense of "covering", neither of which belong to the proposed central uses of prepositional *over*. If nothing else this suggests that *over* is a poor choice for a model of prepositional use and meaning. More importantly, it raises the question of how far the prepositional function is central or primary for the other path morphemes.

5. Path morphemes in adult speech

The next stage of the investigation was to see how the path morphemes behave in adult speech. To do this I used the British National Corpus, which is a collection of 100 million words of contemporary British speech and writing. The corpus has been available to researchers since 1995 and attempts to be representative of a wide range of genres and registers in present-day British English. The spoken component contains about 10 million words of which 7,760,753 words in 672 texts, are dialogue or multi-person conversation.

The corpus has been tagged using the CLAWS tag-set developed at Lancaster University (Garside and Smith, 1997) so that in principle it is possible to count the uses of the path morphemes as adverbs, prepositions, or particles by using the search functions of SARA, the special access software (Aston and Burnard 1998). Unfortunately, there is no information in the corpus documentation (Burnard 1995) as to whether the tagging software was separately trained on spoken texts. Inspection of concordance lines suggests that the assignment of part-of-speech tags to the path morphemes in the spoken texts is somewhat inaccurate, although at present this is no more than a subjective impression. As will be seen from Table 1, the numbers involved are too large to allow manual checking on any scale, but I intend to make a systematic examination of samples in the near future. The subjective impression is that there are more particles tagged as prepositions than vice versa.

Table 1 shows the results for *on* and *over*. *On* is one of the most frequent path morphemes in the Wells Corpus: only *in* occurs more often. Psycholinguistic studies (such as E. Clark 1973) have long suggested that the spatial meanings of these two path morphemes are among the first to be understood by very young children, so *on* was a good candidate for a comparison between adult and child usage. Table 1 clearly shows that *on* occurs proportionately more frequently as a preposition in the BNC than does *over*. There is an important difference between the values for the whole corpus, where nearly 90% of uses are prepositional, and the values for the spoken dialogues, where the figure falls below 70%. If there is a category of prepositions in English, then *on* clearly behaves more like a central member in the written than in the spoken language. Interestingly, the phrasal verb *come on*, which represents the most frequent use of *on* in the Wells Corpus (see below), still accounts for 4% of all uses in the adult spoken data and, more importantly, for nearly 35% of all the particle uses. This suggests that at least some of the fixed expressions learned in the early stages of language acquisition are still playing an important role in adult usage.

The results for *over* confirm the observations from the Wells Corpus. In the corpus as a whole *over* functions less than half the time as a preposition and in the spoken dialogues the figure falls below 30%. Almost as many examples of spoken *over* occur in phrasal verbs as in prepositional phrases. Nearly 8% of all uses are in phrases with *all over (the)* and a large proportion of these are clearly fixed expressions, as the table shows. I have not yet counted the prepositional use with quantities, in the meaning of "excess", such as *over a million pounds*, or the use with time periods and distances, meaning "extent in time or space", such as *over the weekend*. The pilot study showed that, in the small corpus I examined (see Section 4 above), these make up nearly 20% of the prepositional uses of *over*. This suggests that fixed patterns may play an important role in all the uses of this word form in adult language.

Table 1. *Path Morphemes in the British National Corpus*

On	Whole corpus		Spoken dialogue	
	Number	Percent	Number	Percent
1. Adverb	9	0.00	2	0.00
2. Adverb-Particle	49,654	6.87	10,656	17.62
3. Adverb/Preposition	263,792	36.50	6,625	10.96
4. Preposition	646,746	89.48	41,672	68.91
5. Adjective	1	0.00	1	0.00
6. Other	16	0.00	1,513	2.50
Total	7,22,796	100.00	60,469	100.00

Frequent combinations in spoken dialogue:

on top	2,323	*on there*	894
on top of	835	*on here*	283
come on	2,624	*go on*	2,357

Over	Whole corpus		Spoken dialogue	
	Number	Percent	Number	Percent
1. Adverb	23,091	18.55	1,151	13.56
2. Adverb-Particle	20,167	16.20	2,221	26.17
3. Adverb/Preposition	26,398	21.21	1,590	18.73
4. Preposition	53,595	43.06	2,326	27.40
5. Adjective	174	0.14	9	0.11
6. Other	1,029	0.83	1,191	14.03
Total	124,454	100.00	8,488	100.00

Frequent combinations in spoken dialogue:

all over	679	*over there*	336
of which:		*over here*	842
all over the	200		

64% with 6 nouns: *country, county, earth, world, floor, place*

6. *On* in the Wells Corpus

There were over 4,000 examples of *on* in the Wells Corpus, so that it made sense to analyze the data by age bands. This had not been possible for *over*, where there were only between 20 and 40 occurrences for each age band, too few for reliable description. With more than ten times as much data, it was possible to plot the distribution between different types of uses for different speakers and at different stages of the childrens' development.

The occurrences of *on* were classified not only according to function and (in some cases) meaning, but also according to whether they were produced by the target children, the mothers, fathers, siblings, other children who were present, or other adults. In all but the first case, the utterances addressed to the target child and to other individuals were counted and classified separately. It has thus been possible to extract a great deal of information, although at the price of some very laborious counting! It would be impossible in the space of this paper to show the full range of data that can be extracted from this material. I present here data from the first, fourth, seventh, and tenth age-bands only, although some of the examples are from other age bands and this will be indicated.

7. The first recordings

Figure 2 shows the distribution of uses by all speakers in utterances addressed to the children at the time of the first recordings. The distribution is striking and becomes even more so when one knows that over 90% of the 165 phrasal verbs were the fixed expression *come on*. This is used to exhort, to encourage, to chivvy, or to try to persuade a distressed child to stop crying. The meaning of *on* in this expression, the most frequent in the whole of the *on* data, is clearly *not* locative. Indeed the expression is not compositional, and should be regarded as a fully lexicalized idiom. It hardly has anything to do with *coming*, in contrast to *come (over) here*, for instance, which also very frequent. The other phrasal verbs that occur more than once,

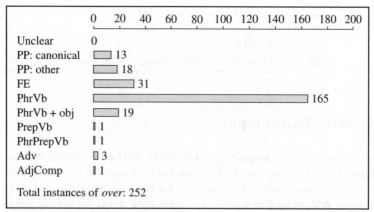

Figure 2. Uses of on *by all speakers to children aged 18 months*

go on, hang on, and (*don't*) *keep on,* also show a non-locative use of *on:* it functions as an intensifier.

Canonical prepositional phrases are those where *on* has its supposedly proto-typical meaning of [+contact, +support] (cf. Bowerman 1996). However, the major-ity of occurrences with this meaning have not been recorded in this category. It soon became clear that there was a fairly small set of prepositional phrases of this type that recurred very frequently, such as *on the/your chair, on the/your potty, on the table, on there, on here.* These are classified as fixed expressions and will be dis-cussed below. 'Other' prepositional uses were in expressions such as *on an aero-plane, on Thursday.* Examples of this type were also included in the fixed expres-sion section, such as *on the television, on the* (*clothes*)*line, on a bus.* These uses were very common, and it seems that children are exposed to them as frequently as the canonical uses.

7.1 Fixed expressions

In order to establish which prepositional phrases to include in the category of fixed expressions, all those with the form *on a*(*n*) *X, on the X, on your X* and *on my X* were counted in the entire corpus. There were 906 of these. The occurrences of candidate prepositional phrases were then expressed as a percentage of the whole. An arbitrary minimum of 1% was set and there were 19 prepositional phrases at or over this level, which together made up 47% of the whole. These are listed in Table 2 (see following page).

There are two grouped categories in this list. One of them is *settee, etc.* Different families use different names for this item of furniture, *settee, sofa* and *couch,* with *settee* (which is often held to be a working-class word) in the majority. The sam-ples in the corpus are very small in proportion to the amount of talk the children actually hear. Since practically every family has such an item of furniture, it seemed reasonable to assume that the real occurrence of the names was even greater and to group the different names in this way. The same argument applies to the group *side, etc.* Every household has a favored 'parking place' for things that need to be put out of the way: in some families it is called *the side,* in some it *is the shelf, the work-top, the counter,* or *the mantelpiece.* I assumed that all these places would be salient locations for the children. They occur with the definite article, but without any further modifiers, suggesting that everybody knows exactly where is meant.

There are a further 18 nouns which are in more than 0.5% but less than 1% of all these prepositional phrases, also listed in Table 2. These make up an additional 13% of the total. Thus, 37 nouns account for 60% of all the prepositional phrases of this type. Given that children in the second half of their second year are acquiring new words every day, it seems plausible to see this very small set of prepositional phrases as a fixed repertoire, which serves as a demonstration of the multiple mean-ings of prepositional *on*. Since most of the nouns only occurred with one or two of the determiners in the chosen set, the maximum number of prepositional phrases that would need to be recognized is less than 100. The basic set of nouns, which all refer

Table 2. *Fixed expression prepositional phrases with* on *in the Wells Corpus*

Total number of prepositional phrases (with *on* and determiner *a(n)*, *the*, *my your*) in Wells Corpus			906
More than 1% (19 nouns)		Between 0.5% and 1% (18 nouns)	
back	1.5	bottom	0.7
bed	3.4	door	0.6
bike	2.4	face	0.6
(game) board	1.2	farm	0.6
bus	1.5	foot/feet	0.9
carpet	1.2	front	0.6
chair	3.1	gate	0.6
fingers	1	ground	0.7
floor	6.8	hand	0.9
knee/lap	1.1	head	0.9
(clothes) line	1	horse(y)	0.9
own	3.2	legs	0.9
plate	1.1	nose	0.8
settee etc.	1.4	road	0.9
side etc.	2.6	seat	0.6
swing	1	tape (recorder)	0.7
stairs/step	1.2	verandah	0.6
table	3.3	way	0.7
television	1.3		
top	1.9		
train	1.2		
wall	3.2		
window	1.4		
Total	47	Total	13.2
Percentage of fixed expressions of this type:			60
Total number of nouns:			37

to salient objects in the child's environment (body parts, furniture, the ever-present potty, the floor and its covering, one or two toys, and some parts of the house and garden), would be an accessible and manageable set of central category members. The important thing in this context is that many of these, such as *bus, clothesline, television*, do not illustrate the supposedly central meaning of prepositional *on*.

The only other uses of *on* that are at all frequent in this age-band are the phrasal verbs with a direct object. Most of these relate to putting on or taking off various items of clothing. There was one instance of *putting on the television*. In the later age bands the children themselves frequently demand to have their favorite programs *on*.

At the time of the first recordings the children themselves were not using *on* very much. There are only three recorded examples. One is of a little girl urging on a toy, in one of the many sequences of speech during solitary play:

(18) *OLI: yyy. *OLI: Come on 2. *OLI: Ah 1 naughty 1. *OLI: yyy 11.
       *OLI: Brum 2. *MOT: Olivia 2. *MOT: What are you doing 4 yyy 2?
       (Age-band 1: Olivia 1;6.0)

There are also two uses of *on there*, one to request the placing of an object and one to direct attention:

(19) *GAR: Want. *TRA: Yes 3? *GAR: Want bread.
       *TRA: Do you want bread ? *TRA: Want some 3?
       *TRA: Your table 5? *GAR: Da da on there.
       (Age-band 1: Gary 1;6.0 with his elder sister)

(20) *NEI: Oh. *NEI: Him on there. *MOT: Father Christmas ?
       *NEI: There 13. *NEI: Up there 15.
       (Age-band 1: Neil 1;6.4).

This is interesting in view of the fact that there are four examples in this age-band of *over there*, all used by the children to direct attention, in a sample that is only 10% of the size of that for *on*. Unlike *over there*, however, *on there* is clearly a prepositional use of *on*, although it is impossible to tell from only two examples which meanings of *on* are intended. Certainly the other speakers use it to refer to a variety of orientations.

7.2 Early developments

Before considering the results for the fourth age-band (Figures 3 and 4 below), I will discuss some examples of early uses of *on*. The earliest comes from the second age-band:

(21) *BEN: on table. *BEN: road.
*MOT: youre not supposed to be on the table.*MOT: its naughty.
*BEN: road. *MOT: its a road yes.
*MOT: but youre not supposed to climb on it 5.

(Age-band 2: Benjamin 1;8,27).

Here we see that Benjamin has left out the article from the prepositional phrase. This might be regarded as a proof that it was already analysed. Since the children seem not to be able to use or attend to articles at this stage, it could just as well represent his perception of the form of the expression—he clearly understands its meaning. The only other (unanalyzed) examples of prepositional phrases in this age-band (in a total of 15 child utterances) are 4 examples of *on there*. There are however 3 utterances that suggest the children are treating a noun group and a following locative adverb as an unanalysed unit:

(22) *MOT: What's that ? *MOT: What are they 4?
*SAM: Socks on. *MOT:Yea

(Age band 2: Samantha 1;9,7 looking at pictures in a mail order catalog.)

It is interesting to note that the mother is clearly asking about some objects in the picture, since she says "What are *they*". When the child refers to them as "socks-on", the mother does not correct the answer. There are other examples of this type of expression in later age-bands.

The next example is from the third age-band and represents a very early attempt to use a prepositional phrase:

(23) *JON: Don't put Bonny. *JON: Your foot 3.
*JON: Don't put on my feet 3.
*MOT: Don't put my feet on Bonny you mean.
*JON: Don't put feet on Bonny.
*MOT: I'm smoothing Bonny with my toes 2.
*JON: No 7.*MOT: You've got shoes on. *MOT: You'll hurt her 2.

(Age band 3: Jonathan 1;11,29. Bonny is the dog)

Jonathan is clearly trying to produce a prepositional phrase, but can't quite manage it, and when he repeats his mother's demonstration he leaves out the possessive. It should be noted that Jonathan is something of a linguistic early developer in this group, producing very complex utterances at a much earlier stage than most of the other children. He produces the first example of a superfluous prepositional object in the whole corpus, more than a year earlier than any of the other children:

(24) *JON: I'm coming 3. *JON: I don't want my sandals on me.
*MOT: Well if you don't have sandals on.

*MOT: You can't go on the verandah can you ?
(Age-band 4: Jonathan 2;2.26)

8. The second stage: greater productivity

In the third set of recordings the children produce only 32 out of 379 utterances with *on*. With the fourth age-band we see their production really expand. They now produce 106 out of 508 utterances, almost 21% of the total.

The children are clearly beginning to use *on* in many of its adult functions and the pattern of use resembles that of the other speakers' utterances addressed to them not only in the earlier months but at the time of this recording (see Figure 4). Fixed expressions and phrasal verbs predominate and 27 of the children's 32 phrasal verbs are instances of *come on*.

The categories adverb and adjective complement are interesting. The former occurs in expressions of the type: *'ve got/get your a/my coat/shoes/socks on*. In British English *'ve got* is frequently used in informal speech, while *have* is felt to be more formal. Since the possessive relation clearly refers to the items of clothing, *on* indicates their location. Unlike *put on*, *get on* seems not to behave fully as a phrasal verb, that is, there is only one example of *on* preceding a direct object noun-group in the whole corpus, produced by one of the mothers:

(25) *MOT: Get on your boots.*GAR: Oh dear 2. Where are they to?
       (Age-band 7: Gary 3;0,4)

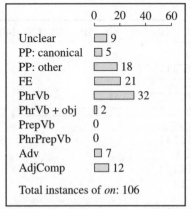

Figure 3. Uses of on *by children aged 2 years, 3 months*

There are 729 examples of *get on* in the spoken dialogue section of the BNC, but no examples of this structural type.

There are also requests to *get on*, referring to a swing, bike, horse or other 'sittable' toy. I am aware that many researchers consider this type of use to be elliptical. I am however not convinced that children in this age-group can be assumed to have thought a prepositional phrase and then not uttered it, especially since so many of the prepositional phrases they do produce are probably as yet unanalyzed. In addition, an inspection of the examples in the BNC suggests that in many cases adults use *get on* as a prepositional verb, that is, the preposition is felt to be as strongly bound to the verb as to the following noun-group, and is frequently "stranded". Since the children only start to use prepositional verbs much later, I have classified these earlier cases as adverbial.

The adjective complement occurs in expressions such as *the light/kettle/telly is on*. Interestingly the target children use this more than the other speakers (see Figure 4), perhaps because they feel more need to comment on the things they see than the others do.

The change in the distribution of uses in the other speakers' production is interesting (cf. Figure 2), and would support the controversial hypothesis that care-givers introduce new forms as soon as the children have mastered the earlier ones (see Snow and Ferguson 1977 for examples of both sides of the argument). As was mentioned in the discussion of Figure 3 above, the total number of utterances with *on* has increased substantially. However the number of utterances addressed to the child has only risen by 14%. There are two reasons for this. First, the children themselves are saying more and, second, the number of utterances not addressed to the

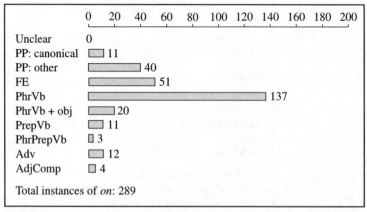

Figure 4. Uses of on *by all speakers to children aged 2 years 3 months*

child has also increased. This is perhaps because the children can be more safely left to play while parents, and other adults and children, carry on their own conversations in parallel. Interestingly, the proportion of canonical uses of prepositional *on* in the other speakers' utterances to the children has actually diminished, while the non-canonical uses have more than doubled in number, although their percentage has only risen from 12% to 14%. What is new in this age band is the use of prepositional verbs in utterances to the children. At this stage there are no examples of these from the children.

8.1 Confusing examples

The children seem at this early stage to be beginning to notice that there sometimes has to be 'one of those little words' in front of the thing they are referring to. What they don't always seem so certain about is which word it should be. Already in the third age-band we see a child using more than one path morpheme at once:

(26) *GAV: Mum+my [=! vocative]. *GAV: On there Mummy [=! vocative][?].
     *GAV: On there Mummy [=! vocative]. *GAV In on there #2.

   (Age-band 3: Gavin 1;11,30 wants to be lifted on to the kitchen table)

Later examples of the same type of use are also found:

(27) *LEE: Sit on car.*LEE: Sit in car 2.
     *LEE: Sit car 2.*LEE: Look. *FAT: I'll break it if I sit on it 2.
     *FAT: He's too small for Dad. *LEE: Not small.

   (Age-band 5: Lee 2;6.1 trying to persuade his father to sit on a toy car)

(28) *MOT: Don't you touch it will you ? *GAV: No. *MOT: xxx germs.
     *GAV: I want to put powder on 1 on 1 up on the toilet.

   (Age-band 6, Gavin 2;10,5 helping his mother to clean the bathroom)

(29) *STE: They had. *STE: That this stands on there.
     *STE: But Uncle John didn't let Jonathan jump in on the stand jump in the swimming pool on the stands.

   (Age-band 8: Stella 3;3,7 telling her mother about a visit to the pool)

This confusion is not surprising, given the wide range of utterances addressed to the children in which there are path morphemes in sequence:

(30) *MOT: Wait a minute Gavin.*MOT: Hey come on off.

   (Age-band 4: Gavin 2;4,4)

(31) *GER: No. *MOT: Yes. *GER: No yes no yes. *MOT: Yes yes yes.
*GER: No yes. *MOT: Come on up you go.

(Age-band 5: Gerald, 2;65, mother lifts him onto her knee, says she'll read
the book and then go and wash up)

(32) *MOT: Now just you sit down on that toilet and do a wee. *HAR: Ah 18.

(Age band 5: Harriet 2;6,1 being unco-operative)

9. The later stages

Figure 5 shows that there are considerable changes by the time the children are 3
years old, in the seventh age-band. There are even greater ones at almost five, in the
tenth age-band, just before the children enter school (Figure 6, below). Wells and
his co-workers did not record all the children at this later stage, 18 months after the
ninth recording. Half of the original sample were to be followed into primary school
and only these were recorded at this stage (Wells 1981: 11). Thus the uses of *on* in
Figure 6 (p. 113) are produced by only 16 children, not 32. In view of this, it is clear
that the overall incidence of *on* in the older children's talk is more than doubled.

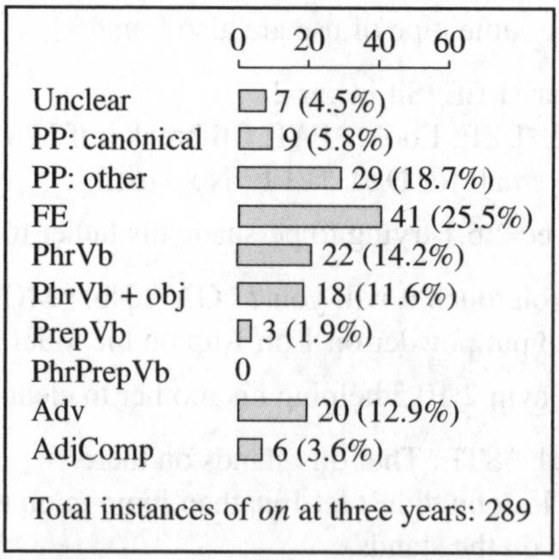

	0 20 40 60
Unclear	□ 7 (4.5%)
PP: canonical	□ 9 (5.8%)
PP: other	▭ 29 (18.7%)
FE	▭ 41 (25.5%)
PhrVb	▭ 22 (14.2%)
PhrVb + obj	▭ 18 (11.6%)
PrepVb	▯ 3 (1.9%)
PhrPrepVb	0
Adv	▭ 20 (12.9%)
AdjComp	□ 6 (3.6%)
Total instances of *on* at three years: 289	

Figure 5. Uses of on *by children aged*
3 years

Comparing Figure 5 with Figure 3 (above), we can see immediately that the number of phrasal verbs without an object has dropped. There are many more phrasal
verbs with an object and prepositional verbs make a first appearance. Obviously the
more complex particle uses of *on* are being mastered. There are also now more
adverbial than adjective complement uses. The most interesting change is in the use

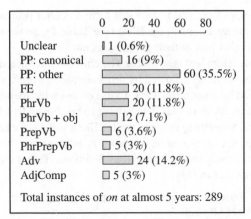

Figure 6. Uses of on *by children aged almost 5 years*

of prepositional phrases. The proportion of all uses which occurs in canonical prepositional phrases has scarcely changed, from 4.7% to 5.8%. Nor has that for the other uses, rising from only 16% to 17%. But the use of fixed expressions has gone up from 19.8% to 26.5%. Clearly the children are now freely talking about all the things that were being so assiduously pointed out to them.

When we look at the graph for the five-year-olds, we see the first use of phrasal-prepositional verbs, and a more even distribution of the other multi-word verb structures, although *come on* has not disappeared. Children can be heard using it with their younger brothers and sisters. But the proportion of multi-word verbs has clearly gone down, from 28% of all uses to 25.4%, in favor of a doubling in the use of non-canonical prepositional phrases, from 17% to 35.5%. The proportion of canonical prepositional phrases has also doubled, but remains only 9.5% of the total. Adverbial uses have fallen slightly, from 18.8% to 14.2 % of all uses. The conclusion is clear: the children have learned how to form prepositional phrases over the two years since the samples in Figure 5. But the ones they are using the most are *not* those where *on* has its canonical meaning, but others, such as *on Christmas Eve*, *on my body*, *on furniture* (as a place to play), *on salmon*, *on the wheel*, *on the balloon*. There are also examples of *on* with a personal pronoun such as *her*, *it*, *me*, and of *on* with a demonstrative or quantifier, as in *on that page*, *on the other book*.

10. Getting from there to here

The children have clearly learned how to use *on* as a preposition by the time they enter primary school. However, their uses of multi-word verbs and of *on* as an adverb, have not disappeared, and in fact still form a greater proportion of the total than in the adult conversations in the BNC (see Table 1). So we may assume that the development in this part of their language is not yet over.

How does this development take place? The children have acquired two types of construction, a verb or noun followed by *on*, as in multi-word verbs (V + *on*, N + *on*) and *on* followed by a noun (*on* + N). To use *on* as an independent grammatical morpheme (whatever its word-class), they have to be able to detach it from both of these types of ELU. Something that was treated like a suffix (cf. example 22 above), or perceived as a prefix (*on the table, on the telly*), is now understood as something else—but without entirely losing its previous functions. This is clear from the persistence of uses like that in (33):

(33) *HAR: And Rosemary did give me my pa [//] my pants on.
     *MOT: xxx? *HAR: Yeh.

    (Age-band 6: Harriet, 2;9,0, discussing who gave her different items of clothing).

In adult usage *on* often seems to function both as the end of one type of construction and the beginning of the other, giving rise to patterns of variation:

(34) a. Put on your socks.
     b. Put them on.
     c. You should put your socks on your feet not your hands.

Since the original transcriptions of the Corpus also recorded intonation contours, it is possible to see the children playing safe, and using both structures, perhaps because they are not yet convinced that one occurrence of a path morpheme can carry more than one function:

(35) *ELL: You [?] put he [= that] on #1 on there #4.
     *ELL: Goes on #1 on there #3.

    (Age-band 8: Ellen 3;3,4, arranging Christmas cards).

The '1' indicates a falling intonation as at the end of a declarative utterance. The repetitions of *on* are not a hesitation: there are two separate intonation contours, one for the multi-word verb and one for the prepositional phrase. The analysis of formerly fixed expressions is a sign that the status of *on* is changing:

(36) *LAU: yes we are on it. *SAR: xxx already on holiday ?
     *SAR: Already on holiday.

    (Age-band 9: Laura 3;6,2, playing with her elder sister Sarah)

The insertion of a second, superfluous object after a phrasal verb might well indicate an over-extension of the "blending" of the two functions of *on*:

(37) *IRI: I'm just going to put her sheet on her for her
*IRI: So she can keep cosy.

(Age band 10: Iris 4;8,4, playing with her doll)

(38) *JAS: Mum. *JAS: Why do I why do I have to have one of these on my
body?
*MOT: Well that's cos you'll get here then.
*JAS: Why do I have these on my body ?
*MOT: Well it's because it's to hear how you talk.

(Age band 10: Jason 5;0,19, asking about the microphone harness—he has
forgotten about it in the 2-year interval).

We also find attempts to form new phrasal verbs, by analogy with the ones that
have been learned earlier (cf. Hopper and Traugott 1993: 56):

(39) *PEN: d(o) you want to try one on?
*PEN: Here you are. [?] *PEN: Right. *PEN: Take these on.
*MOT: You better get them off. *PEN: That's [?] all mudd.

(Age-band 7: Penny 2;11.27, playing with her father's boots).

These examples, and numerous others in the corpus, show the children experiment-
ing with the complex structures that their analysis is revealing to them. They don't
always get it right, of course, but they are learning to cope with the multiple functions of path morphemes by the time they go to school.

11. Conclusions and future research

Figure 7 on the following page shows the changes in distribution of different uses
of *on* over the four samples I have described in detail.

The rise in importance of the non-canonical prepositional phrases can be clearly
seen, as can the initial predominance and later decrease of phrasal verbs and prepositional fixed expressions. The conclusions that can be drawn from the observations
described in Sections 7 to 10 above can be summarized as follows:

(a) Phrasal verbs are acquired before prepositional phrases. This implies that the
use of *on* in phrasal verbs is at least as central as its use as a preposition.

(b) The first uses of *on* in both multi-word verbs and prepositional phrases are *not*
the supposedly central locative ones. In the later stages these certainly occur,
but are still in the minority when the children are about to start school. This
suggests that in present day English the locative meaning is not necessarily
the primary one, whatever the case may have been in earlier periods.

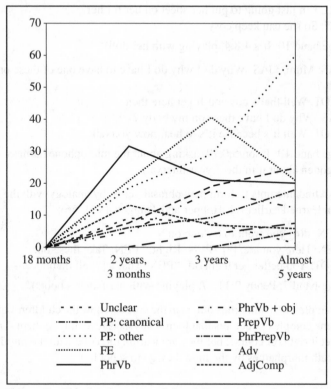

Figure 7. The development of the different uses of on *across four age-bands*

(c) The later development of the different functions of *on* appears to involve a re-organization of the structures acquired earlier on.

The development of the functions of the path morphemes I discuss in this paper is clearly not complete when the children enter school. At this point their usage bears little resemblance to traditional views of how English prepositions function or to the many cognitive models proposed. I believe that adult usage, and adult beliefs about usage, are conditioned by prescriptive teaching, and expect to see evidence of this both in schoolchildren's and in adults' written production.

The evidence from this study also suggests that there is considerable variation in the acquisition and behavior of individual path morphemes. Sinclair (1991a) has convincingly demonstrated that *of* does not function as a preposition in British

English, but can be regarded as the single member of a separate word class. This view has been adopted for the British National Corpus, where there is a special tag for *of* and a different one for prepositions. If, as seems likely, other path morphemes can be shown to have their own individual grammars, this would throw doubt on the status and even the existence of the word-class 'preposition' in present-day English. The process of acquisition is too complex and the adult uses are too varied to justify such a narrowly defined category. The same blindness or distorted vision that afflicts the teaching of English, to native speakers and foreigners alike, has also affected all too many linguistic descriptions. Instead of the Procrustes' bed of traditional categories, we need to make more use of the authentic data which is now so readily available, to establish a classification of attested structures that does justice to the empirical evidence.

Notes

* I would like to thank Joan Bybee, Catie Berkenfield, Mike Stubbs, Andrea Gerbig, Angela Hahn, and Sabine Reich for their helpful comments in the preparation of this paper.

1. The *Collins COBUILD Dictionary of Phrasal Verbs* (Sinclair 1989), which is based on findings from the COBUILD Corpus (Sinclair 1991a), lists 19 (!) structures in order of frequency in the dictionary, with the structures described above as type 2 and type 1 occurring 1267 and 1148 times respectively, and type 3 occurring 581 times. Type 4 is less frequent, occurring 192 times: in fact three other structures are more frequent in the dictionary — that is, there are more *possible* structures of these types. Unfortunately there is no indication of how frequently *particular* examples of a given structure actually occur in the corpus. As is shown in later sections, at least some individual verbs are vastly more frequent than others of the same structural type.

2. Mike Stubbs points out (personal communication) that the expression *all over the place* has an overwhelmingly negative use in the large corpora, i.e. in adult usage.

3. The examples from the Wells Corpus are cited from the CHILDES database, which uses the CHAT format (MacWhinney 1991), but only the main tier, with the transcribed utterances, is given. The children's ages are given in the form Year; Month, Day. Where contextual information is given it was obtained from the commentary tier of the transcription. The CHILDES format has been largely retained, including the punctuation, although often more than one utterance (roughly equivalent to a tone group) is now shown on each line. Transcribers' comments are shown in [square brackets]. The participants' abbreviated names are given in the form *XXX, with *MOT for the target child's mother and *FAT for the father. The numbers in the transcriptions are codes for intonation contours, based on Halliday (1967). The symbols * # < > are also used to indicate hesitations and variations of pitch and loudness. These symbols have been retained from an earlier pre-CHILDES transcription scheme and their significance is mostly irrelevant for my arguments here. However I do discuss evidence from intonation contours in Section 10. Where words in the recordings were indecipherable the transcribers have indicated this with xxx or yyy.

References

Altenberg, B. and Eeg-Olofsson, M. 1990. "Phraseology in spoken English: Presentation of a project". In *Theory and Practice in Corpus Linguistics*. [Language and Computers: Studies in Practical Linguistics 4], J. Aarts and W. Meis (eds.), 1–26. Amsterdam/Atlanta, GA: Rodopi.

Aston, G. and Burnard, L. 1998. *The BNC Handbook: Exploring the British National Corpus with Sara*. [Edinburgh Textbooks in Empirical Linguistics]. Edinburgh: Edinburgh University Press.

Biber, D. 1993. "Representativeness in Corpus Design". *Literary and Linguistic Computing* 8 (4): 242–57.

Bowerman, M. 1996. "The origins of children's spatial semantic categories: cognitive versus linguistic determinants". In *Rethinking linguistic relativity*, [Studies in the Social and Cultural Foundations of Language No. 17], J. J. Gumperz and S. Levinson (eds.), 145–76. Cambridge: Cambridge University Press.

Brugman, C. 1983. *The Story of over*. Trier, Germany: L.A.U.T.

Burnard, L. (ed.). 1995. *Users Reference Guide for the British National Corpus Version 1.0*. Oxford: Oxford University Computing Services.

Bybee, J. 1998. "The emergent lexicon". *CLS 34: The Panels*. Chicago: Chicago Linguistic Society, 421–35.

Cameron, D. 1995. *Verbal Hygiene*. London/New York: Routledge.

Claridge, C. 2000. *Multi-word Verbs in Early Modern English: A Corpus-based Study*. Amsterdam/Atlanta, GA: Rodopi.

Clark, E.V. 1973. "Non-linguistic strategies and the acquisition of word meanings". *Cognition* 2: 161–82.

Clark, H.H. 1973. "Space, time, semantics and the child". In *Cognitive development and the acquisition of language*, T.E.Moore (ed.), 27–63. New York: Academic Press.

Croft, W. 1998. "Linguistic evidence and mental representations". *Cognitive Linguistics* 9 (2): 151–73.

Dirven, R. 1995. "The construal of cause: the case of cause prepositions". In *Language and the Construal of the World*, J. Taylor and R. MacLaury (eds.), 95–118. Berlin: Mouton de Gruyter.

Fillmore, C. 1992. "'Corpus linguistics' or 'Computer-aided armchair linguistics'". In *Directions in Corpus Linguistics*, [Proceedings of Nobel Symposium 82], J Svartvik (ed.), 35–60. Berlin: Mouton de Gruyter.

Francis, G., Hunston, S., and Manning, E. 1996. *Collins COBUILD Grammar Patterns 1: Verbs*. London: HarperCollins.

Francis, W. N. and Kučera, H. 1967. *Computational Analysis of Present-day American English*. Providence, RI: Brown University Press.

Garside, R. and Smith, N. 1997. "A hybrid grammatical tagger: CLAWS4". In *Corpus Annotation: Linguistic Information from Computer Text Corpora*, R.Garside, G.Leech, and A. McEnery (eds.), 102–21. London: Longman.

PATHS TO PREPOSITIONS?   119

Hallan, N. 1996. *Corpus data and semantic structures: The English preposition over*. Unpublished M.A. thesis, Trier University, Germany.

Halliday, M.A.K. 1967. *Intonation and grammar in British English* (Janua linguarum: Series practica; 48). The Hague: Mouton.

Hopper, P. J. and Traugott, E. C. 1993. *Grammaticalization*. Cambridge: Cambridge University Press.

Johansson, S., Leech, G. and Goodluck, H. 1978. *Manual of Information to Accompany the Lancaster-Oslo/Bergen Corpus of British English, for Use with Digital Computers*. Oslo: University of Oslo Department of English.

Johnson, Mark, 1987. *The Body in the Mind: The Bodily Basis of Meaning, Imagination and Reasoning*. Chicago: University of Chicago Press.

Kjellmer, G. 1991. "'A mint of phrases'". In *Corpus Linguistics: Studies in honour of Jan Svartvik*, K. Aijmer and B. Altenberg (eds.), 111–27). London: Longman.

Kučera, H. and Francis, W.N. 1967. *Computational analysis of present-day American English*. Providence Rhode Island: Brown University Press.

Labov, W. 1972. *Language in the Inner City*. Philadelphia: University of Pennsylvania Press.

Labov, W. 1973. "The linguistic consequences of being a lame". *Language in Society* 2: 81–115. Also in *Language in the Inner City*, pp. 255–97.

Lakoff, G. 1987. *Women, Fire and Dangerous Things: What Categories Reveal about the Mind*. Chicago: University of Chicago Press.

Lakoff, G. and Johnson, M. 1980. *Metaphors We Live By*. Chicago: University of Chicago Press.

Lancashire, I. 1992. "Phrasal Repetends in Literary Stylistics: Shakespeare's *Hamlet* III.1". In *Research in Humanities Computing 4: Selected Papers from the ALLC/ACH Conference, Christ Church, Oxford, April 1992*, Nancy Ide (ed.), 34–68. Oxford: Clarendon Press.

Langacker, R.W. 1987. *Foundations of Cognitive Grammar, I: Theoretical Prerequisites*. Stanford: Stanford University Press.

Levinson, Stephen C. 1996. "Relativity in spatial conception and description". In *Rethinking linguistic relativity*, [Studies in the Social and Cultural Foundations of Language No. 17], J. J. Gumperz and S. Levinson (eds.), 133–44. Cambridge: Cambridge University Press.

Lieven, E. V. M., Pine, J. M., and Baldwin, G. 1997. "Lexically based learning and early grammatical development". *Journal of Child language* 24: 187–219.

Louw, B. 1993. "Irony in the text or insincerity in the writer? The diagnostic potential of semantic prosodies". In *Text and Technology*, M. Baker, G. Francis, and E. Tognini-Bonelli (eds.), 157–76. Amsterdam: Benjamins.

MacWhinney, B. 1991. *The CHILDES Project: Tools for Analysing Talk*. Hillsdale, New Jersey: Erlbaum.

Moon, R. 1998. *Fixed Expressions and Idioms in English: A Corpus-Based Approach*. Oxford: Clarendon Press.

Murphy, R. 1994. *English Grammar in Use: A self-study reference and practice book for intermediate students*. Cambridge: Cambridge University Press.

Pawley, A. and Syder, F. H. 1983. "Two puzzles for linguistic theory: nativelike selection and nativelike fluency". In *Language and Communication*, J. C. Richards and R. W. Schmidt (eds.), 191–226. London: Longman.

Rosch, E. 1973. "On the internal structure of perceptual and semantic categories". In *Cognitive development and the acquisition of Language*, T.T. Moore (ed.), 111–44. New York: Academic Press.

Rosch, E. 1978. "Principles of Categorization". In *Cognition and Categorization*, E. Rosch and B.B.Lloyd (eds.), 27–48. Hillsdale, New Jersey: Lawrence Erlbaum.

Sandra, D. and Rice, S. 1995. "Network Analyses of prepositional meanings: Mirroring whose mind—the linguist's or the language user's". *Cognitive Linguistics* 6–1: 89–130.

Schulze, R. 1987. *The Perception of Space and the Function of Prepositions in English: A Contribution to Cognitive Grammar*. Duisburg: L.A.U.D.

Sinclair, J. (ed.). 1989. *Collins COBUILD Dictionary of Phrasal Verbs*. London: Harper Collins.

Sinclair, J. 1991a. *Corpus, Concordance, Collocation*. Oxford: Oxford University Press.

Sinclair, J. (ed.). 1991b. *Collins COBUILD Students Grammar: Self-study Edition with Answer Key*. London: Harper Collins.

Snow, C. E. and Ferguson, C. A. (eds.). 1977. *Talking to children: Language input and acquisition*. Cambridge: Cambridge University Press.

Soars, J. and Soars, L. 1986–97. *Headway*. Oxford: Oxford University Press.

Stubbs, M. 1995. "Collocations and semantic profiles: On the cause of the trouble with quantitative studies". *Functions of Language* 2 (1): 23–55.

Stubbs, M. 1996. *Text and Corpus Analysis: Computer-assisted Studies of Language and Culture*. Oxford: Blackwell.

Taylor, J. 1995. *Linguistic Categorization: Prototypes in Linguistic Theory*. Oxford: Clarendon Press.

Vandeloise, C. 1994. "Methodology and analyses of the preposition *in*". *Cognitive Linguistics* 5 (2): 157–84.

Wells, G. 1981. *Learning through Interaction: The Study of Language Development*. Cambridge: Cambridge University Press.

Wells, G. 1986. *The Meaning Makers: Children Learning Language and Using Language to Learn*. Sevenoaks, England: Hodder and Stoughton.

Part II:
Word-level frequency effects

Lexical diffusion, lexical frequency, and lexical analysis

BETTY S. PHILLIPS

Indiana State University

1. Lexical analysis and lexical frequency

In her 1985 book on *Morphology*, Bybee makes the following connection between word frequency and lexical analysis: "High-frequency words form more distant lexical connections than low-frequency words. In the case of morphologically complex words . . . high-frequency words undergo less analysis, and are less dependent on their related base words than low-frequency words" (118). Suppletive forms such as *go/went* exemplify this principle most dramatically. But the same principle can be seen in the process of linguistic change, where, for instance, frequent words and phrases such as *God be with you, housewife,* and *day's eye* become *good-bye, hussy,* and *daisy,* respectively.

Phillips (1998: 231) draws on this observation to devise the following hypothesis regarding the lexical diffusion of sound change: "For suprasegmental changes, changes which require analysis (e.g., by part of speech or by morphemic element) affect the least frequent words first, whereas changes which eliminate or ignore grammatical information affect the most frequent words first." This statement was a modification of an earlier Frequency-Actuation Hypothesis (Phillips 1984: 336) but left intact the section on segmental changes, namely that "For segmental changes, physiologically motivated sound changes affect the most frequent words first; other sound changes affect the least frequent words first."

The purpose of this paper is to offer a further refinement of this hypothesis, namely that "Sound changes which require analysis—whether syntactic, morphological, or phonological—during their implementation affect the least frequent words first; others affect the most frequent words first." Because this hypothesis links word frequency with the implementation of a change, I call it the Frequency-Implementation Hypothesis.

2. Frequency, analysis, and sound change

The connection between lexical frequency and lexical analysis was originally drawn in Phillips (1998), which attempted to explain why some stress shifts affect the least frequent words first whereas others affect the most frequent words first. That is, Phillips (1984: 333) had shown that in the shift of stress in noun-verb pairs such as *convíct* (noun or verb) becoming *cónvict* (noun) vs. *convíct* (verb), the least frequent words changed first, as displayed in Table 1, where the frequency numbers in the left-hand column (innovations) are consistently lower than those in the right-hand column. This change reflects an emergent generalization that nouns receive initial stress and hence relies on access to material beyond the surface phonetics. Hence, I consider this change as requiring lexical analysis—the lexical entry has to be analyzed to reveal each word's part of speech.

Yet an investigation of the shift in stress in verbs ending in *-ate* found that the most frequent verbs were changing first (Phillips 1998). That is, more frequent verbs like *frustrate* and *dictate* have developed the final-stressed pronunciations

Table 1. *English diatones* (*Phillips 1984: 333*)*

Word group	Average Frequency (according to Carroll *et al.* 1971)	
	Diatonic innovation	Final-stressed
a-	7.4	15.8
con-/com-	10.6	37.1
de-	5.2	8.0
dis-	1.6	4.9
es-	3.1	10.6
ex-	2.5	22.0
pre-	3.7	8.1
re-	8.0	11.1
sur-	5.5	24.3

*Sample words from each group: *áddress/addréss* vs. *advánce*, *cóntent/contént* vs. *concérn*, *décrease/decréase* vs. *declíne*, *díscharge/dischárge* vs. *dispúte*, *éssay/essáy* vs. *estéem*, *éxport/expórt* vs. *expréss*, *prélude/prelúde* vs. *presérve*, *rédress/redréss* vs. *retréat*, and *súrvey/survéy* vs. *surprise*.

frustráte and *dictáte* much sooner than less frequent words like *láctate* and *lústrate*. Table 2 records the progression, as recorded by dictionaries of British English (whose dates are given in the top row), of the shift of stress to the final syllable in British disyllabic verbs in *-ate*, limiting the corpus to those verbs whose first syllable is closed. (This subset was the largest phonetically definable group and showed the clearest lexical diffusion by frequency. Further limitations on this study are discussed in Phillips 1998.) In dramatic contrast to the diatonic stress shift detailed in Table 1, Table 2 shows the progression of the verbal *-ate* stress shift from the more frequent words to less and less frequent words.

The explanation offered in Phillips (1998) for the divergent behavior of the *convíct/cónvict* shift and the *díctate/dictáte* shift was that the former change required close analysis of the words in question—that is, the speaker had to determine first if the word was a noun or a verb before assigning stress. With frequent *-ate* verbs, on the other hand, the suffixal nature of the *-ate* was being ignored, not analyzed as a verbal suffix. That is, the more frequent verbs in *-ate* had lost the analysis of stem + suffix and were being treated like monomorphemic verbs, allowing the stress rules of English to apply automatically, without hindrance. It was this lack of analysis that caused the more frequent words to change first.

This notion of analysis can be extended to illuminate the behavior of segmental changes. That is, the many studies that have shown the most frequent words changing first in a sound change have all to my knowledge involved changes that may be seen as physiologically-induced sound changes—either straightforward assimila-

Table 2. *British English, Disyllables in* -ate *(Phillips 1998)*

Verb	Freq	1755	1780	1824	1872	1917	1937	1988
frustrate	666	+	−	−	+	+	+	+
dictate	233	−	−	−	−	+	+	+
prostrate	39	−	−	−		+	+	+
pulsate	36				−	+/−	+/−	+/−
stagnate	29	−	−	−	−	−/+	−/+	+/−
truncate	15	−	−	−	−	−/+	−/+	+/−
mandate	9						−/+	−/+
lactate	7					−	−	−
palpate	5					−	−	−
filtrate	0	−	−	−	−	−	−	−
gestate	0							−
lustrate	0	−						
testate	0	−						

+ = ultimate stress (*dictáte*); - = initial stress (*díctate*)

tions or reductions (e.g., Fidelholz 1975; Hooper 1976; Phillips 1980, 1984; Rhodes 1996). Typical are the examples provided by Rhodes (1996: 244): flapping in relatively frequent words such as *vanity* and *encounter* vs. un-flapped [t] in the less frequent *amity* and *enchanter* and schwa deletion in *general* and *diamond* vs. schwa retention in the less frequent *ephemeral* and *dialect.*

To take an extended example, the innovative pronunciation in some dialects of the initial *s-* in word-initial *str-* clusters as /ʃ/ (that is, *street* /strit/ becoming /ʃtrit/) seems to affect the more frequent words first. One interesting aspect of this shift is that it involves a shift from one phoneme (in the classical sense) to another, yet most [ʃ] speakers seem unaware of the shift. While this may of course be simply due to the influence of spelling, in any case informants seem almost always unaware of their pronunciation and attach no stigma to it.

My data on this shift includes 30 informants from Georgia, all of whom read a list of 110 words in which were embedded 16 instances of initial *str-* covering a broad range of word frequency. The Signalyze speech analysis software yielded spectra of the two homonyms *straight* and *strait*, *straight* having a word frequency of 145.4 versus *strait*'s frequency of 3.955 according to Carroll *et al.* (1971).[1] As Johnson (1997) points out, "the fricatives [s] and [ʃ] differ substantially. The spectral peak in [ʃ] occurs at about 3.5 kHz, while the spectral peak in [s] is near 8 kHz, although there is also a minor peak at about 4 kHz." Most of the Georgia speakers had either all [s]'s or all [ʃ]'s, but the two who had distinctly different pronunciations of *straight* vs. *strait* both tended toward [ʃ] in *straight* and toward [s] in *strait*. Their highest peaks for *straight* were 4200 Hz and 4700 Hz, whereas their highest peaks for *strait* were 8100 Hz and 8700 Hz.

The theory of lexical analysis helps explain why for these two speakers the more frequent *straight* is the one to exhibit the new, assimilated pronunciation. In the same way that phrases like *C'mon* and *gonna* become units, unanalyzed into their constituent parts, so within words segments may have more or less integrity. This lack of segmental integrity is clearest in cases of reduction, especially of words or morphemes that serve grammatical functions. As Bybee *et al.* (1994: 6) explain, "*phonological reduction* continues to take place throughout the life of a gram . . . Note that this reduction is both *substantive* (the actual articulatory gestures are reduced) and *temporal* (the articulations are compressed so that the temporal duration of the sequence is decreased) (Pagliuca and Mowrey 1987)." But the same mechanism accounts for content words as well: more frequent *straight* is not being analyzed into its constituent parts—its phonemes—as closely as is the infrequent *strait*.

Yet another example comes from Southern American English, where the frequent word *Tuesday*, historically [tjuzdi], is often pronounced with an initial affricate—[tʃuzdi]. What makes this an interesting case is that a competing sound change affects infrequent words such as *tumor*. It too historically began with [t] + [j], [tjumər]—but rather than assimilating the glide, *tumor* and other infrequent words are much more likely to drop the glide, becoming [tumər] etc. (Phillips 1981, 1994) Why should two such similar words behave so dissimilarly? I suggest it is solely due to their word frequency: As a very frequent word, *Tuesday* is not analyzed into its constituent segments as closely as are infrequent words such as *tumor*. The less frequent the word, the more likely it is to be analyzed into separate segments, which anaysis reveals a violation of a sequential contraint against initial /tj/ clusters.

If degree of analysis affects the direction of change for /#str/ and /#tj/ clusters, what are the implications for other sound changes? Similar to /j/ deletion in its affect on the least frequent words first is the merger in early Middle English of /ö(:)/ with /e(:)/. Phillips (1984: 331) shows that this merger has no reductive or assimilatory motivation—the roundedness of the neighboring segments does not influence the vowel —and offers a typological explanation: that languages without high front rounded vowels do not generally have mid front rounded vowels. In fact, only those dialects which had recently lost their high front rounded vowels proceeded to merge these mid vowels as well. That the sound change affected the least frequent words first apparently stems from the need for close lexical analysis: speakers had to access each form from their lexicons and recognize its disfavored /ö(:)/ in order to substitute /e(:)/.

This merger seems to be a perfect example of what Krishnamurti (1998: 213) calls a typologically motivated change, that is, "a change which is motivated by

Table 3. *Middle English /ö(:)/ > /e(:)/ (adapted from Phillips 1984: 328)*

Category	Freq.	Average % innovative ⟨e⟩
Adverbs and function words (Ave. %e = 100)	12–51	100
Non-numerical adjectives (Ave. %e = 70)	2–8	66
	21–36	76
Verbs (Ave. %e = 67)	2–10	69
	11–47	68
	69	52
	355	41
Nouns (Ave. %e = 28)	1–8	49
	21–47	6
	68–82	4
	158	1
Numerals (Ave. %e = 0)	17–45	0

some kind of asymmetry in the phonological system or some need to balance certain parts of the system." Yet Krishnamurti says such a change "tends to be regular," using regular in Labov's sense of "without lexical or grammatical conditioning or any degree of social awareness" (Labov 1994 as quoted by Krishnamurti, p. 194). In direct contrast, the change from rounded to unrounded variants in Middle English clearly has both lexical (by word frequency) and grammatical (by word class) conditioning (Phillips 1984, 1995). Table 3 summarizes the data on the long vowels.

3. Lexical analysis and word class

This example of a sound change with both lexical and grammatical involvement leads to another major consideration: the importance of recognizing word class as an independent factor in sound change. All too often in discussions of changes, authors will attribute the aberrant behavior of a group of words to their word frequency when what is really significant is the group's word class.

For example, about the High German Consonant Shift, Chambers and Wilkie (1970: 112) say that parts of the High German Consonant Shift "are common to all High German dialects, apart from a few common words in Middle Franconian (*that*, *it*, *hwat*)." Yet it is unlikely that word frequency is primarily accountable here since strengthenings such as this typically affect words which receive stronger sentence stress first (Phillips 1983).

Similarly, Rusch (1992: 87), in discussing /æ/-raising in Middle English, says that the most frequent words behave differently, when the main difference is probably word class, since the aberrant forms are all function words. That is, specifically Rusch says, "it may be more prudent . . . to assume that ⟨æ⟩–⟨e⟩ variation in [the] Peterborough Chronicle reflects a lexical diffusion of the sound change . . . . Relevant evidence from the high-frequency words, not yet discussed, dramatically support this hypothesis". The high-frequency words in question turn out to be *wæs* 'was', *þet* 'that,' and the preterite forms of *habban* 'have' (87). Yet Rusch offers no explanation for these spellings beyond their high frequency.

Table 4, adapted and expanded from Phillips (1983), helps clarify how word frequency and word class affect sound changes—and provides a point of departure for a discussion of how foregrounding vs. backgrounding fits into the discussion. Note that the cover term "function words" has been used here to identify that wide range of words which normally receive low sentence stress. Bolinger's (1975: 121–2) list provided the basis for deciding whether to include a word as a "function word" or not: the linking verb *to be*; prepositions; determiners; quantifiers; coordinating conjunctions; relative pronouns; adverbial conjunctions; intensifiers; auxiliary verbs; pronouns, proadverbs, and other prowords. Again, although the cover term "function words" is used, what marks this disparate group as a unit is their characteristically low sentence stress.

The changes labeled X reflect the general tendency of function words to also have high frequency. So, as one might expect, both the function words and the high frequency words have changed first in those sound changes—all either reductions or assimilations. For example, for the deletion in English of final /d/ and /t/ after a consonant, Neu (1980: 53) found "there is a high correlation between frequency of word occurrence and frequency of rule application. This correlation is most striking when the high-frequency items are function words whose only vowel is reducible to schwa." In the Old English translation of Gregory's *Pastoral Care*, "all three scribes . . . consistently write *sint* (299 times) and never the traditional spelling *sind*–despite many other words spelled with final -*nd*, such as *blind*, *find*, *gepynd*, *gescind*, *send*, and *wind*" (Phillips 1983: 488). Similar evidence for /a/ becoming /ɔ/ before nasals is given in Phillips (1980) and below. In fact, Bybee *et al.* (1994: 19) recognize this positive correlation between word class and word frequency when they state: "It is non-controversial that in terms of segmental length, the grams of a language in general tend to be shorter than the lexical items. More systematic observation (e.g. Zipf 1935) informs us that the most frequently used forms of a language are also among the shortest." And they add that one expects grams to be more frequent than typical lexical items. This observation fits with the X sound changes—the reductions or assimilations.

Similarly, Fenk-Oczlon's (1989: 93) emphasis on the ease with which Back-

Table 4. *Word frequency vs. word class* (*adapted and expanded from Phillips 1983*)

Sound change	Most frequent words change		Function words change	
	First	Last	First	Last
/t,d/ deletion (Mod. Eng.)	X		X	
/d/## devoicing (Old Eng.)			X	
a > ɔ / ___ nasal (Old Eng.)	X		X	
/t/ flapping (English)	X			
schwa deletion (English)	X			
/tj/ > /tʃ/ (S. Eng.)	X			
-ate stress shift (English)	X			
/ö(:)/ > /e(:)/ (Middle Eng.)		Y	Y	
/tj/ > /t/ (S. Eng.)		Y		
"convict stress shift (Eng.)		Y		
Vowel leng. (Middle Eng.)				Z

grounding affects frequent words really only works for the X sound changes: "Wo etwas auf Grund hoher Häufigkeit (in einem bestimmten Kontext) geläufig ist und auch beim Kommunikationspartner als geläufig vorausgesetzt werden kann, kann ... am ehesten reduzieren, ohne die Kommunikationsziele zu sehr zu gefährden (Fenk-Oczlon, 1989b)." [Translation: "Where something is familiar because of its high frequency (in a particular context) and also can be surmised by one's communications partner ... one can most easily reduce, without putting in jeopardy the communications goal."]

What is needed, however, is a theory that will account for all types of sound change: X, Y, and Z. Only a theory that incorporates lexical analysis can account

Table 5. *Vowel lengthening in the Orumlum, c.1200 AD (Phillips 1983)*

Consonant cluster	Word classes Changed	Exhibit variation	Unchanged
-ld	verbs adjectives adverbs	nouns	*auxiliaries
-nd	adjectives	verbs nouns	*auxiliaries *conjunction *prepositions adverbs
-mb	verb adjective nouns		adverb
-ng	adjectives *prepositions	verbs adverbs nouns	
-rd		verbs nouns	adjective *auxiliary adverb
-rþ	nouns	verbs adjectives	*auxiliary adverbs
-rn		adverbs verbs adjectives nouns	*auxiliary
-rl		nouns	verb

*Function words and categories

for the sound changes labeled Y. As we have seen, the unrounding of ME /ö(:)/, as a sound change based on typological factors, requires close analysis of the lexical entries in order to implement the change and therefore affects the least frequent words first. But it is also a weakening—a movement from a marked vowel to an unmarked vowel, which affects weakly stressed words sooner than stressed words.

The motivation behind the change labeled Z, lengthening of vowels before certain consonant clusters in Middle English, remains obscure, but if it is phonetically motivated, one would expect it to affect the most frequent words first. As a strengthening, it correlates with Foregrounding and affects the more highly stressed content words first. Table 5 replicates the data from Phillips (1983: 493), which investigated the spelling of the pertinent words in the *Ormulum*, a manuscript known for its scribe's habit of doubling consonants after short vowels, as in *child* 'child' vs. *wolldenn* 'would', *bindenn* 'bind' vs. *annd* 'and', *wrang* 'wrong' vs. *brinngenn* 'bring', *climbenn* 'climb' vs. *ummbe* 'about', and so forth.

One final observation requires an explanation. That is, in studies on word frequency and sound change, if the data base is large enough to yield a substantial number of items covering more than one word class, the frequency effects are clearest within word classes. One example is given above for ME /ö(:)/-unrounding. Another example is /an/ becoming /ɔn/ in West Saxon OE, reflected in spellings such as *befangne/befongne* 'surrounded', *hwane/hwone* 'whom', *sang/song* 'song', *wana/wona* 'deficiency', *cann/conn* 'know', *ðanon/ðonon* 'thence', and so forth. (For a discussion of the phonetics/phonology behind this shift, see Hogg 1982 and 1992: 78, who considers this change primarily a nasalization and who doubts the phonemic status implied by the *-on-* spellings. His stance has no impact on our discussion here, since the change is still an assimilation.) Tables 6 and 7are taken from Phillips (1980) and show the results for Alfred's translation of Gregory's *Pastoral Care*, based strictly on word frequency and word class. Table 8, on the other hand, has not been previously published. It details the effects of frequency *within*

Table 6. *Old English -on- Spellings by Word Frequency (Phillips 1980)*

Word group frequency	Ave. % of -on/-om spellings
1–10	39.4
11–20	49.4
21–30	51.3
31–60	55.3
61–90	95.0
91–400*	64.0
over 400	97.8

*Frequency group 91–400 contains only 3 words, each from a different word class.

Table 7. -on- *Spellings by word class* (*Phillips 1980: 22*)

Word class	Ave. % of -on/-om spellings
Verbs	31.91
Nouns	43.64
Adjectives	44.00
Adverbs and function words	84.29

word classes and shows how word frequency effects can be seen even within word classes (verbs being the only exception).

Is there any reason why this should be the case, that is, that word frequency effects are felt inside of word classes? The answer may be because speakers access word class before they access phonological structure. As van Turennout *et al.* (1998: 572) observe, "data from behavioral studies as well as from neuropsychological studies of patients with language impairment have suggested that a word's semantic and syntactic properties are retrieved before its phonological form is constructed." In their own experiment, van Turennout *et al.* found that "in noun-phrase production it takes . . . about 40 ms to retrieve a noun's initial phoneme once its syntactic gender has been retrieved" (574).

This order of access also perhaps accounts for the behavior of another sound change, one purposefully omitted from Table 4, namely the loss of the initial /h/ in Old English word-initial /hw/. One would expect the function words to change first

Table 8. -on- *Spellings by word frequency within word class*

Word class	Frequency range	Ave. % of -on/-om spellings
Verbs	1–10	31
	11–100	37
	242	26
Nouns	1–10	40
	11–100	49
	745	93
Adjectives	1–10	33
	11–100	58
	113	67
Adverbs/function words	1–10	64
	11–100	87
	over 100	99

for this sound change, since it is clearly a weakening, yet the function words are resistant to the change. Toon (1978: 361) attributes this tenacity of /hw/ to "the fact that it usually occurs in an easily identifiable and grammatically closely related lexical subset"—our modern *"what, when, where, why, which, whether, while*, etc." set. This explanation incorporates what is sometimes called *neighborhood density*, that is, "the number of words that are phonologically similar to a given word" (Vitevitch *et al.* 1998). Vitevitch *et al.* (1998: 327) find that "words occurring in dense similarity neighborhoods were responded to more slowly than those in sparse neighborhoods." Similarly, Wright (1998) reports that "all other things being equal—including lexical frequency—words in a dense neighborhood are more carefully articulated than words in a sparse neighborhood." This careful articulation implies phonological analysis. The implication for sound change is clearly that lexical analysis may include analysis by neighborhood similarity: words in such a phonological subset can resist the direction of a sound change because they are being analyzed phonologically as well as grammatically. They are first recognized as members of a particular grammatical category, allowing the speaker to use that information to influence that category's participation in a sound change, but they are also analyzed by neighborhood similarity, allowing them to behave independently even within their word class.

Neighborhood density might also account for even single aberrant forms that resist a sound change due to an undesirable merger. For example, an aberrant form in the ME /ö/ > /e/ shift might be explained in this way. Table 9 details the change among the short vowels. Although there are not as many or as compelling forms as

Table 9. *Middle English /ö/ > /e/ (adapted from Phillips 1984: 329)*

Category	Freq.	Average % innovative ⟨e⟩
Func. Words	1 (*bineþenn*)	100
(Ave. %e = 76)	48 (*heore > their*)	4
	137 (*sellf*)	100
	347 (*hemm > them*)	100
Verbs	3–39	85
(Ave. %e = 85)		
Non-numerical adjectives	2–15	72
(Ave. %e = 72)		
Nouns	1–2	75
(Ave. %e = 55)	26–90	46
Numerals	2–46	10
(Ave. %e =10)		

for the long vowels (shown in Table 3), the basic pattern of least frequent words changing first is clear among the nouns, the only word class with enough lexemes with a large enough range to feel confident of a conclusion in this regard. And the basic pattern of function words changing first is evident, although there are only four. However, within the function words, the word *heore* 'their' stands out. The other three function words all exhibit the innovative spelling (and one presumes the innovative pronunciation). *Heore* 'their', in contrast, retains its ⟨eo⟩ spelling 96% of the time. An explanation for this aberrant behavior must surely include the phonologically and semantically similar word *here*, meaning 'her'.

4. Conclusion

That sound change is influenced by word frequency, word class, and neighborhood density implies a lexicon rich in detail and rich in interconnections and interdependencies. Whether speed of access itself determines some of the differences in behavior is a tantalizing hypothesis that should be tested further. It does seem that the factor of neighborhood density must be incorporated into a psychologically real model of the lexicon and the effect of sound change upon that lexicon. And it does seem that in determining which words are affected first in a sound change, word class takes precedence over word frequency. Finally, within word classes, sound changes which require fine analysis of the lexical entry (including neighborhood density effects, word class, morphological make-up, as well as phonotactic constraints and typological sound changes in general) affect the least frequent words first. In requiring such analysis, they resemble morphologically motivated, analogical changes, which also affect the least frequent words first (Bybee 1995: 236). In contrast, changes which ignore the phonological integrity of segments and the morphological composition of words affect the most frequent words first. In brief, the Frequency-Implementation Hypothesis does hold: "Changes which require analysis —whether syntactic, morphological, or phonological—during their implementation affect the least frequent words first; others affect the most frequent words first.

Notes

1. The Signalyze software was provided through a University Research Grant from Indiana State University.

References

Bolinger, D. 1975. *Aspects of language*, 2nd Edition. New York: Harcourt Brace Jovanovich.

Bybee, J. 1995. "Diachronic and typological properties of morphology and their implications for representation". *Morphological Aspects of Language Processing*, L.B. Feldman, (ed), 225–46. Hillsdale, NJ: Lawrence Erlbaum.

Bybee, J. 1985. *Morphology: a Study of the Relation Between Meaning and Form*. Amsterdam: John Benjamins.

Bybee, J., Perkens, R., and Pagliuca, W. 1994. *The Evolution of Grammar: Tense, Apsect, and Modality in the Languages of the World*. Chicago: University of Chicago Press.

Carroll, John, et al. (eds.) 1971. *The American Heritage Word Frequency Book*. New York: Houghton Mifflin.

Chambers, W. W., and Wilkie, J.R. 1970. *A Short History of the German Language*. London: Methuen.

Fenk-Oczlon, G. 1989. "Geläufigkeit als Determinante von phonologischen Backgrounding-Prozessen". *Papiere zur Linguistik* 40: 91–103.

Fidelholz, J. 1975. "Word frequency and vowel reduction in English". *Papers from the Eleventh Regional Meeting of the Chicago Linguistic Society*, 200–13. Chicago: CLS.

Hogg, R. 1982. "Was there ever an /ɔ/- phoneme in Old English?" *Neuphilologische Mitteilungen* 83: 225–9.

Hogg, R. 1992. *A Grammar of Old English*. Volume 1: *Phonology*. Oxford: Blackwell.

Hooper, J. 1976. "Word frequency in lexical diffusion and the source of morphophonological change". *Current Progress in Historical Linguistics*, W.M. Christie (ed), 95–105. Amsterdam: North-Holland.

Johnson, K. 1997. *Acoustic and Auditory Phonetics*. Cambridge: Blackwell.

Krishnamurti, B. 1998. "Regularity of sound change through lexical diffusion: A study of s > h > Ø in Gondi dialects". *Language Variation and Change* 10: 193–220.

Labov, W. 1994. *Principles of Linguistic Change, Volume I: Internal Factors*. Oxford: Blackwell.

Neu, H. 1980. "Ranking of constraints on /t,d/ deletion in American English: a statistical analysis". In *Locating Language in Time and Space*, W. Labov (ed), 37–54. New York: Academic Press.

Pagliuca, W. and Mowrey, R. 1987. "Articulatory evolution". In A.G. Ramat, O. Carruba, and G. Bernini (eds.), *Papers from the 7th International Conference on Historical Linguistics*, Amsterdam: Benjamins, 459–72.

Phillips, B. 1980. "Old English *an ~ on*: A new appraisal". *Journal of English Linguistics* 14: 20–3.

Phillips, B. 1981. "Lexical diffusion and Southern *tune, duke, news*". *American Speech* 56: 72–8.

Phillips, B. 1983. "Lexical diffusion and function words". *Linguistics* 21: 487–99.

Phillips, B. 1984. "Word frequency and the actuation of sound change". *Language* 60: 320–42.

136   BETTY S. PHILLIPS

Phillips, B. 1994. "Southern English Glide Deletion Revisited". *American Speech* 69: 115–27.

Phillips, B. 1995. "Lexical Diffusion as a Guide to Scribal Intent: A Comparison of ME ⟨eo⟩ vs. ⟨e⟩ Spellings in the *Peterborough Chronicle* and the *Ormulum*". In H. Andersen (ed.), *Historical Linguistics 1993: Selected Papers from the 11th International Conference on Historical Linguistics*. Amsterdam: Benjamins, 379–86.

Phillips, B. 1998. "Word Frequency and Lexical Diffusion in English Stress Shifts". In R. Hogg and L. van Bergen (eds.), *Historical Linguistics 1995*: Volume 2: *Germanic Linguistics*. Amsterdam: Benjamins, 223–32.

Rhodes, R. 1996. "English reduced vowels and the nature of natural processes". In B. Hurch and R. A. Rhodes (eds.), *Natural Phonology: the State of the Art*. Berlin: Mouton de Gruyter, 239–59.

Rusch, W. J. 1992. *The Language of the East Midlands and the Development of Standard English*. New York: Peter Lang.

Toon, Thomas. 1978. "Lexical diffusion in Old English". In D. Farkas, W.M. Jacobsen, and K.W. Todrys (eds.), *Papers from the Parasession on the Lexicon*. Chicago: Chicago Linguistic Society, 347–64.

van Turennout, M., Hagoort, P., and Brown, C.M. 1998. "Brain activity during speaking: from syntax to phonology in 40 milliseconds". *Science* 280: 572–74.

Vitevitch, M. S. and Luce, P. A. 1998. "When words compete: levels of processing in perception of spoken words". *Psychological Science* 9: 325–29.

Wright, R. 1998. "Factors of lexical competition in vowel articulation". Paper presented at Labphon 6. York, UK, July 1998.

Zipf, G. 1935. *The Psycho-biology of Language*. Boston: Houghton Mifflin.

Exemplar dynamics: Word frequency, lenition and contrast

JANET B. PIERREHUMBERT

Northwestern University

1. Introduction

Over the last decades, a considerable body of evidence has accumulated that speakers have detailed phonetic knowledge of a type which is not readily modelled using the categories and categorical rules of phonological theory. One line of evidence is systematic differences between languages in fine details of pronunciation. For example, it is known that Spanish and English differ systematically in the exact formant patterns typical of their point vowels (Bradlow 1995). Canadian French differs from both Canadian English and European French in the distribution of VOT times of voiced and voiceless stops (Caramazza and Yeni-Komshian 1974). These are just two of many examples, with more reviewed in Pierrehumbert (2000) and Pierrehumbert *et al.* (in press); at this point, it is not possible to point to a single case in which analogous phonemes in two different languages display exactly the same phonetic targets and the same pattern of phonetic variation in different contexts. Exact phonetic targets and patterns of variation must accordingly be learned during the course of language acquisition. The usage-based framework readily accommodates such findings by proposing that mental representations of phonological targets and patterns are gradually built up through experience with speech.

A particularly interesting and challenging result is the discovery that learned phonetic detail may be associated not just with languages or dialects, but even with specific words in the lexicon of a given dialect. This observation is made most convincingly in a series of studies by Bybee which explore the relationship of word frequency to lenition. Bybee (Hooper 1976) explored the process of schwa reduction and desyllabification which applies variably before sonorants such as /r/ and /n/ in English. She found that in high frequency words, such as *every* and the noun *eve-*

ning , the schwa was completely absent and the syllable it originally projected had vanished. In mid-frequency words, such as *memory* and *salary* , the modal outcome is a syllabic /r/. In rare words, such as *mammary* and *artillery* , the modal outcome is a schwa plus /r/. Another example is provided by so-called t/d-deletion, which is widely acknowledged to be a case of variable undershoot of the coronal articulation of the /t/ or /d/. Bybee (2000) found that deletion—defined as the inability of the transcriber to hear the stop on a tape-recording—is more prevalent in high-frequency words than in low-frequency words. The set of double-marked past tense verbs (such as *told* and *left*) provides a way to control for the morphological factors which could play a part in this pattern. Within the set of double-marked pasts alone, Bybee's data showed a statistically significant relationship of word frequency to the rate of /t/ deletion, with the most frequent word (*told*) having /d/ deleted in 68% of cases while the least frequent (*meant*) never had the /t/ deleted. Further documentation of the association between word frequency and leniting historical change is provided in Phillips (1984, this volume).

Although these frequency effects will be the main focus in this paper, is is also important to acknowledge that word-specific allophony has been found in a number of other situations as well. For example, Yaeger-Dror and Kemp (1992) and Yaeger-Dror (1996) demonstrate that words in a particular cultural/semantic field in Montreal French have resisted a historical shift in the vowel system and as a result display idiosyncratic vowel quality. Hay (2000) also presents data relating degree of morphological decomposibility to degree of /t/ lenition in words such as *shiftless*.

These results challenge standard models of phonology and phonetics at two levels. First, in all standard models, the lexicon is distinguished from the phonological grammar. The exact phonetic details of a word's pronunciation arise because the word is retrieved from the lexicon, and processed by the rules or constraints of the grammar whose result (the surface phonological form of the word) is fed to a phonetic implementation component. The phonetic implementation component computes the articulatory and/or acoustic goals which actualize the word as speech. The phonetic implementation component applies in exactly the same way to all surface phonological representations, and the outcome depends solely on the categories and prosodic structures displayed in those representations. As a result, there is no way in which the phonetic implementation can apply differently to some words than to others. If a phonetic implementation rule is variable and gradient, then the same probability distribution of outcomes would arise for all words which meet the structural description of the rule. This generic feature of modular generative models with phonetic implementation rules is developed at more length in Pierrehumbert (1994).

A second challenge arises from the fact that the differential phonetic outcomes relate specifically to word frequency. Standard generative models do not encode word frequency. They treat the word frequency effects which are so pervasive in experiments involving priming or lexical decision tasks as matters of linguistic performance rather than linguistic competence. Thus the intrusion of word frequency into a traditional area of linguistics, namely the conditioning of allophony, is not readily accommodated in the classical generative viewpoint.

If each word corresponded to a completely idiosyncratic phonetic signal, then results such as Bybee's could be readily formalized in a highly transparent scientific model. We would simply assume that holistic gestural or acoustic templates are associated with word meanings. The real challenge arises from the fact that the classical view does provide important insights about the mental representation of phonology. Although a word may have idiosyncratic phonetic properties, it is perceived as made up of units of sound structure which are also shared with other words. The existence of these subparts—whether phonemes, moras, or syllables—is reflected in productive behaviors such as pronunciation of neologisms and loan word assimilations. It is also reflected in the tendency of historical changes to sweep through the vocabulary. Thus, the correct model must describe the interaction of word-specific phonetic detail with more general principles of phonological structure.

In this paper, we will develop a formal architecture which is capable of capturing these regularities. This formal architecture is "generative" in the sense that it provides explicitly for phonological representations and processes; it predicts that some outcomes are possible and others are not. Like a generative grammar, it is informed by the goal of specifying all and only the outcomes which are possible in human language. It represents a considerable departure from generative models, however, in the way the lexical representations are organized and the consequences of lexical representation for speech production. Specifically, the model assumes that detailed phonetic memories are associated with individual words and it implicitly defines word specific probability distributions over phonetic outcomes. Whereas the classic models define a strong separation between the lexicon and the grammar, in the present model these represent two degrees of generalization over the same memories and are thus strongly related to each other. Furthermore, in the present model, frequency information plays an intrinsic role in the system because it is implicitly encoded by the very nature of the memory system.

The general properties of the model all originate from the psychological model of similarity and classification from which the proposal derives, namely exemplar theory. From its origins as a model of perception only, it is extended to be a model of production. By examining the consequences of the perception-production loop over time, we provide a formal framework for thinking about the quantitative predictions of usage-based phonology, as proposed by Bybee. We derive the finding that leniting historical changes are more advanced in frequent words than in rarer ones. Calculations are presented which reveal the interaction of production noise, lenition and entrenchment. A realistic treatment is also provided for the time course of a phonological merger which originates from lenition of a marked category.

2. Exemplar Theory

Exemplar theory was first introduced in psychology as a model of perception and categorization. It was subsequently extended specifically to speech sounds by Johnson (1996) and Lacerda (in press), providing a highly successful model of vowel categorization in particular. Goldinger (1996) also applies the strongly related model of Hintzman (1986) to model the identification and recognition of words. We will adopt some key assumptions from this previous work, indicating briefly the empirical motivation for these assumptions.

In an exemplar model, each category is represented in memory by a large cloud of remembered tokens of that category. These memories are organized in a cognitive map, so that memories of highly similar instances are close to each other and memories of dissimilar instances are far apart. The remembered tokens display the range of variation that is exhibited in the physical manifestations of the category. For example, the remembered tokens of the vowel /ε/ would exhibit a variety of formant values (related to variation in vocal tract anatomy across speakers, variation along the dimension of hypo-hyperarticulation, and so forth) as well as variation in f0 and in duration. The entire system is then a mapping between points in a phonetic parameter space and the labels of the categorization system. The labels constitute a level of representation in their own right, or else they may be viewed as functional links to other levels of representation.

It is important to note that the same remembered tokens may be simultaneously subject to more than one categorization scheme, under such a model. For example, a recollection of the phrase *Supper's ready!* could be labelled as "Mom" and "female speech", in addition to exemplifying the words and phonemes in the phrase.

If every encountered token of a category is stored as a separate exemplar, then frequent categories will obviously be represented by numerous tokens and infrequent categories will be represented by less numerous tokens. The difference in token count is one ingredient of the model's explanations of frequency effects, as we will see below. The mind's capacity for long-term memories of individual examples is in fact astonishingly large, as experiments reviewed in Johnson (1996) indicate. Nonetheless, the volume of speech which a person processes in a lifetime is so great that we would not wish to assume individual memories of every use of every word.

Exemplar theory responds to this problem in two ways. First of all, we assume that memories decay. Memories of utterances that we heard yesterday are more vivid than memories from a decade ago. Second, the parameter space in which the exemplars are represented is assumed to be granularized. Examples whose differences are too fine to show up under the granularization are encoded as identical (see Kruschke 1992). For example, the ear cannot distinguish arbitrarily fine differences in f0. The JND (just noticeable difference) for f0 in any given part of the range is determined by the resolution of the anatomical and neural mechanisms which are involved in encoding f0. Thus, it is reasonable to suppose that speech tokens differing by less than one JND in f0 are stored as if they had identical f0s. Similar constraints on the resolution of all other perceptual dimensions would motivate granularization of the phonetic parameter space as a whole. As a result, an individual exemplar—which is a detailed perceptual memory—does not correspond to a single perceptual experience, but rather to an equivalence class of perceptual experiences.

This said, it becomes reasonable to propose that each exemplar has an associated strength—which may be viewed as a resting activation level. The exemplars encoding frequent recent experiences have higher resting activation levels than exemplars encoding infrequent and temporally remote experiences.

When a new token is encountered, it is classified in exemplar theory according to its similarity to the exemplars already stored. Perceptual encoding of the new token locates it in the relevant parameter space. Its similarity to any single stored exemplar can be computed as its distance from the exemplar in the parameter space. To classify the new token, the most probable labelling given the labelling of the exemplars in the neighborhood is computed. The model implemented here follows the specifics of Lacerda (in press). A fixed size neighborhood around the new token determines the set of exemplars which influence the classification. The summed similarities to the exemplars for each label instantiated in that neighborhood is computed, with the similarity to each given exemplar weighted by the strength (or activation) of that exemplar. Recall that the strength is a function of the number and recency of phonetic tokens at that location in the exemplar space.

Figure 1 illustrates the operation of the choice rule for a hypothetical case in which the labels /I/ and /ɛ/ are being considered for an unknown vowel token. For the sake of exposition only, we assume that the only relevant dimension is f2 (the value of the second formant); this is the x-axis. In a realistic situation, the input would of course have higher dimensionality. The y axis is the activation level for each of the stored exemplars. Exemplars of /ɛ/ are shown with dashed lines towards the left, and exemplars of /I/ with solid lines towards the right, a consequence of the fact that the vowel /I/ generally exhibits higher f2 than /ɛ/. However, one individual token has of /ɛ/ a higher f2 than one token of /I/. This overlap of the phonetic distributions for /ɛ/ and /I/ really does arise in practice, because of dialect differences, speaker differences, and random variation in production. The unidentified vowel

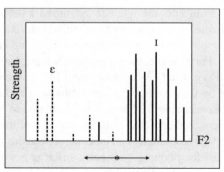

Figure 1.

has an f2 which places it in a region of ambiguity, as shown by the location of the star under the x-axis. The window in which the comparison is being made is shown by arrows. Within this window, there are seven exemplars of /I/, of which six are highly activated. There are only two (less activated) exemplars of /ɛ/. Hence, the winning label is /I/. The equation specifying this classification rule is given in the appendix.

In other approaches (e.g. Kruschke 1992), all exemplars with all labels contribute to the classification, but an exponentially decaying weighting by distance has the result that the exemplars nearest to the stimulus dominate the calculation. As a result, the overall behavior of the model is substantially similar to that of the model reported here. We note also that attentional weights may be imposed to model how different contexts, expectations, and task requirements influence classification; however these effects are not at issue in the present paper.

Note that the labelling depends on the relationship amongst the exemplar clouds in the neighborhood; the winning label is the one which is overall more probable than the competitors. A label which has more numerous or more activated exemplars in the neighborhood of the new token has an advantage in the competition. Given that high frequency labels are associated with more numerous exemplars (whose resting activations are, on the average, higher), they will have more dense and more activated exemplar clouds. In situations involving ambiguity, the model thus predicts a bias towards a high-frequency label. This prediction is supported by the experimental literature.

The classification rules just discussed have no temporal scale, summarizing only the end result of the decision process. Of course this does not mean that the brain has for each perceptual classification process a separate little pocket calculator, which it employs to compute the values of the relevant formuli over the relevant exemplar clouds. Instead, the decision rules may be viewed as representing synoptically the behavior of an activation/inhibition system. The sums of the exemplar strengths represent the fact that exemplars spread activation to labels, so that the activation of any given label is a cumulative function of the number and activation level of the exemplars associated with it. The comparison amongst the scores for different labels reflects the results of reciprocal inhibition amongst labels, with the winning label being the one which succeeds in suppressing the activation of its competitors. The model is consistent with the standard assumption that reaction times for phonological and lexical decisions reflect the time required for activation to build up and cross a decision threshhold. Thus, the model is consistent with, and can even serve to elucidate, results on the speed of phonological and lexical decisions.

To summarize, the exemplar approach associates with each category of the system a cloud of detailed perceptual memories. The memories are granularized as a function of the acuity of the perceptual system (and possibly as a function of additional factors). Frequency is not overtly encoded in the model. Instead, it is intrinsic to the cognitive representations for the categories. More frequent categories have more exemplars and more highly activated exemplars than less frequent categories.

Let us now review the most obvious successes of this approach, as it applies to speech, before passing on to extensions of the model.

Exemplar theory provides us with a way to formalize the detailed phonetic knowledge that native speakers have about the categories of their language. Since exemplar theory stores directly the distribution of phonetic parameter values associated with each label, it provides us with a picture of the "implicit phonetic knowledge of the speaker". The acquisition of this knowledge can be understood simply in terms of the acquisition of a large number of memory traces of experiences. There is no competing model which achieves the same level of descriptive adequacy. Notably, the assumption that there exists a universal symbolic alphabet which provides an interface to a universal sensori-motor phonetic implementation component (as in Chomsky and Halle 1968; Chomsky and Lasnik 1995) provides no means of representing the extremely fine differences across languages in values and probability distributions of phonetic properties. Therefore, it yields no insight into how the knowledge of such details might be acquired.

Another obvious success of the model is its treatment of prototype effects, handling with a single mechanism two major findings. One is the finding that a new token which is well-positioned with respect to a category can actually provide a better example of that category (in being recognized quickly and rated highly) than any actual example of that category that has been previously experienced. This phenomenon, sometimes taken as an argument for the abstraction of prototypes, follows from the exemplar model if "goodness" is interpreted in terms of the probability of the winning label (with the probability arising from the relative score in relation to the scores of competitors). This probability does not necessarily reach a maximum on a position in the parameter space which is actually occupied by an exemplar; a position which is centrally positioned in a dense neighborhood of exemplars will receive a very high probability even if there is no exemplar at that exact point. Thus the abstract prototype need not be explicitly computed and stored in advance. A second success of the model, as noted by Lacerda, is its the ability to explain the fact that extreme examples of phonological categories are sometimes judged to be better than modal examples. For example, as shown in Johnson, Flemming, and Wright (1993) the perceptually best examples of the corner vowels /i/ and /u/ have more extreme formant values than typical productions. This outcome follows from the fact that the probability for a label is influenced both by the activation of exemplars having that label, and by competition from other labels having exemplars in the same area of the cognitive map. Increasing the distance of a novel token from all exemplars with competing labels will thus raise the subjective goodness.

A last strength of exemplar models is that they provide a foundation for modelling frequency effects, since frequency is built in to the very mechanism by which memories of categories are stored and new examples are classified. It is not necessary to posit special frequency counters whose cognitive and neural status are dubious. Indeed, exemplar models can be fleshed out with assumptions about neural encoding so as to capture the main experimental findings about frequency effects, including an understanding of why frequency affects both the outcome of decisions and the speed with which decisions are taken.

3. Production

3.1 Model 1

As is evident from the last section, exemplar models were developed to model perceptual data. Real language use in communication involves both perception and production. In this section, we undertake an extension of the model in order to handle production. By modelling the complete perception-production loop using exemplar theory, we will show that facts about the reflexes of word frequency in production which were discovered by Bybee and Phillips can be modelled. No other current theoretical approach can handle these facts.

In perception, the encoded phonetic character of an incoming stimulus locates it in the parameter space. Activation of exemplars in the neighborhood is passed upwards to the labels, with the most probable label winning in competition with alternatives. Production proceeds in the opposite direction. Following Levelt (1989) and others, we assume that the decision to produce a given category is realized through activation of that label. The selection of a phonetic target, given the label, may be modelled as a random selection of an exemplar from the cloud of exemplars associated with the label. It will not be important here whether the exemplars have a dual acoustic-motor nature, or whether the motor program is computed on the fly in order to match the acoustic goals represented by the exemplar. Similarly, we will not attempt to model the deeper causes which may figure in the choice amongst possible exemplars. Although social and stylistic factors may select for different parts of the exemplar cloud in different situations, the aggregate behavior of the system over all situations may be modelled as a repeated random sampling from the entire aggregate of exemplars. The likelihood that a particular exemplar will be selected is proportionate to its strength. Production is taken to be sensitive to strength in exactly the same way that perceptual classification is. Thus, this first model of production is a minimal extension of previous work on how exemplars function in perception.

Now, a phonetic target is not necessarily achieved exactly. Even for a speaker who is merely talking to himself, one may assume random deviations from the phonetic target due to noise in the motor control and execution. For a community of multiple speakers, there would be random differences amongst the stored memories of different members of the community. Thus if a listener hears a speech token produced by a different speaker than himself, that speech token could be randomly different from the exemplars in his own stored memories. In sum, new tokens being added to an existing exemplar cloud may be viewed (to a first order approximation) as a random sampling from that cloud with added noise.

Figure 2 shows the consequences of this simple approach for the evolution of a single category from a single token to a distribution of exemplars. As in Figure 1, the situation is simplified to one phonetic dimension for expository purposes. The x-axis of the figure represents a relevant phonetic parameter, such as second formant value (if we are considering categories of vowel frontness), or f0 (if we are considering tonal categories). A nominal scale is indicated. The single token of the category which seeded the cloud is located at $x = 1$. That is, the very first speech token which the listener associates with the category label in question displays a phonetic value of 1, and this value serves as the starting point for the development of the new category. (We have said nothing about **why** a listener may posit a new category, as this question involves functional issues which exceed the scope of the paper). The production noise is unbiased with a uniform distribution of width 0.2. The y-axis is the count of memory-weighted count exemplars in each small interval of the phonetic scale. The e-folding time of a memory is 2000 time steps (e.g the parameter controlling the exponential decay of memories is 2000 production/perception iterations. See appendix for further details). Three superimposed curves show the situation after 10,000, 50,000, and 100,000 iterations. Thus, the figure is essentially like three superimposed histograms, except that the area under

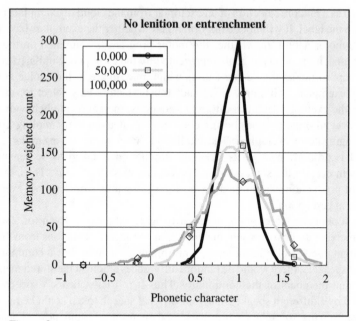

Figure 2.

each curve is not normalized to 1.0 as a probability would be. As discussed above, the total representation of the category is strengthened as more and more memories are stored; temporal decay of older memories, not normalization, is responsible for the gradual lowering of the peak in the figure.

Figure 2 is based on the idealization by which every single production is accurately classified as a member of the category. Note that the variance of the distribution along the phonetic dimension displayed increases with usage. It is important to model this increase in variance, since mature categories do display variation. (They do not have spike-like distributions showing only phonetic properties which correspond exactly to the first token of the category which is internalized by the listener.) The overall shape approaches a Gaussian distribution as the number of tokens increases. This limiting behavior arises from the fact that the production-perception loop is an additive random process.

3.2 Model II: Systematic Bias

Figure 2 showed the case where there is no systematic bias in production. Recent work by Lindblom and colleagues on hypo- and hyper- articulation (Lindblom

1990) argues for systematic production biases. The case which will interest us here is hypo-articulation, or the tendency to undershoot articulatory targets in order to save effort and speed up communication. This tendency is arguably the cause of leniting historical changes, such as schwa reduction and /t/-deletion. Of course, in a complete model of historical change it will be necessary to offer some explanation of why certain languages at certain times begin to permit particular leniting changes while not permitting others. But given that a historical leniting change is in progress, its phonetic consequences may be represented as a systematic bias on the production process in the model we are developing here.

Figure 3 presents results of a calculation identical to Figure 2, except that a systematic bias has been introduced in the production process. The bias applied is −0.01, or leftwards along the phonetic scale which serves as the x-axis. This means that each token is produced slightly lenited compared to the exemplar of the category which has been randomly selected as a production goal. No matter how lenited the production goal may be, the production is that little bit more lenited. This is one concrete interpretation of Lindblom's general observations. Lindblom is claiming that speakers undershoot targets to the extent possible—e.g. to an extent that still permits communication. It would not be consistent with Lindblom's general line of

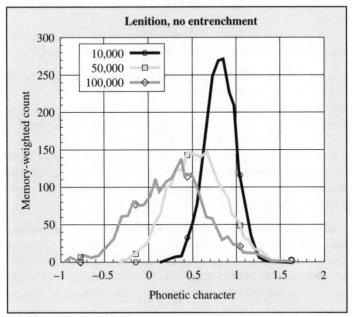

Figure 3.

thought to think that speakers underarticulate to the point that their target words become unrecoverable. As before, the distributions shown represent the results of 10,000, 50,000 and 100,000 interations of the model. By comparing Figure 3 to Figure 2, we see that a systematic lenition bias causes the distribution of exemplars to shift. In addition, it causes an increase in variance, much as a photograph of a moving object shows a blur.

One way to view this figure is diachronically. It shows how the distribution of a category evolves over time after a leniting historical change is first introduced. The mode of the distribution gradually moves towards the left (or lenited) end of the phonetic axis. The graph also has a synchronic interpretation, provided that we add a key assumption—namely, that not just phonemes, but individual words, have associated exemplar clouds. For example, we assume that each of the words *bet*, *bed*, and *bend* has an exemplar cloud, and that the exemplar cloud for the phoneme /ɛ/ is the union of the /ɛ/ sections of the exemplar clouds for these words and for all other words containing an /ɛ/. With this added assumption, the figure may be viewed as displaying a synchronic comparison amongst words of different frequencies which are impacted by the same historical change in progress. Since the high frequency words are used more often than the low frequency words, their stored exemplar representations show more numerous impacts of the persistent bias towards lenition. As a result, they are further to the left on the axis than the low frequency words.

The result displayed in Figure 3 is exactly the result documented by Bybee, Philips, and others. Some detailed predictions of the model include:

1. Each individual word displays a certain amount of variability in production.
2. The effect of word frequency on lenition rates is gradient.
3. The effect of word frequency on lenition rates should be observable within the speech of individuals; it is not an artifact of averaging data across the different generations which make up a speech community.
4. The effect of word frequency on lenition rates should be observable both synchronically (by comparing the pronunciation of words of different frequency) and diachronically (by examining the evolution of word pronunciations over the years within each person's speech.)

The exemplar model is the only current model which has these properties. An additional prediction is that probability distributions for words undergoing a historical change should be skewed, with the extent of the skew being slight or great according to the velocity of the change. Even with recent advances in speech processing technology, it would require an extremely ambitious amount of data analysis to evaluate this prediction.

Two further observations may be made on the cognitive interpretation of this model. First, note that speakers immersed in a new speech environment find that their pronunciation patterns shift over a relatively long time span, of several months or more. (For example, see the longitudinal phonetic study reported in Sancier and Fowler 1997). The time span for historical changes is on the order of decades or more. Thus, the extremely high number of iterations used in making the calculations in the figures is not unrealistic. Consider, for example, a leniting change affecting the vowel in the preposition *of*. The present paper alone has over 200 examples of this word, and 10,000 examples would probably occur in less than one month of speech. Second, it is often noted that historical changes impact the speech of older people less than younger people, so that a change in progress results in a divergence between the speech patterns of different generations. The model suggests two possible factors in this finding. First, older people may have more exemplars than younger ones for the same pattern, so that the parameter values displayed in older exemplars dominate the production statistics. This line of explanation depends on the assumption that memories decay slowly. A second possibility is that older people are less likely to add new exemplars than young ones; because the formation of new memories becomes less rapid and robust with age, the production statistics are dominated by exemplars stored at a younger age. Differences in attention or in feelings of social affiliation could impact formation of exemplar memories in an analogous way. Both of these lines of explanation predict that the speech patterns of older adults could shift to some extent, just not as rapidly as for younger people.

3.3 Model III: Entrenchment

Figure 3 has a serious problem which is already foreshadowed in Figure 2. In a model with production noise, the variance for any given category steadily increases with usage; when there is a systematic production bias, the velocity the bias imparts to this distribution aggravates the spread. However, practice is often reported to have the opposite effect of decreasing the variance, a phenomenon known as "entrenchment". For example, a child who takes up the cello produces highly variable tuning of notes at the beginning, and more and more accurate tuning over years of practice. The phonetic variability associated with a typical phonological category decreases gradually up through late childhood (Lee *et al.* 1999). The bare exemplar model provides no way to model entrenchment. There is no combination of parameter settings for the model which allows a category to fill out after being seeded by a single example, without simultaneously predicting that the spreading out will go on indefinitely.

The model must be further elaborated in order to model entrenchment effects. The model of entrenchment for which we present calculations is broadly inspired by work by Rosenbaum *et al.* (1993) on reaching movements. The understanding of production is modified so that production does not depend only on a single target exemplar (selected at random). Instead, a target location in the exemplar cloud is selected at random, and the exemplars in the neighborhood of this location all contribute to the production plan, to a degree which reflects their activation level. The neural interpretation of this proposal is that a region in the brain, not merely a single point, is activated when planning a production. Activation-weighted averaging over a group of exemplars results in entrenchment, because averaging mathematically causes reversion towards the mean of a distribution.

Calculations of a leniting change in progress which include this treatment of entrenchment are displayed in Figure 4. A neighborhood of 500 exemplars is used in calculating the distributions displayed in this figure. A comparison of Figure 3 and Figure 4 shows that the entrenchment narrows the distributions, so that the distribution width for the case of 100,000 iterations is roughly comparable to that for 10,000 iterations. With the particular parameter settings selected here, the spreading effects arising from production noise and lenition and the anti-diffusive effect of entrenchment have essentially cancelled out in determining the variance. If a larger neighborhood were used in the treatment of entrenchment, then the high count case would have less variance. In a situation involving high production noise

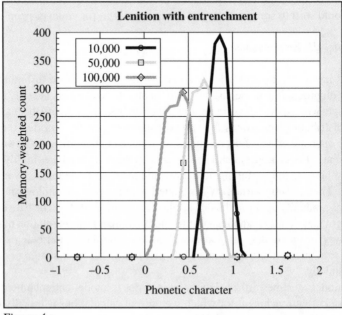

Figure 4.

or a high degree of systematic bias, the high count case would display more variance than the low count case.

The issue of entrenchment is a complicated one, and the treatment we have presented is only one of many possible ones. The Hintzman/Goldinger model proposes an entrenchment effect on the perception side rather than the production side; when any given stimulus is classified, it sets up an "echo" which reflects not only its own properties but also the properties of the exemplars in the stimulus neighborhood which contributed to the classification. The echo is what is stored in memory, not the stimulus itself. Since the echo combines information over a neighborhood, it shows reversion towards the mean just as our production model does. The type of data we are considering here—patterns of historical change—involve the entire perception-production loop and they do not tell us whether entrenchment occurs in perception, in production, or in both.

In the Hintzman/Goldinger model, the neighborhood which influences the echo of a stimulus has a fixed size on the exemplar map. This means that there are few influences on the echo if the neighborhood of the stimulus is sparsely populated. In the production model presented here, the neighborhood contains a fixed number of exemplars; it expands its size in regions which are sparsely populated. The Hintzman/Goldinger treatment has the result that more episodic information is encoded in memory for rare events than for frequent ones; for example, one is more likely to remember that a word was spoken in a particular voice if the word is rare than if it is common. However, we were unable to make a fixed neighborhood work out in the production model since it creates too much instability in the exemplar dynamics at the beginning of the calculation when there are very few examples of a category. This is why an n-nearest-neighbors model is offered here. An integrated model which handles all known neighborhood effects simultaneously remains to be developed.

A third issue is whether entrenchment critically involves feedback from other levels, and if so, what kind of feedback. Notice that self-organizing systems can in principle form and sharpen peaky distributions without any type of feedback at all, much as the lumpiness in the energy distribution after the Big Bang eventually evolved into the universe we know with concentrated physical objects, such as galaxies and viruses. All that is needed is some type of anti-diffusive factor, such as gravity, which causes unevenness in the parameter distributions to become exaggerated. Equally, however, people sharpen categories faster and to a greater degree if they receive feedback, particularly if the feedback provides functionally important rewards or penalties. Speech patterns appear to fall into an intermediate situation, in that people adapt their speech patterns to their speech community even without overt pressures and rewards, but that communicative success and social attunement provide implicit feedback which is certainly important. The model presented here does have feedback, in that it has an informational loop between the stimulus encoding and the abstract level of representation represented by the labelling. If an incoming stimulus is so ambiguous that it can't be labelled, then it is ignored rather than stored. That is, the exemplar cloud is only updated when the communication was successful to the extent that the speech signal was analyzable (As in real life, there is no guarantee that the listener's analysis is the speaker's, however.) In addition, the model automatically generates social accommodation of speech patterns, since speech patterns which are heard recently and frequently dominate the set of exemplars for any given label, and therefore guide the typical productions. This effect arises from the feedback loop from production to classification to production which is set up by the "speech chain" of conversational interaction. To model the more specific feedback effects which occur in different social contexts, it is necessary to introduce attentional weighting as a further factor. For example, if a child emulates the speech patterns of a particularly admired role model, this would be modelled by weighting of the exemplars in that particular voice. This weighting represents the net positive effect of feedback from the other levels of representation involved in the child's understanding of his social situation.

4. Neutralization

In the calculations presented so far, it has been assumed that all productions that are classified at all are classified in the same way. Under this assumption, a leniting change causes an unbounded drift in the phonetic distribution for each word exemplifying a category. In fact, however, historical changes have natural completion states. When the change is complete, the new situation is stable.

To model this situation, we need to look at two labels which are competing over a phonetic parameter range. We consider the case of a marked phonological category competing with an unmarked one. Following Greenberg and others, we take the unmarked category to be more frequent than the marked one (see papers in Greenberg *et al.* 1978). In the calculation presented, the unmarked category is three times as frequent as the marked one. The marked category is also the phonetically unstable one which is subject to a persistent bias. The unmarked one is assumed to be phonetically stable. An example of this situation would be the collapse of a phrase-final voicing contrast. Phrase-final voiced obstruents are typically less frequent than voiceless ones. Lack of articulatory effort results in poor voicing in final position, e.g in tokens which are subject to being misperceived as voiceless. Historically, voiced and voiceless obstruents are reported to collapse to the unvoiced category in this position.

In Figure 5, the right hand distribution represents the marked category which is

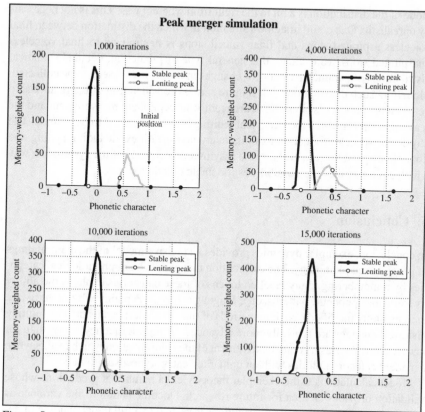

Figure 5.

subject to a persistent leftwards bias. The left hand distribution is a stable unmarked distribution competing for labelling of the same phonetic parameter. The
successive panels represent four time slices in the evolution of the situation. Because the marked distribution is subject to a persistent bias, it drifts to the left. When
it approaches the unmarked distribution, some individual tokens which were intended as examples of the marked case are perceived and stored as examples of the
unmarked case. This happens more often than the reverse. Insofar as it does happen,
the disproportion in frequency between the two categories increases. In the end,
the marked category is completely gobbled up by the unmarked one. Note that the
distribution of the unmarked category does show some influence of the marked
category it absorbed. Although the location of the distribution is still closer to the
original location of the unmarked category than that of the marked category, the

mode of the distribution is a bit to the right from where it was. This is not necessarily unrealistic. One could imagine a situation in which the distinction between final voiceless aspirated stops and final voiced stops is neutralized to final voiceless unaspirated stops. To evaluate this general type of prediction, detailed statistical distributions of parameter values for changes in progress will need to be collected. Modelling such distributions will require serious consideration of the relationship between the phonetic scales which are readily susceptible to measurement and the scale of effort on which the persistent leniting bias is presumed to be defined. The physics of speech production exhibits many nonlinearities, including ceiling and floor effects, and these will shape the assymptotic behavior of the system in a way which circumscribes the possibilities for stable outcomes.

5. Conclusion

In conclusion, exemplar dynamics provides an incisive model of the main findings of usage-based phonology. The assumption that people learn phonological categories by remembering many labelled tokens of these categories explains the ability to learn fine phonetic patterns of a language. It also explains why patterns are incrementally modified over long periods of time in adult speech, and why leniting historical changes are typically more advanced for high-frequency words than for low frequency words. A realistic treatment of the neutralization which results when a marked category collides with an unmarked category is also provided.

Model calculations using exemplar theory yield a number of predictions whose validation provides an area for future research. Documentation of the variance as well as the means of phonetic distributions is critical to a full understanding of entrenchment. Similarly, the documentation of mergers-in-progress is also signalled as an important topic.

Appendix: Model Description

The fundamental entity in our model is the exemplar list $E(L)$, which consists of the list of exemplars $\{e_1^L, \ldots, e_n^L\}$ associated with label L. To decide which label to assign to a new utterance with phonetic characteristic x, we define a score for each label by the equation

$$score(L,x) = \sum_{i=1\ldots n} W(x - e_i^L) \, exp(-\frac{t - T_i}{\tau}) \tag{1}$$

where W is a window function, t is the current time, T_i is the time at which the ith exemplar was admitted to the list, and τ is the memory decay time. Currently we are using a square window function, with $W = 1$ if its argument has absolute value below .05, and $W=0$ otherwise. If, for example there are two labels A and B in contention, we compute $score(A,x)$ and $score(B,x)$ and assign x to the label with the greatest score. In the case of a tie, the utterance is discarded. In the case of the successful classification, x is put at the head of the exemplar list corresponding to its label.

The exemplar list is also used in the production step. First a production target x_{target} is obtained by picking an exemplar randomly from the exemplar list of the desired label. In picking an exemplar, we assign each exemplar a relative probability which decays according to its age, specifically $exp(-(t-T_i)/\tau)$. This implements memory decay in the production process, as old exemplars are only rarely used. Without entrenchment, the token produced is then obtained by adding a performance noise and a lenition bias to the target Thus

$$x = x_{target} + \varepsilon + \lambda \qquad (2)$$

where ε is a random number chosen from a uniform distribution ranging from $-.1$ to .1 and λ is a constant lenition bias. In the one-peak cases shown in Figure 3 and Figure 4, we used $\lambda=-.01$. In the neutralization case shown in Figure 5, we used $\lambda=-.1$ for the (infrequent) leniting peak. Note that the noise and the lenition bias is applied once per utterance, so that infrequent utterances evolve on a slower time base. An additional effect, however, is that if the memory time τ is held fixed for all labels, infrequent labels access an effectively smaller portion of the exemplar list in production and classification, owing to a greater impact of memory decay. In all calculations reported above, we used a fixed memory time $\tau = 2000$ for both production and classification.

To implement entrenchment, the production target was modified as follows, prior to addition of noise and bias. We picked the n_{trench} closest exemplars to the trial x_{target}, using the memory-weighted distance

$$d_i = \left| x_{target} - e_i^L \right| exp(\frac{t - T_i}{\tau}) \qquad (3)$$

and then formed a new target by taking the memory-weighted mean of the n_{trench} values. In the limit of very large n_{trench}, the production target becomes fixed at the memory weighted mean of the exemplar list. The simulations reported above were carried out with $n_{trench} = 500$

In the case of a single label, the production-iteration loop proceeds as follows. First, we seed the exemplar list with a single value. Subsequently, we alternate between producing a new token according the protocol described above, and adding the new token to the exemplar list *provided its score is nonzero*. In the case of two labels *A* and *B*, we seed each exemplar list with a single value, then randomly produce a token *x* of *A* or *B* with probability *p* and 1–p respectively, compute *score(A,x)* and *score(B,x)* and finally append *x* to the exemplar list of the higher scoring label. This procedure generalizes in the obvious way to arbitrary numbers of labels.

Acknowledgments

I'm grateful to Bjorn Lindblom, Stefan Frisch, and Gary Dell for their useful comments during the development of this model. I'm grateful for the stimulating discussion at the symposium from which the present volume results, and I'd also like to thank audiences at University of Arizona, University of North Carolina, and Northwestern University for their feedback after subsequent presentations of the work.

References

Bradlow, A. 1995. "A comparative acoustic study of English and Spanish vowels". *Journal of the Acoustical Society of America.* 97(3), 1916–24.
Bybee, J. 2000. "The phonology of the lexicon; evidence from lexical diffusion". In M. Barlow and S. Kemmer (eds.), *Usage-Based Models of Language.* Stanford: CSLI, 65–85. (See also Hooper).
Caramazza, A. and Yeni-Komshian, G. H. 1974. "Voice onset time in two French dialects". *Journal of Phonetics* 2, 239- 245.
Chomsky, N. and Halle, M. 1968. *The Sound Pattern of English.* New York: Harper and Row.
Chomsky, N. and Lasnik, H. 1995. "The Theory of Principles and Parameters". In Chomsky, N. (ed.) *The Minimalist Program.* Cambridge, MA: MIT Press, 13–128.
Goldinger, S. D. 1996. "Words and voices: Episodic traces in spoken word identification and recognition memory". *Journal of Experimental Psychology: Learning, Memory, and Cognition* 22, 1166–83.
Greenberg, J. H., Ferguson, C. A. and Moravscik, E. A. (eds.) 1978. *Universals of human language.* Stanford University Press, Stanford CA.
Hay, J. B. 2000. "Causes and Consequences of Word Structure". Ph.D. dissertation, Northwestern University.
Hintzman, D. L. 1986. " 'Schema abstraction' in a multiple-trace memory model". *Psychological Review* 93, 328–38.
Hooper, J. B. 1976. "Word frequency in lexical diffusion and the source of morphophonological change". In W. Christie, (ed.) *Current Progress in Historical Linguistics.* Amsterdam: NorthHolland 96–105.
Johnson, K. 1996. Speech perception without speaker normalization. In K. Johnson and Mullennix (eds.) *Talker Variability in Speech Processing.* San Diego. Academic Press.

Johnson, K., Flemming, E. and Wright, R. 1993. "The hyperspace effect: phonetic targets are hyperarticulated". *Language* 69, 505–28.

Kruschke, J.K. 1992 "ALCOVE: An exemplar-based connectionist model of category learning". *Psych. Review* 99, 22–44.

Lacerda, F. In press. "Distributed memory representations generate the perceptual-magnet effect". *Journal of the Acoustical Society of America*.

Lee, S., Potamianos, A. and Narayan, S. 1999. "Acoustics of children's speech; developmental changes of temporal and spectral paramaters". *Journal of the Acoustical Society of America* 105, 1455–68.

Levelt, W. J. M. (1989) *Speaking*. Cambridge MA: MIT Press.

Lindblom, B. 1990. "Explaining phonetic variation: A sketch of the H and H theory". In W.J. Hardcastle and A. Marchand (eds.), *Speech Production and Speech Modelling*. Dordrecht: Kluwer Academic Publishers: 403–40.

Pierrehumbert, J. 1994. "Knowledge of variation". *Papers from the parasession on variation*, 30th meeting of the Chicago Linguistic Society. Chicago: Chicago Linguistic Society, 232–56.

Pierrehumbert, J. 2000. "What people know about sounds of language". *Studies in the Linguistic Sciences* 29(2).

Pierrehumbert, J., Beckman, M. E. and Ladd, D.R. In press. "Conceptual Foundations of Phonology as a Laboratory Science". Burton-Roberts, N. Carr, P., and Docherty, G. (eds. *Phonological Knowledge*, Oxford UK: Oxford University Press.

Phillips, B. S. (1984) "Word Frequency and the actuation of sound change". *Language* 60, 320–42.

Rosenbaum, D. A., Engelbrecht, S. E., Bushe, M. M. and Loukopoulos, L. D. 1993. "A model for reaching control". *Acta Psychologica* 82, 237–50

Sancier, M.L. and Fowler, C.A. 1997 "Gestural drift in a bilingual speaker of Brazilian Portuguese and English", *Journal of Phonetics* 25, 421–36.

Yaeger-Dror, M. 1996. "Phonetic evidence for the evolution of lexical classes: The case of a Montreal French vowel shift". In G. Guy, C. Feagin, J. Baugh, and D. Schiffrin (eds.) *Towards a Social Science of Language*, 263–87. Amsterdam: Benjamins.

Yaeger-Dror, M. and Kemp, W. 1992. "Lexical classes in Montreal French". *Language and Speech* 35: 251–93.

Emergent phonotactic generalizations
in English and Arabic*

STEFAN A. FRISCH, NATHAN R. LARGE,
BUSHRA ZAWAYDEH, and DAVID B. PISONI

University of Michigan, SUNY Buffalo,
Lernout and Hauspie Speech Products, Inc., and Indiana University

1. Introduction

According to generative linguistic theory, the competence of a native speaker of a language includes knowledge of the possible words in the speaker's language. The grammar contains phonotactic constraints that define the set of possible words. The actual words in the language are a subset of the possible words, except, of course, for any exceptions. In generative theories, which are currently based on a notion of constraint violation, the generative system and the set of possible words that it generates are of primary importance. The actual lexical items are relatively unimportant. These items are listed in a lexicon along with any idiosyncratic properties they may have that cannot be generated by rule. By contrast, a view of phonotactics as emergent generalizations over the set of lexical items gives the lexicon crucial importance in determining phonotactic knowledge (e.g., Bybee 1988). In an emergent phonotactics, lexical patterns serve as the primary linguistic data that determine all aspects of a native speaker's phonotactic competence. A growing body of literature provides evidence that phonotactic competence is an emergent property of the mental lexicon (Aslin et al. 1998, Beckman and Edwards 2000, Frisch 2000, Hay et al. 1998, Jusczyk et al.1994, Kessler and Treiman 1997, Ohala and Ohala 1986, Treiman et al. 2000, Vitevitch et al. 1997). A lexicon that is organized so that the common properties across words overlap and become the basis for the phonotactics of the language is also supported by psycholinguistic research on speech perception and production (e.g., Luce and Pisoni 1998, Vitevitch 1997). Given an emergent phonotactics, however, it is not clear exactly how lexical knowledge is used to delimit the space of possible words. Under an abstractionist view, phonotactic patterns across lexical items are abstract constraints adduced from the primary linguistic data (e.g., Coleman and Pierrehumbert 1997, Hayes 1999). In an exemplar model, no abstract constraints are postulated and the collective action of the lexical items restricts the space of possible words via similarity or analogy to the existing words (e.g., Goldinger 1998, Kirchner 1999, Pierrehumbert this volume).

In this paper, the traditional generative account of phonotactics and the two models of emergent phonotactic knowledge (abstract emergent constraints, and similarity-based analogy) are compared. The data to be accounted for are well-formedness judgments for nonwords in English and Arabic. We find strong support for the view of phonotactics as a set of emergent generalizations over the lexicon. Native speaker judgments are variable and gradient, but systematic. The degree of variation and/or gradience is very precisely predicted by statistical patterns in the lexicon. While native speaker judgments do reflect categorical phonotactic constraints, the constraints can predict only the gross patterns and they account for none of the fine detail. In addition, wordlikeness and acceptability judgments for Arabic nonwords show that at least some of the knowledge employed by native speakers in making well-formedness judgments appears to be abstracted away from particular lexical items (exemplars) and, thus, are not entirely similarity-based. However, influences of individual exemplars are also found. Therefore, we conclude that emergent phonotactic grammar is grounded in the lexicon and its effects can be seen at multiple levels of abstraction, from individual lexical items to generalizations across natural classes.

2. English phonotactics

It is often stated in introductory linguistics texts that a native English speaker knows that some nonwords are possible English words, while others cannot be words of English (e.g., Hawkins 1979: 50). However, psycholinguistic studies of well-formedness judgments for novel English words consistently find that there is a much greater degree of variability in well-formedness than just the two dimensions of possible and impossible. Accounts of degrees of well-formedness in generative phonological theory have been given using a variety of formal devices. For example, Chomsky and Halle (1968) proposed that the generality of the rule that is violated by a nonword determines its acceptability. Informally, nonwords that violate very general rules (e.g., stop-nasal sequences cannot be initial clusters in English words) are more unacceptable than nonwords that violate more specific rules (e.g., /tl/ cannot be an initial cluster in English words). One shortcoming of the generative approach to well-formedness judgments is that all of the generative accounts focus entirely on the role of phonotactically illegal sequences. Thus, these accounts make no prediction of the differences in acceptability of possible nonwords (e.g., /blɪk/ versus /yoᴵdʒ/).

An alternative approach to well-formedness considers the composition of the entire nonword in determining its well-formedness. Very common phonological units contribute positively toward well-formedness, while rare or unattested phonological units contribute negatively. Coleman and Pierrehumbert (1997) formalized this approach to well-formedness using a stochastic grammar generated from a dictionary of English words. They examined acceptability judgments for 150 novel words, some of which contained illegal consonant clusters (e.g., /mrupaʃən/). They found that the presence of an illegal cluster did influence acceptability judgments. However, they also found that the composition of the remainder of the nonword played a role in mitigating the influence of an illegal cluster on acceptability. Using their stochastic grammar, in which unattested clusters are given a marginal low probability, they were able to predict a significant amount of the variation in acceptability judgments between different nonwords. The stochastic grammar was an effective predictor of acceptability for nonwords that contained illegal clusters and those that did not.

In the Coleman and Pierrehumbert (1997) analysis, acceptability judgments for each stimulus item were averaged over 12 experimental participants. In most cases, some of the participants accepted a particular nonword while others rejected it, regardless of whether the nonword contained an illegal cluster or not. In an emergent phonotactic grammar, such as the stochastic grammar of Coleman and Pierrehumbert (1997), any novel nonword has a degree of well-formedness associated with its phonotactic probability or similarity to the lexicon. Thus, there is no lower bound on probability or similarity that some particular nonwords will achieve. It is worthwhile to consider how, in this theory, a native speaker decides a nonword is unacceptable. Presumably, the probability or similarity of the nonword is below some threshold, and so the nature of this threshold is of interest. The hypothesis that will be examined in the first part of this paper is that the unacceptability threshold is based on the likelihood that a nonword with a given probability could occur given the experience of the individual making the well-formedness judgment. A proposal put forward in Frisch (1996), foreshadowed in Pierrehumbert (1994), is that the threshold is determined by the size of the lexicon. A nonword that is too unlikely, given the size of the particular lexicon of a native speaker, would be judged unacceptable by that speaker. A prediction that this hypothesis makes is that the acceptability thresholds would be different for speakers with different size lexicons. Speakers with larger lexicons would accept less probable nonwords, as the probability that an item could occur in a larger lexicon is higher than the probability that an item could occur in a smaller lexicon. This hypothesis will be tested by examining individual differences in the well-formedness judgments of the participants in two experiments presented in Frisch, Large, and Pisoni (2000). We first review the results of Frisch, Large, and Pisoni, demonstrating the importance of probability in well-formedness judgments, and then present an analysis of individual differences in these experiments that further support the hypothesis that phonotactic grammar is emergent from the lexicon.

2.1 Well-formedness judgments for English

For the nonwords in the Coleman and Pierrehumbert (1997) analysis that did not contain an illegal cluster, it is clear that low overall probability of the nonword influenced the likelihood that it would be rejected. Frisch *et al.* (2000) replicated and extended this finding. The Frisch *et al.* stimulus set consisted of 144 English nonwords. The nonwords were 2, 3, or 4 syllables in length, and were constructed of attested lexical constituents that spanned a range of probabilities in the Coleman and Pierrehumbert grammar. This grammar uses a lexical representation that parses words into onset and rime constituents, and also differentiates positions of prominence within the word. Constituents are members of eight different prosodic categories: word initial onset, medial onset, medial rime, and word final rime for both stressed and unstressed constituents. All onsets were single consonants (C). The medial rimes were single vowels (V) and the final rimes were vowels plus a single consonant (VC). Thus, the nonword stimuli had an alternating CV pattern with a final consonant. There were no phonotactically illegal sequences according to the descriptive phonotactics of English. All words had initial stress, and the four syllable words had primary stress on the third syllable and secondary stress on the initial syllable. Transcriptions of sample nonword stimuli with relatively high or low probability constituents are shown in (1). A complete list is given in Frisch *et al.* (2000).

(1) High   [sɪ.ʃəp]
     Low   [zu.yɛ.θʊs]
     High   [sɪ.rə.sɛ.nən]

In the Coleman and Pierrehumbert grammar, an overall measure of expected probability for a nonword is computed by taking the logarithm of the product of probabilities of the onset and rime constituents of the nonword. This measure of expected probability was examined in our study as a predictor of well-formedness judgments in two different tasks: wordlikeness judgments (1–7 scale) and acceptability judgments (possible/impossible as a word of English). Two groups each consisting of twenty-four Indiana University undergraduates provided the well-formedness judgments. Productions of the nonwords were recorded in advance and played individually to the participants in a computer-controlled experimental ses-

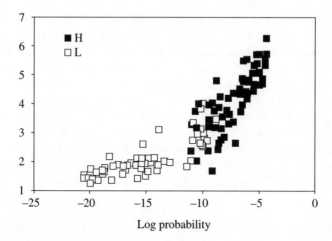

Figure 1. *Mean wordlikeness for English nonwords as a function of expected probability*

sion. The participants' responses were made on custom designed button boxes that were either labeled with the 1–7 rating scale or with two buttons labeled for accept and reject, depending on the task.

Figure 1 shows the mean rating on the wordlikeness scale across participants for each nonword as a function of expected probability in Frisch *et al.* (2000) Experiment 1. Nonwords containing low probability constituents are the open boxes. Nonwords containing high probability constituents are the filled boxes. Mean wordlikeness judgments for these nonword stimuli have an extremely strong relationship with expected probability ($r(142) = .87$, $p < .001$). Identical results were obtained with the acceptability judgments ($r(142) = .87$, $p < .001$). Thus, these experiments provide strong evidence for the relevance of expected probability in well-formedness judgments. The importance of nonword probability in well-formedness judgments supports a theory of phonotactic knowledge that includes probabilistic generalizations over the lexicon.

2.2 Individual differences in well-formedness judgments

In addition to collecting well-formedness judgments for the nonword stimuli, data on individual differences in actual lexical knowledge were collected from the same participants that performed the well-formedness tasks. There is evidence that the extent of an individual's lexical knowledge is an important individual factor in language processing. Lewellen *et al.* (1991, 1993) used lexical knowledge, as measured by a word familiarity test, along with several other scores measuring verbal ability, to differentiate between 'high-verbal' and 'low-verbal' experimental participants. These participants were found to perform differently on several language tasks involving real word stimuli. Some evidence for individual differences in well-formedness judgments are discussed in Large (1998), but the analysis there does not bear directly on the question at hand. In this section, additional evidence for an emergent phonotactic grammar will be provided by modeling individual differences in phonotactic judgments as a function of the actual lexical knowledge of the participants. We find that participants with relatively larger mental lexicons are more likely to judge low probability nonwords as well-formed, suggesting that well-formedness is determined by a lexicon-based probability cutoff.

2.2.1 Methods
To examine the role of lexical knowledge on the processing of nonwords, a measure of lexical knowledge was obtained from the experimental participants based on their relative familiarity with a variety of real words. The familiarity test used to measure lexical knowledge in the participants is a shortened version of the word familiarity test (FAM test) used by Lewellen *et al.* (1991). The FAM test is based on comparing an individual's familiarity with a variety of English words to the norms obtained by Nusbaum *et al.* (1984). Nusbaum *et al.* presented each of the 20,000 entries from the Webster's Pocket Dictionary to a group of participants in a large scale study of lexical knowledge in university undergraduates. Each word in the dictionary was rated for familiarity by 10 undergraduate psychology students on a 7-point familiarity scale. The Lewellen *et al.* FAM test uses the same familiarity task with a subset of 450 words, 150 from each of three broad categories: high familiarity (mean familiarity > 6), Mid familiarity (3 < mean familiarity < 6), and Low familiarity (mean familiarity < 3). Lewellen *et al.* compared their participants' ratings to the Nusbaum *et al.* norms to assess the lexical knowledge of their participants against the general undergraduate population. Our modified version of the FAM test uses 150-items, 50 items at each of the three familiarity levels. A reduced list was used due to time constraints on the experimental session.

The FAM portion of each experiment occurred after the well-formedness judgment task. In the FAM test, each participant was asked to rate each real word based on their 'familiarity' with that item, using the 7-point scale. A rating of '1' corresponded to "I have never seen this word before". A '4' rating corresponded to "I have seen this word, but do not know its meaning". A '7' rating corresponded to "I know this word and know at least one meaning for it well". Ratings of 2, 3, 5, and 6 were described individually, as intermediate points between these extremes. The instructions emphasized that this was a different task from the previous nonsense word studies, and that the task was to rate real words according to a different scale. The procedure was otherwise identical to the one used for the well-formedness judgments for the spoken nonword stimuli, except the real words were presented orthographically.

Following Lewellen *et al.*, FAM scores were computed for each participant using the mean familiarity rating for each 50-word subset, Fam High, Fam Mid, and Fam Low. Replicating their results, we found that Fam High scores did not vary much across participants, so this score was discarded. In order to use the maximum number of words to estimate lexical knowledge along with the maximum variance in scores between participants, we averaged ratings of the Medium and Low-familiarity items together to produce a composite index score, Fam ML. This Medium and Low-familiarity score was used as a measure of an individual's lexical knowledge.

To determine whether participants with greater lexical knowledge found less probable items to be more acceptable, the responses of each participant were modeled with a simple piecewise linear function. For the wordlikeness judgments, the ratings of one representative participant and the corresponding model are shown in Figure 2. The model has upper and lower probability cutoffs. Below the lower cutoff probability (indicated by the arrow) ratings are constant, representing the low wordlikeness rating given to clearly unacceptable items. Above the upper cutoff probability, ratings are also constant. In between the cutoff probabilities the ratings are a linear function of probability. This model captures the roughly S-shaped pattern of responses obtained in the ratings experiment that is shown in Figure 1. For

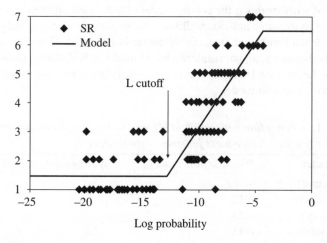

Figure 2.

the experiment that collected acceptability judgments, the model consisted only of one cutoff probability. Below the cutoff probability, the model predicts 'unacceptable' judgments, and above the cutoff probability, the model predicts 'acceptable' judgments. The models were optimally fit to each individual participant's responses using linear programming. If individual lexical knowledge influences the low probability cutoff for ratings and the cutoff for acceptability, we predict that participants with greater lexical knowledge will place these cutoffs at a lower probability than participants with less lexical knowledge.

2.2.2. Results and discussion

The parameters for the models were compared to Fam ML scores for each participant. Table 1 shows correlations between Fam ML and the model parameters across participants. For the wordlikeness judgments, Fam ML is significantly correlated with low cutoff probability ($r(22) = -.46$, $p = .04$). The correlation is negative, indicating that for participants with higher FAM scores, the low probability cutoff was at a lower probability, as predicted. None of the correlations with the other parameters were significant. For the acceptability judgments, the correlation between Cutoff probability and Fam ML is in the predicted direction, but did not reach statistical significance.

The finding of individual differences in well-formedness judgments for low probability stimuli supports the hypothesis that the threshold of acceptability for nonwords is inversely related to lexicon size. The fact that probability in a stochastic grammar was successfully used as a predictor of individual differences appears to support the abstractionist approach to emergent phonotactic constraints. Note that regardless of whether this is the correct model of individual differences or not, the existence of systematic individual differences in well-formedness judgments is further evidence that the phonotactic grammar is emergent. However, we might wonder whether an exemplar, similarity-based model of well-formedness can also account for the increased acceptability of low probability items. This possibility can be tested with a second model.

Table 1. *Correlation between Fam ML and individual model parameters for two well-formedness judgment experiments*

Parameter	Wordlikeness model	Acceptability model
Low cutoff	−.46*	
High cutoff	−.12	
Low score	−.33	
High score	−.11	−.16

*p < .05

In general, the familiarity rating given to a lexical item is highly correlated with usage frequency. It has long been known that low frequency lexical items are composed of more rare phonemes than high frequency lexical items (Frauenfelder *et al.* 1993, Landauer and Streeter 1973). Thus, it might be the case that a lexicon containing more low frequency lexical items will contain more similar exemplars to the low probability stimuli in our corpus, resulting in an increased intuition of well-formedness in the participant. This hypothesis was tested by generating two sets of lexical neighborhoods for the nonword stimuli, to simulate the differences in lexical neighborhoods for individuals with larger and smaller lexicons. A word is traditionally considered a lexical neighbor of a nonword if two-thirds of the phonemes in the word can be matched with corresponding segments in the nonword (Luce and Pisoni 1998). Multisyllabic words and nonwords were aligned so as to maximize the number of shared segments (for details, see Frisch *et al.* 2000). For example, the nonword stimulus item /hɪtənət/ and the word *infinite* /ɪnfənət/ share the vowel in the first two syllables and all three segments in the final syllable. With 5 of 7 segments shared, *infinite* is a neighbor of the nonword /hɪtənət/.

   In one set of lexical neighborhoods for the nonwords, all lexical items in Webster's Pocket Dictionary were potential neighbors for each nonword. In the other set of lexical neighborhoods, only the best known words, with normative familiarity of 6 or higher, were used. Comparing the sizes of the lexical neighborhoods of the nonword stimuli for the larger and smaller lexicons, differences were found only for the shorter, higher probability nonword stimuli. In general, the lower probability items have no lexical neighbors in either lexicon. Thus, it appears that an exemplar, similarity-based model would predict greater individual differences for high probability items rather than low probability items. The individual differences that were found for low probability items are therefore not accounted for by the similarity-based model. The influence of lexicon size on low probability rather than high probability items supports the abstractionist approach and the stochastic grammar over an analogical exemplar approach. Therefore, based on individual differences in well-formedness judgments for English nonwords we conclude that native speaker knowledge must include an abstract, emergent grammar of phonotactics based on the lexicon.

3. Arabic phonotactics

The probabilistic factors that influence well-formedness judgments in English presented above provide strong evidence for the importance of statistical distributions in phonotactics. However, the results presented here involved nonwords that did not contain constraint violations, and so might be criticized for not really tapping into grammar as it is conceived of in linguistic theory. It should be noted that other studies of English nonwords (Coleman and Pierrehumbert 1997, Ohala and Ohala 1986) have demonstrated lexical influences with nonwords containing phonotactically illegal sequences. Once again, criticism could be made of these studies as they are limited to English. For example, Frisch and Zawaydeh (in press) collected well-formedness judgments for Arabic nonwords that contained phonotactic violations. They were unable to demonstrate convincing statistical influences, so it may well be that the emergent characteristics of English are somehow a language specific phenomenon. In this section, we review the results of Frisch and Zawaydeh (in press) and present additional analysis that demonstrates that an emergent grammar provides the best account of the well-formedness judgments they obtained for Arabic nonwords. In the Arabic nonwords, several different factors that influence well-formedness judgments will be presented. These factors range from the presence of a violation of an abstract phonotactic constraint to the existence of particular words in the lexicon that are similar to a novel nonword. The range of factors and their interaction are of particular interest, as they demonstrate that the proper account of well-formedness judgments must be able to explain both linguistic generalizations and individual word effects. We will argue that an emergent grammar that contains generalizations at multiple levels of abstraction is the only theory of phonotactic knowledge that can account for all of these effects.

The phonotactics of Arabic verbal roots have been the topic of a considerable amount of influential research in phonological theory (see McCarthy 1986, 1988, 1994). In the autosegmental analysis of Arabic morphology, a verbal root is an abstract consonant sequence, e.g., /ktb/. The typical Arabic root contains three consonants. The consonants of the root are interleaved with vowels to create words, as in (2):

(2) a. *katab*   'to write'
    b. *kataba*   'he wrote'
    c. *kutib*   'to be written'
    d. *kuutib*   'to be corresponded with'

Arabic verb roots are subject to strong consonant co-occurrence restrictions. The generative account claims that a possible root is any consonant sequence that does not contain more than one consonant from the categories given in (3). These classes are described with combinations of the place of articulation features and manner features for Arabic segments.

(3) Labials = {b, f, m}
    Coronal Obstruents = {t, d, T, D, θ, ð, s, z, S, Z, S}
    Velars = {k, g, q, χ, ʁ}

Gutturals = {χ, ʁ, h, ʕ, ħ, ʔ}
Coronal Sonorants = {l, r, n}

The phonotactic constraint in Arabic has been described as an avoidance of repetition of place features, OCP-PLACE (McCarthy 1988, 1994). However, Pierrehumbert (1993) and Frisch et al. (1997) have demonstrated that the patterns of consonant co-occurrence within the roots of Arabic are subject to systematic exceptions that are quantitative in nature. Pierrehumbert (1993) claimed that combinations of homorganic consonants are avoided "to the extent that they are similar" to one another. The quantitative analyses are based on a comparison of the co-occurrence of consonant pairs that are observed in an Arabic dictionary. Pierrehumbert (1993) used the ratio of the number of consonant pairs observed (O) to the number that would be expected by chance (E) to measure co-occurrence (O/E). Chance is determined by multiplying the probability of each consonant occurring in each position in the root. The expected probability thus takes into account the frequency of occurrence of the consonants involved.

Using expected probability to measure co-occurrence provides some insight into the long standing problem of determining systematic versus accidental gaps. In a typical phonological analysis, when only a few instances of a phonological pattern can be found, whether the low occurrence is considered accidental or systematic is determined entirely by the theoretical account being given. Considering the expected probability of the cooccurring items provides another piece of information about the systematicity of the pattern. A non-occurring consonant pair with high expected probability is a (statistically) unlikely event, and so the gap is likely to be systematic. On the other hand, the non-occurrence of a low probability consonant pair (i.e., where both of the consonants in the pair are of low probability separately) could well be accidental. This measure of the relative frequency of co-occurrence of a consonant pair (henceforth O/E) is also advantageous as it can be used to discover both categorical and quantitative constraints. In general, a constraint is observed in cases where O/E is reliably less than 1 across a natural class. Categorical constraints, including those traditionally recognized as constraints in generative theory, are cases where O/E = 0 (i.e., no co-occurrences), and are thus a special case of O/E less than 1.

3.1 Well-formedness judgments for Arabic

The psychological reality of the OCP-Place constraint was demonstrated by Frisch and Zawaydeh (in press). They asked 30 native speakers of Jordanian Arabic for wordlikeness judgments for 256 novel words. The novel words were presented as citation verb forms of novel root consonant sequences. The novel words were presented orthographically in a fully-vowelled Arabic script form, corresponding to $C_1aC_2aC_3a$. The novel words were rated on a 1–7 wordlikeness scale.

The nonwords used by Frisch and Zawaydeh were conceptually divided into three 'stimulus sets', though the experimental participants were presented with a single list of nonwords that included all of the stimuli from all of the stimulus sets. The three stimulus sets tested three different aspects of the competence of the Arabic speakers. The first stimulus set, consisting of 160 novel verbs, used a three-way factorial experimental design to examine the effects of OCP-Place constraint violation, expected probability of the consonant sequence, and similarity of the novel root to existing roots (measured using lexical neighborhoods, as was done with the English nonwords in Section 2.2.2). In this stimulus set, the presence of an OCP-Place constraint violation was found to be the only robust influence on ratings. The mean rating for OCP-Place violations was 2.6 and the mean rating for nonwords without violations was 3.6, a highly significant difference ($F(1,191) = 63.9$, $p < .001$). There were no effects of expected probability or similarity to existing roots on the ratings.

The measure of probability in the first stimulus set only took into account the frequency of the consonants, and not their frequency of co-occurrence. Thus, it could be that Arabic speakers are not sensitive to an abstract constraint, but rather that they are sensitive to a non-occurring consonant sequence. The second stimulus set, consisting of 40 novel verbs, addressed this distinction. In this stimulus set, contrasting pairs of nonwords were constructed. One nonword contained an OCP-Place violation, and the other contained no violations. The nonwords were equated on the transitional frequency of the consonant pairs involved, so that the violating pair was matched with an equally infrequently occurring consonant pair that was not a constraint violation. For example, the novel verb root */thf/ did not contain an OCP-Place violation. In Wehr's dictionary, there are no roots of the form /thC/, four roots of the form /Chf/, and three roots of the form /tCf/, where C is any consonant. This non-violation root was matched with the novel root */tsb/, containing an OCP-Place violation. In Wehr's dictionary, there are no roots of the form /tsC/, four roots of the form /Csb/, and three roots of the form /tCb/, where C is any consonant. The stimuli were also equated for expected probability and similarity to existing roots. In other words, these stimuli directly contrasted systematic gaps with accidental gaps of equal probability and similarity to other lexical items. The presence of a constraint violation resulted in significantly lower wordlikeness ratings compared to non-violations with equally infrequent consonant sequences. This suggests that an abstract constraint rather than a simple transitional frequency effect was the source of the difference in ratings for violations and non-violations.

The third stimulus set, consisting of 56 novel roots, was designed to test whether Arabic speakers differentiated different degrees of violation of the OCP-Place constraint. This stimulus set contrasted constraint violations with different degrees of similarity between homorganic consonants, directly testing the Pierrehumbert (1993) account and the Frisch *et al.* (1997) model. We found an influence of similarity on wordlikeness judgments as novel roots containing constraint violations with more similar consonant pairs were judged less acceptable than novel roots containing constraint violations with less similar consonant pairs. Overall, Frisch and Zawaydeh (in press) found strong support for the linguistic analysis of the OCP-Place constraint, but little support for the probabilistic influences predicted by an emergent phonotactic grammar for Arabic.

3.2 Lexical influences in Arabic phonotactics

It is possible that the presence of a violation of broad patterns of well-formedness in the Arabic stimuli suppressed the influence of more subtle lexical factors that have elsewhere been found (e.g., Jusczyk *et al.* 1994, Treiman *et al.* 2000). Of course, the OCP-Place constraint itself can be viewed as an emergent generalization over the lexicon, especially given the gradient constraint analysis of Frisch *et al.* (1997). However, to make a strong case for the phonological significance of emergent lexical generalizations, lexical effects should be demonstrated in native speaker judgments. In this section, a reanalysis of the data of Frisch and Zawaydeh (in press) is undertaken to demonstrate that probabilistic and similarity-based lexical factors do influence well-formedness judgments in Arabic.

3.2.1 Methods
In the Frisch and Zawaydeh (in press) experiment, wordlikeness judgments were collected using a 1–7 scale. As they note, the overall wordlikeness ratings given for their stimuli are low, generally four or less, so the amount of variation between stimuli was small. They attribute the low ratings to their attempt to match OCP-Place constraint violations with non-violations of equal probability, so that in general all of the nonwords were low probability, and thus not very wordlike. One reason that subtle lexical effects may not have been found is the small amount of variation in ratings between stimuli. Frisch *et al.* (2000) proposed a method of reanalyzing low wordlikeness ratings that better differentiated ratings for low probability stimuli. This method is to examine the number of ratings of '1' and ratings greater than '1' for each stimulus across subjects in a manner similar to the data collected in an acceptability task. Each '1' is called an "implicit rejection" signifying that it was given the lowest possible rating on the 1–7 scale. The Arabic data were reanalyzed using the implicit rejections measure in order to enhance the difference between low and very low ratings and increase the chance of finding subtle lexical influences.

There is another factor in the Arabic experiment that Frisch and Zawaydeh dis-covered in post-hoc analysis of their data. After the experiment was completed, some participants reported that some of the stimuli sounded very similar to particu-lar real words. While Frisch and Zawaydeh controlled their stimuli for overall similarity to roots in the lexicon, using the measure of lexical neighborhoods, they did not consider whether their nonwords were extremely similar to any particular words. Their analysis of the rating data showed that those nonwords that were extremely similar to particular lexical items were rated significantly higher than the rest of the nonwords. This effect of a highly similar lexical item is the sort of influence that would be expected in an exemplar-based emergent grammar. The influence of a particular lexical item on the ratings may also have obscured other lexical effects, like expected probability, so our reanalysis will take this factor into account.

Finally, the only probabilistic influence that Frisch and Zawaydeh (in press) var-ied across their stimuli was the expected probability of the root (the product of the probabilities of the consonants). They did not systematically vary the transitional probability of the consonants in their stimuli. Transitional probability has been shown to be an important factor in probabilistic syntagmatic patterns (e.g., Bush this volume, Bybee this volume, Treiman et al. 2000). Frisch and Zawaydeh also did not control the O/E of the consonant pairs used for the constraint violations or the non-violations. Since the O/E measure forms the basis of the gradient OCP-Place con-straint in the Frisch et al. (1997) model it is possible that the well-formedness judg-ments would be sensitive to the O/E measure. Accordingly, a post-hoc correlation analysis of the Arabic experiment data was undertaken. A composite measure of transitional probability was generated, by multiplying the C_1C_2 transitional probabil-ity by the C_2C_3 transitional probability for each nonword. A composite O/E measure was also generated for each nonword by multiplying the O/E of C_1C_2 by the O/E of C_2C_3. In cases where a consonant pair was unattested, so that transitional probability or O/E is zero, the zero values were replaced by a marginal low probability using Good-Turing estimation following the procedure of Bod (1998: 84), see also Coleman and Pierrehumbert (1997).

Correlations between the implicit rejections for each nonword and its expected probability, transitional probability, and O/E were examined. For the three probabilistic measures, we used the logarithm of the probability rather than the raw probability, as log probabilities are generally a more accurate reflection of fre-quency and probability effects in psycholinguistic tasks (e.g., Coleman and Pierre-humbert 1997, Eukel 1980). Since particular similar words influenced ratings, as discussed above, a correlation between implicit rejections and the presence or ab-sence of a similar word was also computed. Finally, the correlation between implicit rejections and the number of OCP-Place violations was examined, to see whether a categorical predictor of OCP-Place violation provides a better account of the rating data than the probabilistic measures.

3.2.2 Results and discussion

Table 2 shows the correlation between the number of implicit rejections (ratings of '1') and the predictors just discussed. In addition, correlations for the expected probability and number of lexical neighbors are also given (these are factors that were systematically varied in the experiment). There are a number of significant influences on the judgments: the presence of an OCP-Place violation, the presence of a salient neighbor, the transitional probability of the consonant sequence, and O/E of the consonant sequence. Among these predictors, the O/E measure provided the best prediction of the implicit rejections. The transitional probability is also a significant predictor, but it does not perform as well as O/E. Note that if the mean rating data are examined directly, rather than through the implicit rejections measure, the same qualitative patterns are found. All correlations are lower by .05 to .1, except that the similar word predictor has a somewhat higher correlation with the raw rating data. Apparently the existence of a similar word was more likely to increase a high rating, rather than to change a very low rating to a higher one. This is an interesting result that parallels our prediction that exemplar effects are expected only for higher probability nonwords in the investigation of individual differences on well-formedness judgements for English. Overall then, the implicit rejections analysis appears to have had the desired effect of increasing the amount of variation in the ratings measure for the stimuli that were not very wordlike.

Table 2. *Correlation between the implicit rejections measure and constraint-based, similarity-based, and probabilistic predictors of well-formedness.*

Predictor	Correlation
Constraint-based	
OCP-Place	.46*
Similarity-based	
Similar word	−.27*
Neighbors	−.05
Probability-based	
Log Expected	.03
Log Transitional	−.40*
Log O/E	−.54*
*p < .001	

Given that the O/E measure provided the best prediction of the well-formedness judgments for these stimuli, this renanalysis has shown that emergent probabilistic patterns play an important role in well-formedness judgments based on the phonotactics of Arabic. Since many of the other predictors were also significant, it is worth considering whether multiple factors influenced well-formedness judgments in this experiment. Note that the significant predictors are correlated with one another, so finding several significant effects does not necessarily mean more than one factor is relevant. For example, OCP-Place violations tend to have low O/E. Also, words in Arabic tend not to contain OCP-Place violations, so nonwords with violations are less likely to be highly similar to a real Arabic word. It is possible, then, that only one of these measures is necessary to provide an account of the rating data.

In order to test this possibility, a regression analysis of the experiment data was performed. A stepwise regression procedure was employed so that a variable would be entered into the regression at a particular step only if it was the best contributor in explaining the remaining variation given the variables already in the current model at that step. The regression had available the significant predictors from the correlation analysis: OCP-Place violation, similarity to an existing word, transitional probability, and O/E. The model first added an O/E parameter, then a similar word parameter, and finally an OCP-Place parameter. Transitional probability did not make a significant contribution once O/E was entered into the model, which is not particularly surprising as transitional probability and O/E take some of the same factors into account. The regression model indicates that many factors contributed to the well-formedness judgments given by the Arabic speakers.

Table 3 shows the mean percent of implicit rejections for groups of nonwords in the experiment based on the factors used in the regression model. Stimuli are grouped based on whether they contained one or more OCP-Place violations, had a similar real word, and had a consonant pair that was unattested in the roots of Arabic (O/E = 0). The categories are arranged so that the positive influences on well-formedness are at the top of each group, and negative influences are at the bottom. Nonwords with no OCP-Place violation, a similar real word, and all consonant pairs attested were given an implicit rejection rating of '1' only 14% of the time, while nonwords with an OCP-Place violation, no similar real word, and an unattested consonant pair (probably the OCP-Place violation) were given an implicit rejection 43% of the time. Closer inspection of pairs of entries in Table 3 confirms that all three factors had independent and cumulative influences on the well-formedness judgments.

The influence of lexical patterns on well-formedness judgments in Arabic has been successfully demonstrated, despite a relatively noisy data set with wordlikeness judgments in a limited range. Sensitivity to the relative frequency of consonant pairs in the lexicon was found for novel word forms whether or not they contained

Table 3. *Number of stimuli in the Arabic experiment and the mean percent of implicit rejections for nonwords by OCP-Place violation, existence of a similar word, and O/E*

	N	Implicit rejections
No violation		
Similar word		
O/E > 0	19	14%
O/E = 0	4	22%
No similar word		
O/E > 0	75	20%
O/E = 0	3	40%
OCP violation		
Similar word		
O/E > 0	8	18%
O/E = 0	14	27%
No similar word		
O/E > 0	39	30%
O/E = 0	52	43%

a constraint violation. Thus, the probability of a constraint violating consonant pair clearly plays a role in determining the acceptability of novel words. We find the Arabic data also support an emergent theory of phonotactics despite the presence of a strong phonotactic constraint. The gradient nature of the constraint provides additional evidence that the phonotactic grammar is emergent.

4. Summary and conclusion

A range of influences have been demonstrated for well-formedness judgments in English and Arabic. Assuming that well-formedness judgments reflect the underlying phonotactic competence of the experimental participants, there appear to be a number of factors that play a role in shaping the phonotactic grammar. Well-formedness judgments for English show that the probability of a novel word, given the distribution of phonological constituents in the lexicon, provides a foundation for phonotactic well-formedness. The English nonword stimuli were carefully controlled to eliminate all other lexical and linguistic influences and the predictions of the probabilistic grammar were extremely accurate. The strong influence of the O/E measure on wordlikeness ratings for novel Arabic words demonstrates that the well-formedness of sequences of phonological constituents is determined relative to this baseline of probability. However, the phonotactic grammar does not consist entirely of these shallow statistical generalizations. The additional influence of whether or not a consonant pair with some particular O/E level was an OCP-Place violation indicates that Arabic speakers also have knowledge of natural classes. Since infrequently occurring or unattested consonant pairs that are in a natural class with other infrequently occurring or unattested consonant pairs are what comprise a linguistic constraint, the only conclusion that can be drawn is that traditional notions of phonotactic constraints are psychologically real (Frisch and Zawaydeh in press). However, the phonotactic constraint in Arabic is more complex than a traditional all-or-nothing constraint, as it is probabilistic and lexically-based.

In the case of Arabic, it is difficult to draw a clear line between influences due to the phonotactic grammar and influences due to the use of that grammar in a metalinguistic task. The traditional, conservative distinction in which all constraints are categorical provides no account of the systematic distribution of constraint violations presented in Pierrehumbert (1993) and Frisch et al. (1997). In the traditional view, nearly all of the influences on well-formedness judgments that have been shown here would be labeled as performance factors. This distinction would be arbitrary, solely on the basis that they are probabilistic influences.

The influence of a highly similar word to the well-formedness of a nonword demonstrates that analogical comparisons involving lexical exemplars also play a role in well-formedness judgments. One approach to emergent grammar presented in the introduction was an exemplar only model. The influence of a highly similar word on nonword well-formedness supports this model, but the other categorical and probabilistic effects show that more abstract generalizations over the lexicon are also needed. Overall, it appears that both types of emergent influences are present, representing generalizations at different levels of abstraction. Analogical effects are well-known in historical change, and have been argued to influence synchronic grammar as well (e.g. Kenstowicz 1997, Steriade 2000). Presumably, all the influences on well-formedness judgments that have been presented in this paper are involved in coining new words in a language, adapting loanwords, or creating novel forms by compounding, truncation, or affixation. Therefore, emergent phonotactic generalizations are relevant to our understanding of language and its representation in the minds of speakers.

Notes

*   This research funded in part by NIH Training Grant DC00012 to Indiana University and an Indiana University Grant-in-Aid of Research.

References

Aslin, R.N., Saffran, J.R., and Newport, E.L. 1998. "Computation of conditional probability statistics by 8-month-old infants". *Psychological Science* 9: 321–4.

Beckman, M. and Edwards, J. 2000. "Lexical frequency effects on young children's imitative productions". In *Papers in Laboratory Phonology V: Language Acquisition and the Lexicon*, M. Broe and J.B. Pierrehumbert (eds.), 208–18. Cambridge: Cambridge University Press.

Bod, R. 1998. *Beyond Grammar: An Experience-based Theory of Language.* Stanford, CA: CSLI Publications.

Bybee, J. L. 1988. "Morphology as lexical organization". In *Theoretical morphology*, M. Hammond and M. Noonan (eds.), 119–41. San Diego: Academic Press.

Chomsky, N. and Halle, M. 1968. *The Sound Pattern of English.* Cambridge, MA: MIT Press.

Coleman, J. and Pierrehumbert, J.B. 1997. "Stochastic phonological grammars and acceptability". In *Computational Phonology: Proceedings of the Third Meeting of the ACL Special Interest Group in Computational Phonology*, 49–56. Somerset, NJ: Association for Computational Linguistics.

Eukel, B. 1980. "Phonotactic basis for word frequency effects: Implications for lexical distance metrics". [Abstract] *Journal of the Acoustical Society of America* 68: s33.

Frauenfelder, U. H., Baayen, R. H., Hellwig, F. M., and Schreuder, R. 1993. "Neighborhood density and frequency across languages and modalities". *Journal of Memory and Language* 32: 781–804.

Frisch, S. 1996. "Similarity and frequency in phonology". Unpublished Doctoral Dissertation, Northwestern University. ROA-198, Rutgers Optimality Archive, http://ruccs.rutgers.edu/roa.html.

Frisch, S. 2000. "Temporally organized representations as phonological units". In *Papers in Laboratory Phonology V: Language Acquisition and the Lexicon*, M. Broe and J.B. Pierrehumbert (eds.), 283–98. Cambridge: Cambridge University Press.

Frisch, S., Broe, M., and Pierrehumbert, J. B. 1997. "Similarity and phonotactics in Arabic". Unpublished manuscript, Indiana University and Northwestern University. ROA-223, Rutgers Optimality Archive, http: //ruccs.rutgers.edu/roa.html.

Frisch, S., Large, N. R., and Pisoni, D. B. (2000). "Perception of wordlikeness: Effects of segment probability and length on processing non-words". *Journal of Memory and Language* 42: 481–96.

Frisch, S. and Zawaydeh, B. In press. "The psychological reality of OCP-Place in Arabic". *Language.*

Goldinger, S.D. 1998. "Echoes of echoes? An episodic theory of lexical access". *Psychological Review* 105: 251–79.

Hay, J., Pierrehumbert, J. B., and Beckman, M. Forthcoming. "Speech perception, wellformedness, and the statistics of the lexicon". In *Papers in Laboratory Phonology VI.* Cambridge: Cambridge University Press.

Hayes, B. 1999. "Phonological acquisition in Optimality Theory: The early stages". Manuscript, UCLA. ROA-327, Rutgers Optimality Archive, http: //ruccs.rutgers.edu/roa.html.

Hawkins, P. 1979. *Introducing Phonology*. London: Hutchinson.

Jusczyk, P.W., Luce, P.A., and Charles-Luce, J. 1994. "Infants' sensitivity to phonotactic patterns in the native language". *Journal of Memory and Language* 33: 630–45.

Kenstowicz, M. 1997. "Uniform exponence: Exemplification and extension". Manuscript, MIT. ROA-218, Rutgers Optimality Archive, http: //ruccs.rutgers.edu/roa.html.

Kessler, B. and Treiman, R. 1997. "Syllable structure and the distribution of phonemes in English syllables". *Journal of Memory and Language* 37: 295–311.

Kirchner, R. 1999. "Preliminary thoughts on 'phonologization' within an exemplar-based speech processing system". Manuscript, University of Alberta. ROA-32, Rutgers Optimality Archive, http: //ruccs.rutgers.edu/roa.html.

Landauer, T.K. and Streeter, L.A. 1973. "Structural differences between common and rare words: Failure of equivalence assumptions for theories of word recognition". *Journal of Verbal Learning and Verbal Behavior* 12: 119–31.

Large, N. R. 1998. "Predicting wordlikeness: Phonotactics as statistical perception of sound patterns". Unpublished Honors Thesis, Indiana University.

Lewellen, M.J., Goldinger, S.D., Pisoni, D.B., and Greene, B.G. 1991. "Word familiarity and lexical fluency: Individual differences in serial recall of spoken words". In *Research on Speech Perception, Progress Report 17*, 229–39. Bloomington, IN: Speech Research Laboratory, Indiana University.

Luce, P.A. and Pisoni, D.B. 1998. "Recognizing spoken words: The neighborhood activation model". *Ear and Hearing* 19: 1–36.

McCarthy, J. 1986. "OCP effects: Gemination and antigemination". *Linguistic Inquiry* 17: 207–63.

McCarthy, J. 1988. "Feature geometry and dependency: A review". *Phonetica* 43: 84–108.

McCarthy, J. 1994. "The phonetics and phonology of Semitic pharyngeals". In *Papers in Laboratory Phonology III: Phonological Structure and Phonetic Form*, P. Keating (ed.), 191–283. Cambridge: Cambridge University Press.

Nusbaum, H.C., Pisoni, D.B., and Davis, C.K. 1984. "Sizing up the Hoosier mental lexicon: Measuring the familiarity of 20,000 words". In *Research on Speech Perception, Progress Report 10*, 357–76. Bloomington, IN: Speech Research Laboratory.

Ohala, J. and Ohala, M. 1986. "Testing hypotheses regarding the psychological manifestation of morpheme structure constraints". In *Experimental Phonology*, J. Ohala and J. Jaeger (eds.), 239–52. San Diego: Academic Press.

Pierrehumbert, J.B. 1993. "Dissimilarity in the Arabic verbal roots". In *Proceedings of the North East Linguistics Society 23*, 367–81. Amherst: GSLI Publications.

Pierrehumbert, J.B. 1994. "Syllable structure and word structure: a study of triconsonantal clusters in English". In *Papers in Laboratory Phonology III: Phonological Structure and Phonetic Form*, P. Keating (ed.), 168–88. Cambridge: Cambridge University Press.

Steriade, D. 2000. "Paradigm uniformity and the phonetics-phonology boundary". In *Papers in Laboratory Phonology V: Language Acquisition and the Lexicon*, M. Broe and J. Pierrehumbert (eds.), 313–34. Cambridge: Cambridge University Press.

Treiman R., Kessler, B., Knewasser, S., Tincoff, R., and Bowman, M. 2000. In *Papers in Laboratory Phonology V: Language Acquisition and the Lexicon*, M. Broe and J. Pierrehumbert (eds.), 269–82. Cambridge: Cambridge University Press.

Vitevitch, M. S. 1997. "The neighborhood characteristics of malapropisms". *Language and Speech* 40: 211–28.

Vitevitch, M.S., Luce, P. A., Charles-Luce, J., and Kemmerer, D. 1997. "Phonotactics and syllable stress: implications for the processing of nonsense words". *Language and Speech* 40: 47–62.

Ambiguity and frequency effects in regular verb inflection

MARY L. HARE[a], MICHAEL FORD[b] and WILLIAM D. MARSLEN-WILSON[b]

Bowling Green State University,[a]
MRC Brain and Cognition Unit, Cambridge University[b]

1. Introduction

In the field of psycholinguistics there is increasing evidence that speakers and comprehenders are sensitive to statistical and probabilistic aspects of language. In contrast to theories that assume the general application of rules or heuristics, many current accounts of language processing adopt a constraint-based approach that considers detailed properties of lexical items. This trend results from empirical findings that comprehenders make processing decisions based on such detailed and usage-based information as the lexical frequency of a word (MacDonald 1994) and its contingent frequency in particular syntactic contexts (Juliano and Tanenhaus 1993) in addition to its semantic content (Stowe *et al.* 1991, Spivey-Knowlton *et al.* 1993). While frequency of use is implicated in a number of the on-line processes involved in language comprehension and production, the effects have been most striking and most generally acknowledged in the study of lexical access.

1.1 Word frequency effects in lexical access

Although the exact interpretation of *lexical access* is open to debate (MacDonald *et al.* 1994) we will assume for the present work that it involves the computation or activation of a distributed representation of information in lexical memory. One common task used to study lexical representation and access is lexical decision, in which subjects make speeded judgements about whether a letter (or phoneme) string is a word or not. In this and related tasks, subjects have been found to respond more rapidly to words with a higher frequency of use (Rubenstein *et al.* 1970). The effect occurs even when the less frequent words are correctly recognized, so it does not appear to reflect the subject's knowledge. This word frequency effect is taken to reflect basic properties about how lexical information is acquired, represented, and accessed, and as such it plays a role in all theories of lexical recognition (e.g., Morton 1969).

The robust effect of word frequency in lexical representation can be used to investigate a current question in the developmental and psycholinguistic literature. That is the debate over whether regularly inflected nouns and verbs are mentally represented as such or whether they are computed by rule based on a representation of the stem. The implications of the debate go well beyond the investigation of morphology, since issues of regularity in word classes and, in particular, the question of regular inflection in nouns and verbs have recently become a crucial test case for accounts of productivity in language. There are, for example, a number of ways of forming the past tense of English verbs, yet it is invariably the regular *-ed* form that is used when novel verbs are encountered (Prasada and Pinker 1993). Stephen Pinker has gone so far as to suggest that this productive use of the regular inflection is "perhaps the simplest example of the great human capacity for generating an unlimited number of new linguistic forms" (Pinker 1997).

1.2 Accounts of productivity in regular inflection

At least two broad classes of approach have been taken in accounting for the productive use of regular inflections. On the first, it is claimed that knowledge of language requires at least two mechanisms: a lexical memory to represent known words and a rule-based combinatorial grammar for productive behavior. The most clearly articulated proposal along these lines is the *dual mechanism* model, associated with Pinker and colleagues (Kim *et al.* 1991, Pinker and Prince 1988, Prasada and Pinker 1993, Prasada *et al.* 1990). On this account, irregular past tense verbs like *sang* or *gave* are represented in lexical memory like any other word. Regular inflection, however, results from rule application: the verb stem is accessed, then input simultaneously to both the lexical memory and the rule-based modules. The regular rule will fire unless a corresponding irregular form is accessed, in which case the irregular form blocks production of the regular.

Such an account nicely explains the productive use of the regular past. The rule can apply to all items not otherwise listed as exceptional and, since it operates over symbols with no phonological content, it will apply to novel words and non-words as easily as to known words of the language.

Note that this account predicts clear differences in the representation and access of regularly and irregularly inflected forms. Of particular interest in the present work is the prediction that since irregular past tenses are represented in the lexicon, their frequency of use should affect their speed of access. In contrast this cannot be the case for the regulars, since these are not represented, but rather are generated on-line.

The second class of approach, taken by several current linguistic and psycholinguistic accounts, assumes that both regularly and irregularly inflected forms can be lexically represented. In the *parallel dual-route model* of Baayen and Schreuder (1999), for example, access representations include both full forms and their constituent morphemes. The resting activation of each is based on its relative token frequency and morphologically complex forms are recognized via either full form or constituent representations based on a complex interaction of frequency, access modality, and other factors. Productivity—the recognition of novel complex words—is permitted through the independent constituent representations.

Other models of this class make a less explicit distinction between full forms and constituents. On the morphological theory developed by Bybee (1985, 1988, 1995) all words, even those that are morphologically complex, may be represented lexically, with their frequency of occurrence playing a strong role in how items are represented and processed. Phonological and semantic similarities across words are represented with explicit lexical connections. A general pattern of correlated phonological and semantic connections across words represents a morphological relationship. *Schemas*, or generalizations that can be abstracted over such patterns, can be applied to base verbs, resulting in productive behavior.

A final and influential approach is the connectionist model, first suggested by Rumelhart and McClelland (1986) and developed more recently in a body of other work (e.g., Daugherty and Seidenberg 1992; Hare and Elman 1995; Hare *et al.* 1995; Plunkett and Marchman 1991, 1993). On this account, generally instantiated as a feedforward network employing a learning algorithm, differences in behavior between the two regularity classes develop through a single processor's experience with data that are heterogeneous with respect to item frequency, phonological similarity, and other factors. These networks learn inductively, and are driven to develop a set of weighted connections that associates each input-output pair. As a result, they abstract generalizations from the data. Their subsequent behavior is based on the productive application of such generalizations.

Research on connectionist learning has shown that both learning and the ability to generalize are sensitive to the factors of frequency and consistency (Plaut *et al.* 1996). As a consequence, one important difference between this and a dual-mechanism account is that while the dual-mechanism approach must exclude effects of frequency in the regular verbs, the network approach is obliged to include them. The same holds true for other full-listing models, since all assume (by definition) that regular verbs are represented, and all posit a crucial role for item frequency in processing.

1.3 Frequency effects in regular past tense verbs

The predictions of the two classes of account overlap to a large extent, but as the previous discussion shows, they make very different claims about the role of frequency in regularly inflected verbs. On the connectionist and other full-listing accounts, both regular and irregular past tense verbs are represented in lexical memory, and therefore their frequency of use should have an effect on how quickly both are accessed. The dual-mechanism account agrees as far as irregular past tenses are concerned, but disagrees with respect to the regular past tense verbs, arguing that these are not represented lexically. The frequency of the regular verb stem should have an effect, since the past is computed by rule once the stem has been accessed. The frequency of the past tense form itself, however, cannot possibly affect access time.

Current experimental findings on the question are ambiguous, with some studies reporting effects of frequency only in irregularly inflected forms and others finding frequency effects in regular forms as well. Taft (1984) refers to an unpublished study in which subjects were read a list of words and asked to write what they heard. Half the items in the list were homophones such as /deyz/, where the more frequent member of the pair was a suffixed form (*days*) while its less frequent competitor was monomorphemic (*daze*). The other half of the items were also homophones, but these were items like /nid/, where neither competitor (*need* or *knead*) was suffixed. In non-suffixed condition, subjects responded less often to the lower-frequency item (26% lower-frequency responses), as might be expected. In the suffixed/non-suffixed condition, however, subjects wrote the non-suffixed word 56.67% of the time, despite the fact that this was the lower-frequency form. Taft interprets these results as indicating that suffixed forms like *days* are represented through the stem and, therefore, are more complex to access than morphologically simple items like *daze*. While the suffixed forms used in Taft's study were not necessarily regular inflections, regular inflection in English does invariably involve suffixation, so these results might be taken to argue that frequency is irrelevant in the regular verbs.

There *is* evidence, on the other hand, that past tense frequency is relevant to irregular verbs. In separate experiments, Prasada *et al.* (1990) and Seidenberg and Bruck (1990) presented subjects with verb stems and asked them to name the corresponding past tense form as rapidly as possible. In both experiments the frequency of the verb stem influenced naming latencies for both regular and irregular verbs. By contrast, there was a reliable effect of past tense frequency only for irregular verbs, with longer naming latencies for low frequency than for high frequency items. Again, the results are consistent with the dual-mechanism claim that lexical representation is influenced by regularity. On this interpretation the irregular forms are produced after a search through the lexicon for the appropriate past tense, and, on the standard assumption that the search is ordered by frequency, the more frequent past tense items are accessed more rapidly. For the regular verbs, on the other hand, only stem frequency influences search time. Once the verb stem has been accessed, the addition of the past tense suffix takes a constant amount of time across verbs, so no differences due to past tense frequency are expected.

However, Daugherty and Seidenberg (1992) have shown that the same pattern of effects occurs in a connectionist model, due to the interacting effects of frequency and similarity during learning (Plaut et al. 1996). Regular verbs benefit from the similarity effect, since they share a consistent form of inflection. Consequently the learning of the regular past tense is less dependent on frequency of presentation than the irregular past tenses are, since a regular verb benefits from the existence of the other regular items. In Daugherty and Seidenberg's network model this led to stronger frequency consequences for irregulars than regulars, matching the pattern of results found in the experimental data.

Since the naming data are consistent with both full-listing and dual-mechanism accounts, they do not decide between the two possibilities. To further complicate the picture, other researchers do appear to find effects of past tense frequency among the regular past tense verbs. Bybee (2000) looked at final t/d deletion in English. Loss of a final [t] or [d] after a consonant is more common in high frequency words, leading to a general effect of token frequency on the rate of deletion. Bybee's study finds this to be as true of regularly inflected past tense verbs as of monomorphemic words or irregulars, suggesting that regularly inflected verbs must be represented in a way that allows their frequency of use to be computed. In an analysis of speech errors, Stemberger and MacWhinney (1986) found fewer errors and, in particular, fewer zero-marking errors on high frequency than on low frequency past tense forms. Since high frequency has been shown to protect items from error (Atkinson and Shiffrin 1968, Bybee 1985, Hare and Elman 1995) this suggests again that at least the high-frequency regular pasts are stored. These studies are consistent with recent work of Gordon and Alegre (1999), who found form frequency effects in regularly inflected items whose frequency of occurrence was relatively high, but not in those with a frequency below 7 per million.

Thus the evidence to date cuts both ways. While some studies appear to disprove an effect of past tense frequency, hence arguing against a full-listing account for regularly inflected verbs, others argue in its favor. The goal of the current paper is to contribute more potentially decisive experimental evidence to the debate.

1.4 Frequency and ambiguity resolution

In the experiments to be presented here we rely on a second finding in the literature, the role of relative frequency in lexical ambiguity resolution. Early studies using the cross-modal priming paradigm (e.g., Swinney 1979, Tanenhaus et al. 1979) supported an account in which both meanings of ambiguous words such as *tire* are accessed simultaneously. It has been noted, though, that these studies involved ambiguities whose two meanings were of similar frequency (MacDonald *et al.* 1994). More recent work has shown that when the frequencies of the alternatives differ, this has an effect on the order in which the meanings are accessed. Simpson (1981), using visual priming, presented an ambiguous prime followed by a target word that was associatively related to either the dominant (more frequent) or subordinate (less frequent) meaning of the prime. Subjects making a lexical decision to the target showed significantly facilitated reaction times only to targets related to the prime's more frequent reading. Simpson and Burgess (1985), using the same paradigm but varying the interval between items (stimulus onset asynchrony, SOA) to investigate the time-course of access, found that both meanings were apparently activated, but the rate of activation depended on their relative frequency (though see Onifer and Swinney 1981). In a series of eye-tracking experiments, Rayner and colleagues (Duffy *et al.* 1988, Rayner and Duffy 1986) looked at ambiguous words whose two meanings were equally frequent, and found that in a semantically neutral context, these words led to longer fixation times than unambiguous controls. This supports the position of Swinney (1979) that both meanings were accessed in parallel. However, if one meaning was more frequent, fixation time for the ambiguities was not different from the control. This was interpreted to show that only the more frequent meaning was accessed during the task.

Given this background, one might ask whether frequency effects of this sort are found for morphologically complex ambiguous words as well. The answer to this question would be highly informative on the issue of regularity in lexical representation: If there is an effect of relative past tense/homophone frequency on speed of access for irregular verbs, but not for regulars, it would argue strongly for an account that accords lexical status only to the irregulars. On the other hand, the finding that both regular and irregular verbs display parallel effects of relative frequency would argue for an account in which all inflected verbs are represented and processed in a similar fashion.

2. Experiments

In this work we use an off-line and an on-line task—writing to dictation and cross-modal immediate repetition priming—to investigate the issue.

2.1 Experiment 1–writing to dictation

In the first experiment we use a dictation task, as in the Taft (1984) study, but involving ambiguous past tense verbs. This will allow us to compare Taft's results, which were based on a range of suffixed forms, to effects limited to verb inflection and to compare results in the regulars to effects found in the irregular verbs. In this experiment we assume, following the experimental results reviewed above, that the more frequent meaning of a homophone will be accessed more rapidly than its competitor in a neutral context. We also assume that subjects operating under time pressure will write the first item accessed when the homophone is heard. In the experiment we vary the relative frequency of past tense forms and their homophonic competitors, predicting that subjects will respond with the higher-frequency reading. The question of interest is whether this result will be found only for irregular verbs, which are non-controversially assumed to be represented in the lexicon, or whether it will obtain for regular verbs as well.

2.1.1 Method

Materials. Test items in the experiment included 40 regular and 39 irregular past tense verbs, each of which had a monomorphemic homophone. Both the frequency of the past tense form and the frequency of the verb stem were calculated using the Lancaster-Oslo/Bergen (LOB) norms (Johansson and Hofland 1989) a million-word collection of British English texts. Stem frequency, throughout, is defined as the cumulative frequency of occurrence of a verb stem across all its regularly inflected variants.

It was not possible to straightforwardly manipulate the frequencies of the stem and the past tense form as we would have liked, since we were constrained by the limited number of past tense homophones available in the language. Instead the verbs were classified according to the relative frequency of their past tense form (PT) and homophone (HP) meanings; the important question of stem frequency will be addressed later in the paper. The frequency classifications used were the following:

(a) *PT greater*: Items where the frequency of the past tense form was higher than the frequency of the homophonic reading by a factor of 2:1, as in the regular pair *allowed/aloud* or the irregular pair *made/maid*.
(b) *HP greater*: Items where the frequency of the homophone is higher, by the same factor of 2:1, than the frequency of the past tense. Examples are *fined/find, ate/eight*.
(c) *Approximately equal*: This left a number of verbs where the frequency of the past tense differed by 10 per million or less from the frequency of the homophone. Although we can make no predictions on frequency effects in these *approximately equal* items, they are included in order to measure response tendencies in a competitor situation independent of frequency bias. Examples of this category are the pairs *ducked/duct* or *heard/herd*. The number of items in

each group was not large (see Table 1 under Results) because of the limited data possibilities available in English.

Procedure. The test and filler items were recorded and digitized on PC microcomputers, which played out speech tokens from the disk. Each subject was presented with all items. Words were played out binaurally over closed ear headphones and the subjects' task was to write a phrase or sentence containing each word as they heard it. There was a six second pause following each word to allow subjects to write. The pause was followed by a warning tone alerting subjects that the next word was about to be presented.

The subjects were asked to write a sentence rather than the individual word since many of the irregular homophones are also homographs (e.g., *spoke, ground*) and only context would determine which meaning was intended. Only responses where the intended meaning was clear from the context were scored.

2.1.2 Results
The results presented below are for 21 subjects, all native speakers of British English between the ages of 18 and 45. Data were analyzed in terms of the proportion of past tense responses out of the total number of possible responses. All probability values hold for both the items and subjects analyses, unless stated otherwise. Table 1 gives the mean proportion of past tense responses for each condition.

Anovas. We examined the effects of Verb Type (Regular, Irregular) and Frequency Group (PT greater, HP greater, Approximately Equal) in an analysis of variance taking the proportion of past tense responses as the dependent variable.

As predicted, the proportion of PT responses varied across frequency groups for both Regular and Irregular verbs (see Table 1), resulting in an overall effect of Frequency Group (p < 0.01). Across Regular and Irregular verbs, the proportion of past tense responses was higher in the PT greater than either the HP greater (p < 0.01) or Approximately Equal (p < 0.05) groups and higher in the Approximately Equal than the HP greater group (p< 0.01). Since there was a greater number of past tense responses in the Irregular than the Regular verbs, the analysis also showed a main

Table 1. *Mean proportion of past tense responses, Experiment 1*

	Regular		Irregular	
	Prop. PT	N	Prop.PT	N
PT greater	0.78	9	0.73	15
HP greater	0.20	17	0.44	15
Approximately equal	0.42	14	0.78	9

effect of Verb Type and an interaction of Verb Type with frequency group (p < 0.05).

A second analysis, looking at the Regular and Irregular verbs individually, showed that predicted variation across frequency group held true of both classes of verb. In the Irregulars, there were significant differences between PT greater and HP greater and between Approximately Equal and HP greater (p < 0.05), although the PT greater group did not differ from Approximately Equal. Importantly, the Regular verbs showed the effect of relative frequency as well: there were significantly more past tense responses in the PT greater than the Approximately Equal and HP greater groups (p < 0.01) and significantly more in the Approximately Equal than in the HP greater group (p < 0.05).

Correlations. We then computed the correlation between the proportion of past tense responses given by subjects for each item with the log of the Past tense / Homophone frequency difference for that item. We chose to look at the difference between the past tense and the homophone frequencies (rather than the frequency of either one) since this gives the size and direction of the frequency advantage, which we take to be the crucial factor. This correlation was significant across all items (r = 0.52, df=77, p < 0 .001) as well as individually both for the Regular (r = 0.66, df=38, p < 0.001) and Irregular verbs (r = 0.41, df=37, p = 0.02).

2.1.3 Discussion

The Dictation experiment finds significant effects of relative PT/homophone frequency in both the Regular and Irregular verbs. Subjects reliably responded with more past tense forms when the past tense had a frequency advantage over its homophone and this effect was just as visible in the Regular verbs as in the Irregulars. For the Irregular verbs the proportion of past tense responses drops significantly from the PT greater and Approximately Equal groups to the HP greater. Regular verbs show an even stronger effect, with the proportion of past tense responses dropping significantly across all three frequency groups. Furthermore, the proportion of past tense responses correlates significantly with the size and direction of the frequency advantage, not only for the Irregulars, but for the theoretically important case of the Regular verbs as well.

This is a different pattern of effects than that discussed in Taft (1984). The Taft study contrasted one condition in which suffixed words were more frequent than their non-suffixed homophones (parallel to our Regular PT greater condition) with a non-suffixed homophone condition (parallel to the Irregular PT or HP greater conditions). That study found more low-frequency responses in the first case than the second. Here, by contrast, the low-frequency responses are Equal across the two parallel cases (22% low-frequency responses in the Regular and 27% in the Irregular Past Tense Greater conditions). Thus it does not appear that the earlier results can be extended to argue that item frequency is irrelevant in the regular verbs.

One interesting difference between verb classes in the current experiment was the larger number of verb responses in the irregular groups. An explanation for this difference between the regular and irregular Approximately Equal verbs is given by the correlation results and involves the differences in frequency tendencies of the two verb classes. The frequency classification was only an approximate measure and, in fact, for 7 of the 9 verbs in the Irregular Approximately Equal group the past tense was relatively higher in frequency, while for the majority of the Regular Approximately Equal items the homophone was higher instead. When the Approximately Equal responses are subdivided by frequency class, the numerical pattern is consistent with the general result. As the correlations have already shown, a higher proportion of past tense responses is found for items whose past tense frequency is higher than the frequency of the homophone. The significant increase in homophone responses from the Irregular PT greater to the HP greater group shows that although there may be a verb preference in the irregulars, it is nonetheless affected by relative frequency.

Finally, to rule out the possibility that the sentence-writing task biased subjects toward the verb interpretation, we removed the irregular homographs and re-ran the experiment with a single-word task. Subjects heard the homophone, as before, and wrote only that word. The mean proportions of past tense response did not differ across the two experiments, dispelling the suspicion of a sentence-based verb bias.

2.1.4 Summary of Experiment 1

Prior work on the access of ambiguous words leads us to expect the most frequent meaning of a homophone to be activated most rapidly and, indeed, our subjects, operating under time pressure, reliably chose the more frequent of the two. What is striking about these results is that this was the case not only for the irregular past tense verbs, which are non-controversially expected to show effects of past tense frequency, but also for the more controversial case of the regular verbs. This pattern is predictable under an account assuming that Regulars and Irregulars are processed in similar ways, but more difficult to reconcile with any account that allows past tense frequency to affect access only in the Irregular verbs.

The results to this point leave open questions, however. In the first place, since the first experiment is an off-line task, the results may well have been influenced by factors other than the automatic process of lexical access. In this case the frequency effect for the regulars may have been due to a post-access strategy rather than accurately reflecting the structure of the lexicon. More importantly, although a rule-based account does not predict an effect of past tense frequency per se in the regular verbs, it does predict that speed of access will be affected by the frequency of the verb stem (cf. Prasada and Pinker 1993). It is therefore crucial to eliminate the possibility that the effect in the regular case is due to stem rather than past tense form frequency. In response to two these concerns, and to test the robustness of the frequency effect in the regular verbs, we ran a second experiment using a very different task.

2.2 Experiment 2—primed lexical decision

Experiment 2 uses the *cross-modal immediate repetition priming task* to compare the effects of past tense frequency in regularly and irregularly inflected verbs. In this task the subject hears a spoken prime, for example *spoke*, and immediately at the offset of the prime sees a visually presented target, such as *SPEAK*, which in our case is morphologically related to the prime. The subject makes a lexical decision on this visually presented target. The priming effect is measured as the time to respond following the related prime, minus the time taken to respond to the same target following an unrelated control prime (Marslen-Wilson *et al.* 1993, Marslen-Wilson *et al.* 1994).

Pilot research in our laboratory, using this task to test the ability of irregular past tense verbs to prime recognition of their stems, found evidence of frequency-modulated competition effects among homophones. A subset of the irregular primes in the pilot test were homophones, like *made/maid* or *blew/blue*. Overall, these items showed interference compared to items where the prime was unambiguous (e.g., *sang*). Interestingly, the bulk of the homophone interference effect came from those items where the homophone competitor was the more frequent reading (as in *blew/blue*). If the past tense was the more frequent reading (e.g., *made/maid*), the priming effects did not differ significantly from those in the unambiguous case.

This difference parallels the ambiguity effects outlined in the introduction and one simple explanation is that, when subjects hear the auditory input, the two possible meanings must compete for access and the more frequent has an advantage. This result with irregular verbs is to be expected under any account, since irregular past tense verbs and their stems are both non-controversially considered independent words. The question of theoretical interest is whether such competition effects can also be found in the regular past tense verbs. The following experiment was devised to answer this question.

2.2.1 Methods
Materials. Test items in the experiment included 54 regular and 54 irregular verbs. Although the irregular verbs were not crucial to the question being asked here, they were included for consistency with the pilot experiment. In each verb class, two-thirds (36) of the verbs had a past tense form with an unrelated homophone, as in

Table 2. *Example stimulus set, Experiment 2*

		Prime	Target
Regular	*homophone*	paced (*paste*)	PACE
	unambiguous	jumped	JUMP
Irregular	*homophone*	blew (*blue*)	BLOW
	unambiguous	slept	SLEEP

Experiment 1. For comparison, the final third of the items had unambiguous, non-homophonic past tense forms (e.g., *jumped*). The Homophone and Non-homophone items were matched in frequency.

For each verb the visual target was always the uninflected verb stem, while the prime was either the inflected past tense or an unrelated control. Table 2 gives an example stimulus set.

As in Experiment 1, the homophonic verbs were classified according to the relative frequency of the past tense and homophone readings into PT greater, HP greater, and Approximately Equal groups. The number of items in each condition is given in Table 3.

Table 3. *Frequency conditions, Experiment 2*

	Regular	Irregular
Unambiguous	18	18
PT greater	9	15
HP greater	13	13
Approximately equal	14	8

Control primes were matched to the past tense primes for frequency and syllable length. The control primes were either nouns or verbs and all were inflected—nouns with the regular plural, verbs with the regular past tense. The control primes had no relationship, whether phonological, semantic, or morphological, to the target, which was always an uninflected verb.

Design and procedure. Subjects sat in a carrel facing a computer display screen and wearing closed ear headphones. An auditory prime was played out over the headphones. Immediately at the offset of the prime the visual target was presented on the screen, in upper case, for 200 milliseconds (ms). Subjects made a lexical decision to the target by pressing the button marked YES or NO on a button box in front of them. Subjects were allowed 2000 ms to respond. There was a fixed 3000 ms stimulus–onset asynchrony (SOA), which meant that the interval between the subject's response and the beginning of the next trial varied according to the reaction time and the length of the auditory prime.

2.2.2 Results and analyses

The results are for 48 subjects, all native speakers of British English. Table 4 gives the overall condition means, broken down by prime type and frequency groups within verb type. Figure 1 gives the priming effects for each verb type.

Table 4. *Mean reaction times, Experiment 2*

Verb type	Frequency group	PT mean	Control mean
	No HP	520	568
Regular	PT greater	560	578
	Equal	556	557
	HP greater	600	565
	No HP	546	547
Irregular	PT greater	524	519
	Equal	550	543
	HP greater	578	552

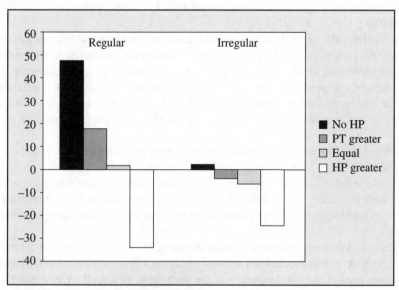

Figure 1. *Priming effects, Experiment 2*

Anovas. In the first analysis of variance we examined the effects of Prime type (Past Tense and Control), Verb type (Regular and Irregular), and Frequency group (Unambiguous, PT greater, HP greater, Approximately Equal). All *p*-values are for both the subjects and items analyses unless stated otherwise.

Priming effects differed across frequency groups, giving rise to a significant interaction between Frequency group and Prime type (p<0.001). Since the main question of the experiment regards the behavior of the Regular verbs with respect to frequency, this interaction will be investigated with separate ANOVAs for the Regular and Irregular verbs, below. In addition to the interaction, there was a marginal effect of Verb Type (F_1, p < .01; F_2, p < 0.07) and a marginal interaction between Verb type and Prime (F_1, p < .05; F_2, p < 0.08). Both were due to the fact that the related prime had a facilitatory effect in the Regular verbs, but not in the Irregulars. The subjects' analysis also showed an overall effect of Frequency group, although again this was not significant by items.

We next investigated the Frequency Group x Prime Type interaction by looking at the factors Prime type (Past Tense and Control) and Frequency group (Unambiguous, PT greater, HP greater, Approximately Equal) in separate ANOVAs for the two classes of verbs.

In the Regular verbs, responses were faster after test than after control primes in the Regular Unambiguous and PT greater conditions (48 and 18 ms facilitation, respectively), but slower after test than control in the HP greater condition (-35 ms). This resulted in a significant interaction between Frequency group and Prime Type (p < 0.01).

In the Irregular verbs there was no main effect of prime type and no interactions, due to the lack of facilitation. Nonetheless these results parallel those of the pilot Lexical Decision study. As in the Regular verbs, responses to the Irregular HP greater verbs were slower after test than control primes (-26 ms). The interference effect was significant by items (p < .05), though not in the subjects analysis, and resulted in a marginal effect of Frequency group (F_1, p < 0.001; F_2, p > 0.1).

Correlations. The results so far are consistent with the claim that the frequency of use of a past tense verb, whether regular or irregular, affects that verb's ability to facilitate recognition of its stem. As such they support an account that predicts that past tense frequency should matter for the Regular verbs and they run counter to the predictions of any account not allowing the frequency of Regular verbs to be computed.

There is, however, an alternative explanation of these data. As pointed out in the Introduction, a dual-mechanism account disallows effects of past tense frequency, but does predict that the frequency of the verb stem should affect how quickly a regular past tense is recognized, since the past tense rule applies only after the stem has been accessed. Because stem and past tense frequencies tend to be inter-correlated, it might be argued that any apparent effect of past tense frequency is simply an artifact of the correlation with stem frequency, with stem frequency as the crucial factor in predicting the effects.

To demonstrate that this is not the case, we computed the partial correlations between priming effects (the Past Tense/control difference) and the differences in frequency between both the stem and the homophone and the past tense and the homophone, for the PT greater and HP greater verbs. This allows us to test whether an advantage in past tense frequency makes a unique contribution in predicting priming effects, once stem frequency has been controlled for. If stem frequency were indeed the crucial factor, then once it has been partialled out of the equation, there should be no significant effect of past tense frequency.

The lack of facilitation in the irregular verbs led the correlations to show no inde-pendent effect of either stem or past tense frequency when looking at the Irregular verbs alone, or the two classes of verbs together. Crucially, however, the Regular verbs do show a reliable independent effect of past tense frequency ($r=.498$, $df=18$, $p < .05$), demonstrating that the Regular PT frequency effect cannot be solely an artifact of stem frequency. Stem frequency also has a reliable effect in the Regular verbs. In this case, however, the slope of the correlation is negative. ($r=-.456$, $df=18$, $p < 0.05$).

2.2.3 Discussion of results
Overall, these results offer a clear answer to the questions being asked in the experi-ment. In the Irregular verbs, despite the lack of facilitation relative to control, we see the same frequency-modulated homophone competition effect as in the prelimi-nary study: Unlike the PT-greater verbs, there is a significant interference effect in the competitor HP-greater condition.

Turning to the main question of the experiment, we see that the Regular verbs show effects across all frequency groups, with significantly larger facilitation in the Unambiguous, PT greater, and Approximately Equal groups than in the competitor HP greater group. The HP greater group, unlike the others, shows interference rela-tive to control. These findings are consistent with the results of Experiment 1 and again suggest that frequency must somehow be accrued for both senses of the ho-mophone, even when one sense is a regular verb.

Although past tense and stem frequencies are intercorrelated, the past tense fre-quency effect is not an artifact of this correlation. As the regression results show, relative PT/homophone frequency has an effect on the reaction time variance that is independent of relative stem frequency. This positive correlation is consistent with previous work on the access of lexical ambiguities, since it indicates that the larger the frequency difference between the prime and the competitor, the more likely that prime is to be accessed, leading to facilitated reaction times to related targets. A final point of interest is that while there is significant priming relative to control for regularly inflected verbs that do not have homophones, the facilitation is greatly reduced for all homophone primes. Even in the PT greater group, responses to the targets are not significantly faster in the Past Tense condition than following control. Thus relative frequency alone does not account for the entire pattern of results, since the simple existence of a competing homophone appears to have an effect that is not completely overridden by differences in frequency.

3. General discussion

The pattern of results found in these two experiments is difficult to reconcile with a model that assumes that frequency effects in the past tense must vary with the regularity of the verb. Both experiments show effects of past tense frequency that are, if anything, stronger in the regularly inflected items than in the irregulars. In addition, the results rule out the alternative explanation that these effects are actually an artifact of stem frequency.

This runs counter to the predictions of a dual-mechanism account, which leads us to expect past tense frequency effects in the irregular verbs, but no effect of past tense frequency in the regulars. Crucial to this model is the assumption that the application of a rule cannot be affected by the identity of the item to which it is applied. Stem frequency should affect the first step in the production of the past tense—the access of the stem—but the subsequent application of the past tense rule should take a constant time. Allowing the frequency of the past tense form to influence the process would suggest that the rule is more easily applied in those cases where it has been applied more often and the rule application should be indifferent to such properties of the specific item involved.

Instead, these results suggest that lexical knowledge is highly redundant, allowing for influence of both the past tense form and the stem, which may well be represented and interconnected in ways that allow them to affect each other. In the interests of cognitive economy, it is also reasonable to represent the items that are used most often. This, along with our experimental results, argues that regular past tense verbs, particularly frequent past tense verbs, are lexically represented in some fashion and, indeed, a number of models of lexical organization are consistent with these assumptions (Butterworth 1983, Baayen and Schreuder 1999, Bybee 1985, Rumelhart and McClelland 1986).

A final interesting fact of our data is the basic difference in priming effects between the regular and irregular verbs found in Experiment 2. Although we find significant facilitation for unambiguous regular verbs, there is no priming effect in the irregulars, even in the unambiguous case. On the face of it, this asymmetry fits more readily into a dual mechanism account, since it appears to reflect a qualitative difference in the representations of regular and irregular verbs. Note, however, that the observed difference is directly opposite to that predicted by a dual mechanism model: the frequency-modulated priming effects are found in the regular verbs, not the irregulars.

Yet, as noted in the introduction, a number of previous studies have found frequency effects in the irregular verbs, so it is somewhat surprising that the cross-modal priming paradigm does not. It would be unreasonable to take the lack of priming effects as evidence that the irregular primes are not lexically represented, given the strong independent evidence to the contrary. Instead we note that frequency effects on speed of access must interact with the effectiveness of a particular item as a prime in the unambiguous case. Both here and in previous work (Marslen-Wilson et al. 1993), we have found that irregular verbs are ineffective at priming their stem in the cross-modal priming paradigm. This contrast also occurs in a distributed connectionist model. Hare and Marslen-Wilson (1997) reproduced this pattern of priming effects with a simple auto-associative architecture, in which the task is to reproduce the input on an output layer. This architecture offers a reasonable approximation to the priming task, since it allows the modeler to view the activation or the verb stem when either that stem or a past tense is input as the prime.

The autoassociator can also be designed to force the network to extract generalizations about the data set. This is done by incorporating an internal processing layer that is smaller than the input and output layers, so that there are not enough resources to simply copy an identity mapping from the input through the internal units to the output. Instead, the network is forced to abstract any generalizations found in the input and use these to reconstruct that input on the output level. In the Hare and Marslen-Wilson model, the dominant generalization involved the close formal relationship between a verb stem and its regular past tense. If the model captured that relationship between these, it saw a large decrease in error. Since error reduction drives the networks, that relationship was indeed well-learned and, consequently, the regular items performed well on the priming task. For the same reason the irregulars, which rarely contain the stem in their past tense form, did badly. Thus the difference in priming performance was due in large measure to the smaller formal difference between the regular past and its stem form, and how this difference influenced network learning and generalization.

4. Conclusion

While earlier studies such as those of Taft (1984) or Prasada et al. (1996) appeared to show a contrast between regularly and irregularly inflected verbs with respect to frequency effects, there is no sign of any such asymmetry in the results of the experiments presented here. These studies give no particular evidence for any account in which regularly inflected forms are generated by rule while irregulars are listed independently. On the other hand, the frequency, priming, and homophone competition effects found here are consistent with lexical models in which full forms can be represented even if they are morphologically regular and provide a set of interesting constraints on accounts of morphological processing and the representation of inflected forms.

References

Atkinson, R.C. and Shiffrin, R.M. 1968. "Human memory: a proposed system and its control processes". In *The Psychology of Learning and Motivation*, K.W. Spence and J.T. Spence (eds.), 90–191. London: Academic Press.

Baayen, H. and Schreuder, R. 1999. "War and peace: morphemes and full forms in a Noninteractive Activation Parallel Dual-Route Model". *Brain and Language* 68 1/2: 27–32.

Butterworth, B. 1983. "Lexical Representation". *Language Production* 2: 257–94. London: Academic Press.

Bybee, J. 1985. *Morphology*. Philadelphia: John Benjamins.

Bybee, J. 1988. "Morphology as lexical organization". In *Theoretical Morphology*, M. Hammond and M. Noonan (eds.). San Diego: Academic Press.

Bybee, J. 1995. "Regular Morphology and the Lexicon". *Language and Cognitive Processes* 10 (5): 425–55.

Bybee, J. 2000. "Phonology of the lexicon". In *Usage-Based Models of Language*, M. Barlow and S. Kemmer (eds.), 65–85. Stanford: CSLI.

Daugherty, K., and Seidenberg, M. 1992. "The Past Tense Revisited", In *The Proceedings of the 14th Annual Meeting of the Cognitive Science Society*. Hillsdale, NJ: Erlbaum.

Duffy, S.A., Morris, R.K., and Rayner, K. 1988. "Lexical ambiguity and fixation times in reading". *Journal of Memory and Language* 27: 429–46.

Gordon, P., and Alegre, M. 1999. "Frequency Effects and the Representational Status of Regular Inflections". *Journal of Memory and Language* 40: 41–61.

Hare, M.L., Elman, J.L., and Daugherty, K.G. 1995. "Default Categorization in Connectionist Networks". *Language and Cognitive Processes* 10(6): 601–30.

Hare, M.L., and Elman, J.L. 1995. "Learning and Morphological Change". *Cognition* 56: 61–98.

Hare, M.L., and Marslen-Wilson, W.D. 1997. "Past Tense Priming in an Auto-Associative Network". In *The Proceedings of the 19th Annual Meeting of the Cognitive Science Society*. Hillsdale, NJ: Erlbaum.

Johansson, S., and Hofland, K. 1989. *Frequency Analysis of English Vocabulary and Grammar*. Oxford: Clarendon Press.

Juliano, C., and Tanenhaus, M. K. 1993. "Contingent frequency effects in syntactic ambiguity resolution". In *The Proceedings of the 15th Annual Conference of the Cognitive Science Society*. Hillsdale, NJ: Erlbaum.

Kim, J.J., Pinker, S., Prince, A., and Prasada, S. 1991. "Why no mere mortal has ever flown out to center field". *Cognitive Science* 15: 173–218.

MacDonald, M. C. 1994. "Probabilistic constraints and syntactic ambiguity resolution". *Language and Cognitive Processes*. 9: 157–201.

MacDonald, M.C., Pearlmutter, N.J., and Seidenberg, M.S. 1994. "Lexical Nature of Syntactic Ambiguity Resolution". *Psychological Review* 101(4): 676–703.

Marslen-Wilson, W.D., Hare, M.L., and Older, L. 1993. "Inflectional Morphology and Phonological Regularity in the English Mental Lexicon". In *The Proceedings of the 15th Annual Conference of the Cognitive Science Society*. Hillsdale, NJ: Erlbaum.

Marslen-Wilson, W.D., Tyler, L.K., Waksler, R., and Older, L. 1994. "Morphology and meaning in the English mental lexicon". *Psychological Review* 101(1): 3–33.

Morton, J. 1969. "The interaction of information in word recognition". *Psychological Review* 76: 165–78.

Onifer, W. and Swinney, D. A. 1981. "Accessing lexical ambiguities during sentence comprehension: Effects of frequency on meaning and contextual bias". *Memory and Cognition* 9: 225–36.

Pinker, S. 1997. "Words and rules in the human brain". *Nature* 387(6633): 547–8.

Pinker, S., and Prince, A. 1988. "On language and connectionism: Analysis of a Parallel Distributed Processing model of language acquisition". *Cognition* 28: 73–193.

Plaut, D.C., McClelland, J.L., Seidenberg, M.S., and Patterson, K.E. 1996. "Understanding Normal and Impaired Word Reading: Computational Principles in Quasi-Regular Domains". *Psychological Review* 103(1): 56–115.

Plunkett, K., and Marchman, V. 1993. "From Rote Learning to System Building". *Cognition* 48: 21–69.

Plunkett, K., and Marchman, V. 1991. "U-shaped learning and frequency effects in a multi-layered perceptron: Implications for child language acquisition". *Cognition* 38: 43–102.

Prasada, S., and Pinker, S. 1993. "Generalization of Regular and Irregular Morphological Patterns". *Language and Cognitive Processes* 8: 1–56.

Prasada, S., Pinker, S., and Snyder, W. 1990. "Some evidence that irregular forms are retrieved from memory but regular forms are rule generated". Paper presented at the 31st meeting of the Psychonomic Society, New Orleans.

Rayner, K., and Duffy, S.A. 1986. "Lexical complexity and fixation times in reading: Effects of word frequency, verb complexity, and lexical ambiguity". *Memory and Cognition* 14: 191–201.

Rubenstein, H., Garfield, L. and Milliken, J.A. 1970. "Homographic entries in the internal lexicon". *Journal of Verbal Learning and Verbal Behavior* 9: 487–92.

Rumelhart, D.E., and McClelland, J. 1986. "Learning the Past Tense of English Words". In *Parallel Distributed Processing, Vol. 2*, Rumelhart, D.E. and McClelland, J. (eds.), 216–71. Cambridge, Mass.: MIT Press.

Seidenberg, M., and Bruck, M. 1990. "Consistency effects in the generation of past tense morphology". Paper presented at the 31st meeting of the Psychonomic Society, New Orleans.

Seidenberg, M.S., and McClelland, J. 1989. "A distributed, developmental model of word recognition and naming". *Psychological Review* 97: 447–52.

Simpson, G. B. 1981. "Meaning dominance and semantic context in the processing of lexical ambiguity". *Journal of Verbal Learning and Verbal Behavior* 20: 120–36.

Simpson, G.B., and Burgess, C. 1985. "Activation and selection processes in the recognition of ambiguous words". *Journal of Experimental Psychology: Human Perception and Performance*, 11: 28–39.

Spivey-Knowlton, M. J., Trueswell, J. C., and Tanenhaus, M. 1993. "Context and syntactic ambiguity resolution". *Canadian Journal of Psychology* 47: 276–309.

Stemberger, J., and MacWhinney, B. 1986. "Frequency and the lexical storage of regularly inflected words". *Journal of Memory and Cognition* 14: 17–26.

Stowe, L., Tanenhaus, M., and Carlson, G. 1991. "Filling gaps on-line: Use of lexical and semantic information in sentence processing". *Language and Speech 34* (4): 319–40.

Swinney, D.A. 1979. "Lexical access during sentence comprehension: (Re)consideration of context effects". *Journal of Verbal Learning and Verbal Behavior* 18: 645–59.

Taft, M. 1984. "Exploring the Mental Lexicon". *Australian Journal of Psychology* 36: 35–46.

Tanenhaus, M.K., Leiman, J., and Seidenberg, M.S. 1979. "Evidence for multiple stages in the processing of ambiguous words in syntactic contexts". *Journal of Verbal Learning and Verbal Behavior* 18: 427–40.

Frequency, regularity and the paradigm:
A perspective from Russian on a complex relation*

GREVILLE CORBETT, ANDREW HIPPISLEY, DUNSTAN BROWN, and PAUL MARRIOTT

University of Surrey and National University of Singapore

1. Introduction

The correspondence between irregularity and high frequency is well known (Bybee 1995, Greenberg 1966). What is not always clear is whether the frequency envisaged is based on the lexeme and all its manifestations, including the irregular word form(s), or just the irregular form(s) alone.[1] For example in the case of English *went*, is it this single word-form that is highly frequent compared to other past tense forms, or is it the lexeme *go* that is highly frequent, in both its regular and irregular manifestations, compared to other lexemes? Bybee (1985: 120) suggests the following:

> the correlation of irregularity with frequency occurs on two dimensions. The first is the lexical dimension . . . where irregularity correlates with frequent lexical entries. The second is within the paradigm.

To investigate further we have examined frequencies of noun lexemes, and their word forms, in a one million word Russian corpus (the Uppsala corpus), together with information on regularity. So as to more finely locate any correspondence between frequency and regularity, the types of irregularity we considered range from full suppletion to minor irregularity in stress.

2. Claims, hypotheses, and statistical method

In Section 2, we briefly discuss the various claims made about the frequency and irregularity relationship, and outline the hypotheses we test to explore this relationship. At the end of the section we give an overview of the statistical method adopted (see also Appendix 1).

2.1 Claims

The most general claim is that there is a relationship between high frequency and irregularity. This is a claim with which almost any linguist would agree. However, the nature of the relationship is so vague as to be untestable. Once we begin to clarify the claim, we find an interesting range of possible relationships. Our strategy will be to suggest that each may be true, and then look for ways to prove or disprove them. The initial claim that we investigated was that there might be a straightforward linear correlation between regularity and frequency; however the data suggested that in fact it was more appropriate to search for a more complex relationship.

Let us start with irregularity and consider its *extent*, i.e., the distribution of irregular forms within a paradigm. Within a given lexeme it might be that every form could be irregular independently; or else it might be that forms come in groups which are regular or irregular together. We have looked at Russian, specifically at nouns. This word class has two numbers and six cases (presented later in Table 1). We can ask whether irregularity concerns a high level split between singular and plural or whether we should consider individual forms. Of course, we shall try both approaches (this is taken further in Section 2.2).

A second question concerns the *degree* of irregularity. Russian *č'elovek ~ l'ud'–i* 'person ~ people' form an irregular relation, but so do *mést-o ~ mest-á* 'place ~ places'.[2] In the first example we have different stems (suppletion) and in the second we have the stress unexpectedly on the ending in the plural (where in the singular it is on the stem). Intuitively, the first type of irregularity is more severe than the second. If we believe there is a relationship between frequency and irregularity, then we might claim that it will be sensitive to *degrees* of irregularity. To test this claim we set up a ranking of irregularity, devised of course without reference to frequency (see Section 4).

Turning now to notions of frequency, as hinted at already this can be viewed in two ways. Suppose we have a noun whose plural is irregular. With what precisely do we expect to find a relationship? It is easiest to see the alternatives if we consider a corpus and look at the tests we might apply. We might compare lexemes, one to another, or we could compare regular and irregular forms within lexemes. For the first approach, we could count up how many times each lexeme occurs in the plural. Since we are counting only plurals (without respect to other forms, i.e., the singular) we call this the *absolute frequency* of a lexeme's plural. We can then compare the *absolute frequency* of plural of different lexemes to see if there is a relationship between irregular plurals and their *absolute frequency*. There is, however, a quite different way to look at the plural (and indeed at any cell or combination of cells in a paradigm), that is we may compare it, within the lexeme, with the other available forms. For a given lexeme, we could count how many times it occurs in the plural as compared to the number of times it occurs in the singular. This is the *relative frequency* of the plural. We can then compare the *relative frequency* of the plural in lexemes where it is irregular with the *relative frequency* in lexemes where it is regular. We consider this question further in the next section.

Since the distinction between *absolute* and *relative frequency* is important, consider a tiny corpus consisting of four lexemes, as in Figure 1.

	Lexeme A	Lexeme B	Lexeme C	Lexeme D
Singular occurrences	10	20	30	40
Plural occurrences	5	5	10	10
Absolute plural frequency	5	5	10	10
Relative plural frequency	0.33	0.2	0.25	0.2

Figure 1. *Absolute and relative frequency*

Lexemes C and D occur in the plural 10 times each. Their *absolute plural frequency* is 10, higher than that of the other two lexemes. But when we turn *to relative plural frequency*, we note that lexeme A has 5 plural occurrences out of a total of 15. Its *relative plural frequency* is therefore 0.33 which is higher than that of any of the other lexemes.

2.2 Terms and hypotheses

We now set out a number of hypotheses to test the relationship between irregularity and frequency. The hypotheses are formulated in such a way that their confirmation or disconfirmation will not only determine whether there is a relationship between irregularity and frequency, but will also answer more specific questions as to what the nature of the relationship is. To determine whether there is a relationship between regularity and frequency we will look for a particular kind of *anomaly* in the corpus. Before looking at the hypotheses, we introduce the terms *plural anomaly* and *cell anomaly*.

2.2.1 Plural anomaly and cell anomaly
The focus of the investigation is specifically on any *anomaly* in the behavior of the plurals in the corpus. Before stating the hypotheses, we need to be clear what we mean by *plural anomaly*. The definition is given in (1):[3]

(1) *Plural anomaly*

Plural *anomaly* can be in terms of absolute or relative frequency

a. *Absolute plural anomaly*
   This is an absolute anomalous frequency of plurals for a given lexeme
b. *Relative plural anomaly*
   This is a relative anomalous frequency of plurals for a given lexeme (the proportion of a lexeme's plurals is anomalous)

What we are saying in (1) is that the *anomaly* in the plurals of the corpus can be viewed in two distinct ways. The first is in terms of an anomalous count of plurals for a lexeme compared to the amount one would expect for a typical lexeme of the corpus (*absolute plural anomaly*). In other words, if a lexeme's count of plural word forms is extreme compared to the distribution of counts of plurals, we would have identified an *absolute plural anomaly*. This is an *absolute anomaly* because what is being compared is an absolute number of plurals for a lexeme with the distribution of the absolute number of plurals in the corpus.

The second way of thinking about the *anomaly* is in relative terms. Here the proportion of instances of the lexeme that are plural is examined for an *anomaly*. The distribution of plural proportions can be calculated for the lexemes of the corpus, and if the given lexeme's proportion of plurals is extreme compared to this distribution, we would have identified a *relative plural anomaly*. (This may be seen as a generalisation of Tiersma's (1982) notion of local markedness.)

So far we have thought of *plural anomaly* generally in terms of the plural half of the lexeme's paradigm. We also wish to allow for the possibility of the *anomaly* being due, as it were, to one of the case and number cells. For this we need the idea of another specific kind of *anomaly*, which we will term *cell anomaly*, as defined in (2):

(2) *Cell anomaly*
   One specific cell has an extreme proportion compared to the distribution of the proportion of that cell throughout the corpus. This can only be stated in relative terms.

In *cell anomaly* the *anomaly* is that a given lexeme has a significantly higher (or lower) than average proportion of word forms for a given cell.[4] For example, the lexeme may have a much higher than average proportion of genitive plurals compared to the corpus in general. Note that it is important to define *cell anomaly* in relative terms only, because formulating it in absolute terms might mean that we would be observing *plural* (or singular) *anomaly* in disguise. In other words, the cell may be above or below the average simply as a consequence of the singular or plural subparadigm being above or below the average.

2.2.2 Hypotheses to be tested

The relationship between regularity and frequency will therefore be seen in terms of *plural* or *cell anomaly*, as just discussed. We now list four hypotheses which we will test. The four hypotheses are discussed in turn.

(3) Hypothesis 1a

There is a relation between *absolute plural anomaly* and irregularity.

If Hypothesis 1a is confirmed, we will have shown that there is a relation between irregularity and frequency and the data analysis will tell us the nature of this relationship.

Note that if we observed *absolute plural anomaly* in certain groups of lexemes, this might still be because the lexeme as a whole was anomalously frequent. We need a test which tells us whether the frequency relationship is with the general lexeme, or whether it is specifically with the lexeme's irregular forms. Recall our original question in the introduction: is frequency related to the lexeme as a whole or to its irregular word forms? We address this question using Hypothesis 1b:

(4) Hypothesis 1b

There is a relation between *relative plural anomaly* and irregularity.

We also need to test whether there is a stronger relationship with irregularity when we combine *plural anomaly* (either absolute or relative, see (1), with the more specific *cell anomaly* (2). In other words, if a lexeme's plural forms occurred more frequently than average and a particular cell in the plural was proportionally more frequent than average, are we right in expecting the form in question to be even more irregular? We address this question using Hypothesis 2, which allows us to look for a stronger (and more fine-grained) relationship between high frequency and irregularity:

(5) Hypothesis 2

If Hypothesis 1a or Hypothesis 1b is true, there is a stronger relationship between irregularity and the combination of *plural anomaly* and *cell anomaly*.

A particular case and number may occur more frequently than average either due to the lexeme occurring frequently or to the fact that the cell occurs unusually out of proportion to all word forms in the corpus (*absolute frequency* of the cell).

Note that if Hypotheses 1a and 1b were disconfirmed, we would need to find out whether there might be any relationship at all between irregularity and frequency. We would do this by looking at the level of individual case and number cells.

(6) *Hypothesis 3*

There is no relation between irregularity of a plural cell and the *absolute frequency* of that cell.

Hypothesis 3 is independent of Hypotheses 1 and 2. It allows us to find the answer to whether or not irregularity of a single cell by itself has a relationship with *absolute frequency*. Hypothesis 3 is there for completeness. As we shall see, Hypothesis 3 proved to be unnecessary and will play only a minor part in the following discussion.

2.3 Statistical method

Using the data extracted from the corpus (see Section 3), we investigated the relationship between irregularity and frequency. This frequency could be in absolute or relative terms.

We extracted subsets of lexemes from the corpus according to the regularity of the lexemes. For all lexemes an appropriate *absolute* or *relative frequency* is calculated. If there were no effect between regularity and frequency then we would expect no statistically significant difference in the measured frequency distributions in the subset and in the full corpus. In order to compare these distributions a simple summary statistic—the median—was chosen. Hence all tests are based on finding statistically significant differences between the median frequency in the subset and in the full corpus. Informal exploratory data analysis was done to investigate the claims. We used box-plots to compare the distributions of frequencies across groups (Daley *et al.* 1995). See for example Figure 2 in Section 5.2 where a box plot is used.

Having formulated the hypotheses in terms of significant differences in median values, it is necessary to use an appropriate statistical test. We decided to use a non-parametric technique, in which we are assuming that the frequency of lexeme use in the corpus is a good representation of their use in the general language. The quantity and quality of the data is sufficiently high that any loss of efficiency in using non-parametric techniques is felt to be unimportant. This small loss is more than compensated for by the simplicity and directness of the non-parametric tests used. For details of the testing procedure see Appendix 1.

3. The data

We tested the hypotheses on the Russian nouns in a corpus. Russian is a good choice for this type of investigation, because noun paradigms have sufficient cells for us to tease apart the irregularity of the lexeme in its entirety and that of one of its word forms. Also, irregularity in Russian is highly varied, ranging from full suppletion to shift in stress.

3.1 Russian nominal inflection

Russian is an East Slavonic language, part of a branch of Indo-European which has been relatively conservative in terms of inflectional morphology. Nouns distinguish number and case, and fall into different inflectional classes. These inflectional classes share some forms between them, so that it is not self-evident how many inflectional classes should be recognized. The traditional answer is three, but other views are possible, as discussed in Corbett (1982), where he argues for four basic inflectional classes. Our analysis is based on these four classes, as shown in Table 1. There are several partially overlapping reasons for recognising these four as major classes. Each is productive, though the productivity of classes III and IV is dependent on a small number of derivational affixes. Each has a significant number of members (at least several thousand, though again there is some disparity). Each is

Table 1. *Major noun classes of Russian*

		I zakón 'law'	II gazéta 'newspaper'	III rúkop'is' 'manuscript'	IV bolóto 'swamp'
Singular	NOM	zakón	gazéta	rúkop'is'	bolóto
	ACC	zakón	gazétu	rúkop'is'	bolóto
	GEN	zakóna	gazéti	rúkop'is'i	bolóta
	DAT	zakónu	gazéte	rúkop'is'i	bolótu
	INST	zakónom	gazétoj	rúkop'is'ju	bolótom
	LOC	zakóne	gazéte	rúkop'is'i	bolóte
Plural	NOM	zakóni	gazéti	rúkop'is'i	bolóta
	ACC	zakóni	gazéti	rúkop'is'i	bolóta
	GEN	zakónov	gazét	rúkop'is'ej	bolót
	DAT	zakónam	gazétam	rúkop'is'am	bolótam
	INST	zakónam'i	gazétam'i	rúkop'is'am'i	bolótam'i
	LOC	zakónax	gazétax	rúkop'is'ax	bolótax

*We use the following abbreviations: NOM—nominative, ACC—accusative, GEN—genitive, DAT—dative, INST—instrumental, LOC—locative.
Notes: (i) forms are given here in phonemic transcription (see note 2). Palatalization (or 'softening') is indicated by '; (ii) there is no overt ending in the nominative/accusative singular in types I and III, nor in the genitive plural of types II and IV.

regular, in that there are mutual predictabilities between certain cells of the paradigm. And, provided these four classes are distinguished, the gender of almost every Russian noun is predictable from information available in the lexicon (Corbett 1982). Thus positing these four classes depends partly on their type frequency, in other words the number of different lexical items, or 'types', found in a dictionary that they apply to (Bybee and Thompson 1997). However, our main interest is the relationship between regularity and token frequency, the number of actual occurrences of a lexical item in running text.

A useful overview of the data can be found in Timberlake (1993: 836–45), and Network Morphology treatments are available in Corbett and Fraser (1993), Brown and Hippisley (1994) and Fraser and Corbett (1995).

3.2 Irregularity in Russian nouns

Russian nouns are ideal for our investigation because they provide numerous types of inflectional irregularity, from the most radical to the very minor. Starting with the most radical cases, we find instances of full suppletion—nouns whose singular and plural stems are quite different. Then there are those cases whose stems are clearly related, but they differ in ways which may be unpredictable or only partly predictable. Stem augments may be found in the singular, the plural, or in both. Then, on the other extreme, we find minor inflectional irregularities, such as the use of forms which typically belong with nouns of another class. And finally we find nouns which would be fully regular if we looked only at segmental phonology, but which are prosodically irregular. There are four main types of stress pattern and then there are minor irregular patterns in addition (Brown et al. 1996).

3.3 The corpus and the dataset

We use the Uppsala corpus, which is a set of Russian sub-corpora of various genres, containing in total about one million words. It is considered the best Russian corpus available, in terms of scope and design. For information on the Uppsala corpus, see Lönngren (1993) and Maier (1994). The dataset which we created is in the form of a Microsoft Excel document where, in addition to regularity information, case, number (singular and plural), and animacy information about the nouns occurring in the Uppsala corpus are given numerical values, corresponding to irregularity indexes, case features, animacy features, and frequency information.

Since we were interested in estimating proportions in different categories, there would be large standard errors in our estimates where observed numbers in each category are small. Large sampling errors would complicate detailed cluster analysis. For this reason we recorded only those lexemes which occur at least five times.

Given this, the dataset contains around 5440 lexemes, accounting for around 243,000 word forms from the entire one million word corpus.[5]

4. Ranking irregularity

As we have said, our aim is to investigate the relationship between irregularity and frequency; we specifically wish to tease apart the irregularity of a lexeme and that of one of its inflectional forms. It is important to be clear what we mean by irregularity, and what we view as the paradigm of the lexeme. This is clarified in 4.1. In 4.2 we outline a number of principles on which an irregularity ranking is based and in 4.3 we carefully show how lexemes are assigned their rank. Further examples are given in Appendix 2. Finally in 4.4, we look at irregularity as treated in the Natural Morphology theory, as a point of comparison.

4.1 Definitions and assumptions

We briefly state what we mean by regularity, and outline our assumptions about the paradigm of Russian nouns.

4.1.1 Regularity and irregularity
We start by giving a notion of regularity for an inflectional language.

Regularity. We expect a regular noun to have:

  (i) a single (unchanging) stem
 (ii) a fixed stress (whether fixed with respect to the stem or with respect to the word-edge)
(iii) a consistent set of endings (i.e., a set of endings which predict each other)[6]

Irregularity. We treat each irregular type as a numerical step away from regularity. Suppletion is the most severe type of irregularity. However, even this does not define an end point, since a noun with suppletive stems *and* irregular inflections is more irregular than a noun with suppletive stems but regular inflections. The question is how much structural difference there is between a given irregular noun and the prototypical regular noun, for example *gazéta* 'newspaper'. How much, and how drastic, is the change required to bring an item to a state of regularity? An irregularity type is therefore viewed in terms of distance from the regular type, and the distance itself is viewed in terms of the nature of the adjustment required to 'restore' the item.

'Structural irregularity'.   We are investigating 'structural irregularity', i.e., irregularity determined by comparing forms according to a set of principles. Since we wish to investigate the relationship with frequency, we must exclude any frequency consideration when determining regularity. Thus a noun with a small deviation from the regular pattern counts as almost regular, even if it is the only noun to behave in that way.

4.1.2 Assumptions about the paradigm and irregularity
We treat all cells of the paradigm as equal (though it might be argued that, say, an irregularity in the nominative singular should be treated as more important than a similar irregularity in another cell). More difficult is the number of cells to recognize.

Assumptions about cells and irregularity
We start with a distributional criterion, that is, we determine how many distinctions are justified by the syntax (Comrie 1986, 1991). We accept the traditional view of six cases and two numbers, hence twelve cells in all.[7] However, if we were simply to assume that each paradigm has twelve cells, this would lead to a counter-intuitive result. The problem is that there are certain cells whose forms must be identical within one or another inflectional class. Consider the contrasting paradigms of *zakón* 'law' and *dom* 'house' in Table 2.

Table 2. *Contrasting paradigms in Russian*

	Singular	Plural		Singular	Plural
NOM	zakón	zakón-i	NOM	dom	dom-á
ACC	zakón	zakón-i	ACC	dom	dom-á
GEN	zakón-a	zakón-ov	GEN	dóm-a	dom-óv
DAT	zakón-u	zakón-am	DAT	dóm-u	dom-ám
INST	zakón-om	zakón-am'i	INST	dóm-om	dom-ám'i
LOC	zakón-e	zakón-ax	LOC	dóm-e	dom-áx

The relevant point is that the accusative plural cannot be a distinct form, in these or any other paradigms; it must be the same as the nominative plural, as here, or as the genitive plural, for animates.[8] We treat *zakón* 'law' as the regular noun (see Table 1, and the points made in Section 3.1). The noun *dom* 'house' has the irregular form *dom-a* 'houses': the inflection is not predictable given the other forms in its paradigm, and forms in another of the classes established in Section 3.1 are wrongly predicted given the ending. If we count twelve cells, then *dom* 'house' is irregular in two cells. However, if the accusative plural were regular *dom-i* while the nominative plural were irregular *dom-a*, that would actually be much more irregular. It would be breaking a fundamental pattern which extends to every noun (and adjective and pronoun) in the language, according to which the accusative plural is identical to the nominative or genitive. It therefore appears more logical to treat the nominative and accusative as one cell here. We do this because there is a 'whole word' referral, that is to say, the forms must be absolutely identical, including in respect to stress (see Brown *et al.* 1996). In a similar way, we do not count the accusative singular for nouns of classes I, III, and IV and we treat the dative and locative singular of class II as syncretic. The result is that there is a maximum of ten distinct cells for any given noun.

Assumptions about number and irregularity.   There are several instances in which singular and plural are contrasted in Russian. Consider the paradigm in Table 3, from a different inflectional class, class IV (see Table 1), in terms of its stress.

Table 3. *Paradigm with singular/ plural split*

	Singular	Plural
NOM	mést-o	mest-á
ACC	mést-o	mest-á
GEN	mést-a	mest
DAT	mést-u	mest-ám
INST	mést-om	mest-ám'i
LOC	mést-e	mest-áx

A perfectly regular paradigm would have the same stress position throughout. In this case, however, we have fixed stem stress in the singular and a different fixed stress in the plural (on the ending). Here it is counter-intuitive to count up cells; the point is that there is a single difference between singular and plural.[9] We treat this as less irregular than a single cell being 'out of line'. We shall see this same pattern in various types of irregularity at different points below.

4.2 Principles

There are six principles on which the irregularity ranking is based and these will be treated in turn. In the examples, the nominative singular is contrasted with the nominative plural unless otherwise stated, with the gloss given for the singular form only.

Principle 1
Stem irregularity ranks above inflectional irregularity:
stem irregularity > inflectional irregularity

Example: *sosed ~ sosed'-i* 'neighbor' > *pleč'-o ~ pleč-'i* 'shoulder'

The first example *sosed* displays stem irregularity in that the stem final consonant /d/ alternates with /d'/ in the plural. The second example *pleč'-o* displays inflectional irregularity: the item switches from class IV in the singular to class I in the plural, as seen in the nominative (refer to Table 1). One motivation for this ranking is that inflectional irregularity may be treated as an abstract (featural) difference in stems. John McCarthy (personal communication) suggests other evidence for the primacy of stems: in vowel harmony systems, either the stem may determine the vowel possibilities of the ending or stem and ending may determine each other, but it is never the case that the ending alone determines the properties of the stem.

Principle 2
Segmental irregularity ranks above prosodic irregularity:
segmental irregularity > stress irregularity

Example: *sosed ~ sosed'-i* 'neighbor' > *óz'or-o ~ oz'ór-a* 'lake'

In the first example the stem final consonant /d/ alternates with palatalized /d'/, a segmental irregularity. In the second example, the alternation concerns stress, from initial to predesinential syllable, a prosodic irregularity.[10] The justification for this principle is that typically there are greater phonological differences available through segmental means than through prosodic means. Note that though stress has a great effect on vowel quality in Russian, such that stress affects the entire word, this effect is 'automatic'.

Principle 3
Within stem irregularity, specifically of the segmental kind, suppletion ranks above irregularity involving augments and augment irregularity, in turn, ranks above simple alternations in the stem:

suppletion > augments > stem alternations

Example: *č'elovek ~ l'ud'–i* 'person' > *tatar'in ~ tatar-i* 'Tatar' > *sosed ~ sosed'-i* 'neighbor'

Note that *tatar'in* represents a noun with an augment in the singular, namely *-'in*, but no augment in the plural. This ranking is based on the degree of similarity among the alternates; augments are closer to full suppletion than alternations, which can be accounted for by rules of allomorphy. In terms of stems, this reflects the difference between indexed stems ('morphomically' distinct, see Aronoff 1994), and stem alternants (morpho-phonologically distinct).

Principle 4
Within segmental stem alternations we distinguish motivated alternations (i.e., mobile vowels) and non-motivated alternations. Unmotivated alternations rank higher than motivated:

unmotivated stem alternation > motivated stem alternation

Example: *sosed ~ sosed'-i* 'neighbor' > *kn'ižk-a* 'book (diminutive)' ~ *kn'ižek* (genitive plural)

Note that in the second example, a mobile vowel appears in the genitive plural, but given the structure of the lexeme this is where it is expected to occur, and is therefore 'motivated'. This principle is based on phonology; motivated alternates are those which are in accord with a phonological principle of the language (sonority in the case of mobile vowels).

Principle 5
Within unmotivated segmental stem alternations we distinguish two broad classes of alternations, those affecting the segment of the stem adjacent to the inflection and others:

non-adjacent segment alternation > adjacent segment alternation

Example: *č'ort ~ č'ert'-i* 'devil' > *sosed ~ sosed'-i* 'neighbor'

In the first example, the alternation concerns the vowels /o/ and /e/, appearing within the form, and not at the edge. Note that this example also has alternation of the stem final segment /t/ and /t'/. This ranking is expressed by treating examples such as *č'ort*, which show ablaut, along with stems which have an augment *x* in the singular and an augment *y* in the plural (see Principle 6). The justification for Principle 5 is that the adjacent stem segment is more easily associated with the inflection than is the non-adjacent stem segment.

Principle 6
Finally, we impose a ranking on the various kinds of augmentation. The several possible outcomes outlined in Section 3.2 are ranked with respect to one another as follows:

augment *x* opposing augment *y* >
   augment in singular opposing lack of an augment in plural >
   augment in plural opposing lack of augment in singular

Example:
kot'onok ~ kot'at-a 'kitten' > *tatar'in ~ tatar-i* 'Tatar' > *brat ~ brat'j-a* 'brother'

Principle 6 could be interpreted in terms of classical notions of markedness (Jakobson 1932). The principles outlined above yield the ranking in (7).[11]

(7) Irregularity ranking[12]
    suppletion irregularity>
      pluralia tantum irregularity>
        stem augments irregularity>
          segmental stem irregularity >
            stress stem irregularity >
              segmental inflectional irregularity >
                stress inflectional irregularity >
                  full regularity

4.3 Natural Morphology and the ranking of irregularity

It should be mentioned that a number of the principles we propose bear some resemblance to those developed independently (and for an entirely different purpose) within the Natural Morphology theory. Indeed, the notion of a scale to express the nature of word structure can be found in Dressler's (1985: 59) scale of 'phonological naturalness'. Here (morpho)phonological rules are distributed on a scale depending on how closely they match a universal set of phonological processes.[13] Moreover there are a number of naturalness principles which have an affinity with our structural principles of irregularity. In other words, to some extent Natural Morphology views structural distance from the norm in terms of naturalness. For us, greater structural distance corresponds to greater irregularity; for Natural Morphology it corresponds to greater unnaturalness. Perhaps the most important principle is that of Morphotactic Transparency, i.e., the less one disturbs the perceptual segmentation of stem and ending, the more transparent the item is (Dressler 1985: 316; 1987: 102–10). The hierarchy is given in (8) with least transparent first.

(8) Morphotactic Transparency
    total suppletion >
      partial suppletion >
        modification by MPRs >
          modification by MPRs (morph. boundary intact) >
            modification by PRs (allophonic) >
              no modification

Another principle found in the Natural Morphology literature is that of System Congruity (Wurzel 1987: 65–6; 1989) which states that it is more natural for a given item to follow generalizations in the morphological system than not to do so. Once inflectional classes have been established, the expectation is that nouns will not deviate from the pattern. Closely connected to this principle is the idea of 'implicative paradigm structure conditions' (Wurzel 1987: 76–7). The example

Wurzel gives is that if in Russian a noun in the nominative singular ends in /a/, its genitive singular will end in /i/. Finally, the Principle of Constructional Iconicity states that 'what is more semantically ought to be constructionally more as well' (Mayerthaler 1987: 25–8). For example, SINGULAR is formally unmarked and 'non-featured', and -SINGULAR is formally marked and therefore 'featured'. For further discussion of Naturalness Principles, see Wheeler (1993).

5. Discussion of results

Our results prove interesting. We find relations between frequency and irregularity and a certain degree of correspondence with the irregularity ranking we outlined in Section 4. We also find evidence for a split between prosodic and non-prosodic morphology. Finally we find one intriguing area related to particular cells, where it appears that there might be a relationship between *cell anomaly* and irregularity of the nominative plural. In fact, this turns out to be *plural anomaly* in disguise.

5.1 Absolute plural anomaly

The first of our hypotheses, Hypothesis 1a, is confirmed. There is a relation between *absolute plural anomaly* and irregularity. Below we give eight groups of nouns from the corpus divided up according to our irregularity ranking in (7). In addition, we make a distinction between two stress patterns which divide the singular and plural and would both, therefore, share the same irregularity ranking. These patterns are, according to the classification in Zaliznjak (1977): pattern C (stem stress throughout

Table 4. *Absolute plural anomaly in eight groups of nouns*

	Type of irregularity	Stress pattern	Median plural count	Observed number of types	p-value[14]
Group 1	end stress pl	C	9	64	< 0.001
Group 2	end stress sg	D	5	80	< 0.05
Group 3	stem stress alternation	n/a	22	2	0.25
Group 4	stem alternation	n/a	96	3	< 0.001
Group 5	stem augment in pl	n/a	10	24	< 0.001
Group 6	stem augment in sg	n/a	15	10	< 0.05
Group 7	stem augment in both	n/a	14	14	< 0.05
Group 8	suppletion	n/a	935.5	3	< 0.001

singular, ending stress throughout plural); pattern D (ending stress throughout singular, stem stress throughout plural). The eight groups are given in Table 4.

For each of the groups in Table 4 the median value for plural occurrences is significantly higher than for the corpus as a whole, with the single exception of Group 3 (see p-values in the table).

If we were to rank each group in increasing order according to the median value, we would get the following: Group 2, Group 1, Group 5, Group 7, Group 6, Group 3, Group 4, Group 8. The data do not support irrefutably such an ordering because, despite the fact that the *anomalies* for seven of the groups are significant, the differences between the groups are in some cases insignificant. This also means that the ordering in (7) has not been disproved: the data here could still be consistent with the principled ordering of the Irregularity Ranking, which is an interesting result. Groups 3 and 4 have small sample sizes which means their place in the ordering suggested by Table 4 should be treated with some scepticism.

What is conclusively shown from our investigation is that both singular augments and plural augments are related to *absolute plural anomaly*. This is significant. While we might argue that singular augments mark the unexpected number with *plural anomaly*, this cannot be the case with plural augments, which mark what is the expected number. In other words, it appears that having an augment throughout a particular number (irrespective of whether it is singular or plural) is related to a lexeme having a high *plural anomaly*. We might have expected an augment in the plural to be associated with higher occurrence of singulars than the average for the corpus. The opposite is the case. In sum there is a relationship between frequency and irregularity in absolute terms, but we must now test our Hypothesis 1b in order to see if this is true in relative terms.

5.2 Relative plural anomaly

Groups 1–8 were tested for the next of our hypotheses. Evidence for Hypothesis 1b turns out to be not as strong as that for Hypothesis 1a. It involves groups of a specific type. We find evidence for Hypothesis 1b for two groups and, arguably, for a third. The stronger evidence is for group 6 (where there is a stem augment in the singular), and group 5 (where there is a stem augment in the plural). The weaker evidence is for group 4 (where there is a stem alternation). In each case the irregularity is segmental rather than prosodic. The results are given in Table 5.

As the data in Table 5 show, there is some evidence that the frequency of occurrence of the irregular forms, and not just frequency of occurrence of the lexeme as a whole *does* relate to irregularity of the forms in question. However, if the irregularity affecting an entire subparadigm is a prosodic one, there is no evidence for a relationship between this irregularity and high relative frequency. In the box plot in

Table 5. *Relative plural anomaly*

Group	Type of irregularity	Median plural proportion	p-value
1	end stress pl	0.2	0.1
2	end stress sg	0.15	0.54
3	stem stress alternation	0.18	0.54
4	stem alternation	0.68	0.06
5	stem augment in pl	0.36	0.03
6	stem augment in sg	0.82	< 0.001
7	stem augment in both	0.32	0.4
8	suppletion	0.62	0.16

Figure 2 the prosodic groups (Groups 1, 2, and 3) have much lower medians than the others.[15]

The median is represented by the white line in the middle of the box; the box itself represents a range of proportions covering the middle 50% of the lexemes in

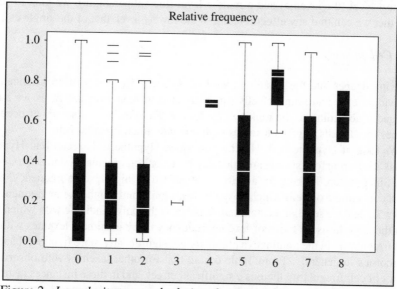

Figure 2. *Irregularity type and relative plural anomaly.*
Key: y axis = proportion of plurals, x axis = irregularity type: 0 = regular,
1 = stress C, 2 = stress D, 3 = stem stress alternation , 4 = stem segment
alternation, 5 = stem augment in plural, 6 = stem augment in singular,
7 = different stem augment in singular and plural, 8 = suppletion

the category; the whiskers cover the remaining 50%, except outliers which are indicated separately with horizontal bars (Daley *et al.* 1995). It is an extremely interesting and important result to find the answer to the question we posed at the beginning of this paper is that *relative frequency* of occurrence in the plural appears to be important where non-prosodic irregularity is concerned, but not where prosodic irregularity is concerned. Thus degree of irregularity is important.

Prosodic irregularities involve a high *absolute plural anomaly* but no *relative plural anomaly*. This means that there is a high number of plurals (*absolute plural anomaly*) and also a high number of singulars to match the plurals (no *relative plural anomaly*). Thus the prosodic irregularity may relate to the frequency of occurrence of the lexeme as a whole (the lexeme's plural must be frequent to give the *absolute anomaly*, and its singular must also be frequent, otherwise it would show *relative plural anomaly*). In contrast, the fact that certain non-prosodic irregularities have significant *relative plural anomalies* indicates that these may be related to the frequency of occurrence of a subparadigm, namely the plural.

Hence we have identified an effect which applies to the lexeme as a whole, and one which applies to the plural subparadigm. Having found effects applying to the highest level (the lexeme) and a middle level (the subparadigm), we look to see whether we can find any effect relating to the lowest level, that of the single cell.

5.3 Cell anomaly

Delving deeper into the paradigm, we look to see if frequency of occurrence of individual case and number cells can be related to their irregularity, as we had gauged it according to the ranking. We look at the *absolute frequency* of occurrences for all cells of given lexemes with one individual irregular cell.[16]

We look at Hypothesis 2. Having confirmed Hypothesis 1, recall that Hypothesis 2 is testing for a stronger relationship based on cell irregularity and *cell anomaly*. Since we are looking for an effect not caused by high lexeme frequency, we must concentrate on cells which do not have a significantly high lexeme frequency. From Table 6 we see that the nominative plural is the only candidate with which to test the hypothesis: in terms of lexeme frequency those inanimate lexemes with a cell irregularity in the nominative plural are not significantly more frequent than in the corpus in general.[17] From Table 6 note that for other lexemes with observed forms of cell irregularity there is a significant effect, and in these instances instead of *cell anomaly* we may be seeing lexeme frequency in disguise. We therefore concentrate on the nominative plural *cell anomaly* as a good candidate to test Hypothesis 2.

In order to compare like with like, we test for *cell anomaly* in the nominative plural of inanimates only. There are two tests. For the first test we find that in the

Table 6. *Cell irregularity and lexeme frequency*

Irregular cell	Median Lexeme Frequency	p-values
Accusative singular	838	< 0.001
Instrumental singular	158	< 0.01
Nominative plural (animates)	15	0.477
Nominative plural (inanimates)	14	0.34
Genitive plural	50	< 0.05
Instrumental plural	2,771	< 0.01

nominative plural cell there is a significantly higher (p < 0.01) proportion of instances of that cell in those lexemes with the cell irregularity. We then need to test if this is due to *relative plural anomaly*. In fact, the increase in the proportion of the nominative plural cell can be explained by the increase in the total plural proportion for those lexemes which have the irregularity. There is no evidence (p = 0.5) for an increase in the cell frequency as a proportion of the plural frequency.[18] In sum, this means that having an odd nominative plural cell seems to be connected with having proportionally more plurals than expected. In other words, we are not observing a *cell anomaly*. Thus we found little evidence confirming Hypothesis 2.

As was expected, Hypothesis 3 is disconfirmed: there is a relationship between irregularity and the *absolute frequency* of the cell which is irregular. See Table 7.

Table 7. *Irregularity and absolute frequency of cell*

Irregular cell	Median cell frequency	p-value
Accusative singular	172	< 0.001
Instrumental singular	16	< 0.01
Nominative plural	2	< 0.01
Genitive plural	2	< 0.05
Instrumental plural	99	< 0.001

Given that Hypothesis 1a is true, our result for Hypothesis 3 is not surprising. The relationship simply falls out from the relationship specified in Hypothesis 1. It was formulated to cover for the case where Hypothesis 1a was disproved.

6. Conclusions

Our Hypothesis 1a, that there is a relation between *absolute plural anomaly* and irregularity, is strongly confirmed. More specifically, nouns which have an irregularity involving a split between singular and plural will tend to be nouns which occur frequently in the plural. There is a less dramatic but still significant effect when only stress is involved. The only instance where we did not find a significant effect was where there was a stress alternation involving the stem only. Apart from that, there are some indications of a relation between the degree of irregularity, as postulated in advance independently of frequency, and the degree of *plural anomaly*, with cases of suppletion being an extreme case.

Hypothesis 1b, that there is a relation between *relative plural anomaly* and irregularity was less strongly confirmed. Recall that here we are concerned with the plural forms of a lexeme as a proportion of all occurrences of the lexeme. For those types where we did observe an effect, where the plural was used in proportion to the singular significantly more frequently than found generally through the corpus, the irregularity was always a segmental one—stress irregularity was not sufficient to produce an effect here. Furthermore whether the irregularity concerns the singular or the plural, we still find a high relative plural frequency (for instance nouns with an augment in the singular still have a high plural *relative frequency*).

When we moved down to examine single cells (Hypothesis 2), we found no evidence that irregularity is related to a high *relative frequency* of a specific cell in the paradigm, once the effects discussed under Hypothesis 1a and 1b are factored out. This is an interesting result, since it implies a structuring of lexical items. It suggests that an individual irregular cell does not stand out from its subparadigm (singular or plural) in terms of frequency. (Hypothesis 3 was included to cover outcomes which did not arise and so needs no further discussion here.)

There are three morphological levels which might be relevant for frequency effects. The first is the level of the lexeme as a whole; the second is the level of the subparadigm of the lexeme; and the third is the level of the individual cell. We found no evidence for an effect relating to the third of these levels. We did find evidence for a relation with the other two. This relation may be sensitive to the type of the irregularity. For the relation with the first level, the lexeme as whole, the clearer evidence comes from prosodic irregularities (as we argued in Section 4.2). For the second of these levels, the number subparadigm, there is evidence from nonprosodic types of irregularity (Figure 2). This shows the importance of looking at languages such as Russian with extensive paradigms. In languages where there is just a singular/plural split, with no other category distinction, we could not separate sub-paradigm from individual cell. Given this we see that the relation between irregularity and high frequency is more intricate than we imagined once we pull apart the notion of irregularity on the one hand, in term of a ranking of irregularity, and frequency on the other, in terms of a distinction between *absolute* and *relative frequency*. The conclusion we draw is that there is a relationship, but the relationship is a complex one which depends on the type of frequency concerned and the degree of irregularity in question.

Appendix 1: Statistics methodology

Testing differences between median values.
In order to test the differences between the median values of two groups, bootstrap testing was used, see Efron and Tibshirani (1993).

Let us suppose that a subset of lexemes S has been extracted from the corpus C according to some linguistic criterion, usually based on regularity. We calculate the median frequency of the distribution of the required frequency. Let us denote this to be m(S) in the subset S and m(C) in the full corpus, C. We need to see if m(S) is significantly different from m(C) assuming the Null Hypothesis that there is no relationship between the extraction criterion (irregularity) and the measure quantity (frequency).

Under this assumption we can evaluate the distribution of m(S) by randomly selecting (with replacement) samples of equal size to S from C, and calculating their median. This procedure is repeated many times and an estimate of the underlying distribution of the median is constructed. This will be the bootstrap distribution of the median under the assumed hypothesis. The actual value of m(S) can then be compared to this bootstrapped distribution to see if it is significantly higher or lower than expected. A p-value can then be directly calculated from the bootstrap distribution. For details of this procedure see Efron and Tibshirani (1993: Ch. 13).

Appendix 2: The Irregularity Scale with examples

The table gives a small number of examples with their irregularity scores.

0	komnata	fully regular
0.1	sad	singular-plural stress difference
0.2	polosá	stress different in one form
0.3	volk	singular-plural stress difference and irregular nominative plural form
0.4	borodá	stress differs in two forms
1.0		
1.1	lič'iko	different inflection (segmental) singular versus plural
1.11	glaz	different inflection (segmental) singular versus plural; and inflectional stress difference singular versus plural

1.2	soldat	irregular inflection (segmental) in one cell (genitive plural)
1.21	dom	irregular inflectional form in one cell (nominative plural); and inflectional stress difference singular versus plural
2.0		
2.1	óz'oro	different stem stress singular versus plural
3.0		
3.1	otec	motivated stem alternation in expected cell
3.201	koleno	unmotivated stem alternation in singular versus plural; different inflection in singular versus plural
3.4	pesn'a	motivated stem alternation in expected cell; plus unmotivated stem alternation in one cell (genitive plural)
4.0		
4.1		
4.10001	nebo	stem augment in plural only; singular versus plural inflectional stress difference
4.2		
4.2004	krestjan'in	stem augment in singular and not plural; irregular inflectional form in two cells (nominative plural and accusative/genitive plural)
4.3001	xoz'ajin	stem augment both in singular and plural; different inflection singular versus plural
4.40002	doč'	stem augment throughout except for one cell (nominative/accusative singular); inflectional stress irregularity in one cell (nominative plural)
5.0		
5.1	vorota	plurale tantum
6.0		
6.1		
6.100002	č'elovek	suppletion singular vs plural; segmental inflectional irregularity in one cell (instrumental plural)
6.2	god	suppletion in one cell (genitive plural)

Notes

* This is a joint paper: Hippisley contributed the lion's share of the corpus work, Marriott is responsible for the statistical analysis, and other aspects were shared. Corbett and Brown are from the Department of Linguistic and International Studies, and Hippisley from the Department of Computing, University of Surrey; Marriott is from the Department of Statistics and Applied Probability at the National University of Singapore. The research reported here was supported by the ESRC (grant no. R000222419, and in part grant no. R000237845); we are grateful for this support. A grant from the University of Surrey Research Promotion Initiative is also gratefully acknowledged. Sections of this research were presented at the ESRC seminar series Challenges for Inflectional Description, University of Surrey, June 24, 1998 and at the Linguistics Association of Great Britain, University of Manchester, April 8–10, 1999. We are grateful to those present there and at the conference 'Frequency effects and emergent grammar' for lively discussion. We would like to thank Alan Timberlake for his valuable input to discussions about ranking of irregularity, Harald Clahsen and Andrew Spencer for bringing useful references to our attention, and Maria Polinsky for sharing her judgements on certain Russian forms. Finally we wish to thank Joan Bybee, Paul Hopper, and Catie Berkenfield for their helpful comments.

1. Using Schreuder and Baayen's terms, do we base the frequency on the 'stem-frequency', i.e., the sum of all word forms, or the 'surface frequency', i.e., the sum of one of the word forms (1997)? They were looking at the effect of subjective frequency and visual perception times, and for them it was important to distinguish a number of different counts: 'surface frequency', 'stem frequency', 'morphological family size' (the number of members of a derivational family), and 'cumulative family frequency' (the stem frequency of all members of the derivational family apart from the base). In their work on derivation, they found that this last frequency had surprisingly no effect, whereas morphological family size did.

2. Russian orthography closely follows phonemic representation and the phonemic transcription we use is, therefore, close to standard transliteration, with a few minor points of difference (based on Corbett and Fraser 1993:fn. 2). For an outline of Russian phonology, see Timberlake (1993: 828–32). The main points are summarized as follows:

Consonants
The set of paired palatalized (soft) and unpalatalized (hard) consonants are distinguished by an acute (') which marks the soft member of the pair. For example, in the minimal pair *l'uk* 'hatchway', and *luk* 'onion' the first form has the soft /l'/. Note that consonants are always soft before the phoneme /e/, hence there is no need to mark them with an acute in this context. For example, the locative singular of *zakón* 'law' is represented as *zakóne* since the stem final /n/ is automatically soft.
    The velars /g/, /k/, and /x/ are hard except when preceding the /i/ and /e/ phonemes; in these contexts they are automatically softened. We therefore do not use an acute on the velars in these contexts since they are automatically softened. Compare the nominative singular form *ruč'ka* 'handle' with the genitive singular *ruč'ki*, where the /k/ is soft before the -*i* ending, but not indicated as such. Note that unpaired soft /č'/ and /šč'/ are redundantly marked with an acute when preceding a vowel, but unpaired soft /j/ is never marked with an acute.

Vowels
We recognize five vowel phonemes (under stress) which are /a/, /e/, /i/, /o/, and /u/. The phoneme /i/, standardly transliterated as '*i*', has an allophone [ɨ], standardly transliterated as '*y*'. The allophone [ɨ] is automatically used when following a hard consonant. The correct version of /i/ will therefore be implied by the nature of the preceding consonant.

3. Absolute singular and relative singular *anomaly* are defined analogously.

4. In this instance and throughout the paper we use the word "significant" to mean statistically significant.

5. The basic dataset is available on the world wide web and can be found at http://surrey.ac.uk/LIS/ SMG, along with a readme file.

6. This notion is akin to Wurzel's concept of "implicative paradigm structure conditions" (Wurzel 1987: 76–8).

7. For simplicity the few instances of the second genitive in -*u* and the second locative in -*ú*, available for class I nouns only, were treated with the corresponding named cases. These can be thought of as 'sub-cases' realized by a small minority of nouns in specific contexts. The second locative occurs with the locational prepositions *v* 'in' and *na* 'on', as for example in *v sneg-ú* 'in the snow'; the second genitive is used in partitive constructions such as *ja ne vip'il č'aj-u* 'I didn't drink any tea'. See the discussion in Timberlake (1983: 838) for details.

8. In these paradigms the nominative and accusative singular are also identical, but this is not so for all inflectional types in Russian (see Table 1).

9. Where stress is expected on the ending, and yet there is no ending (as in the genitive plural *mest* 'places'), the stress automatically falls on the last syllable of the stem. Since this is fully automatic we do not count it as an irregularity.

10. We use 'prosodic' to cover tone, pitch, and stress. Of these only stress is relevant for Russian.

11. It should be noted that in order to investigate a more fine grained relationship between irregularity and high frequency, the ranking in (7) was converted into a numerical scale to provide for all instances of irregularity, including combinations such as stress and inflectional irregularity. Though nothing significant emerged from the finer-grained rankings, we include the scale with examples in Appendix 2 for completeness.

12. We take suppletion, pluralia tantum, and stem augments to be irregular by definition.

13. For example one such universal process is assimilation, phonologically natural because it "eases articulatory effort by allowing inertia to prevail and smoothing transition from one segment to another" (Dressler 1985: 49). Russian word final devoicing matches this universal process perfectly, and therefore receives the score 1 for phonological naturalness (1985: 59). For full details of all scores, see Dressler (1985: 59–66).

14. The p-value represents the probability that a median value more extreme than that observed could have occurred purely by chance. A value < 0.05 is reasonable evidence that there is a relationship between *anomaly* and irregularity. A value < 0.01 is strong evidence that there is a relationship.

15. Recall that for Hypothesis 1a this does not exclude a relationship between *absolute frequency* and irregularity for these prosodic irregularities.

16. This includes lexemes for which the cell in question is the only irregularity, as well as lexemes for which the cell irregularity is accompanied by a singular-plural irregularity defined independently of that cell irregularity. For example, the lexeme *dom* 'house' has a change in stress between the singular and plural (a singular-plural irregularity). In addition, it has an unexpected nominative plural ending -*a*. This is an irregularity in a single cell which accompanies another irregularity.

17. As discussed in Section 4.1.2 we treat nominative plural and accusative plural of inanimates as one cell. This means that we must restrict our comparison to inanimates only, and exclude animates. When we use the terms 'nominative plural' for inanimates we mean the cell which includes what are, in fact, distributionally accusative plurals.

18. We have also checked the ten inanimates from this group which only have the cell irregularity. There is no significant difference between these and the inanimates as a whole with regard to *cell anomaly* (p=0.2).

References

Aronoff, M. 1994. *Morphology by Itself: Stems and Inflectional Classes*. Cambridge, MA: MIT Press.

Brown, D., Corbett, G. G., Fraser, N. M., Hippisley, A., and Timberlake, A. 1996. "Russian noun stress and Network Morphology". *Linguistics* 34(1): 53–107.

Brown, D. and Hippisley, A. 1994. "Conflict in Russian genitive plural assignment: A solution represented in DATR". *Journal of Slavic Languages* 2: 48–76.

Bybee, J. 1985. *Morphology: a Study of the Relation between Meaning and Form*. Amsterdam/Philadelphia: John Benjamins.

Bybee, J. 1995. "Regular morphology and the lexicon". *Language and Cognitive Processes* 10(5): 425–55.

Bybee, J. and Thompson, S. 1997. "Three frequency effects in syntax". *BLS*.

Comrie, B. 1986. "On delimiting cases". In *Case in Slavic*, R. D. Brecht and J. S. Levine (eds.), 86–106. Columbus, Ohio: Slavica.

Comrie, B. 1991. "Form and function in identifying cases". In *Paradigms: the Economy of Inflection*, F. Plank (ed.), (Empirical Approaches to Language Typology 9), 41–55. Berlin/New York: Mouton de Gruyter.

Corbett, G. 1982. "Gender in Russian. an account of gender specification and its relationship to declension". *Russian Linguistics* 6(2): 197–232.

Corbett, G. G. and Fraser, N. M. 1993. "Network morphology: A DATR account of Russian inflectional morphology". *Journal of Linguistics* 29: 113–42.

Daley, F., Hand, D., Jones, C., Lunn, D., and McConway, K. 1995. *Elements of Statistics*. London: Addison-Wesley.

Dressler, W. 1985. *Morphonology: the Dynamics of Derivation*. Ann Arbor: Karoma.

Dressler, W. 1987. "Word-formation as part of natural morphology". In *Leitmotifs in Natural Morphology*, W. Dressler (ed.), 99–126. Amsterdam/ Philadelphia: John Benjamins.

Efron, B. and Tibshirani, R. J. 1993. *An Introduction to the Bootstrap*. New York/London: Chapman and Hall.

226   CORBETT, HIPPISLEY, BROWN, AND MARRIOTT

Fraser, N. and Corbett, G. 1995. "Gender, animacy and declensional class assignment: a unified account for Russian". In *Yearbook of Morphology 1994*. G. Booij and J. van Marle (eds.), 123–50. Dordrecht: Kluwer.

Greenberg, J. 1966. *Language Universals, with Special Reference to Feature Hierarchies*. The Hague: Mouton.

Jakobson, R.1932. "Zur Struktur des russischen Verbums". In *Charisteria Gvilelmo Mathesio qvinqvagenario a discipulis et Circuli Lingvistici Pragensis sodalibus oblata*, 74–84. Prague: Pražký Lingvistický Kroužek. [Reprinted in Jakobson's *Selected Writings* II, 3–15]. The Hague: Mouton.]

Lönngren, L. 1993. *Častotnyj slovar' sovremennogo russkogo jazyka*. (Acta Universitatis Upsaliensis, Studia Slavica Upsaliensis 33). University of Uppsala: Uppsala.

Maier, I. 1994. "Review of Lennart Lönngren (ed.) Častotnyj slovar' sovremennogo russkogo jazyka". *Rusistika Segodnja* 1: 130–6.

Mayerthaler, W. 1987. "System-independent morphological naturalness". In *Leitmotifs in Natural Morphology*, W. Dressler (ed.), 25–58. Amsterdam/Philadelphia: John Benjamins.

Schreuder, R. and Baayen, H. 1997. "How complex simplex words can be". *Journal of Memory and Language* 37(1): 118–39.

Tiersma, P. 1982. "Local and general markedness". *Language* 58(4): 832–49.

Timberlake, A. 1993. "Russian". In *The Slavonic Languages*, B. Comrie and G. Corbett (eds.), 827–86. London/NewYork: Routledge.

Wheeler, M. W. 1993. "On the hierarchy of naturalness principles in inflectional morphology". *Journal of Linguistics* 29: 95–111.

Wurzel, W. 1987. "System-dependent morphological naturalness in inflection". In *Leitmotifs in Natural Morphology*, W. Dressler (ed.), 59–96. Amsterdam/Philadelphia: John Benjamins.

Wurzel, W. 1989. *Inflectional Morphology and Naturalness*. Dordrecht: Kluwer.

Zaliznjak, A. A. 1977. *Grammatičeskij slovar' russkogo jazyka*. Moscow: Russkij jazyk.

Data sources

1. For the Uppsala corpus, see Lönngren (1993).
2. The basic dataset referred to in note 5 is available at http://surrey.ac.uk/LIS/SMG, along with a readme file.

Part III
Phrases and constructions

Probabilistic relations between words:
Evidence from reduction in lexical production

DANIEL JURAFSKY, ALAN BELL,
MICHELLE GREGORY, and WILLIAM D. RAYMOND

University of Colorado, Boulder

1. Introduction

The ideas of frequency and predictability have played a fundamental role in models of human language processing for well over a hundred years (Schuchardt 1885; Jespersen 1923; Zipf 1929; Martinet 1960; Oldfield and Wingfield 1965; Fidelholz 1975; Jescheniak and Levelt 1994; Bybee 2000). While most psycholinguistic models have thus long included word frequency as a component, recent models have proposed more generally that probabilistic information about words, phrases, and other linguistic structure is represented in the minds of language users and plays a role in language comprehension (Bybee and Scheibman 1999; MacDonald 1993; McRae *et al.* 1998; Narayanan and Jurafsky 1998; Trueswell and Tanenhaus 1994) production (Gregory *et al.* 1999; Roland and Jurafsky to appear), and learning (Brent and Cartwright 1996; Landauer and Dumais 1997; Saffran *et al.* 1996; Seidenberg and MacDonald 1999).

In recent papers (Bell *et al.* 1999; Gregory *et al.* 1999; Jurafsky *et al.* 1998), we have been studying the role of predictability and frequency in lexical production. Our goal is to understand the many factors that affect production variability as reflected in reduction processes such as vowel reduction, durational shortening, or final segmental deletion of words in spontaneous speech. One proposal that has resulted from this work is the *Probabilistic Reduction Hypothesis*: word forms are reduced when they have a higher probability. The probability of a word is conditioned on many aspects of its context, including neighboring words, syntactic and lexical structure, semantic expectations, and discourse factors. This proposal thus generalizes over earlier models which refer only to word frequency (Zipf 1929;

Fidelholz 1975; Rhodes 1992; Rhodes 1996) or predictability (Fowler and Housum 1987).

In this paper we focus on a particular domain of probabilistic linguistic knowledge in lexical production: the role of local probabilistic relations between words. Our previous research as well as research by others (Bush 1999; Bybee and Scheibman 1999; Krug 1998) suggests that words which are strongly related to or predictable from neighboring words, such as collocations (sequences of commonly cooccurring words), are more likely to be phonologically reduced.

This paper extends our earlier studies of reduction, arguing that these probabilistic relations between words should be interpreted as evidence for emergent linguistic structure, and more specifically as evidence that probabilistic relations between words are represented in the mind of the speaker. Testing the claim requires showing that probabilistic relations are represented very generally across words. We therefore examine probabilistic relations with function words as well as with content words, with frequent words as well as with infrequent words. It is also crucial to understand the exact nature of these probabilistic effects. We thus study various probabilistic measures of a word's predictability from neighboring words, and test the effects of each on various types of reduction. Our conclusions support the Probabilistic Reduction Hypothesis; more probable words are more likely to be reduced. The results suggest that probabilistic relations between words must play a role in the mental representation of language.

Our experiments are based on two distinct datasets, each drawn from 38,000 words that were phonetically hand-transcribed from American English telephone conversations (Greenberg et al. 1996). The first dataset consists of 5,618 of the 9,000 tokens of the ten most frequent function words: I, and, the, that, a, you, to, of, it, and in. The second focuses on 2,042 of the 3,000 content word tokens whose lexical form ends in a t or d. Each observation is coded with its duration and pronunciation as well as contextual factors such as the local rate of speech, surrounding segmental context and nearby disfluencies. We use linear and logistic regression to control for contextual factors and study the extent to which various probabilistic measures of lexical predictability account for reduction of word forms, as indicated by vowel reduction, deletion of final t or d, and durational shortening. Throughout this paper we will use the term 'reduced' to refer to forms that have undergone any of these processes.

2. Measures of probabilistic relations between words

The Probabilistic Reduction Hypothesis claims that words are more reduced when they are more predictable or probable. There are many ways to measure the probability of a word. This section discusses a number of local measures that we have studied, although we will mainly report on two measures: the conditional probability of the target word given the preceding word and the conditional probability of the target word given the following word.

The simplest measure of word probability is called the *prior probability*. The prior probability of a word is the probability without considering any contextual factors ('prior' to seeing any other information). The prior probability is usually estimated by using the *relative frequency* of the word in a sufficiently large corpus. The relative frequency is the frequency of the word divided by the total number of word tokens in the corpus:

$$P(w_i) = \frac{C(w_i)}{\sum_j C(w_j)} = \frac{C(w_i)}{N} \tag{1}$$

The relative frequency is thus a normalized version of word frequency similar to information in frequency dictionaries such as Francis and Kučera (1982). Throughout the paper we use the term *relative frequency* rather than prior probability, although the reader should keep in mind that frequencies are estimates of the probability of a word's occurrence independent of context. We also consider the relative frequencies of the preceding and following words.

Probability can also be measured with respect to neighboring words. We use two measures (the *joint probability* and the *conditional probability*) of the predictability of a word given the previous word. The *joint probability* of two words $P(w_{i-1}w_i)$ may be thought of as the prior probability of the two words taken together, and is estimated by just looking at the relative frequency of the two words together in a corpus:

$$P(w_{i-1}w_i) = \frac{C(w_{i-1}w_i)}{N} \tag{2}$$

This is a variant of what (Krug 1998) called the *string frequency* of the two words.

The *conditional probability of a word given the previous word* is also sometimes called the *transitional probability* (Bush 1999; Saffran *et al.* 1996). The conditional probability of a particular target word w_i given a previous word w_{i-1} is estimated from a sufficiently large corpus by counting the number of times the two words occur together $C(w_{i-1}w_i)$, and dividing by $C(w_{i-1})$, the number of times that the first word occurs:

$$P(w_i|w_{i-1}) = \frac{C(w_{i-1}w_i)}{C(w_{i-1})} \tag{3}$$

The difference between the conditional and joint probability is that the conditional probability controls for the frequency of the conditioning word. For example, pairs of words can have a high joint probability merely because the individual words are of high frequency (e.g., *of the*). The conditional probability would be high only if the second word was particularly likely to follow the first. Most measures of word cohesion, such as conditional probability and mutual information, are based on such metrics which control for the frequencies of one or both of the words (Manning and Schütze 1999). In addition to considering the preceding word, the effect of the following word may be measured by the two corresponding probabilities. The *joint probability of a word with the next word* $P(w_i w_{i+1})$ is estimated by the relative frequency of the two words together:

$$P(w_i w_{i+1}) = \frac{C(w_i w_{i+1})}{N} \tag{4}$$

Similarly, the *conditional probability of the target word given the next word* $P(w_i|w_{i+1})$ is the probability of the target word w_i given the next word w_{i+1}. This may be viewed as the predictability of a word given the word the speaker is about to say, and is estimated as follows:

$$P(w_i|w_{i-1}) = \frac{C(w_i w_{i+1})}{C(w_{i+1})} \tag{5}$$

Finally, we mention briefly four other measures that played a smaller role in our analyses. We considered a number of *trigram probability* measures. Two of these were the conditional probability of the target given the *two previous* words $P(w_i|w_{i-2}w_{i-1})$, and the conditional probability of the target given the *two following* words $P(w_i|w_{i+1}w_{i+2})$. Neither of these turned out to predict reduction after we controlled for the (bigram) conditional probabilities of the previous and following words. The conditional probability of the target given the *two surrounding* words is the probability of the target given one word preceding and one word following the target $P(w_i|w_{i-1} \ldots w_{i+1})$. This measure was a significant predictor in some analyses. It is estimated as follows:

$$P(w_i|w_{i-1} \ldots w_{i+1}) = \frac{C(w_{i-1} w_i w_{i+1})}{C(w_{i-1} \ldots w_{i+1})} \tag{6}$$

Table 1 contains a summary of the probabilistic measures and some examples of high probability items from the dataset for each measure. The reader can obtain some idea of the ways that these different measures of local predictability rank word combinations in Tables 6–8 in Appendix 2.

The actual computation we used for estimating these probabilities was somewhat

Table 1. *Summary of probabilistic measures and high probability examples*

Measure		Examples
Relative Frequency	$P(w_i)$	just, right
Joint of Target with Next Word	$P(w_iw_{i+1})$	**kind** of
Joint of Target with Previous	$P(w_{i-1}w_i)$	a **lot**
Conditional of Target given Previous	$P(w_i|w_{i-1})$	Supreme **Court**
Conditional of Target given Next	$P(w_i|w_{i+1})$	**United** States
Conditional of Target given Surrounding	$P(w_i|w_{i-1} \ldots w_{i+1})$	little **bit** more

more complex than the simple explanations above. Since our 38,000 word corpus was far too small to estimate word probabilities, we used the entire 2.4 million word Switchboard corpus (from which our corpus was drawn) instead. See Jurafsky *et al.* (1998) for details about the backoff and discounting methods that we used to smooth the estimates of very low frequency items. We then took the log of these probabilities for use in our regression analyses.

In this paper we report mainly the effects of conditional probabilities. In general, however, we find that most of the measures (conditional probability, joint probability, various relative frequencies of words) show some effect on reduction. Given their definitional interdependence, this is not surprising. If one wishes to pick a single measure of probability for convenience in reporting, it makes sense to pick one which combines several independent measures, such as mutual information (which combines the joint, the relative frequency of the target, and the relative frequency of the neighboring word) or conditional probability (which combines joint probability and the relative frequency of the neighboring word). We chose conditional probability because for this particular data set it was a better single measure than joint probability.

In Gregory *et al.* (1999) we considered the *mutual information* (Fano 1961) of the target word and the following word. There we showed that mutual information produces very similar results to the conditional probability of the target word given the following word. For this reason, and because mutual information turns out to be an inappropriate metric for our analyses of function words,[1] we report on conditional probability rather than mutual information in this paper.

In general, the most predictive model of any data is obtained by using a combination of (independent) measures rather than one single measure. Thus, for example, in some cases we found that a combination of conditional probability, joint probability, and relative frequency all play a role in reduction. See Appendix 1 for further discussion of the relationships between conditional probability, joint probability, and relative frequency of the previous word.

3. Effects of predictability on function words

Our first experiment studied the ten most frequent English function words in the Switchboard corpus. (These are also the ten most frequent words in the corpus.)

3.1 The function word dataset

The function word dataset was drawn from the Switchboard corpus of telephone conversations between strangers, collected in the early 1990s (Godfrey *et al.* 1992). The corpus contains 2430 conversations averaging 6 minutes each, totaling 240 hours of speech and about 3 million words spoken by over 500 speakers. The corpus was collected at Texas Instruments, mostly by soliciting paid volunteers who were connected to other volunteers via a robot telephone operator. Conversations were then transcribed by court reporters into a word-by-word text.

Approximately four hours of speech from these conversations were phonetically hand-transcribed by students at UC Berkeley (Greenberg *et al.* 1996) as follows. The speech files were automatically segmented into pseudo-utterances at turn boundaries or at silences of 500 ms or more, and a rough automatic phonetic transcription was generated. The transcribers were given these utterances along with the text and rough phonetic transcriptions. They then corrected the phonetic transcription, using an augmented version of the ARPAbet, and marked syllable boundaries, from which durations of each syllable were computed.

The phonetically-transcribed corpus contains roughly 38,000 transcribed words (tokens). The function word dataset consists of all instances of the ten most frequent English function words: *I, and, the, that, a, you, to, of, it,* and *in.* This subcorpus

Table 2. *Common pronunciations of the ten function words by vowel type*

	Full	Reduced
a	[eɪ] [ʌ],[ɪ]	[ə],[ɨ]
the	[ði],[i],[di] [ðʌ],[ðɪ],[ʌ]	[ðə],[ðɨ], [ə]
in	[ɪn],[ɪ],[ɪr̃], [ɛn],[ʌn],[æn]	[ɨn],[n̩],[ən]
of	[ʌv],[ʌ],[ʌvv] [ɪ],[i],[ɑ]	[ə],[əv],[əf]
to	[tu],[tʉ],[ɾu] [tʊ],[tɪ],[tʌ]	[tə],[tɨ],[ə]
and	[æn],[ænd],[ær̃] [ɛn],[ɪn],[ʌn]	[ɨn],[n̩],[ən]
that	[ðæ],[ðæt], [æ] [ðɛ],[ðɛt],[ðɛr]	[ðɨt], [ðɨ], [ðɨr]
I	[aɪ] [ɑ],[ʌ],[æ]	[ə]
it	[ɪ],[ɪt],[ɪr] [ʉt],[ʉ],[ʌ]	[ɨ],[ə],[ət]
you	[yu],[u],[yʉ] [yɪ],[ɪ],[i]	[yɨ],[y],[ɨ]

contained about 9,000 word tokens. Our analyses are based on the 5,618 tokens remaining after excluding various non-comparable items (see Section 3.3).

Each observation was coded for two dependent factors reflecting reduction:

- *Vowel reduction*. We coded the vowel of each function word as *full* or *reduced*. The full vowels included basic citation or clarification pronunciations, e.g. [ðɪ] for *the*, as well as other non-reduced vowels. The reduced vowels that occurred in the function words were [ə] and [ɨ].[2] Table 2 shows full and reduced-vowel pronunciations of the function words, while Figure 1 shows the relative proportions of each vowel type by function word.
- *Duration in milliseconds*. The duration of the word in milliseconds.

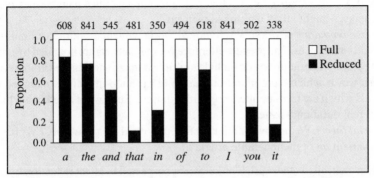

Figure 1. *Proportion of full and reduced forms for the ten function words. Total occurrences appear above.*

3.2 The Regression Analysis

We used multiple regression to evaluate the effects of our predictability factors on reduction. A regression analysis is a statistical model that predicts a *response variable* (in this case, the word duration, or the frequency of vowel reduction) based on contributions from a number of other *explanatory factors* (Agresti 1996). Thus when we report that an effect was significant, it is meant to be understood that it is a significant parameter in a model that also includes the other significant variables. In other words, after accounting for the effects of the other explanatory variables, adding the explanatory variable in question produced a significantly better account of the variation in the response variable. For duration, which is a continuous variable, we used ordinary linear regression to model the log duration of the word. For vowel quality, which is a categorical variable, we used logistic regression.

3.3 Control factors

The reduction processes are each influenced by multiple structural and performance factors that must be controlled to assess the contribution of the probability measures to reduction. We briefly review these factors here and our method of controlling for them. First, we excluded tokens of function words based on the following three factors:

- *Planning problems.* We removed function words which are immediately followed by disfluencies indicative of 'planning problems' (pauses, filled pauses *uh* and *um*, or repetitions), since they tend to have less-reduced pronunciations (Fox Tree and Clark 1997; Jurafsky *et al.* 1998; Bybee and Scheibman 1999; Shriberg 1999). We also removed words that were preceded by filled pauses since preceding pauses might affect durational patterns.
- *Phrase boundary position.* We removed words which are initial or final in our pseudo-utterances. The pseudo-utterances of our datasets are bounded by turns or long pauses, although they do include multiple intonational phrases in some cases. Thus words which were initial or final in our pseudo-utterances included most words which are turn- or utterance-initial or final. Such words are known to have different durational patterns.
- *Special forms.* We removed cliticized function words (e.g., *you've*, *I've*, *it's*) and the variant *an* of the indefinite article *a*.

We then controlled other variables known or suspected to affect reduction by entering them first in the regression model. Thus the base model for an analysis was a regression on the following set of control factors:

- *Rate of speech.* Speech researchers have long noted the association between faster speech, informal styles, and more reduced forms. For a recent quantitative account of rate effects in Switchboard, see Fosler-Lussier and Morgan (to appear). We measured rate of speech at a given function word by taking the number of syllables per second in the smallest pause-bounded region containing the word. Our regression models included both log rate and log squared rate.
- *Segmental context.* A general fact about reduction processes is that the form of a word is influenced by the segmental context—for example, consonant deletion is favored when a segment is preceded by or followed by a consonant. We controlled for the class (consonant or vowel) of the following segment.
- *Syllable type of target.* We coded the target word for syllable type (open or closed) (e.g., *it* vs. *a*). This variable interacts closely with segmental context.
- *Reduction of following vowel.* The prosodic pattern of the utterance plays a crucial role in reduction. Since our current dataset does not mark stress or accent, the only prosodic control was whether the vowel in the syllable following the

target word was reduced or full. (This partially controls for stress since the reduction of the following vowel should correlate with its stress level, and hence the stress level of the target word.)

We also included a number of terms for the interactions between these variables.

Several factors that have been reported to influence reduction were not controlled in this study. First, our definition of words was quite simplified; we assume that anything bounded by spaces in the text transcriptions was a word. Thus *Supreme Court* and *most of* were each considered two words, although we controlled for this simplification in the experiments described in Section 4. Other factors not controlled included additional aspects of the preceding segment environment (e.g., vowel identity and coda identity), prosodic structure (including position and metrical prominence) and social variables (register, age, gender, race, social class, etc.). We did control for some of these social variables in our earlier work (Bell *et al.* 1999) and still found robust effects of the predictability measures. Control of reduction of the following vowel and of pseudo-utterance position in our analyses partially controls effects of prosodic structure, stress, and accent.

The fact that the ten words in this dataset were all very frequent limited our ability to study relative frequency. (The most common word, *I*, is about 3 times more frequent than the least common word *in*, compared to an overall ratio of probability of about 100,000 to 1 for the highest and lowest frequency words in the entire corpus.) What variation there is, moreover, is inextricably confounded with the effects of form and patterns of combination of the individual items. Since it is consequently not possible to obtain useful inferences about the effects of relative frequency with the function words dataset, this variable is omitted from the analyses.

3.4 Results

3.4.1 Vowel reduction in function words

We first tested the relationship between the target word and the previous word, by adding the conditional probability of the target word given the previous word $P(w_i|w_{i-1})$ to the regression equation after a base model that included the control variables. Predictability from the previous word was a significant predictor of reduction ($p < .0001$). The higher the conditional probability of the target given the previous word, the greater the expected likelihood of vowel reduction in the function word target.

The predicted likelihood of a reduced vowel in words which were highly predictable from the preceding word (at the 95th percentile of conditional probability) was 48 percent, whereas the likelihood of a reduced vowel in low predictability words (at the 5th percentile) was 24 percent.

Reduction of the target word is also affected by its probabilistic relations with the following word. Higher conditional probabilities of the target word given the following word $P(w_i|w_{i+1})$ were again a predictor of a greater likelihood of reduction ($p = .002$).

The predicted likelihood of a reduced vowel in words which were highly predictable from the following word (at the 95th percentile of conditional probability) was 42 percent, whereas the likelihood of a reduced vowel in low predictability words (at the 5th percentile) was 35 percent. Note that the magnitude of the effect was a good deal weaker than that with the previous word.

Even after accounting for the individual effects of the conditional probability of the preceding and following words, there is a small additional significant effect of the preceding and following words together, as measured by the conditional trigram probability given the two surrounding words ($P(w_i|w_{i-1} \ldots w_{i+1})$) ($p < .02$).

3.5 Function word duration

We found similar effects of predictability on function word duration. The conditional probability of the target word given the previous word $P(w_i|w_{i-1})$ was a significant predictor of durational shortening ($p < .0001$). The higher the conditional probability of the target given the previous word, the shorter the target word. High conditional probability tokens (at the 95th percentile of the conditional probability) have a predicted duration of 92 ms; low conditional probability tokens (at the 5th percentile) have a predicted duration of 118 ms.

A similar effect on shortening was found for the relationship of the target word with the following word. The conditional probability of the target word given the following word $P(w_i|w_{i+1})$ was again a strong predictor of shortening; the higher the probability of the target word given the following word, the shorter the target was ($p < .0001$). Tokens which were highly probable given the following word (at the 95th percentile of the conditional probability) have a predicted duration of 99 ms; tokens with low probability given the following (at the 5th percentile) have a predicted duration of 123 ms.

As with vowel reduction, there is a small additional significant effect of the preceding and following words together, as measured by the conditional probability given the two surrounding words ($p < .0001$).

3.6 Independence of duration and vowel reduction

The fact that the vowels in function words are reduced when the words are more predictable could be modeled as a categorical, non-gradient effect. That is, based on predictability, speakers could be making some sort of categorical choice in lexical production between two possible vowels, one full and one reduced. But the results on durational shortening cannot be modeled categorically. The effect of predictability on shortening is a gradient, non-categorical one.

It is possible, however, that the shortening effects that we observe for function words might be solely a consequence of the vowel reduction effects, since reduced vowels are indeed durationally shorter than full vowels. If shortening was only a consequence of vowel selection, there might be no evidence for a gradient effect of probability on reduction. In order to test whether the effects of probability on shortening were completely due to vowel reduction, we added a variable to the base model for duration that coded whether the function word's vowel was reduced or full.

We found that all the probabilistic variables remain robustly significant predictors of duration, even after controlling for vowel reduction. That is, predictability not only affects vowel reduction, but has an additional independent non-categorical effect on word duration.

As further confirmation, we looked at the full and reduced vowels separately to see whether the shortening effects occurred in words with full vowels as well as words with reduced vowels. Indeed, higher probability predicted durational shortening both in the words with full vowels and words with reduced vowels. For words with full vowels and words with reduced vowels, those that had higher conditional probabilities (given either the previous or following word) were significantly shorter than those with lower conditional probabilities ($p = .0001$).

These results confirm that there is an effect of predictability on reduction that is continuous and not purely categorical, suggesting that the domain of applicability of the Probabilistic Reduction Hypothesis includes linguistic levels that allow continuous phenomena.[3]

3.7 The function word dataset: discussion

The results for the function word dataset show that function words that are more predictable are shorter and more likely to have reduced vowels, supporting the Probabilistic Reduction Hypothesis. The conditional probability of the target word given the preceding word and given the following one both play a role, on both duration and deletion. The magnitudes of the duration effects are fairly substantial, in the order of 20 ms or more, or about 20 percent, over the range of the conditional probabilities (excluding the highest and lowest five percent of the items).

The fact that there are effects of predictability on duration in addition to the effects on vowel reduction, and that they affect both full and reduced vowels, suggests that some of the effects of predictability on reduction are continuous and non-categorical. Under one possible model of these effects, the categorical vowel reduction effects could be the result of lexicalization or grammaticalization leading to segmental changes in the lexicon or grammar, while the continuous duration effects are on-line effects, perhaps mediated in part by prosodic structure, but not represented in lexicalized differences. Our results do not allow us to make any conclusions about such a possible model. Indeed, while our results, like many results on variation phenomena, could arise from two qualitatively different processes, one applying more generally across items and processes and one the result of lexicalizations and grammaticalizations, these need not map cleanly into categorical and non-categorical reductions. At least some vowel reduction may be gradient, and it is conceivable that some of the duration effects demonstrated above could arise from lexicalization. Thus the actual delineation of a model of the effects of predictability on reduction remains to be done.

4. Lexical versus collocation effects

So far we have shown that the conditional probability of a function word given the surrounding words is a significant predictor of reduced vowels and shorter durations. Shortening effects seem to provide strong evidence that probabilistic links between words are represented in the mind of the speaker.

But an examination of the high probability word pairs in Tables 6–8 (Appendix 2) raises a potential problem. Many of these pairs (like *sort of* or *kind of*) might be single lexical items rather than word pairs (*sorta, kinda*). This classification as high-probability word pairs would then stem from the fact that we rely on a purely orthographic definition of a word (i.e., words are separated by white space). Perhaps our results concerning the effect of predictability on reduction are merely facts about such recently emergent words like *sorta*, and not facts about probabilistic relations between words that are accessed separately. That is, perhaps our results are purely lexical rather than syntactic (e.g., word-order) facts about reduction.

In order to test this hypothesis, it is necessary to show that higher predictability is associated with increased reduction even in word combinations that are not lexicalized. Based on the intuitions that many pairs of words with high conditional probability may be lexicalized (see the top half of Tables 7 or 8) and word pairs with low conditional probabilities are likely not (see the bottom half of Tables 7 or 8), we split the function word observations into two groups of high and low conditional probabilities. Table 3 shows the ten sequences with the highest conditional probabilities from the **lower** half of the range. Looking at these tables, these words are less likely to be lexically combined with their neighbors, and yet their duration is still affected by both the conditional probability given the preceding and the conditional probability given the following word. The higher the probability of the word given its neighbor, the shorter the word.

Table 3. *The ten most probable function word sequences in context from the lower half of the probability range, according to two probability measures. Function words in this lower range did show effects of durational shortening due to higher probability.*

Conditional probability given previous word $P(w_i|w_{i-1})$	Conditional probability given next word $P(w_i|w_{i+1})$
Top ten of lower half	Top ten of lower half
them **and**	**a** chocolate
sometime **in**	**a** law
differences **of**	**a** crime
bet **that**	**the** old
homes **that**	**the** gun
does **that**	**you** must
where **the**	**the** Mastercard
been **a**	(oil) **and** filter
with **a**	**the** north
fine **and**	**I** do

For each of these groups, we tested the effects of conditional probability given the previous word on both vowel reduction and durational shortening. Each test was then repeated for the conditional probability given the following word. Since lexicalized sequences of words should have high conditional probabilities, if the effects we find are limited to lexicalizations, we should find that our effects only hold for the upper halves of the conditional probabilities.

Considering first the effects of the preceding word, we found that there was no significant effect of conditional probability on vowel reduction in the low group, but there was a significant effect of conditional probability in the high group. These results lend some support for the influence of lexicalization. For duration, however, conditional probability of the preceding word had a significant effect for both groups, although it did appear to be somewhat stronger for the high group.

The results for following word effects did not support the lexicalization hypothesis. Conditional probability of the following word was just as good a predictor of vowel reduction in the low probability group as in the high probability group.

We were surprised to find that the duration of tokens in the high group was *not* affected by conditional probability given the following word, even though durations in the low group were shorter for higher conditional probabilities. This suggests that there may be a ceiling that limits its effect on duration.

While these results are preliminary, and invite further analysis, they suggest two conclusions. First, more predictable words are more reduced even if they are in a low probability group and unlikely to be lexically combined with a neighboring word. Thus we find clear evidence for probabilistic relations between words. Second, particularly for the predictability from the previous word, the high group shows a stronger effect of predictability on reduction. This suggests that there is some reduction in duration may be due to the lexicalization of word pairs.

5. Effects of predictability on final-t/d content words

Our previous results show that function words which are very predictable from neighboring words (i.e., have high conditional probability given the previous or following word) are more reduced. Even though these results show that probabilistic relations hold over the full range of predictabilities for function words, it is possible that they would not hold for content words. This might be true, for example, if function words are more likely to cliticize, lexicalize, or collocate with neighboring words than content words, or if probabilistic relations between words were to only apply at the higher ranges of predictability that are more typical of function words. Because content words have a much wider range of frequencies than function words, they also allow us to investigate the role of target word frequency. We therefore turn to content words to see if they are also reduced when they are more probable.

5.1 The final-t/d content word dataset

The final-t/d content word dataset is again drawn from the 38,000 word phonetic-ally-transcribed Switchboard database. (See 3.1 for details.) The database contained about 3,000 content words ending in t or d. Eliminating observations to control for factors discussed below left 2,042 word tokens in our analyses. Table 4 shows some common examples, together with frequencies per million words from the entire 2.4 million word Switchboard corpus.

Each observation was coded for two dependent reduction factors:[4]

- *Deletion of final consonant.* Final t-d deletion is defined as the absence of a pronounced oral stop segment corresponding to a final t or d in words. A final t or d was coded as deleted if in the Greenberg *et al.* (1996) transcription the t or d was not transcribed as phonetically realized. For example, the phrase 'but the' was often pronounced [bəðə] in the dataset, with no segment corresponding to the t in *but.* Table 5 shows examples of full and t/d-deleted forms.
- *Duration in milliseconds.* The hand-coded duration of the word in milliseconds.

Table 4. *The 30 most frequent words in the final-t/d dataset, with counts from the 2.4 million word Switchboard corpus, but renormalized (divided by 2.4) to be counts-per-million*

Word	Frequency	Word	Frequency	Word	Frequency
want	12,836	last	887	read	604
just	8,781	bit	863	part	585
lot	3,685	first	834	fact	585
good	3,225	thought	826	heard	523
kind	3,103	need	826	made	521
put	1,226	sort	823	start	484
said	1,190	old	818	least	461
went	1,153	great	793	point	460
used	941	bad	669	state	452
most	899	quite	628	let	442

Table 5. *Examples of full (including tapped) and reduced (i.e., deletion of final t or d) forms from the final-t/d dataset*

Word	Full and Tapped Forms	Forms with Deleted t or d
mind	[maɪnd]	[maɪn], [maɪ]
about	[əbʌd],[baʊt]	[bæ]
made	[maɪd], [meɪɾ]	[meɪ]
most	[moʊst], [moʊt]	[moʊs] [m]
lot	[lɑt], [lɑɾ]	[lɑ]

5.2 Control Factors

As with the function word analyses, we excluded tokens of words which occurred in disfluent contexts, or initially or finally in pseudo-utterances. We also excluded polysyllabic words from the duration analyses to make the items more comparable.

Other factors were controlled by including them in the regression model before considering the predictability factors. They included variables already discussed—rate of speech, rate of speech squared, whether the next vowel was reduced or not, following segment type (consonant or vowel), and whether the word coda included a consonant cluster.

The base model also included the following additional factors:

• *Inflectional status.* Fasold (1972), Labov (1972), Bybee (2000) and others noted

that a final t or d which functions as a past tense morpheme (e.g., *missed* or *kept*) is less likely to be deleted than a t or d which is not (e.g. *mist*).
• *Identity of the underlying segment.* We coded the identity of the underlying final segment (t or d).
• *Number of syllables.* The number of syllables in the word is of course correlated with both word frequency and word duration (for the deletion analysis only, since the duration analysis was limited to monosyllabic words).

5.3 Results

Using multiple regression, the predictability measures were tested on the two shortening variables of deletion and duration by adding them to each of the regression models after the base model. Recall that in the function word experiment we did not include the relative frequency of the target word as a factor. For the content words, however, this factor was included. Note that while targets are content words, preceding and following words may be function words.

5.4 Duration

The duration analysis was performed on 1,412 tokens of the final-t/d content words. We found a strong effect of the relative frequency of the target word ($p < .0001$). Overall, high frequency words (at the 95th percentile of frequency) were 18% shorter than low frequency words (at the 5th percentile).

The conditional probability of the target given the next word significantly affected duration: more predictable words were shorter ($p < .0001$). Words with high conditional probability (at the 95th percentile of the conditional probability given the next word) were 12% shorter than low conditional probability words (at the 5th percentile).

Both the conditional probability of the target given the previous word ($p = .0009$) and the joint probability of the target with the previous word ($p = .046$) significantly affected duration. This instance is complicated in that no one factor adequately represents the effects on duration.

5.5 Deletion

The deletion analysis was performed on 2,042 tokens of t/d-final content words. Again, we found a strong effect of relative frequency ($p < .0001$). High frequency words (at the 95th percentile) were 2.0 times more likely to have deleted final t or d than the lowest frequency words (at the 5th percentile).

The conditional probability of the target given the previous word did not significantly affect deletion. The only previous word variable that affected deletion in target words was the relative frequency of the previous word. More frequent previous words lead to less deletion in the target word ($p = .007$).

We had found in earlier work (Gregory *et al.* 1999) that deletion was not sensitive to predictability effects from the following word. This result was confirmed in our current results. Neither the conditional probability of the target word given the next word nor the relative frequency of the next word predicted deletion of final t or d.

5.6 Final-t/d content word dataset: discussion

Content words with higher relative frequencies (prior probabilities) are shorter and are more likely to have deleted final t or d than content words with lower relative frequencies. As is the case with all of our results, this is true even after controlling for rate of speech, number of syllables, and other factors. The effect of target word frequency was the strongest overall factor affecting reduction of content words, and provides support for the Probabilistic Reduction Hypothesis.

In addition to the effect of relative frequency, we also found an effect of conditional probability. Content words which have a higher conditional probability given the following word are shorter, although not more likely to undergo final segment deletion.

Overall, however, the effects of conditional probability on reduction are much weaker in content words than in function words. Conditional probabilities of the targets given either the following or the previous word had no effect on deletion. Failure to find effects may be due to the smaller number of observations in the content word dataset or the general lower frequencies of content words.

The only effect on deletion was an effect of previous-word relative frequency. High-frequency previous words led to *longer* target forms and *less* final-t/d deletion. Unlike the effects of joint and conditional probabilities which plausibly represent the predictability of the target word, the effect of previous (or following) word frequency has no immediate interpretation. We are currently investigating two possible explanations for the role of previous-word frequency. One possibility is based on the fact that the previous-word frequency is in the denominator of the equation defining the conditional probability of the word given the previous word (Equation 3; see also Appendix 1). Perhaps the effect of previous word frequency is really a consequence of conditional probability, but the size of our content-word dataset is too small to see the effects of the numerator of Equation 3. This could be due to the fact that the counts for any two-word combinations are lower than the counts for single words.

Another possibility is that the lengthening of content words after frequent previous words is a prosodic effect. For example, if the previous word is frequent, it is less likely to be stressed or accented, which might raise the probability that the current word is stressed or accented, and hence that it is less likely to be reduced.

Prosodic effects might also explain the asymmetric effect of surrounding words (i.e. preceding words played little role in final deletion). This likely illustrates that not all reduction processes are affected in the same way by probabilistic variables. (Gregory *et al.* (1999), for example, found a different pattern for tapping of final t and d.) The asymmetry of this particular case is perhaps understandable from the fact that final deletion is a word edge effect, in the terminology of the phonological of prosodic domains. It would be worth investigating whether such edge processes are systematically less sensitive to the probability conditioning effects of material across the prosodic boundary they mark.

6. Conclusion

The fundamental result of these analyses is that we find evidence for the Probabilistic Reduction Hypothesis. In general, more probable words are reduced, whether they are content or function words. Predictability from neighboring words played a strong role in the high-frequency function words. The content words exhibited weaker effects of surrounding context, but strong effects of relative frequency. Thus all of our measures of local predictability play a role in at least some reduction processes, and all the reduction processes are influenced by some predictability measures. By showing that probabilistic factors influence lexical production, our results also provide general support for probabilistic models of human language processing (Jurafsky 1996; Seidenberg and MacDonald 1999).

Our analyses also show that predictability links between words are a key factor in such probabilistic models. We showed, using several kinds of evidence, that the effect of the neighboring word on reduction was not necessarily due to lexicalization. This includes evidence that the effect of predictability on reduction applies both to content and function words, and that the effect of predictability applies both to the higher and to the lower ranges of predictability. The fact that the shortening effects are independent of vowel reduction also tends to support this hypothesis, since such gradient processes are more likely at production processing levels after lexical items have been merged into a prosodic frame.

This is an ongoing research effort, and we are currently extending these results in a number of directions, including further examination of the slightly different effects on context versus function words, use of larger and more general datasets, and effect of other measures of collocation and predictability.

Acknowledgements

This project was partially supported by NSF IIS-9733067. Thanks to Eric Fosler-Lussier for supplying us with the N-gram probability distributions and collaborating on many earlier related projects, Cynthia Girand for helping with the construction of the original function word database and collaboration on related projects, Joan Bybee for inspiring this line of research and for useful feedback and comments, Matthew Dryer and David Perlmutter for (independently) suggesting that we check more carefully if the effects of predictability were confined to the lexicon, and to the audiences of various talks, including the CMU workshop and the linguistics department at UC San Diego.

Appendix 1: Joint versus Conditional Probability

In the body of this paper we reported on the conditional probability as a measure of word predictability. This appendix summarizes a slightly different way of looking at conditional probability.

Recall that the conditional probability of the target word given the previous word is estimated from two counts:

$$P(w_i|w_{i-1}) = \frac{C(w_{i-1}w_i)}{C(w_{i-1})} \qquad (7)$$

An alternative computation substitutes probabilities for the counts, since the probabilities are just the counts divided by a normalizing constant, and the normalizing constants cancel:

$$P(w_i|w_{i-1}) = \frac{P(w_{i-1}w_i)}{P(w_{i-1})} \qquad (8)$$

Thus the conditional probability is made up of two probabilities: the *joint probability with the previous word* $P(w_{i-1}w_i)$ (which may be thought of as the 'relative frequency of the two words occurring together') and the *relative frequency of the previous word* $P(w_{i-1})$. This means that instead of using the conditional probability in the regression equation to predict reduction, we can add in the two relative frequencies instead as independent factors.

Adding in these two factors to the regression (directly after the base model, i.e., without the *conditional probability given previous* variable) showed that both play a role in vowel reduction ($p < .0001$).

Probability	Equation	Regression Coefficient
Joint probability of target with previous word	$P(w_{i-1}w_i)$	−.503
Relative frequency of previous word	$P(w_{i-1})$	+.724

The *regression coefficient* gives the weight that the regression assigned to each factor. The negative coefficient for the joint probability means that the higher the joint, the more likely the word's vowel is reduced. By contrast, the coefficient is positive for previous word probability. This means that a higher previous word probability predicts **less reduction**. This is what we would expect from the probabilistic model, since the prior probability of the previous word is in the denominator in Equation 8.

The difference between the analyses is that the conditional probability essentially holds the relative weights of the joint and preceding word probabilities equal, whereas in the second analysis they are free to vary. The regression is essentially telling us, for this set of data, that the joint probability should be weighted somewhat less heavily than the previous word's relative frequency. We can see the relationship a different way by combining the conditional probability with the joint.

Probability	Equation	Regression Coefficient
Conditional probability of target given previous	$P(w_{i-1}|w_i)$	−.724
Joint probability of target with previous	$P(w_{i-1}w_i)$	+.221

It is not a coincidence that the coefficient of the conditional probability (−.724) is the same magnitude as the coefficient of the previous word's relative frequency in the first analysis. The first analysis gives the relative weights of the two basic (log) probabilities. Since the weight of the relative frequency must be .724, and in the second analysis its only expression is through the denominator of the conditional probability, the conditional probability must have a weight of −.724. Thus the coefficient of the joint probability (+.221) in this regression exactly compensates for the difference between the joint and the prior probabilities in the first analysis (−.503 +.724).

These results (and similar ones for the conditional probability of the target given the following word) suggest that the components of conditional probability may be playing slightly different roles in reduction, and reflect different causes. This is clearly an area that calls for further study.

Appendix 2: Examples of conditional probabilities

Table 6. *The function word contexts with the highest conditional probabilities, according to three probability measures. Target function words are in boldface. Note that* of *and* to *are most likely to collocate with the previous word, while* I, the *and* a *tend to collocate with the following word. To *is most predictable from the surrounding two words*

Highest probability given previous word	Highest probability given next word	Highest probability given surrounding word
$P(w_i\|w_{i-1})$	$P(w_i\|w_{i+1})$	$P(w_i\|w_{i-1} \ldots w_{i+1})$
rid **of**	**I** guess	going **to** be
supposed **to**	**I** mean	well **I** guess
tends **to**	**the** midwest	know **I** mean
ought **to**	**a** lot	have **a** lot
kind **of**	**a** shame	do **a** lot
able **to**	**the** Kurds	supposed **to** be
sort **of**	**the** wintertime	used **to** be
compared **to**	**in** terms	matter **of** fact
kinds **of**	**the** same	quite **a** bit
tend **to**	**the** United	kind **of** thing

Table 7. *Effects of the previous word. The final-t/d content words with the highest and lowest conditional probabilities given the previous word, and the highest and lowest joint probabilities with the previous word. The target word is in boldface*

Highest probability given previous word	Highest joint probability with previous word
supreme **court**	a **lot**
Amsterdam **Holland**	i **get**
doctoral **student**	i **just**
sesame **street**	a **good**
capital **punishment**	it's **just**
Harrison **Ford**	little **bit**
German **shepherd**	i **thought**
awful **lot**	was **just**
backyard's **great**	it **just**
raters **loved**	my **husband**
Lowest probability given previous word	Lowest joint probability with previous word
and **punished**	non **colored**
and **proceed**	blind **sided**
and **shred**	tongue **pressed**
and **disinterested**	Arizona **used**
and **sauerkraut**	girls **kind**
and **closed**	Lehrer **report**
and **gold**	student **discount**
and **touched**	tomatoes **next**
and **ironside**	soccer **filed**
and **bloomed**	families **end**

Table 8. *Effects of the following word. The final-t/d content words with the highest and lowest conditional probabilities given the next word, and the highest and lowest joint probabilities with the next word. The target word is in boldface*

Highest probability given next word	Highest joint probability with next word
United States	**kind** of
good heavens	**lot** of
last resort	**want** to
east coast	**sort** of
need trimming	**used** to
Burt Reynolds	**need** to
called crier	**just** a
government entities	**most** of
good fellas	**part** of
grapefruit citron	**went** to
Lowest probability given next word	Lowest joint probability with next word
threatened i	**eight** engines
hold i	**installed** the
ragged i	**harmed** you
indoctrinated i	**engaged** to
England i	**unemployment** insurance
liberated i	**determined** and
road the	**filmed** in
draft the	**blind** sided
misclassed the	**dependent** you
installed the	**homemade** pasta

Notes

1. This is because mutual information includes the relative frequency of the target word. Since the function word analysis was based on only ten types of function words, this relative frequency component will merely act to distinguish the ten items, rather than to represent their frequencies, as it would with a larger sample.

2. In general we relied on Berkeley transcriptions for our coding, although we did do some data cleanup, including eliminating some observations we judged likely to be in error; see Jurafsky *et al.* (1998) for details.

3. In order to ensure that the durational effects have some continuous component, we would also need to control for presence or absence of consonants. While we couldn't do a full analysis here, we did examine the durations of a subset of 2,878 items in which all consonants were present. Even after

controlling for these categorical factors (vowel quality and consonant presence), target words were still shorter when they had a high conditional probability given the following word, or a high joint probability with the previous word.

4. Our earlier work also considered other reduction factors; see Jurafsky *et al.* (1998) for our results on deletion of coda obstruents in function words (*it, that, and, of*) and Gregory *et al.* (1999) on tapping in final-t/d words.

References

Agresti, A. 1996. *An Introduction to Categorial Data Analysis.* New York: John Wiley & Sons.

Bell, A., Jurafsky, D., Fosler-Lussier, E., Girand, C. and Gildea, D. 1999. "Forms of English function words—Effects of disfluencies, turn position, age and sex, and predictability". In *Proceedings of ICPhS-99*, I.395–8.

Brent, M. R. and Cartwright, T. A. 1996. "Distributional regularity and phonotactic constraints are useful for segmentation". *Cognition* 61: 93–125.

Bush, N. 1999. *The Predictive Value of Transitional Probability for Word-Boundary Palatalization in English.* Master's thesis, University of New Mexico, Alberquerque, NM.

Bybee, J. L. 2000. "The phonology of the lexicon: evidence from lexical diffusion". In M. Barlow and S. Kemmer (eds.), *Usage-based Models of Language*, 65–85. Stanford: CSLI.

Bybee, J. and Scheibman, J. 1999. "The effect of usage on degrees of constituency: the reduction of *don't* in English". *Linguistics* 37(4): 575–96.

Fano, R. M. 1961. *Transmission of information; a statistical theory of communications.* Cambridge, MA: MIT Press.

Fasold, R. W. 1972. *Tense marking in Black English.* Center for Applied Linguistics, Washington, D.C.

Fidelholz, J. 1975. "Word frequency and vowel reduction in English". In *CLS-75*, 200–13. University of Chicago.

Fosler-Lussier, E. and Morgan, N. To appear. "Effects of speaking rate and word frequency on word pronunciation in conversational speech". *Speech Communication.*

Fowler, C. A. and Housum, J. 1987. "Talkers' signaling of 'new' and 'old' words in speech and listeners' perception and use of the distinction". *Journal of Memory and Language* 26: 489–504.

Fox Tree, J. E. and Clark, H. H. 1997. "Pronouncing 'the' as 'thee' to signal problems in speaking". *Cognition* 62: 151–67.

Francis, W. N. and Kučera, H. 1982. *Frequency Analysis of English Usage.* Houghton Mifflin, Boston.

Godfrey, J., Holliman, E., and McDaniel, J. 1992. "SWITCHBOARD: Telephone speech corpus for research and development". In *IEEE ICASSP-92*, 517–20. San Fransisco: IEEE.

Greenberg, S., Ellis, D., and Hollenback, J. 1996. "Insights into spoken language gleaned from phonetic transcription of the Switchboard corpus". In *ICSLP-96*, S24–7. Philadelphia, PA.

Gregory, M. L., Raymond, W. D., Bell, A., Fosler-Lussier, E., and Jurafsky, D. 1999. "The effects of collocational strength and contextual predictability in lexical production". In *CLS* 35: 151–66. Chicago: University of Chicago.

Jescheniak, J. D. and Levelt, W. J. M. 1994. "Word frequency effects in speech production: Retrieval of syntactic information and of phonological form". *Journal of Experimental Psychology: Learning, Memory and Cognition* 20: 824–43.

Jespersen, O. 1923. *Language*. New York: Henry Holt.

Jurafsky, D. 1996. "A probabilistic model of lexical and syntactic access and disambiguation". *Cognitive Science* 20: 137–94.

Jurafsky, D., Bell, A., Fosler-Lussier, E., Girand, C., and Raymond, W. D. 1998. "Reduction of English function words in Switchboard". In *ICSLP-98*, vol 7, 3111–14. Sydney.

Krug, M. 1998. "String frequency: A cognitive motivating factor in coalescence, language processing, and linguistic change". *Journal of English Linguistics* 26: 286–320.

Labov, W. 1972. "The internal evolution of linguistic rules". In R. P. Stockwell and R. K. S. Macaulay (eds.), *Linguistic Change and Generative Theory*, 101–71. Bloomington: Indiana University Press.

Landauer, T. K. and Dumais, S. T. 1997. "A solution to Plato's problem: The Latent Semantic Analysis theory of acquisition, induction, and representation of knowledge". *Psychological Review* 104: 211–40.

MacDonald, M. C. 1993. "The interaction of lexical and syntactic ambiguity". *Journal of Memory and Language* 32: 692–715.

McRae, K., Spivey-Knowlton, M. J., and Tanenhaus, M. K. 1998. "Modeling the influence of thematic fit (and other constraints) in on-line sentence comprehension". *Journal of Memory and Language* 38: 283–312.

Manning, C. D. and Schütze, H. 1999. *Foundations of Statistical Natural Language Processing*. Cambridge, MA: MIT Press.

Martinet, A. 1916. *Elements of General Linguistics*. Chicago: University of Chicago Press.

Narayanan, S. and Jurafsky, D. 1998. "Bayesian models of human sentence processing". In *COGSCI-98*, 752–7. Hillsdale, N.J.: Lawrence Erlbaum.

Oldfield, R. C. and Wingfield, A. 1965. "Response latencies in naming objects". *Quarterly Journal of Experimental Psychology* 17: 273–81.

Rhodes, R. A. 1992. "Flapping in American English". In W. U. Dressler, M. Prinzhorn, and J. Rennison (eds.), *Proceedings of the 7th International Phonology Meeting*, 217–32. Turin: Rosenberg and Sellier.

Rhodes, R. A. 1996. "English reduced vowels and the nature of natural processes". In B. Hurch and R. A. Rhodes (eds.), *Natural Phonology: The State of the Art*, 239–59. Berlin: Mouton de Gruyter.

Roland, D. and Jurafsky, D. 2000. "Verb sense and verb subcategorization probabilities". In P. Merlo and S. Stevenson (eds.), *The Lexical Basis of Sentence Processing: Formal, Computational and Experimental Issues*. Hillsdale, N.J.: Lawrence Erlbaum.

Saffran, J. R., Aslin, R. N., and Newport, E. L. 1996. "Statistical cues in language acquisition: Word segmentation by infants". In *COGSCI-96*, 376–80.

Schuchardt, H. 1885. *Über die Lautgesetze: Gegen die Junggrammatiker*. Berlin: Robert Oppenheim. Excerpted with translation in Theo Vennemann and Terence H. Wilbur, (eds.), *Schuchardt, the Neogrammarians, and the Transformational Theory of Phonological Change*. 1972. Frankfurt: Athenaeum Verlag.

Seidenberg, M. S. and MacDonald, M. C. 1999. "A probabilistic constraints approach to language acquisition and processing". *Cognitive Science* 23: 569–88.

Shriberg, E. 1999. "Phonetic consequences of speech disfluency". In *Proceedings of the International Congress of Phonetic Sciences (ICPhS-99)*, vol. I, 619–22. San Francisco.

Trueswell, J. C. and Tanenhaus, M. K. 1994. "Toward a lexicalist framework for constraint-based syntactic ambiguity resolution". In C. Clifton, Jr., L. Frazier and K. Rayner (eds.), *Perspectives on Sentence Processing*, 155–79. Hillsdale, NJ.: Lawrence Erlbaum.

Zipf, G. K. 1929. "Relative frequency as a determinant of phonetic change". *Harvard Studies in Classical Philology* 15: 1–95.

Frequency effects and word-boundary palatalization in English

NATHAN BUSH

University of New Mexico

1. Introduction

Phonological reduction in naturally-occurring discourse tokens appears to be a highly-variable phenomenon subject to a multitude of factors. Bloomfield (1933: 386) epitomizes the belief, widely held amongst scholars of language variation, that "no permanent factor . . . can account for the specific changes which occur at one time and place and not another," and that the myriad dynamic sociolinguistic variables which potentially affect phonological reduction often render "the causes of sound change . . . unknown". The potential complexity to this issue does not stop here. Beyond these sociolinguistic factors, one must realize " . . . that language, while existing to serve a social function (communication), is nevertheless seated in the minds of individuals" (Guy 1980: 1). The approach of this paper will be to momentarily cast aside a collective of sociolinguistic factors, and focus more on a single, more "permanent" (to borrow Bloomfield's term) factor that arises as we ". . . separate the variation due to change from the variation due to social factors . . . from the variation due to internal factors" (Labov 1994: 26).

To illustrate the minimal, yet essential, role played by phonetic conditioning environments in the occurrence of word-boundary palatalization, examine the following utterances (examples taken from Carterette and Jones 1974/MacWhinney 1995):[1]

(1) . . . they didn't talk good you know.
 [ðedɪəntɔkgʊd͡jəno]

(2) Would you like me to teach you how to swim?
 [wʊd͡ʒəlaʔmidətitʃjəhautəswɪm]

The /d/ and /j/ sequence in *would you* as found in (2) regularly palatalizes to [wʊdʒə] at its medial juncture, while the same combination in *good you*, as in (1), typically does not. Therefore, the predictability of word-boundary palatalization in English must be contingent upon other factors beyond the oversimplified, text-book conclusion that "such palatalization processes usually happen in the environment of high front sounds such as /i/ or /j/" (Akmajian *et al.* 1995: 102).

In this paper, a statistical analysis of individual word boundaries where pala-talization does and does not occur, including the text frequency of the collocated lexical elements, reveals the following: word-boundary palatalization is more likely between two words if those words occur together with high frequency. I will argue that such a predisposition towards word-boundary palatalization is indicative of a cognitively-motivated chunking phenomenon which causes frequently-used se-quences of lexical material to acquire lexical storage as single, agglutinated mental representations (cf. Boyland 1996, Bybee and Scheibman 1999).

2. The data

The corpus for this paper consists of naturally-occurring discourse extracted from a large body of material originally recorded and transcribed in Carterette and Jones (1974). This same corpus has since been reproduced on CD-ROM as part of the MacWhinney (1995) CHILDES project. Two subsets of the Carterette and Jones (1974) data, as they appear in MacWhinney (1995), entered into the analysis: the 'adult' corpus and the 'fifth grade' corpus, for a total of approximately 40,000 words.[2] I selected these two corpora because their speakers constitute a maximally representative sample of adult-like phonology with respect to word-boundary palatalization phenomena while they also provide a more conclusive quantity of data than the adult corpus would offer on its own.[3] The data for both the adult and fifth-grade subcorpora were recorded from natural (i.e., largely non-directed) conversa-tions of three-person conversation groups. A total of eight separate conversation groups were used for the adult-speech corpus and sixteen groups constituted the fifth-grade corpus. The students within both groups, if they did not already know each other, were introduced to each other informally on a first-name basis and basi-cally left to develop casual conversation of their own design. Most subjects in the fifth-grade corpus were from the same classrooms and were generally not in need of introductions. The text was subsequently transcribed according to the Trager and Smith (1951) system with some modifications suggested by Peter Ladefoged specif-ically for the purposes of the Carterette and Jones study (Carterette and Jones 1974: 18). Four phoneticians used this customized phonetic alphabet to complete the final phonemic transcriptions of the text and, in so doing, they fortunately captured certain phonetic details such as word-boundary palatalization (as evidenced by the transcription of the alveopalatal affricates /tʃ/ and /dʒ/).[4]

In an attempt to gather all pertinent examples of potential word-boundary palatalization environments in the corpus, I used a computer-aided search of the Carterette and Jones (1974)/MacWhinney (1995) data using the *Monoconc for Windows* concordance/text analysis program (Barlow 1997).[5] For the purposes of the data search, I targeted those word pairs (i.e., *word dyads*) that juxtaposed a word-final alveolar stop in the first word with a word-initial palatal glide in the second word, which thus created the appropriate environment for word-boundary palatalization to occur.[6] The *Monoconc* program allowed for the automatic retrieval of all orthographic *t* + *y* and *d* + *y* combinations that occurred across word boundaries in the CHILDES/ Carterette and Jones (1974) corpus. The searches resulted in the retrieval of 404 tokens of the word-boundary *t* + *y* and *d* + *y* combinations, including 124 different word dyads of varying frequencies that fit the orthographic criteria.

3. The analysis

It has long been known (but not generally accepted) that high-frequency discourse items tend to reduce faster than lower-frequency items (Hooper 1976, Phillips 1984, Zipf 1929). More recently, similar hypotheses have been extended to multi-word strings of lexical information. Several researchers have concluded that the frequency of co-occurrence of two words reflects the degree to which the lexical items are likely to 'grammaticize' (Bybee *et al.* 1994), 'coalesce' (Krug 1998), or 'morphologize' (Boyland 1996). Krug (1998: 301) asserts that a simple statistic that he refers to as 'string frequency' offers a metric that correlates to the likelihood that morphological fusion, or coalescence, has taken place within co-occurring lexical items, such as the familiar contractions of pronominal subjects and their frequently-paired auxiliary verbs (e.g., *she is → she's*). This notion of string frequency simply extends the more conventional concept of token (or text) frequency to two-word collocations whose text frequency is assessed as a single unit. In light of Krug's findings, an attempt to correlate token-frequency-based effects such as string frequency on the one hand and word-boundary palatalization rates on the other forms the methodological point of departure for this research.

Table 1 lists the dyads from the corpus and includes for each dyad the string frequency of the word pair in the first column of numerical data.

In an attempt to follow Krug's (1998) lead and correlate string frequency with phonological output, I also tally the number of times that word-boundary palatalization either occurred or did not occur for a given dyad; these figures are in the second and third columns of numerical data in Table 1. It is important to note that

Table 1. *An alphabetical index and analysis of all potential candidates for word-boundary palatalization from the Carterette and Jones (1974)/MacWhinney (1995) corpus (FCE = Frequency of the conditioning environment; SOP = Success of palatalization in tokens with the appropriate conditioning environment; '+' = Occurs; '–' = Does not occur)*

Dyadic palatalization candidate (X+Y)	FCE	SOP +	SOP –	Dyadic palatalization candidate (X+Y)	FCE	SOP +	SOP –
about you	2	2	0	kind you'd	1	0	1
and you	1	0	1	last year	6	3	3
at you	3	1	2	least you	1	0	1
at your	2	1	1	let you	2	1	1
at U.C.L.A.	1	0	1	lot you	1	1	0
backyard you	1	0	1	married yesterday	1	0	1
bad you	1	0	1	meet you	1	0	1
band you're	1	1	0	not yet	1	0	1
bet you	1	1	0	out you	1	0	1
bright yellow	1	0	1	playground yesterday	1	0	1
but yet	1	0	1	pregnant you	1	0	1
but you	3	1	2	put your	4	1	3
but you'd	1	1	0	said yeow	1	0	1
but you're	1	1	0	said yes	1	0	1
can't you	1	0	1	said you	3	1	2
cat you	1	0	1	second year	1	0	1
could you	2	1	1	slot your	1	0	1
did you	69	46	23	started young	1	0	1
didn't you	7	4	3	that year	1	0	1
dissect your	1	0	1	that you	7	5	2
don't you	11	10	1	thought you	1	1	0
eat you	1	0	1	told you	5	4	1
eight yard	1	0	1	tried you	1	0	1
eight yards	1	0	1	what year	1	0	1
eight years	1	0	1	what you	10	6	4
get you	2	1	1	what your	1	0	1
get yourself	1	1	0	what you've	1	1	0
good you	1	0	1	what'd you	4	2	2
got you	1	0	1	what'd your	1	0	1
had yesterday	1	0	1	where'd you	2	2	0
had you	1	0	1	would you	10	8	2
how'd you	1	0	1	wouldn't you	1	1	0
kid yeah	1	0	1				

the string frequency totals listed for each item in the first column of Table 1 are 'adjusted' totals for the following reason: some instances of dyads encountered prior phonological reduction (such as final [t]/[d] deletion in which the word-final [t] or [d] of the first word of the pair reduces to zero) which consequently precluded the onset of word-boundary palatalization. Therefore, I list the string frequency totals in Table 1 instead as 'Freq. of the conditioning environment,' even though this column of data is essentially an application of Krug's string frequency statistic. In so doing, I have effectively eliminated those dyads that encountered prior reduction of the necessary phonological conditioning environment from the analysis.

Looking again at Table 1, it is clear that the word *you* is by far the most common lexical item to form the *y*-position member of the *x+y* dyads that enter into the word-boundary palatalization process. It should also be noted, however, that other *y*-position members, such as the word *year* in *last year*, also palatalize at a relatively high rate, invalidating either of the following erroneous assumptions: (1) *y*-position members with low token frequency (e.g., *year* as opposed to *you*) tend to inhibit the palatalization process (as deduced in Cooper *et al.* 1978), or (2) this word-boundary phenomenon occurs only with the word *you* or derivatives thereof.

Throughout this paper, I refer to an individual performance of a phonologically appropriate word-dyad which retains (i.e., does not reduce to zero) the word-final alveolar stop of the first word in the pair (and similarly avoids other inhibitory prior phonological reduction) as an *independent palatalization trial*.[7] Therefore, only 65 of the 124 different word dyads located in the course of the orthographic *t* + y/*d* + y word-boundary searches enter into palatalization trials with a frequency ≥ 1 and are thus listed in Table 1 as *dyadic palatalization candidates*.

A positive correlation emerges in Table 1 between those word dyads which enter into palatalization trials frequently and those which palatalize frequently.[8] The word-searches that produced the orthographic *t* + y/*d* + y dyads were compared with their 'phonemic' transcriptions, so that the incidence of each phonologically-appropriate collocation could be assessed for presence versus absence of a voiced or voiceless alveopalatal affricate. Based on this test, it was decided whether word-boundary palatalization had or had not occurred (see again second and third columns of numerical data in Table 1).

In Table 2, I tabulate the palatalization success or failure of each independent palatalization trial of each word dyad in Table 1. It is from the string frequency-based 'Freq. of the conditioning environment' column of Table 1 that independent trial results are assigned to the 'high-' versus 'low-' frequency columns in Table 2.

The chi-squared test of significance in Table 2 confirms an extremely high degree of interdependence (p-value < .001) between the frequency of particular word dyads and the likelihood that these word dyads will palatalize at their word boundary.

For the purposes of Table 2, I assign the cut-off between dyads with

Table 2. *Chi-squared test of significance which suggests an interdependence*
between co-occurrence factors and word-boundary palatalization rates[9]

	Frequency of the Conditioning Environment		
	Dyads w/high-frequency conditioning environments	Dyads w/ low-frequency conditioning environments (including dyads which simply co-occur infrequently)	Total
No. of instances ('trials') in which palatalization DID occur	86	23	109
No. of instances ('trials') in which palatalization DID NOT occur	39	52	91
Total	125	75	200

Chi-Sq =   4.690 + 7.817 +
              5.618 + 9.363   = 27.488
Degrees of Freedom   = 1
P-value   = **<.001**

'high-frequency' and 'low- frequency' conditioning environments (see again 'Freq. of the conditioning environment' column of Table 1) to be between four and five tokens of a given word dyad with the necessary conditioning environment, or 'candidacy' status, retained. The important point that underlies Table 2 is not where the break between 'high-frequency' and 'low-frequency' optimally occurs, but rather that such a distribution of the word dyads (with concomitant palatalization occurrence and 'Freq. of the conditioning environment' values) results in a strong correlation with a very high degree of confidence.[10] Thus the group of word dyads that retain word-boundary palatalization candidacy with 'high-frequency' (according to Table 2) is comprised of the collocations *did you, didn't you, don't you, last year, that you, told you, what you,* and *would you,* while the 'low-frequency' group consists of all other remaining word dyads listed in Table 1. If the actuation of word-boundary palatalization were not sensitive to frequency-based factors, then the proportion of 'occur' versus 'did not occur' outcomes should remain the same across the two columns of data in Table 2. Instead, we find that if two words commonly co-occur, then the palatalization trials for these specific word dyads will be successful (i.e., 'occur') far more often than not, and vice versa.

    It may be useful to reinterpret the data by removing *did you* from the corpus because of its potential, as an extreme outlier (see again 'Freq. of conditioning environment' column of Table 1), to skew the data and the aforementioned correlation between co-occurrence frequency (of the necessary conditioning environment) and palatalization rate. Nonetheless, deleting such a high-frequency item from the database does little to detract from the lack of independence between co-occurrence factors and palatalization rates suggested by Table 2. An χ^2 value of 21.339 is still achieved ($p < .001$), underscoring the fact that a strong correlation exists between factors of frequency and phonological reduction.

3.1 Beyond string frequency: transitional probability

String frequency, as it is stated in Krug (1998), is hypothesized to be the indicator of the amount of cognitive coalescence which has occurred in multi-word strings of lexical material and "the most important *motivation* in phonological and morphological changes that result in the cliticization and merger of two adjacent items" (Krug 1998: 309, my emphasis). But Krug does not specify the actual mechanism by which string frequency encourages phonetic change. Clearly one possibility is that words which are frequently used together can be chunked as a single unit in memory and behave like a single word for phonetic purposes. Since palatalization of /t/ and /d/ commonly occurs word-internally, it will also occur inside these chunks (cf. Bybee 2000, Bybee to appear).

However, in addition to the simple co-occurrence measured by string frequency, other perspectives of the emergent relationship between two words can be taken. Consider, for example, the effect of the sequential nature of two-word dyads, such as those that naturally occur in the lexical string *what did you ask*. What special statistical property characterizes high-frequency word dyads (such as *did you* in this example) that is not, for instance, also shared by the component items (*what + did*) or (*you + ask*)? The answer: the power of prediction. The word *did* is, statistically speaking, an excellent predictor of the word *you*, while the words *what* and *you* are followed by a much more widely distributed range of lexical possibilities. This predictive relationship is referred to as *transitional probability* (cf. Hunltzen *et al.* 1964, Morgan and Saffran 1995, Saffran *et al.* 1996, Saffran *et al.* 1996) and it is especially applicable to those phenomena that are prone to being processed in a serial-order fashion, such as auditory speech perception and spoken language production. Furthermore, the degree to which certain words phonologically reduce (in terms of length, vowel quality, and final obstruent deletion) has recently been shown to be based at least in part upon the degree to which certain lexical items may be predictable from previous words in discourse (Jurafsky *et al.* 1998: 3). These findings warrant a similar test of some probability-based factor in our investigation of word-boundary palatalization.[11]

Token-frequency-based trends in phonologically- or morphologically-reductive processes such as 'Zipf's law' and, more recently, grammaticization theory (Bybee *et al.* 1994, Haiman 1994), have often been discussed in terms of a trade-off between speaker- and hearer-based economy and other functional constraints (Krug 1998, Lindblom 1992, Zipf 1949). In regards to our word-boundary palatalization dilemma, however, transitional probability points to an alternative, and potentially less limited, motivation, deeply rooted in considerations of a more cognitive bent. Stated in maximally generic terms, transitional probability is simply the statistical likelihood that, given the occurrence of phenomenon *x*, phenomenon *y* will follow. Many of the most basic human cognitive processes exploit this type of frequency-motivated relationship: mental association, prediction/foreshadowing, inferencing, cause-and-effect reasoning, classical conditioning, priming effects, etc.[12] The common denominator underlying these general cognitive operating principles is that we, along with a large number of physiologically more simple organisms, maintain an ability to associate a stimulus with its frequently-encountered context(s) in memory. Emergent from these powers of stimulus-context association is an aptitude that allows us to *predict* a context for a frequently-encountered stimulus, or to predict one stimulus given another stimulus situated in that same shared context. Transitional probability is therefore not only a statistical notion, but it also may be interpreted as being a cognitive correlate whereby the strength of an associative bond in memory is reflective of the degree to which one stimulus is a predictor of another stimulus of shared context. In other words, this statistic might serve not only as an indicator of the amount of 'bondedness' between two phenomena in the objective world, but as an equally reliable predictor of the degree to which the two representations of these phenomena may be 'bound' in memory (cf. Bybee and Scheibman 1999 for a specific linguistic application of this proposal). Moreover, the notion of transitional probability appears to be equally applicable to both linguistic and non-linguistic phenomena, as in the basic human cognitive processes (e.g., mental association, classical conditioning, etc.) cited above. In light of this discussion, I will now argue that transitional probability points to an alternative explanation as to how frequency-based factors condition the occurrence of word-boundary palatalization and thus motivate the actuation of this phenomenon.

In accordance with Saffran *et al.* (1996: 610), I define transitional probability for the purposes of this paper as the token frequency of word dyad *x+y* divided by the token frequency of word *x* alone (i.e., (trans. prob.) = freq. $_{[x,y]}$/freq. $_{[x]}$). Looking at these mathematical terms, we see that transitional probability involves a frequency-based relationship, much like string frequency. Transitional probability departs from string frequency, however, in the sense that it additionally compares the token frequency of a word dyad with the token frequency of the *x*-position member alone of that same word dyad. If we are to contrast string frequency and

Table 3. *An alphabetical index of the palatalization candidates from the Carterette and Jones (1974)/MacWhinney (1995) corpus, comparing (1) the transitional probability for each dyad, and (2) the number of palatalization 'successes' or 'failures' for each instance of each dyad that preserved the necessary phonological conditioning environment for word-boundary palatalization to potentially occur (TP = Transitional probability; SOP = Success of palatalization in tokens with the appropriate conditioning environment; '+' = Occurs; '−' = Does not occur)*

Dyadic palatalization candidate (X+Y)	TP	SOP +	SOP −	Dyadic palatalization candidate (X+Y)	TP	SOP +	SOP −
about you	.0176	2	0	kind you'd	.0222	0	1
and you	.0385	0	1	last year	.1490	3	3
at you	.0308	1	2	least you	.1111	0	1
at your	.0154	1	1	let you	.1111	1	1
at U.C.L.A.	.0385	0	1	lot you	.0156	1	0
backyard you	.5000	0	1	married yesterday	.1000	0	1
bad you	.0476	0	1	meet you	.3333	0	1
band you're	.1667	1	0	not yet	.0083	0	1
bet you	.3333	1	0	out you	.0146	0	1
bright yellow	.3333	0	1	playground yesterday	.2000	0	1
but yet	.0039	0	1	pregnant you	1.000	0	1
but you	.0311	1	2	put your	.0615	1	3
but you'd	.0039	1	0	said yeow	.0135	0	1
but you're	.0078	1	0	said yes	.0135	0	1
can't you	.0556	0	1	said you	.1216	1	2
cat you	.0483	0	1	second year	.0526	0	1
could you	.0740	1	1	slot your	.5000	0	1
did you	.4900	46	23	started young	.0357	0	1
didn't you	.1042	4	3	that year	.0019	0	1
dissect your	.3333	0	1	that you	.0444	5	2
don't you	.0578	10	1	thought you	.0294	1	0
eat you	.1667	0	1	told you	.1724	4	1
eight yard	.0435	0	1	tried you	.0625	0	1
eight yards	.0435	0	1	what year	.0036	0	1
eight years	.0435	0	1	what you	.0500	6	4
get you	.0167	1	1	what your	.0036	0	1
get yourself	.0056	1	0	what you've	.0036	1	0
good you	.0137	0	1	what'd you	.5000	2	2
got you	.0051	0	1	what'd your	.1250	0	1
had yesterday	.0042	0	1	where'd you	1.000	2	0
had you	.0127	0	1	would you	.1692	8	2
how'd you	1.000	0	1	wouldn't you	.0833	1	0
kid yeah	.1000	0	1				

transitional probability in a real-data situation, we find these two statistics some-times behave in very different ways. In fact, seemingly any combination of figures with respect to these two statistics may be found in the analysis of the text (see now Table 3): (a) both the dyad token frequency and the transitional probability between the individual component items (word x and word y) are high (e.g., 'did you');[13] (b) the dyad token frequency is high, but the transitional probability between the com-ponent items is comparatively low (e.g., 'and you'); (c) both the dyad token fre-quency *and* the transitional probability between the components are low (e.g., 'but yet'); and (d) the dyad token frequency is low, but the transitional probability be-tween the component items is comparatively high (e.g., 'pregnant you').[14,15] This independence between string frequency and transitional probability within the dyad should make it possible to test which one is the best statistical predictor of phono-logical fusion.

3.2 Transitional probability as a predictor of phonological reduction

Again using a chi-squared test of significance, it is possible to investigate the possi-ble interdependence between the occurrence of word-boundary palatalization and, this time, not the token frequency, but rather the transitional probability (computed using the Saffran *et al.* 1996 method described earlier) of each dyad as it enters into

Table 4. *Chi-squared test of significance which suggests an interdependence between transitional probability and word-boundary palatalization rates*[16]

	Dyads w/ high trans. prob. (**y** has high trans. prob. given **x**)	Dyads w/ low trans. prob. (**y** has low trans. prob. given **x**)	Total
No. of instances ('trials') in which palatalization DID occur	97	12	109
No. of instances ('trials') in which palatalization DID NOT occur	66	25	91
Total	163	37	200

Chi-Sq = 0.750 + 3.306 +
             0.899 + 3.960 = 8.915
Degrees of Freedom   = 1
P-value   = **<.01**

Table 5. *A numeric index of all 'high' versus 'low' transitional probability word dyads as designated for the purposes of the chi-squared distribution in Table 4, listed in terms of decreasing transitional probabilities for each column. Boldface items are those dyads that were also deemed to have a high frequency of the environment necessary for word-boundary palatalization to occur (see Table 1) (TP=Transitional probability; FCE = Freq. of the conditioning environment)*

Dyadic palatalization candidate (X+Y)	TP	FCE	Dyadic palatalization candidate (X+Y)	TP	FCE
how'd you	1.000	1	**that you**	.0435	**7**
pregnant you	1.000	1	eight yard	.0435	1
where'd you	1.000	2	eight yards	.0435	1
backyard you	.5000	1	eight years	.0435	1
slot your	.5000	1	and you	.0385	1
what'd you	.5000	4	at U.C.L.A.	.0385	1
did you	**.4900**	**69**	started young	.0357	1
bet you	.3333	1	but you	.0311	3
bright yellow	.3333	1	at you	.0308	3
dissect your	.3333	1	thought you	.0294	1
meet you	.3333	1	kind you'd	.0222	1
playground yesterday	.2000	1	about you	.0176	2
told you	**.1724**	**5**	get you	.0167	2
would you	**.1692**	**10**	lot you	.0156	1
band you're	.1667	1	at your	.0154	2
eat you	.1667	1	out you	.0146	1
last year	**.1490**	**6**	good you	.0137	1
what'd your	.1250	1	said yeow	.0135	1
said you	.1216	3	said yes	.0135	1
least you	.1111	1	had you	.0127	1
let you	.1111	2	not yet	.0083	1
didn't you	**.1042**	**7**	but you're	.0078	1
kid yeah	.1000	1	get yourself	.0056	1
married yesterday	.1000	1	got you	.0051	1
wouldn't you	.0833	1	had yesterday	.0042	1
could you	.0740	2	but yet	.0039	1
tried you	.0625	1	but you'd	.0039	1
put your	.0615	4	what year	.0036	1
don't you	**.0578**	**11**	what you've	.0036	1
can't you	.0556	1	what your	.0036	1
second year	.0526	1	that year	.0019	1
what you	**.0500**	**10**			
cat you	.0843	1			
bad you	.0476	1			

a given independent speech trial. The results of this chi-squared test are found in Table 4. Much like in Table 2, it was necessary to designate an arbitrary cut-off point solely for the purpose of performing the chi-squared analysis, where those dyads with a transitional probability ≥ .0444 are considered 'high' transitional-probability dyads, and those with a transitional probability of ≤ .0435 are considered 'low.' The resultant distribution of the individual word dyads, categorized according to their 'high' versus 'low' transitional probability, appears in the Table 5.

Turning back to the chi-squared test in Table 4, the transitional probability of word dyads also appears to be an excellent indicator of the likelihood for word-boundary palatalization phenomena to occur (p-value < .01).[17]

While the quantifiable statistical significance for this test based on transitional probability is slightly less than that for string frequency (see again Table 2, where p < .001), it is worthwhile to now mention several factors that should be taken into consideration when interpreting these results.

As seen in Table 5, the eight dyads that were originally determined to have relatively high frequency of the conditioning environment necessary for word-boundary palatalization to occur (i.e., *did you, didn't you, don't you, last year, that you, told you, what you,* and *would you*) are all found in the 'high transitional probability' column of this table. Thus (1) the frequency of the conditioning environment necessary for word-boundary palatalization to occur and (2) transitional probability are high for the same dyads in most cases. An example of a dyad with high frequency (with respect to the necessary conditioning environment) but low transitional probability is *and you,* since a large class of items can follow *and.* However, because the /d/ in *and* deletes (thus making the stop unavailable for palatalization), this pair cannot be used to test the difference between the predictions of frequency effects related to string frequency versus those based on transitional probability.[18] In addition, some non-palatalizing examples such as *pregnant you* exhibit a transitional probability of 1.000, or 100%, simply due to the fact that the word *pregnant* occurs in the corpus only once, and the one time that this word does appear, it is followed by the word *you.* Such examples detract from the perceived predictability of transitional probability with respect to low-frequency dyads, or more specifically, dyads in which the x-position member occurs only once.[19],[20]

4. Phonological rules and their limited domains of applicability

Traditionally, palatalization phenomena have not been explained in terms of frequency-based effects, but rather using formal phonological rules that operate within words, such as the derivation of [tʃ] or [dʒ] from "underlying" /t/ or /d/ in lexical items like *actual* and *gradual* (Chomsky and Halle 1968: 230). Chomsky and

Halle (1968: 163ff, 230) offer the following palatalization rule in their attempt to formalize the palatalization process within the framework of their "Word-level phonology":

$$(3) \quad \#\# \ldots \begin{bmatrix} -\text{sonor} \\ +\text{cor} \end{bmatrix} \rightarrow \begin{bmatrix} -\text{ant} \\ +\text{strid} \end{bmatrix} / \underline{\quad} \begin{bmatrix} -\text{back} \\ -\text{voc} \\ -\text{cons} \end{bmatrix} \begin{bmatrix} -\text{cons} \\ -\text{stress} \end{bmatrix} \ldots \#\#$$

A common aspect of formal systems typified by (3) above is the manipulation of *minimal* units of linguistic representation (e.g., individual phonemes, morphemes, or words), where " . . . each terminal string that enters the phonological component is uniquely and exhaustively analyzed as a sequence of words" (Chomsky and Halle 1968: 163). In this type of approach, word boundaries are lexically represented according to the following general convention:

> The boundary # is automatically inserted at the beginning and end of every string dominated by a major category, i.e., by one of the lexical categories "noun," "verb," "adjective," or by a category such as "sentence," "noun phrase," "verb phrase," which dominates a lexical category.   (Chomsky and Halle 1968: 366)

In an effort to rectify discrepancies involving the mappings of word-internal phonological rules onto larger-scope syntactic constituents such as the word-boundary phenomenon under investigation here, Chomsky and Halle (1968: 9–10) posit the notion of "readjustment rules." These rules subdivide complex expressions into "phonological phrases" that subsequently serve to define the scope of rule-based phonological processes. The particulars of this proposed interface between phonology and syntax have not gone unnoticed in more recent literature. Rules that were originally derived in response to specific word-level behavior have now been adapted to operate at the phrase level (Kenstowicz and Kisseberth 1990: 194). Word-boundary rules have been reformulated in terms of "domain-limit rules" that affect the left or right terminus of phonologically- or prosodically-based constituents, including words or more complex phrases (Hyman 1990: 109). Furthermore, these higher-order phonological principles appear to operate within a variety of syntactic contexts (Kenstowicz and Kisseberth 1990: 194). Indeed, we have witnessed the occurrence of word-boundary palatalization *with high frequency* in "a variety of syntactic contexts"—contexts that appear to defy parsimonious description according to any syntactic or phonological criteria other than possibly high/low stress pattern, including *did you* and *would you* (AUX + PRO), *didn't you* and *don't you* (AUX + NEG + PRO), *that you* and *what you* (COMP + N), and *told you* and *get yourself* (V + N). Even more inexplicably for traditional generative-type approaches, word-boundary palatalization *occasionally* transpires in independent trials of other dyads whose similarities are even less conducive to any categorization whatsoever, such as *about you* (PREP + N), *band you're* (N + COMP), *but you'd* (CONJ + N), *last year* (ADJ + N), and *put your* (V + ADJ). In spite of these wide-ranging examples of environments in which word-boundary palatalization actually occurs in running speech, the generally received answer to this problem has remained as follows: " . . . as soon as the domain of application of a phonological rule involves a string of two or more words, syntax must be called upon to determine what types of words may be involved and how these words must be related to each other" (Vogel and Kenesei 1990: 340). Hence, a debate continues in the literature concerning whether syntactic structures feed phonological rules directly or whether, perhaps, some more indirect relationship exists between syntactic constituents and phonological output. In the latter case, it has been proposed that phonological principles access syntactic structures only indirectly via an intermediate prosodic hierarchy (Kaisse 1990: 128).

I contend that it is instead the non-random distribution of natural speech that develops chunks of stored information out of frequently-used, multi-word strings, consequently forming segments that represent single, agglutinated phonological domains (cf. Bybee 1998, Bybee this volume, Bybee and Scheibman 1999). Before going into a more in-depth discussion regarding the storage of frequency-based chunks of information within the lexicon, it may first be helpful to further define what is meant by the "chunking" of lexical material.

4.1 The frequency-based chunking of lexical information

Chunking is a resource-conserving principle of information storage (cf. Miller 1956) whereby complex representations undergo a reduction in information complexity once higher-level generalizations are (a) abstracted from the code and (b) subsequently mapped onto reorganized, simplified expressions in memory. A similar reorganization of linguistic code typically occurs with strings of information that collocate frequently (Haiman 1994), presumably because it is more likely that these complexity-reducing generalizations will be gleaned from a repetitious sequence of stimuli presentations than from fewer exposures to the same type of information (cf. Bellezza and Young 1989).

In the theoretical framework of gestural phonology (cf. Browman and Goldstein 1992), the representation of articulatory linguistic code exists, at least in part, as phonological mappings of learned phonetic motor programs. A discussion of the chunking principle as it applies to these motor programs is subsumed in Boyland (1996) under the rubric of *skill learning*. In Boyland's model, a precondition for skill acquisition—namely, the recurring usages of particular action sequences in a given context—results in lower-level compositional stimuli being compiled into simplified hierarchical information structures.[21] Similar to the way in which a written signature often fails to fully represent the original, independent orthographic components, so do frequently-uttered speech strings gradually reduce in information complexity, *regardless of the nature of the units* (phonemes, morphemes, words, etc.). Essentially, the effect of repetition upon the storage of lexical information is that, in high-frequency situations, collocations of minimal units develop fused representations of amalgamated (and, hence, simplified) expression. When one attempts to randomly extract the decontextualized individual components from the chunked form, however, meaning (in the broad 'information' sense) is inevitably lost.[22] For reasons already explained in some detail earlier in this paper, transitional probability is a more consistent index of the degree of exclusive distributional interrelatedness between two discourse items than is string frequency. I would like to further propose that transitional probability can also serve as a statistical correlate that reflects the inherent potential that two lexical items may chunk, thus forming an autonomous unit stored separately from the two components that originally contributed to its development.

4.2 The development of lexical structure based on transitional probability

The notion of transitional probability is not an *ad hoc*, unfounded concept created in response to an attempt to explain the phonological trends central to this paper. Current research in the field of child language development has called into question the validity of any *a priori* (cf. Hopper 1987) lexical categories and corresponding word boundaries that conveniently serve to delimit the segments upon which rules like the Chomsky and Halle (1968) formula reproduced in (3) operate (cf. Saffran *et al.* 1996). More precisely, any traditional syntactically-based method by which each word segment might gain autonomous representation in a child's developing lexicon is motivationally inadequate, since infants must initially acquire word boundaries from largely continuous (i.e., phonetically unsegmented or unparsed) speech stream inputs. Much commonplace evidence exists in support of the argument that lexical categories and word boundaries are in a constant state of flux. Children, for instance, typically under-analyze continuous streams of speech that include components with high co-occurrence potential, such as when the words *give* and *me* are represented as simply *gimme*.[23] Adults are prone to similar analytical mistakes in regard to their own word-recognition processes, commonly misinterpreting, for example, the idiomatic expression *for all intents and purposes* as being instead *for all intensive purposes*. (cf. discussion of "perceptual grouping" in Boyland 1996: 11ff.). This learning problem with respect to lexical segmentation has been addressed in recent literature which demonstrates that humans, including mere infants, are able to infer word boundaries solely from distributional information—theoretically speaking, the transitional probabilities between syllables (Morgan and Saffran 1995, Saffran *et al*. 1996, Saffran *et al*. 1996). These related studies conclude that while suprasegmental information will certainly enhance subjects' online ability to infer word boundaries from unbroken streams of speech, the nonrandom distribution of syllables in natural language alone provides sufficient cues to word segmentation during listeners' attempts to process completely foreign, continuous speech inputs when all suprasegmental information, including pauses between words, are removed from the speech stream.

What emerges from this type of statistically-based language learning is a lexicon whose component units have their size and structure functionally determined by the distributional patterning of chunks of linguistic information, regardless of whether these chunks are comprised of functionally indivisible syllables, words, or more inclusive multi-unit collocations (cf. Bybee 1998). Saffran *et al*. (1996: 609) note a striking parallel between this type of learning mechanism for word boundaries and that which is understood to operate in the visual modality for object recognition: as an object begins to move within the visual field, stronger spatial correlations develop between the different parts of the moving object as compared to those correlations that exist between the object and its surrounding visual context. Studies in both human infant and primate visual object recognition (e.g., Kellman *et al*. 1987, Kellman and Spelke 1983, Spelke 1990, Spelke *et al*. 1989, Sejnowski and Nowlan 1995) implicate coordinated motion as being a primary cue in the proper integration and assembly of even noisy signals to form a single, perceived object.

Figure 1 demonstrates how even preverbal infants apparently engage in object recognition based upon the unified motion of incongruous visual signals. The infants did not attend to the scenario presented in Figure 1a for a significant length of

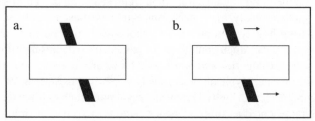

Figure 1. *Two separate stimuli presented to infants, where (a) is a stationary rod (or two rods, since ambiguity here is intended) grounded against a rectangle, and (b) is a rod that is presumed to be a single object interrupted by the rectangle because the visually-discontinuous portions of the rod are seen to move in unison. Adapted from Spelke (1990)*

time when the rectangle was removed from the stimulus and the stationary rod was discovered to be two non-connected, independent objects. In Figure 1b, however, the rods were moved back and forth in unison, causing the infants to ascribe object singularity to the upper and lower portions of the rod. When the intervening rectangle was removed, the infants attended significantly longer to the scenario when, to their surprise, the rods were discovered to be two distinct entities, despite their coordinated movement. According to Spelke (1990), infants' conceptualization of objects is defined by the following constraints: (1) the bodies must be connected; (2) the bodies must move independently of their environment; and (3) bodies must move on connected paths. With transitional probability or some other measure of coordinated word movement, it is possible to assess how unified object recognition of co-occurring lexical items may proceed along similar, principled lines. Furthermore, an explanation of word segmentation and, consequently, lexical-item recognition that employs a parsing mechanism cognitively analogous to that of visual-object recognition certainly achieves an amount of theoretical parsimony above and beyond more traditional accounts of language acquisition that require some type of highly specialized language acquisition apparatus.

4.3 The palatalization rule revisited

The segmentation of speech strings based primarily upon the processing of frequency-sensitive, probabilistic patterns of lexical material will obviously hold implications for word-boundary phonological processes such as palatalization. Following from this redefinition of lexical structure is the likelihood that high-frequency word collocations such as *would you* and *did you* may be stored as agglutinated chunks of information due to the strong distributional correlations that link the component units.[24] Figure 2 presents a re-examination of the generative account of word-level palatalization as it might apply to *would you* versus *good you* (our original examples (1) and (2)), given the sharp contrast that exists between these two dyads' transitional probabilities (see again Table 3 or Table 5).[25] We now find this rule applying to two disparate phonological input strings, whose representation is segmented in the lexicon in radically different fashions based upon the frequent co-occurrence and high transitional probability of *would* (but not *good*) with the segment *you*.

In this type of scenario, *would you* can be stored in the lexicon as a single, readily-accessed chunk of information due to its frequent co-occurrence potential (string frequency of *would you* = 11 per approximately 40,000 words; however, see again note 24), while the two lexical components of *good you* (string frequency = 1 per approx. 40,000 words) remain stored separately. Therefore, the boundaries which define these lexical segments interface with the palatalization rule in Figure 2 with different results, with *would you* now palatalizing *internally* (similarly to

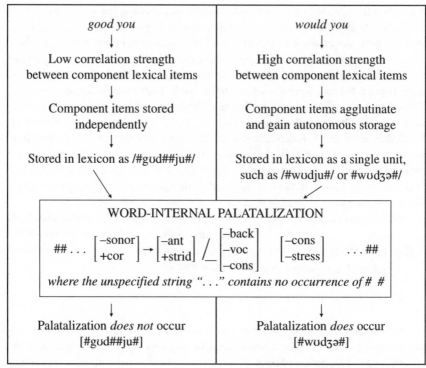

Figure 2. *The role of transitional probability in the word-boundary palatalization success of good you versus would you. 'Word-Internal Palatalization' rule reproduced from Chomsky and Halle (1968: 230)*

actual or *gradual*) due to a "word"-internal phonological process (because *would you* is stored functionally as a unitary "word"), while the separately-defined components of *good you* are not subject to the same rule because their junctural boundaries remain intact.[26]

Perhaps not surprisingly, the discourse distributions reflected in transitional-probability statistics are emergent syntactic constituents in and of themselves (cf. Bybee 1998, Bybee and Scheibman 1999).[27] In theory, the same lexical bonds which develop between two words of high transitional probability effectively structure these same items into single, functional, constituent phrases, and it is these probabilistically-determined phrases that serve to segment and define the input for a given phonological rule. Conversely, it may therefore be possible to predict the constituent breaks of these syntactic structures from the low-transition-probability junctures between particular lexical items (or planning units; cf. Jurafsky *et al.* 1998: 2), as proposed in Figure 3.

Taking into account the high degree of predictability of *you* given *would* (but not *good*), we observe the conditions for palatalization are now met for *would you*, but not for *good you* (see again Figure 2), due to the different ways in which these dyads are lexically structured via the aforementioned frequency-dependent chunking process. The fact that *would you* exhibits a very high transitional probability as a collocated pair (and is consequently chunked), in contrast with the comparatively loose probabilistic relationship between *good* and *you* (which results in no lexical agglutination), provides a plausible causal *motivation* for the actuation of word-boundary palatalization beyond the simple phonetic conditioning environments. Furthermore, this motivation may explain the fact that, in the corpus, it appears as though certain individuals *sometimes* palatalize high-transition-probability dyads such as *would you*, but other times they do not. Specifically, the inflexibility inherent in a typical generative description of palatalization might be eased by the realization that, on occasion, the input(s) to such a formalism require the access of one of two possible distinct lexical options for an individual: *would* separate from *you*, or a single chunked form such as /#wʊdju#/ or /#wʊdʒə#/. The consequence of maintaining two such types of representation, one with the two components agglutinated together (as in /#wʊdju#/) and the other with the two forms stored separately (e.g., /#wʊd##ju#/), is a possible [wʊd] [ju] versus [wʊdʒə] alternation in the phonological output, dependent on which type of form is initially activated in the lexicon and input to the palatalization rule (cf. Bybee 1998, Bybee and Scheibman 1999). It is in this way that the constituent boundaries emerge from the non-random patterning inherent in natural language and give rise to the following three distinct lexical entries: /wʊd/ 'would'; /ju/ 'you'; and a third, chunked item, /wʊdju/

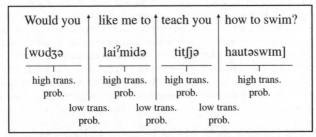

Figure 3. *The relationship between transitional probability and emergent constituent structure in naturally-occurring discourse (utterance taken from the Carterette and Jones 1974/MacWhinney 1995 corpus).*

'wouldya' or 'wouldja', that is especially prone to palatalization in its new "word"-*internal* environment. The original requirement that the Chomsky and Halle (1968: 230) palatalization rule must invariably operate within a word-internal environment is now relaxed by a redefinition of 'word' to mean a 'unitary chunk of lexical information.' What used to be a word-boundary juncture between *would* and *you* is now, as a result of the chunking effect, a word-medial (or syllable-boundary) domain, similar to that of *actual* and *gradual*. No longer must we rely upon *a priori* syntactic structure in some instances or prosodic criteria in others to limit the domains of applicability for phonological processes; rather, the distributional characteristics of the words themselves make this determination for us.

Notes

1. The word-boundary palatalization discussed here should not be confused with word-internal, or "lexical" palatalization (in words like *gradual*) that, in comparison, appears invariable (cf. Zsiga 1995).

2. 'Adult' corpus was exclusively college-age undergraduates sampled from a southern California junior college.

3. The two other, similarly-transcribed corpora from the Carterette and Jones (1974) portion of the CHILDES CD-ROM, consisting of a third-grade and also a first-grade sample, were not included as part of this data set due to the fact that the phonology was less representative of adult-like speech.

4. I have referred to the transcription of the Carterette and Jones (1974) data as *phonemic* because this is the term that these researchers used to describe their transcription process used in this study. However, it is obvious that some important *surface* representational information was captured fairly accurately using this "phonemic" (underlying representational) system. Specifically, the palatalization of word-boundary phenomena was routinely reflected in the text, which is one reason why palatalization was chosen in particular for this study as a highly ostensible form of word-boundary reduction since the sheer volume of word-boundary palatalization represented in the transcription makes me confident that this *was*, in fact, a distinction that the phoneticians consistently attended to. On the other hand, flapping, for instance, was sporadically reflected in the text without the use of a separate phonemic or phonetic character, represented using an occasional /d/ for the surface realization (flapping) of voiceless /t/. Presumably, the necessity of symbols used to represent the voiced and voiceless alveopalatal affricate in the repertoire of these phoneticians' quasi-phonemic alphabet allowed for the extension of these phonemes to surface phenomena such as the word-boundary palatalization under discussion here.

5. The CD-ROM used for the manipulation of the database for this paper is entitled "The CHILDES Database," and is accompanied by a user's manual, "The CHILDES Project: Tools for Analyzing Talk" (Second Edition). For full reference information, consult MacWhinney (1995).

6. It is important to realize that the term 'word dyad,' as it is used for the purposes of this paper, applies

to *any* two consecutive words, regardless of frequency, so that there always exists an $[n-1]$ number of possible word dyads for any utterance or phrase consisting of *n* words. All word dyads referred to in this paper juxtapose a word-final alveolar stop with a word-initial palatal glide, unless otherwise specified.

7. The "independent" nature of each *independent palatalization trial* stems from the probabilistic notion that each event (where palatalization either occurs or does not) acts according to a fixed probability rate whose outcome is not dependent on the results of prior trials. Using the analogy of the flip of a coin, the probability of getting "tails" is 50% and the fact that it is possible for the coin to land on "tails" three times in a row does not necessarily increase the chances of getting "heads" on the fourth trial — the theoretical probability of getting "tails" (or "heads," for that matter) on the fourth trail remains 50%.

8. At first glance, it may not seem intuitively informative to note that words that commonly enter into *independent palatalization trials* also display a high propensity for word-boundary palatalization. One might guess that words that have "more of an opportunity" would also "have better luck," so to speak. However, the *independent* nature of these trials must be kept in mind: "more opportunity" does not translate into "better luck," if all other factors (here, the requisite phonologically-conditioned combinations) are held equal, in which case the probability (i.e., rate) of word-boundary palatalization should be the same for all word dyads (again, see Table 1 for a list of those items under consideration). It is the "other factors" (beyond those of simply preserving the necessary phonological conditioning environment) that will be of interest to this discussion — those factors (such as co-occurrence frequency and other related emergent phenomena like transitional probability) that might cause the probability of palatalization for some word dyads to increase, and for others, to comparatively decrease.

9. "Yates correction" for this 2 × 2 chi-squared test has minimal impact, reducing χ^2 value to 25.976; *p*-value remains < .001.

10. In fact, my positing the existence of a cut-off point for the distribution of word dyads whose conditioning environments are maintained with "high-frequency" versus "low-frequency" is purely for the convenience of statistical analysis. In actuality, the existence of this type of binary, categorical distribution is highly improbable. My belief is that such a correlation between palatalization occurrence and frequency-based factors is likely operative along some type of gradient continuum, precluding the existence of any lexical correlate to this arbitrary break between "high" and "low" frequency.

11. While transitional probability is perhaps the most simple (and therefore, easily testable) expression of conditional probability, other statistical measures exist which may prove to be even more accurate indicators of the degree to which the occurrence of one lexical item intimates the likelihood for the occurrence of another item nearby. See note 20 for a discussion of some more advanced statistics which suggest the need for computational analyses of corpora much larger than that which is analyzed here.

12. The question as to the exact nature of the relationship between transitional probability and priming effects is an interesting one. More specifically, it seems intuitive to posit a functional (and possibly evolutionarily adaptive) relationship that may exist between transitional probability, priming effects, and lexical search space, the details of which are a matter best left to further empirical research.

13. In fact, of the 145 instances of *did* in the corpus, the word *you* immediately followed the word *did* nearly 50 percent of the time, i.e., 'Freq. of [x+y]' for *did you* = 71.

14. The actual context for this unusual dyad from the Carterette and Jones (1974)/MacWhinney (1995) corpus is as follows: "That the more pregnant you are...its proven that its the retention of water."

15. The fact that the 'pregnant you' example has a transitional probability of 100% serves as a reminder that the transitional probability derived from low-frequency dyads is a largely unreliable statistic, basically in the sense that "Y always follows X" is still a largely untested hypothesis — theoretically testable, though, given a larger database.

16. "Yates correction" for this chi-squared data (again, even without the benefit of *did you* figured into the equation) produces an χ^2 value of 7.857, *p*-value < 0.01.

17. Preliminary indications from my statistical analysis suggest that a binary logistic regression that plots the transitional probability for each dyad from Table 3 against the probability that palatalization will occur for that dyad may be useful in assessing "predictive" values, such that, given any one transitional probability figure for any word dyad, a statistical likelihood for palatalization to occur may be either interpolated or extrapolated from the data to-date. This type of statistic essentially offers a "best fit" linear relationship between these two variables.

18. It is interesting to note that the conjunction *et*, which is highly frequent in French and has (like *and*) a very low transitional probability with the next word, never enters into liaison (Bybee this volume).

19. This shortcoming again points to the necessity of testing the predictions of transitional probability on a much larger database. However, there will, unfortunately, always be combinations of words that occur only once, and some of these will undoubtedly have a transitional probability of 100%. In a larger database, these local anomalies would contribute less, proportionally, to the overall phonological predictability of transitional probability, or lack thereof.

20. Gregory *et al.* (1999) argue for the notion of *mutual information* as being the most reliable statistically-significant predictor of phonological reduction. This notion mathematically incorporates statistics similar to transitional probability (i.e., Gregory *et al.*'s 'conditional probability' or 'collocational probability') and also token frequency ('prior probability'). Gregory *et al.* define mutual information as $MI = p(x, y)/p(x) p(y)$, where (x, y) is our 'word dyad' and p is 'probability of.' Transitional probability was found to be a significant factor in some, but not all, of their tests on the predictability of phonological reduction. More importantly, Gregory *et al.* demonstrate that string frequency alone ('joint bigram probability') is not a factor in word shortening, and therefore, they claim, it is not a sufficient indicator of the amount of cohesion between two words. Additionally, Clear (1993) invokes a related definition of mutual information as a means toward a different goal: recognizing significant co-occurrence relationships between words, not necessarily adjacent to each other, in an attempt to mathematically determine when certain combinations of lexemes warrant lexicographic differentiation as separate senses of a target word within a dictionary entry. Both of these studies point toward a potentially bi-directional, associative influence cast upon words not only following a target lexeme, but also preceding it. While such mutual influences are more than likely to exist (and may, therefore, underscore the need for further analysis of this database in search of these reciprocal effects), the unidirectional nature of transitional probability nonetheless makes significant contributions in and of itself towards assessing the mutual exclusivity shared by two or more words.

21. Boyland (1996) cites two skill acquisition theories, Anderson (1983) and Rosenbloom *et al.* (1989), that implicate the chunking mechanism as being central to the interface between frequency of stimulus presentation and information storage.

22. Pollack and Pickett (1964) illustrate the altered information content of chunked linguistic motor programs in the following experiment: subjects were asked to identify individual words which had either been (1) recorded from a list of randomly-presented words or (2) spliced at random from a continuous stream of spoken language. The subjects were largely unable to identify the segments randomly spliced from running speech due to these items' reduced articulatory detail. Presumably, this lack of articulatory detail is the result of the chunking principle which supplements the reduced information complexity of the chunked code with contextual information that preserves significant meaning. Without some type of contextualized presentation, the spliced segments were basically unrecognizable, thus evidencing the necessary lexical mapping which occurs between chunked information and the context with which it is indexed.

23. Note that the VERB + PRONOUN chunk *gimme* often coexists within the developing lexicon as an autonomous unit alongside separate entries for both *give* and *me*, as it did for a period during the author's own child-language development.

24. Note that the storage of chunked forms that incorporate multiple components of lexical material does NOT preclude the storage elsewhere in the lexicon of the forms in their separate, uncompressed state.

25. The simplicity of lexical representation suggested by Figure 2 is probably overstated. Instead, evidence suggests that minute variations in the perceived and produced forms of a word (such as that type of variation that distinguishes /#wʊdju#/ from /#wʊdʒə#/ and from any intermediate forms) are registered in the lexicon, akin to the "usage-based" model discussed in Bybee (1996).

26. But cf. Gregory *et al.* 1999. These researchers conclude that, given their probabilistic model, positing such structural changes to lexical entries to account for predictable phonological reduction is not entirely necessary.

27. Landauer and Dumais (1997: 235) allude to the theoretical potential for the existence of a mechanism able to analyze distributional patterns in discourse and, in the process, acquire syntactic knowledge therefrom.

References

Akmajian, A., Demers, R.A., Farmer, A.K., and Harnish, R.M. 1995. *Linguistics: An Introduction to Language and Communication*. Cambridge, Mass: MIT Press.

Anderson, J.R. 1983. *The Architecture of Cognition*. Cambridge, Mass: Harvard University Press.

Barlow, M. and Neumann, S. 1997. *Monoconc for Windows*. A PC-based computer concordance program. Houston: Athelstan. Further information available @ http://www.athel.com.

Bellezza, F.S. and Young, D.R. 1989. "Chunking of repeated events in memory". *Journal of Experimental Psychology: Learning, Memory, and Cognition* 15 (5): 990–7.

Bloomfield, L. 1933. *Language*. New York: Henry Holt.

Boyland, J.T. 1996. *Morphosyntactic Change in Progress: A Psycholinguistic Treatment.* Ph.D. Dissertation, University of California, Berkeley.

Browman, C.P. and Goldstein, L.M. 1992. "Articulatory phonology: An overview". *Phonetica* 49: 155–80.

Bybee, J. 1996. "Usage-based phonology". Paper presented at the Symposium on Formal and Functional Theories, University of Wisconsin, Milwaukee.

Bybee, J. 1998. " The emergent lexicon." *Chicago Linguistics Society* 34.

Bybee, J. This volume. "Frequency effects on French liaison".

Bybee, J. 2000. "Lexicalization of sound change and alternating environments." In *Papers in Laboratory Phonology V: Acquisition and the Lexicon*, M. Broe and J. Pierrehumbert (eds.), 250–68. Cambridge: Cambridge University Press.

Bybee, J. To appear. *Phonology and Language Use.* Cambridge: Cambridge University Press.

Bybee, J., Perkins, R., and Pagliuca, W. 1994. *The Evolution of Grammar: Tense, Aspect, and Modality in the Languages of the World.* Chicago: University of Chicago Press.

Bybee, J., and Scheibman, J. 1999. "The effect of usage on degrees of constituency: the reduction of *don't* in English". *Linguistics* 37: 575–96.

Carterette, E., and Jones, M.H. 1974. *Informal Speech: Alphabetic & Phonemic Texts with Statistical Analyses and Tables.* Berkeley: University of California Press.

Chomsky, N., and Halle, M. 1968. *The Sound Pattern of English.* New York: Harper and Row.

Clear, J. 1993. "From Firth Principles". In *Text and Technology*, M. Baker, G. Francis, and E. Tognini-Bonelli (eds.), 271–92. Amsterdam: John Benjamins.

Cooper, W.E., Edigo, C., and Paccia, J.M. 1978. "Grammatical control of a phonological rule: palatalization". *Journal of Experimental Psychology: Human Perception and Performance* 4 (2): 264–72.

Gregory, M., Raymond, W.D., Bell, A., Fosler-Lussier, E., and Jurafsky, D. 1999. "The effects of collocational strength and contextual predictability in lexical production". *Chicago Linguistic Society* 35: 151–66.

Guy, G.R. 1980. "Variation in the group and the individual: the case of final stop deletion". In *Locating Language in Time and Space*, W. Labov (ed.), 1–36. New York: Academic Press.

Haiman, J. 1994. "Ritualization and the development of language". In *Perspectives on Grammaticalization*, W. Pagliuca (ed.), 3–28. Amsterdam: John Benjamins.

Hooper, J.B. 1976. "Word frequency in lexical diffusion and the source of morphophonological change". In *Current Progress in Historical Linguistics*, W. Christie (ed.), 96–105. Amsterdam: North Holland.

Hopper, P.J. 1987. "Emergent grammar". *Berkeley Linguistic Society* 13: 139–57.

Hunltzen, L.S., Allen,, J.H.D. Jr., and Miron, M.S. 1964. *Transitional Frequencies of English Phonemes.* Urbana: University of Illinois Press.

Hyman, L.M. 1990. "Boundary tonology and the prosodic hierarchy". In *The Phonology-Syntax Connection*, S. Inkelas and D. Zec (eds.), 109–25. Chicago: University of Chicago Press.

Jurafsky, D., Bell, A., Fosler-Lussier, E., Girand, C., and Raymond, W. 1998. "Reduction of English function words in switchboard". As reprinted at the following website address: http://www.colorado.edu/ling/faculty/jurafsky/icslp98red.ps. Also in Proceedings of ICSLP-98. Sydney.

Kaisse, E.M. 1990. "Toward a typology of postlexical rules". In *The Phonology-Syntax Connection*, S. Inkelas and D. Zec (eds.), 127–43. Chicago: University of Chicago Press.

Kellman, P.J., and Spelke, E.S. 1983. "Perception of partly occluded objects in infancy". *Cognitive Psychology* 15: 483–528.

Kellman, P.J., Gleitman, H., and Spelke, E.S. 1987. "Object and observer motion in the perception of objects by infants". *Journal of Experimental Psychology: Human Perception and Performance* 13: 586–93.

Kenstowicz, M. and Kisseberth, C. 1990. "Chizigula tonology: The word and beyond". In *The Phonology-Syntax Connection*, S. Inkelas and D. Zec (eds.), 163–94. Chicago: University of Chicago Press.

Krug, M. 1998. "String frequency: a cognitive motivating factor in coalescence, language processing, and linguistic change". *Journal of English Linguistics* 26 (4): 286–320.

Labov, W. 1994. *Principles of Linguistic Change: Internal Factors*. Oxford: Blackwell.

Landauer, T.K. and Dumais, S.T. 1997. "A solution to Plato's problem: the latent semantic analysis theory of acquisition, induction, and representation of knowledge". *Psychological Review* 104 (2): 211–40.

Lindblom, B. 1992. "Phonological units as adaptive emergents of lexical development". In *Phonological Development: Models, Research, Implications*, C.A. Ferguson, L. Menn, and C. Stoel-Gammon (eds.), 131–64. Timonium, MD: York Press.

MacWhinney, B.. 1995. *The CHILDES Project: Tools for Analyzing Talk*. Hillsdale, NJ: Lawrence Erlbaum.

Miller, G.A. 1956. "The magical number seven, plus or minus two: some limits on our capacity for processing information". *Psychological Review* 63: 81–97.

Morgan, J.L., and Saffran, J.R. 1995. "Emerging integration of sequential and suprasegmental information in preverbal speech recognition". *Child Development* 66: 911–36.

Phillips, B.S. 1984. "Word frequency and the actuation of sound change". *Language* 60: 320–42.

Pollack, I. and Pickett, J.M. 1964. "Frequency importance function for isolated words and for conversation of female talkers". *Language and Speech* 7: 71–5.

Rosenbloom, P.S., Laird, J.E., and Newell, A. 1989. The chunking of skill and knowledge. In *Working Models of Human Perception*, B.A.G. Elsedoorn and H. Bouma (eds.), 391–410. London: Academic Press.

Saffran, J.R., Aslin, R.N., and Newport, E.L. 1996. "Statistical learning by 8-month-old infants". *Science* 274: 1926–8.

Saffran, J.R., Newport, E.L., and Aslin, R.N. 1996. "Word segmentation: The role of distributional cues". *Journal of Memory and Language* 35: 606–21.

Sejnowski, R.J., and Nowlan, S.J. 1995. "A model of visual motion processing in area MT of primates". In *The Cognitive Neurosciences*, M. Gazzaniga (ed.), 437–49. Cambridge, MA: MIT Press.

Spelke, E.S. 1990. "Principles of object recognition". *Cognitive Science* 14: 29–56.

Spelke, E.S., von Hofsten, C., and Kestenbaum, R. 1989. "Object perception in infancy: Interaction of spatial and kinetic information for object boundaries". *Developmental Psychology* 25: 185–96.

Trager, G.L., and Smith, H.L. 1951. *An Outline of English Structure*. Norman, Oklahoma: Battenburg.

Vogel, I., and Kenesei, I. 1990. "Syntax and semantics in phonology". In *The Phonology-Syntax Connection*, S. Inkelas and D. Zec (eds.), 339–63. Chicago: University of Chicago Press.

Zipf, G.K. 1929. Relative frequency as a determinant of phonetic change. *Harvard Studies in Classical Philology* 15: 1–95.

Zipf, G.K. 1949. *Human Behavior and the Principle of Least Effort: an Introduction to Human Ecology*. New York: Hafner.

Zsiga, E.C. 1995. An acoustic and electropalatographic study of lexical and postlexical palatalization in American English. In *Phonology and Phonetic Evidence: Papers in Laboratory Phonology IV*, B. Connell and A. Arvaniti (eds.), 282–302. Cambridge: Cambridge University Press.

The role of frequency
in the realization of English *that**

CATIE BERKENFIELD

University of New Mexico

1. Introduction

The nature of phonological category structure and its relationship to linguistic storage has been an issue of utmost theoretical importance to linguists in recent years (Browman and Goldstein 1992; Bybee 1988; Lindblom 1990; Lindblom *et al.* 1984; Mowrey and Paguliuca 1995; Ohala 1997; Pierrehumbert 1990). The purpose of the research presented here is to address the nature of phonological category structure and representation in the theory of lexicon and grammar by studying speech data from recorded conversations.[1] In particular, I investigate phonetic properties of the different functional categories that are instantiated by the English word *that*. These categories are Demonstrative pronoun, Demonstrative adjective, Relative clause marker, and Complementizer. The phonetic properties I measure are the duration of the vowel /æ/ and first formant (F1) values for this vowel. I also measure the degree of correlation for these two properties. The analyses indicate that each function of *that* is represented independently in the phonological system, in terms of phonetic vowel properties. The findings suggest that a usage-based approach to language structure and diachronic development, which takes into account low-level phonetic properties of the speech signal and the frequency of repeated constructions in speech, may be a principled way of addressing the correspondence of form and meaning for this data.

Interestingly, the synchronic representation of phonological structure may indicate contrastive function of phonetic properties for Demonstrative adjectives and Complementizers. In addition, the degree of correlation of vowel duration and centralization seems to be most robust for Complementizers, a correlation which is predicted by the usage-based framework. However, in terms of the relative frequency of Complementizers compared to other frequent categories, this correlation is anomalous. Most interesting is the notion that centralization for the vowel /æ/ displays both allophonic, predictable information and potentially phonemic, contrastive information in the synchronic grammar. Finally, it becomes clear that the study of phonetic factors in isolation from meaning may yield a reduced and artificial picture of the interaction between phonetics, phonology, and semantics. Repeated constructions will show reductive change in both meaning and form which is sensitive to diachronic development and token frequency, but is also unpredictable in specific ways.

Jurafsky *et al.* (1998) looked at several variables as they pertain to the reduction of function words (including *that*). These variables included speech rate, planning problems, lexical context, and predictability, all of which showed strong, independent effects on reduction. More recently, Jurafsky *et al.* (this volume) tested a Probabilistic Reduction Hypothesis, showing that with several measures of frequency, "more probable words are reduced, whether they are content or function words."

My approach uses the theoretical notion of token frequency to describe the categorical boundaries of the varieties of *that* in the lexicon and grammar. This study provides evidence that the vowel in *that* may not be a monolithic phonological category—low front vowel, because its phonetic properties provide a basis for contrast in meaning for two functions. This is consistent with a usage-based approach. This approach also supports the phonetic analysis of diachronically related material, showing that variation is the rule rather than the exception and that phonetic properties can illuminate functional change. It also indicates that analyses of stress variables need not be confined to highly lexical words, because there is variation even among diachronically related function words.

First, I will provide background discussion for some of the theoretical issues at stake: a characterization of the exemplar model, a discussion of phonetic reduction and frequency, and, finally, the artificial privileging of phonological contrasts over phonetic gradation. In the main body of the paper, I will first introduce the research topic and discuss why the data has the potential to yield interesting results. After situating the reader with an understanding of the issues and the impetus for the analyses, I will discuss the nature of the data and the procedures I used to collect it. The three analyses will be discussed in three separate sections. Finally, I synthesize the results and show how phonetics and phonology can be linked in complex ways, indicating that an understanding of both categorical and gradient structure is crucial to an accurate model of the lexicon and grammar. Now that I have given a brief overview of the paper, I introduce some of the theoretical constructs that frame the current study.

2. Theoretical constructs and considerations

2.1 The exemplar model

Characterizations of categorical structure have, for the majority of Western intellectual history, been grounded in the notion that categories are discrete with individual entities (either concrete or abstract) belonging or not belonging to a given category (but see Lakoff 1987 for a critical synopsis of objectivism). This take on categorical structure has influenced the study of linguistics throughout its development as a scientific field. In fact, much of modern linguistic analysis is predicated on the early structuralist approaches to categorization, especially analyses of phonological categories, which relegated the elements of speech to "either/or" characterizations.

The notion of binary categorical contrasts formed the basis for the articulatory features which Chomsky and Halle outlined in *The Sound Pattern of English* (1968). During the development of the generative theory of grammar, gradient acoustic phenomena were put aside as factors related to "performance" in the Chomskyan sense. Thus, the fine-grained details of the speech signal, regardless of whether they were acoustically or articulatorily based, were not taken into account in establishing phonological categories.

More recently, philosophical writings and psycholinguistic research have motivated linguists to reevaluate the notion of categories as either/or phenomena. From Wittgenstein (see Givón 1984 for discussion) to Nosofsky, we see attempts in the literature to deal with the boundaries of categories. New philosophical and psycholinguistic evidence supports the notion that human beings are able to maintain flexible and gradient category structure (see Bybee to appear; Givón 1984; and Lakoff 1987). Two of the strongest empirically based theories to emerge in recent years are the prototype theory (Mervis and Catlin 1976; Rosch and Mervis 1975; Rosch *et al.* 1976; Varela *et al.* 1991) and the exemplar theory (Nosofsky 1988; Nosofsky *et al.* 1992) of categorization. I will assume an exemplar-based model in this study since the exemplar model explicitly takes into account the effect of token frequency on categorization.[2] It is further assumed that different kinds of categorization coexist in the lexicon and grammar, consistent with a network model (cf. Bybee 1998). I do not specifically rule out a prototype approach. However, the methodology presented in this study more closely approaches what is known about exemplars.

Nosofsky reports that "the summed-similarity exemplar model is not simply a disguised prototype model . . . when exemplar information is summed to form a prototype, information is lost concerning individual component dimensions" (707). This statement draws an important distinction between the exemplar and prototype models, indicating a higher-level, more abstracted category structure for a prototype. The prototype of a category more closely approximates what has been posited as phonological in the classical sense; it is an abstraction which enables the language user to ignore low-level phonetic detail in the categorization of a token. On the other hand, the exemplar model explicitly stores the finer detail of the acoustic signal such that if a language user needs additional information to decode a message, that information is available from memory as well.

How is this distinction useful for the purposes of this research? If exemplar storage maps "individual component dimensions" of tokens, e.g., the variety of phonetic properties in the speech signal which together indicate token function or the discourse meaning of particular exemplars, the exemplar model is the better model to study the on-line language processing factors which drive the emergence of linguistic constructions, an important factor being repetition or frequency of occurrence.

In an exemplar model of linguistic storage, individual tokens of linguistic forms are stored in the lexicon and grammar. A token is a particular instance of any linguistically meaningful use (e.g., a morpheme, a syntactic pattern, etc). When language users perceive a novel linguistic token, they compare it to the tokens already stored in memory in order to evaluate whether it belongs to a particular category and then they store the novel token in that category, if it is sufficiently similar, reinforcing the category (Nosofsky 1988: 700).

The exemplar model also allows for the notion of fuzzy or gradient category structure. Miller (1994) addresses the internal structure of phonetic categories and concludes that language users take advantage of multiple acoustic cues to categorize tokens, with some of those tokens being better examples of the category than others, indicating gradient category structure. While Miller does not directly address the question of exemplar vs. prototype structure, her findings are consistent with an exemplar-based approach.

Recently, Bybee's work in phonological representation indicates that analysis of fine phonetic detail can help predict and explain phonological change (in press). She argues that frequency of use affects the phonetic details of individual words. She writes "there is no necessity to sort exemplars into prototypes and discard the memory of the particular token. In fact, if tokens of experience are not stored in memory, at least for a while, no prototype could be formed, since categorization depends upon the comparison of multiple individual percepts" (42). Thus, actual experience of language, in addition to users' abstractions of that experience, is responsible for the state of the language and the kinds and directions of language change.

The present study assumes gradient category structure for individual grammatical functions which allows for variation in phonetic properties; we see indications of vowel variation within the category as well as evidence of category boundaries, which are predictable on the basis of function of English *that*. The study also recognizes that variation is the source of and force directing categorical change.

Now that we have looked at the issues of the exemplar model, I turn to a discussion of reduction, which I will use in this study to describe phonetic properties of the speech signal, and frequency, which is a crucial component of my methodology.

2.2 Reduction and frequency

Browman and Goldstein (1992) have discussed reduction of articulatory gestures as a result of stress and sentence position prosodic variables, as well as being a result of register variation on a casual to formal continuum. They write "gestures shrink in space and time in some contexts. This . . . kind of variation is quite constrained—it scales the metric properties of a gestural event, but does not alter the composition of articulatory components out of which it is assembled" (167). Mowrey and Pagliuca (1995) have discussed sound change in terms of reduction also. In fact, they posit language internal sound change as either temporal reduction or substantive reduction (108). Mowrey and Pagliuca do allow exceptions to this trend but indicate that exceptions are "statistically insignificant relative to reduction" (109). The notion that sound change is almost always reductive highlights the importance of the frequency of particular strings of sounds and automatization. Boyland (1996), drawing on Anderson (1993) and Rosenbloom *et al.* (1993), has argued that repetition of behavior leads to automation, i.e., repetition of action leads to *knowing how* to perform a behavior without having to think about the component parts of the behavior. The streamlining of gesture, in articulatory phonology, seems to be an interesting case for procedural knowledge, which may result in articulatory reduction. Repetition of units has been shown to correspond to reduction in linguistic form. I turn to that discussion next.

In this paper, token frequency refers to the number of times speakers use the word *that* in running text. Each token is counted individually even if the *kind* of token is similar to other tokens. Other authors have found relationships between reduction and token frequency. Hooper (1976) found that schwa deletion was more likely to occur in frequent lexical items in English than in less frequent items. For example, it is more likely that the word *memory* will undergo schwa deletion than the word *armory* since *memory* is more frequent. She proposed that "infrequent items are the most resistant to phonetically motivated change" (95). Phillips (1984), following Hooper, argued that physiological factors in speech production (i.e., ease of articulation) led to raising of Old English /a/ before nasals in the most frequent words. Jurafsky *et al.* (1998) provide empirical evidence that highly frequent function words in English (including, incidentally, *that*) show reduction as a result of speech rate, segmental context, and predictability. Token frequency is clearly important to an exemplar model of language representation because a token *is* an exemplar and, therefore, is stored as such in the lexicon and grammar.

2.3 *Privileging of phonological features*

The discussion of theoretical constructs to this point has set the stage for the main thesis of this paper. I argue that the division between phonological categorical structure and measurable phonetic properties is artificial. Gradualness of change and variation in usage contribute to how functions emerge in grammar. Within the context of this paper, I look at phonetic substance in terms of vowel duration, discussing the durational effects of reduction of /æ/ in Section 4 (analysis 1). I then look at vowel quality with reference to reduction in Section 5 (analysis 2). In Section 6 (analysis 3), I look at the degree to which these two reductive processes are correlated.

I will use the word *phonetic* to refer to gradient, quantitative, and measurable signals in the speech stream of the data collected for this study. While some of these phonetic properties may have *phonological* or categorical import, I will refrain from making such judgements until the conclusion (Section 7) of the paper.

3. Functional distribution of English *that* and the historical source of modern *that* functions

3.1 *Functional distribution of English that*

Native speakers of English use the word *that* frequently. Examples (1)–(5) illustrate the main functions encoded by tokens of Present Day English (PDE) *that*. Each example is followed in parentheses by a notional characterization of the function as defined by the *Oxford English Dictionary* (OED):

(1) Demonstrative pronoun function.

'I would think that it would be important for us to obtain *that*.' (nominally oriented referent; *c*.888[3])

(2) Demonstrative adjective function.

'And in the aftermath of *that* speech, he had calls from something over 20 leaders, countries around the world.' ("simple demonstrative"; *c*.1,200)

(3) Demonstrative adverb function.[4]

'It's not *that* serious.' ("to that extent or degree"; *c*.1,450)

(4) Complementizer function.[5]

'But I I do think *that* due process—but an expeditious consideration of all these facts—since we really are pretty cognizant now of what the facts are—is is warranted and and would do a real service to the country and to this particular issue.' ("introducing dependent substantive clause as subject, object, or other element of principal clause"; *c*.888)

(5) Relative clause marker function.

'And some of the the work *that* would need to be done to identify sensitive materials can be carried out by staff.' ("introducing restrictive clause"; *c*.825)

Examples (1)–(5) are from a small corpus of conversational speech taken from *The Newshour with Jim Lehrer*, on PBS. The token *that* was used 305 times (out of 10,640 words), constituting approximately 3% of the data. Table 1 shows the distribution of the functions of English *that* within the single genre used as the foundation for this study—professional, political commentary—and within larger corpora comprising data from numerous genres of spoken and written data.

Unfortunately, neither the Switchboard Corpus of American English nor the Brown Corpus of Written English distinguishes between the Demonstrative pronoun and Demonstrative adjective categories. This issue is addressed in Section 4, analysis 1.

It appears, from the information in Table 1, that the spoken and written genres of the English language show considerable variation in the distribution of the functions of *that*. Because this study stems from a usage-based approach to language, I will assume that the Switchboard Corpus distribution of tokens, since it represents speech over a wide variety of topics, is the most accurate representation of *that* functions in conversational American English. The numbers to keep in mind for the purposes of the current research are those numbers indicating the relative frequency of each category in the Switchboard Corpus. Now that I have shown the synchronic distribution, we turn briefly to the historical appearance of each function.

Table 1. *Comparative distribution of* THAT *functions in a specific speech genre, in the Switchboard Corpus of American Speech, and in the Brown Corpus of Written English*[6]

Function	Newshour transcripts 10,640 words speech data N (% of total)	Switchboard Corpus 2,400,355 words speech data N (% of total)	Brown Corpus 1,014,232 words text data N (% of total)
Demonstrative pronouns	83 (28%)	21,028 (56%)	2,455 (23%)
Demonstrative adjectives	29 (10%)		
Complementizers	107 (36%)	7,470 (20%)	6,468 (60%)
Relative clause markers	82 (27%)	8,395 (22%)	1,810 (17%)
Total tokens	301 (100%)	37,574 (98%)[7]	10,733 (100%)

3.2 Historical source of modern that functions

Relative clause markers and Complementizers developed out of the Demonstrative pronoun (Traugott 1992 and O'Neil 1977, respectively). Demonstrative adjectives are also shown to have developed from this source (OED 1971: 868). Given these historical relationships, I propose to take the Demonstrative pronoun category as a base category against which to compare the other categories. This basis of comparison is somewhat artificial since it might appear to assume that the phonetic form of Demonstrative pronouns has remained static over the centuries. I would prefer to take the view that all of the categories have changed over the centuries. But because the category of Demonstrative pronouns is the semantic and phonological source for the other categories, it is the only available constant against which to measure the phonetic form of other functions of English *that* in PDE.

The Demonstrative pronoun function is the least grammaticized of the four categories in question. These pronouns point to previously mentioned referents in a discourse. More grammatical in function are the Demonstrative adjectives whose constituency within an NP still allows them to point toward a referent, but where they do not represent a referent themselves. In other words, their meaning is more bleached in that they are more "functional" and less "meaningful" than their historical source. More grammatical too are the Relative clause markers and the Complementizers, which function to introduce a restrictive relative clause or a dependent, subordinated clause in the discourse, respectively.[8]

An important issue that arises here is that Demonstrative pronouns are the most frequently occurring category of any under consideration in The Switchboard Corpus of American Speech. If Demonstrative pronouns are so frequent, why do we find them to have unreduced vowels in general? There may be several reasons for this. One reason may be the function itself. As I pointed out in the previous paragraph, Demonstrative pronouns refer to either things or events which an interlocutor has introduced in the discourse. Thus, these pronouns are less semantically bleached than other kinds of tokens, in that there is some entity to which they refer, and they are predicted to have a fuller articulation due to a stronger lexical or content status.

Another reason for the maintenance of a fully articulated vowel may be that they are the only kind of token which occurs at the end of a syntactic or discursive unit, where speech is most likely to slow in rate, resulting in vowel lengthening. While I argue for the substantive properties of phonetics in this work, I also allow that other issues of distribution may factor into determining the nature of the phonetic signal. Most notably, prosody of the vowel can often be linked to syntactic placement. A *that*-construction may range from functioning as an collocationally independent unit like Demonstrative pronoun to functioning as a collocationally dependent unit like conjunctive Complementizer.[9] Demonstrative pronoun tokens which constitute a construction in and of themselves are likely to be more fully articulated whereas the more syntagmatically dependent constructions will have a greater temporal distribution of articulatory energy over the larger construction. The lexical participants in the syntagmatically dependent *that*-constructions tend to have more articulatory energy concentrated in them while the grammatical participants have less.

Given this historical background, I turn to the substance of the current work—the phonetic analyses which help describe and explain the current state of English *that* usage and representation in the lexicon and grammar.

4. Analysis 1

The purpose of the first analysis is to see whether there is any correlation between phonetic reduction and grammatical function of tokens of English *that*. More specifically, I wanted to find out if tokens from a category with a high frequency in corpus text compared to the Demonstrative pronoun function tokens—the historical source category—have a shorter mean vowel duration. I am taking shorter mean vowel duration as evidence of phonetic reduction.

We might expect reduction in a variety of phonetic properties of English *that*, ranging from ð-deletion to final stop deletion in addition to changes in the length and quality of the vowel. In fact, for much of the data in this corpus, other kinds of phonetic reduction co-occur with shortness of vowel duration.[10] Umeda (1975) found that /æ/ shows the greatest standard deviation in duration (14–20 milliseconds) among English vowels in function words including *that*.[11] Looking at English *that* has the potential to illuminate frequency effects since the low front vowel /æ/ shows the greatest potential for variation in vowel duration according to Umeda's analysis.

4.1 Data source

The data are taken from a series of recorded television conversations. A conversation is defined as involving at least two people engaged in verbal turn-taking. Each participant had to be, in my judgement, a native speaker of English. There were thirteen speakers. Because the data are all recorded from interviews on *The Newshour with Jim Lehrer* on PBS, they are not intended to be representative of all registers. I selected 301 tokens from the 305 occurrences of the word *that* as usable in the 10,640 word corpus.

4.2 Methodology

I measured vowel duration as an indicator of phonetic reduction. I used *Sound-*

Effects shareware for Macintosh to measure duration. The process consisted of sampling speech recorded on videotape in *SoundEffects* at a rate of 22,050 Hertz (Hz) and displaying a speech waveform for each token. The visual representation was sufficient to gauge duration in milliseconds (ms). I recorded duration values starting with the second trough apparent in the vowel wave and measured the wave up to a return to the baseline position indicating stop closure for final /t/. Where stop closure did not occur, I measured the wave until visual cues in the waveform indicated a transition to another vowel or non-stop consonant.

4.3 Hypothesis 1

Let us turn to a concise version of my first hypothesis. The first hypothesis is:

Hypothesis 1_0

There is no relationship between the token frequency of the *that* construction and vowel duration reduction when the mean vowel duration of *that* in a function is compared to other *that*-functions which developed out of the same source category.

The statistical test applied to evaluate the hypothesis is the two-tailed t-test. We can predict, from a usage-based perspective, that the more frequent the construction involving *that* in the data, in comparison to other uses of *that* which developed out of the Demonstrative pronoun source, the more reduced the phonetic representation of the token will be.[12]

4.4 Results

4.4.1 Data distribution

Table 2 shows the frequency of the functional categories from the corpus.

4.4.2 Statistical test results

The results of the t-tests applied, in order to compare Demonstrative pronouns with all other categories, are given in (6a–c).

(6) a. Demonstrative pronouns (n = 83) have a longer mean vowel duration than Complementizers (n = 107), p < .01
   b. Demonstrative pronouns (n = 83) have a longer mean vowel duration than Relative clause markers (n = 82), p < .01
   c. Demonstrative pronouns (n = 83) have a longer mean vowel duration than Demonstrative adjectives (n = 29), p < .01

Table 2. *Mean duration and distribution of categories for* that *tokens*[13]

Function	Tokens	Mean vowel duration	Switchboard Corpus 2,400,355 words speech data N (% of total)
Demonstrative pronouns	83	133 ms	18,084 (48%)[14]
Demonstrative adjectives	29	97 ms	2,944 (8%)
Complementizers	107	84 ms	7,470 (20%)
Relative clause markers	82	63 ms	8,395 (22%)
Total	n = 301		37,574 (98%)

4.5 Discussion

We can see from these results that the grammaticization, or development of grammatical material out of less grammatical material, is measurable in terms of vowel duration for all three constructions. As *that* moves out of the semantic domain of Demonstrative pronoun, its meaning becomes more grammatical and its phonetic properties, in this case the duration of the vowel, parallel the change by differing from the source category in a statistically significant way, such that the more grammaticized functions have a shorter duration.

Relative clause markers are the most frequent category, in the Switchboard Corpus, of those uses that developed out of the Demonstrative pronoun source. These tokens have the shortest mean vowel duration of any function, at 63 ms. Then, as predicted, Complementizers are the next most frequent use with a mean vowel duration of 84 ms. Finally, Demonstrative adjectives are the least frequent and show the longest mean vowel duration with values clustering around 97 ms. In visual form, we might characterize these relationships as shown in Figure 2.

Both Relative clause markers and Complementizers have grammaticized along a pathway that led to more extreme semantic reevaluation—their semantic scope has widened and they occur with a larger number of syntactic patterns—and phonetic reduction. Not surprisingly, they occur in sentence positions characterized by a lack of stress. The wider range of phrasal collocations for Relative clause markers is demonstrated by the fact that these tokens occur at the boundaries of NP's, whereas

As token frequency in corpus speech increases, mean vowel duration in ms decreases

+	8,395 tokens	Relative clause marker	63 ms	−
	7,470 tokens	Complementizer	84 ms	
−	2,944 tokens	Demonstrative adjective	97 ms	+

Figure 2. *Tendency for non-source categories to have shorter mean durations as their token frequency increases in corpus text*

the Demonstrative pronoun tokens constitute, by default, NPs. Relative clause markers can occur in the type of syntactic contexts shown in (7a–d), among others.

(7) a. Relative clause marker *that* + NP [function: OBJ of NP]
    . . . *the deposition* that *the President gave* . . .

 b. Relative clause marker *that* + VP [function: SUBJ of S]
    . . . *the standard* . . . *is conduct* that *threatens our constitutional form of government* . . .

 c. Relative clause marker *that* + copula + adj [function: SUBJ of S]
    . . . *a process* that *is thoughtful, deliberative, and fair.*

 d. Relative clause marker *that* + aux V + past participle [function: SUBJ of S]
    . . . *one thing* that's *mentioned in the independent counsel's report* . . .

Likewise, the Complementizer tokens can occur in a range of phrasal contexts like those shown in (8a–d), which are all subsumed within the schema [Complementizer *that* + S]:

(8) a. Complementizer *that* + S
    . . . *the wires have been discussing the fact* that *Judiciary Committee members are discussing the videotape.*

 b. Complementizer *that* + PP
    . . . *I will say* that *in judging the credibility of a witness, it can be very valuable to observe the demeanor of that witness* . . .

 c. Complementizer *that* + ADV
    . . . *it's likely* that *tomorrow or the next day there will be a meeting* . . .

 d. Complementizer *that* + CONJ
    . . . *I suspect* that *if a poll were done strictly in San Diego County* . . .

However, Demonstrative adjectives tokens are restricted to occurring in the positions, as shown in (9a–c).

(9) a. Demonstrative adjective *that* + N
   . . . *we should only withhold* that *information which is needlessly embarrassing to third parties* . . .

   b. Demonstrative adjective *that* + Adj + N
   . . . *the Senate has removed* that *same federal judge for perjury* . . .

   c. Demonstrative adjective *that* + ADV +Adj + N
   . . . *And what did all this do to his job approval,* that *most important benchmark?*

The wider range of potential syntactic phrase collocations for Relative clause markers and Complementizers shows us that these functions have followed qualitatively different grammaticization paths than the Demonstrative adjectives, in that their distribution is less constrained. Therefore, we might think of them as having a broader, more general conceptual scope. In spite of the broader syntactic collocation potential or the notion that more types of syntactic construction are available for collocation, the lexical type becomes more restricted for the more grammaticized elements. In other words the elements that fill the lexical slot following *that* come from closed classes. For example, in my data when they appear in sequences occurring with a frequency greater than 1, Complementizers are followed by only the personal pronouns or by words indicating location (e.g., *here, there,* and *in*) (See Berkenfield 2000 for elucidation of this topic). Low token frequency sequences tended to include words from open classes .

Indeed, when we compare the vowel duration of all *that* uses, the only pairwise comparison which does not show statistically significant vowel duration differences is Complementizers in comparison to Demonstrative adjectives ($p < .06$), as demonstrated in (10) a–c:

(10) a. Relative clause markers (n = 82) have a shorter mean vowel duration than Complementizers (n = 107), p = 0.0000

   b. Relative clause markers (n = 82) have a shorter mean vowel duration than Demonstrative adjectives (n = 29), p = 0.0000

   c. Complementizers (n = 107) have a shorter mean vowel duration than Demonstrative adjectives (n = 29), p = 0.062 but this is not significant

This overlap in durational means for these two functions may be further confounded by ambiguity in syntactic cues used to indicate function for Demonstrative adjectives and Complementizers, in a few cases. One of the places where ambiguity of function between Complementizers and Demonstrative adjectives seems to result is when a token of *that* occurs preceding an NP in a Complementizer token. Examples (11) and (12) show where this ambiguity may occur:

(11) Ambiguous Complementizer token.
But I I do think *that* due process—but an expeditious consideration of all these facts—since we really are pretty cognizant now of what the facts are—is is warranted and and would do a real service to the country and to this particular issue. ("introducing dependent sb. clause as subject, object, or other element of principal clause"; *c*.888)

In (11), we have a potential ambiguity if the token is categorized as a Demonstrative adjective modifying the NP *due process*; this ambiguity seems particularly plausible given the distance between the NP and the rest of the subordinate clause as well as the fact that the parenthetical *but an expeditious . . .* could be taken as the subject of *is is warranted . . .* , with the first eight lexical items in the utterance interpreted as a kind of false start.

In contrast, in (12), the simplicity of the syntactic structure lends itself to interpreting the token as a Demonstrative adjective.

(12) Ambiguous Demonstrative adjective token.
Help us understand what *that* kind of thing means. ("indicating one thing as distinguished from another"; 1,551)

If this interpretation is correct, we see multiple pressures from frequency of use and syntactic position operating on the phonetic form of English *that*. There appear to be frequency-driven constraints on phonetic form and at the same time the syntactic representation appears to mediate the range of possible mean vowel durations. Since syntax in part determines the processing of *that*, it is not surprising that the phonetic representation shows overlap in terms of vowel duration. That is, since syntactic constructions aid language users in categorizing particular tokens and syntactic constructions do not frequently show formal overlap, it is not too surprising that the prosodic duration differences are not significant for the two functions. However, this apparent ambiguity in the analysis of form will be addressed in section 5, analysis 2.

We now turn to an examination of reduction in vowel quality for a subset of the data presented in the first analysis.

5. Analysis 2

The purpose of the present analysis is to examine the formant values of the vowels in the corpus of English *that* tokens. In this analysis, I take another look at what the nature of phonetic reduction is with regard to the English *that* data. That is, in addition to reduction in vowel duration, are there other concomitant changes in the acoustic signal? In this analysis, I look at vowel centralization. I test two independent hypotheses using the empirical data from the corpus of *Newshour* speech.

5.1 Data source

Out of the thirteen speakers for the first analysis of English *that*, I chose the three speakers who had the highest number of tokens. Each of the speakers was male, which was useful in attempting to control for pitch variation by gender. Otherwise, I selected this subset of speakers in order to control for inter-speaker variation, since formant frequencies vary considerably from speaker to speaker. The data from the three speakers are idealized in a number of ways. First, I eliminated from consideration any token of *that* which involved a speech error or an instance of turn-taking negotiation where it was impossible to separate the phonation of one speaker from another. I further eliminated any tokens of *that* which occurred in the context of a pause, either before or after the token, including discourse chunk pauses, pauses between sentences, and phrase and clause-internal pauses. A pause is defined as a cessation of phonation of at least 150 ms. These criteria resulted in a token count of 128 usable examples from the three speakers.

The distribution of the data by speaker is broken down in Table 3.

Table 3. *Distribution of token functions by speaker*

Function	Speaker #1	Speaker #2	Speaker #3	Totals
Demonstrative pronouns	7 tokens	9 tokens	12 tokens	28 tokens
Demonstrative adjectives	6 tokens	6 tokens	0^{15}	12 tokens
Complementizers	9 tokens	14 tokens	24 tokens	47 tokens
Relative clause markers	11 tokens	19 tokens	11 tokens	41 tokens
Totals	33 tokens	48 tokens	47 tokens	n = 128

5.2 Methodology

Phonetic reduction was measured in terms of F1 frequency values. I transferred the sound files that I sampled at 22,050 Hz in *SoundEffects* to *Macquirer* software. I used the 256-point window in *Macquirer* to take Fast Fourier Transform (FFT) measurements of each token. The FFT was measured 30 ms from the beginning of each vowel unless the duration of the vowel was 30 ms or shorter. If the duration was 30 ms or shorter, I halved the duration and took the measurement at the mid-point. F1 and F2 values were charted in *Plot Formants*, separated by token function and speaker and averaged by speaker.

5.2.1 Data distribution.
Table 4 shows the range, mean, and standard deviation of the data by function for Speaker #1.

Table 4. *F1 ranges, means, and standard deviations by function for Speaker #1*

Speaker #1	F1 Range	Mean	SD	# of tokens
Demonstrative pronouns	611–53 or 42 Hz	638 Hz	15 Hz	n = 7
Demonstrative adjectives	586–680 or 94 Hz	635 Hz	39 Hz	n = 6
Complementizers	395–589 or 194 Hz	523 Hz	57 Hz	n = 9
Relative clause markers	448–576 or 128 Hz	502 Hz	32 Hz	n = 11

Table 5 shows the range, mean, and standard deviation for the different functions' values for Speaker #2.

Table 5. *F1 ranges, means, and standard deviations by function for Speaker #2*

Speaker #2	F1 Range	Mean	SD	# of tokens
Demonstrative pronouns	502–784 or 282 Hz	632 Hz	89 Hz	n = 9
Demonstrative adjectives	506–656 or 150 Hz	587 Hz	56 Hz	n = 6
Complementizers	308–609 or 301 Hz	444 Hz	96 Hz	n =14
Relative clause markers	313–513 or 200 Hz	394 Hz	59 Hz	n = 19

Table 6 shows the range, mean, and standard deviation for the data by function for Speaker #3:

Table 6. *F1 ranges, means, and standard deviations by function for Speaker #3*

Speaker #3	F1 Range	Mean	SD	# of tokens
Demonstrative pronouns	552–674 or 122 Hz	631 Hz	31 Hz	n = 12
Demonstrative adjectives	N/A	N/A	N/A	N/A
Complementizers	381–634 or 253 Hz	534 Hz	66 Hz	n = 24
Relative clause markers	297–582 or 285 Hz	496 Hz	84 Hz	n = 11

5.3 Hypotheses 2

Hypothesis 2 is given here:

Hypothesis 2_0

There is no relationship between the token frequency of a *that* construction and F1 reduction of the vowel when the F1 values of one function are compared to others which developed out of the same source.

The second hypothesis is based on results from the earlier analysis. We predict on a usage-based approach that, in tokens belonging to categories with increased frequency in corpus text in comparison to other categories which also developed out of the Demonstrative pronoun source, the vowels will tend to have lower values of F1, corresponding to a more centralized vowel quality.

5.3.1 Statistical test results.

First, I compared each of the diachronically related categories to the source category for the three speakers together. The results of the t-tests are given in (13a–c).

(13) a. Demonstrative pronouns (n = 28) tend to have higher F1 values than Demonstrative adjectives (n = 12), but this difference is not significant, $p < .24$

b. Demonstrative pronouns (n = 28) do have significantly higher F1 values than Relative clause markers (n = 41), $p < .01$

c. Demonstrative pronouns (n = 28) do have significantly higher F1 values than Complementizers (n = 47), $p < .01$

5.3.2 Discussion.

These tests indicate that Relative clause markers and Complementizers show significantly lower F1 values than the Demonstrative pronoun category. Demonstrative adjectives also have a lower mean F1 than the source, which might be useful in predicting vowel movement toward centralization for this function in the future development of English, as characterized by Givón (1984: 418), although the difference is not statistically significant.

The next evaluation consists of a comparison of the mean F1 values by category across speakers. These values are given in Table 7.

Totally consistent with the results of the first analysis on vowel duration, Relative clause markers—the most frequently occurring function in corpus speech—show the lowest or most centralized mean F1 values of the three categories which appeared after the Demonstrative pronoun function historically. Complementizers follow and Demonstrative adjectives do not show significantly lower differences, although they do show centralization away from the Demonstrative pronoun source.

Table 7. *Mean values of F1 for all speakers and functional category distribution in the Switchboard Corpus of American English*

Functional category	Mean value of F1 for all speakers	Switchboard Corpus 2,400,355 words speech data N (% 37,574)
Demonstrative pronouns	633 Hz	18,084 (48%)
Demonstrative adjectives	611 Hz	2,944 (8%)
Complementizers	505 Hz	7,470 (20%)
Relative clause markers	450 Hz	8,395 (22%)
		37,574 (98%)

Of course, this finding is based on limited data and should be tested on a larger data set.

Thus we reject hypothesis 2_0 for Relative clause markers and Complementizers although not for Demonstrative adjectives.

5.4 Hypothesis 3

Hypothesis 3 is given here:

Hypothesis 3_0

There is no difference in the F1 values of Demonstrative adjectives and Complementizers, which could help disambiguate them, when they occur in the same apparent syntactic environment.

The second question that I raise in the current analysis, which I hope will clarify the potential ambiguity of Demonstrative adjectives and Complementizers when they occur immediately before an NP, is whether there are qualities of the acoustic signal which might help language users to distinguish between the two categories (cf. Section 4, analysis 1). Since these categories were the only ones not to show statistically significant differences in vowel duration in the first two analyses, do we assume that speakers rely on post-processing decisions about function, or is there information present in the acoustic signal which helps to disambiguate the function of the token on purely phonetic grounds?

5.4.1 Statistical test results.
There were Demonstrative adjective tokens available to address this question from only two speakers, Speaker #1 and Speaker #2. The t-test result is given here as number (14).

(14) Demonstrative adjectives (n = 12) have significantly higher F1 values than Complementizers (n = 47), p < .01.

5.4.2 Discussion.
Demonstrative adjectives have a mean F1 value of 611 Hz while Complementizers have a mean F1 value of 505 Hz. Thus we reject hypothesis 3, showing that there are acoustic cues to the syntactic function. Another way of looking at this result is in terms of synchronic phonemic contrast. If we ignore the diachronic facts which indicate that the Demonstrative adjective and the Complementizer developed out of the Demonstrative pronoun source, we have no means of predicting the meaning of a particular token on the basis of vowel duration, since the range of vowel duration for these two functions shows some overlap (cf. Section 4). In other words, what may be diachronically predictable may not be synchronically predictable and should be considered for inclusion in the phonological model. On the other hand, there are significant differences between the two categories in the degree of centralization, such that Complementizers are realized with more reduced vowel quality than Demonstrative adjectives. However, both categories are coded using a low front vowel and both categories can occur in overlapping syntactic distribution as demonstrated in Section 4, analysis 1. We can argue that centralization of the vowel in Complementizers serves a contrastive function, to differentiate these tokens from Demonstrative adjectives.

We now address the question of whether phonetic reduction along one parameter is paralleled by reduction along other parameters.

6. Analysis 3

The purpose of this next section is to see whether reduction in one phonetic property is paralleled by reduction in another phonetic property. The idea is to clarify whether one measure of reduction will serve in place of another for all functional categories. We have seen reduction both in duration and vowel quality for both Relative clause markers and Complementizers. The results for Demonstrative adjectives only hold for duration, although we might predict their realizations to move toward centralized vowels in the future development of English, all other variables being equal.

6.1 Data source

The data were the same as those used in Section 5, analysis 2.

6.2 Methodology

Correlations of vowel duration and vowel centralization were plotted in Excel. Then, I tested the statistical significance of these correlations.

6.3 Hypothesis 4

The fourth hypothesis is given here:

Hypothesis 4_0

There is no correlation between vowel duration and F1 value for all uses of *that* for three speakers.

Hypothesis 4 predicts no correlation between F1 formant reduction on the vertical axis and the decrease in vowel duration, regardless of the evolution of categories out of the source category. In other words, where we see evidence of reduction along one acoustic parameter—vowel duration—we do not expect to see reduction of other kinds. These correlations are based on a small number of tokens and the results should be taken as preliminary. Results of plotting paired measurements of F1 values and vowel durations in charts reveals intra-speaker variation in terms of the fourth hypothesis as well.

6.4 Statistical test results

Table 8 shows the correlation, test statistic, and significance value for each speaker's vowel duration and F1 value by function.

6.5 Discussion

The clearest examples of significantly correlated relationships, of the sort tested by hypothesis 4, appear in the correlations for all speakers for the Complementizer category, with Speaker #2's correlation showing a slightly wider distribution. Speaker #3's Relative clause markers show some significant correlation and so does Speaker #2's, if the two shortest and two longest tokens are removed from the sample as outliers, although their proximity to the main distribution might rule this out (this is indicated in the p value in Table 8). Otherwise, there appears to be either scattered distribution (e.g., Speaker #1's Demonstrative pronouns and Adjectives) or a strong maintenance of the F1 value across duration (e.g., Speaker 1's Relative clause marker category and Speaker #3's Demonstrative pronoun category).

The results of this section indicated that there are statistically significant cor-

Table 8. *Statistical test results for correlations of vowel duration and F1 value by speaker*

Speaker	Category	Correlation of vowel duration and centralization	Test statistic	Significance value
Speaker #1	Demonstrative pronouns (n = 7)	r = .3227	T = .7624	p = .2401
	Demonstrative adjectives (n = 6)	r = .0457	T = .0915	p = .4927
	Complementizers (n = 9)	r = .6300	T = 3.2449	**p = .0025**
	Relative clause markers (n = 11)	r = .1829	T = .5581	p = .2952
Speaker #2	Demonstrative pronouns (n = 9)	r = .2280	T = .6195	p = .2776
	Demonstrative adjectives (n = 6)	r = .5903	T = 1.4626	p = .1087
	Complementizers (n = 14)	r = .6411	T = 2.894	**p = .0067**
	Relative clause markers (n = 19)	r = .2934	T = 1.2654	p = .1114
Speaker #3	Demonstrative pronouns (n = 12)	r = .3959	T = 1.3633	p = .1013
	Complementizers (n = 11)	r = .7646	T = 5.5644	**p = .0000**
	Relative clause markers (n = 24)	r = .6019	T = 2.2612	**p = .0250**

relations between F1 value and vowel duration for the Complementizer category but not for Relative clause markers in two out of three cases and never for Demonstrative adjectives.

Now I turn to a summary of the findings and interpret the resulting picture.

7. Conclusion

7.1 Summary of analyses

The three phonetic analyses which form the main body of this paper, indicate that the phonetic form of English *that* is shaped by a complex of influences. In analysis 1, we saw that vowel duration of tokens decreases as the functional category of the token becomes more frequent in speech corpus counts. Then in analysis 2, we found F1 values for all non-source categories moving toward centralization. We also found that the acoustic signal disambiguates functional category information in the F1 values of Demonstrative adjectives and Complementizers, disambiguating these kinds of tokens where their occurrence is potentially unresolvable from other cues. In the third analysis, we saw a tendency for the Complementizer F1 values to correlate with duration in reduction. These first three analyses provide evidence for the notion that each categorical function of *that* is represented independently in the usage-based lexicon and grammar, with a range of internal variation but predictable category boundaries. The boundaries are predictable using the frequency counts. All other things being equal, the diachronic development of functional categories is mirrored by the phonetic properties of classes of tokens.

We may wish to include phonetic information in a model of phonology which specifically deals with historical change. However, specification of some of these facts would be redundant in a diachronic grammar. In the second analysis, we found that F1 values are significantly different and may be sufficient enough a signal to disambiguate Demonstrative adjectives and Complementizers from one another, whereas the differences in duration alone (Section 4, analysis 1) were not significant. From a synchronic point of view, the point of view of the speaker, vowel centralization may function contrastively to indicate grammatical category. The final finding with import for the phonological representation indicates that as reduction along one phonetic parameter—duration—occurs in Complementizers, so will reduction along another—vowel centralization.

7.2 Discussion

If we assume that linguistic categories are subject to change, then the exploration of diachronically related material should yield insights into how speakers reanalyze and subsequently organize phonetic material. Thus, the description and testing of diachronically related material, as it occurs in real speech situations, offers avenues of analysis into reduction effects which have previously been looked at mostly in experimental settings. Furthermore, the evidence presented here (as well as in Jurafsky *et al.* this volume) supports the notion that function words are worthy of phonetic analysis, for the insights that this can yield. While the duration phenomenon is predictable within the theoretical framework, I argue that it should have the status of a phonological "feature." Exemplar tokens contribute to a prototype generalization about a category, which perhaps should be given phonological status in the grammar. But the individual phonetic percepts cannot be discarded. If we simply assign duration to a predictable consequence of syntactic distribution—a type of "allophonic variation," we fail to capture the processes of language change and how syntactic functions and sequences of items give rise to new patterns or constructions. Browman and Goldstein (1992), in their theory of articulatory phonology, structure their presentation in terms of gestures which contain an inherent durational dimension. However, from a diachronic perspective, the representation of a single value for the duration of each gesture, disregarding the function of the construction in which the gesture occurs, leaves something to be desired. The same would be true of representing a unitary value for vowel centralization for both Complementizers and Relative clause markers. Finally, it appears that representing the correlation between duration and centralization for Complementizers could be done at one level of abstraction, but these reductive effects are less linked for Relative clause markers and Demonstrative adjectives. Showing this quantitative and qualtitative difference in behavior yields insights into the complexity of reduction. This linkage is not directly tied to frequency since we would predict that Relative clause markers, being most frequent in the Switchboard Corpus, would have the most extreme case of reduction along both the parameters of duration and centralization. The only phonological model that allows for this level of complexity is the exemplar model of storage within a usage-based approach to language. Additionally the exemplar model is the only current model that allows for gradual change in representation.

7.3 Conclusion

It becomes clear, through empirical observation, that language users are capable of coding and decoding remarkably complex information in the acoustic and visual signals, not all of which is predictable. Arguments to the effect that human beings have finite cognitive storage are perhaps overrated. The evidence in this study shows that the properties of phonetic categories and, potentially, their phonological representation are multidimensional and are probably stored at various levels of abstraction: both particular exemplars and generalized prototypes are stored.

This study adds to the growing body of research that argues that the distinction between phonetics and phonology is somewhat artificial. The gradient nature of phonetic detail allows for specification both of particular synchronic details about usage-based structure and for the diachronic processes that bring about such change.

In order to model linguistic change through time as well as the synchronic facts, the phonological representation of categories should have both gradient phonetic and categorical prototype levels, acknowledging that repetition of sequences results in the reduction of the phonetic substance. This substance is sensitive to diachronic development and token frequency but some properties of substance are also unpredictable.

In order to be successful, a usage-based model of phonology, which seeks to explain both synchronic variation and diachronic change, must allow for the specification of phonetic properties and the trends which phonetic properties instantiate. The representation of phonological categories must reference the gradient signal as well as categorical boundaries, taking advantage of the phonetic factors which embody, drive, and explain the evolution of phonological/semantic categories in language.

Notes

* I would like to thank Paul Hopper, Joan Bybee, Caroline Smith, and Melissa Axelrod for their comments on various drafts of this paper. Any errors of analysis or interpretation are my own.

1. Throughout this paper, I will refer to the "lexicon and grammar". This is not meant to imply an unprincipled division of the two from one another. In fact, the material presented in this paper should support the argument that a division of lexicon and grammar is, in any realistic sense, one of degree (cf. Bybee 1988 and Langacker 1991a, 1991b).

2. See Frisch et al. (this volume) for an interesting characterization of the difference between prototype and exemplar-based storage and discussion of different types of effects in English and Arabic.

3. The date after the semicolon in parentheses is the first date of attestation in the OED. The date given is not meant to imply that the function or form did not exist before this date of attestation.

4. The category for Demonstrative adverbs was infrequent in my sample. For this reason, the category will not be considered in the paper.

5. The OED refers to the Complementizer function as a "conjunction" category.

6. Percentages in Table 1 reflect rounding variation.

7. Percentages in this column do not add up to 100% because the function of some 681 tokens in the Corpus could not be categorized in one of the functions under investigation in this paper.

8. I found only three non-restrictive relative clauses in the data. This small number is consistent with Fox and Thompson (1990) who found no tokens of non-restrictive relative clauses in their analysis of spoken English.

9. Paul Hopper (personal communication) has noted that Demonstrative pronouns cannot really be characterized as syntagmatically independent, given their *dependence* on prior mention of the lexical referent in discourse. So I define dependence, for this study, as how a particular function (like Complementizer) requires not only the presence of the sequence /ðæt/ but also other items participating in the construction. Conversely, independence simply means that the Demonstrative pronoun function is characterized by a simple NP coded by /ðæt/, which requires no other material in a local or sentential sequence for its completion. This simplification may not get at the whole picture of the relationship between the phonetic signal and semantic structure but it is useful for the purposes of this paper. See Berkenfield (2000) for discussion of collocations and functions in the *Newshour* Corpus and calculations of string frequency and transitional probability.

10. See Jurafsky *et al.* (1998) and Jurafsky *et al.* (this volume) for discussion of other factors that contribute to reduction in frequent English words including *that*.

11. Umeda's definition of a function word is any word up to the 50th rank in Francis and Kučera (1967).

12. Stepwise regression analysis indicates that immediate syllabic environment, realization of a token as [ðæt] vs. [ðæts], and membership of words preceding and following a token in an open vs. closed grammatical class do not influence the values of vowel duration. But these results should be verified with a larger data set.

13. Percentages in Table 2 reflect rounding variation.

14. As mentioned in Section 3.1, the Switchboard Corpus of American English does not have tags that distinguish between Demonstrative pronoun and Demonstrative adjective tokens. In order to come up with a basis for comparison between the Switchboard and my own *Newshour* corpus, I did a sample count from the Switchboard Corpus of the first 100 tokens of *that* and found that 49 were Demonstrative pronoun tokens while only 8 were Demonstrative adjectives. So the token values for Demonstrative pronouns and Demonstrative adjectives in Table 2 under the Switchboard heading are an extrapolation, based on dividing the total number of the tokens in the Switchboard 100-token sample representative of these two functions (n = 57) by the number of Demonstrative pronoun and Demonstrative adjective tokens in the *Newshour* corpus. Thus the extrapolated numbers came out with 86% of the Switchboard tokens being Demonstrative pronouns and 14% as Demonstrative adjectives. But the percentages which follow the token numbers in Table 2 are based on the total number of tokens in the corpus (n = 37574).

15. Each speaker had to have at least six tokens of a particular function for me to make generalizations based on his data. One speaker had only 3 tokens of Demonstrative adjectives. I felt this number was too small to base generalizations upon, so the corresponding formant values were omitted.

References

Anderson, J.R. 1993. *Rules of the Mind*. Hillsdale, NJ: Lawrence Erlbaum.

Berkenfield, C. 2000. "The role of syntactic constructions and frequency in the realization of English *that*". Master's Thesis, University of New Mexico.

Boyland, J. T. 1996. "Morphosyntactic change in progress: a psycholinguistic treatment". Doctoral Dissertation, UC Berkeley.

Browman, C. P. and L. Goldstein. 1992. "Articulatory phonology: an overview". *Phonetica* 49: 155–80.

Bybee, J. 1998. "The emergent lexicon". *CLS* 34.

Bybee, J. In press. *Phonology and Language Use.* Cambridge: Cambridge University Press.

Chomsky, N. and Halle, M. 1968. *The Sound Pattern of English.* New York: Harper and Row.

Fox, B. A. and Thompson, S. A. 1990. "A discourse explanation of the grammar of relative clauses in English conversation". *Language* 66(2): 297–316.

Francis, W. N. and Kučera, H. 1967. *Computational Analysis of Present-day American English.* Providence, RI: Brown University Press.

Frisch, S., Large, N. R., Zawaydeh, B., and Pisoni, D. B. This volume. "Emergent generalizations in English and Arabic". In *Frequency and the Emergence of Linguistic Structure*, J. Bybee and P. Hopper (eds.). Amsterdam: John Benjamins.

Givón, T. 1984. *Syntax: a Functional-Typological Introduction, Volume 1.* Amsterdam: John Benjamins.

Hooper, J. (Bybee). 1976. "Word frequency in lexical diffusion and the source of morphophonological change". *Current Progress in Historical Linguistics*, W. Christie (ed.), 96–105. Amsterdam: North Holland.

Jurafsky, D., Bell, A., Fosler-Lussier, E., Girand, C., and Raymond, W. 1998. "Reduction of English function words in Switchboard". *Proceedings of ICSLP-98*, Sydney.

Jurafsky, D., Bell, A., Gregory, M., and Raymond, W.D. This volume. In *Frequency and the Emergence of Linguistic Structure*, J. Bybee and P. Hopper (eds.). Amsterdam: John Benjamins.

Lakoff, G. 1987. *Women, Fire, and Dangerous Things: What Categories Reveal About the Mind.* Chicago: The University of Chicago Press.

Langacker, R. 1991a. *Concept, Image, and Symbol: the Cognitive Basis of Grammar.* Berlin: Mouton De Gruyter.

Langacker, R. 1991b. *Foundations of Cognitive Grammar, Volume 2, Descriptive Application.* Stanford, California: Stanford University Press.

Lindblom, B. 1990. "Explaining phonetic variation: a sketch of the H and H theory". *Speech Production and Speech Modelling*, W.J. Hardcastle and A. Marchal (eds.), 403–39. Netherlands: Kluwer Academic.

Lindblom, B., MacNeilage, P., and Studdert-Kennedy, M. 1984. "Self-organizing processes and the explanation of phonological universals". *Explanation for Language Universals*, B. Butterworth, B. Comrie, and Ö. Dahl (eds.), 181–203. New York: Mouton.

Mervis, C. B. and Catlin, J. 1975. "Relationships among goodness-of-example, category norms, and word frequency". *Bulletin of the Psychonomic Society* 7: 283–4.

Miller, J. L. 1994. "On the internal structure of phonetic categories: a progress report". *Cognition* 50: 271–85.

Mowrey, R. and Pagliuca, W. 1995. "The reductive character of articulatory evolution". *Rivista di Linguistica* 7: 37–124.

Nosofsky, R. M. 1988. "Exemplar-based accounts of relations between classification, recognition, and typicality". *Journal of Experimental Psychology: Learning, Memory, and Cognition* 14: 700–8.

Nosofsky, R. M., Kruschke, J.K., and McKinley, S.C. 1992. "Combining exempar-based category representations and connectionist learning rules". *Journal of Experimental Psychology: Learning, Memory, and Cognition* 18: 211–33.

Ohala, J. J. 1997. "The relation between phonetics and phonology". *The Handbook of Phonetic Sciences*, W.J. Hardcastle and J. Laver (eds.), 674–94. Oxford: Blackwell.

Oxford English Dictionary, Compact Edition. 1971. Oxford: Oxford University Press.

O'Neil, W. 1977. "Clause adjunction in Old English". *General Linguistics* 17: 199–211.

Phillips, B. S. 1984. "Word frequency and the actuation of sound change". *Language* 60: 320–42.

Pierrehumbert, J. 1990. "Phonological and phonetic representation". *Journal of Phonetics* 18: 375–94.

Rosch, E. and Mervis, C.B. 1975. "Family resemblances: studies in the internal structure of categories". *Cognitive Psychology* 7: 573–605.

Rosch, E., Mervis, C.B., Gray; W.D., Johnson, D.M., and Boyes-Braem, P. 1976. "Basic objects in natural categories". *Cognitive Psychology* 8: 382–439.

Rosenbloom, P.S., Laird, J.E., and Newell, A. Eds. 1993. "The soar papers: research on integrated intelligence". *Artificial Intelligence*. Cambridge: MIT Press.

Traugott, E. C. 1992. "Old English syntax". *The Cambridge History of English, Volume I: Old English*, Hogg, R. (ed.), 168–289. Cambridge: Cambridge University Press.

Umeda, N. 1975. "Vowel duration in American English". *Journal of the Acoustical Society of America* 58: 434–45.

Varela, F. J., Thompson, E. and Rosch, E. 1991. *The Embodied Mind*. Cambridge: The MIT Press.

Frequency, iconicity, categorization:
Evidence from emerging modals*

MANFRED G. KRUG

University of Freiburg

1. Introduction

In this paper, I discuss the ways in which discourse frequency, categorization, and iconicity interact during the early stages of grammaticalization. The empirical evidence comes primarily from the domain of English modal constructions. In order to place the present study within its wider field of research, it may be important to note that such a focus on *constructions* in grammaticalization reflects a recent trend in this branch of linguistics in general (e.g., Bisang 1998; Bybee forthcoming, 1999; Heine 1999; Lehmann 1999; Tabor and Traugott 1998; Traugott forthcoming).

There is widespread consensus that fundamental changes are currently affecting the English auxiliary system (see, for instance, the programmatic remarks in Bolinger 1980: 6, Bybee and Dahl 1989: 60, Croft 1990: 190, Givón 1993: 187, or Traugott 1997: 193). But despite a vast literature on the central modals, detailed accounts of the often-cited "wholesale reorganization" (Bolinger 1980: 6) are virtually non-existent. Basing my claims on synchronic analyses (diachronic aspects are dealt with in Krug 2000), I propose in this paper that structures like BE GOING TO, HAVE GOT TO, HAVE TO, and WANT TO are changing their categorial status. More specifically, I propose that we are witnessing the rise of a new focal point, that is, a new category on the main verb—auxiliary cline.[1] For the recency of these items, for the transformation which they are currently subjected to, and for their overall movement toward (more) grammaticalized behavior, I believe that *emerging modals* is the most appropriate term for this new category.

I begin by showing that there is a strong correlation between the discourse frequency of verbal expressions and grammatical status. From an emergent grammar point of view, this fact lends support to a grammaticalization hypothesis for the items under investigation. Subsequently, I discuss the question of whether iconicity and economy are necessarily competing forces in language change (my answer is No). Falling out from the same discussion is the formulation of an 'Iconicity of Grammatical Categories Principle', which states that grammaticalization, in particular the creation of a new category, tends to destroy syntagmatic iconicity but may create paradigmatic iconicity.

2. The rise of a new grammatical category

2.1 The correlation between frequency and grammatical status

Table 1 shows the discourse frequency of the 30 most common verbal expressions as found in the spontaneous speech of the British National Corpus.[2] The present list is drawn from Krug (2000), which is based on an investigation of a total of 130 verbs.[3]

To render the observed incidences in more accessible relations: on standard estimates (e.g., Biber *et al.* 1999: Ch. 5) one occurrence per thousand words, i.e., the incidence exceeded by the top 30 verbs translates roughly into one occurrence in ten minutes. According to the same estimator, BE would occur on average some 6 times per minute, GET roughly once per minute, and GOING TO once in three minutes. These figures refer to the average number of words produced in natural conversation (which includes speech pauses etc.). Notice, therefore, that this is a low estimate. If we carry out a calculation in terms of speech production (roughly six syllables or three words per second are a standard measure, cf. Aitchison 1994: 7), the

Table 1. *The 30 most frequent verbs in spontaneous speech in the BNC (exceeding a discourse frequency of one occurrence per thousand words)*[4]

Discourse frequency Occurrences per thousand words	Items
> 50	BE
> 10	DO, HAVE, GET
> 5	GO, SAY, KNOW, CAN, THINK, 'LL
> 2.5	SEE, COME, MEAN, **GOING TO/GONNA**, WOULD, LOOK, WILL, PUT
> 1	TAKE, COULD, MAKE, **HAVE TO**, TELL, **WANT TO/WANNA**, WANT (+ NP), GIVE, **GOT TO/GOTTA**, 'D (MODAL), LIKE, SHOULD

incidence would be roughly twice as high. Notice further that the discourse frequencies of the individual verbs as found in the BNC are remarkably congruent with those obtained by Biber *et al.* (1999: Ch. 5f) from a different British corpus. This congruence suggests that given a sufficiently large spoken corpus, frequency distributions of very common verbs will be recurrent, irrespective of the topics of individual discourse samples. This in turn seems to permit the interpretation of frequency patterns in terms of general cognitive and functional importance.

Let us, therefore, turn to a brief discussion of the corpus findings. Among the top 30 verbs, modal verbs form the largest group: *can, will, would, could, should* (plus their clitic forms *'ll, 'd*). The most frequent verbs are the primary verbs (BE, DO, HAVE), and GET. GET also functions as both a lexical and an auxiliary verb. Another prominent group is formed by modal constructions—the focus of the present investigation: GOING TO, HAVE TO, GOT TO, and WANT TO. These are the chief emerging modals (see Krug 2000 for detailed discussion). Only a few lexical verbs are found among the top 30 verbs of English spontaneous speech (many of which, in fact, are prominent in pragmatic functions, so that their lexical status is often debatable: cf. *you know, I mean, I see*). Insofar as they qualify as lexical verbs, they fall into the following natural semantic classes:

(a) verbs pertaining to the world of reasoning and/or perception such as KNOW, SEE, THINK, MEAN, LOOK
(b) verbs of saying, feeling and reporting (overlapping with the preceding group): MEAN, SAY, TELL, THINK
(c) verbs that are commonly used in equative (copular) patterns: GET, LOOK
(d) highly generalized verbs of motion: COME, GO
(e) generalized dynamic verbs for expressing thematic roles such as benefactive, patient or agent: GIVE, MAKE, PUT, TAKE
(f) volitional verbs: LIKE, WANT (+ NP)

It seems worthwhile to briefly discuss the import of Table 1 for the relationship between discourse frequency and grammatical status. For the sake of convenience and simplicity, I consider as *grammatical* all those items which, according to Quirk *et al.* (1985: 120–46) have at least a loose connection to the English auxiliary complex. In Quirk *et al.*'s classification (1985: 137; reproduced in Appendix A), these forms include the central modals, primary verbs, marginal modals, semi-auxiliaries, and modal idioms. For illustration, it seems helpful to set out the proportions of auxiliary verbs in tabular form (see Table 2). It is striking that the proportion of auxiliary verbs (when measured in groups of ten) progressively decreases from the first ten verbs to the next ten, and so on. The proportion drops sharply after the top thirty verbs from 40% to 20% (Krug 2000). This is the ratio for the 4th and 5th groups. After these 50 most frequent English verbs, grammatical items crop up

Table 2. *Proportions of auxiliary verbs among the*
80 most frequent verbs in spontaneous spoken English

High-frequency verbs	Proportion of auxiliary verbs
1–10	50%
11–20	40%
21–30	40%
31–40	20%
41–50	20%
51–60	0%
61–70	0%
71–80	10%

rather sporadically (less than 1 in ten on average, see Krug 2000). In other words, there is a striking correlation between high frequency and auxiliary status: among the top thirty verbs almost 50% enjoy auxiliary status. And at 20% the correlation between auxiliary status and the 31st to 50th verb is much lower but still significant.

It is expected, then, that BE GOING TO, HAVE TO, WANT TO, and GOT TO, which semantically qualify as modal expressions, are today among the top 30 verbs in spontaneous conversation. It is further noteworthy that these constructions have acquired their high discourse frequency only during the last century or so (Krug 2000). Hopper's framework of emergent grammar assumes that "structure, or regularity, comes out of discourse and is shaped by discourse" (1987: 142). From this perspective, therefore, we seem to witness several fine examples of the acquisition of grammatical status on frequency and semantic grounds alone. Such a claim will be supported and refined in the remainder of this study, primarily by advancing phonological evidence. Finally, I will offer arguments involving the concepts of iconicity, economy, and isomorphism.

2.2 Iconicity and economy: competing motivations?

This section argues against the common view that iconicity and economy are always competing forces in language change. I accept the view that economy and ritualization increase grammaticalization (Haiman 1994a, 1994c). In proposing that economy and ritualization do not necessarily lead to the loss of iconicity, however, I diverge from most previous research.[5] We will see that in the field of emerging modals the reverse is true: here economy and ritualization actually seem to be *creating* iconicity. As will become clear, reconciliation with previous research is possible especially if we distinguish between syntagmatic and paradigmatic iconicity. More specifically, therefore, I shall argue that grammaticalization typically has two concomitants: loss in syntagmatic iconicity and gain in paradigmatic iconicity. Even though Haiman is not the founding father of the linguistic study of iconicity (predecessors include Peirce, Jakobson, Ullmann, and Lyons), it was certainly primarily through him that work on iconicity gained fresh impetus in the 1970s and 1980s. Thus his iconicity axiom, stating that *"recurrent similarity of form must reflect similarity in meaning"* (1985: 26; italics original), serves as a convenient starting point for the present discussion. Proceeding from this assumption, studies in iconicity claim that language structure reflects affinities between concepts. Witness a recent definition of diagrammatic iconicity:

> Although the component parts of a diagram may not resemble what they stand for, the relationships among those components may approximate the relationships among the ideas they represent. (Haiman 1994b: 1629)

Compare also a definition of Haiman's 'Iconic Principle of Interpretation' (1994c: 1636): "formal closeness reflects conceptual closeness of elements" or, stated negatively: "difference in form [e.g., of near synonyms] iconically reflects their difference in meaning" (1994c: 1636).[6] Much work within the functionalist tradition has been devoted to exploring the roles of economy and iconicity. The history of this line of research is summarized in Haiman (1983: 814) and DuBois (1985: 358). Terminology varies considerably. Scholars like Saussure (1916), Zipf (1949), Malkiel (1968), Givón (1979, 1995), Plank (1979), Haiman (1980), Horn (1984), and Goldberg (1995) have suggested the following pairs:

(1) Competing motivations—competing terms:

iconicity	vs. economy
(form-meaning) isomorphism	vs. least effort
Q-Principle	vs. R-Principle
perceptual separation	vs. ease of articulation
transparency (or clarity)	vs. opacity
minimal coding	vs. maximal coding

Terminology and focus may vary but there is wide-spread agreement that these pairs represent opposing forces in language change. Witness for instance Haiman (1985: 18):

> [T]here is an inverse correlation between iconicity and economy . . . I believe that the tendencies to maximize iconicity and maximize economy are two of the most important motivations for linguistic forms in general.

A consequence of the opposing-forces view is that as grammaticalization proceeds, opacity increases and iconicity is destroyed. This assumption is concisely expressed by Haiman (1985: 259):

[T]he functionalist . . . recognizes the existence of competing motivations, in particular, iconic and economic motivations. At any stage of any natural language, there will be areas in the grammar where originally iconically motivated structures have become grammaticalized, and there will be others where they have not.

More recently, Haiman has drawn attention to the wider concept of ritualization. It is akin to economy since it is taken to include all instances of, *inter alia*, erosion and grammaticalization (1994c: 1633, 1635). The basic assumption regarding the relationship between economy and iconicity (in his recent work the latter notion is subsumed under the label of motivation), however, has not changed:

> The standard traditional position on language change and motivation . . . is that sound change—which is regular—destroys semantic motivation (of which iconicity . . . is one major type), while analogical processes—which are irregular—tend to restore it. In fact, both major types of change tend equally to destroy motivation, which may be semantic, pragmatic, phonetic, or syntactic. Insofar as they do, they can be seen as aspects of one fundamental tendency, that of ritualization.   (Haiman 1994c: 1633)

Against this backdrop let us consider the evidence of progressive univerbation for the items investigated here:

(2) *want to*   > *wanta*   > *wanna* /'wɒnə/
(3) *is/am/are going to* > *'s/'m/'re going to* > *gonna* /'gɒnə/
(4) *have/has got to*   > *'ve/'s got to*   > *gotta* /'gɒtə/[7]

I argue that (2) to (4) are instances of ongoing grammaticalization—more exactly, auxili(ariz)ation—and that the phonological variants represent different stages in the evolution of new auxiliaries.[8] This situation can be regarded as evidence of the persistence of older syntactic variants (cf. *will* and *'ll*). The leftmost column lists three rather different structures. WANT is often regarded as a main verb (e.g., Biber *et al.* 1999: 362, Quirk *et al.* 1985: 146, Radford 1997: 50); the other two are periphrastic constructions involving an auxiliary (BE GOING TO and HAVE GOT TO). Significantly, after different reduction processes like assimilation, cliticization, and deletion, the results are three instances of univerbation, which are highly similar: first, all have two syllables and a Germanic stress pattern (i.e., first stem syllable stressed) and then the vowel of the second, reduced syllable is schwa. We can go into further detail for prototypical pronunciations: each of them has four phonemes whose structure is /CVCə/, where C stands for consonant and V for vowel. Admittedly, HAVE TO does not fit into this paradigm. As far as phonology is concerned, therefore, it does not conform to the prototype. But many other items do. We may add that *had better* has travelled very much the same path via auxiliary encliticization to auxiliary omission:

(5) *had better* > *'d better* > *better, betta*   /'betə/

It would be interesting to investigate whether the word-final /r/ in modal *better* is always pronounced in generally rhotic accents. Common /r/ deletion would strengthen the case for advocating iconicization and auxiliarization. *Need to* has the same phonemic structure: /'ni:tə/. If we allow for different nonfinite complementation patterns (infinitive perfect), contractions like *coulda* /'kʊdə/, *woulda* /'wʊdə/, *shoulda* /'ʃʊdə/ and *mighta* /'maɪtə/ can be included in what appears to be an emerging paradigm. Notice that while these constructions are very heterogeneous as regards their etymology, they have in common a semantic affinity with the modal domain. Other items are very similar to the /'CVCə/ pattern but diverge from it by one phoneme, e.g., *oughta* /'ɔ:tə/, *tryta* /'traɪtə/, and *tryna* /'traɪnə/ (< *trying to*; cf. *gonna*). Quantitative or qualitative divergence by one phoneme is found for items like *hafta* /'hæftə/, *hasta* /'hæstə/, and *usta* /'ju:stə/.[9]

As regards *wanna*, *gonna*, and *gotta*, considerations of phonological similarity can be taken two steps further: in British English the full vowel is typically [ɒ] for all three items.[10] Moreover the second consonants /n/ and /t/ are homorganic: both are alveolar. The above developments conform with general phonological concomitants of morphologization. As Hopper and Traugott (1993: 145) inform us, these surface on two levels:

(a) A quantitative ('syntagmatic') reduction: forms become shorter as the phonemes that comprise them erode.

(b) A qualitative ('paradigmatic') reduction: the remaining phonological segments in the form are drawn from a progressively shrinking set. This smaller set of phonemes tends to reflect the universal set of unmarked segments. They tend especially to be apical (tongue tip) consonants such as [n], [t], and [s], the glottal consonants [ʔ] and [h], and common vowels . . . The result is that from a synchronic perspective grammatical morphemes tend to be composed of 'unmarked' segments.

Three out of the four phonemes in the /CVCə/ structure qualify as unmarked: /n/ and /t/ (including the flapped allophone) are apical; vowels are generally unmarked; and schwa is the most unmarked phoneme of all. The first phoneme, by contrast, which tends to differentiate the items, is typically marked (e.g., /g/, /w/, /b/, /k/).

To return to the question of whether in the cases investigated here grammaticalization strengthens or weakens iconicity, the answer is that it does both. As grammaticalization proceeds, the items lose in (syntagmatic) iconicity to the extent that the transparency of the constructions in (2) to (4) decreases from left to right: /'gɒnə/for instance is quite detached from /gəʊ/ both phonologically and semantically and traces of movement in *gonna* are rather opaque. Similarly, the original possessive semantics of HAVE GOT can be ruled out for modal *gotta*. For *wanna* the argument is more complex. Consider:

(6) This room wants cleaning. ('lack' only)
(7) They want money. ('desire' and possibly 'lack')
(8) I wanna go. ('desire' only)

The original 'lack' semantics is retained only in some lexical uses, notably with gerundial complements as in (6). The typical lexical usage with an NP complement (7) is desiderative, but a backgrounded 'lack' reading is often possible. In the modal usage (8), however, no trace of the original 'lack' meaning is present. This could be considered evidence of a partial semantic split between the lexical and modal usage, despite much common volitional ground. Hence, for *gonna*, *gotta*, and *wanna*, the present data in general underpin Haiman's claim (1994c: 1633) that "ritualization *emancipates* forms from whatever motivation they once may have had." On the other hand, as the discussion of the phonological properties has revealed, grammaticalization has also led to gains in (paradigmatic) iconicity insofar as the rightmost items in (2) to (4) are very much alike structurally.[11] Their similarity in form thus reflects functional and conceptual closeness, i.e., membership in a new modal category.

Different from the majority of researchers, who have variously described the pairs in (1) as competing motivations', 'clashing forces', 'antinomic principles', or 'rival determinants', Givón appears to subscribe to a model of change in which economy is prior to iconicity and should indeed be granted motivational status since it is taken to promote the emergence of iconic forms:

> ultimately one may wish to view economy as a major *mechanism* which shape [*sic*] the rise of iconic representation in language.   (Givón 1985: 190)

In the face of the evidence presented here, Givón's dynamic understanding seems more helpful in accounting for developments in the modal domain and, probably, also elsewhere (cf. Croft 1990: 256f). The competing-forces view, however, can be saved if the notion of iconicity is understood in a restricted sense, i.e., if it is seen as confined to *syntagmatic* iconicity. To sum up, I have thus far proposed that the process of grammaticalization need not exclusively lead to de-iconicization. It may in fact increase iconicity or even *create* a new type of (paradigmatic) iconicity. As will become clearer from what follows, the emerging formal resemblance of the items discussed here indicates their affinity with an emerging category.

Even though Fischer (1999) is primarily concerned with lexical items, his work on *associative phonological iconicity* (also known as phonaesthesia, secondary onomatopoeia, or secondary iconicity) lends strong support to the claim just made, viz. that the observed phonological similarity indicates conceptual closeness and thus hints at the development of a new verbal category. To begin with, Fischer (1999: 131) considers associative iconicity to be diagrammatic: "it is motivated not by individual meaning-form relationships, but by relations between forms all expressing a particular meaning." In the present context, this meaning is modal, i.e., an abstract, grammatical notion. Fischer (1999: 129–31) further distinguishes between primary and secondary associative iconicity and describes the relationship that holds between them:

> [S]peakers associate certain sounds or sound combinations with certain meanings (primary association), but they do so partly (primarily?) because they mentally associate these words with others that also contain these sounds or sound combinations (secondary association) . . . .The latter criterion (secondary association) may well be more important . . . .[P]rimary association is supported and strengthened by . . . secondary association, i.e., the association of words sharing a certain form (here: sound combination) and certain meanings with other such words.

Notice that he also points to the intimate relationship between associative iconicity, productivity, and categorization:

> The existence of . . . phonaesthetically associated words . . . may cause more such words to be created, and phonaesthetic word clusters thus have a tendency to perpetuate themselves and to grow larger . . . . *Association is thus a form of category building,* . . . [A]ssociative iconicity manifests explicitly (i.e., iconically) marked linguistic categories (categories of form as well as meaning) . . . (129–32; emphasis added)

Doubtless, the productivity of grammatical constructions is much more restricted than that of lexical items. Furthermore, new modal constructions cannot be created *ad hoc*, in contrast to lexical phonaesthetic neologisms like *bash, clash, dash, gash, slash, smash* etc. (see Fischer 1998: 129 for further relevant examples). It nonetheless appears that those items that by regular assimilation processes may develop a phonological variant with the 'appropriate' phonemic structure have a better chance of either being adopted into a grammatical category or of surviving in such a category than others. An instance of obsolescence that may be partly due to 'inappropriate' phonological structure is *uton* 'let's'. This was certainly the structurally (and semantically) most idiosyncratic item in the early Middle English inventory of preterite present verbs, from which essentially all PDE central modals are recruited.

An instance of the assumption of category membership that may be partly due to phonological structure is WANT, whose development from a lexical verb with nonmodal ('lack') semantics in Middle English into a central member of the emerging modals is something of a mystery. There was certainly no way of predicting this development in Middle English. The rise of WANT would seem to contradict the common observation that the morphs generally serving as sources for grammatical morphemes are characterized by very frequent use. WISH had a much better starting position for a variety of reasons. For one thing, it was initially more frequent than WANT, simply because it is older. For another, WISH already had desiderative semantics in Old English, which WANT fully developed only in the 18th century. It is important to note, therefore, that frequency is not the only criterion which determines whether an item enters into grammaticalization. Bybee *et al.* (1994: 10) state that there is additionally "the reference plane of basic, irreducible notions, whether they concern existence or movement in space or psychological or social states, perspectives, and events, which serves as the basis for grammatical meaning in human languages." 'Lack', the original meaning of WANT, is surely such a basic notion. It remains a problem in the domain of volitional semantics, however, that an entirely new construction developed and spread at the expense of one that existed prior to it.

Phonological form and, therefore, ultimately iconicity, might possibly be a motivating force. WANT TO is structurally more similar to GOT TO and GOING TO than the older WISH or other rival candidates like DESIRE or INTEND. Perhaps this helps to account for why WANT TO has become the new English volitional modal after the departure of *will* to the future. But this is rather speculative and the motivations for the rise of WANT TO will have to await further investigation such as inquiries into field-internal developments. In any case, Fischer's claims as well as my statement of iconicization by grammaticalization require more refined considerations on categorization. This is the topic of the ensuing sections.

2.3 Why introduce a new category?

In terms of categorization, the simplest account would be to assume that the highly frequent constructions investigated here (BE GOING TO, HAVE TO, WANT TO, HAVE GOT TO) are currently becoming members of the category of central modal verbs. While the overall direction of change certainly is toward the central modals, I prefer a slightly different line of argument. I submit that we are seeing the rise of a new category, which I call *emerging auxiliaries* or, more exactly, *emerging modals.* On theoretical grounds it is important to note that I do not propose the rise of a major verbal category, but the rise of a subcategory within the higher-level class of modal verbs. Thus I embrace a prototype view of modal status, which is similar to Heine's (1993) perspective. Consequently the emerging modals are regarded as proper modal auxiliaries, the unifying criterion being their modal function and semantics. Brinton (1988: 237), Hopper and Traugott (1993), and Traugott (1997) share this view. It would not seem helpful to exclude all verbs taking infinitival *to* complements from auxiliarihood simply because they do not share the syntactic properties of the central modals. In fact, adopting a purely morpho-syntactic model of categorization would obscure ongoing developments. Few languages seem to have a class of modal verbs that are as rigidly grammaticalized as the English central modals *will, may, should*, etc. (Heine 1993: 72f). Even in cognate languages such as German, the same modals have not developed the formal idiosyncrasies of their English counterparts. Items like WANT TO, GOING TO, or GOT TO and, in particular, their contracted forms would easily qualify as modal verbs in many languages. Bybee and Dahl (1989: 60) have pointed out that many of the properties of the central modals are due to diachronic coincidence, that is, they are consequences of verbal behavior that was prevalent in the period when these verbs grammaticalized. Modern English (neo)auxiliarization must be different.

Various subcategories have been suggested in the literature on auxiliaries before. Heine (1993: 14f) provides a good summary. Probably most wide-spread is the pretheoretical use of *quasi-auxiliaries*. Others have suggested the terms *semimodals, secondary auxiliaries*, or a more refined taxonomy which includes such subcategories as *semi-auxiliaries, marginal modals*, and *modal idioms* but which also includes *main verbs* that take *to* complements (Quirk *et al.* 1985; cf. Appendix A). I do not wish to invalidate such taxonomies because they are usually consistent within the respective frameworks. Still I believe that these classes are either too all-encompassing (such as *quasi-modal*) or too strictly morphosyntactic (hence too narrow) for the present purposes and thus prevent us from identifying an evolving but, nonetheless, rather concisely definable class of verbs. The core members of the new category are recruited from the classes identified in previous research, which attests to the usefulness of these classes. It is here that the present study overlaps with Pullum's (1997) otherwise very different treatment, because by calling the items he investigates (*wanna, gonna, usta, hafta, gotta, ougtha, sposta*) 'therapy verbs' he implicitly recognizes a new category as well.

Occam's razor is a maxim stating that categories must not be needlessly multiplied. I shall therefore present arguments for why the introduction of a new class in the English auxiliary domain is not a needless proliferation of categories. Note first of all that most reductions that lead to the observed phonological similarity are perfectly regular. Take for instance the reductive effect which stable stress on *want*, *go(-ing)*, or *got* has on the following unstressed infinitival marker, irrespective of the answer to the isochrony debate. But some items are much more drastically reduced than others (cf. *going to* > *gonna* vs. *want to* > *wanna* or *need to* > *neeta*). There is, it appears, no *a priori* reason for the items to converge on a similar phonetic structure. Hence it seems difficult to explain the structural similarity solely on phonological grounds.[12] More speculatively, one might invoke the notion of gravitation at this point: several regular erosive developments affect different items to different extents and thus result in similar phonological forms. Some kind of (gravitational) force appears to slow down the process of erosion at a non-arbitrary point, thus temporarily preventing the items from diverging. This force, then, apparently leads to the emergence of a semi-stable intermediate step on the grammaticalization path of these items from constructions to affixes.

In addition, we can resort to cognitive principles such as Rosch's 'cognitive economy', which predicts that "the task of category systems is to provide maximum information with least effort" (1978: 28). Despite definitional problems, cross-linguistic work has demonstrated that the term *modal* is indeed a helpful label (Bybee *et al.* 1994: *passim*, Heine 1993: Ch. 1f, Palmer 1986: Ch. 1). It is generally understood as a non-affixal grammatical item which has certain semantic properties: deontic or epistemic meanings, often both.[13] Language-internally and cross-linguistically, then, modals tend to be perceived as similar semantically and functionally. Further, language-internally, modals tend to be similar from a morphological and syntactic point of view (take for instance the Germanic inventories of erstwhile preterite-presents).[14] This existence of a grammatical modal category both across and within languages makes it plausible to assume that speakers of a given speech community have at least one mental category for the expression of modality in their language. In English, due primarily to the semantic erosion of the old inventory—probably the ultimate *raison d'être* for the universal principle of layering which leads to the constant renewal of the grammatical inventory of any one language—we are now seeing the emergence of just such a new modal layer.

Finally, positing the emergence of a new category with formally similar items ties in neatly with Lehmann's theoretical discussion of one of his six parameters of grammaticalization, viz. paradigmaticity:

> [P]aradigmaticity is gradually reached in the process of grammaticalization . . . . The process of paradigmatic integration or *paradigmaticization* leads to a levelling out of the differences with which the members were equipped originally. (1995 [1982]: 134f; emphasis original)

Lehmann (1995 [1982]: 132f) points to the well-known fact that highly grammaticalized paradigms tend to be smaller than less grammaticalized ones. Significantly, from the relatively open class of verbs that can take *to* infinitives not all can serve as hosts to cliticized *to* (cf. **intenna*, **attemma* from *intend to* and *attempt to*, respectively).[15] The number of members participating in this paradigm, therefore, is rather restricted and hence its members are obviously more grammaticalized than the group of verbs taking *to* infinitives. Granting the emerging modals categorial status, then, is also a taxonomical reflection of precisely this observation.

2.4 An 'Iconicity of Grammatical Categories Principle'

It is received wisdom that grammaticalization occurs in very localized contexts. Consider for instance Hopper's 'Principle of Divergence':

The Principle of Divergence, or Split, as Heine and Reh call it . . . , refers to the fact that when a lexical form undergoes grammaticization, for example to an auxiliary, clitic or affix, the original form may remain as an autonomous lexical element . . . The Principle of Divergence results in pairs or multiples of forms having a common etymology, but diverging functionally.   (Hopper 1991: 24)

It is entirely consistent with this principle that for the items under investigation, form-meaning isomorphism is being created by grammaticalization: modal *gonna*, *gotta*, and *wanna* with a phonemic structure /'CVCə/ typically take infinitives, while NP complements tend to follow the fuller, older forms as in *going to the cinema*, *got to the house*, or *want a book*.[16] Observing this is tantamount to stating emerging isomorphism (compare also the notion of 'natural grammar' discussed by Heine *et al.* 1991: 118–22). The trend toward isomorphism can also be accommodated by two processes described in more recent research (Bybee and Thompson 2000, Haiman 1994a): chunking and lexical autonomy. This takes us from a purely phonological level to psychological and syntactic reasons for positing a new category. Chunking describes the automatization of frequently recurring sequences as single processing units. It renders them amenable to phonological attrition, as is commonly pointed out in grammaticalization theory (e.g., *going to* > *gonna*). Lexical autonomy refers to the progressive widening of the semantic and functional gaps between a parent lexeme, e.g., WANT, and its more grammaticalized descendant (*wanna*). In Krug (2000), for example, it is argued that *want to* and *wanna*, even though both are followed by the infinitive, actually possess partially different syntactic properties. Or take the fact that *gotta* occurs with supportive DO in questions and negation (Pullum 1997: 89). This instantiates both chunking and lexical autonomy to the extent that it proves the independent status of the new item.

Emerging isomorphism for *gonna* can indeed be inferred from a study in apparent time based on the spoken component of BNC. Table 3 gives the proportions of modal *going to* (i.e., followed by the infinitive) when measured against all instances of *going to* (i.e., followed by a noun phrase or infinitive). It shows that the two youngest groups have a significantly higher proportion of NP complements after *going to* than the remaining groups.[17] Together with the much higher incidence of

Table 3. *Modal* going to *as proportions of all* going to *sequences compared with the incidence of the word-form* gonna: *a study in apparent time*[18]

Age groupings	1–14	15–24	25–34	35–44	45–59	60+
(1) Sum *going to*	420	432	1150	1178	2,213	1,105
(2) within which are modal	71%	71%	78%	81%	85%	80%
(3) within which + NP	29%	29%	22%	19%	15%	20%
(4) *gonna* per million words	2369	2452	1727	1570	1166	553

contracted *gonna* (row 4), this suggests that the youngest two age groups have further progressed in the functional split towards isomorphism. The emerging distinction is that between modal (or futural) *gonna* + infinitive and spatial *going to* + NP. It is obvious from the data that this is an incipient development. Even for the youngest groups, modal *going to* still accounts for some 70% of all occurrences.

While it is fascinating to spot such incipient developments, their observation is not entirely surprising. On theoretical grounds, isomorphism is what Givón (1985: 189) would have predicted to develop without even having to look at textual evidence. Witness his 'Iconicity Meta-Principle':

(9)   All other things being equal, a coded experience is easier to *store, retrieve* and *communicate* if the code is maximally isomorphic to the experience.

Hopper and Thompson (1985: 151) have formulated the 'Iconicity of Lexical Categories Principle'. It seems possible to adapt their principle to grammatical domains. Note first the phrasing of the original principle:

(10) The more a form refers to a discrete discourse entity or reports a discrete discourse event, the more distinct will be its linguistic form from neighboring forms, both paradigmatically and syntagmatically.

Here I propose a somewhat more ambitious (and maybe somewhat more controversial) 'Iconicity of Grammatical Categories Principle'. Its wording is largely the conversion of Hopper and Thompson's formulation for lexical categories:

(11) Other things being equal, the more a form refers to what is crosslinguistically realized as a grammatical morpheme, the more distinct will be its linguistic form from neighboring forms and from its source construction syntagmatically, and the more similar will it be to related forms paradigmatically.

This principle emphasizes a point made above, viz. that iconicity, just like grammaticalization (cf. Lehmann 1995 [1982]: Ch. 4), has a syntagmatic and a paradigmatic dimension. The 'Iconicity of Grammatical Categories Principle', then, proposes that grammaticalization typically involves loss of *syntagmatic* iconicity, which is the emancipation from the etymological source of a given item, as well as increased distinctness from its co-text. For the emerging modals, this is to say that while grammaticalizing they are becoming different from their source constructions (e.g., HAVE GOT TO) on the one hand, and from their neighboring forms in the syntagm (i.e., lexical verbs) on the other. This loss in syntagmatic iconicity, however, tends to be accompanied by gains in *paradigmatic* iconicity, that is to say, the development of formal resemblance with items belonging to the same, potentially emerging, paradigm (here: the class of emerging modals).[19] It is important to note, however, that this principle enjoys greater validity for free grammatical morphemes developing roughly in sync than for layers from very different historical stages. The latter tend to include such heterogeneous items as affixes and free complex constructions, which necessarily differ greatly. Therefore, only when the condition of approximate diachronic coincidence is met will other things be equal enough for the above principle to apply.

That frequently expressed notions tend to grammaticalize is one tenet of functionalism. This is made explicit in, for instance, Bybee's (forthcoming) new definition of grammatic(al)ization:

> which recognizes the crucial role of repetition . . . and characterizes it as the process by which a frequently-used sequence of words or morphemes becomes automated as a single processing unit.

The above 'Iconicity of Grammatical Categories Principle' is therefore partly inspired by, very generally, Hopper's notion of emergent grammar or, more specifically, by Givón's 'Principle (27)':

> The notion of Emergent Grammar is meant to suggest that structure, or regularity, comes out of discourse and is shaped by discourse in an ongoing process . . . .The notion of emergence . . . takes the adjective emergent seriously as a continual movement towards structure . . . (Hopper 1998: 156f [1987: 142])

> The more important an item is in the communication, the more *distinct* and *independent* coding expression it receives. (Givón 1985: 206)

The statement of (11) would not deserve the label 'principle' if it were restricted to the few items discussed in the present study. It is therefore important to note that, synchronically, many grammatical categories, in particular categories that contain *free* grammatical morphemes, have several prototypical members which tend to be structurally similar.[20] Take for instance English uncased personal pronouns (*I*, *you*, *she*, etc.): six out of seven consist of two phonemes (it is probably no coincidence that the monophonemic *I* is also the most frequent pronoun). Further, six out of seven end in a (rather close) vowel, five out of seven begin in a consonant (fricative or glide). The situation for English personal pronouns with objective case is similar.

Another case in point is the French system of uncased personal pronouns, as shown in Table 4. This is even more homogeneous than the English or German systems in that each pronoun consists of two phonemes. If we compare its Latin etymological sources, we see that the French system has regularized (hence iconicized) the Latin inconsistencies following the two-phoneme principle.

Many other pronoun systems could be invoked such as the highly iconic Italian accusative paradigm with its items *ci*, *vi*, *li*, *le*, *si*.[21] Interestingly, obligatory (and thus frequently used) items seem to result in more iconic paradigms than paradigms with optional (hence rarer) items, even when both paradigms share essentially the same etymology. This fact points to the intimate relationship between frequency, erosion, and iconicity. The French system of nominative personal pronouns given in Table 4 compares for instance with far less homogeneous counterparts in Italian or Spanish (particularly striking is Spanish with structurally relatively complex pronouns such as *nosotros* 'we' or *ellos* 'they'). This seems to underpin the claim that much paradigmatic iconicization comes about by erosion due to frequent use.

Table 4. *Latin vs. French personal pronouns*

Person	Latin sg.	French sg.		Latin pl.	French pl.	
1st	*ego*	*je*	/ʒə/	*nos*	*nous*	/nu/
2nd	*tu*	*tu*	/ty/	*vos*	*vous*	/vu/
3rd m.	*ille/illum*	*il*	/il/	*illi/illos*	*ils*	/il/
3rd f.	*illa/illam*	*elle*	/el/	*illae/illas*	*elles*	/el/

To take a category which is more closely related to the present investigation, let us consider the rather homogeneous set of present-day English central modals. To recall, it is probably no coincidence that the idiosyncratic *uton* was lost from the inventory of preterite present verbs (cf. Warner 1993: 186). Further, today the historical preterite forms of three (out of four) central modals (*would, could,* and *should*) have the structure /Cʊd/, where C stands for consonant. Historically, their (stem) vowels were not identical. They are now. It must be admitted that the development of each of these stem vowels is by no means exceptional.[22] Nevertheless, discourse frequency aside perhaps, there is no genuinely phonological principle predicting the shortening of each individual stem vowel in these items. More significantly, as their orthography indicates, *would* and *should* had originally an additional phoneme /l/, unlike the analogical respelling *could*. Phonotactically the consonant cluster /-ld/ has remained part of English, as *pulled, child,* and *fold* show. Simplification of consonant clusters as such is not unusual either, but the result that three central modals have become formally nearly identical is certainly noteworthy.[23] And even the remaining central modals which at a glance look rather different are not that different on closer inspection: *can, will, shall* and *might* can be seen as forming another subgroup of modals with a /CVC/ structure, where, just like in the cases of *could, would,* and *should,* the last phoneme is alveolar. In fact, *mus(t)* too belongs to this group since its final consonant cluster is usually reduced. In other words, only one central modal, viz. *may,* is radically different phonologically from the remaining eight members of its category, if one can speak of radical differences when the difference consists of the absence of one phoneme. Finally, their overall structural coherence can be demonstrated by the fact that all nine central modals share a set of at least twelve morphosyntactic idiosyncrasies not shared by lexical verbs (see Quirk *et al.* 1985: 137).

To consider a different category, prototypical prepositions in English or German consist of two phonemes and share a locative and directional semantics (e.g., English *in, on, at, to*; German *in, an, auf, zu*). English prepositions like *under, over, above*, and *across* follow in terms of core membership, and it seems a comparatively long way to such items as *with regard to*. Significantly, such tendencies are not restricted to Germanic or Indo-European languages but are indeed valid crosslinguistically. As Kortmann and König (1992: 682f) note:

> in a wide variety of languages, a core group of highly frequent, monosyllabic, highly versatile primary adpositions can be distinguished from typically disyllabic, less versatile secondary ones and so on, down to one or several layers of marginal and peripheral groups.

A final example can be provided from the domain of adverbial subordinators (e.g., *since, if, while*). Based on a typological study of 50 European languages (Kortmann 1997), this is probably the most weighty piece of evidence invoked so far. For adverbial subordinators, then, the same tendency obtains as for the domain of adpositions just quoted. More intriguing still, over the course of time the adverbial subordinators of English have become more similar structurally to the cross-linguistically valid monosyllabic prototype.

Generalizations from such research seem possible. First, historically not all members of a category start out from a position of formal resemblance to the prototype. Further, progressive development of shared properties, which is typical in the formation of new categories (e.g., Rosch 1978), is not restricted to the morphosyntactic level: phonology is involved as well. Neither of these observations is new. Hence, the developments in the realm of emerging auxiliaries are by no means exceptional. It is remarkable, though, that the prototype in the case of emerging modals is not attested in older stages of the language, but that economy and concomitant grammaticalization seem to be triggering the emergence of just such an iconically motivated prototype.

2.5 Categorization in grammaticalization and related frameworks

The above considerations are grounded in cognitive principles that appeal to iconicity, isomorphism, and prototype theory, all of which are related to grammaticalization theory. I will now discuss the hypothesis of a newly emerging category in the light of some fundamental tenets concerning categorization in grammaticalization theory proper. Building on work by Givón, Hopper and Traugott (1993: 7) have established a cline of grammaticality which has several focal points where linguistic forms or structures may cluster:

(12)   content item > grammatical word > clitic > inflectional affix

They point out that "it is often difficult to establish firm boundaries between the categories represented on clines," and indeed they note that "the study of grammaticalization has emerged in part out of a recognition of the general fluidity of so-called categories" (1993:7). Significantly, in language change "forms do not shift abruptly from one category to another, but go through a series of gradual transitions, transitions that tend to be similar in type across languages" (Hopper and Traugott 1993: 6).[24] In other words, the above cline of grammaticality is valid for both the synchronic categorization and the historical development of words and constructions.

Bybee *et al.* (1994: 8) note that "it is also typical of grammatical or closed classes to reduce further in size. Individual members are lost, usually by one member generalizing to take over the functions of other members." They cite *will* replacing *shall* in the auxiliary domain, a development, it must be said, that has been going on for centuries. Positing that WANT TO etc. are currently becoming central modals would therefore present a problem to the reduction-of-members hypothesis. This problem is resolved by stating the evolution of a new category. Bybee and Dahl (1989: 60) seem to strengthen this position:

> Since . . . lexical morphemes can become grammatical, it would seem to follow that new closed classes items may be added to a language. While this is true, it is also the case that new grams are rarely added to existing closed classes, rather, as they grammaticize, they create new closed classes.

It is not doubtful that the emerging modals investigated in the present study are moving towards the upper focal point of the main verb—auxiliary verb cline as proposed by Quirk *et al.* (1985: 137, cf. Appendix A). On the other hand, it seems equally clear that most of them will not reach this focal point. Present-day syntax is simply different from Old and early Middle English syntax, which is partly fossilized by the central modals. Good examples of the preservation of older syntax are subject-verb inversion in interrogatives and NOT negation. Both features, I believe, are due precisely to the high discourse frequency of relevant strings such as *will you* and *should not* (and their older forms, of course).[25] Strong entrenchment of such sequences probably made them immune to change—different from the infrequent sequences of *lexical* verbs followed by NOT or personal pronouns, which developed DO support (cf. Bybee forthcoming). In sum, these facts at least partially explain two of the auxiliaries' most salient properties and they also reveal one reason why today new auxiliaries cannot develop the criteria NOT negation and operator inversion: there are no frequent strings such as WANT TO *not* or GOT TO *you* . . . ? Productive patterns like DO-support and semi-productive infinitival *to* complements (or their phonological traces) will fossilize on emerging auxiliaries, a fact that will only become apparent once new ways of infinitival marking (such as *on -ing*) have become more productive.

Not all of the emerging modals take DO support (GOING TO hardly ever, GOT TO only in colloquial American styles and in some British dialects). The notion of *prototype* enters crucially at this point. Developed by the psychologist Eleanor Rosch (e.g., 1978), this model of categorization has become popular within the domain of cognitive linguistics (see Taylor 1995 for a general introduction). Its value for the typology of auxiliaries has been stressed by, among others, Warner (1993), Heine (1993), and Traugott (1997). For convenience, I quote Heine's (1993: 113) concise summary of the prototype approach to classification:

> Prototypes differ from classical categories in that they cannot be defined by means of necessary and sufficient properties; rather they have the following attributes in particular . . . :
> • Not every member is equally representative of its category.
> • Prototypical members share a maximum of attributes with other members and a minimum with members of contrasting categories.
> • The structure of categories takes the form of a set of clustered and overlapping attributes.
> • Categories are blurred at the edges; they have fuzzy boundaries.

Compare Traugott (1997: 192) on auxiliaries:

> The positions on this continuum are to be thought of as "cluster points", magnets, as it were, where iron filings (in this instance source verbs) coalesce; or, to use more familiar terminology, they represent clusters of prototypical properties.

While the magnet metaphor may be helpful, a frequentative approach suggests an alternative model: cluster points probably do not arise as immaterial magnets; rather, I believe, the actually existing most frequent source verbs function as magnets and attract other less common constructions.[26] A case in point would be the gradual long-term increase in the use of DO support and *to* (rather than bare) infinitives with NEED and perhaps OUGHT and DARE, a development which I interpret as a movement toward the new focal point of emerging modals (Krug 2000).

3. Conclusion

In proposing that a new (verbal) category is currently emerging, I have by no means added a novel principle to grammaticalization theory.[27] I hope to have contributed, however, to a better understanding of the initially quoted commonplace according to which a 'wholesale reorganization' is currently affecting the English auxiliary system. To conclude, let us integrate some of my empirical results into Heine's discussion of frequency, erosion, and iconicity. Heine (1993: 111f) maintains that "it is the pragmatic factor of frequency of use that appears to be most immediately responsible for erosion." I tend to agree with this position (notice, for instance, that of the items under investigation here, the most frequent one, BE GOING TO, is also generally the one most drastically reduced). It is noteworthy, however, that Heine himself anticipates a more complex interaction with iconic factors:

> The sequence [Desemanticization > High frequency > Loss of information value > Erosion] does not account for all the forces that can be held responsible for erosion; the question as to how this sequence relates to the parameter of iconic coding, for example, remains entirely open to further research.   (Heine 1993: 111f)

This issue should have become somewhat more clear through the present study. I have suggested that iconic coding and erosion need not necessarily be counter-forces. For the items under investigation, different reduction processes are leading to very similar products of univerbation. On this basis and on the basis of Fischer's (1999) considerations on associative iconicity, it was argued that erosion may give rise to a new, more abstract type of iconicity. Rather than betray the etymological origin of an item, the newly developed type of paradigmatic iconicity indicates category membership. Further, in the field of emerging modals, grammaticalization does not only lead to increased paradigmatic iconicity: by identifying early signs of a functional split (e.g., modal *gonna*, *gotta* + infinitive vs. spatial, nonmodal *going to*, *got to* + NP), it is also possible to show incipient isomorphism.

In the early phase after the revival of grammaticalization theory in the 1980s, work focused on formal aspects (i.e., morphological, phonological, and syntactic). Since the late 1980s, attention has shifted to semantic and pragmatic aspects of grammaticalization (e.g., Brinton 1988, Bybee *et al.* 1994, Bybee and Dahl 1989, Heine *et al.* 1991, Sweetser 1990, Traugott 1988). While I accept the importance of semantic-pragmatic aspects and of all three formal levels, I here wish to stress the role of phonology and discourse frequency in grammaticalization (cf. Bybee this volume, Bybee and Thompson 2000). If the present data are significant for the over-all framework of grammaticalization, then phonetic variation and phonological developments must not be considered epiphenomena. Performance (i.e., speech production and perception) and, in particular, frequency and phonetic variation ought to be recognized as major forces in the early stages of category formation. By this I do not wish to imply that overt phonetic form is the only relevant domain in the creation of new categories. As this study has shown, cognitive principles (such as iconicity) also apply, if probably at a later stage. A rather speculative sketch based on the present investigation would be approximately as follows: discourse, i.e., actual physical input, produces phonetic variation. This variation is not entirely random, though. Frequency of use facilitates such variation as is manifest in more and less eroded forms. In an iconicity-driven cognitive process, structurally similar variants are selected, which leads to a convergence of items belonging to a category.

The result may be a rather homogeneous representation of a (potentially new) grammatical category.

Appendix A: The auxiliary verb—main verb scale (from Quirk *et al.* 1985: 137)

(one verb phrase)	(a)	Central modals	*can, could, may, might, shall, should, will/'ll, would/'d, must*
	(b)	Marginal modals	*dare, need, ought to, used to*
	(c)	Modal idioms	*had better, would rather/sooner*, BE *to*, HAVE *got to*, etc
	(d)	Semi-auxiliaries	HAVE *to*, BE *about to*, BE *able to*, BE *bound to*, BE *going to*, BE *obliged to*, BE *supposed to*, BE *willing to*, etc.
	(e)	Catenatives	APPEAR *to*, HAPPEN *to*, SEEM *to*, GET + *-ed* participle, KEEP + *-ing* participle, etc.
(two verb phrases)	(f)	Main verb + nonfinite clause	HOPE + *to*-infinitive, BEGIN + *-ing* participle, etc.

Notes

* I would like to thank the participants of the symposium for a stimulating discussion. Special thanks are due to Joan Bybee, Verena Haser, and Bernd Kortmann for their valuable comments on earlier versions of the written paper.

1. In this study I will generally distinguish between word forms such as *has* and paradigms such as HAVE. The paradigm WANT TO, then, covers all word forms of WANT followed by *to*, plus the form *wanna*. Phonological transcriptions like /'gɒtə/ and phonetic transcriptions like ['gɒɾə] are given according to the IPA.

2. The British National Corpus (BNC) contains 100 million words of current British English, 90 million of which are written, 10 million of which are spoken. The spoken component divides into two subcorpora of roughly equal size: one contains more formal speech (council meetings, speeches etc.), while the other contains spontaneous conversation (see Aston and Burnard 1998 for details).

3. Biber *et al.* (1999: ch. 5) provide two helpful inventories of common lexical verbs. For the present study, fresh corpus research seemed necessary since Biber *et al.* limit their searches to lexemes, whereas I needed to include constructions.

4. The figures for HAVE, GET, GO, WANT and LIKE do not include forms of HAVE TO, HAVE GOT TO, GOING TO, WANT TO and LIKE TO. The table generally provides phrase searches in the BNC, which is a sufficient estimator for most items. However, frequent word forms that are ambiguous between verbal and nominal, adjectival, or prepositional status (such as *being, thought, like/s*) were disambiguated with the help of the part-of-speech option.

5. Very recently, however, Fischer (1999a, 1999b) has expressed a related idea, viz. that increased iconicity and isomorphism often accompany grammaticalization.

6. Haiman refers only to causatives and coordinate constructions. I will try to show that this principle enjoys wider currency.

7. A discourse factor probably plays a role in the deletion of the auxiliaries BE and HAVE in BE GOING TO and HAVE GOT TO. Deletion in the latter is facilitated by the fact that the string *I got* by itself is grammatical and frequent. This contrasts with *I going*, which is not grammatical in unmarked and frequent statements but only attested in rare interrogatives or even rarer inversions after semi-negatives like *hardly*.

8. The term *auxiliation* was coined by Benveniste (1968). I follow the tradition of most European-based studies in grammatic(al)ization, which use the longer terms. For the sake of simplicity, groups of phonological variants are given above as orthographic variants. While this is a crude simplification, more phonetic detail will be provided below.

9. The last three examples are not empty respellings; the devoicing of the verb-final consonants is an assimilation process typical of word-internal sound sequences.

10. American English is slightly different: the quality of the full vowel is rather [ɑ], its length varies, and it is usually more nasalized in *gonna* and *wanna*; /t/ is generally flapped. Bybee *et al.* (1994: 6) and Bybee and Thompson (2000) use schwa for the stressed vowel in *gonna*, which might indicate that *gonna* in this variety is more advanced on its way to morphologization. Ambiguous statements in pronunciation dictionaries, however, demonstrate that more detailed phonetic studies are necessary (cf. Windsor-Lewis 1992; Wells 1990; Jones 1997: *s.v. gonna*).

11. Related to this concept of iconicity is the much older notion of analogy, which Bußmann (1996: *s.v. analogy*) defines as the "synchronic or diachronic process by which conceptually related linguistic units are made similar (or identical) in form."

12. There probably exists a frequency reason, though: the assimilation processes found between the verb forms *want, going, got* and the following infinitival marker *to* are typical of word-internal sound sequences or of highly frequent word sequences (which presumably themselves are single processing units and thus akin to single words). It seems certain, for instance, that mainstream American speakers more commonly flap their /t/s in *want to* than in *winter* or even *rent to*. This, then, at least partially explains why, within the set of emerging modal constructions, the most drastic reductions (viz. from *going to* to *gonna*) are found for the most frequent sequence.

13. See Palmer (1986, 1989) for discussion; or Bybee *et al.* (1994: ch. 6) for an alternative, if broadly related, semantic classification. As will become clear from note 20 below, it is important to stress the non-affixal property of modals at this point.

14. It needs to be borne in mind that the modals in the Germanic languages have not developed in step, not even in individual languages. Nevertheless, the overall direction of their changes, best documented for English (e.g., Warner 1993), seems to be towards more coherent classes.

15. Discourse frequency of the sequences [VERB — *to*] evidently plays a major role here, with high frequency favoring, low frequency disfavoring cliticization (cf. Krug 1998).

16. It must be conceded, though, that due to a different source construction *want a* and particularly *got a* seem less likely to diverge drastically from the modal usage.

17. As for statistical significance, a chi-square test rejects the null hypothesis (H_0: Different age groups use both modal and nonmodal forms of GOING TO alike) at the 0.1% confidence level.

18. Percentages were extrapolated from two random samples of 100 instances each. The standard deviation was always below 2.1.

19. Within the limits of the present paper, I can discuss little more than phonological aspects. Krug (2000) also discusses incipient morphological and syntactic convergence for the emerging modals.

20. Ultimately, one would need to corroborate this claim by more typological work. A starting point is a crosslinguistic study by Bybee (1986) on bound grammatical morphemes (verbal inflections). She has shown that semantically coherent verbal affixes (expressing tense, aspect, or mood) are not structurally similar, at least not as far as their position relative to the verb is concerned. In other words, she finds that there is no correlation between the structural criterion 'affix position' (post- or pre-verbal) and semantic class (e.g., tense or mood). In order to obtain a fuller picture of the presence or absence of structural similarity for bound and/or free grammatical morphemes, however, we would require comparative studies of further formal properties, i.e., of phonological, morphological, and syntactic properties.

21. Cf. also Lehmann's (1995[1982]: 134) discussion of the formal and functional homogeneity of many grammatical paradigms.

22. The vowels in *would* and *should* underwent the Great Vowel Shift from /o:/ to /u:/ (their originally short vowels had been lengthened because of the following consonant cluster /ld/). The stem vowel in all three items was later shortened and centralized from /u:/ to /ʊ/, a development which not all related items underwent, though. It is not inconceivable that a frequency factor plays a role here, too. There are certainly only a few high-frequency words which did not take part in the laxation of the vowel (cf. *good, should, could, would*, with *food, goose, lose, shoe*, and *fool*). And the few high-frequency words like *you* that still retain a long /u:/ have developed weak-form variants like /jʊ, jə/. This fact, and other ambivalent cases like *room* or *roof*, actually seem to indicate that this change is still in progress.

23. It must be conceded, however, that postvocalic /IC/ seems prone to change generally. Consider the loss of /l/ in other (again, usually frequent) words like *walk* and *talk*; or *alright, already*, and *almost* (in the last three examples, where /l/ deletion is optional, the two phonemes are not part of the same syllable, though). Or consider the loss of /l/ in words like *palm* or, finally, the trend for [ɫ] to become vocalized in Estuary English (e.g., *milk, help*).

24. This is widely agreed upon. A notable exception is Lightfoot (1979), who argues for cataclysmic change in the development of the central English auxiliaries.

25. While I do not have hard statistical evidence for this claim, a cursory look at the Middle English component of the Helsinki Corpus shows that verbs preceding NOT (and its variants like *noht*, *nought*, etc.) are almost always modals or, of course, HAVE and BE. These are the only verbs that have retained NOT negation. It also appears that a similar tendency holds in Middle English for what we today call operator inversion (cf. Krug 1998 on the theoretical outline of and empirical support for the concept of string frequency).

26. A related analogy to the natural sciences is one in terms of gravitation theory (see Krug 2000 for discussion).

27. Compare, for instance, Meillet (1912), Bybee and Dahl (1989), or Hopper's (1991) Principle of Layering.

References

Aitchison, J. 1994 [1987]. *Words in the Mind: an Introduction to the Mental Lexicon*. Oxford: Blackwell.
Aston, G. and Burnard, L. 1998. *The BNC Handbook: Exploring the British National Corpus with SARA*. Edinburgh: Edinburgh University Press.
Benveniste, É. 1968. "Mutations of linguistic categories". In *Directions for Historical Linguistics: a Symposium*, W. Lehmann and Y. Malkiel (eds), 85–94. Austin: University of Texas Press.
Biber, D., Johansson, S., Leech, G., Conrad, S., and Finegan, E. 1999. *The Longman Grammar of Spoken and Written English*. London: Longman.
Bisang, W. 1998. "Grammaticalization and language contact, constructions and positions". In *The limits of grammaticalization*, A. G. Ramat and P. Hopper (eds), 13–58. Amsterdam: Benjamins.
Bolinger, D. 1980. *Language: the Loaded Weapon*. London: Longman.
Brinton, L. 1988. *The Development of English Aspectual Systems: Aspectualizers and Postverbal Particles*. Cambridge: Cambridge University Press.
Bußmann, H. 1996. *Routledge Dictionary of Language and Linguistics*. G. Trauth and K. Kazzazi (trans and eds). (German original: *Lexikon der Sprachwissenschaft*, 1990.) London; New York: Routledge.
Bybee, J. 1986. "On the nature of grammatical categories: a diachronic perspective". *Eastern States Conference on Linguistics* 2: 17–34.
Bybee, J. 1999. "Fusion in grammaticalization: automatization and the suffixing preference". Paper given at the conference *New directions in grammaticalization*, Potsdam, June 1999.
Bybee, J. Forthcoming. "Mechanisms of change in grammaticization: the role of frequency". In *Handbook of historical linguistics*, B. Joseph and R. Janda (eds). Oxford: Oxford University Press.

Bybee, J. and Dahl, Ö. 1989. "The creation of tense and aspect systems in the languages of the world". *Studies in Language* 13(1): 51–103.

Bybee, J., Pagliuca, W., and Perkins, R. 1994. *The Evolution of Grammar: Tense, Aspect, and Modality in the Languages of the World.* Chicago: University of Chicago Press.

Bybee, J., and Thompson, S. 2000. "Three frequency effects in syntax". Berkeley Linguistic Society 23: 378–88.

Croft, W. 1990. *Typology and Universals.* Cambridge: Cambridge University Press.

DuBois, J. 1985. "Competing motivations". In *Iconicity in Syntax*, J. Haiman (ed), 343–65. Amsterdam: Benjamins.

Fischer, A. 1999. "What, if anything, is phonological iconicity?" In *Form Miming Meaning: Iconicity in Language and Literature*, M. Nänny and O. Fischer (eds), 123–34. Amsterdam: Benjamins.

Fischer, O. 1999a. "On the role played by iconicity in grammaticalisation processes". In *Form Miming Meaning: Iconicity in Language and Literature*, M. Nänny and O. Fischer (eds), 345–74. Amsterdam: Benjamins.

Fischer, O. 1999b. "Grammaticalization and iconicity: two interacting processes". Paper given at the conference *New directions in grammaticalization*, Potsdam, June 1999.

Givón, T. 1979. *On Understanding Grammar.* New York: Academic Press.

Givón, T. 1985. "Iconicity, isomorphism and nonarbitrary coding in syntax: iconicity in syntax". In *Iconicity in Syntax*, J. Haiman (ed), 187–220. Amsterdam: Benjamins.

Givón, T. 1993. *English Grammar: a Function-based Introduction* (2 volumes). Amsterdam: Benjamins.

Givón, T. 1995. *Functionalism and Grammar.* Amsterdam: Benjamins.

Goldberg, A. 1995. *Constructions: a Construction Grammar Approach to Argument Structure.* Chicago: University of Chicago Press.

Haiman, J. 1980. "The iconicity of grammar: isomorphism and motivation". *Language* 56(3): 515–40.

Haiman, J. 1983. "Iconic and economic motivation". *Language* 59(4): 781–819.

Haiman, J. 1985a. *Natural Syntax: Iconicity and Erosion.* Cambridge: Cambridge University Press.

Haiman, J. 1994a. "Ritualization and the development of language". In *Perspectives on grammaticalization*, W. Pagliuca (ed), 3–28. Amsterdam: Benjamins.

Haiman, J. 1994b. "Iconicity". In *The Encyclopedia of Language and Linguistics* (10 volumes), R.E. Asher (ed), 1629–33. Oxford: Pergamon.

Haiman, J. 1994c. "Iconicity and syntactic change". In *The Encyclopedia of Language and Linguistics* (10 volumes), R.E. Asher (ed), 1633–7. Oxford: Pergamon.

Heine, B. 1993. *Auxiliaries: Cognitive Forces and Grammaticalization.* Oxford: Oxford University Press.

Heine, B. 1999. "On the role of context in grammaticalization". Paper given at the conference *New Directions in Grammaticalization*, Potsdam, June 1999.

Heine, B., Claudi, U., and Hünnemeyer, F. 1991. *Grammaticalization: a Conceptual Framework.* Chicago: University of Chicago Press.

Hopper, P. 1991. "On some principles of grammaticization". In *Approaches to grammaticalization*. (2 volumes), E. Traugott and B. Heine (eds), I: 17–35. Amsterdam: Benjamins.

Hopper, P. 1998. "Emergent Grammar" (revised version of Hopper 1987, *Berkeley Linguistics Society* 13, 139–57). In *The Psychology of Language: Cognitive and Functional Approaches to Language Structure*, M. Tomasello (ed), 155–75. Mahwah, New Jersey: Erlbaum.

Hopper, P. and Thompson, S. 1985. "The iconicity of the universal categories *noun* and *verb*". In *Iconicity in Syntax*, J. Haiman (ed), 151–83. Amsterdam: Benjamins.

Hopper, P. and Traugott, E. 1993. *Grammaticalization*. Cambridge: Cambridge University Press.

Horn, L. 1984. "Toward a new taxonomy for pragmatic inference: Q-based and R-based implicature". In D. Schiffrin (ed.), 11–42.

Jones, D. 1997 [1917]. *English Pronouncing Dictionary*. Cambridge: Cambridge University Press.

Kortmann, B. 1997. *Adverbial Subordination: a Typology and History of Adverbial Subordinators Based on European Languages*. Berlin: Mouton de Gruyter.

Kortmann, B., König, E. 1992. "Categorial reanalysis: the case of deverbal prepositions". *Linguistics* 30: 671–97.

Krug, M. 1998. "String frequency: a cognitive motivating factor in coalescence, language processing and linguistic change". *Journal of English Linguistics* 26(4): 286–320.

Krug, M. 2000. *Emerging English Modals: a Corpus-based Study of Grammaticalization*. Berlin; New York: Mouton de Gruyter.

Lehmann, C. 1995 [1982]. *Thoughts on Grammaticalization* [*Lincom Studies in Theoretical Linguistics* 1]. Munich: Lincom Europa.

Lehmann, C. 1999. "New reflections on grammaticalization and lexicalization". Paper given at the conference *New directions in grammaticalization*, Potsdam, June 1999.

Lightfoot, D. 1979. *Principles of Diachronic Syntax*. Cambridge: Cambridge University Press.

Malkiel, Y. 1968. "The inflectional paradigm as an occasional determinant of sound change". In *Directions for historical linguistics*, W. Lehmann and Y. Malkiel (eds), 21–64. Austin: University of Texas Press.

Meillet, A. 1912. "L'évolution des formes grammaticales". *Scientia (Rivista di Scienza)* 12(6): 384–400.

Palmer, F. 1986. *Mood and Modality*. Cambridge: Cambridge University Press.

Palmer, F. 1989 [1979]. *Modality and the English Modals*. London: Longman.

Plank, F. 1979. "Ikonisierung und De-Ikonisierung als Prinzipien des Sprachwandels". *Sprachwissenschaft* 4: 121–58.

Pullum, G. 1997. "The morpholexical nature of *to*-contraction". *Language* 73: 79–102.

Quirk, R., Greenbaum, S., Leech, G., and Svartvik, J. 1985. *A Comprehensive Grammar of the English Language*. London: Longman.

Radford, A. 1997. *Syntactic Theory and the Structure of English: a Mnimalist Approach*. Cambridge: Cambridge University Press.

Rosch, E. 1978. "Principles of categorization". In *Cognition and categorization*, E. Rosch and B. Lloyd (eds), 27–48. Hillsdale: Erlbaum.

Saussure, F. de. 1916. *Cours de Linguistique Générale*. Paris: Payet.

Sweetser, E. 1990. *From Etymology to Pragmatics: Metaphorical and Cultural Aspects of Semantic Structure*. Cambridge: Cambridge University Press.

Tabor, W. and Traugott, E. 1998. "Structural scope expansion and grammaticalization". In *The Limits of Grammaticalization*, A.G. Ramat and P. Hopper (eds), 229–72. Amsterdam: Benjamins.

Taylor, J. 1995 [1989]. *Linguistic Categorization: Prototypes in Linguistic Theory*. Oxford: Clarendon.

Traugott, E. 1988. "Pragmatic strengthening and grammaticalization". *Berkeley Linguistics Society* 14: 406–16.

Traugott, E. 1997. "Subjectification and the development of epistemic meaning: the case of *promise* and *threaten*". In *Modality in Germanic Languages: Historical and Comparative Perspectives*, T. Swan and O. Westvik (eds), 185–210. Berlin: Mouton de Gruyter.

Traugott, E. Forthcoming. "Constructions in grammaticalization". In *Handbook of historical linguistics*, B. Joseph and R. Janda (eds). Oxford: Oxford University Press.

Warner, A. 1993. *English Auxiliaries: Structure and History [Cambridge Studies in Linguistics 66]*. Cambridge: Cambridge University Press.

Windsor-Lewis, J. 1972. *A Concise dictionary of British and American English*. London: Oxford University Press.

Wells, J. 1990. *Longman Pronunciation Dictionary*. London: Longman.

Zipf, G. 1949. *Human Behavior and the Principle of Least Effort: an Introduction to Human Ecology*. New York: Hafner.

Frequency effects on French liaison

JOAN BYBEE

University of New Mexico

1. Phonology-syntax interface

A mainstay of the debates concerning the phonology-syntax interface are phenomena of external sandhi, that is, phonological alternations whose conditioning environment is across a word boundary.[1] A recurrent problem in this area is the fact that it is usually impossible to motivate a purely syntactic account of such alternations. This has led to the widespread consensus that the relation between syntax and phonology is indirect and often seemingly arbitrary (Inkelas and Zec 1995; Nespor and Vogel 1986; Vogel and Kenesei 1990). In this paper, I propose a solution to the problem of predicting the sites for external sandhi and I pose certain questions that are seldom raised in such discussions, in particular, how is it that syntactic structures can condition phonological alternations and how is it that such alternations can develop and be maintained?

It is important first to distinguish between phonetically conditioned processes that operate across word boundaries and those lexicalized instances that occur only within fixed phrases or constructions.[2] Phonetically-conditioned processes are observable within pause groups, wherever their conditioning environment occurs, both inside of words and across boundaries, allowing for some variation. Examples are Spanish s-aspiration at early stages of development, the spirantization of voiced stops in Spanish, vowel coalescence in Spanish, English flapping of coronal stops, French *enchaînement* (resyllablification), just to name a few. Phonetically-motivated processes sometimes give rise to word-level alternations, that is, cases of a single morpheme with two variants in two different words. I have argued (Bybee 2000a) that while morphemes commonly develop alternations, words tend *not* to develop variants; rather there is a strong tendency for a single word to have a single variant or small range of variation. Yet sometimes alternations *do* develop such that a single word will have more than one stable variant. In this case, we get the second type of external sandhi, which is no longer phonetically-conditioned, but rather applies across word boundaries in particular constructions. I will claim that this only happens in high frequency phrases and constructions and that the establishment of such alternations provides evidence that, indeed, these phrases and constructions are stored in memory just as invariant words are.

In the case of French liaison, which we will discuss here, it is often claimed that liaison occurs most commonly in phrases with 'greater syntactic cohesion' and yet there are no definitions of this cohesion that correctly predict all cases of liaison. I will demonstrate that this syntactic cohesion is a direct result of frequency of co-occurrence: words that are used together more often tend to seem more fused and also tend to have more liaison. I will argue against a mismatch between syntactic and phonological structure and will argue instead that the phonology provides good evidence for storage and processing units. Since I do not see the need to posit any grammatical structure that is independent of processing and storage, I will argue that the phonology provides excellent evidence for the nature of the syntactic structure.

2. French liaison

French liaison is one of the best-studied cases of alternations between versions of the same word under putative syntactic conditions. Liaison is the name for the appearance of a word-final consonant before a vowel-initial word in words that in other contexts end in a vowel. Thus, the third singular copula *est* is pronounced [ɛt] in example (1a and b) and as [ɛ] in example (2a and b) (the *s* is never pronounced). Examples from Green and Hintze (1988).

(1) a. . . . le climat est [t] également très différent.
       'The climate is also very different'
    b. C'est [t] encore un refuge de notables.
       'It's still a refuge for famous people'

(2) a. C'e(st) le meurtre.
       'It's murder'
    b. le Conseil Régional qui e(st) donc son assemblée délibérante . . .
       'The Regional Council which is thus their deliberative assembly'

The phonological condition for the appearance of the liaison is before a vowel-initial word, but only under certain syntactic conditions. In (3) and (4), the presence of the plural liaison is obligatory for the definite article *les*. However, in the noun phrase in (3), the plural morpheme on the noun may variably appear before a vowel-initial adjective, while in (4) the presence of [z] on this same noun is not possible, as the construction involves an NP subject and its verb.

(3) le[z] enfant[z] intelligent   'the intelligent children'

(4) le[z] enfan(ts) arrivent.   'the children arrive'

Moreover, in cases such as (1) and (3) where liaison is possible, there is currently considerable variability. In the databases studied by Ågren (1973) and by Green and Hintze (1988), speakers at times also omitted the consonant before a vowel. Such omissions are taken as evidence that liaison is disappearing in some contexts.

In the next section I will examine the evolution of liaison from its initiation as a phonetically-conditioned consonant deletion to its present state as attested in conversation, in which it is highly lexically and morphologically governed, as argued by Baxter (1975), Green and Hintze (1988), Klausenberger (1984), Morin and Kaye (1982) and Tranel (1981). I will argue that the morphosyntactic and lexical contexts in which liaison became established occurred with high frequency and were thus sequences that could be stored in memory. Currently, as liaison is being lost, we see that it is maintained in the contexts that are most frequently occurring (Ågren 1973; Delattre 1966). Please note that the treatment of liaison offered here is illustrative only and not by any means exhaustive.

3. Final consonant deletion in French

The source of the liaison alternations is the deletion of word-final consonants before another consonant. It is important to note that this was only a specific instance of the more general deletion of syllable-final consonants, which was entirely phonetically conditioned. The first wave of such deletion occurred very early in French, when consonants that had been final in Latin were lost, e.g., Latin *pŏntem* 'bridge' and *caput* 'chief' lost their final consonants. A subsequent development was the loss of final post-tonic vowels, which created another full set of final consonants (giving e.g., *pont, chef* from the Latin words given above). The stops and fricatives in final position developed two or sometimes three alternates in the environments before a pause, a consonant or a vowel. Harris (1988: 213) gives the example of *dix* 'ten' which is pronounced [dis] before a pause, [di] before a consonant (*dix femmes* 'ten women') and [diz] before a vowel (*dix élèves* 'ten pupils'). More commonly today, where the alternations persist, the only two variants are the presence and absence of the consonant. However, it is interesting that while this consonant deletion was in progress, the preconsonantal and prepausal conditions were distinguished. The deletion occurred earlier in preconsonantal position than before pause (Klausenberger 1984). This fact suggests that an important phonetic condition for the deletion was the masking provided by a following consonant, and that the spread of deletion to prepausal position was due to the restructuring of the lexical representations.

The result of this phonetic change was that many words, notably nouns and some adjectives, lost their final consonants completely. For instance, nouns such as *haricot* 'kidney bean', *buffet* 'sideboard', *bois* 'forest', *goût* 'taste', *tabac* 'tobacco' and *sirop* 'syrup' are pronounced without a final consonant. However, words that occurred frequently in particular grammatical or idiomatic conditions that placed them before a vowel, tended to develop an alternation. Word-internally such conditions existed before the feminine suffix, which was vocalic and thus yielded alternations between masculine and feminine nouns and adjectives, such as found in [pəti] 'small (masc.)' and [pətitə] 'small (fem.)', which today, with the loss of final schwa, yields the alternation [pəti], [pətit].

In French of the 16th and 17th centuries, when final consonant deletion was being implemented, there was a strong tendency, as there is today (Green and Hintze 1988), for forward resyllabification in case a final consonant was followed by a vowel. This process, known as *enchaînement*, makes a final consonant syllable-initial when a vowel follows within the same pause group. As I argued in Bybee (2000a), there is a strong tendency towards a single representation for individual words, the result of which was that many words simply lost their final consonants. However, for grammatical words and grammatical morphemes multiple representations according to the constructions they frequently occur in are possible, so that many such words or morphemes that frequently occurred in constructions that put them in prevocalic position maintained their liaison consonant in those constructions (Berkenfield this volume; Bybee and Scheibman 1999; Jurafsky *et al.* this volume). Examples are shown in (5)—(12), based on Morin and Kaye (1982) and Tranel (1981: 233). The use of the liaison consonant in (5), (6), and (7a and b) are considered obligatory, while in the remaining contexts liaison is variable in spoken French.

(5) Determiners
  a. *vos* [z] *enfants*   'your children'
  b. *les* [z] *autres*   'the others'
  c. *un* [n] *ancien ami*   'an old friend'

(6) Clitic pronouns
  a. *nous* [z] *avons*   'we have'
  b. *ils* [z] *ont*   'they have'

(7) Person/number endings
  a. *allons* [z]-*y*   'let's go'
  b. *chante-t-il*   'does he sing?'
  c. *nous vivons* [z] *à Paris*   'we live in Paris'
  d. *ils chantent* [t] *en choeur*   'they sing in chorus'

(8) Plural /-z/ in noun-adjective constructions
   a. *enfants* [z] *intelligents*   'intelligent children'
   b. *des découvertes* [z] *inquiétantes*   'worrisome discoveries'

(9) A small set of masculine singular adjectives that occur before their nouns
   a. *un petit* [t] *écureuil*   'a little squirrel'
   b. *un gros* [z] *amiral*   'a fat admiral'
   c. *un long* [g] *été*   'a long summer'

(10) The plurals of the same
   a. *deux petites* [z] *histoires*   'two short stories'
   b. *quelques* [z] *années plus tôt*   'a few years earlier'

(11) Prepositions, adverbs, particles
   a. *dans* [z] *un mois*   [dãzɛ̃mwa]   'in a month'
   b. *pendant* [t] *un mois*   [pãdãtɛ̃mwa]   'for a month'

(12) Fixed phrases
   a. *c'est* [t] *à dire*   'that is to say'
   b. *pas* [z] *encore*   'not again'

Despite the variety of morpheme or word types included in this list, it is important to note that there are no purely lexical, or open class items, that exhibit liaison; rather the items range from suffixes, e.g., for plural, to grammatical classes, such as prepositions and small closed classes, i.e., the prenominal adjectives (see Section 5 for further discussion of this small class). Two relevant points can be made about such forms: first, they are all of relatively high frequency, especially in the constructions or phrases in which the liaison consonant appears; and second, they all occur in very specific grammatical constructions. No liaison consonant appear independently of a specific construction. The situation of liaison consonants within specific constructions will be discussed in the next section.

4. Grammatical constructions and liaison

The roles of morphology, syntax, and lexicon have been widely recognized in accounts of French liaison, but the relative contribution of each has been debated in the literature and very little has been said about the role of frequency in establishing and maintaining liaison consonants. Perhaps the most monolithic approach is that of Selkirk (1974) which attempts to derive liaison contexts by reference to the placement of word boundaries (#, ##) according to the principles proposed in Chomsky and Halle (1968), which place single word boundaries around members of lexical categories, but not around members of grammatical categories. These principles define a phonological word as the material between instances of two word boundaries (##). Selkirk proposes that liaison occurs only within the phonological word. Because of the way #'s are placed, the effect of these principles is to say that liaison occurs when grammatical and not lexical morphemes are involved. This analysis works well for most cases, but because it treats all instances of liaison as involving grammatical morphemes, it leaves open the question of how prenominal adjectives will be treated, since they are technically lexical in generative theory. Kaisse (1985) proposes that liaison takes place in a sequence *ab* if *b* is the head of the phrase and c-commands *a* (that is, if *a* is in the phrase of which *b* is the head). The data we will examine in this section and the next shows that the variability of liaison is highly affected by the very specific location of the grammatical element in a construction and that all cases of liaison do not have the same status in terms of their productivity and degree of entrenchment, indicating that a single syntactic principle is not likely to be successful in predicting liaison contexts.

The syntactic principles proposed so far are adequate for the obligatory liaison in examples (5) and (6), which involve determiners with their nouns and clitic pronouns with their verbs, but it is not possible to successfully extend either of these proposals to cases where liaison is considered variable. Indeed, any syntactic proposal referring to the head of a phrase is going to have trouble applying to both noun-adjective combinations (example [8]) and adjective-noun combinations (examples [9] and [10]) (de Jong 1990). In fact, proposals based on traditional assumptions about constituent structure run into difficulties with the fact that liaison occurs 98.7% of the time in a sequence *est* [*t*] *un* + NOUN '3rd Sg. is a NOUN' but about 47% of the time in the sequence *je suis un* + NOUN 'I am a NOUN', which presumably has the same constituent structure; similarly *est* + PAST PARTICIPLE has an extremely high rate of liaison, 98.6%, while *je suis* + PAST PARTICIPLE has only 57% liaison (data from Ågren 1973).

Another approach is to postulate a level of prosodic organization and stipulate that liaison applies within units so organized, i.e., phonological words or phrases (de Jong 1990; Selkirk 1986). Such proposals were tested in the experiments of Post (2000), but her attempts to find a correspondence between the prosodic unit of phonological word, and the occurrence of liaison failed to produce significant results.

Most other authors (Baxter 1975; Green and Hintze 1988; Klausenburger 1984; Morin and Kaye 1982; Tranel 1981) have offered an analysis that refers to both morpho-syntactic and lexical factors. Like other alternations that have become lexicalized or morphologized, what was a unitary phonological change has become associated with particular grammatical contexts and is no longer unitary (cf. Bybee 2001, Chapter 5). The account offered here is based on these previous treatments and will only mention some of the liaison environments, as the main point will be to underscore the role of frequency and phonological material situated in constructions. I will assume that frequency of use played a major role in the establishment of these alternations, and I will argue on the basis of modern data that frequency of use plays a major role in preserving liaison alternations. In particular, I will argue that the 'degree of syntactic cohesion' that is often mentioned in studies of liaison is a direct result of the frequency with which the two items surrounding the liaison consonant occur in sequence.

Evidence in support of the view that liaison is morphologized or lexicalized is the fact, pointed out in various studies, most explicitly in Encrevé (1983), Morin and Kaye (1982) and Post (2000), but also in Ågren (1973) and Green and Hintze (1988), that liaison consonants can occur both before and after a pause, or with and without forward syllabification or *enchaînement*. In other words, while liaison originally depended upon forward resyllabification, it is not now restricted to occurring within a phonological word. On the other hand, *enchaînement*, which is still a viable process in Modern French, occurs only within pause groups and not across them.

The current approach to liaison takes the construction as the basic unit, and since constructions often contain very specific lexical and grammatical material, attributes the liaison consonant to the construction itself. Constructions are repeated sequences of morphemes or words which bear a particular semantic or functional relation to one another when used together in a construction which they do not necessarily have outside that construction. Constructions have different degrees of conventionalization, as they come to be established in a language through repeated use. The mechanisms for the establishment of constructions are (i) automation of chunks of linguistic material due to repetition, and (ii) categorization of the items occurring in particular positions in these larger chunks. Because repeated use is a major factor in the formation of constructions, it will *not* necessarily be the case that constructions have unpredictable meaning—they can simply be oft-used chunks of language. However, owing to the autonomy that accompanies repetition and frequency of use, constructions will often take on non-transparent meanings.

On one end of a continuum involving constructions are fixed phrases, such as *I don't know* and *c'est à dire* 'that is to say', nearer the middle are constructions with some grammatical material and a slot that is more open, e.g., the preposition *dans* with its NP object, and on the most general end, a construction such as [NOUN + PLURAL + ADJECTIVE], with two slots which take open class items. It seems useful to restrict the term 'construction' to sequences that include a more-or-less open slot and to classify phrases without open slots, such as *c'est à dire* as fixed phrases. The open slots in constructions are subject to categorization in terms of semantic features (such as 'motion verb') or grammatical features (such as pronoun). Since constructions arise from frequently-used stretches of speech, it is not necessary for the organization of items in a construction to correspond to traditional notions of constituency, as we will see in examining some liaison contexts. It is important to bear in mind, however, that traditional notions of constituency are also derivable from frequency of co-occurrence, since items that go together in a semantic sense tend to occur together in discourse.

One construction that is much discussed in the liaison literature involves a plural noun followed by an adjective which begins with a vowel. In some cases, a [z] occurs between the noun and adjective, a remnant of the plural marking that has been deleted when a consonant follows. The examples from (7) are repeated here as (13).

(13) a. *enfants [z] intelligents*   'intelligent children'
     b. *des découvertes [z] inquiétantes*   'worrisome discoveries'

Ågren (1973) reports that liaison in such contexts is considered obligatory in certain frequent phrases, some of which are proper nouns: *affaires [z] américaines* 'American affairs', *Champs [z] Elysées, Nations [z] Unies* 'United Nations', *Jeux [z] Olympiques* 'Olympic Games', and so on. Among the optional contexts, liaison only occurs in 26% of cases with a plural noun followed by an adjective. Most authors regard this construction with liaison as somewhat productive, however, owing to the existence of examples such as these offered by Morin and Kaye (1982), in which the [z] liaison occurs for plural but at some remove from its etymological site:

(14) a. *des chefs d'Etat [z] africains*   'African heads of state'
     b. *les chemins de fer [z] anglais*   'the English railways'

Morin and Kaye (1982) argue that the plural liaison does not just occur in lexicalized expressions, but also applies productively in these cases.

The data suggest two constructions for plural noun-adjective expressions. The more general one contains a plural determiner followed by an unmarked noun and adjective.

$$(15) \begin{bmatrix} les \\ ces \\ des \\ \text{etc.} \end{bmatrix} \begin{matrix} \text{NOUN ADJECTIVE} \\ \\ \text{plural} \end{matrix}$$

A second, more restricted construction, applies only to vowel-initial adjectives:

$$(16) \begin{bmatrix} les \\ ces \\ des \\ \text{etc.} \end{bmatrix} \begin{matrix} \text{NOUN -z- [Vowel]-ADJECTIVE} \\ \\ \text{plural} \end{matrix}$$

Besides the second construction (16) being restricted to vowel-initial adjectives, there is another difference between them: the first construction (15) applies to more items, that is, it has a higher type frequency, which make it more productive than the second one. Thus it is not surprising that there is variation in the data resulting from speakers choosing the more general schema even for vowel-initial adjectives in most cases. Still, the more specific schema with the [z] before vowel-initial adjectives is available and is sometimes used. Thus the loss of liaison resembles regularization of irregular verbs: if the specific schema is not easily accessed, then the more general one, which is stronger and easier to access, is used.

In addition to the schemas in (15) and (16) there might also be more specific schemas for adjectives that are frequently used with the [z], such as *anglais*, or *américain*:

(17) $\begin{bmatrix} les \\ ces \quad \text{NOUN} \; \text{-z-} \; anglais \\ des \\ \text{etc.} \end{bmatrix}$ plural

The examples in (14) result from the phrasal nouns *chefs d'Etat* and *chemin de fer* occurring in the NOUN position in the constructions (16) or (17).

Another plural construction that results in cases of 'false liaison' consists of the cardinal numbers plus [z] and a noun. As reported in Tranel (1981: 214–16), liaison is frequently maintained with the cardinal numbers *deux* [døz] 'two' and *trois* [trwaz] 'three' before vowels when in the same construction as the following noun and when plurality is indicated. Thus *les deux* [z] *amis* 'the two friends' has liaison, but *le deux octobre* 'October 2nd' does not. The viability of the [z] as a plural marker in this construction is evidenced in the widely-reported use of cardinal numbers without etymological final [z] in this construction. Tranel (1981: 216) gives the following examples:

(18) a. *quatre enfants*   [katzãfã]   'four children'
     b. *huit épreuves*   [ɥizeprœv]   'eight events'
     c. *neuf oeufs*   [nœfzø]   'nine eggs'
     d. *vingt-cinq années* [vẽtsẽkzane]   'twenty-five years'
     e. *trois mille évêques* [trwamilzevɛk] 'three thousand bishops'

Not only do these examples show the intrusion of a non-etymological [z], but examples (c) through (e) also show that the other final consonant of the number is present. Thus this construction goes beyond the function of creating optimal syllable-structure to a truly morphological use, where the [z] is signaling plurality.

On the basis of examples such as those in (18), Tranel (1981), Morin and Kaye (1982), and Klausenberger (1984) argue for an analysis which inserts the liaison consonant in certain contexts before a vowel, rather than deleting it before a consonant. The solution proposed here is neutral with regard to insertion or deletion. It simply states that a construction exists which contains the [z] after a number and before a vowel-initial noun. This construction could be formulated as in (19):

(19)   [NUMBER -z- [vowel]- NOUN]$_{\text{plural}}$

The construction in (19) is a generalization from the conservative usage, in which *deux, trois, six,* and *dix* were the only numbers that had [z] before vowel-initial nouns. The forms in (18), then, provide positive evidence for the tendency to extract generalized or more schematic constructions from more specific instances of use.

As mentioned above, Ågren (1973), Morin and Kaye (1982), and Green and Hintze (1988) all report that the liaison consonant can appear even if a pause or hesitation syllable occurs between the two words of the construction. Green and Hintze (1988: 159) found an example with the number *quatre* in their data:

(20)   *quatre euh . . . [z] obligations*   'four uh . . . obligations'

Such examples show that it is possible to pause or hesitate in the middle of a construction, just as it is possible to pause in the middle of a word. Since the words of a construction are usually associated with other instances of the same word, their identity as words is known and the point between two words is a possible place to pause. The position of the pause in this and other examples reported in these works suggests that the liaison consonant is more associated with the second word, where it begins the first syllable, than with the first, which was its historical source.

Another illustration of the close association of particular liaison consonants with particular constructions is in the reciprocal construction, discussed in Morin and Kaye (1982). These authors report that liaison is optional after *l'un* 'the one', but only when used in the reciprocal construction; elsewhere liaison is not possible. Thus in (21) liaison with [n] is an option, but in (22) it is not:

(21)   a. *Il les a confundus l'un [n] avec l'autre.*
       'He took them for each other'
       b. *Ils se ressemblent l'un [n] à l'autre.*
       'They look like each other'

(22)   *Ils sont venus, l'un avec sa mère, l'autre avec son père.*
       'They came, one with his mother, the other with his father'

These examples in particular show that grammatical morphemes are highly entrenched in the constructions in which they appear, not just in French, but in all cases. A grammatical morpheme is identified as such because of its appearance in certain well-defined grammatical constructions. The history of grammatical morphemes shows that if they occur in different constructions, they move away from one another in phonological shape, meaning, and distributional properties (Heine and Reh 1984; Hopper 1991; see also Berkenfield, this volume, for a study of the beginnings of such a process with English *that*). In French there are several grammatical morphemes deriving from *un*, which originally was only the numeral 'one': *l'un* 'the one', as in example (20), where liaison is not possible; the reciprocal, as in (19), where liaison is optional; and the indefinite article *un/une*, in which liaison is considered obligatory.

5. Loss of liaison as regularization

Studies of optional liaison, such as Ågren (1973), show a tendency for the loss of liaison in many contexts. As mentioned above, the observation is often made that liaison is maintained in cases of 'tighter syntactic cohesion' (Tranel 1981); however, no one has offered a definition of this syntactic cohesion that is detailed enough to make correct predictions across the numerous constructions involved in liaison. It has been noticed and amply documented in Ågren (1973) that uses with higher frequency maintain a higher level of optional liaison than those that are less frequently used (see also Booij and de Jong 1987). However, no one has yet zeroed in on frequency of use as a causal factor in the establishment, maintenance or loss of liaison.

My proposal is that French consonant liaison, though it takes place between traditional 'words' rather than word-internally, is very similar to morphologically and lexically conditioned alternations that occur word-internally: it was established with an original phonetic motivation and the alternations gradually came to be associated with certain morpho-syntactic and lexical contexts. Like other morpho-lexical alternations it is subject to both extension to new contexts in cases of productivity and leveling or loss of the alternations. The frequency factors affecting these ongoing changes are the same as in the cases of word-internal alternations. High type frequency of a construction spurs productivity. Unproductive alternations are gradually leveled or regularized, with low frequency forms being leveled first and high token frequency resisting the leveling for the longest time.

What makes this case of special interest is the fact that the units in which the alternations occur are larger than traditional words. For arbitrary alternations to become established and to be maintained in such units, these units must constitute units of storage, just as words do. Thus the facts of French liaison and other cases of external sandhi are valuable in that they provide evidence for the nature of storage units beyond the traditional word. The evidence presented so far strongly suggests that frequent fixed phrases are storage and processing units, as are constructions containing grammatical morphemes. Among the latter, more specific and more general constructions compete, leading to the gradual loss of the more specific construction, which in this case is the one with liaison.

I have already mentioned that grammatical morphemes are entrenched in constructions; to describe this situation, I have proposed that grammatical constructions contain these grammatical morphemes as explicit phonological material. Thus the same grammatical morphemes in different constructions are independent of one another. The more frequently used a construction is, the greater likelihood that its form will be maintained, rather than being replaced by some more productive construction (Bybee and Thompson 1987). It is not surprising, then, that certain liaison contexts, in particular those involving articles and their noun (see examples [5]) and those involving clitic pronouns and their verb (examples [6]), are obligatory by all accounts and not tending towards loss of liaison. These constructions are those that are apparently regarded as having the tightest syntactic cohesion, a cohesion that could be attributed to frequency of co-occurrence. No relative frequency counts are available to prove this point, but given the fact that almost all NPs have either a definite or indefinite article and in spoken language subject and object clitic pronouns are used redundantly (Harris 1988: 231–2, 235–6), the high frequency of these construction cannot really be in doubt.

Other reasons exist for regarding [ARTICLE + NOUN] constructions and [CLITIC + VERB] constructions as storage and processing units in Modern French. The maintenance of gender distinctions, which are overtly signaled primarily in the singular article suggest the storage of the article, both singular and plural, with the noun. Studies of spoken French usage demonstrate that the subject and object clitic pronouns are now almost obligatory accompaniments to the verb, behaving perhaps more like prefixes than clitics, again suggesting lexical status (Harris 1988: 232).

The special treatment of articles with *h-aspiré* words also points to lexical representation of articles with nouns. These are words which are vowel-initial but do not take a liaison consonant, even in the obligatory contexts. Thus *des haricots* 'the beans' is pronounced [dɛariko] in standard French. If *h-aspiré* words behaved as though they were consonant initial with respect to liaison from all sources and with respect to elision (vowel deletion at the end of the preceding word), then it would make sense to treat them as though they were consonant-initial. However, Tranel (1981) reports that the exceptional status of these words is maintained most strongly in those contexts in which the syntactic constituency is tighter (p. 300–1, n. 4).

If frequency of co-occurrence is the main factor governing the appearance of the liaison consonant, then we would not expect to find such consonants between any two randomly selected lexical items whose probability of co-occurrence is extremely low. Indeed, we do not. One case that might appear to contradict this claim is the small class of prenominal adjectives that link to a following vowel-initial noun, even in the masculine.

(23) a. *un petit* [t] *écureuil*   'a little squirrel'
    b. *un gros* [z] *amiral*   'a fat admiral'
    c. *un long* [g] *été*   'a long summer'

The important point about the construction represented by these examples is that it is restricted to a small set of adjectives, many of which have a different meaning when used pre-nominally rather than in the more common post-nominal position. They are, in a sense, partially grammaticized and not fully lexical in this construction. Still, the frequency of such adjectives in this construction and their resulting 'syntactic cohesion', must be less than some of the other fully grammatical morphemes exhibiting liaison. It is thus predicted that liaison in this context will be maintained less than in other contexts.

(24) Prenominal adjectives that condition liaison
    bon   'good'
    long   'long'
    nouveau 'new'
    mauvais   'bad'
    grand   'great, big'
    gros   'fat'
    petit   'little'

A real test of the frequency hypothesis is possible with the data reported in Ågren (1973), where different inflectional forms of the same word with different frequencies and the same word in different constructions with different frequencies can be compared for the maintenance of liaison. First consider the forms of the copular verb, *être*. Ågren points out that the presence of liaison is directly related to the token frequency of these forms. He gives the data in Table 1, which shows the number of cases of liaison (L) and non-liaison (NL) and the number of times each item was used in the data he analyzed, listed according to the percentage of cases of liaison.

The correspondence between token frequency and percentage of liaison is quite close, except for two important exceptions, both of which are explained by Ågren. The first is the high percentage of liaison for the not-so-frequent Present Participle, *étant*. Here Ågren points out the high percentage of occurrence of liaison in the construction *étant* + *Past Participle*, which has liaison in seven out of eight cases in his data. Four of these cases are the fixed phrase *étant entendu* 'being understood, given that'.

The other exception is the 1st Singular Present Indicative form *suis*, which has

Table 1. *Number of instances of liaison for the forms of the verb* être

	L	NL	Total	Percentage of liaison
est (3rd Sg. Pres. Ind.)	2,591	77	2,668	97%
sont (3rd Pl. Pres. Ind.)	242	38	280	86%
étant (Pres. Part.)	22	7	29	76%
était (3rd Sg. Impf.)	272	95	367	75%
êtes (2nd Pres. Ind.)	24	10	34	71%
étaient (3rd Pl. Impf.)	36	21	57	63%
sommes (1st Pl. Pres. Ind.)	43	31	74	58%
suis (1st Sg. Pres. Ind.)	65	74	139	47%
serait (3rd Sg. Fut.)	17	24	41	41.4%
soit (3rd Sg. Pres. Subj.)	22	32	54	40.7%
j'étais (1st Sg. Impf.)	6	23	21	21%

fewer instances of liaison than predicted by its token frequency. For this case, Ågren observes that it is common to reduce the sequence *je suis* 'I am' to [ʒsɥi]. In fact, further reduction of this sequence is often noted, even to [ʃɥi]. In Ågren's data this reduced form tends to occur without liaison. In other words, the new contraction of *je suis* does not end in [z], possibly because the reduction of this phrase, which is originally a casual speech phenomenon, is not compatible with liaison, which is more common in more formal styles. This example shows that the reduction of high frequency sequences in casual speech can lead to the establishment of competing constructions. The reduced form can then spread to contexts in which it would not have originally occurred, i.e., before a vowel-initial word.

In addition, there is a general tendency for liaison in verbs to involve the consonant [t] and liaison for noun plural to involve [z]. Thus all verb forms ending in [z] tend to have a lower percentage of liaison than those of comparable frequency involving [t]. This fact suggests the possibility of a more schematic representation that associates liaison [t] with verbs and [z] with noun plurals (Klausenberger 1984).

The wide range of variance for liaison with the forms in Table 1 is especially interesting because these forms are all inflected forms of the same verb, and yet they behave quite differently under liaison conditions.[3] Their usage is regularizing, with the low frequency forms more likely to undergo regularization than the high frequency forms. The mechanism by which this occurs is parallel to the way in which irregular inflected forms such as *weep/wept* regularize. As a low frequency verb, its irregular Past may not be as easy to access as a high frequency verb would be. Thus a new Past can be made for it by using the base form and the regular Past tense construction.

All of the forms of *être* listed in Table 1 occur in two variants, one with and one without a final consonant. The variant without a final consonant is the more commonly occurring. Thus in any given use of these forms there is competition between a construction that is more specific—the one for a word before a vowel-initial word —and the more general construction—the one for the word before a consonant-initial word. The latter construction will apply more often, since consonant-initial words are more common than vowel initial ones (by at least two to one). The more specific construction can be preserved by frequency which increases its lexical strength, but there is always the option of using the more general construction, the one without liaison.

The token frequency of the first element alone will not predict the occurrence of liaison, nor should we expect it to; rather the important variable is how often the two elements that are linked occur together and, perhaps also, the transitional probability between the first and second element. For instance, Ågren counted the frequency of liaison with the auxiliaries *aller* 'to go', *falloir* 'to be necessary', *pouvoir* 'to be able to', *devoir*, 'to have to', and *vouloir* 'to want'. When these are compared to one another, their frequency of occurrence does not correspond neatly with their percentage liaison. Part of this lack of correspondence is due to certain high frequency forms such as *je voudrais* not participating in liaison because (i), final *s* in verb forms shows less liaison and (ii), because as a fixed expression it has become invariable. However, much of the variation among the auxiliaries is due to different rates of occurrence in specific constructions. All of these auxiliaries occur with a following infinitive; the most frequent infinitive to follow them is *être* 'to be' accounting for 226 out of 604 infinitives after an auxiliary. The second most frequently occurring infinitive was *avoir* 'to have', which occurred 71 times. We would thus expect

Table 2. *Ågren's findings for the auxiliaries and following infinitives*

	avoir		être + PP		être + other word		Other infs	
	L	NL	L	NL	L	NL	L	NL
aller	3	3	5	2	2	6	5	16
devoir	9	7	47	3	39	2	19	16
falloir	2	3	1	1	10	4	42	23
pouvoir	18	20	41	4	40	13	60	59
vouloir	3	3	3		2	1	14	53
Total	35	36	97	10	93	26	140	167
% liaison	50%		91%		78%		46%	

the highest rates of liaison to occur with *être*, and indeed this is what is found, as shown in Table 2. In fact, occurrences of *être* can be divided into those that comprise the passive construction and those that are more copular in function. Ågren found a different percentage of liaison in the two cases.[4]

A frequency effect is evident here, in that *être* is the most common infinitive to follow these auxiliaries and the most common site for liaison. These findings are particularly clear with *devoir* and *pouvoir* which occur very frequently with *être*.

The very high percentage of liaison with *devoir* and *pouvoir* with *être* + *Past Participle* suggests very specific constructions for these modals and the passive. The differences between this and the other uses of *être* confirms our statement that grammatical morphemes are very much entrenched in the particular constructions in which they occur. Considerations of function also play a role. When *devoir* and *pouvoir* are used with the passive, their subjects are not the agents of the main verb and, therefore, their subjects cannot be the agents for whom obligation or ability is being predicated. Consider (25) from Ågren 1973: 83:

(25) *Marie-Claire, est-ce que vous pensez que l'homme et la femme doivent* [*t*]
      être placés sur le même plan intellectuel et social?
      'Marie-Claire, do you think that man and woman should be put into the
      same intellectual and social level?'

This example illustrates the 'root obligation' sense, as no specific source for the obligation is expressed. It expresses only a very general sense of obligation. Similarly (26) expresses 'root possibility'—general conditions exist for the possibility of completing the predication (Ågren 1973: 86). Both root obligation and root possibility are more grammaticized functions than the obligation and ability meanings from which they arise (Bybee *et al.* 1994; Nordquist 1999).

(26) *Ça prouve, enfin qu'il y a, qu'il y a des choses extraordinaires qui peuvent*
      [*t*] *être faites encore.*
      'This proves finally that there are, there are extraordinary things that could
      be done still.'

Note that in these cases, the auxiliary will ordinarily be in the third person. Thus the sequences [*doi*[*t*] *être* + *PP*] and [*peu* [*t*] *être* +*PP*] and their plural counterparts are constructions which have particular semantic readings that differ slightly from those of the same modals in active constructions. These functions may reinforce the autonomy of the construction. The viability of the liaison [t] in these constructions is supported by the overgeneralization reported in Morin and Kaye (1982):

(27) *Ça doit bien t-être cuit, maintenant*   'It must be cooked by now'

In this example the modal is fulfilling an epistemic functions, which is a further development from the root obligation reading.

Another interesting difference to observe in Table 2 is the difference between the cases where *être* is the following infinitive and those cases, which are pooled to-gether, in which a variety of lexical infinitives occur. While, in all, there are more of the latter, neither type frequency nor frequency of the construction as a whole are the relevant variables. Since the maintenance of liaison is comparable to the mainte-nance of irregularity in inflected forms, it is the token frequency of the particular sequence that is operable in resisting regularization.

On the other hand, liaison *is* still used with lexical infinitives about half the time in the data analyzed. This means that forms such as 3rd Singular *doit* or *peut* occur in constructions that supply the liaison consonant in case the next word begins with a vowel. That is, there are two constructions for *doit* (besides the ones mentioned above)–(28a) is the more general construction that is used with a greater variety of infinitives, while (28b) is the less general one. The more general schema is gradu-ally taking over and replacing the less general one, except in very specific sequences with high token frequency.

(28) a. [[dwa] INFINITIVE]_{obligation}

     b. [[dwa] -t- [vowel]- INFINITIVE]_{obligation}

6. Transitional probability

A possibility to consider in this case of two-word combinations is that transitional probability might be a better predictor of cohesion and thus liaison than simple string frequency (Bush this volume, Jurafsky *et al.* this volume). Transitional proba-bility is the probability that in any occurrence of one word, a particular second word will follow. It is calculated by dividing the number of occurrences of XY in a text by the number of occurrences of X (Saffran *et al.* 1996). Very often, string fre-quency and transitional probability make the same predictions, but in some cases where string frequency is high, but transitional probability is not so high due to the occurrence of a wide variety of other elements after X.

A chance to distinguish string frequency and transitional probability is afforded by the data in Table 2, which may point to transitional probability as an important factor in cohesion. As shown in Table 3 (based on Table 2), the rate of liaison before *être* is lower after *pouvoir* than after *devoir*, especially when *être* is followed by a non-Past Participle word. This could be related to the fact that *pouvoir* is followed by other infinitives much more often than *devoir* is. The fact that *pouvoir* is used with many other infinitives lowers the transitional probability for *être* after *pouvoir*.

Table 3. *Item following* devoir *and* pouvoir *(Ågren 1973)*

	être + PP		être + other word		Other infinitives		Total
	L	NL	L	NL	L	NL	
devoir	47	3	39	2	28	23	142
pouvoir	41	4	40	13	78	79	254

We can use the figures in this table to calculate the transitional probability for the combinations *devoir* + *être* and *pouvoir* + *être*, as shown in Table 4. Note that the number of tokens of these sequences are approximately the same, but that *pouvoir* is used much more often before other infinitives than *devoir* is.[5]

Table 4. *Comparison of the rate of liaison and transitional probability for* devoir *and* pouvoir

	être + PP		être + other word	
	Percentage of L	TP	Percentage of L	TP
devoir	94%	.35	95%	.29
pouvoir	91%	.18	75%	.21

The lower transitional probability for *être* + *PP* after *pouvoir* does not have much of an effect on this construction, possibly because of its grammatical status as passive. But for *pouvoir* with *être* followed by some other word, the low transitional probability relative to *devoir* corresponds to a lowered rate of liaison, though the differences in transitional probability are small and may not be significant given the number of instances available.

What would be the causal mechanism that is reflected in the relation between liaison and transitional probability? Two possibilities present themselves. First, the frequent co-occurrence of X+Y leads to a strong sequential connection between these units, but if X also occurs before other items frequently (thus having a lowered transitional probability before Y), the connection between X and Y often has to be suppressed, which could weaken the connection. A second possibility refers more to type frequency than transitional probability. Since an item such as *peut* occurs before many different infinitives, the construction used with consonant-initial infinitives will have a higher type frequency and thus be more likely to cause regularization than the construction with *doit*, which would have a lower type frequency.

Further evidence for transitional probability must be sought in cases that would differentiate between these mechanisms.

Other evidence for the workings of transitional probability in French liaison is the fact that the coordinating conjunction *et* never conditions liaison. This is a very high frequency morpheme, and undoubtedly occurs in some high frequency combinations. However, the fact that virtually any word of the language can follow *et* gives any particular word a rather low transitional probability, possibly explaining why there is no liaison with this item.

7. Syntactic cohesion as frequency of co-occurrence

The data examined here concerning French liaison supports the view that what has been called 'syntactic cohesion' is frequency of co-occurrence, the factor which determines the strength of the association between the first element and the second one. These connections are stored in memory and reinforced by frequent use. The evidence for their memory storage is that the principles that we have established for morpho-lexical alternations are operable at what has been taken to be this higher level of organization as well. In particular, the higher the frequency of the phrase or construction, the more likely it is to preserve liaison; the lower its frequency, the more likely it is to lose liaison by the application of a more general construction.

Collocations of words that are used frequently have strong memory representations. Just as morphologically complex words that are high frequency are more autonomous from their own paradigms and paradigms of other words, so high frequency phrases grow more autonomous. That is, the connections between the words and morphemes of such phrases and other instances of the same words or morphemes in other constructions become weaker. The potential loss of association is heightened by phonetic and semantic or functional change. The extreme outcome of this process is seen in grammaticization, where parts of grammaticized constructions are no longer associated with their lexical sources, e.g., the difficulty English-speaking children have when they begin to read of identifying the form they know as *gonna* with the three morphemes, *go*, *ing* and *to*. In most liaison contexts this loss of internal structure is not so extreme, but the 'syntactic cohesion' referred to operates by this same mechanisms: frequent sequences are processed together and this unity breaks down their connections with related items.

8. Taking the phonology seriously

It is common practice to try to predict French liaison, English *don't* reduction, and other cases of words that have variants by reference to syntactic constituency and relations. However, all such attempts leave some cases unaccounted for and many such analyses still require special mention of certain lexical items or grammatical morphemes. Many researchers have thus concluded that the relation between syntactic structure and phonological rule application is indirect (Vogel and Kenesei 1990 among others). Interestingly, a position that is not often taken is that the relation between syntax and phonology is quite direct, but that we are not operating with the correct syntax. In other words, it is not usually argued that phonological evidence suggests different syntactic structures, except at the most surface level. In contrast, in determining morphological structure, phonological evidence is often taken into account. Deciding whether or not a grammatical morpheme is an affix or not often involves some consultation of the phonological fusion between the proposed affix and stem. What would be the consequences of letting the phonological tail wag the syntactic dog?

In many cases, of course, nothing would change. In French, as liaison indicates, determiners go with nouns and clitic pronouns go with verbs. The only innovation I have proposed is that [DETERMINER + NOUN] and [CLITIC PRONOUN + VERB] sequences are stored in memory. Similarly, [ADJECTIVE + NOUN] and [NOUN + PLURAL + ADJECTIVE] sequences are constituents syntactically. However, English sequences of [PRONOUN + AUXILIARY], such as *I'll* and *I'm*, are not usually considered constituents. In fact, the highest-level syntactic break within a clause—that between subject NP and VP occurs within this sequence. Yet it is undeniable that auxiliaries contract and fuse with subject pronouns, not with the following verb, even though the auxiliary and verb are in the same constituent. The reason proposed (Bybee and Scheibman 1999; see also Krug 1998) is that specific instances of [PRONOUN + AUXILIARY] are of extremely high frequency, much higher than any particular sequences of [AUXILIARY + VERB]. The phonological and usage facts, then suggest an analysis of English much like that of Quileute, where the forms of subject pronouns are determined by modal functions (Andrade 1933: 203ff).

Another interesting case of French liaison concerns the copular verb in 3rd Singular, *est*. In Ågren's data, 47% of the uses of *est* occur in the construction [*est* + *un* + noun] 'is a noun'. In this sequence, liaison occurs 98.7% of the time, much more than with any other uses of *est*. This strongly suggests a construction in which *est* [*t*] *un* is a constituent that precedes a noun. A comparable claim about English would be to say that *is a* is a constituent because of the frequency of use of these two items together. Of course, to say that *est un* or *is a* is a constituent is not to say that *un* + *noun* and *a* + *noun* are not also constituents. There is no reason why two constructions cannot overlap, giving ambiguous constituent analyses in cases such as these.

If we take usage as the determinant of constituency and syntactic hierarchy such that items frequently used together are constituents, then phonology is a valid indicator of constituency, since the same property—frequent co-use—conditions phonological alternations.

9. Conclusion

In a model in which memory storage includes not just individual words, but also phrases and constructions, lexicon and grammar are not strictly separated, but are integrated and subject to the same organizational principles (Bybee 1998; Langacker 1987). Any repeated stretch of speech can be stored in memory and placed into categories with identical and similar units. Categorization occurs at multiple levels. Exemplars of the same word or phrase are mapped onto a single representation. Tokens of the same construction are similarly mapped onto a representation and the items in the variable positions of the construction contribute to the formation of categories based on their semantic properties. Thus in the English construction X is going to Y, the occurring tokens contribute to the formation of the categories X and Y. In the French construction [NUMBER + z + [vowel]-NOUN], the occurring tokens create the categories NUMBER and NOUN.

While this paper is superficially about phonology-syntax interactions, the main goal has been to argue that constructions have many of the same properties as morphologically-complex words. Elements (both phonemes and morphemes) within constructions frequently co-occur and can undergo phonological reduction and fusion just as material inside of words can. Then alternations can be preserved inside of constructions which are of high frequency. Alternations are also subject to leveling if some other more general construction produces a new, regularized way of saying the same thing. Alternations in lower frequency constructions and phrases are then leveled first, with the more entrenched alternations remaining. Thus constructions that encompass more than one word are more entrenched (resistant to change) if they have high token frequency, and more productive if they have high type frequency. These properties all imply that constructions are storage and processing units just as words and fixed phrases are.

Notes

1. I gratefully acknowledge the help of Jennifer Hayes in researching this topic, and Dawn Nordquist and Caroline Smith for comments and suggestions. The material in this chapter also appears as Chapter 7 of Bybee 2001.
2. Kaisse (1985) and Hayes (1990) also make this distinction.
3. Ågren found the same pattern among the inflected forms of the auxiliary *avoir* 'to have' and the semi-auxiliaries (as he calls them) *aller* 'to go', *falloir* 'to be necessary', *pouvoir* 'to be able to', *devoir*, 'to have to', and *vouloir* 'to want'.

358   JOAN BYBEE

4. In Ågren's chart *être* + *Past Participle* is distinguished from *être* + *autre mot* 'other word'. I am assuming that most of the cases of the latter are not also passives, though they could be in case the 'other word' is followed by the Past Participle.
5. The reason for this seems to be that *falloir*, which is very similar in meaning to *devoir* is commonly used with other infinitives instead of the third person forms of *devoir*, see Table 2.

References

Ågren, J. 1973. *Etude sur quelques liaisons facultatives dans le français de conversation radiophonique: frequence et facteurs*. Uppsala: Acta Universitatis Upsaliensis.

Andrade, M. J. 1933. *Quileute*. New York: Columbia University Press.

Booij, G. and de Jong, D. 1987. The domain of liaison: theories and data. *Linguistics* 25.1005–25.

Bybee, J. 1998. The emergent lexicon. *CLS 34: The Panels*, 421–35.

Bybee, J. 2000a. Lexicalization of sound change and alternating environments. In Michael Broe and Janet Pierrehumbert (eds.) *Papers in Laboratory Phonology V: Acquisition and the Lexicon*. Cambridge: Cambridge University Press, 250–68.

Bybee, J. 2000b. Phonology of the lexicon. In Michael Barlow and Suzanne Kemmer (eds.) *Usage-based models of language*. Standord: CSLI, 65–85.

Bybee, J. 2001. *Phonology and language use*. Cambridge: Cambridge University Press.

Bybee, J. and Scheibman, J. 1999. The effect of usage on degree of constituency: the reduction of *don't* in American English. *Linguistics* 37.575–96.

Bybee, Joan and Sandra A. Thompson. 2000. Three frequency effects in Syntax. *Berkely Linguistic Society* 23: 378–88.

Chomsky, N. and Halle, M. 1968. *The sound pattern of English*. New York: Harper and Row.

Delattre, P. 1966. *Studies in French and comparative phonetics*. The Hague: Mouton.

Encrevé, P. 1988. *La liaison avec et sans enchaînement: Phonologie tridimensionnelle et usage du français*. Paris: Seuil.

Green, J. N. and Hintze, M. 1988. A reconsideration of liaison and enchainement. *Occasional Papers*. University of Essex: Department of Languages and Linguistics, 136–68.

Harris, M. 1988. French. In Martin Harris and Nigel Vincent (eds.) *The Romance Languages*. Oxford: Oxford University Press, 209–45.

Hayes, B. 1990. Precompiled phrasal phonology. In Inkelas and Zec (eds.) 85–108.

Inkelas, S. and Zec, D. 1990. *The phonology-syntax connection*. Chicago: University of Chicago Press.

Inkelas, S. and Zec, D. (eds.). 1995. Syntax-phonology interface. In J. Goldsmith (ed.) *The Handbook of Phonological Theory*. Cambridge, MA: Blackwell, 535–49.

Kaisse, E. 1985. *Connected speech: the interaction of syntax and phonology*. San Diego: Academic Press.

Klausenberger, J. 1984. *French liaison and linguistic theory*. Stuttgart: Franz Steiner Verlag Wiesbaden GMBH.

Krug, M. 1998. String frequency: a cognitive motivating factor in coalescence, language processing and linguistic change. *Journal of English Linguistics* 26.286–320.

Langacker, R. 1987. *Foundations of Cognitive Grammar, Vol. 1. Theoretical Prerequisites.* Stanford: Stanford University Press.

Morin, Y. and Kaye, J.D. 1982. The syntactic bases for French liaison. *Journal of Linguistics* 18.291–330.

Nespor, M. and Vogel, I. 1986. *Prosodic Phonology.* Dordrecht: Foris.

Nordquist, D. 1999. A synchronic study of *have to* and *got to* with diachronic implications. Paper presented at the Second Annual High Desert Linguistic Society Student Conference, University of New Mexico.

Post, B. 2000. *Tonal and phrasal structures in French intonation.* The Hague: Thesus.

Saffran, J. R, Newport, E. L., and Aslin, R. N. 1996. Word segmentation: the role of distributional cues. *Journal of memory and language* 35.606–21.

Selkirk, L. 1974. French liaison and the X̄-notation. *Linguistic Inquiry* 5.573–90.

Tranel, B. 1981. *Concreteness in generative phonology. Evidence from French.* Berkeley and Los Angeles: University of California Press.

Vogel, I. and Kenesei, I. 1990. Syntax and semantics in phonology. In Inkelas and Zec (eds.), 339–63.

The role of frequency in the specialization of the English anterior*

K. AARON SMITH

University of New Mexico

1. Introduction

In Modern English, the Perfect is expressed with the auxiliary verb *have* and the Perfect Passive Participle (PP) of the main verb.[1] The Perfect occurs in the present (Present Perfect), as in the example in (1a), or in the past (Past Perfect) as in the example in (1b), the former having the auxiliary in the present tense and the latter with the auxiliary in the past.[2]

(1) The Modern English Perfect
   a. one of the kids was asking me about a baseball Game and I said, *have* you ever *seen* a baseball game. (MacWhinney 1995, adult data)
   b. we uh *had played* the bowl Liberty Bowl that year it was around Christmas (MacWhinney 1995, adult data)

In earlier stages of the English language, the anterior constructions in (1a) and (1b) competed with another construction, consisting of the auxiliary *be* + PP. The sentences in (2a) and (2b) show present tense and past tense examples of this construction from Old English.

(2) Old English Perfect[3]
   a. Nu *is* se dæg *cumen* (Beowulf, line 2644)
      now is the day come
      'now the day has come'
   b. ða *wæs* winter *scacen* (Beowulf, line 1136)
      when was winter departed
      'when winter had departed'

According to grammars of Old English and works on the history of English tense/aspect, these two Old English constructions were distributed by syntactic or semantic verb type. Some of these accounts indicate that the *be* + PP construction was used with mutative verbs, i.e., verbs involving a change in state, and the *have* + PP construction with non-mutative verbs, i.e., verbs not involving a change of state (Traugott 1972). Others propose that the *be* + PP construction was used with intransitive verbs of motion, while *have* + PP was used with non-motion transitive verbs (Davis 1913; Mitchell and Robinson 1992). As with these studies, and nearly all other treatments of the two auxiliary constructions, they attempt to capture the distribution of *be* and *have* in terms of argument structure or semantics.

In contrast, this study assumes that such accounts of the *be* and *have* auxiliaries are not adequate for a description of their use in older periods of English because the data show "irregularities" in the use of *be* + PP among these verb classes from even our earliest texts. Furthermore, since the distribution of these two constructions changes over the history of English such that more and more intransitive verbs of motion came to be used with the *have* auxiliary, it seems appropriate to consider the OE distribution of these auxiliaries as a step in that replacement. Therefore, I take a different approach in this paper and present data on the history of the *be* + PP and *have* + PP constructions, investigating the nature of the process by which the *have* construction came to take over the older uses of the *be* construction. This process, where competing forms or constructions are lost to a competing member of a class, has come to be known as specialization (Bréal 1892 [1991], Hopper 1991). Specialization applies universally in the process of grammaticization as forms within a given construction move from a less grammatical to a more grammatical status. In this paper, I offer data from the history of English showing that the specialization of competing syntactic constructions in language proceeds, at least in some respects, by the same forces that have been shown to drive morphophonemic leveling within paradigms: frequency of occurrence and the effects of frequency on the mental representation of linguistic items. In this paper, I will also show two other effects of frequency that can occur in both morphophonemic leveling and syntactic specialization: split and entrenchment. More broadly, the effects of frequency on the *be/have* constructions will also provide evidence that these constructions are stored directly in memory and that specific verbs are stored within those constructions in their mental representation.

2. Type/token frequency

For this study, two kinds of frequency will be distinguished: type and token frequency. Token frequency, also called text frequency, refers to the total number of occurrences of a particular form or construction in running text. For example, *have* + PP occurs a total of 39 times in the entire poem *Beowulf*. We say then that the *have* + PP construction has a token frequency of 39 in that poem.

Type frequency refers to the dictionary frequency of a particular pattern (Bybee 1995). For example, in addition to counting the total number of times the *have* or *be*-construction occurs in a text, we could also count all of the different verbs used in the *have* + PP construction versus the *be* + PP construction. Doing so, we find that in the OE poem *Beowulf*, there is a total of 11 different verbs that occur in the *be*-construction and 57 different verbs in the *have*-construction. Thus, we would say that the *have*-construction has the greater type frequency of the two in *Beowulf*. Given these definitions of token and type frequency, we can now turn to the role of frequency in morphosyntactic leveling.

3. The role of frequency in morphosyntactic leveling

The term *analogy*, and its role in linguistic change, was first proposed in the 19th century. The Neogrammarians, working in the latter part of that century, spoke of "analogical leveling" which they used to capture a system-internal pressure on the forms in language to develop in ways parallel to related forms (Pedersen 1959).[4] Since the days of the Neogrammarians, so-called analogical change has figured prominently in historical linguistics and one need only peruse a sampling of historical linguistics textbooks to glean the popular linguistic view of this process:

> Leveling consists in the complete or partial elimination of morphophonemic alternations with paradigms. The motivation for the development has been plausibly captured by the slogan one meaning—one form. Alternations which do not seem to signal (important) differences in meaning therefore tend to be eliminated. (Hock 1993: 168)

In the quote from Hock, then, we find the rather common view of analogical change, characterizing it as a cognitive or functional force that drives speakers of a language to regularize forms across paradigmatic alternations.

Traditionally, analogy has been treated as if it were the mechanism behind morphophonemic leveling and the role of frequency and its effects have rarely been discussed as factors involved in that process. For example, no mention of the role of frequency appears in Lehmann (1992) and, even in historical linguistics textbooks where it is mentioned, it is quickly tied into more traditional mechanisms that are believed to drive language change, such as child language acquisition, as seen below in the quote from Bynon (1977):

> Perhaps [the] stability [of irregular morphological forms] and [their] resistance to change is due to their very high frequency of occurrence in discourse and to the fact

that their forms are therefore acquired by the child at an early stage before the respective grammatical rules have been acquired.   (Bynon 1977: 43)

While frequency does affect storage and retrieval of items (to be elaborated on
below), it is not necessary to view this process solely in terms of acquisition and,
therefore, rely too heavily on child acquisition as a cause for linguistic change. Such
an assumption may, in fact, be misleading. Indeed, adults store and retrieve linguistic items also and Bybee and Slobin (1982), for example, show evidence that language innovation noted in older school-age children and even adults is a good predictor of linguistic change. Furthermore, they found that no special relation exists
between small childrens' innovation and morphophonemic change.

Some early linguists did, however, recognize the importance of frequency in the
process that had come to be known as analogy:

> . . . it is natural that by the aid of proportions, groups should often be created which
> were before common in language.   (Paul 1970 [1890]: 102)

Paul seems to be saying that the frequent patterns (i.e., those 'common in language')
will be the ones selected for extension. Throughout his work, Paul makes other
statements suggestive of frequency's role in the "analogical" formation of linguistic
items. Actually in this quote, Paul seems to be tapping into the importance of type
frequency in determining the productivity of a spreading linguistic form. As I will
discuss later, type frequency is very important in determining the productivity of the
have + PP construction as it spread to verbs which had formally been used with the
be auxiliary.

However, in successive waves of linguistic schools, few data were accumulated
in order to study how frequency might work as a factor underlying "analogy".
Only since the mid-70's, and really only rigorously in the last decade or so, has
frequency been seriously studied as a determining factor for the spread of and/or
the resistance to a spreading linguistic form. Hooper (1976) studied the role of
frequency in the formal leveling of English strong verbs to weak verb forms. She
found that less frequent strong verbs were the first to succumb to regularization
and, conversely, that the most frequent strong verbs were longest in resisting such
change. Hooper later expanded these findings in Bybee (1985, 1988, 1995) where
she offers the Network model of language storage. In the Network model, the
mental representation of linguistic items is involved in a complex web-like series
of connections with other linguistic forms based on factors such as phonetic similarity and semantic affinity. These representations are also affected directly by
frequency. Items of greater frequency become entrenched and are able to build
up strong independent representations. The more entrenched a form is, the less
likely it is to be replaced by some frequent pattern. On the other hand, items of
lesser frequency have weaker representations in memory and therefore are more

likely to be replaced by more productive morphophonemic patterns. The mechanism by which this works is to be found in the storage of linguistic items and the retrieval of those items from storage. For example, if a speaker of English is attempting to retrieve the simple past strong form of a high frequency verb, like *spoke*, then that simple past form will be readily available. In other words, the high frequency of that form will have created a strong independent representation in the mind and its frequent use will ensure that it is in a more or less primed state, ready for use. Conversely, the simple past form of a less frequent verb, like *dreamt*, will not be located as easily in the process of retrieval and the speaker may extend a more frequent pattern of past tense formation, like the weak *-ed* suffix, yielding *dreamed*. In this way then, the spread of some morphophonemic pattern will affect lower frequency items first, and higher frequency items last.

Hooper (1976) also found that "the more frequent pattern" could be captured by counting the type frequency of a given construction (see also Bybee 1995). In her study, she found that the token frequency of weak and strong verbs is roughly the same, but the type frequency of the weak verb construction is much higher than any of the strong verb constructions. That is, a greater number of different verbs occur with the weak *-ed* suffix. Since several of the strong verb construction types are of a very high frequency, the overall token frequency of all of the strong verb constructions together approximates the token frequency of all weak verbs. Thus, since the token frequencies of the two constructions equal one another, type frequency must be the determinant of productivity in this case.

The productivity of a frequent type is to be found in storage and retrieval of linguistic items as well. Not only is the strength of a word directly affected in memory by frequency, but a given morphophonological pattern (and as I argue here, a syntactic pattern) can also have varying strengths in memory depending on its frequency. Thus, among constructions used to build the simple past of verbs in English, it is the weak simple past *-ed* suffix that is most frequent in the language. It is for this reason that when the simple past form of a low-frequency verb, like *dreamt*, cannot be retrieved, the frequent type pattern *-ed* will replace it, again yielding *dreamed*. In this way, the actual process of what we call analogy can be viewed mechanistically, affected directly by the language-user's experience with the morphophonemic forms in question.

As I have already mentioned, I will argue that frequency plays a role in the specialization of the *have* auxiliary construction similar to the role it plays in morphophonemic leveling. This study tests two hypotheses. First, it is predicted that even at the earliest stages, the *have* construction had a higher type frequency, which made it the more productive of the two constructions, thus becoming the member of the competing group to specialize over the other. Secondly, it is hypothesized that as the *have* construction spread, it first took over verbs of the *be* construction with the lowest token frequency and that verbs used in the *be* construction of a relatively high frequency were the longest in resisting the spreading *have* construction.

4. Data collection and methodology

In selecting texts for the analysis of the *be* and *have* auxiliary constructions, it was determined that the periods represented by the texts should be close enough in time to capture the relevant developments of the phenomenon in question. For this reason, texts were selected at two hundred-year intervals, starting with the Old English period and extending into the 19th Century. The list in (3) shows the periods of English investigated and the texts used to represent each period. The total word count for each text is also given in (3).

(3) Texts for counting the frequency of English Anteriors

Period and Text	Date	Word count
Old English—*Beowulf/Anglo-Saxon Chronicles*	*c*.700–1000[5]	33,900
Early Middle English—*Brutus' Layamon*	*c*.1200	112,766
Later Middle English—*Sir Gawain and the Greene Knight*	1385	21,679
Early Modern English—*Arte Poesie*	1569	96,180
19th Century—*Wuthering Heights*	1847	118,262

It deserves to be mentioned that little attempt was made to control for the dialectal differences of the authors of the texts in (3). In part, this was a practical decision. Given the methodology used here, it was more efficient to use electronic texts and, therefore, the study had to be limited to those texts available from the World Wide Web or from some other electronic media. This restriction notwithstanding, it would be difficult to find continuous textual documentation of a single dialect in English to carry out the type of longitudinal study proposed here.

Nevertheless, using differing dialects for the study of the phenomenon discussed here should yield accurate results because, as far as I am aware, no dialect of English has ever differed significantly in the use of the *have* or *be* auxiliary in these constructions. In order to test for this, I collected additional data for the Later Middle English Period from Geoffrey Chaucer's poem, *Crysede and Troilus*. Chaucer represents London speech from around 1400 while *Sir Gawain*, the text used for this study, represents a Midland dialect of Middle English of about the same time. Comparing the type frequency of the *be* construction to the *have* construction from the two poems, we find that the ratio of the *be* construction types compared to the *have* construction types is 1: 6.263 in *Crysede and Troilus* as compared to 1:7 in *Sir*

Gawain. Thus, no appreciable difference exists between the dialects concerning the two constructions under study here. It appears safe to extend this assumption to the other periods of English in (3) as well.

Data for this study was collected using the Monoconc concordancing program. With Monoconc, it is possible to search for a form within an electronic text, along with the various collocations in which that form appears. In this way, it was possible to call up all of the occurrences of *have* or *be* in a given text, and then determine which of the occurrences were being used in an auxiliary + PP construction. Both present and past forms of the auxiliary were included in this study. From these instances, I tallied a token and type frequency count of each construction from each work listed in (3). For the *be* + PP construction it was also necessary to separate out instances of that construction used to show anterior (or resultative, see Section 4.0) from those used to signal a passive meaning, cf. He *was told* of the horrible accident over the phone. *Be* + PP was determined to be passive if there was direct or implied agency in the context expressed by an argument other than the grammatical subject.

Finally, since the size of the texts used to collect data, shown in (3), vary in length, it is not possible, or even desirable, to compare the total occurrences of the *have* or *be* construction in one period to the total occurrence of those constructions in another period. Beowulf, for example, has a word count of 33,900 while Wuthering Heights has a word count of 118,262. To compare absolute frequencies between these two periods would really only capture the fact that the one source is larger than the other. Instead, I am concerned here with the proportional distribution of the two constructions relative to one another and not with their absolute frequencies within the specific text. Thus, the data is presented by showing the percentage of *have* + PP compared to the percentage of *be* + PP out of the total number of both combined. In this way, we can capture the proportion of each construction used to signal anterior for each period and observe how that relationship changed over the history of English.

5. Old English *be/have* + PP: Resultative or anterior? An excursus into emergence

Before turning to a presentation of the data, it will be useful to look briefly into the diachronic semantic development of these constructions and the importance of those developments for this study. Several studies have attempted to account for whether the *be/have* + PP constructions represented resultative or anterior meanings in Old English. (See Endnote 1 for a definition of anterior aspect. Resultative is defined here as an action beginning in the past and producing a state that persists into the present [Bybee *et al.* 1994: 318]). In this section, I will review some of the literature on this topic, which argues for a chiefly resultative meaning in Old English and for the development of anterior meaning between the Old and Middle English periods. I will then offer evidence suggesting that the two competing constructions did not develop from a resultative into an anterior meaning at the same rate. Instead, the *have* + PP was first to express anterior senses while *be* + PP remained a resultative category longer.

Carey (1994, 1996) presents evidence that in Old English the *have* + PP construction was chiefly a resultative. Her results are based on frequency data in which she counts the types of verbs occurring in the *have* + PP construction as well as the types of temporal adverbs that co-occur with that construction. Her findings indicate that from the Old English to the Middle English period, there is a steady increase in the use of adverbs compatible with an anterior meaning and, perhaps more interestingly, a sharp decrease in the use of present state adverbs like *still*. For example, in the Alfredian period of Old English (850AD), 38.8% of the tokens of the *have* + PP construction occur with present state adverbials, but never once with anterior adverbials. Example (4) shows the *have* + PP used with the present state adverbial, *nu* 'now', in Old English, taken from Carey (1994).

(4) Ða cwæð se Wisdom: Nu ic hæbbe ongiten þine ormodness
     Then Wisdom says: Now I have understood your unhappiness . . . (*Boethius* 5.13.15)

By the ME period, 14.9% of the tokens of the *have* + PP construction in her database occur with anterior adverbials but not once with a present state adverbial. Example (5) illustrates *have* + PP used with the anterior adverbial, *3ore* 'before' in the Middle English period, taken from Carey (1994).

(5) Me reoweþ sore gultes þat y ha wroþt 3ore.
     I repent myself grievously of the bad deeds that I have done before.

Carey also finds an increase in the use of stative verbs with the *have* + PP construction. In the Old English period, there is not a single token where a stative verb occurs with *have* + PP whereas, by the ME period, 10.6% of the *have* + PP constructions occur with a stative verb. This provides good evidence for the interpretation of the Old English *have* + PP as a resultative since resultative forms, which focus on the resultant state of some activity, universally do not co-occur with stative verbs due to the incongruency of stative and resultant state meaning (Bybee and Dahl 1989; Bybee *et al.* 1994; Dahl 1985). However, by Middle English, the *have* + PP construction had come to be used in anterior senses.

Slobin (1994) finds parallels in the historical development of the English anterior and the acquisition of the anterior by English speaking children. Investigating the fact that the *have* + PP construction can have resultative and anterior uses in Modern English, he finds evidence that children acquire the resultative senses of the English Present Perfect first and only later the strict anterior senses. Slobin points out that although phylogeny recapitulates ontogeny in this case, the mechanisms for the parallel development are very different. His point is that the development of the anterior in English out of a resultative is not due to children wrongly acquiring a misanalyzed resultative as an anterior, but instead, children acquire the resultative first and the anterior last due to cognitive limitations of the developing human mind. On the other hand, the development of an anterior from a resultative in the history of a given language is due to mechanisms that operate in the process of grammaticization, notably inference (Slobin 1994 and Traugott 1989) and semantic generalization (Bybee 1985, Bybee et al. 1994, Dahl 1985). Slobin (1994) brings up a very interesting and important issue when characterizing the semantic coordinates of a form over time in a single language, that is the effects of grammaticization.

A few works on the universal developments in tense and aspect have shown that resultatives commonly develop into anteriors during the grammaticization of a given form (Bybee 1985, Bybee et al. 1994, Bybee and Dahl 1989 and Dahl 1985). As Bybee et al. (1994: 67 ff.) point out, the most common scenario of a resultative becoming an anterior involves a stative verb in combination with some non-finite form of the verb, such as a past participle. Such a development has occurred in Romance and Germanic languages and, according to the data given in Bybee et al. (1994), this development likely occurred in some other languages, such as Kui (Dravidian) and Maithili (Indo-Iranian). Given, then, the universal validity of the resultative to anterior development of the stative verb + non-finite main verb construction, it is quite reasonable to assume that the have + PP and be + PP constructions were resultatives at some earlier stage of English and that the two constructions later developed into anteriors.

However, it is probably rarely the case that competing constructions ever really grammaticize at exactly the same rate and it seems that the have + PP construction was slightly ahead of the be + PP construction in expressing anterior aspect. One piece of evidence for this is the split between the meanings of the verb go in the have and be constructions. In every period of English, including our earliest English source, go is found used in both constructions. In Modern English, however, there is a difference in the meaning between have + gone and be + gone in that the former expresses anteriority and the latter resultative meaning. Examples of the be + gone (resultative) and have + gone (anterior) constructions, taken from Emily Brontë's Wuthering Heights are given in (6a–b).

(6) a. It was a fever, and it is gone; (Wuthering Heights, p. 64)
   b. I have always gone to his little parlour since that night . . . (Wuthering Heights, p. 254)

If *have* + PP became an anterior earlier than *be* + PP, then that would account for the two meanings of the two constructions with *gone*. *Have* + *gone* would develop normally into an anterior meaning while *be* + *gone*, because of its high frequency, would become entrenched with the older resultative meaning. The use of *go* in both constructions in the subsequent periods of English would essentially entrench this split, building up strong mental representations of both instances of *gone*. Thus, when a speaker wants to express either resultative or anterior for *go*, they have both constructions readily available.

Another piece of evidence that suggests that *have* + PP became an anterior before *be* + PP is the fact that the token proportion of *be* to *have* in the earliest period of English (See Table 2 of Section 6) is not in keeping with the trends seen in the subsequent periods of English. In Old English, the token proportion of the *be* + PP construction for resultative is lower than in the following Early Middle English period. This is not what we would expect if the *be* + PP and *have* + PP were undergoing parallel grammaticization developments, with *have* + PP gradually replacing *be* + PP. Carey (1994, 1996), mentioned above, shows that it was precisely during this period that the first instances of *have* + PP as an anterior begin to show up. So, if some tokens of the *have* + PP occurrences in Old English express both anterior and resultative meanings while the *be* + PP tokens are only expressing resultative, that would account for the fact that the token proportion between the two constructions in the Old English period is not in keeping with the subsequent periods of the language. Once *be* + PP comes to signal anterior meaning after the Old English Period, the specialization would proceed in a gradual and unidirectional fashion, which is what we find in the data.

For now, we can simply note that the *be* + PP and *have* + PP constructions did develop from resultatives into anteriors and keep in mind that the rate of grammaticization for the two constructions may have been slightly different. For this reason, in order to capture the dynamic quality of these two entities over the history of English, I will refer to the semantics of the *be* + PP and the *have* + PP constructions as resultative → anterior.

6. Data presentation

In this section, I will present the specific data from the periods of English given in (3) to show that the specialization of the *have* construction over the *be* construction proceeded in a gradual manner where it first affected lower frequency verbs that were formally used in the *be* construction and that verbs of a high frequency used in the *be* construction were the longest in resisting the spreading *have* auxiliary. The first set of data concerns the type frequency of each construction for expressing resultative → anterior meaning. This was achieved by counting the number of distinct verbs used with *be* or *have*. Thus, Table 1 shows the proportional distribution of the *be*-construction versus *have*-construction out of the total number of types of the resultative → anterior category. The number in parentheses shows the total number of types for each construction in the text used to collect data for that period.

Table 1. *Proportion of the types of be-constructions and have-constructions for the resultative → anterior category*

Period of English	Number of anterior types	Proportion of be-construction types	Proportion of have-construction types
Old English	68	16% (11)	84% (57)
Early Middle English	104	11% (12)	89% (92)
Later Middle English	79	11% (9)	89% (70)
Early Modern English	125	8% (10)	92% (115)
19th Century	319	3% (8)	97% (311)

Likewise, Table 2 shows the proportional distribution of the *be*-construction versus the *have* construction for the total tokens of the resultative → anterior construction. The number in parentheses shows the total number of tokens for each construction from the text used to collect data for each period.

Table 2. *Proportion of the tokens of the be-construction and the have-construction for the resultative → anterior category*

Period of English	Number of anterior tokens	Proportion of be-construction tokens	Proportion of have-construction tokens
Old English[6]	103	21% (18)	79% (85)
Early Middle English	283	24% (69)	76% (214)
Later Middle English	108	11% (12)	89% (96)
Early Modern English	332	4% (13)	96% (319)
19th Century	877	4% (38)	96% (839)

7. Discussion of the data

In this section, I argue that the data in Tables 1 and 2 provide evidence that frequency affected the storage and retrieval of verbs used in the *be* + PP or *have* + PP constructions such that as *have* replaced *be*, it first came to be used with low fre-

Table 3. *List of verbs used in the be + PP construction for resultative → anterior construction*

Verb	Meaning	Frequency
alumpen	'happen'	1
gang (gegongan)	'go'	7
scacen (sceacen)	'pass, come about'	4
scofen	'rise'	1
scynded	'hasten'	1

quency verbs and last with high frequency verbs. I also argue that it was the high type frequency of the *have* construction which fueled its productivity and led to the selection of *have* as the member of the competing set to specialize over *be*.

As I discussed in the introduction of this paper, traditional treatments of these two constructions have attempted to capture their distribution in terms of argument structure or semantics of the main verb. The following quote from Mitchell and Robinson (1992: 111) is typical of the description of the *be* + PP construction in Old English: "The verb *to be* is also found with the past participle forming the perfect and pluperfect of intransitive verbs . . ." Similar formulations are found also in Davis (1913) and Traugott (1972).

The data from Tables 1 and 2 show that the *be* construction was really never all that frequent in English and, in *Beowulf*, one of the sources of data for the Old English period, we find that a rather small set of verbs is used with the *be*-construction. The list of verbs used in the *be* construction in *Beowulf* and their frequency in that work are given in Table 3.

Indeed, the verbs in Table 3 do fit the syntactic/semantic characterization given in Old English grammars. However, in *Beowulf*, we also find verbs fitting the description "intransitive, motion, or mutative" used with the *have* auxiliary as well; those verbs are given in Table 4.

Table 4. *Mutative/Intransitive verbs used with have in Beowulf and their frequencies*

Verb	Meaning	Frequency
gemealt	'melted down'	1
geworden	'become'	1
gewaden	'advanced'	1
gebiden	'lived'	1
gedrogen	'passed through'	1
gegan	'go'	1

From Table 4, we find that the frequency of the intransitive/mutative verbs used with the *have* auxiliary is quite low, with none having more than one occurrence in the entire poem.[7] Now, if we assume at some earlier period of English (possibly Proto-Germanic) that the syntactic/semantic characterization given in Old English grammars had some productive reality (that is, that intransitive verbs were used with *be* and that transitive verbs were used with *have*), then the facts regarding intransitive/mutative verbs from *Beowulf* indicate that by the Old English period, strict verb class characterizations are no longer tenable and that the specialization of the *have* auxiliary had already begun affecting relatively lower frequency intransitive verbs.

The above data from *Beowulf* already suggest a replacement of the *be* construction from an earlier time when the *have* and *be* auxiliaries may have had a stricter syntactic/semantic distribution. We find, however, that the same pattern of frequency is observed in each of the periods of English listed in (3). Over the history of English we go from a high of 16% of the resultative → anterior construction types used with *be* to 4% by 19th Century English. In other words, over time in English, more and more types came to be used with the *have* auxiliary. To gain a better idea of how frequency interacts with the specialization process, consider the types of verbs used with the *be* auxiliary in 19th Century English.

Table 5 lists all of the verbs used with the *be* auxiliary in *Wuthering Heights* along with their frequency. Indeed, frequency seems to be an important factor in determining which verbs continued to be used with the *be* auxiliary because the *be* auxiliary persists among such high frequency verbs in *Wuthering Heights* as *come* and *go*. In fact, *go* is the verb with the highest frequency in that work, after the copulative verb *be*, and *come* is only superseded in frequency by *be*, *go*, and the verb *see*. We do find some verbs of a rather low frequency also used in the *be* construction, such as *adjourn* and *vanish*, but this is due not to the productivity of that construction in 19th Century English but rather to the fact that such verbs in

Table 5. *Verbs in Wuthering Heights used with the be auxiliary*

Verb	Frequency
adjourn	1
come	11
depart	1
go	17
grow	1
pass	2
settle	1
vanish	1

Wuthering Heights are used in contexts where there basic meaning is *come* or *go*, as in *I am adjourned to my study* (*Wuthering Heights*, p. 30).[8] In effect, then, the high frequency verbs, *come* and *go*, have become entrenched in the *be* construction by 19th Century English. We have already had occasion to mention the relationship between high frequency and entrenchment of morphophonological forms and the entrenchment of verbs in the *be* construction is the syntactic parallel to this phenomenon, suggesting that high frequency verbs are directly stored in that construction in memory. I will discuss in more detail the mechanism by which entrenchment of verbs in the *be* + PP construction comes about a little later in this paper.

Another way that the data suggest a pattern of replacement, similar to the type of morphophonemic leveling discussed in Hooper (1976) and Bybee (1995) and discussed in Section 3, is the relationship of type to token percentages between the periods of English from Tables 1 and 2. For example, we find that in Early Modern English 8% of the resultative → anterior types were expressed with the *be* auxiliary and 92% of the types with the *have* auxiliary. This compares to 3% and 97% respectively for the 19th Century English period. Now, if we compare the percentages of type proportions from these two periods of English to the corresponding token proportions of the *be* and *have* constructions, we find that Early Modern English had a 4% to 96% token proportion ratio for the two constructions and that 19th Century English had a 4% to 96% token proportion ratio as well.

In other words, while the *be* to *have* type ratio shows an increase of the *have* construction types from Early Modern English to 19th Century English, the *have* to *be* token ratio remains constant. This means that, from Table 1, the 3% of the *be* auxiliary types in 19th Century English must be more frequent than the 8% of *be* auxiliary types from the immediately preceding period because the token frequency ratios, from Table 2, remain constant between these two adjacent periods. Again, this is reminiscent of the pattern of morphophomemic leveling discussed in Section 3 because we find that high frequency items, the 3% of the *be* types in 19th Century English, resist replacement by the *have* construction.

The data also support the claim that it is high type frequency that led to the productivity of the *have* auxiliary. First, *have* + PP always had a higher type frequency, even in the texts for our earliest period. In addition, we notice from Table 2 that the token proportions for the *be* and *have* constructions do not change from Early Modern English to 19th Century English where we have a 4% to 96% proportion ratio respectively for both periods. The type frequency of these constructions as seen in Table 1, however, does change from a proportion in Early Modern English of 8% to 92% to 3% to 97% in 19th Century English. Therefore, for these periods, it is the type frequency relation that provides the continuing productivity of the *have* + PP; otherwise, we might expect a stall-out of the specialization of the *have* construction with certain high frequency intransitives like *come*. In other words, the strong type frequency of the *have* construction throughout the history of the language served as the on-going impetus for the productivity of that construction with the result that it has essentially replaced all instances of *be* + PP for anterior expression in Present-Day English. Furthermore, such effects of frequency on these constructions suggests that they are stored in memory such that frequent tokens (cf. *go*) and frequent types (cf. the *have* auxiliary type) are stronger in mental representation, resisting replacement in the former case and taking over older *be* auxiliary uses in the latter.

We can note one final interesting empirical point to come out of the data. Specifically, there is a steady increase in the use of the *be* + PP and *have* + PP constructions throughout the history of English, with a total of 877 occurrences in the 118,262 word text *Wuthering Heights* compared to 283 occurrences in the Early Middle English text of comparable size (112,766 words). This increase in overall frequency is due to the on-going grammaticization of the constructions. As a construction grammaticizes, it becomes more general semantically, in this case as it moves from resultative to anterior. Since an anterior is applicable in a greater number of contexts than is a resultative, the increase in the absolute frequency of the constructions is expected.

8. Mechanisms of change in the specialization of the *have* + PP construction

Earlier in this paper, I discussed the mechanism by which frequency affects the leveling of some morphophonemic set and in the previous section I showed data that suggest a similarity in the way that morphophonemic leveling and specialization proceed. I claim that the similarities between morphophonemic leveling and specialization are not coincidental, but instead result from the fact that frequency plays a crucial role in both types of change; in the same way that specific verbs are stored with particular morphophonemic patterns, specific verbs are also stored within particular syntactic constructions. For example, in the same way that a person does not call up strong simple pasts for infrequent verbs, a person wishing to express anteriority does not call up an instance of an infrequent verb used in the *be* construction. The speaker "draws a blank" so to speak. Therefore, that speaker will express anteriority for that infrequent verb using the most frequent anterior-building pattern in the language. Again, the most frequent pattern will be that which occurs across the most types, in this case the *have* + PP construction.

However, whereas in the leveling of a morphophonemic pattern we have the spread of a morphophonological alternate to other alternates in a paradigm (or morphological constructions), in the specialization of the *have* and *be* auxiliaries, we are dealing with two syntactic constructions. However, these two syntactic constructions are not totally independent of one another in that they share a number of associations, both semantic (resultative → anterior) and formal (aux. + PP). A further association between the two constructions arises from their pre-English distribution across transitive/non-mutative versus intransitive/mutative verb types.[9] These associations allow us to think of the *be* and *have* constructions as constituting a sort of "syntactic paradigm" (Rydén 1991), where the constructions are formal alternates in the expression of some semantic category (i.e., resultative → anterior). In this way, the process of leveling of a morphophonemic set and the specialization of competing syntactic structures is not really different and the data from this study may actually point to how similar some syntactic and morphological processes can be.

9. Beyond English

The pattern of specialization, exemplified in this paper by the English anterior, is not limited to this one case. It is in fact a universal pattern. In this section, I provide data showing the universal robustness of specialization in the process of grammaticization along the path involving the shift from resultative → anterior meaning. These cross-linguistic data will then give the specialization of the resultative → anterior in English a universal significance.

To achieve this, I was able to use the Gramcats database (Bybee *et al.* 1994: 27 and 303), a stratified probability sample of 76 languages with extensive information on grammatical morphology (mostly verbal), consistently coded according to phonological shape and semantic content, as well as some other grammatical properties. Gramcats is constructed so as to be first, an accurate reflection of the world's languages and second, a sample relatively free from genetic bias; thus, with the information from Gramcats, it is possible to get both semantic and formal information about verbal morphology in the world's languages in order to investigate hypotheses about synchronic and diachronic properties of a set (or sets) of grammatical morphemes.

Specifically as it relates to this paper, the data from Gramcats can provide data about the process of specialization. Given the phenomenon of specialization, we would expect less grammaticized categories on a path of development to have greater competition than more grammaticized categories on that path, just as the competition between the *have* and *be* auxiliaries was greater when they signaled a younger resultative meaning in earlier periods of English. Here, I show specialization on one path of grammaticization, one which involves the resultative → anterior development. I refer to this path, taken from Bybee *et al.* (1994), as the "anterior" path, given in Figure 1.

Table 6 shows the trends of specialization, by showing the total number of grams

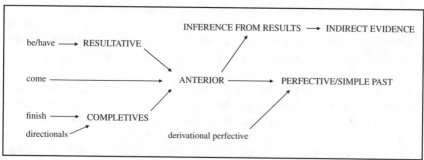

Figure 1. *Anterior path of grammaticization (the categories to the left are younger than those to the right on the path)*

out of the Gramcats sample that compete at that meaning label in the same language with another gram of the same meaning. The final column of Table 6 gives the percentage of grams that compete with another gram in the same language for each of the meaning categories. Note that the meaning categories are arranged in the table in descending order from less grammaticized to more grammaticized, where the difference between "young anteriors" and "old anteriors" in the table is that young anteriors are grams with anterior as their only meaning, and old anteriors are anterior grams with additional uses indicative of a more advanced semantic development (Bybee *et al.* 1994: 105).

The data from Table 6 show clearly the trend for specialization on the anterior path since more grammaticized categories (those at the bottom of the table) have less competition among forms than less grammaticized categories (those at the top of the table). It is interesting to note that in Table 6, the earliest semantic age, completive, has less competition among forms than the next semantic age, which

Table 6. *Specialization by grams for the anterior path (Smith 1998)*

Anterior path

Cluster area on path	No. of grams in sample	No. of grams that compete with another gram of the same meaning in the same language	Ratio
Completive	36	14	38%
Young anterior	57	30	52%
Resultative	22	10	44%
Old anterior	30	9	30%
Perfective	38	14	37%
Simple past	25	5	19%

appears counter to what we would expect. We can attribute this to the fact that completive grams are very young and are often still very lexical or even derivational in nature. They may simply not have been reported as grammatical by the writers of the reference grammars used to code data for Gramcats and therefore not included in the database.

Now, if we can extrapolate the facts about frequency from the development of the English anteriors in this study to the universal tendencies of specialization shown in Table 6, then we can begin to understand one of the important factors that drives the specialization process. Specifically, we can predict that in the specialization of competing forms along the "anterior path" of grammaticization, and likely along other grammaticization paths as well, the construction with the highest type frequency will be the one to specialize over other members of the competing set. Furthermore, we can also predict that high frequency tokens of the less frequent competing types will be the last to succumb to the specialization process.

This last point accounts for why we find relic constructions of non-productive morphological and syntactic patterns of a high token frequency. For example, while the strong past form *spoke* is, in effect, a relic morphological form of a once productive pattern for showing past tense, *be gone* is a relic syntactic pattern of a once productive means of building resultative. In other words, individual instances of a construction can be preserved through frequency in the same way that high frequency morphological forms can persist in a language long after its productivity has ceased to operate, again an indication that specific verbs are stored in certain constructions in memory.[10]

10. Conclusion

In this paper, I have attempted to show that the extension of a syntactic construction to replace competing constructions with the same or closely related meanings proceeds in a way similar to the extension of a morphophonological form over other forms in the same or closely related paradigms. Thus, processes at work in the formation of morphological patterns are not so different from those that shape syntactic patterns. To be sure, many studies have shown that morphology is, in many instances, a diachronic reflex of a more grammaticized syntax (Bybee 1985; Bybee *et al.* 1994; Givón 1971), and so it is not so surprising to find such similarities between the two components.

The analogous developments in morphosyntactic leveling and syntactic specialization is due to the same underlying forces, the frequency of linguistic items and the effect of those frequencies on mental storage and retrieval. The broader theoretical significance of this study is that the effect of frequency on syntactic behavior suggests that entire syntactic constructions are stored in memory (Bybee this volume; Bybee and Thompson 2000). The effect of type frequency gives rise to dynamic patterns of syntactic ordering and token frequency directly affects levels of syntactic representation with specific verbs.

Notes

* I am grateful to Joan Bybee and Catie Berkenfield for helpful comments on this paper. I would especially like to thank Dawn Nordquist not only for reading the several drafts of this study as it progressed, but also for hours of stimulating discussion on the ideas and data in this paper.

1. In this paper, I will follow the convention of using capital letters to refer to language specific grammatical categories and lower case to refer to categories in a universal sense. Also note that while the English Perfect is commonly used to encode anterior aspect (a situation occurring before reference time and relevant to reference time [Bybee *et al.* 1994: 318]), scholars debate whether it is, in fact, an aspectual category, a tense category or a combination of tense and aspect (Comrie 1976: 52).

2. In English, anterior aspect can be combined with progressive forms in the present and past tenses as in, *He has been living in Seattle for five years*. These forms, while certainly interesting for a study of the development of the English tense/aspect system, fall beyond the scope of this paper.

3. There is some debate in the literature as to whether the Old English *have* + PP and *be* + PP formed a resultative or anterior category. That issue is discussed in Section 4.

4. The Neogrammarians were most interested in analogy as a means of explaining why certain sound changes did not follow regular sound laws. Considering that the Neogrammarians did not allow for exception to sound change, it was inevitable that analogy would, for some linguists, operate as a sort of linguistic *deus ex machina* which could be invoked whenever developments were found that would have forced the linguist to admit exception in a sound change. This paper will not deal specifically with the interaction between frequency and sound change. However, for recent treatments of the role of frequency in sound change and "analogy", see Hooper (1976), Bybee (1995), and Philips (1984).

5. Because of the difficulty in dating Old English works, I have chosen to treat Old English as a single period and did not to attempt break the period into later and earlier sub-periods. For an example of the debate surrounding the dating of *Beowulf*, one of the texts used in this study, see Klaeber (1950).

6. For a discussion of why we find a lower *be* token frequency for the Old English Period than in the subsequent period of English, see Section 5.

7. *Gegan* 'go' is of course the exception here as it is used once with the *have* auxiliary in *Beowulf*. The effects of the use of *go* in both construction was discussed in Section 5. The fact that such a high frequency intransitive/mutative verb could be used in the *have* construction in Old English underscores the rather advanced stage in the specialization of *have* by the Old English period.

8. The use of the lower frequency verbs in the *be*-construction is most likely a conscious decision of the author of *Wuthering Heights*, Emily Brontë, who was linguistically aware, and she would have made certain decisions about the use of the *have* versus *be* auxiliary based on semantic criteria that were not in the popular use of the language at that time. This is a danger of using literary texts for the discovery of historical data. At times, the linguistic awareness of the author will interfere with the phenomenon under study. We can also note that all of the verbs used with the *be* auxiliary in *Wuthering Heights* are used with the *have* auxiliary. I take these facts to be indicative of the advanced stage of the specialization of the *have* auxiliary for the resultative → anterior construction.

9. In fact, it seems likely that as *have* + PP grammaticized, it affected the grammaticization of *be* + PP due to these associations. In other words, although *have* + PP may have become a resultative first, its development may have influenced the grammaticization of the *be* + PP construction since the two constructions were related via their earlier meaning and their distribution over certain verb types.

10. See also Bybee and Thompson (2000) for a similar analysis of the subjunctive in French.

References

Bréal, M. 1991 [1882]. *The Beginings of Semantics; Essays, Lectures and Reviews*. G. Wolf (trans and ed). Stanford: Stanford University Press.

Bybee, J. L. 1985. *Morphology: A study of the Relation between Meaning and Form*. Philadelphia: Benjamins.

Bybee, J. L. 1988. "Morphology as lexical organization". In *Theoretical Morphology*, M. Hammond and M. Noonan (eds.), 119–41. San Diego: Academic Press,

Bybee, J. and Slobin, D. I. 1982. "Why Small Children Cannot Change Language on their Own: Suggestions from the English Past Tense". In *Papers from the 5th International Conference on Historical Linguistics*, A. Ahlqvist (ed.), 29–37. Amsterdam: John Benjamins.

Bybee J. L. and Dahl, Ö. 1989. "The creation of tense and aspect systems". *Studies in Language* 13: 51–103.

Bybee, J., Perkins, R. and Pagliuca, W. 1994. *The Evolution of Grammar: Tense, Aspect and Modality in the Languages of the World*. Chicago: University of Chicago Press.

Bybee, J. and Thompson, S. 2000. "Three frequency effects in syntax". In *Berkeley Linguistics Society* 23: 378–88.

Bybee, J. 1995. "Regular morphology and the lexicon". *Language and Cognitive Processes* 10(5): 425–55.

Bynon, T. 1977. *Historical Linguistics*. Cambridge: Cambridge University Press.

Carey, K. 1994. "The grammaticalization of the Perfect in Old English: an account based on pragmatics and metaphor". In *Perspectives on Grammaticalization*, W. Pagliuca (ed.), 103–18. Amsterdams: John Benjamins.

Carey, K. 1996. "Subjectification and the development of the English Perfect". In *Subjectivity and Subjectivisation*, D. Stein and S. Wright (eds.). Cambridge: Cambridge University Press.

Comrie, B. 1976. *Aspect*. Cambridge: Cambridge University Press.
Comrie, B. 1985. *Tense*. Cambridge: Cambridge University Press.
Dahl, Ö. 1985. *Tense and Aspect Systems*. Oxford: Blackwell
Davis, N.1913. *Sweet's Anglo-Saxon Primer*. Oxford: Clarendon Press.
Givon, T. 1971. "Historical syntax and synchronic morphology: an archeologist's field trip". *Chicago Linguistic Society* 7: 394–415.
Hock, H. H. 1993. *Principles of Historical Linguistics*. Berlin: De Gruyter.
Hooper, J. B. 1976. "Word frequency in lexical diffusion and the source of morphophonological change". In *Current Progress in Historical Linguistics* W. Christie (ed.), 96–105. Amsterdam: North Holland.
Hopper, P. 1991. "On some properties of grammaticization". In *Approaches to Grammaticalization. 2 volumes*, E. Traugott and B. Heine (eds.),. Amsterdam: Benjamins.
Klaeber, F. 1950. *Beowulf and the Fight and Finnsburg*. Lexington, MA: D.C. Heath and Company.
Lehmann, W. P. 1992. *Historical Linguistics*. New York: Routledge.
MacWhinney, B. 1995. *The CHILDES Project: Tools for Analyzing Talk*. Hillsdale, NJ: Lawrence Erlbaum.
Mitchell, B. and F. C. Robinson. 1992. *A Guide to Old English*. Oxford: Blackwell.
Paul, H. 1970 [1890]. *Principles of the History of Language*. H.A. Strong (trans). College Park, MD: McGrath Publishing Co.
Pedersen, H. 1959. *The Discovery of Language: Linguistic Science in the Nineteenth Century*. Bloomington, IN: Indiana University Press.
Phillips, B. S. 1984. "Word frequency and the actuation of sound change". *Language* 60: 320–42.
Rydén, M. 1991. "The *Be/Have* variation with instranstives in its crucial phases". In *Historical English Syntax*, D. Kastovsky (ed.). (Topics in English Linguistics Series). Berlin: Mouton de Gruyter.
Slobin, D. I. 1994. "Talking perfectly: discourse origins of the Present Perfect". In *Perspectives on Grammaticalization*, W. Pagliuca (ed.), 119–34. Amsterdam: John Benjamins.
Smith, K. A. 1998. "Regrammaticization". Unpublished manuscript. Universtity of New Mexico.
Tottie, G. 1991. "Lexical diffusion in syntactic change: frequency as determinant of linguistic conservatism in the development of negation in English". In *Historical English Syntax*, D. Kastovsky (ed.). (Topics in English Linguistics Series). Berlin: Mouton de Gruyter.
Traugott, E.C. 1972. *A History of English Syntax*. New York: Holt Rinehart and Winston.
Traugott, E.C. 1989. "On the rise of epistemic meanings in English: an example of subjectification in semantic change". *Language* 65: 31–55.

Electronic literary texts for the periods of English

Anglo-Saxon Chronicle, Manuscript A. Anonymous. Electronic version prepared by T. Jebson. 1995. http://aj@wg.icl.co.uk.

Beowulf. Anonymous. Electronic text prepared by T. Jebsen. 1993. http://www.georgetown. edu/labyrinth/library/oe/beo-ms.html.

Layamon's Brutus. Anonymous. Original publication 1200. Electronic text prepared by E. Gaynor. 1994. http://etext.virginia.edu/mideng.browse.html, LayBruO

Sir Gawain and the Green Knight. Anonymous. Electronic version prepared by J.A. Law. 1993. http://etext.virginia.edu/mideng.browse.html, AnoGawa.

The Arte of English Poesie. E. Spenser. Original publication 1569. Electronic version prepared by G. Puttenham. http://triggs@bellcore.com.

Troilus and Criseyde. G. Chaucer. Original Publication 1400. Electronic version prepared by J.D. Burnley. 1993. http://etext.virginia.edu/mideng.browse.html.

Wuthering Heights. E. Brontë. Original Publication 1848. Electronic version prepared by D. Gants, 1992. http://etext@virginia.edu.

Hypercorrect pronoun case in English?
Cognitive processes that account for pronoun usage*

JOYCE TANG BOYLAND

Alverno College and University of Wisconsin, Milwaukee

1. Introduction

The patterns of usage associated with the pronominal case system in English are often discussed as if they are simply instances of hypercorrection. For example, listeners and readers frequently encounter utterances like "the possible misunderstanding between you and I" and "Thanks to all whom helped me" (COBUILD 1999), which clearly display prestige forms like *I* and *whom*, but in non-standard syntactic contexts. To look no further, however, sets one in danger of missing both significant linguistic regularities and evidence for the cognitive processes responsible for them.

This paper argues, on the basis of two different cases of presumed hypercorrection in the use of English case forms, that examining the frequency-based cognitive processes at work illuminates some open questions in the literature. First, there is still some question as to whether only "certain kinds of socially mobile groups" display hypercorrect usage, and if not, who else does (Giles and Williams 1992). Second, there also remains the question of what the factors are that predict when hypercorrect usage is most likely to occur.

The first half of the paper concerns compound subjects and objects that incorporate a first person pronoun, a construction hereafter referred to as *X and I*. The section consists of two sub-parts: a survey of speakers' attitudes towards *X and I* and a corpus study of *X and I*. Together they demonstrate that the usual sociolinguistically motivated hypercorrection does occur but cannot explain all the regularities observed. These studies do however suggest that frequency can explain the remaining regularities.

The second half of the paper concerns *whom* and is an examination of the specific syntactic contexts in which *whom* is used hypercorrectly. A corpus study reveals a strong contextual influence on case selection from various units of analysis within the sentence. The patterns of influence are consistent with a frequency-based explanation. Results in the *who* vs. *whom* section elaborate and extend previous work by describing new pathways along which innovations spread.

The hypothesis that emerges in the end is that a significant factor determining when a prestige form will spread to new, non-standard contexts is its frequency in its original context. The spread to new contexts is manifested along a number of dimensions. First, prestige speakers, who otherwise would not have used a form in a particular non-standard context, begin to use the form in that context under the influence of other speakers' linguistic patterns. Second, when hypercorrection does occur, it is the most frequently occurring variant that will preferentially be over-generalized. Third, in complex sentences, a form must play multiple functional roles at different levels of analysis, only one of which is presumed to be relevant to the choice of a syntactic form. But hypercorrect usage often occurs when levels presumed to be irrelevant in fact intrude. In such cases, it appears that the prescribed form is outweighed by frequently occurring patterns at other competing levels of analysis.

2. Hypercorrection of personal pronouns in *X and I*

Because of the prevalence of hypercorrection involving forms like *whom* and *you and I*, pronoun case in English is a natural domain in which to investigate the claims of hypercorrection and the limits of those claims. It is agreed, prescriptively speaking, that *X and I* is grammatical as a subject but not as an object (Quirk *et al.* 1985: 338). Descriptively speaking, the appearance of *X and I* as object is recognized as grammatical for some speakers. The process through which this has occurred is usually thought to be some combination of explicit correction and subsequent hypercorrection (Hock and Joseph 1996). As Quirk *et al.* (1985) put it, "prescriptive bias in favour of subjective forms appears to account for their hypercorrect use in coordinate NPs in 'object territory'," where by object territory they refer to the position immediately following the main verb. Let us consider some issues that arise out of this explanation.

Bennett (1994) writes, "The example of hypercorrection given by Hartmann and Stork (1972) . . . is the well-known one of *between you and I* for *between you and me*." When linguists say that "between you and I" is a classic or well-known case of hypercorrection, what exactly are they saying?

Labov (1966) characterizes the natural impetus for hypercorrection as coming from the linguistically insecure lower middle class (LMC) as they attempt to emulate upper middle class (UMC) speakers of the prestige dialect. Vernacular speakers of the LMC latch onto a linguistic form that is used by prestige speakers (e.g., *X and I*), but they use it in contexts where prestige speakers would not (e.g., in object position). Rapid spread of the change is accomplished by LMC mothers and especially schoolteachers carefully and insecurely setting hypercorrect examples for their charges (Labov 1966: 101). Given the overgeneralized pattern as a model, the young speakers who are being taught, whatever their social class, grow up with the intuition that the prestige form (in this case, *X and I*) is the correct form in all contexts (in this case, either subject or object). This model, then, comprises three groups: prestige speakers, the original hypercorrectors, and, at the end, native speakers of a new vernacular who were taught by the original hypercorrectors. Key features of this model include linguistic insecurity and overly general metalinguistic beliefs in the original hypercorrectors. For speakers of the "new vernacular," it is important to note that hypercorrect distribution of prestige forms is grammatical for them. The insecurity of the original LMC hypercorrecting generation is not implicated in this generation, although these speakers may retain the metalinguistic beliefs of their teachers.

Hock and Joseph (1996) make a related but slightly different point in their textbook account of *X and I*. Onto a background of hypercorrection, they add the factor of explicit correction. In accord with the common wisdom, and perhaps personal experience, Hock and Joseph remark that young speakers who uttered sentences like "Me and Charlie went to the movies" were reprimanded and were made to substitute "Charlie and I" for "Me and Charlie." (For discussion of the origins of "me and Charlie," see Rispoli 1994.) These young speakers, indoctrinated thus, overgeneralize this correction and believe that "me and Charlie" is always prescriptively incorrect and "Charlie and I" is always correct. Note that this explanation does not specify whether this generation takes the correction to heart and considers these forms intuitively grammatical (in which case, incidentally, competence would be showing vulnerability to negative evidence), or whether the correction only creates insecure speakers whose beliefs about prescriptive correctness are at odds with their native competence.

The sources described above actually give rise to two explanations of hypercorrect *X and I*. In one, speakers who were corrected by their elders would grow up to become native speakers of the new vernacular for whom "me and Charlie" would be ungrammatical under any circumstance. In an alternative view, these speakers would grow up to become insecure speakers who may retain their native intuition that says "me and Charlie" is grammatical but will also hypercorrect, thus inducing the *next* generation to grow up as native speakers of the new vernacular for whom "me and Charlie" is ungrammatical under any circumstance. Regardless of which generation is the first whose intuitions shift, however, both these scenarios involve three basic categories of speakers: the original LMC hypercorrectors, the unaffected UMC prestige speakers, and the younger generation who natively acquired the new vernacular variety. The question remains of whether these categories account for all hypercorrect usage.

3. *X and I* survey study

Despite the unquestionable usefulness of the existing theories, they are, like any explanation, incomplete. Some contemporary writers on hypercorrection have pointed to new possibilities unexplored by the standard explanation. Labov's model does not, for example, address the possibility that prestige speakers may be affected by or may participate in hypercorrection, thus constituting a fourth category of prestige speakers who hypercorrect. Giles' Communicative Accommodation Theory (CAT) (Giles *et al.* 1987) can account for prestige speakers joining the bandwagon of "hypercorrection", in performance even if not in competence. CAT extends the model of hypercorrection in that it encompasses the mere use of prestige forms in hypercorrect context for pragmatic reasons, regardless of insecurity or meta-linguistic belief. (To maximize clarity, the phrase "hypercorrect usage" will be used when it is important to include hypercorrect performance regardless of socio-linguistic or metalinguistic considerations.) Thus Giles and Williams (1992) ask, specifically, "Do we all hypercorrect under certain circumstances, or is it the pre-rogative of certain kinds of socially mobile groups?" Giles would say that social psychological forces could result in hypercorrect usage by speakers who would normally be classified as prestige speakers. In this paper I aim to give evidence for cognitive forces that produce the same effect.

To address these issues, a first step is to find out what kinds of speakers partici-pate in each of the phases of hypercorrection and what their attitudes are.

3.1 Procedure

A pencil and paper survey was done of 24 college educators and 24 childcare work-ers, a sample chosen to maximize the number of prestige speakers and vernacular speakers, respectively. 22 of the college educators and 12 of the childcare workers completed their surveys according to instructions. Due to the low rate of response by childcare workers, results from that population will be mentioned but not empha-sized in this article.

The first question in the survey asked respondents to fill in the blanks to complete a sentence with a compound object. In the remainder of the survey, the respondents were each given four sentences to rate. The four sentences covered the four possibilities generated by having *X and I* and *X and me*, each in turn filling the subject and the object position. The sentences were printed in random order. The respondents were asked to rate the sentences along two dimensions: grammaticality ("Does it sound natural to you?", with the two possible choices being "Sure, sounds okay" and "Doesn't sound natural"); and prescriptive acceptability ("Would your English teachers approve?", with the possible answers being "She'd say it's fine," "She'd say it's incorrect," and "I have no idea"). The respondents were also asked to choose between "I could see myself saying that" (a conservative measure of grammaticality for the speaker on nonprestige forms), and "I'd never say that" (a conservative measure of ungrammaticality for the speaker on prestige forms).

3.2 Results

Three of the 12 childcare workers who completed the survey match the profile of a LMC hypercorrector. That is, they showed linguistic insecurity about prescriptively correct pronoun usage, judging "Joel has already met my brother and me" as sounding natural but incorrect. One of these respondents even marked every sentence that sounded natural to her as being incorrect according to English teachers and every sentence acceptable to English teachers as something that sounded unnatural. These insecure speakers, consistent with the accepted model of hypercorrection, also marked object *X and I* as being prescriptively correct, judging "Joel has already met my brother and I" to be acceptable to English teachers. Only one of the 22 college educators fit this description. Table 1 represents the choices of these speakers. These data illustrate the defining characteristics of a LMC hypercorrector, namely insecurity and willingness to hypercorrect.

The survey data show further that, among the 22 college educators, 8 fit the description of a prestige speaker. That is, they judged that *X and I* as subject and *X and me* as object were both grammatical in their dialect and to the best of their knowledge prescriptively correct. On every measure, these 8 college educators chose sentences like "Joel and I have already met" and "Joel has already met my brother and me." Table 2 (p. 388) depicts the pattern of choices that define these speakers.

Table 1. *Intuitions of hypercorrectors*

	X and I	*X and me*
As subject	(varies)	(varies)
As object	? natural (varies)	+ natural
	+ correct	− correct
N = 4 (= 3 /12 LMC + 1 /22 UMC)		

Table 2. *Intuitions of prestige speakers*

	X and I	X and me
As subject	+ natural	– natural
	+ correct	– correct
As object	– natural	+ natural
	– correct	+ correct

N = 8 /22 UMC

Of the remaining 12 who did not fit the profile of a prestige speaker, 4 fit in to the standard model of hypercorrection in a different way; these 4 showed the signs of being native speakers of the new hypercorrected vernacular, choosing *X and I* as grammatical for their dialect in both object and subject position, with no sign of insecurity. That is, they chose sentences like "Joel has already met my brother and I" as sounding more natural than "Joel has already met my brother and me." Incidentally, these native speakers of the new vernacular came in both the naive and the sophisticated variety. The sophisticated speaker accepts *X and I* in object position as grammatical for his or her own dialect, but realizes (probably through explicit teaching) that it is not prescriptively correct in the standard dialect. The naive speaker accepts object *X and I* as both grammatical and prescriptively correct. Table 3 represents the choices of these speakers.

Table 3. *New vernacular speakers*

	X and I	X and me
As subject	+ natural	– natural
	+ correct	– correct
As object	+ natural	– natural
	+ correct	– correct: naive
		(or + correct: sophisticated)

N = 4 /22 UMC

So, survey respondents confirmed the existence of the three types of speakers in the classic theory of hypercorrection: LMC hypercorrectors and UMC prestige speakers, and also native speakers of the new pattern of *X and I* in object position. The remaining 8 respondents, however, did not fit any of the three profiles available in the standard model of hypercorrection. Unlike speakers of the prestige dialect, they tolerate *X and I* in object position, judging "Joel met my brother and I" as sounding natural. Unlike the LMC hypercorrectors they showed no insecurity about sentences like "Joel met my brother and me". And unlike the speakers of the "new" vernacular these "other" speakers ordinarily use (or at least, claim to use) *X and I* as subject and *X and me* as object, while being satisfied with the prescriptive acceptability of these standard choices (see Table 4).

Table 4. *"Other" (speakers not conforming to standard theory)*

	X and I	X and me
Subject	+ natural and + correct	– natural and – correct
Object	+ natural (4) or + correct (2) or + actually used to fill in blank (2)	+ natural and + correct

N = 8 /22 UMC

In addition, another informant (a linguist) volunteered that he specifically remembers being a native speaker of the prestige dialect, with regard to pronouns, and being shocked to discover himself "hypercorrecting" by using *X and I* in object position. Again, this is a situation that would not be predicted by the standard theory of hypercorrection. This informant (if his memory is correct) and the 8 "other" speakers present a puzzle for the theory. What factor exists that can override even a person's native competence as well as sociolinguistic sensibilities that would dictate the use of *X and me* in object position? How would such a factor work?

3.3 Discussion

The data do basically uphold Labov's initial model of hypercorrection; there are insecure LMC speakers using hypercorrect forms, UMC prestige speakers, and younger speakers (including UMC speakers) who have acquired their native competence from hypercorrecting speakers. However, the data also confirm the suspicion that there are also other speakers who display hypercorrect usage.

To take Giles and Williams' question, "Do we all hypercorrect under certain circumstances?", the answer here is a qualified yes. What is interesting is that there is a substantial proportion of speakers who do not fit Labov's model, who do fit Giles' model, and whose response patterns reveal cognitive factors in addition to sociolinguistic causes. Specifically, a large proportion of speakers who would otherwise fit the description of prestige speakers, when confronted with *X and I* in object position, either used it or judged it as natural sounding or judged it as correct. Giles' CAT model, because it accounts for hypercorrect usage without requiring insecurity or mistaken metalinguistic belief, could countenance prestige speakers being willing to use hypercorrect *X and I*.

Giles' model, however, does not provide an explanation for how prestige speakers could come to see *X and I* as correct or acceptable in their own dialect, since CAT only explains changes in performance, not competence. A more adequate theory would have to explain changes in speakers' intuitions. A clue is found in the observation that those speakers who depart from Labov's model have one thing in common. Their responses all involve adding an "extraneous" construction (object *X and I*) to a person's grammar (a grammar that already has *X and me* in place for object position and does not "need" *X and I* to perform that function). This extraneous construction is one that has already gained some currency. That is, even if their intuitions provide *X and me* for objective case, speakers frequently hear *X and I* as object, and have to process these sentences when they hear them. This pattern suggests that an attractive theory to explain this late-developing acceptance of object *X and I* would involve a speaker picking up frequently encountered constructions and adding them to their grammars. Note that this explanation would be able to account for not just hypercorrect usage but also hypercorrect intuitions. But is there any evidence that this mechanism is psychologically plausible?

The suggestion that frequent exposure to a construction can actually change a person's grammar does have psychological support. Luka and Barsalou (1998), one of the few accounts in the literature that explains shifting of grammaticality judgments within individual adults (but see Winters 1994), show that frequent exposure to a construction changes adults' intuitive judgments. A cognitive process behind this effect is likely to be priming. Each time a prestige speaker hears a construction, such as object *X and I*, that construction is primed and activation increases (Bock 1986, Boyland and Anderson 1997, Potter and Lombardi 1998), and it becomes more natural sounding to that person, and they become more likely to produce that construction. To the degree that other speakers in their environment regardless of class use the hypercorrect construction, prestige speakers pick up that usage. From a cognitive psychological point of view, the fact that an utterance must be parsed increases the activation of the grammatical construction, and thus its likelihood of being uttered, even if sociolinguistically speaking there is no motivation to use that construction (Boyland and Anderson 1998), or even motivation against using it. Thus there is a natural mechanism, syntactic priming, through which frequency has an effect on syntactic choices.

The pattern of results suggests that the change of intuition associated with hypercorrection may occur not only in discontinuous transmission from generation to generation (e.g., from LMC teacher to UMC child), but instead may occur as a result of a change in mental representation within individual speakers of the prestige dialect. Frequency of exposure is a likely factor, mediated by the mechanism of priming.

A survey of individual speakers' attitudes does not provide quantitative evidence for the essentially quantitative question of whether frequency has an observable effect on grammatical behavior. The remainder of this set of studies is an attempt to find out whether frequency could indeed be a viable explanation for cases like those described above, and whether it could be one of the factors accelerating the progress of hypercorrection.

4. *X and I* corpus study

The survey study sets the scene for a more quantitative study. If "we all hyper-correct under certain circumstances," what exactly are the "certain circumstances" under which we hypercorrect? As Janda and Auger (1992) point out, there are few studies detailing how specific factors contribute to the occurrence of hypercor-rection. They write of their hope for more studies that "quantify the frequency with which such (qualitative) hypercorrection occurs [and] determine with precision the stylistic and other social factors which govern its occurrence" (1992: 192). In other words, what are the specific factors that govern whether a prestige form will be hypercorrected, by either Labov's or Giles' definition? Certainly there are stylistic and other social factors, but frequency and other cognitive factors are also worth investigating and are the focus here.

The corpus study described here attempts to address some of these issues by answering a few basic questions about the specific construction *X and I*. What is thedistribution, hypercorrect and otherwise, of *X and I*? A corpus study answers this question of the contexts that determine the usage of *X and I*, by examining the specific forms that are hypercorrected, looking at the distribution of hypercorrect *X and I*, and finding the distinguishing features of the contexts in which hyper-correction does occur.

A corpus study was conducted to seek evidence as to whether frequency predicts the acceptability of *X and I* constructions. It is commonly recognized (Quirk *et al.* 1985) that the use of *I* as an object occurs especially, or only, when it forms the second part of a compound object, i.e., *X and I*. Judging whether frequency makes a difference in the acceptability of the construction, however, requires a closer anal-ysis. Specifically, it is necessary to make distinctions between strings with different *X*s filling the slot. Once we know which *X and I* string is most frequent and which one has gained the most acceptance, it becomes possible to ask whether frequency can predict acceptability.

4.1 Procedure

The raw data for this study were collected from spontaneous communication on the internet. All traffic in the medium of "usenet newsgroups" (open public discussion groups such as alt.atheism or rec.video) was sampled for 36 hours and a corpus was constructed from all instances of *X and I* and *X and me*. One tenth of the sentences (a total of 2040 or so) were selected at random and were screened such that repeated sentences and sentences in which *X and I* did not form a constituent were discarded. The remaining approximately 225 sentences were then manually coded along three dimensions: a) Did the grammatical context call for a subject or an object? b) Was the subject form, *I*, or the object form, *me*, used? c) was *X* a full NP, a proper noun, you, or a 3rd person pronoun?

The question of interest was "Are more frequently occurring strings overextended more to generate hypercorrections, when compared proportionally to less frequent strings?" A frequency-based theory would predict that more frequent strings would be at the leading edge of innovation.

4.2 Results

The data supported this prediction. The chart below shows the number in each category. Table 5 shows that, of a total of 218 instances of the coordinate NP *X and I*, the most frequently occurring compound NP was *you and I*, followed by *he and I*.[1] *X and me* was not analyzed further in this study because its use is rarely if ever hypercorrect.

Table 5. *Most frequent colloca-*
tions in standard (subject) X and I

X and I	# standard (i.e., as subject)
you and I	40
he and I	8
Jim and I	4
Mulder and I	4
she and I	3
Jeff and I	3
John and I	3
Lyn and I	3
all others	1 or 0 each
Total	218

Table 6 shows the strings most often occurring in the context in which *X and I* would be considered a hypercorrection (subject form in object position). *You and I* leads that list as well.

Table 6. *Most frequent collocations in hypercorrect (object)* X and I

X and I	# hypercorrect (i.e., as object)
you and I	5
she and I	1
Alden and I	1
Ed and I	1
Kat and I	1
all others	0
Total	9

These two facts are not particularly meaningful in themselves. It could well have been the case that *you and I* occurs frequently as a hypercorrection only because it is the favored form regardless of context. Without further analysis, these data would not show that *you and I* has any special role in the spread of hypercorrection. There would just be the tautology that the most frequent form is the form that appears most often. An argument from frequency would have to show that high string frequency (Krug 1998) of *X and I* in the usual context (as subject) *increases* the likelihood of its occurring in hypercorrect context (as object).

This is indeed what the data show, as Table 7 lays out. What we find is that the most frequent form in the standard context did not come to be used with equal frequency in a hypercorrect context. What makes the juxtaposition of these two frequency patterns meaningful is that it shows that the likelihood of *X and I* occurring in hypercorrect contexts is increased relative to baseline. In standard usage, *you* is indeed the most frequent word to precede *and I*, but even so it was used on only 40 occasions; in the other 178 utterances of *X and I*, *X* was a proper noun, full NP, or 3rd person pronoun, for a total of 18%. In contrast, out of the 9 cases of hypercorrection, 5 involved the string *you and I*, for a total of 55%. If the high rate of hypercorrect *you and I* is merely a reflection of the overall frequency of *you and I*, the expected frequency would be (40+5) / (218+9) = 20%. Instead, more than half of the *X and I* hypercorrections are from *you and I*, more than doubling the rate. The highest frequency variant *you and I* in standard contexts becomes the first variant available for hypercorrect contexts and, thus, predominates in the hypercorrect context. This is a regularity that is not predicted by the usual model of hypercorrection, but that is predicted by a frequency model.

Table 7. *Frequency of* you and I *in standard vs. hypercorrect usage*

	Standard (as subject)	Hypercorrect (as object)	Sub-totals	% Hyper-correct
You and I	40	5	45	11%
All other *X and I* combined	178	4	182	2%
Subtotals	218	9	227	4%
% you and I / total X and I	18%	55%	20%	

A directional chi-square test gives a value of 7.5, which would normally give $p < .005$. However, the total number of hypercorrected items is small, so these results should only be taken as suggestive.

The very fact that the number of hypercorrect items is small, however, itself addresses Janda and Auger's concern that there need to be studies that quantify the rate of qualitative hypercorrection, such as object *X and I*. As Table 7 brings out, the rate of hypercorrection of all *X and I*, excluding *you and I*, is only 2%, while the rate of hypercorrection of *you and I* is 11%. Both these figures are relatively low.

Statistical analysis of *X and me* was not carried out because the number of sentences using *X and me* was only one-seventh as many as those using *X and I*, and because the results would not be directly applicable to hypercorrection. However, inspection of the data (Table 8) suggests that the most common non-standard instantiation of *X and me* is as *you and me*, again in line with the notion that the most frequently co-occurring strings are the ones that gain license to appear in non-standard usage.

Table 8. *Frequency of* you and me *in standard vs. nonstandard usage*

	Standard (as object)	Non-standard (as subject)	Sub-totals	% Non-standard
You and me	18	7	25	28%
All other *X and me* combined	12	2	14	14%
Subtotals	30	9	39	23%
% you and me/total X and I/me	60%	78%	64%	

4.3 Discussion

Examining frequency data alerts us to empirical facts that intuitive judgment alone could not. Intuitive judgments did correctly suggest that hypercorrection involving *I* in object position occurred preferentially in coordinate NPs of the form *X and I* and not with *I* alone. However, it took frequency data to reveal that not only are these *I* hypercorrections limited to coordinate NPs in general, but that a specific string, *you and I*, is the primary vehicle for this development.

This data are comparable to those presented by Tottie (1991) and Ogura (1993), both of whom show that syntactic constructions behave like lexical items, specifically in the way they diffuse through the language during lexical diffusion. A construction (e.g., periphrastic *do*) is at first instantiated in a limited number of contexts (as in "I do not hear it") and then extended to others (as in "I do not know/say/like it"). Likewise, object *X and I* seems have started in inclusive first person plural prepositional phrases like "between you and I" and spread to other contexts, as in "people like you and I" and "between Ben and I." Tottie and Ogura use the term "lexical diffusion in syntax" to describe the process, presumably in order to highlight the gradual instantiation of a change as it spreads from speaker to speaker and from context to context. The most frequent variant will "snowball" in popularity (Ogura 1996) not only in overall frequency, as S-shaped curves of propagation describe, but also by expanding into new contexts where the form was previously not allowed. A fine-grained comparison between the frequency data in this paper and in their papers yields interesting contrasts that at first seem contradictory but then complementary, but this comparison is somewhat beyond the scope of this paper.[2]

My interpretation of these data is that frequent usage of a phrase in standard usage makes the phrase cohere and become a unit. As the unit grows in strength, it becomes more and more automatized and is more and more likely to be chosen as the way of expressing the speaker's communicative intention. Boyland (1997) and Boyland and Anderson (1998) flesh out this argument in detail. The point to be made here is that such a process leads not only to the kinds of language change characterized by automatization (*viz.*, grammaticalization), but can contribute to other linguistic phenomena such as hypercorrection, normally considered to fall within the purview of sociolinguistics.

This claim of automatization is similar to many that exist in the literature, but its application to the hypercorrect pronoun case extends each in one way or another. For example, Bybee (1985) argues that the history of morphologically complex word forms can be understood partly as the process of tying together the representations of frequently co-occurring morphemes. The situation under consideration here though (and in Bybee, this volume) represents an earlier stage of development in which distinct words first began to develop an affinity for each other. Perhaps not coincidentally, Bybee (this volume) also discusses the coherence of multi-word sequences as an important factor in language change. The use of *you and I* in English is certainly an example of this. Indeed, Quirk *et al.* (1985: 338) write: "*X and I* is felt to be a polite sequence which can remain unchanged." What the present research adds is the idea that one polite sequence has precedence and that the polite sequence with precedence is determined by frequency in normal contexts. Finally,

Fowler, the well-known prescriptivist, also wrote of case errors due to "the temptation to regard *he-who* or *they-who* as a single word that surely cannot need to have
the question of case settled twice over for it" (Fowler 1926: 68, emphasis mine).
However, he did not support his assertion with quantitative data.

The survey and the corpus studies of *X and I* together have accomplished both
empirical and theoretical goals. The initial survey study uncovered a class of speakers whose judgments do not fit the predictions of the usual model of hypercorrection
in that they accepted both *X and me* and *X and I* in object position. What is the
significance of the fact that some speakers' judgments do not fit the predictions of
the standard model? These speakers' judgments do submit to an explanation in
terms of frequency. Further investigation of frequency data brought to light the
additional discovery that *you and I* specifically, not *X and I* in general, is the context
in which *I* is most commonly used hypercorrectly as an object. The pattern present
in the data suggests that string frequency is one of the factors at work in the normalizing of *I* as object. So we have seen, in the two studies so far, that frequency promotes spread of a form through the language. A form's frequency in hypercorrect
context can increase the number of speakers who use the form hypercorrectly and
a form's frequency in normal contexts can increase the rate at which that form is
used in hypercorrect contexts.

5. *Hypercorrection of who* vs. *whom*

Whom in subject position is another hypercorrection of case that demonstrates, in
a different way, how the frequency of a form in one context promotes the use of the
form in another context. It does so by generating forces within individual sentences
that compete with the usual determinants of case in relative pronouns, leading to
sentences like "I take pleasure in indulgences of imagination about those whom
once lived here" (McGoey 1997).

The usage of *who* and *whom* is a familiar and well-discussed topic. The basic
facts of the matter are well-known. In speech, *who* is used almost exclusively except
after prepositions. *Whom* is seen as the formal variant of *who* and thus also appears
as a hypercorrection for *who*. This asymmetry is long-standing (Buchanan 1762).
Taking these basic facts as a starting point, the recent literature on *who* and *whom*
includes more nuanced discussions, detailing specific circumstances in which *who*
and *whom* are used. The articles discussed below (as well as Thompson and Hopper,
this volume), indicate that, contrary to popular perception, *whom* is not dead and
there are specific contexts in which it occurs with regularity.

Walsh and Walsh (1989) show that *whom* is alive and well, at least in some social
and syntactic contexts. Specifically, they found, through a questionnaire, that the use
of *whom* is "the result of the interaction of two different kinds of rules," which at

times conflict. One of these rules gives *who* as the default but requires *whom* after prepositions, regardless of syntactic function. The other rule, the standard prescriptive rule, requires *who* for subjects and *whom* for objects. They found that when the two rules were in conflict usage varied, but when both rules agreed selection of *who* as well as of *whom* was consistent.

As mentioned above, many writers, including both Quirk *et al.* (1985) and Fowler (1926) have observed that hypercorrection occurs when functional roles at different levels of analysis compete over a relative pronoun's case. These observations have not, however, linked these facts with frequency.

Bennett (1994) documents a particular class of such cases in which *whom* is regularly used that has not heretofore been considered prescriptively correct. This context is exemplified by the sentence "It was never our intent to offend or distress Mrs. P., whom we accept behaved properly." Bennett labels clauses such as these containing *whom* as the Accusative-and-Finite clause, where *whom* acts both as an object of *accept* and as a subject forming a finite clause with *behaved properly*. The use of *whom* appears at first, he argues, to be a hypercorrection, but now occurs with enough regularity that it should be considered grammatical.

Addressing similar claims by Jesperson (1954) and Howard (1986), Aarts (1994) conducted a corpus study. In particular, that study paid attention to this same type of context described by Bennett, bringing in alternative terms—for example, the term *long movement* (Haegeman 1991) to describe the type of relative clauses that Bennett calls *Accusative-and-Finite* and the term *pushdown* (from Quirk *et al.* [1985])—to describe the kind of small clause that interrupts the long-movement clause. That study did find differences in usage of *whom* across syntactic contexts, but the data did not support the specific claim that *whom* is now grammatical in that particular type of context. Acknowledging that the answer is to be found in quantitative research, Aarts examined the corpora that were then available and concluded that there was at that time not enough empirical evidence to support the claim that a pushdown clause licenses the use of *whom*.

Based on this literature, and given the more widespread availability of more speech-like computerized text, another corpus study was conducted and is described here. The results support the position of Jesperson, Bennett, and Howard. The results also suggest that frequency within a combination of different contexts is a primary determinant of when hypercorrection does and does not occur.

6. Who *vs.* whom *corpus study*

In addition to the issues raised above, about relative pronouns, the question quoted above by Janda and Auger (1992) about hypercorrection still stands: Whenever there is hypercorrection or what might appear to be hypercorrection, what is the mechanism? Are the factors governing its occurrence only social and stylistic or are there other factors?

The primary goals for this portion of the current study were, first, to quantify the use of *who* vs. *whom* in different kinds of clauses, including pushdown clauses, and second, to gather evidence for mechanisms that might be responsible for whatever quantitative patterns might emerge.

6.1 Procedure

A database was constructed similar to that used in the *X and I* study; 24 hours of traffic on the usenet news were sampled, in which were approximately 31,000 instances of *who* and 860 of *whom*, of which a subset were found to be relative rather than interrogative pronouns. From these subsets, a random 200 of each were coded further. In addition, all the instances in the corpus of hypercorrect *whom* were also coded fully (N=43). All the coded sentences were labeled according to whether *who/whom* served as subject or object in the matrix (embedding) clause and in the relative clause and whether there was a pushdown (embedded) clause (for which it would serve as an object). Because of the sampling scheme, comparisons should only be made between relative frequencies of the uses of each pronoun; they should not be made between raw frequencies of *who* and *whom*.

6.2 Results

Table 9 shows the distribution of *who* and *whom* as a function of clause types. Notice that speakers, perhaps to a surprising degree, do still have control of case (see Thompson and Hopper, this volume). Both non-standard *who* and hypercorrect

Table 9. *Frequency of correct and hypercorrect relative* who *and* whom

	Who		Whom	
	Raw frequency	%	Raw frequency	%
Used as subject	193	96.5%	15	7.5%
As direct object	3	1.5%	64	32.0%
As object of preposed preposition	1	0.5%	108	54.0%
As other oblique case	3	1.5%	13	6.5%
Total	200	100%	200	100%

$\chi^2 = 314.9$ (3 d.f.), $p < 0.001$

Table 10. *Frequency of subject* who *and* whom *as a function of element of matrix clause modified*

	Who (subject)		*Whom* (subject)	
	Raw frequency	%	Raw frequency	%
Modifying subject of matrix clause	49	25%	4	9%
Modifying direct object of matrix	35	18%	6	14%
Modifying object of preposed preposition in matrix	71	37%	25	58%
Modifying other oblique cases in matrix	38	20%	8	19%
Total	193	100%	43	100%

χ^2 = 8.37 (3 d.f., 1-tailed), p < 0.025

whom are rare. For example, it is harder to find a non-standard sentence like "I recommended the guy who I consider the best locksmith in town" or a hypercorrect sentence like "Allow me, a layman whom haven't kept up with QED-development" and much easier to find a correct sentence like "Hatred corrodes those against whom it is directed."

Table 10 breaks down the first (shaded) row of Table 9, the subject relatives, according to what element in the matrix clause the relative clause modifies. It shows that the most frequent context for *whom* in the relative clause is carried over as a risk factor for hypercorrect *whom* use. When the relative pronoun modifies the subject of the matrix clause, as in "Someone whom is worth listening to has convinced him," hypercorrect *whom* use is low, compared to *who* (9% vs. 25%). When the subject relative modifies the direct object of the matrix clause, as in "*I have a friend* whom had a power surge," hypercorrect *whom* use is comparable to use of *who* (14% vs. 18%). The most typical hypercorrection, however, occurs when the the relative clause modifies the object of a preposition in the matrix clause; hypercorrect *whom* use there is greatly elevated relative to *who*, as in "The low carb idea is for people whom have a problem with carbs" (58% vs. 37%). To maximize the N of the subject *whom*s, all 43 instances from the 24-hour corpus were used, not only the 15 that were found among the first 200 instances of relative *whom*.

What Table 11 (p. 400) displays is the information in the shaded row of Table 9 broken down according to a different criterion, namely, whether the subject relative participates in a "pushdown" clause embedded within a relative clause. Notice that the relative pronoun can serve in a pushdown clause only as an object. An example of a pushdown clause appears in the following sentence: "Many people who should be there are not, people whom I know are living at a certain address." Table 11 shows that when the subject relative serves as the object of an embedded (pushdown) clause, *whom* use is greatly elevated relative to the use of subject relative *whom* when there is no pushdown clause. In fact, all of the 4 subject *whom*s at the top of the third column of Table 10 (modifying the matrix subject) are instances involving pushdown clauses, and the example sentence listed above as "Someone whom is worth listening to has convinced him" in reality occurred as "Someone whom he feels is worth listening to has convinced him."

Table 11. *Subject relative whom use as function of embedded clause*

	Subject *who*	Subject *whom*
No pushdown clause	193	23
As object of pushdown clause	0	20
$\chi^2 = 97.6$[3]		

We see that there is indeed regularity in the overextension of *whom*, over a variety of contexts. Its incidence is particularly evident in the context of pushdown clauses, disconfirming the conclusion drawn by Aarts from similar but less extensive data, and confirming the claims made by Bennett and Jesperson without quantitative data. When a relative clause does contain a pushdown clause, a speaker will almost certainly use *whom* rather than *who* as the subject relative; when there is no pushdown clause, speakers are only 1/10 as likely to use *whom* as subject relative as they are to use *who*.

In addition to that salient result, there are several other regularities, that, when seen together, reveal an overall pattern. In addition to being influenced by its function in the embedded pushdown clause, and the prescription based on its function in the relative clause itself, the choice of *who* vs. *whom* is also subject to a pronounced influence from the matrix clause in which the relative clause is embedded. As Tables 9–11 show, in each case, functioning as an object in *any* of these clauses (either the embedding (matrix) clause or the embedded (pushdown) clause) made it equally or more likely for the speaker to choose *whom* than *who*. In all cases, being the subject of the clause in question depressed *whom* use while, in all cases, being the prepositional object of the clause in question raised *whom* use.

6.3 Discussion

If pronoun case were deterministically assigned on the basis of being the subject vs. the object of a finite relative clause, there would be no such variability apparent in each context. There would be no particular reason for these patterns to exist. Instead, however, it appears that the human speaker's mental representation determines the case assignment of the relative pronoun, not just by consulting its function within the unit of the relative clause, but also within the smaller unit comprising the pushdown clause and the larger unit comprising the matrix clause. A crucial fact tying together these observations is that the frequency of *who* vs. *whom* in main clauses and in normal relative clauses reflects the same pattern—*whom* appears most often after prepositions, intermediately as direct object and least often as subject—and this baseline frequency provides the pattern. So the frequency pattern found in normal relative clauses determines the pattern in other associated clauses. This would not necessarily be expected.

A plausible interpretation of this situation is that frequent exposure increases the activation of multiple syntactic options, which in turn leads to variability in expressed form. Indeed, this variability reflects the overall frequency with which each variant appears and thus the activation of each variant. This explanation makes sense cognitively as well. A cue-based theory like Bates and MacWhinney's (1987) Competition model could account for the observed pattern. The point of interest though is that it is the frequency of *whom* in different kinds of contexts that determines non-standard use of *whom*, where the frequency is proposed to have its effect through the mechanism of priming, as described in Boyland and Anderson (1998). Activating competing representations is phenomenologically experienced as uncertainty and behaviorally expressed as variability. So we can predict, based on facts of frequency, where uncertainty will begin. And uncertainty, though it may not constitute change *per se*, is a seed of variation from which change may arise.

We now have specific information on when *whom* occurs as a subject relative pronoun. We have found empirically that the use of subject relative *whom* occurs with regularity when pushdown clauses are present, as Aarts and others discussed but did not have the data to support, as well as with increased likelihood when the relative clause modified an object rather than the subject of the matrix clause. Both the study of hypercorrection and the study of relative pronouns have benefited from attention to frequency. We also have a cognitively plausible mechanism. A speaker's cognitive system attends simultaneously to multiple units of different sizes within which a form may occur. Within each unit, patterns (like *whom* as prepositional object) that occur more frequently are more heavily primed and thus more highly activated.

7. Conclusion

We see then that situations (object *X and I*, subject *whom*) that appear to be explained simply by hypercorrection cannot be understood quite so simply. Rather, looking at pronouns with frequency in mind illuminates both our empirical knowledge and also our theoretical understanding. A survey of different speakers' intuitions answered, affirmatively, the question of whether hypercorrect forms are used by speakers other than those proposed by Labov. The two corpus studies answered the call for more quantitative data on hypercorrection, both to find the actual rate of hypercorrect usage, and to find factors that influence the rate of hypercorrect usage.

The *X and I* survey showed that sociolinguistically-motivated hypercorrection and explicit correction or instruction alone do not tell the whole story of who uses hypercorrect *X and I*. Rather, some of the speakers showed signs of being influenced (despite "prestige" intuitions) by the hypercorrect speech of others around them, in a way that was not predicted by either Labov's classic model of hypercorrection nor by Giles' Communicative Accommodation Theory. It was hypothesized that these speakers' judgments can, however, be explained by frequency in input speech, and thus that frequency is one of the factors determining the occurrence of hypercorrection. The *X and I* corpus study followed up on this idea. Finding that the string occurring with highest frequency in normal contexts (*you and I*) became the string most likely to appear in new contexts, it was suggested that speakers created pre-analyzed syntactic units (much as described in Bybee, this volume), available to be recruited for new, hypercorrect contexts.

The *whom* corpus study supports arguments that *whom* is grammatical when followed by a pushdown clause (for which it is always an object). The *who* vs. *whom* corpus study provided insight into the power of the ways in which multiple competing cues at different levels of analysis together determine the form, sometimes hypercorrect, of an utterance, where the strength of each cue is related to the frequency with which each cue is associated with each particular form.

We have also seen that hypercorrection has been a useful though limited concept through which to understand variation in pronoun usage. The notion of hypercorrection could profitably be extended by allowing for hypercorrect usage to come not only from sociolinguistic motivation but also from cognitive processes like priming. More frequently encountered and thus more highly activated constructions are more likely to be used subsequently, by other speakers, in other utterances, and in other clauses. In each case, frequency has been an organizing force governing the spread of a form from standard to hypercorrect contexts, where we find that they have been firmly established in our grammars.

Notes

* Special thanks to Joan Bybee, David Tuggy, Noel Rude, Margaret Winters, William Bennett, Gunnel Tottie, Richard Janda, Matthew Rispoli, the UW-Milwaukee Cognitive Science group, and the faculty, staff, and administration of Alverno College, Milwaukee. All errors are my own.

1. Part of the reason that the X slot is most often filled by *you* is probably that the pronouns are closed class, while the other potential fillers of the slot are open class and thus could fill the slot in an infinite number of different ways.

2. Basically, they show that the most frequent words are the last to undergo the change to *do*-support. But that is because the most frequent words are used most frequently in the old simple (not periphrastic) forms, which thus hinders change. With pronominal case, the most frequent are the first to change (e.g., *you and I* being used as object). This is, however, for the same reason, namely that multi-word units that have coalesced are preferred over strings that must be constructed anew. Thus, a frequent string like *"Knowest thou?"* resists change to "Dost thou know?", while a frequent string like "you and I", unanalyzed, takes over all cases of the inclusive first person plural. In both cases, the most frequent strings (e.g., *Knowest thou?* , or *you and I*) have coalesced and resist separation, while more loosely connected strings suffer no such pressure.

3. The statistically astute may notice that the data in the bottom part of Table 11 cannot be analyzed using an ordinary chi-square test with the usual p values, since a chi-square analysis yields one expected cell count of 4, which is less than the conservative minimum of 5. Thus a p value is not listed for the table. However, even if we apply a 10-fold correction factor, p is still < 0.01.

References

Aarts, F. 1994. "Relative *who* and *whom*: prescriptive rules and linguistic reality". *American Speech* 69(1): 71–9.

Bates, E. and MacWhinney, B. 1987. "Competition, variation, and language learning". In *Mechanisms of language acquisition*, B. MacWhinney (ed), 157–93. Hillsdale, NJ: Lawrence Erlbaum.

Bennett , W. 1994. "A case of syntactic change in English". *Studia Anglica Posnaniensia* 29: 31–8.

Boyland, J. T. and Anderson, J. R., 1997. "Comprehension and production as avenues of syntactic priming". In *Proceedings of the Nineteenth Annual Meeting of the Cognitive Science Society*, M. G. Shafto and P. Langley (eds), 871. Mahwah, NJ: Lawrence Erlbaum.

Boyland, J. T. and Anderson, J. R., 1998. "Evidence that syntactic priming is long-lasting". In *Proceedings of the Twentieth Annual Meeting of the Cognitive Science Society*, M. A. Gernsbacher (ed), 1205. Mahwah, NJ: Lawrence Erlbaum.

Buchanan, J. 1762/1968. *The British Grammar*. Menston, Yorks: Scolar.

Bybee, J. 1985. *Morphology*. Amsterdam: John Benjamins.

COBUILD, 1999. *Bank of English* [Electronic corpus]. Birmingham: Harper Collins.

Fowler, H. W. 1926. *A Dictionary of Modern English Usage*. Oxford: Oxford University.

Giles, H., Mulac, A., Bradac, J. J., and Johnson, P. 1987. "Speech Accommodation Theory: the next decade and beyond". In *Communication Yearbook 10*, M. McLaughlin (ed), 13–48.

Giles, H. and Williams, A. 1992. "Accommodating Hypercorrection: A Communication Model". *Language and Communication* 12 (3/4): 343–56.

Haegeman, L. 1991. *Introduction to Government and Binding Theory*. Oxford: Oxford.

Hartmann, R. R. K. and Stork, F. C. 1972. *Dictionary of Language and Linguistics*. New York: Wiley.

Hock, H. H. and Joseph, B. D. 1996. *Language History, Language Change, and Language Relationship : an Introduction to Historical and Comparative Linguistics*. [Trends in Linguistics. Studies and monographs 93]. New York : Mouton de Gruyter.

Howard, P. 1986. *The State of the Language: English Observed*. Harmondsworth: Penguin.

Janda , R. and Auger, J. 1992. "Quantitative evidence, qualitative hypercorrection, sociolinguistic variables—and French speakers' 'eadhaches with English h/0". *Language and Communication* 12(3/4): 195–236.

Jesperson, O. 1954. *A Modern English Grammar on Historial Principles*. Part III and Part IV. London: Allen.

Krug, M. 1998. "String Frequency: A Cognitive Motivating Factor in Coalescence, Language Processing, and Linguistic Change". *Journal of English Linguistics* 26(4): 286–320.

Labov. W. 1966. "Hypercorrection by the lower middle class as a factor in linguistic change". In *Sociolinguistics: Proceedings of the UCLA Sociolinguistics Conference, 1964*. W. Bright (ed), 84–113. [Janua Linguarum (All Series), Bloomington, IN Ser. maior 20.] The Hague: Mouton.

Luka, B. and Barsalou, L. 1998. "The Role of Sentence Priming on the Implicit Memory of Syntactic Structures". In *Proceedings of the Twentieth Annual Meeting of the Cognitive Science Society*, M.A. Gernsbacher (ed), 1240. Mahwah, NJ: Lawrence Erlbaum.

McGoey, E. 1997. "Enduring Worthiness". *Shady Ave*. 1(2): 28.

Ogura, M. 1996. "Snowball Effect in Lexical Diffusion: The development of -s in the third person singular present indicative in English". In *English Historical Linguistics 1994*, D. Britton (ed), 119–41. [Papers from the 8th International Conference on English Historical Linguistics (8 ICEHL, Edinburgh, 19–23 September, 1994), Amsterdam Studies in the Theory and History of Linguistic Science IV: Current Issues in Linguistic Theory (CILT) 135]. Amsterdam: John Benjamins.

Ogura, M. 1993. "The development of periphrastic *do* in English: A case of lexical diffusion in syntax". *Diachronica* 10(1): 51–85.

Potter, M. and Lombardi, L. 1998. "Syntactic Priming in Immediate Recall of Sentences". *Journal of Memory and Language* 38(3): 265–82.

Quirk, R., Greenbaum, S., Leech, G., and Svartvik, J. 1985. *A Comprehensive Grammar of the English Language*. London: Longman.

Rispoli, M. 1994. "Pronoun Case Overextension and Paradigm Building". *Journal of Child Language* 21: 157–72.

Tottie, G. 1991. "Lexical diffusion in syntactic change: frequency as a determinant of linguistic conservatism in the development of negation in English". *Historical English Syntax*, Kastovsky, Dieter (ed), 439–67. [Topics in English Linguistics 2]. Berlin: Mouton de Gruyter.

Walsh, T. and Walsh, N. 1989. "Patterns of *who/whom* usage". *American Speech* 64(3): 284–86.

Winters, M. 1994. "Who Are You Talking to? Or, Whom Shall I Say Is Calling? Language Change in the Adult Grammar". *Rivista di Linguistica* 6(2): 365–82.

Variability, frequency, and productivity in the irrealis domain of French*

SHANA POPLACK

University of Ottawa

1. Introduction

In its view of grammar as anchored in concrete utterances, its quest for regularities in the repetition of such utterances in discourse, indeed in its characterization of grammar as ultimately "social" in nature (Hopper 1987), Emergent Grammar intersects in many largely unacknowledged ways with another seemingly very disparate framework for linguistic analysis—that of linguistic Variation Theory. Variation Theory (Labov 1969; Sankoff 1988a; Sankoff and Labov 1985), like Functional Linguistics, seeks to account for grammatical structure in discourse, paying particular attention to form-function asymmetry. The alternation of two or more variant forms in fulfilling a single function, so characteristic of discourse, is a major focus. The working hypothesis of Variation Theory is that within a given locus of variability, or *variable context*, each of two or more competing variants will occur at greater or lesser rates depending on the features that constitute the context. The expected proportion of each variant is the resultant of the combined contributions of the independent features defining its context.

The large corpora of spoken discourse which are the data of the variationist approach, coupled with its quantitative methodology, facilitate tests of alternative hypotheses as well. In this paper I make use of the data of natural conversation and the analytical tools of Variation Theory to shed light on the role of frequency in discourse, paying special attention to its relationship to productivity, ritualization (Haiman 1994) and the retention of archaic linguistic structures. The variationist apparatus is ideally suited to testing such developments. The multivariate analytical techniques of variable rule analysis (Sankoff 1988b) enable us to ascertain which are statistically significant and to disentangle their effects, if any, from those of the other crosscutting linguistic and extra-linguistic factors simultaneously at play during variant production.

In what follows I investigate the extent to which usage data support the theory that type frequency is a major determinant of productivity and that token frequency may actually detract from productivity (Bybee 1985, 1995; Bybee and Thompson 1997; Langacker 1988). Illustrating with three sets of form-function asymmetries in the irrealis domain of spoken Canadian French, I show that the relationship between token frequency, type frequency and productivity are not as straightforward as a frequency-based approach would imply. In one of the contexts examined, the predictions of the model dovetail well with the facts of variable usage; in the second, the fit between data and theory is less good, but the patterning of variability suggests a possible explanation. In the third case, they fail to account for the data, raising, if not answering, questions about the properties of contexts hospitable to frequency effects.

2. The irrealis domain of French

By irrealis, I refer to the domain of imagined, projected, predicted or otherwise unreal situations or events, following, for example, Bybee (1998: 264). Most, if not all, such situations are conventionally assumed to be expressed in French by the invariant selection of one of the *subjunctive* (SUBJ) mood, as in (1), the inflected *future* (IF) "tense", as in (2), and *conditional* (COND) modality, as in (3).

(1) Elle a attendu que ses enfants *seyent* (SUBJ) assez grands pour aller travailler. (047/1939)[1]
    'She waited until her children *were* old enough to go to work.'

(2) Dans bible ça dit, "Et les hommes *auront* (IF) la terre, ils *feront* (IF) la terre de [sic] quelque chose de bon". (001/622)
    'In the Bible it says, "And man *will have* the earth, he *will make* of the earth something good".'

(3) Si c'*était* (IMP) à mon choix, je les *enlèverais* (COND) de là. (025/657)
    'If it *were* up to me, *I'd get* them out of there.'

In ordinary speech, however, the irrealis sector is host to considerable variability. This results in rampant form-function asymmetry, even in contexts in which a specific form is prescribed as obligatory. Thus both the indicative (IND) or the conditional may appear in contexts "requiring" the subjunctive, as in (4a and b), the periphrastic future (PF) has virtually replaced its inflected counterpart in all but a few future temporal reference contexts (5), and the conditional in -*rais* is ousting the prescribed imperfect (IMP) in protases of hypothetical conditional complexes (6).

(4) a. Faut je lui *dis* (IND) c'est vrai. Faut je lui *dise* (SUBJ) c'est la vérité
        (064/356–69)
        'I have to *tell* him it's true ... I have to *tell* him it's the truth.'
    b. Faut au moins que je *serais* (COND) bien obligée. (067/78)
        'At I'*d* least *have to be* really forced.'

(5)   Ce soir, on *va* te *ramener* (PF) puis tu y *alleras* (IF) à soir à cinq heures.
        (071/584)
        'Tonight, we'*re going to bring* you *back* and you'*ll go* there tonight at 5: 00.'

(6)   Si mon petit *allait* (IMP) à l'école là, s'il *serait* (COND) à l'école puis
        qu'il *reviendrait* (COND) puis qu'il *dirait* (COND), "Un professeur m'a
        tapé dans face là", il *aurait* affaire à moi. (037/437)
        'If my kid *went* to school, if he *would be* at school, and he *would come*
        back, and he *would say*, "a teacher slapped me across the face", he'*d have*
        to deal with me.'

The facts illustrated in (1)–(6) furnish an interesting test of the relationship between frequency and productivity. The replacement of both the subjunctive by the indicative and the imperfect by the conditional are thoroughly non-standard, while the incursion of the periphrastic variant into the domain of the inflected future is generally considered colloquial. Moreover, historical research (LeBlanc 1999; LeBlanc and Poplack 1999a,b; Poplack 1992; Poplack and Turpin 1999) indicates that this variability is sufficiently longstanding and widespread as to have attracted the attention of the prescriptive and descriptive enterprise—each of these cases has been described, "explained" or denigrated by the French grammatical tradition from the 1600s through to the present. Indeed, the situation of the (Canadian) French irrealis domain qualifies as "emergent" par excellence, in the sense of Hopper (1987), insofar as it reflects centuries of prior, and as yet, unresolved variability.

The grammarian typically responds to such situations by attempting to factor out the variability, either by (1) ignoring it, (2) condemning the offending variant, or (3) attempting to redress the form-function asymmetry, typically by assigning to each form a preferred "reading" or function. In the latter effort they are abetted by the symbiotic relationship between members of the irrealis sector and the various domains of modality (especially epistemic modalities involving speaker commitment to the truth value of the proposition). This makes it possible to attribute the variability to such unobservables as speaker intent, and thereby explain it away. The abiding distaste of grammarians (and many linguists) for inherent variability, coupled with the important interpretive component they assign to speaker commitment and hearer inference, conspire in the observations—with which the literature is rife—that each variant form fulfills a specific semantic task. Thus selection of the indicative in place of the subjunctive is often (and as we shall see, incorrectly) explained by the assertion that the speaker did not wish to commit herself to the reality, probability or truth value of the complement proposition (e.g., Grevisse 1986). Selection of the periphrastic future was associated by grammarians with proximity for centuries, but since the 1930s has been justified (again erroneously) by the opportunity it purportedly affords the speaker of envisaging the future eventuality in a more engaged, immediate, certain, committed and affective way than its inflected counterpart (e.g., Confais 1995; Deshaies and Laforge 1981; Fleischman 1982; Leeman-Bouix 1994). After an auspicious, though short-lived début (Maupas 1625), use of the conditional in protases has alternately been ignored or vilified, with remarkably little effect on its rapidly-increasing usage (Section 7).

What is the current role of these variant forms in discourse and why have they coexisted for so long? Does each perform the semantic task(s) claimed for it, or are some simply historical residue of erstwhile distinctions? If the latter, what accounts for their retention? Are they used indifferently with all eligible verbs or is the survival of some due rather to frequent repetition and sedimentation in grammar? In what follows I assess which account best fits the facts of spontaneous usage.

3. The network model of usage-based grammar

Bybee's (1985, 1988, 1995) network model claims that two factors are central in determining productivity, defined as the ability of a pattern to apply to novel items. The first is type frequency, or the number of different lexical items to which a particular pattern or construction is applicable. The more such items there are, the greater the likelihood that the pattern will also apply to novel items. This prediction is illustrated by Guillaume's (1927/1973, cited in Bybee 1995) demonstration that the widespread tendency of French children to generalize "first conjugation" verb morphology to other verbs is due, not to the greater token frequency of -er verbs, as is commonly assumed, but rather to their elevated type frequency (Table 1).

Table 1. *Token and type frequency of French verbs according to conjugation class (adapted from Guillaume 1927/73, cited in Bybee 1995)*

	Conjugation class	Token frequency	Type frequency
(I)	*Chanter*	36%	**76%**
(II)	*Finir*	6%	6%
(III)	*Vendre*	**57%**	18%

The other determinant of productivity, according to this model, is "schema strength", which is also based on type frequency. Schemas are generalizations about sets of words with similar patterns of semantic and phonological connections. If the defining properties of the schema are highly restrictive, it will not apply to many new forms. Thus the past tense formation pattern *string/strung* is not fully productive, since most English verbs do not meet the phonological description of *string*. Only an "open" schema, such as that of the English past tense *-ed*, can attain full productivity, since there are no restrictions on the forms to which it can apply (Bybee 1995: 430).

High token frequency, on the other hand, is not consistent with productivity. Bybee (1995: 434) explains this apparent contradiction as follows: Frequent forms can be learned by rote, without undergoing internal analysis or participating in schemas. This results in increased *lexical strength* (Bybee 1985) or *entrenchment* (Langacker 1987). Highly frequent entrenched words or phrases, according to these authors, tend to be stored unanalyzed , and are accessed more rapidly than their lexically weaker counterparts. Such items are also said to resist analogical levelling, resulting in the conservation of archaic structures. This "Conserving Effect" explains why high-frequency sequences (phonological, morphological or syntactic) are able to resist change toward newer more productive patterns (Bybee and Thompson 2000: 381).

The data of the French irrealis sector offer an appropriate testing ground for these claims, since as we shall see in Sections 5, 6, and 7, the three variables constituting it can be contrasted according to token frequency, type frequency and schema strength, among other factors, and these can be related to their productivity in actual usage.

4. Method and data

4.1 Data

The data I report on were all extracted from the *Corpus du français parlé à Ottawa-Hull* (Poplack 1989), a massive compendium of the highly informal conversation of a representative sample of 120 francophones native to the national capital region of Canada. This corpus of natural speech contains thousands of repetitions of each of the grammatical structures of interest to us, but no judgements, opinions or replies to queries concerning them. As such it is ideally suited to examining language as it is used unreflectingly, and to situating these uses in linguistic, social and historical context. At approximately 3.5 million words, the corpus is large enough to enable meaningful study of the kinds of frequency and usage questions that are the focus of this volume. In each of the areas under study the same lexical types recur, used in the same conversations by the same speakers, though not necessarily at the same frequency levels, nor in the same morphological categories. In particular, verbs with suppletive morphology in the subjunctive and future sectors have regular conjugations in the imperfect. These circumstances enable us to disentangle purely lexical effects from those due to frequency of occurrence and morphological irregularity, an important check since these factors tend to be so highly correlated (Bybee and Thompson 2000; Poplack 1992). For example, an effect due to lexical identity can be expected to manifest itself by like behavior of the lexical item across variables; if morphological irregularity is determinative, effects should differ from variable to variable.

4.2 Method

Recognizing that the same linguistic "function" may at times be realized by different "forms", variationists seek to explain why one is actually chosen in a given context over another. The selection process is construed as resulting from the complex contribution of environmental factors, linguistic and social (plus a degree of inherent variability), which may conspire or conflict in the production of the form. This process is modelled by operationalizing hypotheses about selection constraints as *factors* in a multivariate analysis. Making use of a program for variable rule analysis (Rand and Sankoff 1990; Sankoff 1988b), I ascertain which of these factors contribute statistically significant effects to variant choice when all are considered simultaneously, as well as their relative magnitude with respect to each other.

The hypotheses I consider here relate to the contributions of token frequency, type frequency, schema strength and semanticity to productivity. As is standard in variationist research, it is first necessary to define the *variable context*, or locus of variability. The alternation between subjunctive and indicative, for example, is only relevant to specifically "subjunctive-selecting" contexts, since the reverse situation (subjunctive supplied in indicative contexts) is vanishingly rare (Poplack 1992). *Token frequency* is a count of the number of times a variant occurred in running speech (sometimes normalized as a percentage of all tokens being analyzed in a context). *Lexical identity* distinguishes the lexical types with which it co-occurred. *Lexical strength* refers to the proportion a given lexical type represents out of all lexical types in its cohort (e.g., the proportion the verb *falloir* represents of all matrix verbs used in the corpus). Due to discrepancies between the traditional accounts of these phenomena and the facts of usage detailed here, I distinguish *prescribed* type frequency or lexical schema (the class of lexical items to which the phenomenon is prescribed to apply) from *observed* type frequency or schema strength, i.e., the items (or contexts) in which a variant form actually occurred.

Productivity is a more elusive notion to operationalize. In the network model, it is defined as the ability to apply to novel items. By far the most important source of novel lexical material in Ottawa-Hull French is that originating from English, a phenomenon that has been thoroughly quantitatively studied (Poplack 1985, 1988; Poplack and Meechan 1998; Poplack et al. 1988). This work documents the strong tendency towards integration of borrowed material into the morphological and syntactic structures of French, due to which novel verb forms behave indistinguishably from the remainder of the verb paradigm. Similarities between established and nonce forms extend to the constraint hierarchies governing variability. The criterion of applicability to novel items is therefore less relevant here. For the purposes of this exercise, then, a variant will be considered *productive* if it fulfills the weaker requirement of occurring at a substantial, and relatively *homogeneous*, rate across all lexical items and contexts forming its domain.

An additional measure of productivity is *semanticity*, or the extent to which variant choice is associated with the nuances typically ascribed to it. If a morphological form performs a semantic task, it should occur freely with any lexical item which predicates a proposition consistent with that task, and this occurrence should be unhampered by restrictions imposed by lexical type, frequency and/or other morphosyntactic considerations. Productivity, as already observed by Bybee and Thompson (1997), is of course gradient. I class as *fully productive* the occurrence of a variant, in fulfillment of a specific semantic task, at comparable rates across (1) all lexical items and (2) all eligible subcontexts within its variable context. In what follows I examine how these categories interact with the expression of irrealis in three areas of French grammar.

5. The subjunctive

Standard French requires subjunctive morphology on every verb embedded under the set of "subjunctive-selecting" matrices.[2] Since at least 1698, however, it has been noted that the indicative sometimes appears in such contexts (Templery 1698), resulting in the type of variability illustrated in (4). Notwithstanding, unambiguous subjunctive morphology is currently quantitatively robust, appearing in a full 77% of verbs embedded under subjunctive-selecting matrices. But closer inspection reveals that its use is actually highly restricted and largely lexically determined. This is because the lexical types with which the subjunctive co-occurs, whether matrix or embedded, are highly restricted. Table 2 shows that a single verb—*falloir* 'must' —accounts for nearly 2/3 of the subjunctive-selecting matrices, and with a rate of 89%, displays a preternaturally high association with subjunctive morphology. This imbalance is compounded by two other verbs, *vouloir* 'want' and *aimer* 'like', which are also frequent and display equally strong associations with the subjunctive. *Falloir, vouloir* and *aimer* together account for nearly 3/4 of all the subjunctive governors in the corpus. All the other matrix verbs are as likely to co-occur with the subjunctive as not (Poplack 1992).

Table 2. *Distribution of frequent matrix verbs according to lexi-cal strength and propensity to select subjunctive morphology*

	Token frequency (N)	Lexical strength (% of all matrix verbs)	% Subjunctive morphology
Falloir	1,669	62	89
Vouloir	273	10	91
Aimer	86	3	67
Total N	**2,694**		

Moreover, though all French verbs are theoretically eligible to take the subjunctive so long as they are embedded under a subjunctive-selecting matrix, resulting in a prescribed lexical schema which is wide open, only four do so with any regularity (Table 3).

Table 3. *Distribution of frequent embedded verbs according to lexical strength and propensity to select subjunctive morphology*

	Token frequency (N)	Lexical strength (% of all embedded verbs)	% Subjunctive morphology
Être	659	24	65
Aller	390	14	87
Avoir	386	14	66
Faire	358	13	86
Total N	**2,694**		

As with the matrix verbs, the individual token frequency of these four embedded verb types is again extremely high, as is their lexical strength: together they represent 65% of all embedded verbs in the corpus. The next most frequently occurring verbs only account for an additional 3%, and there are only three of them (*prendre* 'take', *venir* 'come', *mettre* 'put'). The vast majority of embedded verbs each occurred one or two times, with associated lexical strengths of well under 1%.[3]

Although such overwhelming effects of lexical type are difficult to reconcile with the selection of subjunctive morphology to express modal nuances of doubt, non-assertion and the like, a significant proportion of French grammars has endorsed this position for centuries. The variable rule analysis in Table 4 examines the conditioning of variant choice according to a number of factors which could contribute to a non-factual reading of the utterance, and compares their contribution to choice of the subjunctive with that of factors of a morphosyntactic nature. I then relate these to measures of frequency and ritualization, some of which are analyzed independently. Fully productive use of the subjunctive should be relatively impervious to the dictates of processing, priming, distance or purely morphosyntactic considerations.

(7) Factors considered in the analysis of variant choice in subjunctive-selecting contexts

    Modal:
        Indicators of non-factual modality
        Structure of matrix clause
        "Semantic" class of matrix verb
    Syntactic:
        Overtness of complementizer *que*
        Distance between matrix and embedded verb
    Measures of frequency and ritualization:
        Lexical identity
        Token frequency
        Type frequency
        Conjugation class
        Priming

Table 4 displays the factors selected by the variable rule analysis as statistically significant to the probability that subjunctive morphology will be selected under "subjunctive-selecting" matrices other than *falloir*. As these do not entertain the same overriding lexical associations with the subjunctive, they are more likely to feature productive use. Yet no factors relevant to the putative meaning of the subjunctive were retained as significant by the stepwise multiple regression procedure incorporated in the variable rule program, indicating that semantic considerations do not play a role. (Selection of the factor incorporating the traditional categorization of matrices into "semantic" classes is an artifact of the inclusion in each of some (relatively) high-frequency verbs with high (or, as in the case of negated verbs of opinion, low) rates of subjunctive). The operative *independent* influences involve priming—the tense of the matrix verb tends to be copied to the embedded verb, processing—presence of the (variably deleted) complementizer *que* favors selection of subjunctive morphology, and a combination of morphological suppletion and high token frequency of the embedded verb. These results are entirely consistent with the strong lexical effects described above.

Table 4. *Variable rule analysis of the contribution of factors selected as significant to the choice of subjunctive morphology in embedded clauses governed by verbs other than* falloir *(from Poplack 1992)*

Overall tendency:	.526
"Semantic" class	
Volitive	.77
Emotive	.66
Opinion	.09
Tense of matrix verb	
Imperfect	.65
Present	.51
Passé composé	.42
Periphrastic Future	.38
Conditional	.25
Presence of *que*	
Overt	.52
Absent	.47
Morphological form/frequency of embedded verb	
Suppletive/frequent	.56
Regular/rare	.36

Summarizing this section, although the token frequency of the standard subjunctive variant is elevated, virtually all its uses are concentrated among a handful of highly favoring matrix verbs collocated with a small cohort of frequent and irregular embedded verbs. Outside of these few contexts, in which its use has become ritualized, selection of the subjunctive is very rare. Thus despite an open prescribed schema (admitting all verbs embedded under the class of subjunctive-selecting matrices), the *observed* lexical strength of this variant is highly restricted. I have also ruled out semanticity as a contributor to variant choice. I therefore categorize it as low to nil in terms of productivity. The French subjunctive clearly exemplifies the Conserving Effect of high token frequency, coupled with very low type frequency. Bybee and Thompson (1997) have explained this by observing, correctly, in my opinion, that the "high-frequency expressions have maintained their traditional (subjunctive) form despite general changes which allow the construction of sentences with indicative forms in comparable, but less frequent, contexts".

6. The future

Consider next the expression of future temporal reference, for which three morphological variants have been competing since the thirteenth century: the periphrastic (PF), inflected (IF) and futurate present (P) forms, illustrated in (8a–c).

(8) a. Bien *demain*, tu *vas aller* (PF) au Bingo, tu *vas gagner* (PF). (065/2301)
   '*Tomorrow* you'*re going* to go to Bingo and you'*re going to win*.'
   b. J'ai dit, "Laisse faire, on *ira* (IF) à messe *demain* matin". (070/686)
   'I said, "Forget it, we'*ll go* to Mass tomorrow morning".'
   c. Il dit, "J'y *vas* (P) *demain* matin chez vous". (119/861)
   'He says, "I'*m going* to your house *tomorrow*".'

As in the case of the subjunctive, variants are generally claimed to be chosen according to distinctions in the way the speaker envisages the future eventuality. Typically, however, there is little consensus as to what those distinctions are nor which variants are capable of expressing them. From 1753 to 1935 grammarians were virtually unanimous in ascribing to the periphrastic form a reading of proximity (belied by the usage examples in (7)); subsequently the epistemic readings cited in Section 2 above gain favor. Aside from these semantic associations, the prescribed lexical schema for the future variants is totally open: each is (theoretically) equally felicitous with any verb in the language. Nonetheless, Table 5 shows that variant distribution is once again highly skewed: The periphrastic form features the highest token frequency by far, accounting by itself for nearly 3/4 of all future temporal reference expression. The inflected form (traditionally considered the default variant) appears from Table 6 to occur no more than 20% of the time; as we shall see below, it is in fact a good deal less frequent than this, at least in productive uses.

Table 5. *Distribution of major variant expressions of future temporal reference*

	%	N
Periphrastic future	73	2,627
Inflected future	20	725
Futurate present	7	242
Total		3,594

I again investigate the conditioning of variant occurrence, using factors meant, as previously, to capture lexico-semantic and morphosyntactic properties of the contexts in which they appear. These are listed in (9).

(9) Factors considered in the analysis of variant choice in future temporal reference
     contexts

Modal:
   Contingency
   Temporal distance
   Imminence
   Polarity
   Stativity
   Person and number of subject

Discourse:
   Adverbial specification

Measures of frequency and ritualization:
   Lexical identity
   Token frequency
   Type frequency
   Conjugation class
   Priming

Table 6 displays the results of a variable rule analysis of the contribution of the
above factors to the choice of the inflected future. Only three of these factors con-

Table 6. *Variable rule analysis of the contribution
of factors selected as significant to the choice of
inflected (IF) morphology in future temporal reference contexts* (from Poplack and Turpin 1999)

	IF
Overall tendency:	.145
Total N (/variant)	725
Type of adverbial specification	
Non-specific	.85
No adverbial	.47
Specific	.37
Grammatical person	
Formal *vous*	.81
Other	.49
Polarity	
Negative	.99
Affirmative	.36

tribute statistically significant effects, and as in the case of the subjunctive, none is relevant to the meanings generally ascribed to this variant.

These include a functional effect of adverbial specification, promoting the inflected variant in the context of a non-specific time adverbial, as in (10), thereby avoiding the habitual reading that would result from use of the futurate present.

(10) Tôt ou tard il*s reviendront* (IF). (023/659)
'Sooner or later they'*ll come back.*'

A second factor, meant to test the purported association of the periphrastic variant with the more "subjective" 1st person subjects, shows instead that the inflected future is favored with the (rarely used) formal pronoun of address *vous*. This is consistent with the strong association of this variant with frozen and formulaic expressions, such as those in (11).

(11) a. Dieu a toujours dit, 'Aide-toi et le ciel t'*aidera* (IF).' (113/855)
'God has always said, "Heaven helps those who help themselves".'
b. C'est comme qu'ils disent, hein? 'Qui a bu *boira* (IF).' (101/1315)
'It's like they say, eh? "A leopard can't change its spots".'

But by far the greatest effect on variant choice is contributed by negation of the future eventuality. The inflected future is overwhelmingly preferred (and the other variants correspondingly eschewed) in negative contexts, as in (12).

(12) Dire que dans quatre cents ans d'ici il *va avoir* (PF) encore des Asselin, puis ils *vont* encore *parler* (PF) français. Qu'ils *parleront* (IF) *pas* l'anglais. (004/3611)
'To think that 400 years from now, there *are* still *going to be* Asselins, and they'*re* still *going to speak* French. That they *won't speak* English.'

This spectacular contribution of negation to the selection of the inflected variant has been amply attested in empirical analyses of usage (e.g., Lesage 1991; Sundell 1991), especially oral (e.g., Chevalier 1994; Deshaies and Laforge 1981, Emirkanian and Sankoff 1985; Lorenz 1989; Zimmer 1994). It remains largely unacknowledged in other contemporary studies of French (with the notable exceptions of Franckel 1984 and Vet 1993). Nor was the negative effect noted in a single one of the 130 prescriptive and descriptive grammars of French dating from the 1600s to the present that we have consulted (Poplack *et al.* in preparation). It comes as no surprise that the retention of the inflected future in this context has as yet received no convincing explanation. Whatever the reason, negative contexts are now the only loci in which the inflected future variant is used productively in spoken Canadian French.

What of the lexical effect? Given that the same frequent, morphologically irregular verbs that retained the subjunctive also have irregular inflected futures (*serai* < *être, irai* < *aller, aurai* < *avoir, ferai* < *faire*), they should exert a conserving effect here as well. But when the effect of negation is factored out, as in the middle portion of Figure 1 (Section 8), no association between lexical form and variant choice can be detected. On the contrary, all verbs, when negated, are overwhelmingly conjugated with the inflected variant, regardless of lexical type. Verbs in the affirmative, on the other hand, occur with it only rarely, again regardless of token or type frequency, conjugation class or purely lexical considerations. The only exception involves the few uses that are formal in nature or entrenched in conventionalized expressions. When these are removed from the data, truly productive uses of the inflected form (as in 8b) fall to fewer than 6% of the data. Even these are slowly receding, since they are preferred by speakers over 70 (Poplack and Turpin 1999).

Summarizing, the prescribed lexical schema for the inflected future is wide open, since there are no restrictions on the lexical items with which it can co-occur. Examination of usage confirms that variant selection is indifferent to token frequency, lexical identity, lexical strength, conjugation class or any other property relating to the verb. Nonetheless, its observed schema is highly restricted—selection of the inflected variant is basically limited to negative and some formulaic contexts, which themselves account for only 10% of the future temporal reference data. This explains the very low overall token frequency of this variant. Its restricted productivity is corroborated by the results of the multivariate analysis (Table 6), which reveals that the choice between competing variants is not made to effect the semantic tasks usually ascribed to it. Retention of the inflected future does not appear to be motivated by operation of the frequency effects predicted by the network model.

7. The conditional

The protasis of hypothetical *si*- complexes represents another locus of long-term variability. The requirement that the standard imperfect (or pluperfect) indicative be employed in this context is often flouted in favor of the non-standard conditional, as in (6). This usage, first recorded by grammarians in 1625 (when the conditional was last considered to "go well" with *si* [Maupas 1625]), has continued to flourish: its token frequency now exceeds that of the standard imperfect in Ottawa-Hull French, as can be seen in Table 7.

What are the factors that encourage retention of the imperfect? Unlike the other two domains of the irrealis system, where form-function asymmetry has been

Table 7. *Distribution of variants in the protases of hypothetical si complexes*

	%	N
Conditional	53	766
Imperfect	47	687
Total		1,453

persistently—if controversially—ascribed to modal or semantic differences, no such explanation has ever been offered for the choice between imperfect and conditional in the protasis. Nonetheless, drawing on observations of actual usage, LeBlanc (1999) and LeBlanc and Poplack (1999a,b) examined the conditional complexes according to traditional (Latin) semantic classifications invoking the likelihood that the condition in the apodosis would be realized. We distinguished possible or potential conditions, as in (13), from impossible or counterfactual ones, as in (14). Variable rule analysis compares, as previously, their contributions to variant choice with those of factors of a syntactic nature, which can then be related to the effects of frequency and ritualization. These are listed in (15).

(13) Si votre père *serait* (COND) mort puis la petite vous *dirait* (COND) quelque chose comme ça, que c'est vous *feriez*? (018/486)
    'If your father *would be* dead and the kid *would tell* you something like that, what *would* you *do*?'

(14) Si j'*avais* (IMP) des jeunes puis *fallait* (IMP) je travaille là, je pense que ça l'*arriverait*. (114/1334)
    'If I *had* youngsters and I *had* to work, I think that that *would happen*.'

Aside from a priming effect, whereby the tense/mood of one verb is copied to successive verbs in coordinate protases, exemplified in (6) above, Table 8 (p. 420) shows that *none* of the factors hypothesized to play a role in the retention of the imperfect was selected as significant by the stepwise multiple regression procedure. The one notable exception, in striking contrast to the behavior of the subjunctive and the inflected future variants, as well as to prescribed usage, involves the semantic value of the condition. If the realization of the condition is viewed as possible, as in (13), the conditional is favored in the protasis; if it is viewed as counterfactual, as in (14), the imperfect is more likely. This effect, a replica of that operating in Latin, has not been attested in prescriptive or descriptive grammars of French.

(15) Factors considered in the analysis of variant choice in the protases of conditional *si* complexes.

Modal:
Semantic reading
Polarity of protasis and apodosis
Person of subject (protasis)

Syntactic:
Embedding of conditional complex
Linear order of protasis and apodosis
Distance between protasis and apodosis

Measures of frequency and ritualization:
Lexical identity
Token frequency
Type frequency
Conjugation class
Priming

Table 8. *Variable rule analysis of the contribution of factors selected as significant to the choice of IMPERFECT morphology in the protases of si complexes (from Leblanc 1999)*

Overall tendency:	.473	
Total N:	1,406	
Semantic reading:		N
Counterfactual	.55	379
Potential	.43	361

Most cases of linguistic variability result in neutralization of semantic distinctions in well-defined discourse contexts. Conditional complexes represent one of the comparatively rare cases where inherent variability *introduces* a semantic distinction (detailed in Poplack and LeBlanc 1999a,b). This extends speakers' highly productive usage of conditional morphology in its exponentially more frequent main-clause uses so as to align form with function in protases of conditional *si* complexes as well.

What of the lexical effect? The disparities in distribution of lexical types familiar from the other variables are equally operative in conditional complexes. For the most part they involve the same irregular verbs that we have seen to have played such an important role in choice of the subjunctive, although the suppletive morphology characteristic of the subjunctive and future is not at issue with the imperfect, which derives from an infinitival base (e.g., *étais* < *être, allais* < *aller, avais* < *avoir, faisais* < *faire*). The two lexical types *avoir* 'have' and *être* 'be', for example, constitute a full third of verbs occurring in protases. As with the inflected future, however, neither these, nor a second tier of 10 somewhat less frequent verbs accounting for another third of the data, display any particular association with either of the variant forms. In particular, none of the frequent forms displays a greater propensity to preserve the archaic (in this context) imperfect than its less frequent counterparts. On the contrary, Figure 1 shows that all lexical types feature the same rate of imperfect usage, regardless of token frequency, type frequency or schema strength.

Summarizing this section, despite a restricted variable context involving only protases of conditional complexes, the prescribed lexical schema for the imperfect is again wide open in terms of permissible lexical hosts. And in contrast to the subjunctive and the inflected future, the imperfect does in fact occur freely not only across all lexical items, but also in all contexts constituting its domain; it is the preferred variant in counterfactual conditions. This despite the fact that it is rapidly losing ground in protases. Even its apparently moderate rate in Table 7 is artificially inflated by inclusion in the calculation of all 120 speakers constituting the *Corpus du français parlé à Ottawa-Hull*. When speakers are distinguished according to age (LeBlanc 1999; LeBlanc and Poplack 1999a,b), the variants are seen to be involved in vigorous change in progress, with the imperfect again retained mainly in the speech of those currently aged over 70.

8. Summary of effects

8.1 The effect of token frequency on variant choice

Bybee and Thompson (2000) have suggested that high token frequency leads to two types of outcome: 1) reductive changes including loss of internal structure and semantic bleaching, and 2) conservation of older forms in high-frequency contexts while other forms prevail in comparable, but less frequent contexts. According to these authors, this is because the more frequently a form is used, the more its representation is strengthened, making it easier to access in the same form the next time, and resulting in a "lexically arbitrary residue of formerly productive patterns" (Bybee and Thompson 2000: 384).

Figure 1 summarizes the effects of token frequency, or lexical strength, and lexical identity on choice of subjunctive, inflected future and imperfect morphology in

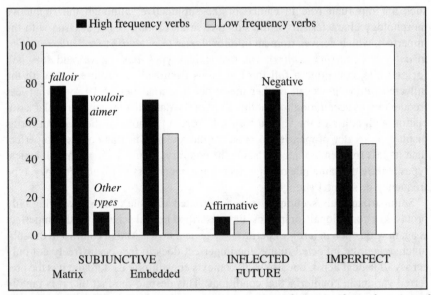

Figure 1. *The effect of token frequency on variant choice in three domains of French grammar. Vertical axis measures percentage of subjunctive, inflected future or imperfect variants, with frequency class indicated by shading*

each of their respective variable contexts. As noted earlier, high token frequency clearly plays a major role in the retention of the French subjunctive in the expected direction, as does lexical identity, since the subjunctive prevails specifically with three frequent matrix and four frequent embedded verbs; it is far rarer in the context of less frequent verbs. In neither case is it selected to perform any particular semantic work, consistent with the reductive bleaching effects also associated with high token frequency. In the case of the inflected future and imperfect variants, however, the very same verbs whose lexical strength contributed so much to the conserving and reduction effects operating on the subjunctive, play no role in variant choice. This is true whether they are considered individually, or aggregated according to frequency, as in Figure 1.

8.2 The relationship between type frequency and productivity

As noted above, type frequency should determine degree of productivity, since the more lexical items co-occur with a pattern or construction, the less likely it will be associated with any one of them in particular (Bybee and Thompson 1997: 7). High type frequency is also said to ensure high token frequency, which in turn increases lexical strength, making the construction more accessible for further uses.

Table 9 depicts the relationship between token frequency, prescribed and observed type frequency and productivity in our data.

Despite restricted domains of application in the case of the subjunctive and the imperfect, every one of the morphological forms studied here has a high prescribed type frequency, or open schema, insofar as it is free to co-occur with any verb in the language. With neither the inflected future nor the conditional, however, is token frequency correspondingly high. Nor does observed type frequency necessarily correlate with prescribed type frequency, as illustrated by the behavior of the subjunctive. Neither the subjunctive nor the inflected future were found to convey, in usage, any of the meanings usually attributed to them. While the inflected future is virtually restricted to negative contexts, it carries no negative connotations outside of that context. The imperfect, on the other hand, does perform a semantic task in protases of hypothetical *si* complexes, albeit one which to my knowledge has never been reported. And while the low productivity of the subjunctive is perhaps predictable from its low type frequency, the same can certainly not be said of the other two variants. Thus, insofar as these data are concerned at least, the relationship among token frequency, type frequency and productivity is not straightforward.

Table 9. *The relationship between token frequency, type frequency and productivity in the French irrealis domain*

Morphological variant:	Subjunctive	Inflected Future	Imperfect
Variable context:	"Subjunctive-selecting matrices	All future temporal reference	Protasis of hypothetical *si*-clause
Prescribed:			
Type frequency	Very high	Very high	Very high
Observed:			
Frequency (token)	Very high	Very low	Low and decreasing
Frequency (type)	Very low	Very high	Very high
Semanticity	–	±	+
Productivity	Low and unchanging	Restricted and decreasing slowly	Restricted and decreasing rapidly

9. Discussion

In this paper I have brought a variationist perspective to bear on the tenets of frequency-based models that type frequency and schema strength result in increased productivity. I have argued that the variationist framework provides a particularly apt test of these claims, for a number of reasons. First the variationist focus on natural speech furnishes a representative data base on unreflecting usage, quantitatively important enough to allow meaningful analysis of a variety of frequency effects. Second, since the same verbs, uttered by the same speakers during the same interactions, figure in each of the analyses, we can control for the (highly correlated) relationship between lexical identity, morphological irregularity and frequency. Regardless of which predominates, its effects should be parallel across all variables.

Three areas of the irrealis domain in which two or more forms compete for the expression of a single function were selected for analysis. Inherent variability has been attested here for centuries, and in each case, token frequencies are currently highly skewed in favor of one of the variants, prompting us to seek the factors responsible for retention of the other(s). This involved operationalizing various proposals for variant choice as factors in a multivariate analysis, including the predictions of frequency-based models, and testing them in usage. The analytical tools of Variation Theory enable us not only to detect frequency and lexical effects, where operative, in a large corpus of conversational data, but also to distinguish their effects from the competing contributions of other (linguistic and social) factors.

In the case of the subjunctive, results show that a frequency-based analysis provides a good account of the facts (despite the existence of a small cohort of highly frequent matrix verbs which *disfavor* the subjunctive). For the other two variables, however, neither type frequency, token frequency nor schema strength is fully predictive of productivity, even using the weaker definition I have proposed here. In the case of the future, the network model would predict that some verbs— high frequency, morphologically irregular or lexically strong—should retain the older inflected variant, even in affirmative contexts. This prediction is not borne out. Instead we find a situation where variant usage has become highly differentiated according to polarity. However, this unexpected distribution, the motivation for which is still unclear, may well be implicated in the lack of frequency effect. The network model requires that the (putative) replacement form have the same meaning or function as the pre-existing form, as with the English past tense forms *-ung* and *-ed*. In the case of the French future, erstwhile variant expressions of a single function have now become functionally differentiated.[4] This entails selection of the form associated with the function, and the magnitude of this effect on the inflected and periphrastic futures may have obliterated any effect due to lexical identity or frequency.

What of the imperfect? As the clearly archaic and receding form in protases of conditional complexes, it too should have been retained on high-frequency verbs, according to the network model. This is not the case. Unlike the future, however, here the moderate semantic distinction fulfilled by the competing variants is compatible, within the variationist model, with the frequentist claim for lexically-based differentiation in rates.[5] Variable rule analysis could thus detect a frequency effect if one were operative. At this stage I can only speculate on why none appears. I noted earlier that the morphology of the imperfect is regular, in contrast to the other two cases, where frequent verbs are suppletive. This suggests that high type frequency may not operate independently of morphological (ir)regularity in the determination of productivity.

Another possibility is that frequency effects are most visible when the original variable context is lexically determined. We have seen that, as a function of the interaction of frequency with morphological effects, the list of subjunctive-selecting matrices is narrowing to a (much) smaller list. Similar results obtain with the ongoing regularization of the auxiliary *être* 'be' to *avoir* 'have' affecting the perfect tenses of the lexically-determined set of "*être*-verbs". Here as well, type frequency is clearly a major determinant of the uneven retention of the receding *être* (Willis 1999, 2000; see also Smith this volume). Of course a frequency-based explanation also accounts nicely for the verbs embedded under subjunctive-selecting matrices, which have no list basis. Nevertheless this is a promising line of study, which we are currently pursuing further. It is hoped that future research taking account of the kinds of complex patterning I have demonstrated to be operating here will help distinguish the preferred domains of application of frequency effects.

Notes

* The work reported here forms part of the project on Variation, Prescription and Praxis: Contact and Evolution of Grammatical Systems, generously funded by the Social Science and Humanities Research Council of Canada. Their support is gratefully acknowledged here. Carmen LeBlanc and Lauren Willis collaborated in constituting the *Historical French Grammars Resource* (Poplack *et al.* in preparation) from which the historical information reported here is drawn.

1. Codes refer to speaker number and line number in the *Corpus du français parlé à Ottawa-Hull* (Poplack 1989). Examples are reproduced verbatim from speaker utterances.

2. Here I report on the set of (approximately 67) verbal matrices which co-occurred at least once with the subjunctive, considering embedded verbs displaying unambiguous subjunctive morphology only. For discussion of subjunctive usage with non-verbal matrices, see Poplack (1997).

3. The same skewed distribution is observed with non-verbal subjunctive-selecting matrices, such as *avant que* 'before', *pour que* 'so that' (Poplack 1997).

4. Whether they are also semantically distinct is debatable; at this stage the inflected future conveys no nuance of negation except when collocated with a negative particle.

5. The contribution of the lexical item combined with the contribution of the meaning would yield the probability of variant usage with each lexical item.

References

Bybee, J. 1985. *Morphology: A Study of the Relation Between Meaning and Form*. Amsterdam and Philadelphia: John Benjamins.

Bybee, J. 1988. "Morphology as lexical organization". In *Theoretical Morphology*, M. Hammond and M. Noonan (eds.). San Diego, CA: Academic Press.

Bybee, J. 1995. "Regular morphology and the lexicon". *Language and Cognitive Processes* 10(5): 425–55.

Bybee, J. 1998. "Irrealis as a grammatical category". *Anthropological Linguistics* 40(2): 257–71.

Bybee, J., and Thompson, S. 2000. "Three frequency effects in syntax". *Berkeley Linguistics Society* 23: 378–88.

Chevalier, G. 1994. "L'emploi des formes du futur dans le parler acadien du Sud-Est du Nouveau-Brunswick". Paper read at Colloque Les Acadiens et leurs langues, at Université de Moncton.

Confais, J.-P. 1995. *Temps Mode Aspect: Les Approches des Morphèmes Verbaux et Leurs Problèmes à L'Exemple du Français et de L'Allemand*. Toulouse: Presses Universitaires du Mirail.

Deshaies, D., and Laforge, E. 1981. "Le futur simple et le futur proche dans le français parlé dans la ville de Québec". *Langues et Linguistique* 7: 23–37.

Emirkanian, L., and Sankoff, D. 1985. "Le futur simple et le futur périphrastique dans le français parlé". In *Les Tendances Dynamiques du Français Parlé à Montréal*, M. Lemieux and H. Cedergren (eds.), 189–204. Québec: Gouvernement du Québec.

Fleischman, S. 1982. *The Future in Thought and Language: Diachronic Evidence from Romance*. Cambridge: Cambridge University Press.

Franckel, J.-J. 1984. "Futur 'simple' et futur 'proche' ". *Le Français dans le Monde* 182: 65–70.

Grevisse, M. 1986. *Le Bon Usage*. 12th edition ed. Paris: Duculot.

Guillaume, P. 1927/1973. "The development of formal elements in the child's speech". In *Studies of Child Language Development*, C.A. Ferguson and D.J. Slobin (eds.), 240–51. New York, NY: Holt, Rienhart and Winston.

Haiman, J. 1994. "Ritualization and the development of language". In *Perspectives on Grammaticalization*, W. Pagliuca (ed.), 3–28. Amsterdam and Philadelphia: John Benjamins.

Hopper, P.J. 1987. "Emergent grammar". *Berkeley Linguistics Society* 13: 139–57.

Labov, W. 1969. "Contraction, deletion, and inherent variability of the English copula". *Language* 45(4): 715–62.

Langacker, R.W. 1987. *Foundations of Cognitive Grammar, Volume 1: Theoretical Prerequisites*. Stanford, CA: Stanford University Press.

Langacker, R.W. 1988. "A usage-based model". In *Topics in Cognitive Linguistics*, B. Rudzka-Ostyn (ed.), 127–61. Amsterdam and Philadelphia: John Benjamins.

LeBlanc, C. 1999. *Du Conditionnel dans les Propositions Hypothéques en si: Cet Intrus*. M.A. thesis, University of Ottawa.

LeBlanc, C.L., and Poplack, S. 1999a. "Conditions sur le conditionnel". Paper read at LSRL, at University of Michigan.

LeBlanc, C.L., and Poplack, S. 1999b. "Prescription vs. praxis: Conditional usage in French hypothetical si-clauses". Paper read at NWAVE 28, at Toronto.

Leeman-Bouix, D. 1994. *Grammaire du Verbe Français: Des Formes au Sens: Modes, Aspects, Temps, Auxiliaires*. Paris: Nathan.

Lesage, R. 1991. "Notes sur l'emploi du présent à valeur de futur dans les quotidiens Québécois". *Revue Québécoise de Linguistique Théorique et Appliquée* 10 (3): 117–31.

Lorenz, B. 1989. *Die Konkurrenz Zwischen dem Futur Simple und dem Futur Périphrastique im Gesprochenen Französisch der Gegenwart* Vol. 2. Münster: Kleinheinrich.

Maupas, C. 1625. *Grammaire et Syntaxe Françcoise*. Rouen: J. Cailloué.

Poplack, S. 1985. "Contrasting patterns of code-switching in two communities". In *Methods V: Papers from the Fifth International Conference on Methods in Dialectology*, H. Warkentyne (ed.), 363–86. Victoria: University of Victoria Press.

Poplack, S. 1988. "Language status and language accommodation along a linguistic border". In *Language Spread and Language Policy: Issues, Implications and Case Studies, GURT 87*, P. Lowenberg (ed.), 90–118. Washington, D.C.: Georgetown University Press.

Poplack, S. 1989. "The care and handling of a megacorpus: The Ottawa-Hull French Project". In *Language Change and Variation*, R. Fasold and D. Schiffrin (eds.), 411–51. Amsterdam and Philadelphia: John Benjamins.

Poplack, S. 1992. "The inherent variability of the French subjunctive". In *Theoretical Studies in Romance Linguistics*, C. Lauefer and T.A. Morgan (eds.), 235–63. Amsterdam and Philadelphia: John Benjamins.

Poplack, S. 1997. "The sociolinguistic dynamics of apparent convergence". In *Towards a Social Science of Language, Volume 2: Social Interaction and Discourse Structures*, G. Guy, C. Feagin, D. Schiffrin and J. Baugh (eds.), 285–309. Amsterdam and Philadelphia: John Benjamins.

Poplack, S., LeBlanc, C., and Willis, L. in preparation. The Historical French Grammars Resource. Manuscript, University of Ottawa.

Poplack, S., and Meechan, M., (eds.) 1998. *Instant Loans, Easy Conditions: The Productivity of Bilingual Borrowing; Special Issue, International Journal of Bilingualism*. Vol. 2 (2). London: Kingston Press.

Poplack, S., Sankoff, D., and Miller, C. 1988. "The social correlates and linguistic processes of lexical borrowing and assimilation". *Linguistics* 26(1): 47–104.

Poplack, S., and Turpin, D. 1999. "Does the FUTUR have a future in (Canadian) French?". *Probus* 11: 133–64.

Rand, D. and Sankoff, D. 1990. GoldVarb. A variable rule application for the Macintosh. Centre de recherches mathématiques, Université de Montréal, Montreal, Canada.

Sankoff, D. 1988a. "Sociolinguistics and syntactic variation". In *Linguistics: The Cambridge Survey*, F.J. Newmeyer (ed.), 140–61. Cambridge: Cambridge University Press.

Sankoff, D. 1988b. "Variable rules". In *Sociolinguistics: An International Handbook of the Science of Language and Society*, U. Ammon, N. Dittmar and K.J. Mattheier (eds.), 140–61. Berlin: Walter de Gruyter.

Sankoff, G., and Labov, W. 1985. "Variation theory". Paper presented at NWAVE 14, at Georgetown University.

Sundell, L.-G. 1991. *Le Temps Futur en Français Moderne*. Uppsala: Textgruppen i Uppsala AB.

Templery, J.D. 1698. *Remarques sur la Langue Françoise*. Paris: Martin et George Jouyenei.

Vet, C. 1993. "Conditions d'emploi et interprétation des temps futurs du français". *Verbum* 4: 71–84.

Willis, L. 1999. "Être ou ne plus être: Auxiliary alternation in Ottawa-Hull French". Paper read at NWAVE 28, at Toronto.

Willis, L. 2000. "Être ou ne plus être: Auxiliary alternation in Ottawa-Hull French". M.A. Thesis, University of Ottawa.

Zimmer, D. 1994. "'Ça va tu marcher, ça marchera tu pas, je le sais pas' (71: 15): Le futur simple et le futur périphrastique dans le français parlé à Montréal". *Langues et Linguistique* 20: 213–26.

Part IV
General

Familiarity, information flow, and linguistic form

GERTRAUD FENK-OCZLON

University of Klagenfurt

1. Introduction

"Geläufigkeit und sprachliche Form" (Familiarity and Linguistic Form) was the general title of my cumulative habilitation thesis. All of the articles forming this thesis (Fenk-Oczlon 1989a, 1989b, 1990a, 1990b, 1991) deal with the influence of *frequency* on *linguistic form* via "intervening variables" of *cognitive representation*, such as familiarity, accessibility, predictability, and (subjective) information. To contribute to a symposium on "Frequency Effects and Emergent Grammar" ten years later gives me the feeling that this approach is still modern and offers considerable potential for many linguistic questions not yet discussed from this point of view. It encourages me and gives me the opportunity to outline the above mentioned papers which are, with only one exception (1989a), published in German, so that their "familiarity" for a predominantly North American audience is not too high.

This outline will be supplemented with some comments on additional literature. I start with theoretical considerations (Section 2) regarding the role of cognitive mechanisms mediating between frequency and linguistic structure and I illustrate the superiority of frequency-based explanations of certain linguistic structures.[1] Subsequent sections deal with empirical results regarding different levels of linguistic description: phonology (Section 3), morphology (Section 4), and syntax (Section 5). Sections 3 and 4 summarize results (from Fenk-Oczlon 1989b and 1990b) regarding the way in which token frequency affects reduction processes. These results confirm Bybee's (1994: 297) general claim "that differential reduction due to frequency is pervasive throughout the forms of a language . . ." And Section 5 reports results (from Fenk-Oczlon 1989a) concerning effects of frequency on word order. The influence of frequency on reduction processes and therefore on the length of linguistic forms as well as its influence on word order, seem to contribute to a relatively constant flow of linguistic information.

2. Frequency, "cognitive costs", and the constant flow of linguistic information

2.1 Frequency and cognitive costs

Frequency of linguistic segments (e.g., syllables, words, phrases . . .) does not exert any *direct* effect on language structure, but affects, first of all, cognitive processes: Higher frequency of use of such a segment results in higher *familiarity* of this segment, while the *cognitive costs* necessary for producing and/or perceiving these segments decrease. Cognitive processes are of course involved in all the processes (programming, articulatory, perceptual) of active and passive use of language. The so-called "speaker", for instance, is always also the "hearer" of his own language production. And the vocabulary of a certain subject is not only reactivated in overt language behavior but also in internal monologues, in the internal testing of different drafts of formulations, and in subvocal memorization. Our working memory's "phonological loop" (Baddeley *et al.* 1998) seems to play a special role when we are learning novel phonological forms of new words.

The concept of familiarity is associated with availability and accessibility (e.g., Ertel 1977). High familiarity, including high familiarity within a certain context, manifests itself in faster and more accurate retrieval processes, in faster and more accurate identification and recognition of stimulus patterns, and in higher speed and accuracy of both psychomotor action and anticipation and prediction. Despite a rather afrequentistic conceptualization of *prototypicality* in Rosch (e.g., 1978) these indications of familiarity can be seen as indications of prototypicality too, and higher frequency can be seen as an underlying factor of prototypicality in three respects (Fenk-Oczlon 1987/1988): Frequency of the features determining family resemblance, relative frequency within a certain context; and "frequency of instantiation" (Barsalou 1985: 631), i.e., the frequency in which subjects "have experienced an entity as a member of a particular category". Nosofsky (1988) provided further evidence for a "frequency-sensitive" model of prototypicality.

Familiarity also results in better recall: Immediate free recall after presentation of a list of bisyllabic words is better if these words are more familiar to the subjects, i.e., if their "subjective information" is lower (Fenk 1977). Quantifications of "familiarity" and "cognitive load" are possible in terms of information theory (cf. Fenk 1986, Fenk and Vanoucek 1992), and these terms ("subjective information" and "redundancy") are again closely related with the "(relative) frequency" of elements and of combinations of elements. Goldinger (1998) mentions, apart from "idiosyn-cratic" context-specific effects investigated in laboratory tests, other effects in word perception which

> arise across virtually all procedures or participants. Examples of such robust effects are word frequency, semantic priming, and benefits of context . . . .word frequency and semantic priming effects should be supported by a groundswell of all stored traces. By experiencing a word in many contexts, a person will come to appreciate its high-fre-quency status, syntactic roles, and associative links to other words. A basic assumption in cognitive psychology is that sources of redundant information may trade-off in per-ception and memory (Neisser 1967). By storing words in variable contexts, a person will amass myriad routes back to those words.   (Goldinger 1998: 268)

Obviously, frequency and familiarity are central factors in cognitive performance. It is no wonder that one can find evidence for direct representations of these vari-ables in our cognition. Our cognitive apparatus and its incidental learning show some special sensitivity to frequency. It constructs automatically, without any spe-cific instruction or demand, a representation of the context-relevant relative frequen-cies of events or elements. The fit between subjective and objective frequency dis-tribution is not really perfect and is characterized by systematic failures (Kahnemann et al. 1982). But the fit is higher than was expected in early calibration studies (for a short overview see Fenk-Oczlon 1991: 365 f).

Certain parameters of event-related potentials (ERPs) in our EEG can be regarded as representations of familiarity too. In conditioning experiments the amplitude of the contingent negative variation (CNV) covaries with the relative frequency in which a first (indicative) stimulus is followed by a second (imperative) stimulus (Walter 1964; see also Rockstroh et al. 1982: 14). It varies, in other words, with the transitional probability between the two stimuli. And late components of evoked potentials do again vary with the predictability of stimuli: In highly unpredictable stimuli the P300 component of the wave pattern—a "wave trough" appearing circa 300 milliseconds after the (onset of the) presentation of the stimulus—is more pro-nounced, corresponding to the lower subjective probability or higher information of the stimulus (Rockstroh et al. 1982: 8) The amplitude of this component is often interpreted as a measure of the amount of attention allocated especially to unex-pected and rather surprising events. The N400 component—a negative component with a latency of about 400 milliseconds—seems to be specific for language pro-cessing and seems to co-vary with "lexical access".[2] In a study by Kutas and Hillard (1980), ERPs were recorded for subjects as they read seven-word sentences, pre-sented one word at time. Some of the sentences were completed with words that were either "physically deviant" (bold-faced) or semantically inappropriate, as in "*He spread the warm bread with socks.*" These two types of deviations were associ-ated with distinctly different ERP components—a late negative wave (N400) for semantic deviations and a late positive complex for "physical deviations" (Kutas and Hillard 1980: 99). Moreover, words which elicit large N400s are more poorly remembered than those with smaller N400s (Neville *et al.* 1986). And in lexical decision experiments low frequency words yielded a larger N400 component than high frequency words (Smith and Hallgren 1987).

But frequency is not only reflected by amplitudes of event-related potentials. Osterhout *et al.* (1997: 143) tested the hypothesis that differences in the latency of negative components of ERPs are attributable to word-class effects against the hypothesis that they "are attributable to quantitative differences in word length and frequency." They concluded from their results "that the latency of these negativities is a function of word frequency and length, rather than word class . . . ." (Osterhout 1997: 163). I would like to add here that one of these two "independent" variables, the length of words, can for its part be described as dependent on the variable "frequency" (see Section 4).

Figure 1 illustrates the indirect connection between frequency and linguistic form. In our diagram (Figure 1) illustrating the indirect influence of token frequency on linguistic form, the mediating instance is called "cognitive costs" in order to indicate that these dependencies are governed by economy principles in cognition and communication. All the findings to be reported in the following sections can be understood from the point of view of such economy principles.

But terms like *cognitive costs, difficulty, ease, familiarity* and *subjective information* are *relative* concepts. They refer to a relation between certain items on the one hand and certain (populations of) subjects on the other hand. A certain item which is unfamiliar (or difficult, or surprising, or informative) for a person X may be just the opposite (easy, expected, redundant) for a person Y or for person X at a later point in time. Such concepts can be operationalized only in psychological investigations with restricted numbers of subjects. If the aim is to investigate linguistic form

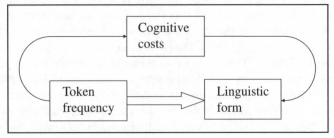

Figure 1. *Relationship between cognitive costs, token frequency, and linguistic form*

as dependent on frequency, we have to neglect these cognitive variables. The only available and quantifiable *independent* variable is frequency (see the short and direct arrow from frequency to linguistic form in Figure 1). But it would be a mistake to exclude the cognitive view from our modeling of the interrelationships and from generating empirical hypotheses about the quality of these interrelationships.

Markedness Theory and Naturalness Theory are also approaches of theoretical linguistics which refer to concepts such as cognitive costs (Mayerthaler 1982) and cognitive ease. As to the extralinguistic foundations of linguistic (e.g., morphological) naturalness, proponents of this approach (Dressler *et al.* 1987) mention (neuro)psychological limitations of perception and limitations of memory. "At this point 'more or less natural' (with respect to universals) corresponds to 'more or less easy' for the human brain" (Dressler *et al.*: 1987: 11f). But for some reason, these authors do not take into account (or even deny) that the *frequency* of a construct is a relevant factor determining its *cognitive costs*.

"Heuristic sources" that are assumed to indicate "naturalness/markedness" are, for example, that the *less marked* is in aphasia normally affected later than the more marked, is earlier acquired in language acquisition, is more frequent in type and token, and is the first element in freezes, i.e., in conventionally ordered pairs (Dressler *et al.* 1987: 11f).

I attempted to turn this line of argumentation upside down and demonstrate that in the "sources of markedness" the term "markedness" can easily be replaced by "frequency". In cases where markedness and frequency diverge, frequency proved to be the better predictor variable, (Fenk-Oczlon 1991). Again, the authors mentioned above did not consider frequency as a relevant factor for those anomalies, which they call "markedness-reversals". But these phenomena are not anomalies and are nothing more than "frequency-reversals" (cf. also Greenberg 1966 and Tiersma 1982).

Frequency is, moreover, a tangible empirical variable whereas markedness is a theoretical construct. So we may say that relatively independent of its degree of markedness, that which is more frequent because of its natural salience and/or cultural importance:

a. is earlier acquired by children
b. is less affected in aphasia
c. is perceived and decoded more easily
d. survives better in neutralization
e. survives better in paradigm regularization
f. is more irregular
g. is encoded in shorter morphological form
h. occupies initial position in freezes

Empirical results regarding the morphological rule (g) and the word order rule (h) are discussed in Sections 4 and 5.

2.2 Frequency and the constant flow of linguistic information

If communication is to be effective, an upper limit on the information transmitted per unit of time, determined by the constraints of cognitive resources, should not be exceeded. On the other hand a very high degree of redundancy would not only waste cognitive capacity, but would also mean an uneconomical expenditure of signs, time, and energy. From this results a lower limit. In an effective and economical communication system, the changes in the flow of information should not be too pronounced and the average level of information transmitted should be adapted to our capacity limits.

"The more frequent, the shorter" is a regularity which contributes to our languages' tendency toward a relatively invariant flow of linguistic information. High frequency means, in terms of information theory, low informational content. An element carrying a small amount of information can be processed within a shorter time. Thus we expected that there would be a proportionality function between the information contained by a word and the length of this word. This hypothesis could be confirmed on the basis of Fucks' (1956) statistical data about relative frequency of various word-lengths in 9 different languages (Fenk and Fenk 1980): The more information the longer and, therefore, a relatively constant flow of linguistic information. A set of crosslinguistic correlations (Fenk and Fenk-Oczlon 1993, Fenk-Oczlon and Fenk 1999) between four variables—size of syllables measured in phonemes, size of words measured in syllables, and size of clauses measured in syllables and in words -computed across 34 languages shows the tendency of all these languages to a restricted variation of the duration of clauses, of the information of clauses, and of the information flow within clauses.

3. Word frequency as a determining factor in phonetic reduction

The observation that frequent words reduce faster than infrequent words has been documented in numerous works (e.g., Bybee 1994, Fidelholtz 1975, Hooper 1976, Mańczak 1980, Phillips 1984, Zipf 1929).

Natural Phonologists (e.g., Donegan and Stampe 1979, Dressler 1984) however argue that phonological lenition or backgrounding processes, such as vowel reduction, lenition and deletion of consonants, monophthongization, and assimilation processes that ease articulation are typical for casual or rapid speech and are phonostylistic variants. Again, frequency arguments are not taken into consideration.

In Fenk-Oczlon (1989b) the attempt was made to show that backgrounding affects frequent words first and that token frequency is a key-factor for backgrounding processes. In casual or rapid speech, reduction is again restricted to the most frequent words. Examples from the literature on lexical diffusion were analyzed in terms of frequency. When for instance analyzing the examples which Kypriotaky (1973) gave for aphaeresis in rapid speech by American students, a clear correspondence between the lexical item's frequency and its "deletion proneness" could be found. In words which belonged to the 1000 most frequent words in English like *about, because, around, suppose, remember, American, enough, before, almost, expect,except, instead, escape, explain* the initial syllable tends to be deleted in rapid or casual speech far more often than in less frequent words. The same holds for Russian. Barinova's (1971) examples for deletion of vowels, consonants or even syllables show that although reduction processes occur first in casual speech, not all items are deletion-prone to the same extent. Again, the most frequent words reduce first. For example, *tebja* [t'ia] you (Acc.), *chodit* [choit] he, she walks, *vidit* [v'iit] he, she sees, *nič ego* [n'čo] nothing, *segodnja* [s'odn] today. All these words belong to the 204 most frequent words in Russian (Josselson 1953).

Other empirical results concerning the role of frequency in phonetic reduction are a by-product of an investigation analyzing the word order in freezes. In Fenk-Oczlon (1989a, see also Section 5) arguments were presented and empirically tested to support the view that the principle "more frequent word before less frequent word" is superordinate to older phonological rules proposed e.g., by Malkiel (1959), Cooper and Ross (1975), and Ross (1980), such as "the first word has fewer syllables than the second word", "the first word has fewer initial consonants and fewer final consonants", "the first word has less obstruent (more sonorant) initial consonants but more obstruent final consonants", and "the first word has shorter vowels".

For Ross (1980) these phonological rules are an expression of the length contrast

Table 1. *The relative frequency of initial consonant clusters (CC, CCC) as dependent on word frequency. (Frequency data for Russian from Josselson 1953: 43–124, and for English from Thondike and Lorge 1944: 267–70)*

Russian		Frequency list 1 (the 204 most frequent words)	Frequency lists 2–5 (the 1993 next frequent words)
	CC	36 words, 17.6 %	555 words, 27.8%
	CCC	2 words, 1%	49 words, 2.5%
English		Frequency class 1–500	Frequency class 500–1000
	CC	37 words, 7.4%	86 words, 17.2%
	CCC	2 words, 0.4 %	6 words, 1.2%

438   GERTRAUD FENK-OCZLON

"short/long". Fewer syllables, shorter vowels, and fewer initial and final consonants all contribute to a shorter word. But the phonological rules can also be an expression of the higher frequency of the first word as compared to the second word. Lesser obstruency of the initial consonant may be associated with frequency as well. Some examples from Fenk-Oczlon (1989a) are figured in Table 1. It illustrates that initial consonant clusters are relatively rare within the class of the most frequent words.

3.1. Frequency and consonant weakening: Why does the first word in freezes, at least in English, tend to have a less obstruent initial consonant?

As far as the lesser obstruency of the initial consonants in the first word is concerned, Ross (1980) admits that he could not find any link to shortness. Again, frequency can be introduced as an explanatory factor. An analysis (Fenk-Oczlon 1989a, 1989b) of the relationship between the degree of obstruency (using Ross's 1980 obstruency scale) and the frequency of initial consonants in English, which I carried out on the basis of frequency data from Thorndike and Lorge, gave the following results (1989a: 524): If we take all the words that begin with one of the glides [y], [w], [h] as our basis for 100%, then their share in the highest frequency grouping of Thorndike and Lorge—'AA' (100 or more per million)—is 11.5% (see Table 2) For the words beginning with a liquid, a nasal, or a fricative, the percentages calculated in the same way are noticeably lower, namely 6.3% (=5.5% for liquids, 6.5 % for nasals, and 6.6% for fricatives; within the fricatives, [θ] and [ð] are conspicuous by their percentage of 15.5%). Of the words that begin with a stop, that is, with the most obstruent sound, only 4.5% are to be found in the highest frequency stage. Thus, in the highest frequency class the frequency distribution of initial consonants (Table 2) differs considerably from the overall distribution: In the class AA the share of obstruents is much lower and the share of non-obstruents much higher than in the overall distribution.

Table 2. *The percentage of words beginning with glides, liquids, nasals, fricatives and stops in the highest frequency grouping of Thorndike and Lorge - 'AA' (Percentage which occurs 100 or more times per million).*

For words beginning with:	
glides	11.5% (16.7 % for [y] 10.7% for [w] and 7.1 % for [h])
liquids	5.5%
nasals	6.5%
fricatives	6.6% (but: [θ] and [ð] 15.5%)
stops	4.5%

Table 3. *The distribution of weak initial conso-*
nants in the two highest frequency classes (from
Fenk-Oczlon 1989b, slightly modified)

Initial consonant	Frequency class 1–500	Frequency class 500–1000
[y]	1.4%	0.8%
[w]	5.0%	3.0%
[h]	7.4%	3.4%
[θ]	4.0%	1.4%
[ð]	2.6%	0.5%

And if one looks at the 1000 most frequent words in English, it can be seen in Table 3 that the share of the weak initial consonants [y], [w], [h], [θ], [ð] drastically decreases from the frequency class 1–500 to the frequency class 500–1000 in Thorndike and Lorge.

There is a clear correspondence between weak initial consonants and frequency in English: the more frequent a word, the weaker its initial consonant. Bybee (1994) argued that theories of weakening should include among the language-specific phonetic factors the distribution of consonants in frequent versus infrequent words.

It might also be interesting that the number of words beginning with a vowel decreases within the 1000 most frequent words in English (1–500 = 16.8%; 500–1000 = 13.2%). It is at least conceiveable that the words start with a vowel because formerly initial consonants have already been deleted. Similarly, in modern English, the deletion of /y/, /w/, /ð/ is observed in words like *yesterday, woman, wood, the, them* . . . (cf. Hughes and Trudgill 1979, cited in Alexander 1988)

It is striking that initial [ð], which is weaker than [θ], appears only in extremely frequent pronominal words such as *they, the, them, their, that, this, these, then etc.* despite the fact that these words had a former initial [θ] (Jespersen 1933: 550).

In some Austrian dialects weakening of initial /s/ to /h/ can be observed. Although the process is not very productive, again it is observed only in high frequency words such as *san* (*sind*) to [*han*] : [*Mir han gwen*] *wir sind gewesen* ("we have been").

4. Frequency and the length of forms: Is the length of morphological forms motivated by economy or iconicity?

In Natural Morphology it is explicitly stated that frequency is only an epiphenomenon of "semantic markedness", i.e., less semantically marked units are more frequent, but it does not have any explanatory power concerning the length of morphological forms (Mayerthaler 1981). The decisive factor for the length of morphological forms is "semantic markedness". The "more semantically marked" a form, the longer.

Haiman (1985: 150) however feels "... from even the briefest consideration ... that morphological complexity is not only an iconic measure of semantic complexity, but an economically motivated measure of pragmatic familiarity." Based on the economy principle, frequently used words should be shorter, and less used forms longer.

4.1 Length of aspect forms in Russian

In order to shed more light on the issue of whether the length of words is motivated by economy or iconicity, an attempt was made to determine which of the two relevant dimensions—*semantic markedness* versus *usage frequency*- is the more capable predictor of the length of aspectual forms and case forms in Russian (Fenk-Oczlon 1990). For this purpose, 67 Russian aspectual pairs were first characterized in terms of their frequency (frequency data from Šteinfeld and Zasorina, cited in Breu, 1980) and then for word length based on these findings. In 50 out of the 67 aspectual pairs the more frequent partner, perfective or imperfective, was also the shorter one. In six cases the inverse relationship held, in eleven cases no decision could be made. In (1) are some examples (from Fenk-Oczlon 1990b: 58f.).

(1) Perfective shorter

Imperfective	Perfective	Gloss
a. davat'	dat'	'give'
b. načinat'	načat'	'begin'
c. pokupat'	kupit'	'buy'
d. ložit'sja	leč'	'lay down'
e. stanovit'sja	stat'	'become'
f. sadit'sja	sest'	'sit down'

(2) Imperfective shorter

Imperfective	Perfective	Gloss
a. moč'	smoč'	'can'
b. igrat'	sigrat'	'play'
c. dumat'	podumat'	'think'
d. slušat'	poslušat'	'listen'
e. starat'sja	postarat'sja	'try'
f. videt'	uvidet'	'see'

In (1) the perfective form is more frequent, in (2) the imperfective form. In all these examples the more frequent form is also the shorter one. In the examples (d)–(f) in (1) the more frequent partner does not even show the reflexive affix -*sja*. This reminds us of Haiman's (1983: 804) postulate that the more predicted reflexive tends to be reduced: e.g., Russian sebja > -sja. In our examples this could mean that the most predictable suffix even has zero expression. The historical data show that, for instance, the verb *sedati—sesti*, "sit down", did not have the reflexive affix on either aspect in the seventeenth century (time of the Smuta, Mayo 1985), but developed only in the less frequent imperfective.

In addition, the often stated correspondence between irregularity and frequency can be documented in our examples. In 32 pairs out of our 67 aspectual pairs, one aspect partner belonged to an unproductive verb class and this was, in 30 of the 32 pairs, the more frequent one. Only in two cases does the opposite hold. Lack of productivity of flectional types is, according to Isačenko (1968: 25), closely connected to irregularity and high frequency. Thus, the unproductive verb classes in Russian seem to be comparable with the Strong Verbs in English or German.

Markedness theory has many more problems with defining which aspect should be shorter. According to e.g., Jacobson (1939/1971) and Maslov (1958), the perfective is the marked aspect and the imperfective the unmarked aspect. According to the principle of iconicity the perfective should therefore be morphologically more complex. As we have seen, this does not hold. "Languages do not show one aspect as clearly unmarked and the other marked . . ." (Bybee 1985: 147). The more a grammatical category is bound to a word in terms of meaning components, the more difficult it is to determine universal markedness weights. (cf. also Tiersma 1982) The use of a certain aspect depends to a great extent on the meaning of the verb. The more dynamic a verb, the more it tends to be used in the perfective aspect (Breu 1980). And the more frequently it is used, the more likely it is to be shorter. Semantic unmarkedness and high frequency usually will converge. But when they diverge, frequency is the factor determining the length of forms. Frequency also seems to be a better predictor of the length of caseforms than universal markedness assignments. The more frequent a case in a particular language, the more it tends toward zero coding.

4.2 The Russian genitive plural

It is often claimed, for instance by Greenberg (1966), that direct cases (nominative, accusative) have, as compared to oblique cases, zero expression. This suggests "that direct cases comprise an unmarked category" (38). Similarily Haiman states: "In no language will the morphological bulk of a direct case affix *exceed* that of the oblique case affixes, as a general rule. There will be languages, however, in which the morphological bulk of oblique case affixes exceeds that of direct case affixes" (Haiman 1985: 137).

An exception to this general rule is the Russian genitive plural of the feminine and neuter, which has zero expression:

Nominative singular	Genitive plural	Gloss
ruka	ruk	'hand'
komnata	komnat	'room'
nedelja	nedel'	'week'
selo	sel	'village'

The zero expression of the genitive plural cannot be explained by its semantic markedness, but could be explained by its high frequency. The Russian genitive plural has many functions and is therefore an extremely frequent case (cf. Šteinfeld 1963). Great length would be uneconomical with signs that are used so frequently. Thus, contraiconic zero-coding of the Russian genitive plural is in any case an economical coding.

One could ask why the masculines have lost the zero-coding they had in Old Russian. A possible *functional* explanation being, there are always competing tendencies in language change, for instance the tendency to be clear and the tendency to be economic. After the emergence of the "genitive/accusative", the animate accusative got a genitive ending, a process which was complete by the end of the 18th century, the zero coding of the genitive plural would have made no distinction between male animate accusative objects in the plural and male animate subjects in the singular. And it was about this time that the marked coding -ov of the genitive plural arose. But the morphologically marked coding of the genitive plural with -ov did not extend to all masculine forms. Again, the exceptions are found in words in which the genitive plural form is used very frequently (Fenk-Oczlon 1990b: 66).

Similar problems of universal markedness assignments become apparent when attempting to explain the different morphological coding of the agent in nominative/accusative vs. ergative languages. In nominative-accusative languages nominative subjects (e.g., agents) are prototypically morphologically unmarked (Givón 1984: 149) while in ergative languages ergative subjects (agents) are prototypically morphologically marked. How could this be explained by semantic markedness? For Mayerthaler (1981) the universally less marked subject is the agent. But why should the agent (subject) be semantically unmarked in nominative-accusative languages and marked in ergative languages? Again it can be seen that universal markedness definitions are quite difficult and frequency arguments can offer a simpler explanation for these facts: the most frequent cases are the morphologically unmarked ones. In nominative-accusative languages the most frequent case is the nominative, because every complete sentence with a nominal subject contains, whether the sentence is transitive or intransitive, a nominative subject. In ergative languages, on the other hand, the absolutive is found in every complete sentence (transitive or intransitive) and is therefore more frequent than the ergative, which occurs only in transitive sentences. Frequency explains why nominative and absolutive case forms tend to be morphologically unmarked and ergative subjects are prototypically morphologically marked.

5. More frequently used units tend to be placed before less frequently used units

There are several mechanisms contributing to a relatively constant flow of linguistic information. For instance, as already mentioned in Section 2, the regularity notion of "the more frequent the shorter". Another mechanism seems to compensate for the successive reduction of information within clauses and sentences. In general, as a sentence continues, the remaining words get more and more predictable—the number of possible and plausible continuations decreases, and so does the (subjective) information. Thus, the first positions of sentences—particularly of isolated sentences and of the first sentence of a longer text—are associated with the lowest predictability or highest information. To place informationally rich elements in a position which is per se characterized by high information, would produce peaks of cognitive overload. An appropriate strategy to avoid such peaks is the tendency to begin a sentence with those words having a higher predictability in this context. For instance with (groups of) words referring to (groups of) words of the preceding sentence, and with terms coding concepts activated by this preceding sentence.

This tendency would explain, among other things, the rule "old before new" or "topic before comment". This doesn't exclude the possibility that there exist tendencies running in opposite direction, such as Givón's principle of the "more important or urgent" to be placed first in the string (cf. Givón 1984, 1990). From the debate (e.g., Chafe 1994, Siewierska 1988) evoked by Givón's suggestion, I would conclude that both tendencies are involved in the programming of speech acts and writing: Cases supporting "old before new" are longer strings of sentences, especially when "programmed" and produced by the very same person. Cases supporting Givón's principle may be impromptu speech, as in a vehement dispute or in rather isolated sentences.

5.1 Word frequency and word order in freezes

In the context of "freezes", the above stated tendency to place informationally poorer elements at the beginning of a string means placing more frequent words before less frequent words (Fenk-Oczlon 1989a). In freezes, i.e., frozen conjoined expressions or binomials, such as *knife and fork*, *peak and valley*, *salt and pepper*, convention lays down the order of the words. Many rules and principles have been suggested to explain the word order in freezes. The suggestions range from those based on the particular language in question to universal principles (e.g., Cooper and Ross 1975, Malkiel 1959, Sobkowiak 1993).

In a former study (Fenk-Oczlon 1989a) arguments were presented to support the view that the rule "more frequent before less frequent" represents a principle that is superordinate to rules previously proposed by others. Cooper and Ross for instance emphazise the importance of a semantic "me first" principle: concepts and qualities that describe the prototypical speaker, or best apply to him, tend to occupy first position in freezes. Freezes, for which no semantic explanations seem to apply, are explained by Cooper and Ross on the basis of phonological constraints. But the phonological rules are, as shown in Section 3, an expression of the higher frequency of the first word as compared to the second. And the prototypical speaker is the statistically normal case, i.e., the more frequent one. (Although it is very interesting to discover the reasons for the greater frequency of particular speaker characteristics, be they of a biological, psychological, or sociocultural nature).

I tested the new rule "more frequent before less frequent" on 400 freezes from English, Russian and German, using statistical data and comparing it with four other rules that have been proposed: "short before long", "the first word has fewer initial consonants than the second", "front vowel before back vowel" , and "semantic principles" (such as the me-first principle). The frequency rule was found to achieve the highest predictive accuracy, with 84% correct predictions. The next best rule (rule "semantic") failed to apply to more than 60% of the freezes, and this despite the fact that this rule actually stood for a whole group of rules ("semantic principles"). The rule "short before long" was even less successful, although it is closely connected with our rule in that the more frequent is mostly encoded as the shortest. The rule "short before long" could not even be applied to 244 freezes since the first word and the second word, measured in terms of the number of syllables were equally long. The rule "front vowel before back vowel" applied to 28% of the freezes, and the rule "the first word has fewer initial consonants than the second" to 17.5%. To explain freezes that represent exceptions to the frequency rule, such as *rise and fall*, *birth and death*, *past and present*, *upstairs and downstairs*, *ascending and descending* recourse was taken primarily to the iconic coding of spatial–temporal relationships.

According to Cooper and Ross words which are "easier to process" tend to occupy the first place in freezes. The results outlined above specify those conditions under which a unit is "more easily processed": it is above all more easily processed if it has—at least in similar contexts—become familiar as a result of frequent use.

6. Conclusion

Relative frequency—overall token frequency as well as relative frequency within specific contexts—has strong effects on cognitive processes which on their part influence diachronic changes such as phonetic reduction and linguistic variables such as length of morphological forms or word order in freezes. These wide ranging effects have in common that they contribute to a rather even distribution of information over the time, i.e., to a relatively constant flow of linguistic information. An upper limit on the fluctuation of the information flow seems to result from cognitive capacity limits (e.g., the psychological present) of language users, and a lower limit from economy principles avoiding too much redundancy in communication. Thus, the effects and regularities described underscore the economy and efficiency of linguistic communication.

Notes

1. These theoretical considerations, including the examples illustrating the explanatory power of frequency arguments, are, with the exception of a paragraph concerning neurophysiological arguments, a synopsis of relevant passages in Fenk-Oczlon (1990a and 1991).
2. In the technical jargon of EEG-studies the "wave crests" appearing in EEG-recordings are referred to as "negative components", and the "wave troughs" as "positive components".

References

Alexander, J. D. 1988. "Aphesis in English". *Word* 39: 29–65.
Baddeley, A., Gathercole, S. and Papagno, C. 1998. "The phonological loop as a language learning device". *Psychological Review* 105(1): 158–73.
Barinova, G. A. 1971. "Redukcija vypadenie intervokal'nych soglasnych v razgovornoj reči". In *Fonologič eskie podsistemy*, S. S. Vygotskij *et al.* (eds.), 117–27. Moskau: Nauka.
Barsalou, L. W. 1985. "Ideals, central tendency, and frequency of instantiations as determinants of graded structure in categories". *Journal of Experimental Psychology: Learning, Memory, and Cognition* 11: 654–92.
Breu, W. 1980. *Semantische Untersuchungen zum Verbalaspekt im Russischen*. München: Sagner.
Bybee, J. L. 1985. *Morphology*. Amsterdam/Philadelphia: John Benjamins.
Bybee, J. L.1994. "A view of phonology from a cognitive and functional perspective". *Cognitive Linguistics* 5(4): 285–305.
Chafe, W. (1994). *Discourse, Consciousness, and Time*. Chicago/London: University of Chicago Press.
Cooper, W. and Ross, J. R. 1975. "World order". In *Papers from the Parasession on Functionalism*, R. E. Grossman, *et al.* (eds.), 11–63. Chicago: Chicago Linguistic Society.

446   GERTRAUD FENK-OCZLON

Donegan, P. and Stampe, D. 1979. "The study of Natural Phonology". In *Current Approaches to Phonological Theory*, D. Dinnsen (ed.), 126–73. Bloomington: Indiana University Press.

Dressler, W. U. 1984. "Explaining Natural Phonology". *Phonology Yearbook* 1: 29–50.

Dressler, W. U., Mayerthaler, W., Panagl, O. and Wurzel W. U. 1987. *Leitmotifs in Natural Morphology*. Amsterdam/Philadelphia: John Benjamins.

Ertel, S. 1977. "Where do the subjects of the sentences come from?". In *Sentence Production Developments in Research and Theory*, S. Rosenberg (ed.), 141–68. Hillsdale, N.J.: Lawrence Erlbaum.

Fenk, A. 1977. "Zum Einfluß von Sinnesmodalität und Informationsgehalt von Zeichen auf den Ablauf kognitiver Prozesse". In *Bericht über den 30. Kongreß der DGfP in Regensburg 1976*, W. H. Tack (ed.), 114–16. Göttingen: Hogrefe.

Fenk, A. 1986. "Informationale Beschränkungen der Wissenserweiterung". *Zeitschrift für experimentelle und angewandte Psychologie*, 32(2): 208–53.

Fenk, A. and Fenk, G. 1980. "Konstanz im Kurzzeitgedächtnis—Konstanz im spachlichen Informationsfluß?". *Zeitschrift für experimentelle und angewandte Psychologie* 27: 400–14.

Fenk, A. and Fenk-Oczlon, G. 1993. "Menzerath's law and the constant flow of linguistic information". In *Contributions to Quantitative Linguistics*, R. Köhler and B. B. Rieger (eds.), 11–31. Dordrecht: Kluwer Academic Publishers.

Fenk, A. and Vanoucek, J. 1992. "Zur Messung prognostischer Leistung". *Zeitschrift für experimentelle und angewandte. Psychologie* 39(1): 18–55.

Fenk-Oczlon, G. 1987/1988. "Prototypentheorie und Frequenz". *Klagenfurter Beiträge zur Sprachwissenschaft*, 13/14: 138–50.

Fenk-Oczlon, G. 1989a. "Word frequency and word order in freezes". *Linguistics* 27: 517–56.

Fenk-Oczlon, G. 1989b. "Geläufigkeit als Determinante von phonologischen Backgrounding-Prozessen". *Papiere zur Linguistik* 40: 91–103.

Fenk-Oczlon, G. 1990a. "Ökonomieprinzipien in Kognition und Kommunikation". In *Spielarten der Natürlichkeit—Spielarten der Ökonomie*, N. Boretzky, W. Enninger, T. Stolz (eds.), 37–50. Bochum: Brockmayer.

Fenk-Oczlon, G. 1990b. "Ikonismus versus Ökonomieprinzip. Am Beispiel russischer Aspekt- und Kasusbildungen". *Papiere zur Linguistik* 40: 46–69.

Fenk-Oczlon, G. 1991. "Frequenz und Kognition—Frequenz und Markiertheit". *Folia Linguistica* 25: 361–94.

Fenk-Oczlon, G. and Fenk, A. 1999. "Cognition, quantitative linguistics, and holistic typology". *Linguistic Typology* 3(2): 151–77.

Fidelholtz, J. L.1975. "Word frequency and vowel reduction in English". *Papers of the Chicago Linguistic Society* 11: 200–14.

Fucks, W. 1956. "Die mathematischen Gesetze der Bildung von Sprachelementen aus ihren Bestandteilen". *Nachrichtentechnische Fachberichte* 3: 7–21.

Givón, T. 1984. *Syntax: A Functional-Typological Introduction*. Volume1. Amsterdam/ Philadelphia: John Benjamins.

Givón, T. 1990. *Syntax: A Functional-Typological Introduction.* Volume 2. Amsterdam/ Philadelphia: John Benjamins.

Goldinger, S. D. 1998. "Echoes of echoes? An episodic theory of lexical access". *Psychological Review* 105(2): 251–79.

Greenberg, J. H. 1966. *Language Universals.* The Hague: Mouton.

Haiman, J. 1983. "Iconic and economic motivation". *Language* 59: 781–819.

Haiman, J. 1985. *Natural Syntax: Iconicity and Erosion.* Cambridge: Cambridge University press.

Hooper, J. L. 1976. "Word frequency in lexical diffusion and the source of morphonological change". In *Current Trends in Historical Linguistics,* W. M. Christie Jr. (ed.), 96–105. Amsterdam: North Holland.

Hughes, A. and Trudgill, P. 1979. *English Accents and Dialects.* Baltimore: University Park Press.

Isačenko, A. V. 1968. *Die russische Sprache der Gegenwart. Teil I. Formenlehre.* München: Hueber.

Jakobson, R. 1939/1971. "Zur Struktur des russischen Verbums". In *Roman Jacobson Selected Writings II,* 3–15. The Hague: Mouton.

Jespersen, O. 1933. "Voiced and voiceless fricatives in English". In *Selected Writings of Otto Jespersen,* 346–426. London: G. Allen and Unwin Ltd.

Josselson, H. 1953. *The Russian Word Count.* Detroit: Wayne University Press.

Kahnemann, D., Slovic, P. and Tversky, A. 1982. *Judgement under Uncertainty: Heuristics and Biases.* New York/Cambridge: University Press.

Kutas, M. and Hillyard, S. A. 1980. "Event-related brain potentials to semantically inappropriate and surprisingly large words". *Biological Psychology* 11: 99–116.

Kypriotaki, L. 1973. "Aphaeresis in rapid speech". *American Speech* 45: 69–77.

Malkiel, Y. 1959. "Studies in irreversible binomials". *Lingua* 8: 113–60.

Mańczak, W. 1980. "Frequenz und Sprachwandel". In *Kommunikationstheoretische Grundlagen des Sprachwandels,* H. Lüdtke (ed.), 37–79. Berlin/New York: Walter de Gruyter.

Mandelbrot, B. 1954. "Structure formelle des textes et communication. Deux etudes". *Word* 10: 1–27.

Maslov, J. S. 1958. *Rol' tak nazyvaemoj perfektivacii i imperfektivacii v processe voznikovenija slavjanskogo glagol'nogo vida.* Moskva.

Mayerthaler, W. 1981. *Morphologische Natürlichkeit.* Wiesbaden: Athenaion.

Mayerthaler, W. 1982. "Markiertheit in der Phonologie". In *Silben, Segmente, Akzente,* T. Vennemann (ed.), 205–46. Tübingen: Niemeyer.

Mayo, P. J. 1985. *The Morhology of Aspect in the Seventeenth Century Russian.* Columbus/Ohio: Slavica Publishers.

Neisser, U. 1967. *Cognitive Psychology.* New York: Appleton-Century-Crofts.

Neville, H. J., Kutas, M., Chesney G. and Schmidt, A. L. 1986. "Event-related potentials during initial encoding and recognition memory of congruous and incongruous words". *Journal of Memory and Language* 25: 75–92.

Nosofsky, R. M. 1988. "Similarity, Frequency, and Category Representations". *Journal of Experimental Psychology: Learning, Memory, and Cognition* 14: 54–65.

Osterhout, L. Bersick, M., and McKinnon, R. 1997. "Brain potentials elicited by words: word length and frequency predict the latency of an early negativity". *Biological Psychology* 46: 143–68.

Phillips, B. S. 1984. "Word frequency and the actuation of sound change". *Language* 60: 320–42.

Rockstroh B., Elbert, T., Birbaumer, N. and Lutzenberger, W. 1982. *Slow Brain Potentials and Behavior*. Baltimore and Munich: Urban and Schwarzenberg.

Ross, J. R. 1980. "Ikonismus in der Phraseologie". *Zeitschrift für Semiotik* 2: 39–56.

Rosch, E. H. 1975. "Cognitive representations of semantic categories". *Journal of Experimental Psychology. General* 104: 192–233.

Siewierska, A. 1988. *Word order Rules*. London/New York/Sydney: Croom Helm.

Smith, M. E. and Hallgren, E. 1987. "Event-related brain potentials during lexical decision: Effects of repetition, word frequency, pronounceability, and concreteness". In *Current Trends in Event-Related Potential Research. EEG Suppl. 40*, R. Johnson Jr., J. W. Rohrbaugh and R. Parasuraman (eds.), 417–21. Amsterdam: Elesevier Science Publishers.

Sobkowiak, W. 1993. "Unmarked-before-marked as a freezing principle". *Language and Speech* 36: 393–414.

Šteinfeld, E. 1963. *Russian Word Count*. Tallin.

Thorndike, E. L. and Lorge, I. 1944. *The Teachers Word Book of 30000 Words*. New York: Columbia University.

Tiersma, P. M. 1982. "Local and general Markedness". *Language* 58: 832–49.

Walter, W. G. 1964. "The contingent negative variation. An electrical sign of significance of association in the human brain". *Science* 146: 434.

Zasorina, L. N. 1977. *Častotnyj slovar' russkogo jazyka*. Moskau.

Zipf, G. K. 1929. "Relative frequence as a determinant of phonetic change." *Harvard Studies in Classical Philology* 40: 1–95.

Emergentist approaches to language

BRIAN MACWHINNEY

Carnegie Mellon University

1. Introduction

It is easy to understand why many linguists are becoming attracted to the view of language as an emergent behavior. For over forty years, syntacticians have worked to establish a fixed set of rules that would specify all the grammatical sentences of the language and disallow all the ungrammatical sentences. Similarly, phonologists have been trying to formulate a fixed set of constraints that would permit the possible word formations of each human language and none of the impossible forms. However, neither language nor human behavior has cooperated with these attempts. Grammars keep on leaking, language keeps on changing, and humans keep on varying their behavior. Frustrated by these facts, linguists have begun to question the methodology that commits them to the task of stipulating a fixed set of rules or filters to match a specific set of data. Searching for more dynamic approaches, they have begun to think of language as an emergent behavior.

Some linguists worry that emergentism can distract us from the hard work of linguistic description. It would certainly be a mistake to abandon structured linguistic description without providing a solid mechanistic alternative. Emergentism is fully committed to providing empirically testable, mechanistic descriptions. However, discovering the exact shape of emergent mechanisms is no small task and it would be foolhardy to abandon traditional linguistic description before solid emergentist alternatives have been formulated. We need to understand what emergentism can offer us, while maintaining a certain skepticism regarding its immediate applicability. In order to begin to organize our thinking about emergent processes in language, the first question that we need to ask is "Emergence from what?" In other words, we need to be able to see how linguistic behavior in a target domain emerges from constraints derived from some related external domain. For example, an emergentist account may show how phonological structures emerge from physiological constraints on the vocal tract. This account invokes external determination, since the shape of one level of description is determined by patterns on a different level. Similarly, an emergentist syntactic account may show how variations in word order arise from patterns of morphological marking.

Emergence plays an important role in all of the physical and biological sciences. Consider the formation of the honeycomb. When a bee returns to the hive after collecting pollen, she deposits a drop of wax-coated honey. Initially, each of these honey balls is round and of approximately the same size. As these balls get packed together, they take on the familiar hexagonal shape that we see in the honeycomb. There is no gene in the bee that codes for hexagonality in the honeycomb, nor is there any overt communication regarding the shaping of the cells of the honeycomb. Rather, this form is an emergent consequence of the application of packing rules to a collection of honey balls of roughly the same size, as suggested in Figure 1.

Nature abounds with examples of emergence. The outlines of beaches emerge from interactions between geology and ocean currents. The shapes of crystals emerge from the ways in which atoms pack into sheets. Weather patterns like the Jet Stream or El Niño emerge from interactions between the rotation of the earth, solar radiation, and the shapes of the ocean bodies. Biological patterns emerge in much the same way. For example, the pattern of a leopard's spots is laid down in the first two days of embryonic development by the diffusion of two morphogens across the surface of the embryo. Variations in the patterns of stripes and dots on the skin emerge as consequences of the developing geometry of the embryo. Using a single-parameter reaction-diffusion physical model of a cylindrical embryo of varying sizes, Murray (1988) was able to simulate the emergence of marking patterns on the

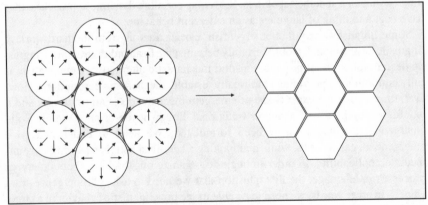

Figure 1. *The emergence of hexagons in a honeycomb from the packing of spheres*

tails of the leopard, cheetah, jaguar, giraffe, zebra, and genet. The only parameter required for these simulations was the shape of the prenatal tail at 40 days. Similarly, Murray could model the shape of spots on the necks of different species of giraffe using what is known about variations in the shape of the embryo at 40 days.

Similar forces determine the emergence of patterns in the brain. For example, Miller *et al.* (1989) have shown that the ocular dominance columns described by Hubel and Weisel (1963) in their Nobel-prize-winning work may emerge as a solution to the competition between projections from the different optic areas during synaptogenesis in striate cortex, as in Figure 2.

Figure 2. *The emergence of ocular dominance columns from Miller et al. (1989)*

Emergentist accounts of brain development provide useful ways of understanding the forces that lead to neuronal plasticity, as well as neuronal commitment. For example, Ramachandran (1995) has shown that many aspects of reorganization depend upon the elimination of redundant connectivity patterns. Moreover, Quartz and Sejnowski (1997) have shown that plasticity may also involve the growth of new patterns of connectivity. On the macro level, recent fMRI work (Booth *et al.* 1999) has shown how children with early brain lesions use a variety of alternative developmental pathways to preserve language functioning.

2. Levels of emergence

The emergentist accounts developed in the current symposium have focused on how frequency determines linguistic structure. In order to better understand the psychological bases of these analyses, we need to conduct a fundamental analysis of the types of emergent processes and the ways in which each is subject to the pressures of frequency, reliability, and other measures of cue validity. To begin this process of analysis, we can distinguish six separate temporal frames or levels for emergence.

a. Evolutionary emergence. The slowest moving emergent processes are those which are encoded in the genes. These processes, which are subject to more variability and competition than is frequently acknowledged, are the result of glacial changes resulting from the pressures of evolutionary biology. We can refer to this type of emergence as "evolutionary emergence". Language is a species-specific ability that depends, in part, on unique genetic patterns that have developed across the last five million years. However, it is unlikely that these emergent patterns directly code specific linguistic structures. Rather, all of these patterns have their effects filtered by the second level of emergence—epigenetic emergence.

b. Epigenetic emergence. Differential expression of embryonic DNA triggers a further set of processes from which the structure of the organism emerges (Gilbert 1994). Some physiological structures are strictly specified by particular genetic loci. For example, the recessive gene for phenylketonuria or PKU begins its expression prenatally by blocking the production of the enzymes that metabolize the amino acid phenylalanine. Although the effects of PKU occur postnatally, the determination of this metabolic defect emerges prenatally in terms of the production of particular enzymes. Other prenatal emergent anatomical structures involve a role for physical forces in the developing embryo. The formation of leopard spots is an example of this type. Epigenetic effects continue after birth, as the processes of gene expression interact with the ongoing physical and neurological changes in the organism. Some of these late-emerging processes may have important implications for the development of language. For example, the myelinization of neurons (Lecours 1975) or the commitment of cerebral areas to stimulus processing (Blakemore and van Sluyters 1974, Julesz and Kovacs 1995) are effects that arise epigenetically.

Emergentist accounts formulated on these first two scales are not fundamentally different from explanations that have figured in nativist theories. However, nativist theories have often failed to view these processes as emergent and have seldom distinguished between evolutionary and epigenetic emergence. By formulating nativist theory in emergentist terms, we gain a richer picture of the actual dynamic processes that shape human development. The next four levels of emergentist accounts also rely heavily on biology as the underpinning for self-organization. However, they allow for the unfolding of biological forces in more flexible and interactive fashions than those envisioned in the first two time scales.

c. Emergence from local maps. Accounts on this level emphasize the ways in which linguistic structures emerge from the local architectures of neural networks. We know that the cells of the cortex are organized into a series of columnar processing units including perhaps 100,000 cells in each unit. Within each processing unit, the organization of information obeys strict map-like patterns. Visual information is organized retinotopically, auditory information tonotopically, and motor information by individual limbs and digits. The formation of these local neural architectures is an emergent phenomenon, determined by processes such as inductance, the preference for short connections, cell differentiation, cell migration, competition for input, and lateral inhibition. Self-organizing feature maps (SOFM) provide a particularly useful way of expressing our current knowledge of this local level of neural structure. Many properties of human language emerge from the ways in which input is processed by local feature maps. Clear examples of this type of emergence include the Pierrehumbert model of phonetic entrenchment (this volume), the Bybee model of morphological entrenchment (this volume), or the various connectionist models of the acquisition of morphology. Models on this level deal with issues such as chunking, dual-processing, gang effects, and exemplar-based processing.

d. Emergence from functional circuits. High-level cognition arises from the interaction of local processing units across long distances in the brain. Cortical processing in local maps is gated and amplified by signals from the thalamus, hypothalamus, hippocampus, amygdala, cerebellum, and basal ganglia. Within the cortex, frontal areas such as the cingulate, the dorso-lateral prefrontal cortex, and Broca's area work to modify the processing of posterior language areas in the temporal and parietal lobes. As patterns are transmitted across longer distances in the brain, temporal constraints start to place limits on information storage and retrieval. In order to deal with these limitations, systems such as the phonological loop (Gathercole and Baddeley 1993) or the output monitor (Shattuck-Hufnagel 1979) use functional neural circuits to maximize performance. Properties of these functional circuits determine many aspects of the shape of human language, particularly on the levels of syntax and discourse. Examples of models based on the operation of these circuits include Baddeley's (1992) articulatory loop, the Just and Carpenter CC-CAPS model of language processing (1992), Anderson's rational model of cognition (1993), or the Competition Model (MacWhinney and Bates 1989).

e. Grounded emergence. Although models based on local maps and functional circuits are well-grounded in neuronal terms, they cannot express the ways in which language functions in a real social context (Goffman 1974, Vygotsky 1962). Nor can they capture effects that are determined by the fact that the speaker has a real body (MacWhinney 1999). The groundings provided by the social context and the body provide two further sources for the emergence of language structure. Social forces and the shape of the ongoing conversation embed language in a framework of givenness, topicality, backgrounding, coreference, and shared knowledge that facilitates successful communication (Givón 1979). Accounts that explore these forces include conversation analysis, discourse analysis, and much of sociolinguistics. At the same time, we use the projection of our own perspectives onto the experiences around us to extract personalized meaning from social interactions (MacWhinney 1999). By taking and shifting perspectives, we can assimilate objects, space, time, causation, and social frames to our own physicalist mental models. Accounts that explore these forces include Cognitive Grammar (Bailey *et al*. 1997) and various new developments in psychology that could be called Embodiment Theory.

f. Diachronic emergence. The changes that languages undergo across centuries can also be viewed in emergentist terms. Some diachronic processes tend to level distinctions and contrasts, others introduce new forms and contrasts (Bybee 1988). Just as erosion and orogeny work together to determine the geologic landscape, forces of leveling and innovation work together to determine the changing linguistic landscape. Among the most important processes are regularization (Bybee 1985), entrenchment (Brooks *et al*. 1999), attraction of new forms to gangs (Hare and Elman 1995), lexical innovation (Clark and Clark 1979), semantic bleaching, and phonological neutralization (Pierrehumbert this volume).

This paper will focus on these last four types of emergence. These are the levels of emergence that have figured most prominently in recent psycholinguistic research and modeling.

3. Emergence from local maps

Connectionist models use nodes, connections, and activation to model the processing of information in local networks. These models come in many types, including Boltzmann machines, back propagation nets, recurrent nets, Hopfield nets, and Kohonen nets (Fausett 1994). Although the bulk of work in the modeling of language processes has used back propagation nets, there are some known limitations to this particular architecture (Grossberg 1987). An interesting alternative to back propagation is the Kohonen network or self-organizing feature map (SOFM) (Miikkulainen 1993).

The most important feature of the self-organizing feature map is its ability to encode lexical items in an emergentist, but still localist fashion. Although the position of a lexical item in a field is determined by a distributed pattern of features in a sparse matrix, these features still reliably activate a consistent node or area of nodes in the map. Figure 3 shows how the semantic fields for a few common nouns become self-organized. In this figure, we see that words that share semantic features are close to each other in the semantic map. For example, the verb *hit* is close to *broke* and the noun *lion* is close to *dog*. On the phonological or lexical map, monosyllables are grouped together on the right and disyllables on the left. This pattern-

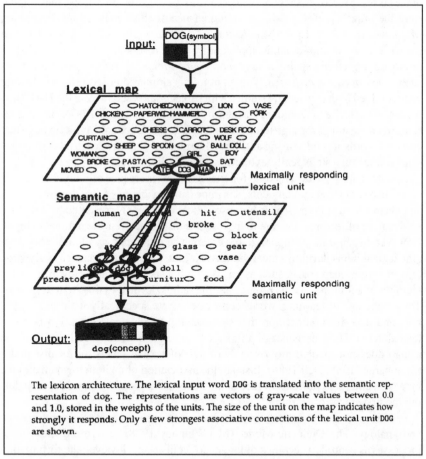

The lexicon architecture. The lexical input word DOG is translated into the semantic representation of dog. The representations are vectors of gray-scale values between 0.0 and 1.0, stored in the weights of the units. The size of the unit on the map indicates how strongly it responds. Only a few strongest associative connections of the lexical unit DOG are shown.

Figure 3. *From Miikulainen (1993), this map illustrates the emergent activation of the phonological form of the word dog on the lexical map and the meaning of dog on the semantic map*

ing is a consequence of the phonological coding chosen for this particular simulation. If another system of phonological features has been used, a different pattern of similarity would have emerged. The important point is that proximity of any two items on the map is determined by the similarity of their featural representations.

Miikkulainen (1993) has shown how a wide range of linguistic phenomena, from polysemy to the parsing of relative clauses, can be explained within the framework of the self-organizing feature map. Feature maps rely on a system of lateral inhibition between nodes that closely mimics actual biological processes found in many areas of the cortex. Moreover, these networks can also be constructed in a way that emphasizes the brain's preference for the maintenance of short connections. Extending Miikkulainen's work, Li and MacWhinney (1999) have shown how these maps can learn the meaning and semantic applicability of the reversive prefixes in English to produce correct forms such as *disassemble* or *unbutton* as well as overgeneralizations such as *unappear* or *disfasten*. The input to this simulation used semantic feature codes derived both from rating studies with subjects and vectors from the HAL (Hyperspace Analogue to Language) database of Burgess and Lund (1997). HAL represents word meanings through multiple lexical co-occurrence constraints in large text corpora. Words are coded using a string of 100 numbers in which each number represents a value on a statistically-extracted semantic dimension.

Feature maps provide a method for encoding the emergence of individual lexical items. In back propagation models, it is impossible to identify a structure that corresponds to a lexical item. This is because lexical items are represented by a distributed pattern of features. Feature maps also use distributed representations as input. However, because they emphasize the emergence of a topology of similarity, specific lexical items develop a clear identity. At first, a word may match a fairly large area in feature map space, such as an area with a six-unit radius. However, as the learning of additional words progresses, the radius devoted to that item decreases. Toward the end of learning, words come to compete specifically with their neighbors and it is this competition that sharpens the topological separation between lexical items. The emergence of a linkage between lexical items and a position on a map does not involve any overt "writing" of lexical labels on localist nodes (Stemberger 1985, Dell 1986). Instead, the association of an item to an area in the map is an emergent process. In fact, some items move around a bit on the map during the first stages of learning.

Feature maps can control the three basic linguistic processes of rote, combination, and analogy. The Dialectic Model (MacWhinney 1978) recognized these three processes as central to accounts of language acquisition. However, the formulation of a neural network model that deals with each of these three processes has proven difficult. First let us consider how feature maps deal with the process of rote learning.

Unlike many other neural network systems, feature maps are capable of "one-shot" associative learning. This means that they can learn a new word on a single trial without unlearning earlier forms. Feature maps share their ability to handle one-shot learning with a few other neural network architectures, such as SDM (Kanerva 1988) and ART (Grossberg 1987). The ability to handle one-shot learning is crucial, because it permits exemplar-based learning. Exemplar-based learning models are superior in various ways to those that do not make a clear encoding of examples (Corrigan 1988, Goldberg 1999, Tomasello 1992). For example, Kruschke's (1992) ALCOVE model of concept learning is grounded on the learning of examples. Taraban and Palacios (1993) have shown how an exemplar-based model is needed to capture the earliest stages of the learning of Russian gender marking or the learning of new forms in a Miniature Linguistic System. Similarly, Matessa and Anderson (in press) have compared ACT-R and the Competition Model. They show that, in miniature linguistic system experiments by McDonald and MacWhinney (1991), as well as in a new experiment designed specifically to compare the two models, ACT-R does a better job of predicting the order of cue acquisition. The reason for the better performance of ACT-R is that it focuses learning on one cue at a time, whereas the Competition Model processes all cues at all times during learning. This cue focusing allows ACT-R to quickly acquire frequent cues and to initially block learning about less frequent cues. In this way, ACT-R does a better job of modeling actual human learning.

The ability to model one-shot learning allows a network to model much of what we have begun to learn about the role of frequency in promoting rote, chunking, and entrenchment. As Bybee, Corbett *et al.* (this volume), Frisch (this volume), Hare (this volume), MacWhinney, Marchman, Pierrehumbert, Plunkett, and many others have argued, high frequency allows forms to become entrenched. However, as Corbett *et al.* (this volume) and Frisch (this volume) have shown, neural network models must assign correct values to the contrasting effects of token frequency, type frequency, construction frequency, and paradigm frequency. In order to model frequency effects on each of these levels, our models have to provide a role for each of these levels of structure. However, these levels themselves should be viewed as emergent. For example, the development of a unique phonology for phrasal chunks such as *I don't know* (Bybee and Scheibman 1999) underscores the importance of mechanisms for acquiring frequent phrasal units.

The second major process invoked by the Dialectic Model (MacWhinney 1978) is combination. One of the simplest types of combination is the attachment of a suffix to a stem to mark a category such as plural or past in English. In recent years, Pinker (1991), Marslen-Wilson (Marslen-Wilson and Tyler 1998), Clahsen (1999), and others have underscored the importance of default patterns in morphology. Attempts to model even this basic level of combination in neural networks have met with mixed results. The problem is that the formulation of a model that includes rote, analogy, and combination in a single architecture requires more complexity than can be found on a local map. We will discuss ways of constructing such an architecture when we examine the joining of local maps into functional neural circuits.

The third major process invoked by the Dialectic Model (MacWhinney 1978) is analogy. Because of the distributed nature of their input representations, feature maps do a good job of modeling analogic processes. Because neighborhood structure is based on featural similarity, feature maps can model the various prototype effects and gang effects that are usually captured by neural network models.

Before leaving the topic of local maps, it is important to mention the potential role for neuronal recruitment and reorganization in emergentist models. Following a suggestion of Miikkulainen (1993), Ping Li and I have been exploring an extension of feature maps based on the notion of map sprouting as a result of competition. The idea is as follows: as the child learns more and more words, the principal lexical feature map starts to become overcrowded. To deal with this competition, words that are close competitors project their competition to a secondary neural area which

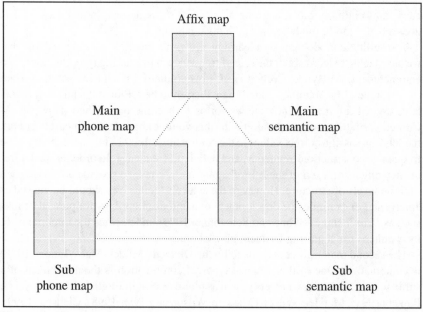

Figure 4. *The emergence of secondary processing areas to resolve cohort competition*

is designed specifically to handle competitions between smaller sets of words. For example, the cohort of words beginning in /kæ/ could project to a single area. These would include *cat, catalog, catastrophe, cab, California, candle* and *cattle*. Although these words would still have a representation on the main feature map, the importance of that representation would diminish over time as the secondary map takes over the competition. All that the main map would continue to process would be the basic onset syllable structure or BOSS (Taft 1981). This same type of recruitment of secondary arenas for competition can occur on both the semantic and phonological level, as illustrated in Figure 4. A mechanism of this sort can help us understand how phonological and semantic categories emerge during the normal course of word learning.

4. Chunking

Neural network models make no claims regarding the shape of phonological and semantic inputs. They assume that the shape of these inputs is determined by perceptual mechanisms that lie outside of the scope of the core simulation. However, changes in the shape of the input can radically alter the outcome of learning in neural networks. One aspect of input representations that needs to be carefully explored is the extent to which speakers process words in terms of phrasal chunks, rather than more analytic morphemes. The tendency of both children and adults to process high frequency phrases as units has been discussed in terms of the process of chunking by researchers such as Bybee, Boyland, Bush, and Scheibman (this volume). Although it is clear that chunking plays a major role in language learning and processing, it is important to clarify several issues that arise in these discussions.

(a) The term "chunk" can refer to unitization in perception, production, or memory. In models such as ACT-R (Anderson 1993) or SOAR (Newell 1990), chunks are the basic units of declarative encodings. However, these models make clear internal distinctions between chunks in perception, production, and memory. When we are operating outside of the explicit framework of these models, it is probably confusing to use a single term for all three levels of unitization. Instead, we can consider using terms such as "Gestalt" or "perceptual chunk" for units in perception and "avalanche" or "motoric chunk" for units in production. The term "Gestalt" is tightly linked to perceptual processes. The term "avalanche" (Grossberg 1978, Gupta and MacWhinney 1997) refers to a series of units that have been chained together for output production. Avalanches are serial strings of behaviors in which the triggering of the beginning of the string leads to the firing of all its component pieces. Thus, the avalanche is used to control production of words or even phrases.

(b) We may believe that chunks arise both through perceptual chunking and ava-
      lanche formation. One fact that argues for this analysis is the observation that
      the exact shape of reductions is often highly lexically specific. For example, in
      the phrase *I don't know*, the deletion of the first flap is specific to this particular
      phrase. Similarly, the reduction of *What's up with you?* to /sʌptʃu/ relies heavily
      on a precise mapping to the original phrasal form. One way of explaining this
      assumes that reductions first arise through simplificatory processes in produc-
      tion, but are then stored by perceptual processes that are unique to the phrasal
      item. The crucial assumption here is that feature maps can use whole perceptual
      chunks as their inputs. This form of processing would be used to account not
      only for phrases such as *I don't know* but also for common nominal phrases or
      constructions of the type that show lexical effects for French liaison (Bybee this
      volume). Neural networks have not yet been used to model these effects.
(c) The reductions that occur in avalanches can have negative perceptual con-
      sequences. For example, Vroomen and de Gelder (1999) have shown that
      phoneme monitoring for initial segments is more difficult in words that have
      been resyllabified in fluent speech. Given this, listeners must develop ways of
      dealing with the problems caused by chunking effects in production. The prob-
      lem is that many phrases appear in both a fluent unitized form and a more ana-
      lytic, less chunked form. This means that the perceptual system needs to be able
      to recognize both forms when required. Recognition of unitized forms is facili-
      tated by the fact that they are typically high in frequency.

5. Emergence from functional circuits

The consolidation of information in chunks in local maps is an important component
of language learning and processing. However, no small set of local maps can process the rich complexity that is contained in even the simplest sentences. In order
to develop more complex neural circuitry, the brain must have ways of connecting
local maps into larger functional circuits. Hebbian learning provides one way of
establishing such connections. For Hebbian learning to work properly between local
maps, it is necessary that the maps be as least partially interconnected. We can refer
to these interconnections between local maps as long distance connections. In
Hebbian learning, long distance connections will be strengthened when the units to
which they are connected fire at the same time. This means that connections between nodes that do not fire together will weaken and disappear over time. This type
of learning works well for the formation of links between feature maps. For example, the /kaet/ node in the phonological map will tend to fire at the same time as the
cat node in the semantic map. This will lead to the strengthening of the connection

between the two nodes on the two maps. The presence of the connection is a given, but its relative strength is emergent. Moreover, there is reason to believe that the connection itself could emerge when needed (Quartz and Sejnowksi 1997). This type of long distance mapping probably involves connections between temporal auditory areas and temporo-parietal semantic areas. When the child comes to linking up words to potential articulations, even more distant connections must be established to frontal areas in motor cortex and Broca's area for speech planning.

5.1 Three models

One example of a model that deals with the formation of these connections between areas is the Gupta and MacWhinney (1997) model of the development of articulatory forms in the child. This model links together the concept of an articulatory plan or "avalanche" (Grossberg 1978) with the notion of a feature map. The architecture of the model is given in Figure 5. In this figure, words are represented as stored

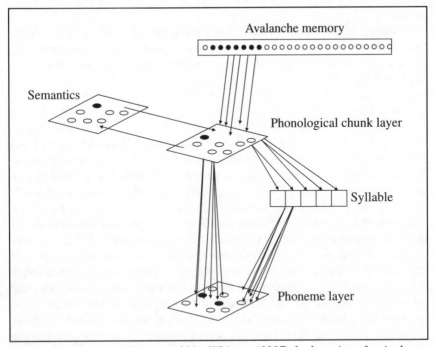

Figure 5. *The model of Gupta and MacWhinney (1997) for learning of articulatory forms*

strings or avalanches. The phonological chunk layer is a feature map with pointers to each individual avalanche. It also maintains connections to the phoneme layer that facilitates the recognition of syllabic templates. As in the model of Figure 3, a layer of semantic connections organizes phonological processing.

A model developed by Plaut and Kello (1999) provides another example of how a language form emerges from connections between processing areas. This model shows how articulatory form emerges from attempts to match input phonology during babbling and the learning of the first words. In this system, a series of six connections between processing areas are used to allow the sounds of words to train the formation of articulations.

A third model (MacWhinney 1999) explains how syntactic processing can be derived from more distant connections between local feature maps. That model uses a core structure in which the semantic and phonological maps of Figure 3 are dependent on a third map of central lexical forms. From these central lexical forms, there are then connections not only to the semantic map, but also to an output phonology map (as in Figure 5) and an input phonology map. In addition, lexical items have connections to phrases or constructions in another map. This model is not yet implemented.

All three of these models link local processing fields into larger functional circuits. As they stand, all three models are preliminary and incomplete. However, they illustrate how complex functional circuits can be built up using local maps as their components.

5.2 Processing effects

Current models of sentence processing focus on the ways in which lexically-based constructions provide cues for role assignments. The assignment of sentence elements to particular grammatical roles is performed through a competitive process based on the relative strength of the cues involved (MacWhinney and Bates 1989). The Competition Model uses various measures of cue reliability to predict cue strength in experiments in which cues are placed in competition. The notion of reliability developed in this work is essentially the conditional probability of an interpretation, given a cue. If the interpretation is always correct when the cue is present, this probability approaches 1.0. For example, in the Italian sentence, "Il spaghetti mangia Giovanni" (The spaghetti eats Giovanni), the noun *spaghetti* competes with the noun *Giovanni* for the role of subject of the verb *mangia*. The cue that favors *spaghetti* is its initial positioning in the NVN order, whereas the cue that favors *Giovanni* is its animacy. In Italian, animacy is a stronger and more reliable cue than word order and so the sentence is given an OVS interpretation. In English, the opposite is true, since word order is more reliable than animacy. Thus, in English, we end up with an implausible interpretation of an event in which some animated spaghetti wants to eat Giovanni.

The basic result of Competition Model work has been that the most reliable cues in a language are also the strongest ones in sentence processing. The relative dominance order of cues varies markedly across languages and is closely tuned to reliability. In addition, cue strengths function additively, so that an array of interacting weak cues can sometimes dominate over one cue with medium validity. However, no combination of weak cues can ever dominate a strong and reliable cue. These patterns have been observed in dozens of studies in children, adults, aphasics, and bilinguals speaking 15 different languages. The view of sentence processing as dependent on cue validity has since been widely supported by other recent work in psycholinguistics (MacDonald 1999, MacDonald *et al*. 1994, Tanenhaus *et al*. 1989, Trueswell and Tanenhaus 1994).

Recent psycholinguistic work has supported the probabilistic and competitive assumptions of the Competition Model; it has also underscored the extent to which syntactic competition emerges directly from individual lexical constructions. For example, MacDonald *et al*. (1994) show how a lexically-based version of the Competition Model can be used to account for the processing of lexical ambiguities, including prepositional phrase attachment, main verb vs. reduced relative competitions, and direct object vs. complement clause ambiguity. Consider the processing of the ambiguity in the garden-path sentence *The horse raced past the barn fell*. Initially, *raced* is interpreted as a main verb in the past tense. However, the suffix *-ed* has a secondary reading as a marker of the past participle. When the verb *fell* is encountered, the interpretation of *raced* as the verb of the main clause encounters competition. To resolve this competition, the past perfect reading of—*ed* is strengthened and a reduced relative interpretation is constructed.

Although reliability is an excellent predictor of eventual sentence interpretation, we now know that the actual on-line processing of syntactic cues is also strongly influenced by the forces of frequency or availability. Listeners come to rely initially on cues that are always present, even if they are not uniformly reliable. For example, in Russian, listeners are willing to wait for the eventual case cue, since it will be reliable when it is encountered (Kempe and MacWhinney 1999). In German, on the other hand, listeners just decide to go with what they have, since no single cue is all that reliable or universally available.

5.3 Frequency effects

The contrast between reliability and frequency effects discussed in the previous section underscores the importance of paying careful attention to the exact shape of frequency effects in sentence processing and language change. Although frequency effects are pervasive throughout language, the targets of these effects need to be carefully specified. Consider these issues:

(a) It is generally accepted that a form becomes stronger when it occurs more frequently. However, for this to work, the system has to detect new instances of a form as related to old instances. This means that the system must perform a similarity match. If a new input closely resembles a previous input, it will activate as the winner its closest match in the map. If the input lies between two currently strong nodes, the system has to be tuned to allow it to emerge as a new center of activation or new lexical item. These effects work in a similar fashion on both segmental and lexical levels. Thus, categorization emerges as a property of the design of neural networks and the way that they process frequency information. This issue arises particularly when the system is attempting to deal with phrasal simplifications such as *supchu* or the reduced form of *I don't know*. If it attempts to map these items onto their component pieces, it may end up misperceiving in other less idiosyncratic cases.

(b) Should our counting of frequency apply to tokens, types, or collocations? Within the context of feature map theory, both types and tokens must be counted. Tokens have their effect through repeated activation of the same type nodes. Types have their effects through neighborhood activation. For example, a given conjugational pattern may be frequent in terms of the types of verbs to which it applies, but not particularly frequent in terms of the actual number of tokens to which it applies. This will occur when the pattern applies to a large number of fairly infrequent stem types. Most neural network models have not yet dealt with frequency effects that are due to constructions. In order to capture such effects, it will be necessary to elaborate the view of these models in terms of functional neural circuits, as discussed earlier.

(c) What is the effect of frequency on pattern productivity? The debate about the status of default inflections as "rules" (Bybee 1995) may reduce to a discussion of the technical parameters that need to be set in a neural network model to model productivity for patterns with a high type applicability.

(d) To what extent can frequency preserve old structures? On the one hand, old structures are preserved against leveling by frequency. On the other hand, the fact that these resistant forms are no longer in accord with new patterns tends to open them to semantic reinterpretation, as in the development of *went* as the past tense of *go*.

(e) What is the effect of transitional probability on fusion, contraction, and affixation? The merger of highly frequent combinations in production leads, over time, to their reinterpretation and acquisition as single forms over time.

(f) What is the effect of frequency on sound change? Sound change has typically been viewed as operating across the board. Flege (in press) has recently shown that sound changes in second language learning also work in this way. However, Phillips (this volume) has shown that sound change affects high frequency items first. What are the mechanisms driving this relation?

(g) What is the effect of frequency on semantic bleaching or other functional changes? According to the Competition Model (MacWhinney 1989, MacWhinney and Pléh 1997), each grammatical device is a coalition of functional motives or pressures that co-exist in a peacefully. While the subject of an English sentence might express definiteness 75% of the time, it might also express perspective 95% of the time. However, if other forces start to tip this balance, we could see a progressive association of subjecthood with definiteness. Over time, subject marking could be identified not as a way of coding perspective, but as a way of coding definiteness. Other examples of reinterpretation include the fusion of *what*, *is*, and *up* to form *sup*. In these cases, as it becomes impossible to extract the original morphemes, the meaning of the merged unit starts to shift. Forms like *goodbye* or even *zounds* represent the end result of this process of reinterpretation of merged forms.

6. Grounding

Local neural maps can account for many fundamental effects in language usage. If we supplement these local mechanisms with functional neural circuits, we can account for still more aspects of parsing, syntax, and language production. Although this neural circuitry provides many of the mechanisms that support cognition and language, a full account must go beyond neurons and circuits. Much of the actual content of cognition is grounded in our bodies and our social lives. Meaning arises from the fact that our minds are embedded in our bodies that experience motion, vision, hearing, and emotions through our sensory organs and muscles. At the same time, we act as social agents who are embedded in ongoing conversations that determine and facilitate the shape of cognition.

MacWhinney (1999) examines the issue of symbol grounding by linking linguistic form to perspective-taking. According to this analysis, when we listen to sentences, we engage in an active process of role-taking by assuming the perspective of the grammatical subject. From this perspective, we begin to interpret the actions, objects, and positions involved in the sentence. Grammatical devices such as relativization, passivization, topicalization, pronominalization, and switch-reference all serve to direct the process of perspective-taking through various perspective shifts. On the lowest level, these processes involved deictic (Ballard, Hayhoe *et al.* 1997) identifications of objects in memory. We process these objects in terms of their physical affordances (Gibson 1977). We use perspective-switching to coordinate multiple perspectives and frames in space and time that are marked through aspectual and spatial language. Perspective also allows us to interpret the causal actions involved in transitive constructions (Hopper and Thompson 1980).

Social perspective-taking allows us to shift between competing social frames (Fauconnier and Turner 1996). In both narrative and conversation, we attempt to coordinate a wide array of referents into a set of coherent perspectives. We then shift back and forth between these perspectives in order to construct social reality. These effects are illustrated in Thompson and Hopper's account (this volume) of the actual usage of transitive markings in conversation, as well as Sheibman's examination (this volume) of perspectival effects on person-marking in conversation.

Functional accounts of perspective-shifting have a variety of antecedents (Chafe 1974, Firbas 1964, Langacker 1995, MacWhinney 1977). However, recent advances in cognitive neuroscience (Kosslyn *et al.* 1995, Rizzolatti *et al.* 1996) are now showing us exactly how perspective-taking is implemented in the brain. As our understanding of these mechanisms grows, we will develop a clearer idea of how language emerges from physical and social perspective-taking.

7. Summary

Our tour of the different levels of emergentist accounts has helped us examine three basic issues:

(a) *Emergence from what*? We have seen that the use of emergentist theories depends very heavily on the temporal level of the processing involved. Some accounts refer to child language development; others refer to language processing; yet other refer to language change. For each of these types of emergence, very different forces are at work.

(b) *Frequency of what*? We have seen that neural networks are able to encode a wide variety of frequency effects. Some of these effects apply to articulations; others apply to lexical items; yet others apply to constructions. These effects include chunking in production, reinterpretation, overgeneralization, and resistance to overgeneralization.

(c) *Integration*. Our models of language usage need to integrate levels, although many phenomena can be addressed on a single level. Integrated models will need to derive frequency effects from the deeper processes of grounding in social relations, perspective-taking, consciousness, and the movements of the human body.

The articulation of emergentist accounts provides us with exciting new ways of linking linguistic theory to the rest of the human sciences.

References

Anderson, J. 1993. *Rules of the Mind*. Hillsdale, NJ: Lawrence Erlbaum Associates.

Baddeley, A. 1992. "Working memory: the interface between memory and cognition". *Journal of Cognitive Neuroscience* 4: 281–8.

Bailey, D., Feldman, J., Narayanan, S. and Lakoff, G. 1997. "Modeling embodied lexical development". *Proceedings of the 19th Meeting of the Cognitive Science Society.*

Ballard, D. H., Hayhoe, M. M., Pook, P. K. and Rao, R. P. 1997. "Deictic codes for the embodiment of cognition". *Behavioral and Brain Sciences* 20: 723–67.

Blakemore, C. and van Sluyters, R. 1974. "Reversal of the physiological effects of monocular deprivation in kittens: further evidence of a sensitive period". Journal of Physiology 237: 195–216.

Booth, J. R., MacWhinney, B., Thulborn, K. L., Sacco, K., Voyvalic, J. and Feldman, H. 1999. "Functional organization of activation patterns in children: whole brain fMRI imaging during three different cognitive tasks". *Progress in Neuropsychopharmocology and Biological Psychiatry* 23: 669–82.

Brooks, P. J., Tomasello, M., Dodson, K. and Lewis, L. B. 1999. "Young children's overgeneralizations with fixed transitivity verbs". *Child Development* 70: 1325–37.

Burgess, C. and Lund, K. 1997. "Modelling parsing constraints with high-dimension context space". *Language and Cognitive Processes* 12: 177–210.

Bybee, J. 1985. *Morphology: a Study of the Relation between Meaning and Form*. Amsterdam: John Benjamins.

Bybee, J. 1995. "Regular morphology and the lexicon". *Language and Cognitive Processes* 10: 425–55.

Bybee, J. and Scheibman, J. 1999. "The effect of usage on degrees of constituency: the reduction of *don't* in English". *Linguistics* 37: 575–96.

Bybee, J. L. 1988. "Semantic substance vs. contrast in the development of grammatical meaning". *Berkeley Linguistics Society* 14: 247–64.

Chafe, W. 1974. "Language and consciousness". *Language* 50: 111–32.

Clahsen, H. 1999. "Lexical entries and rules of language: a multidisciplinary study of German inflection". *Behavioral and Brain Sciences* 22.

Clark, E. V. and Clark, H. H. 1979. "When nouns surface as verbs". *Language* 55: 767–811.

Corrigan, R. 1988. "Who dun it? The influence of actor-patient animacy and type of verb in the making of causal attributions". *Journal of Memory and Language* 27: 447–65.

Dell, G. 1986. "A spreading-activation theory of retrieval in sentence production". *Psychological Review* 93: 283–321.

Fauconnier, G. and Turner, M. 1996. "Blending as a central process of grammar". In *Conceptual Structure, Discourse, and Language*, A. Goldberg (ed.),113–30. Stanford, CA: CSLI.

Fausett, L. 1994. *Fundamentals of Neural Networks*. Englewood Cliffs, NJ: Prentice Hall.

Firbas, J. 1964. "On defining the theme in functional sentence". *Travaux Linguistiques de Prague* 1: 267–80.

Flege, J. E., Frieda, E., Wallay, A. and Randazza, L. 1998. "Lexical factors and segmental accuracy in second-language speech production". *Studies in Second Language Acquisition* 20: 155–87.

Gathercole, V. and Baddeley, A. 1993. *Working Memory and Language*. Hillsdale, NJ: Lawrence Erlbaum.

Gibson, J. J. 1977. "The theory of affordances". In *Perceiving, Acting, and Knowing: Toward an Ecological Psychology*, R. E. Shaw and J. Bransford (eds.). Hillsdale, NJ: Lawrence Erlbaum.

Gilbert, S. F. 1994. *Developmental Biology. 4th edition*. Sunderland, MA: Sinauer.

Givón, T. 1979. "From discourse to syntax: grammar as a processing strategy". In *Syntax and Semantics: Discourse and Syntax*, T. Givón (ed.), 81–114. New York, Academic Press. 12

Goffman, E. 1974. *Frame analysis*. New York: Harper and Row.

Goldberg, A. E. 1999. "The emergence of the semantics of argument structure constructions". In *The Emergence of Language*, B. MacWhinney (ed.), 197–213. Mahwah, NJ: Lawrence Erlbaum.

Grossberg, S. 1978. "A theory of human memory: self-organization and performance of sensory-motor codes, maps, and plans". *Progress in Theoretical Biology* 5: 233–374.

Grossberg, S. 1987. "Competitive learning: From interactive activation to adaptive resonance". *Cognitive Science* 11: 23–63.

Gupta, P. and MacWhinney, B. 1997. "Vocabulary acquisition and verbal short-term memory: Computational and neural bases". *Brain and Language* 59: 267–333.

Hare, M. and Elman, J. L. 1995. "Learning and morphological change". *Cognition* 56: 61–98.

Hopper, P. J. and Thompson, S. A. 1980. "Transitivity in grammar and discourse". *Language* 56: 251–99.

Hubel, D. and Weisel, T. 1963. "Receptive fields of cells in striate cortex of very young, visually inexperienced kittens". *Journal of Neurophysiology* 26: 994–1002.

Julesz, B. and Kovacs, I. eds. 1995. *Maturational Windows and Adult Cortical Plasticity*. New York: Addison-Wesley.

Just, M. and Carpenter, P. 1992. "A capacity theory of comprehension: individual differences in working memory". *Psychological Review* 99: 122–49.

Kanerva, P. 1988. *Sparse Distributed Memory*. Cambridge, MA: MIT Press.

Kempe, V. and MacWhinney, B. 1999. "Processing of morphological and semantic cues in Russian and German". *Language and Cognitive Processes* 14: 129–71.

Kosslyn, S. M., Thompson, W. L., Kim, I. J. and Alpert, N. M. 1995. "Topographical representations of mental images in primary visual cortex". *Nature* 378: 496–8.

Kruschke, J. 1992. "ALCOVE: an exemplar-based connectionist model of category learning". *Psychological Review* 99: 22–44.

Langacker, R. 1995. "Viewing in grammar and cognition". In *Alternative Linguistics: Descriptive and Theoretical Models*, P. W. Davis (ed.), 153–212. Amsterdam: John Benjamins.

Lecours, A. R. 1975. "Myelogenetic correlates of the development of speech and language". In *Foundations of Language Development: a Multidisciplinary Approach*, Volume 1, E. H. Lenneberg and E. Lenneberg (eds.), 121–36. New York: Academic Press.

Li, P. and MacWhinney, B. 1999. "Generalization, representation, and recovery in a self-organizing neural network of language acquisition". In *Proceedings of the 21st Annual Meeting of the Cognitive Science Society*, M. Hahn and S. C. Stoness (eds.), 308–13. Mahwah, NJ: Lawrence Erlbaum.

MacDonald, M. 1999. "Distributional information in language comprehension, production, and acquisition: three puzzles and a moral". In *The Emergence of Language*, B. MacWhinney (ed.), 177–96. Mahwah, NJ: Lawrence Erlbaum.

MacDonald, M. C., Pearlmutter, N. J. and Seidenberg, M. S. 1994. "Lexical nature of syntactic ambiguity resolution". *Psychological Review* 101(4): 676–703.

McDonald, J. L. and MacWhinney, B. 1991. "Levels of learning: a microdevelopmental study of concept formation". *Journal of Memory and Language* 30: 407–30.

MacWhinney, B. 1977. "Starting points." *Language* 53: 152–68.

MacWhinney, B. 1978. "The acquisition of morphophonology." *Monographs of the Society for Research in Child Development* 43(1): 1–123.

MacWhinney, B. 1989. "Competition and lexical categorization". In *Linguistic Categorization*. R. Corrigan, F. Eckman, and M. Noonan (eds.), 195–242. New York: Benjamins.

MacWhinney, B. (ed.). 1999. *The Emergence of Language*. Mahwah, NJ: Lawrence Erlbaum.

MacWhinney, B. 1999. "The emergence of language from embodiment". In *The Emergence of Language*, B. MacWhinney, 213–56. Mahwah, NJ: Lawrence Erlbaum.

MacWhinney, B. and Bates, E. (eds.). 1989. *The Crosslinguistic Study of Sentence Processing*. New York: Cambridge University Press.

MacWhinney, B. and Pléh, C. 1997. "Double agreement: role identification in Hungarian". *Language and Cognitive Processes* 12: 67–102.

Marslen-Wilson, W. and Tyler, L. K. 1998. "Rules, representations, and the English past tense." *Trends in Cognitive Sciences* 2: 428–35.

Matessa, M. and Anderson, J. In press. "Modeling focused learning in role assignment". *Language and Cognitive Processes*.

Miikkulainen, R. 1993. *Subsymbolic Natural Language Processing*. Cambridge, MA: MIT Press.

Miller, K., Keller, J. and Stryker, M. 1989. "Ocular dominance column development: analysis and simulation". *Science* 245: 605–15.

Murray, J. D. 1988. "How the leopard gets its spots". *Scientific American* 258: 80–7.

Newell, A. 1990. *A Unified Theory of Cognition*. Cambridge, MA: Harvard University Press.

Pinker, S. 1991. "Rules of language". *Science* 253: 530–5.

Plaut, D. C. and Kello, C. T. 1999. "The emergence of phonology from the interplay of speech comprehension and production: a distributed connectionist approach". In *The Emergence of Language*, B. MacWhinney, 381–416. Mahwah, NJ: Lawrence Erlbaum.

Quartz, S. R. and Sejnowksi, T. J. 1997. "The neural basis of cognitive development: a constructivist manifesto". *Behavioral and Brain Sciences* 20: 537–96.

Ramachandran, V. S. 1995. "Plasticity in the adult human brain: is there reason for optimism? " In *Maturational Windows and Adult Cortical Plasticity*, B. Julesz and I. Kovacs (eds.), 179–98. New York: Addison-Wesley.

Rizzolatti, G., Fadiga, L., Gallese, V. and Fogassi, L. 1996. "Premotor cortex and the recognition of motor actions". *Cognitive Brain Research* 3: 131–41.

Shattuck-Hufnagel, S. 1979. "Speech errors as evidence for a serial-ordering mechanism in sentence production". In *Sentence Processing: Psycholinguistic Studies Presented to Merrill Garrett*, W. E. Cooper and E. C. T. Walker (eds.). Hillsdale, N. J.: Lawrence Erlbaum.

Stemberger, J. 1985. *The Lexicon in a Model of Language Production*. New York: Garland.

Taft, M. 1981. "Prefix stripping revisited". *Journal of Verbal Learning and Verbal Behavior* 20: 289–97.

Tanenhaus, M., Carlson, G. and Trueswell, J. C. 1989. "The role of thematic structures in interpretation and parsing". In *Parsing and Interpretation*, G. T. M. Altmann (ed.), 211–34. Hove: Lawrence Erlbaum Associates.

Taraban, R. and Palacios, J. M. 1993. "Exemplar models and weighted cue models in category learning". In *Categorization by Humans and Machines*, G. Nakamura, R. Taraban, and D. Medin (eds.). San Diego, Acdemic Press.

Tomasello, M. 1992. *First Verbs: a Case Study of Early Grammatical Development*. Cambridge: Cambridge University Press.

Trueswell, J. C. and Tanenhaus, M. K. 1994. "Toward a lexicalist framework for constraint-based syntactic-ambiguity resolution". In *Perspectives in Sentence Processing*, J. C. Trueswell and M. K. Tanenbaus (eds.), 155–79. Hillsdale, NJ: Lawrence Erlbaum.

Vroomen, J. and de Gelder, B. 1999. "Lexical access of resyllabified word: evidence from phoneme monitoring". *Memory and Cognition* 27: 413–21.

Vygotsky, L. 1962. *Thought and language*. Cambridge: MIT Press.

Inflationary effects in language and elsewhere

ÖSTEN DAHL

Stockholm University

Inflation is a well-known phenomenon to most of us. Together with unemployment, inflation is one of the diseases typical of modern economies. However, inflationary processes are not restricted to the economic sphere in the proper sense. Consider for instance the English words *gentleman* and *lady*, which in their original meaning denoted persons from the nobility, which today are often used synonymously to *man* and *woman*. Similar stories can be told about titles in many languages. In Swedish, a number of different words are used for unmarried women, such as *jungfru, fröken, mamsell*; they all seem to have been used initially for high-status women, but later became general titles for unmarried women and, in some cases, they have finally even obtained a derogatory character. Intuitively, we may say that titles tend to lose their "value" over time, but exactly what is the parallel with monetary value here?

Many titles such as *lord* or *professor* are connected with a certain status in society; they guarantee the bearer certain rights and privileges and the respect of others. If, for instance, a king confers a title on one of his subjects, the effects are similar to the ones that would obtain if the king gave him or her a piece of land or a sum of money. But there is a crucial difference between the piece of land on one hand and the title or the money on the other. The value connected with the title and the money is purely conventional. That is, there must be something in the world that corresponds to the title or to the sum of money, but what that is depends on a convention. In some cases, the lack of a real-world counterpart to an object with a conventional value will lead to an immediate crisis. If I try to sell two-hundred tickets to a theater with one hundred seats I will quite soon be in serious trouble. When the relationship between the object and what it "buys" in the world is less direct, however, there is always a temptation to multiply the conventionally-valued objects to obtain a short-term gain. A king may thus buy the loyalty of a number of people by making them into, say, "Grand Dukes". But if the number of Grand Dukes in the country doubles, the value of that title is bound to decrease.

Conferring a title, or doing other similar things, such as giving medals and orders, is usually "cheap" for the person who does it. Similarly, it is always tempting for someone who controls the issuing of banknotes in a country to get short-term advantages by printing more money. Such actions, however, are basically self-destructive in that the increase in the number of bearers of a title, or in the amount of money in circulation, influences the value of the "symbolic commodity", resulting in inflation.

Similar things are going on in everyday communication. Thus, titles are not necessarily conferred by kings but are used by people all the time in talking to and about each other. Although the use of titles is normally governed by conventions to a large extent, there is often leeway for the choice between different ways of addressing or referring to people. Also, there is usually a "penalty" for using a title that is too low, but while more rarely a "penalty" for using a title which is too high. On the contrary, you may sometimes "buy" a positive reaction from someone by over-titling him or her. In fact, such over-titling is sometimes conventionalized. When academic titles were more commonly used in Sweden than they are today, it was customary to "promote" academics when addressing them. Thus, a person with the lower "licentiate" degree would quite regularly be called "Doctor". In the long run, however, such policies inevitably lead to the depreciation of titles and thus to the introduction of new ones.

The use of evaluative expressions like *excellent* and *good* may work in a similar way. A teacher may want to give her students positive feedback and she tells them their work is "excellent". But if such an expression is used indiscriminately, that is, if everyone is told their work is excellent, the expression loses its informational value and eventually has to be replaced by another expression.

As noted by Haspelmath (forthcoming), inflation is an "invisible-hand phenomenon", to use a term originating with Adam Smith and made popular in linguistics by Keller (1994). This means that inflation is the unintended result of intentional actions. Inflationary phenomena depend on a conflict between the short-term interests of agents and the long-term functioning of the system. Inflation thus is a clear example of a counter-adaptive process: elements of a system become less functional over time and eventually have to be replaced (e.g., by currency reform or the introduction of new titles, etc.) At the same time, it governs the life-cycles of symbolic entities such as currencies and titles.

Inflationary phenomena are readily observable in grammaticalization processes. Let us look at a particularly straightforward case. In Mandarin Chinese, scalar predicates such as *kuài* 'fast' are quasi-obligatorily modified by the intensifier *hěn*, whose traditional meaning is 'very' (Ansaldo 1999: 93). Thus, while (1) is felt to be rather odd except in some special contexts, (2) is now the normal way of saying 'He is fast':

(1) Tā kuài
    he fast

(2) Tā hěn kuài
    he very fast

In fact, when asked to translate English sentences containing the word *very*, speakers tend to resort to other intensifiers such as *fēicháng* 'extremely'. The word *hǎn* has thus undergone a shift, in which it has moved from being an intensifying modifier to being an obligatory part of the scalar predicate construction. It is plausible to assume that the initial driving force of such a process is speakers' desire to maximize the rhetorical effect of their statements. Saying that *x is very fast* is *ceteris paribus* bound to be more interesting, newsworthy, astonishing, etc. than the plain statement that *x is fast*. But again, this may lead to unintentional long-term effects. If some speakers start using stronger expressions, others may have to follow suit, in order not to be left behind in the rhetorical game. This may explain why a modifier such as *hěn* becomes obligatory. Also, since the over-use of expressions leads to a loss in rhetorical strength, new expressions have to be invented for the cases when a strong effect is really needed.

Another type of inflationary effect is observed in the "devaluation" of emphatic constructions. A very general tendency behind a number of common types of grammaticalization processes is for emphatic constructions of various kinds to be over-used in the sense that they come to replace their non-emphatic counterparts. The most famous of these is perhaps "Jespersen's Cycle", the process by which emphatic negation constructions such as French *ne . . . pas*, with the original meaning 'not a step', become the standard way of negating sentences, with the ensuing loss of the original emphatic force. This motivates, on one hand, the phonetic reduction of the morphemes entering into the negation construction, on the other, the introduction of new emphatic constructions to fill the functional gap.

Often, however, we may observe "devaluation" of expressions of a slightly different kind, where it is less obvious that the notion of inflation as used in economics is applicable. Let us first look at a non-linguistic parallel.

Once upon a time alcoholic beverages could not be served in Swedish restaurants if they were not part of a meal, that is, you had to order some food with your drink. The natural strategy on the part of a thirsty guest was of course to miminize the meal that had to be ordered. It is said that special "token sandwiches" were introduced for this purpose. One may imagine that these were not exactly culinary wonders.

What this example illustrates is what happens when a rule of some sort interferes with an agent's cost-benefit calculations. I go to the restaurant because I am thirsty; I am prepared to pay the price that is demanded for the drink I order. However, the state forces me to also pay for some food that I do not really want. From my point of view, this regulation is tantamount to taxation: I simply have to pay more for the drink than if the regulation did not exist. My reaction, as we have seen, is to reduce the extra cost as much as possible—I do not care if the sandwich I get is edible or not, I don't want it anyway.

Returning now to linguistics, a suitable area to look for the effects of con-ventionalization is that of politeness phenomena, which are more obvious in hierar-chically-structured societies. When speaking to superiors, a person of lower rank may be expected to add the title of the person s/he is speaking to, not just once in a conversation but all the time. Thus, in pre-revolutionary Russia, the word *sudar'* 'sir' was routinely added after an utterance in this way. After a while, speakers started to pronounce this word less distinctly and, in the end, it was reduced to a single fricative -*s*: *da-s* 'yes, sir'. But politeness phenomena are not the only place where similar processes take place. A persistent feature of grammaticalization is that linguistic items come to be used in contexts where they are redundant in the sense of not contributing any information that is new to the listener or they are irrel-evant in the sense of not being part of the intended message. For instance, posses-sive markers are obligatory with certain types of relational nouns (body part terms and kinship terms) in many languages, although precisely with these nouns the identity of the possessor tends to be predictable (Dahl and Koptjevskaja-Tamm 1998): thus, in English a possessive pronoun is obligatory in a construction such as *I hurt my leg*, although the same message would be readily understandable without the possessive and indeed is expressed in that way in many other languages. Tense morphemes give information about temporal reference even when that information is derivable from previous context or even indicated by an adverbial in the same sentence, etc.

A somewhat different example of the development of a redundant pattern in lan-guage is provided by "synonymic compounds", that is, compound nouns in which the components are synonymous and thus express the same information. Such com-pounds are common in many languages and appear to be an areal phenomenon characteristic of the eastern part of the Eurasian continent (Wälchli manuscript). Some examples from Uzbek are *toat-ibodatda* 'worship-worship > worship', *to'la-to'kis* 'full-full > full', and *oziq-ovqat* 'food-food > food' (where the second com-ponent is from Arabic). Apparently what has happened is that such patterns become conventionalized and become the normal way of expressing certain concepts.

To see the parallel between the linguistic examples and the "token sandwich" in Swedish restaurants, we have to consider what kind of "cost-benefit calculation" a speaker makes. The speaker of an utterance usually wants to convey a certain amount of information—the "message". In order to do so, s/he has to spend a cer-tain amount of resources—time and energy. A politeness "rule" like the one that forces him/her to add an extra element to the utterance, whether or not it is needed for the message, increases the "cost"—the amount of time and energy spent—without necessarily giving any extra benefits. In the same way as the thirsty Swede tried to get away with the least costly meal possible, the speaker reduces the time and energy spent on the politeness item, leaving only what is necessary for him/her still being considered to having uttered it.

In this connection, it may be relevant to mention the quote from Schlegel (1818) in Heine et al. (1991),[1] which shows an early example of the money metaphor in discussing processes of grammaticalization. Schlegel says that some words are deprived of their semantic force and left with a nominal value; they thus become a kind of "paper money", which "facilitates their circulation". Although the formulation is suggestive, it is not entirely clear (to me at least) what kind of mechanism Schlegel was talking about. However, what comes to mind here is what economists call "Gresham's Law", or the principle that "bad money drives out good": if two objects have the same conventional value assigned to them, an agent in a commercial exchange will prefer to use the one with the lower "real" value. This eventually leads to the disappearance of the more highly valued items from circulation. The parallel to what goes on in communication is that if there are two ways of saying the same thing, the one which is less "costly", that is, in the normal case, shorter and easier to pronounce, will win.

In the study of animal communication, the term "ritualization" is used for the use of behaviors disconnected from their original purpose, in particular, for the development of "display behavior", such as when an animal signals its intention to perform an action (e.g., an attack) by making the initial movements of that action. Since the point is no longer to perform the action but just to display an intention "conventionally", the cost in terms of physical effort and possible damage may be reduced to a minimum. Again, an agent gets away with the cheapest possible way of attaining a conventional value.

That there are parallels between ritualization as understood by ethologists and grammaticalization in natural languages has been suggested before, notably by Haiman (1994). According to Haiman, the factor that is crucial to ritualization is repetition, which, according to him, drives processes such as emancipation (from the original function), habituation, and automatization. Similarly, Bybee (forthcoming), referring to Haiman's discussion of ritualization, proposes that phonological changes of reduction and fusion are conditioned by the frequent repetition of items that undergo grammaticalization (grammaticization). She attributes an important role in this to processes of habituation and automatization of sequences of units in speech. Without denying the relevance of these factors, I would like to emphasize that the mechanism I am talking about here is slightly different.[2] What I want to argue is that the parts of an utterance that are most likely to be reduced are those that contribute least to the intended message—those which have the lowest information load or value.

Consider a simple example. I am writing this in 1999; the phrase *in 1999* is thus something that I say very often and no doubt it is highly routinized for me and for other speakers. Its will also tend to have a reduced pronunciation; people may even prefer to say just *ninety-nine* pronounced something like [nɔ̃ti'nɔin]. But suppose now that the number of my office telephone extension is 1999. It may well be that I have to say this several times every day; still, the chances are that I will go on pronouncing this very distinctly, preserving all the syllables and stresses: ['naintiːn nainti'nain]. The obvious reason is that in contrast to the number of the year, the extension number is wholly unpredictable for my listeners and any reduction might put comprehension in danger.

What this example illustrates is the principle of *redundancy management* (my translation of the term *Redundanzsteuerung* from Lüdtke [1980]), by which we keep a balance between two separate strivings: to minimize the cost of a message and to maximize its chances of being properly delivered (i.e., understood), keeping in mind that a secure delivery demands a certain degree of redundancy. Redundancy management is what makes us pronounce telephone numbers distinctly and the number of the current year sloppily; in general, it ensures that every expression gets the resources it deserves. In the development of lexical and grammatical patterns, it restrains the tendencies to reduce the resources spent on the expression of a pattern.

The term "information load" conflates several different but related phenomena. To start with, we have the information-theoretical consideration that a high degree of unpredictability demands a more elaborate message expression, since the receiver needs more help in choosing between the alternative interpretations. This is what lies behind redundancy management. But there is an additional dimension in human communication, that is the prominence that is given to a message or parts of it. Prominence is used by speakers to guide the attention of listeners to elements that are worth paying attention to—important news items get fatter headlines. In speech, prosodic mechanisms have an essential role to play in the process of what I would like to call *prominence management*, to introduce a parallel term to "redundancy management". In actual practice, it is often difficult to keep redundancy and prominence management apart. Highly unexpected news items also tend to be those that are worth paying attention to. Redundancy and prominence management have in common that they both operate on listeners' expectations.

It follows that an expression is most likely to undergo reduction in a situation where a discrepancy has arisen between the cost of a message and its information load. One case in point is the use of expressions for politeness reasons that we saw examples of. But we can see that the routine use of an intensifying modifier, as in Mandarin Chinese, will have the same effect: the modifier no longer carries the information load that it did originally.

There is an obvious relation to frequency here in that high-frequency items are likely to have a lighter information load. In the literature, this is often expressed in terms of enhanced predictability. It should be pointed out, though, that the relationship between high frequency and predictability is less straightforward than is sometimes thought. The reason is that we have to distinguish the predictability of a linguistic item from the predictability of the information it carries. Consider, for instance, the old principle of journalism which says that when a dog bites a man, it is not news, but when a man bites a dog, it is. This is based on the empirical observation that dogs bite humans more frequently than vice versa. Thus, the content of the message 'man bites dog' has a higher information value than that of 'dog bites man'. But precisely for this reason it is more likely to show up as a headline in a newspaper, which means that in fact 'man bites dog' may be more frequent as a linguistic item. Similarly, when speaking, we tend to leave out items that carry predictable information. This presents a challenge for anyone who wants to explain grammaticalization and similar processes. Grammatical markers tend to carry little or no information that is relevant to the message, yet they may be retained as high-frequency items in a language for millennia. In the case of politeness items such as Russian -s, it is obvious that it is not the intrinsic information load of the expression that keeps them in the language but rather the external pressure on speakers not to violate norms that are considered important for the preservation of a hierarchical society.[3] Likewise, in the Swedish restaurant example, there was an external norm that forced the guests to order food with their drinks.

Explaining the persistence of grammatical markers by the existence of a norm looks like begging the question, however, as long as there is no independent motivation for the norm itself. Eventually, the theory has to provide such a motivation; for the time being, the most important thing may be to realize that it is needed.

In this paper, I have used the notion of inflation, as understood in economics, as a starting-point for a discussion of some processes by which the information load of linguistic expressions and constructions decreases. In another paper (Dahl forthcoming) I introduced the term *rhetorical devaluation* for those processes. As we have seen, rhetorical devaluation, in its different forms, is involved in grammaticalization in essential ways:

1. An expression which expresses a strong value of some parameter may be used even when a weaker value is called for.
2. A construction whose function is to draw attention to an element whose content

is counter to expectation is also used for elements which are not counter to expectation.

3. An expression may be used even when the information it carries is irrelevant (does not belong to the intended message) or predictable (presupposed or inferrable).

All these devaluations have the effect that they change the cost-benefit calculation that a speaker makes, paving the way for reduction and condensation processes.

The question now arises: are there also processes that work in the opposite direction—"linguistic deflation" or "rhetorical revaluation"? The original examples I gave of linguistic inflation were due to the short-term advantages of over-using certain kinds of expressions such as evaluative adjectives. Clearly, in some situations, it may be advantageous for a user to avoid too strong expressions, especially in connection with negative evaluations. If you hear someone say *It may be a little difficult* you may well conclude that the intended meaning is *What you propose is totally impossible*. In "understatement" cultures, the tendency to avoid strong words may extend also to positive statements. Thus, an utterance like *That's not so bad* may in fact be the highest possible praise. It seems clear that phrases of this kind may be lexicalized, as in the expression *not half* 'extremely'. Consider also the conversational implicature 'average → not too good', which seems to have been conventionalized in the word *mediocre*, which in spite of sharing its root with words like *medium* is defined by Merriam-Webster as "of moderate or *low* [my italics] quality, value, ability, or performance". In fact, it has been argued that "pragmatic enrichment", which would involve precisely the conventionalization of conversational implicatures, plays a significant role particularly in the early stages of grammaticalization (cf. Traugott and König 1991, Hopper and Traugott 1993, and, for that matter, my own discussion of conventionalization of implicatures Dahl 1985: 11[4]). Traugott and König (1991) even use the term "strengthening of informativeness" in this connection. A standard example is the development from temporal to causal connectives, as in English *since*. It is tempting to make the following generalization about these cases and the ones discussed earlier in this paper: sometimes a speaker means more than s/he says, sometimes less. In the end, however, it is what the listener actually gets out of the utterance—what it "buys" him/her—that matters. On the other hand, in the same way as inflation is more common than deflation in economics, the general tendency seems to be toward decrease rather than increase in pragmatic or rhetorical strength over time.

Notes

1. Regrettably, I have not had access to the original French text.

2. In the example of display behavior mentioned in the main text the reduction of the action is indeed a necessary condition for the emancipation to go through. The message sent to the enemy is "Go away, or I'll attack you". Essentially this is an offer of a peaceful solution of the conflict, which would be directly contradicted by an actual attack. At least in this particular type of example, habituation and automatization thus seem less relevant for the explanation of reduction processes. Haiman and Bybee do not mention this aspect of the problem.

3. A nice example of how rather a different kind of norm can give rise to the need for redundant expression is given in the Dilbert cartoon reproduced in Haiman (1994: 23).

4. Hopper and Traugott (1993: 75) ascribe to me the view that "present relevance" is a secondary meaning of the English perfect that has arisen in this way. Actually, in the place quoted, I am talking about "inferential" interpretations of the perfect, not about present relevance.

References

Ansaldo, U. 1999. *Comparative constructions in Chinese. Areal Typology and Patterns of Grammaticalization.* Ph.D. Thesis, Department of Linguistics, Stockholm University.
Bybee, J. L. Forthcoming. 'Mechanisms of change in grammaticization: the role of frequency'. In *Handbook of Historical Linguistics*, R. Janda and B. Joseph (eds.). Oxford: Blackwell Publishers.
Dahl, Ö. 1985. *Tense and Aspect Systems.* Oxford: Blackwell.
Dahl, Ö. Forthcoming. 'Grammaticalization and the life-cycles of constructions'. To be published in a volume in the series RASK Supplement Volumes, Carl-Erik Lindberg (ed.). Odense: Odense University Press.
Dahl, Ö. and Koptjevskaja-Tamm, M. 1998. 'Alienability splits and the grammaticalization of possessive constructions'. In *Papers from the 16th Scandinavian Conference of Linguistics. Publications of the Department of Finnish and General Linguistics of the University of Turku 60*, T. Haukioja (ed.), 38–49. Turku: University of Turku.
Haiman, J. 1994. 'Ritualization and the Development of Language'. In *Perspectives on grammaticalization*, W. Pagliuca (ed.), 3–28. Amsterdam: Benjamins.
Haspelmath, M. Forthcoming. 'Why is grammaticalization irreversible?' *Linguistics.*
Heine, B., Claudi, U., and Hünnemeyer, F. 1991. *Grammaticalization: A Conceptual Framework.* Chicago: University of Chicago Press.
Hopper, P. J. and Traugott, E. 1993. *Grammaticalization.* Cambridge: Cambridge University Press.
Keller, R. 1994. *Language Change: The Invisible Hand in Language.* London: Routledge.
Lüdtke, H. 1980. 'Auf dem Wege zu einer Theorie des Sprachwandels'. In *Kommunikationstheoretische Grundlagen des Sprachwandels*, H. Lüdtke (ed.), 182–252. Berlin: de Gruyter.

Schlegel, A. W. von. 1818. *Observations sur la Language et Littérature Provençales*. Paris: Librairie Grecque-Latine-Allemande.

Traugott, E. C. and König, E. 1991. 'The semantics-pragmatics of grammaticalization revisited'. In *Approaches to Grammaticalization*, E. Traugott and B. Heine (eds.), 189–218. Amsterdam/Philadelphia: John Benjamins.

Wälchli, B. Manuscript. 'Towards a Typology of Co-Compounds and Natural Coordination'. Department of Linguistics, Stockholm University.

Subject index

Name index

In the series TYPOLOGICAL STUDIES IN LANGUAGE (TSL) the following titles have been published thus far:

1. HOPPER, Paul J. (ed.): *Tense-Aspect: Between semantics & pragmatics.* 1982.
2. HAIMAN, John & Pamela MUNRO (eds): *Switch Reference and Universal Grammar. Proceedings of a symposium on switch reference and universal grammar, Winnipeg, May 1981.* 1983.
3. GIVÓN, T.: *Topic Continuity in Discourse. A quantitative cross-language study.* 1983.
4. CHISHOLM, William, Louis T. MILIC & John A.C. GREPPIN (eds): *Interrogativity: A colloquium on the grammar, typology and pragmatics of questions in seven diverse languages, Cleveland, Ohio, October 5th 1981-May 3rd 1982.* 1984.
5. RUTHERFORD, William E. (ed.): *Language Universals and Second Language Acquisition.* 1984 (2nd ed. 1987).
6. HAIMAN, John (Ed.): *Iconicity in Syntax. Proceedings of a symposium on iconicity in syntax, Stanford, June 24-26, 1983.* 1985.
7. CRAIG, Colette (ed.): *Noun Classes and Categorization. Proceedings of a symposium on categorization and noun classification, Eugene, Oregon, October 1983.* 1986.
8. SLOBIN, Dan I. & Karl ZIMMER (eds): *Studies in Turkish Linguistics.* 1986.
9. BYBEE, Joan L.: *Morphology. A Study of the Relation between Meaning and Form.* 1985.
10. RANSOM, Evelyn: *Complementation: its Meaning and Forms.* 1986.
11. TOMLIN, Russel S.: *Coherence and Grounding in Discourse. Outcome of a Symposium, Eugene, Oregon, June 1984.* 1987.
12. NEDJALKOV, Vladimir (ed.): *Typology of Resultative Constructions. Translated from the original Russian edition (1983). English translation edited by Bernard Comrie.* 1988.
14. HINDS, John, Shoichi IWASAKI & Senko K. MAYNARD (eds): *Perspectives on Topicalization. The case of Japanese WA.* 1987.
15. AUSTIN, Peter (ed.): *Complex Sentence Constructions in Australian Languages.* 1988.
16. SHIBATANI, Masayoshi (ed.): *Passive and Voice.* 1988.
17. HAMMOND, Michael, Edith A. MORAVCSIK and Jessica WIRTH (eds): *Studies in Syntactic Typology.* 1988.
18. HAIMAN, John & Sandra A. THOMPSON (eds): *Clause Combining in Grammar and Discourse.* 1988.
19. TRAUGOTT, Elizabeth C. and Bernd HEINE (eds): *Approaches to Grammaticalization, 2 volumes (set)* 1991
20. CROFT, William, Suzanne KEMMER and Keith DENNING (eds): *Studies in Typology and Diachrony. Papers presented to Joseph H. Greenberg on his 75th birthday.* 1990.
21. DOWNING, Pamela, Susan D. LIMA and Michael NOONAN (eds): *The Linguistics of Literacy.* 1992.
22. PAYNE, Doris (ed.): *Pragmatics of Word Order Flexibility.* 1992.
23. KEMMER, Suzanne: *The Middle Voice.* 1993.
24. PERKINS, Revere D.: *Deixis, Grammar, and Culture.* 1992.
25. SVOROU, Soteria: *The Grammar of Space.* 1994.
26. LORD, Carol: *Historical Change in Serial Verb Constructions.* 1993.
27. FOX, Barbara and Paul J. Hopper (eds): *Voice: Form and Function.* 1994.

28. GIVÓN, T. (ed.) : *Voice and Inversion.* 1994.
29. KAHREL, Peter and René van den BERG (eds): *Typological Studies in Negation.* 1994.
30. DOWNING, Pamela and Michael NOONAN: *Word Order in Discourse.* 1995.
31. GERNSBACHER, M. A. and T. GIVÓN (eds): *Coherence in Spontaneous Text.* 1995.
32. BYBEE, Joan and Suzanne FLEISCHMAN (eds): *Modality in Grammar and Discourse.* 1995.
33. FOX, Barbara (ed.): *Studies in Anaphora.* 1996.
34. GIVÓN, T. (ed.): *Conversation. Cognitive, communicative and social perspectives.* 1997.
35. GIVÓN, T. (ed.): *Grammatical Relations. A functionalist perspective.* 1997.
36. NEWMAN, John (ed.): *The Linguistics of Giving.* 1998.
37. RAMAT, Anna Giacalone and Paul J. HOPPER (eds): *The Limits of Grammaticalization.* 1998.
38. SIEWIERSKA, Anna and Jae Jung SONG (eds): *Case, Typology and Grammar. In honor of Barry J. Blake.* 1998.
39. PAYNE, Doris L. and Immanuel BARSHI (eds.): *External Possession.* 1999.
40. FRAJZYNGIER, Zygmunt and Traci S. CURL (eds.): *Reflexives. Forms and functions.* 2000.
41. FRAJZYNGIER, Zygmunt and Traci S. CURL (eds): *Reciprocals. Forms and functions.* 2000.
42. DIESSEL, Holger: *Demonstratives. Form, function and grammaticalization.* 1999.
43. GILDEA, Spike (ed.): *Reconstructing Grammar. Comparative Linguistics and Grammaticalization.* 2000.
44. VOELTZ, F.K. Erhard and Christa KILLIAN-HATZ (eds.): *Ideophones.* n.y.p.
45. BYBEE, Joan and Paul HOPPER (eds.): *Frequency and the Emergence of Linguistic Structure.* 2001.
46. AIKHENVALD, Alexandra Y., R.M.W. DIXON and Masayuki ONISHI (eds.): *Noncanonical Marking of Subjects and Objects.* n.y.p.
47. BARON, Irene, Michael HERSLUND and Finn SORENSEN (eds.): *Dimensions of Possession.* n.y.p.